Personnel
Management

Personnel Management:
A New Approach

2nd Edition

Derek Torrington
and
Laura Hall

PRENTICE HALL

New York London Toronto
Sydney Tokyo
Singapore

First published 1991 by
Prentice Hall International (UK) Ltd
66 Wood Lane End, Hemel Hempstead
Hertfordshire HP2 4RG
A division of
Simon & Schuster International Group

© Prentice Hall International (UK) Ltd, 1991

Typeset in 10/12 pt Palatino
by VAP Publishing Services, Kidlington, Oxford

Printed and bound in Great Britain at
the University Press, Cambridge

Library of Congress Cataloging-in-Publication Data

Torrington, Derek, 1931–
    Personnel management : a new approach / Derek Torrington and Laura Hall.
    — 2nd ed.
        p.   cm.
    Includes bibliographical references and index.
    ISBN 0–13–658667–8
    1. Personnel management.   I. Hall, Laura, 1952–   . II. Title.
    HF5549.T675 1991
    658.3—dc20   90–27400
                                                                                          CIP

British Library Cataloguing in Publication Data

Torrington, Derek 1931–
    Personnel management. – 2nd. ed.
    1. Personnel Management
    I. Title   II. Hall, Laura 1952–
    658.3

    ISBN 0–13–658667–8

---

3 4 5   95 94 93 92

This book is for:
Barbara   Mark   Helen
Ian   Sally
Tim   Alex   Greg
Dorothy   Stewart

Contents

Part VI Pay   569

Preface

Although this is the second edition of *Personnel Management: A New Approach*, which was published in 1987, it is also a successor to *Personnel Management* by John Chapman and Derek Torrington, which was published in 1979, with a second edition in 1983. There is thus a continuity of publication in four volumes over twelve years. The remarkable sales success of the book over such a period makes one cautious about changes, especially as our programmes of empirical research among personnel managers in the mid-1980s produced so many variations of insight and interpretation that a completely different treatment of the subject was necessary in the 1987 edition.

Changes in this edition are modest but important. We have taken further the significance of the human resources management approach, as this has consolidated in recent years, and have attempted to work the implications through at all stages of the text. Chapter 3, Personnel Policy, is now Personnel Policy and Strategy, and a single chapter on Manpower Planning has been replaced by two on Human Resource Planning, which are also repositioned in the text to demonstrate the change in emphasis on both strategy and planning. The chapters on organization and communication have both been divided in two, and further developed.

Part III of the book remains the largest and has been retitled Employee Resourcing instead of Manpower Administration. We are not particularly happy with that title, but it seemed important to get away from the term 'administration' and its prosaic connotations. For Part VI we have obstinately refused to change the title from Pay, remaining unconvinced that 'reward', 'compensation' or 'remuneration' can adequately cover the range of topics. The material in Part VI has, however, been much altered to take account of the innovations in the area. All chapters have been updated and rewritten where necessary.

There are many references to 'our recent research'. This was funded by the Leverhulme Trust with the support of the Institute of Personnel Management

and UMIST. It was a questionnaire survey of personnel practice in 350 establishments, followed by interviews with sixty-two senior personnel managers in 1984
and 1985. The emphasis on that research is less in this edition than in the last,
due to the changes that have taken place in personnel practice recently. For our
understanding and interpretation of developments since the mid-1980s we have
drawn obviously on our own, everyday experience in and around personnel
management, and on the grass-roots accounts of life at the sharp end (which
often seems remarkably blunt), which are found in our work as examiners for
the Institute of Personnel Management. Over a thousand examination scripts
each July provide enough material for several books on personnel management.
There has been further invaluable help from a programme of research from 1987
to 1991 under the auspices of the Science and Engineering Council's Teaching
Company Scheme examining aspects of personnel and industrial relations policy
in a large engineering company.

We acknowledge the following permissions: from The Institute of Personnel
Management for permission to use Figures 9.1, 12.2 and 34.5; Pitman Publishing
Ltd for Figure 4.2; Century-Hutchinson Ltd for Figure 27.2; Equal Opportunities
Commission for Figure 21.3; *Academy of Management Journal* for Figure 26.1 and
Table 26.1; Ralph Windle for the poem that opens Chapter 13, reprinted from *The
Bottom Line* by Bertie Ramsbottom (Century-Hutchinson, 1985); and Gower
Publishing Company for Figure 25.1 and for permission to use some material in
Chapter 30, that also appears in their *Personnel Management Handbook* (1987).

Organization of the book

The material of this book deals with the personnel process in organizations that can lead to the effective management of human resources, as well as providing an effective management service to resourceful humans. The figure overleaf interrelates the various chapters to provide an overall picture of the subject matter.

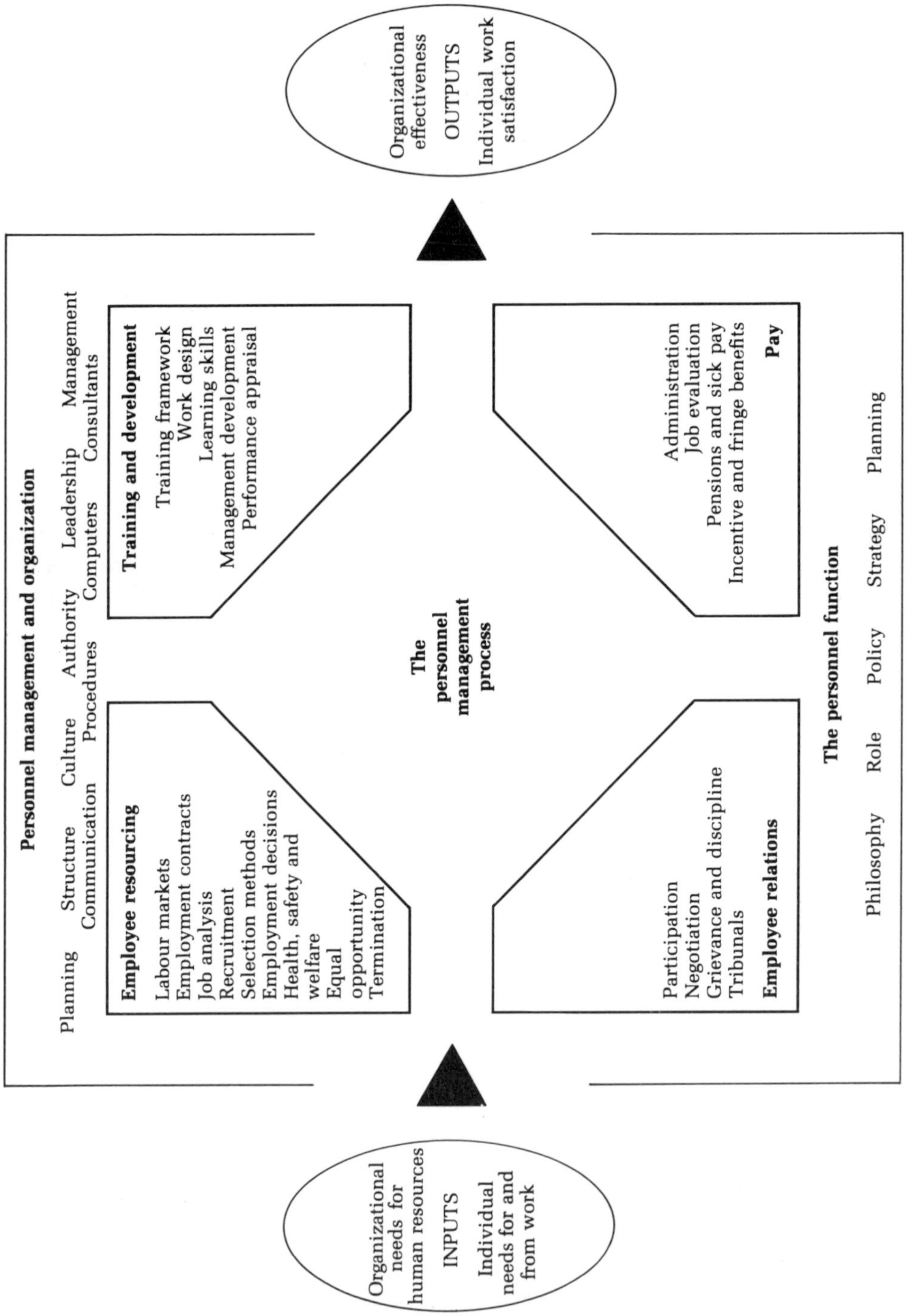

Organizational
effectiveness
OUTPUTS
Individual work
satisfaction

Personnel management and organization

Planning   Structure   Culture   Authority   Leadership   Management
Communication   Procedures   Computers   Consultants

Training and development
Training framework
Work design
Learning skills
Management development
Performance appraisal

Pay
Administration
Job evaluation
Pensions and sick pay
Incentive and fringe benefits

**The
personnel
management
process**

Employee resourcing
Labour markets
Employment contracts
Job analysis
Recruitment
Selection methods
Employment decisions
Health, safety and
welfare
Equal
opportunity
Termination

Employee relations
Participation
Negotiation
Grievance and discipline
Tribunals

The personnel function

Philosophy   Role   Policy   Strategy   Planning

Organizational
needs for
human resources
INPUTS
Individual
needs for and
from work

Figure 0.1   *Human resource management and the person process*

Part
I

The Nature of
Personnel
Management

1

The philosophy of personnel management

That rock-hard, steely-eyed film star Clint Eastwood has appeared in several films as tough cop Harry Callaghan, whose approach to law and order is to shoot first and not bother asking too many questions afterwards. On one occasion he had killed rather a lot of people even by his own high standards, so that he was becoming politically embarrassing to the authorities. Something had to be done. The Chief of Police nerved himself and called Harry into his office, taking care that there was a large table between them, and gave him the news that he was being transferred – to personnel. There was a moment of electric silence. A nervous tic flickered briefly on Harry Callaghan's right cheek. His jaw locked and those famous cold blue eyes gave the Chief a look that could have penetrated armour plate as he hissed his reply through clenched teeth: 'Personnel is for assholes.' Whereupon he left the room, slamming the door with sufficient vigour to splinter the woodwork in several places.

Being a man of few words, Harry Callaghan did not explain further, but we can interpret his view as being the common one that personnel work is not for the people who can and do, but for the people who can't and don't. It is regarded as the easy option for those who shirk the hard, competitive world of marketing, the precision of finance, or the long hours and hard knocks of manufacturing. It is soft, ineffectual and unimportant.

A more benign version of that stereotype is that personnel is the human face of management, still avoiding the ruthless cut and thrust, but an important aspect of making the organization work effectively and ensuring that employees are well looked after. It is this second view that attracts many aspirants to this area, people who feel that they could not cope with social work, but want to do something that is worthwhile and 'working with people'. Personnel management seems to offer all that, and perhaps a company car as well, without the taint of the rat race.

In between those two extremes there lies the reality that personnel managers experience and the ideal they try to achieve. We begin our account of contemporary personnel management by working through a series of personnel stereotypes before putting forward a philosophy for personnel managers to adopt or to modify in the light of their own experience and their own working context. We start the book this way in order to help the reader set up a personal attitude towards the subject. Before considering what personnel management is, what do you think it is for?

Historical development

Although we cannot attribute any particular ideology to a complete group of people at any one time, it is possible roughly to show the development of the personnel function by suggesting a general self-image, which obtained at different periods.

The social reformer

Before personnel emerged as a specialist management activity, there were those in the nineteenth century who tried to intervene in industrial affairs to support the position of the severely underprivileged factory worker at the hands of a rapacious employer. The Industrial Revolution had initially helped people to move away from the poverty and hopelessness of rural life to the factories and the cities, but the organization of the work soon degraded human life and dehumanized working people. In the words of William Wordsworth:

> Men, maidens, youths,
> Mothers and little children, boys and girls,
> Enter, and each the wonted task resumes
> Within this temple, where is offered up
> To Gain, the master idol of the realm,
> perpetual sacrifice.

Free enterprise, the survival of the fittest and the ruthless exploitation of the masses were seen as laws of nature, and it was the social reformers like Lord Shaftesbury and Robert Owen who produced some mitigation of this hardship, mainly by standing outside the organization and the workplace, offering criticism of employer behaviour within and inducing some changes. This was aided by the more general social commentary of Dickens' novels and the observations of Friedrich Engels.

We need to trace the evolution of personnel management to this type of person, as it was their influence and example that enabled personnel managers to be appointed, and provided the first frame of reference for the appointees to work within. It would also be incorrect to say that this type of concern is obsolete. There are regular reports of employees being exploited by employers flouting the law, and the problem of organizational size remains a source of alienation from work. In one large company an inscription was printed on a report stating that it should not be bent, twisted or defaced. A group of employees in the same company made a muted complaint about their lack of identity by producing lapel badges saying: 'I am a human being, do not bend, twist or deface'.

The acolyte of benevolence

The first people to be appointed with specific responsibility for improving the lot of employees were usually known as welfare officers; they saw their role as dispensing benefits to the deserving and unfortunate employees. The motivation was the Christian charity of the noble employer, who was prepared to provide these comforts, partly because the employees deserved them, but mainly because he was disposed to provide them.

The leading examples of this development were the Quaker families of Cadbury and Rowntree, and the Lever Brothers' soap business. All set up progressive schemes of unemployment benefit, sick pay and subsidized housing for their employees during the latter part of the nineteenth century. Although later accused of paternalism, these initiatives marked a fundamental shift of employer philosophy. Seebohm Rowntree became a renowned sociologist as well as being chairman of his company for sixteen years and putting into practice the reforms he advocated in his writings. Cadbury Schweppes and Unilever remain among the most efficient and profitable businesses in the United Kingdom a hundred years after the foundation of the Bournville village and Port Sunlight.

In other instances the philosophy was perverted by relatively cheap welfare provisions being offered as a substitute for higher wages, and was used extensively to keep trade unions at bay.

The Institute of Welfare Officers was established in 1913 at a meeting in the Rowntree factory in York and the welfare tradition remains strong in personnel management, although it keeps re-emerging in different forms. There is constant comment on the provision of facilities like childcare and health screening, as well as the occasional discussion about business ethics (for example, Pocock 1989). The extent to which contemporary working practices for professional and executive employees make unreasonable demands of time and inconvenience is receiving increasing attention, as is the need for employees of all types to balance work and domestic responsibilities:

> Care-friendly employment practices will be the phenomenon of the
> future. Only by addressing the needs of employees caring for
> children, dependants with disabilities and the elderly, will employers
> be able to attract and retain the non-traditional sectors of the
> workforce which are forecast to form the workforce of the 1990s.
> (Worman 1990)

The humane bureaucrat

The first two phases were concerned predominantly with the physical environment of work and the amelioration of hardship among 'the workers'. We now
come to the stage where employing organizations were taking a further step in
increasing their size, and specialization was emerging in the management levels
as well as on the shopfloor. This led to the growth of personnel work on what is
loosely called staffing, with great concern about role specification, careful
selection, training and placement. The personnel manager was learning to
operate within a bureaucracy, serving organizational rather than paternalist–
employer objectives, but still committed to a basically humanitarian role.

For the first time there was a willingness to look to social science for support.
Much of the scientific management philosophy of F. W. Taylor informed
personnel thinking:

> First. Develop a science for each element of a man's work, which
> replaces the old rule-of-thumb method.
>
> Second. Scientifically select and then train, teach, and develop the
> workman, whereas in the past he chose his own work and trained
> himself as best he could.
>
> Third. Heartily co-operate with the men so as to insure all of the work
> being done in accordance with the principles which have been
> developed.
>
> Fourth. There is an almost equal division of the work and the
> responsibility between the management and the workmen. The
> management take over all work for which they are better fitted than
> workmen, while in the past almost all of the work and the greater part
> of the responsibility was thrown upon the men. (1911, pp. 36–7)

Work was to be made more efficient by analysis of what was required and the
careful selection and training of the workman, who would then be supported by
the management in a spirit of positive co-operation.

The Frenchman Henri Fayol considered not the workman but the management process, and his analytical framework for management is sometimes

known as scientific administration, as his approach had much in common with Taylor's.

The humane bureaucracy stage in the development of personnel thinking was also influenced by the Human Relations school of thought, which was in many ways a reaction against scientific management, or a reaction against the way in which scientific management was being applied. Just as the high ideals of the Cadburys and Rowntrees had been adulterated by some of their imitators, so Taylor found his managerial philosophy was seldom fully appreciated, and scientific management became identified with hyper-specialization of work and very tight systems of payment.

The human relations approach appealed immediately to those who were concerned about industrial conflict and the apparent dehumanizing potential of scientific management. The main advocate was Elton Mayo (1933) and the central idea was to emphasize informal social relationships and employee morale as contributors to organizational efficiency.

It was during this stage of development that personnel managers began to develop a technology as well as an approach, and many of the methods developed at this time, remain at the heart of what personnel managers do; the idea of fitting together two sets of requirements is a theme to which we shall return.

The consensus negotiator

Personnel managers next added expertise in bargaining to their repertoire of skills. The acolytes of benevolence had not been numerous or strong enough to satisfy employee aspirations as a result of employer voluntary provision. In the period after the Second World War there was relatively full employment and labour became a scarce resource. Trade unions extended their membership and employers had to change firm, traditional unitarism as the reality of what Allan Flanders, the leading industrial relations analyst of the 1960s, was to call 'the challenge from below' was grudgingly recognized. Where the personnel manager could at best be described as a 'remembrancer' of the employees, the trade union official could be their accredited representative.

Trade union assertiveness brought a shift towards bargaining by the employer on at least some matters. There was a growth of joint consultation and the establishment of joint production committees and suggestion schemes. Nationalized industries were set up, with a statutory duty placed on employers to negotiate with unions representing employees. The government encouraged the appointment of personnel officers and set up courses for them to be trained at universities. A personnel management advisory service was set up at the Ministry of Labour, and this still survives as the first A in ACAS.

The trend began during the early 1940s but received a major boost when the sellers' market of the immediate post-war period began to harden and international competition made more urgent the development of greater productive efficiency and the elimination of restrictive (or protective) practices. The personnel manager acquired bargaining expertise to deploy in search of a lost consensus.

Organization man

Next came a development of the humane bureaucracy phase into a preoccupation with the effectiveness of the organization as a whole, with clear objectives and a widespread commitment among organization members to those objectives. The approach was also characterized by candour between members and a form of operation that supported the integrity of the individual and provided opportunities for personal growth. There was an attempt to understand the interaction of organizational structures between, on the one hand, the people who make up the organization and, on the other, the surrounding society in which it is set.

This development was most clearly seen in the late 1960s and is most significant because it marks a change of focus among personnel specialists, away from dealing with the rank-and-file employee on behalf of the management towards dealing with the management and integration of managerial activity. Its most recent manifestation has been in programmes of organization and management development, as companies have subcontracted much of their routine work to peripheral employees, and concentrated on developing and retaining an elite core of people with specialist expertise on whom the business depends for its future.

Manpower analyst

The last of our historical stereotypes is that of manpower analyst, associated with the term 'management of human resources'. A development of the general management anxiety to quantify decisions has been a move towards regarding people as manpower or human resources. A relatively extreme form of this is human asset accounting, which assigns a value to individual employees in accounting terms and estimates the extent to which that asset will appreciate or depreciate in the future, so eventually everyone is written off in more ways than one.

More widespread is the use of manpower planning, which is:

> a strategy for the organization, utilization and improvement of an organization's human resources. It comprises three main activities:
> (a) assessing what manpower of what different grades, categories and skills will be needed in the short term and long term (i.e. manpower demand); (b) deciding what manpower an organization is likely to

have in the future, based on current trends and anticipated external circumstances (i.e. manpower supply); and (c) taking action to ensure that supply meets demand (e.g. training, retraining, recruitment). (Message 1974)

Although originally based on an assumption of organizational expansion, manpower planning was reshaped during organizational contraction to ensure the closest possible fit between the number of people and skills required and what is available. The activity has been boosted by the advent of the computer, which makes possible a range of calculations and measurements that were unrealistic earlier.

The six stereotypes we have identified have all blended together to make the complex of contemporary personnel management. Although they have emerged roughly in sequence, all are still present to a varying degree in different types of personnel post and the nature of personnel work today can only be understood by an appreciation of its varied components.

Review topic 1.1

Which of those six stereotypes do you personally find most attractive as describing the sort of job you would like to do? Which one, or combination, of the six most accurately describes the job you have?

Four other features have emerged, but have not established a lasting, dominant place in the complex of personnel work. *Social engineering* is a concern with the social role of work and the use of the workplace to solve social problems. *Legal wangling* became dominant in the 1970s, when a plethora of legislation protecting the rights of workers and trade unions gave managers a considerable fright; but managerial concern about legislation has much reduced since 1980. *Industrial democracy* was a heady concept, which has also receded, but there are moves towards greater employee participation still proceeding. Now, however, talk is more of involvement and briefing rather than participation or control. *Labour market analysis* improves the understanding of the setting of the organization in the structure of society with the influences that society therefore exerts. There is a whole range of questions stemming from the nature of the labour force and the way it is changing, as well as the way in which the employment being offered is changing. Interest in this area has increased considerably with concern about the changing demographic trends and the implications of the single European market.

The latest stereotype is undoubtedly that of the *human resources manager*, an idea that took the personnel world by storm in the 1980s and which may be the most significant change in emphasis in the last fifty years. The human resources approach is considered in the next chapter.

The deviant or conformist innovator

The most perceptive analysis of the personnel role in organizations was produced by Karen Legge, when she identified two alternative methods of personnel people seeking power in organizations (Legge 1978, pp. 67–94). First was *conformist innovation*, whereby personnel specialists identify their activities with the objective of organizational success, emphasizing cost benefit and conforming to the criteria of organizational success adopted by managerial colleagues, who usually have greater power. In contrast are the *deviant innovators*, who identify their activities with a set of norms or values that are distinct from, but not necessarily in conflict with, the norms of organizational success. They will emphasize social values rather than cost benefit, in a similar way to the company doctor, for example, whose power derives from an independent, professional stance for dealing with managerial clients.

This dichotomy is, of course, a method of analysis rather than a pair of pigeon-holes into which to place any personnel manager, but it is very revealing about the personnel tradition. Each of the six personnel stereotypes has had its devotees who adopted the flavour of the month enthusiastically in order to achieve a state of independence, shirking the rat race and the hard knocks referred to at the beginning of the chapter. Personnel work has its share of social reformers, acolytes of benevolence, and so forth, who have taken up that stance as an end in itself.

Some aspects of humane bureaucracy have been professionalized, so that there are occupational and organizational psychologists operating under those labels both within organizations and as consultants to organizations. There was a time when training specialists in companies became so committed to training that they spoke of creating learning communities within their organizations as if they were oases in the desert. These, with some of the cult worshippers of organization development, all bore the marks of the deviant innovator.

Total commitment to conformist innovation is, however, a way to lose identity, unless there is some distinctive, expert contribution, no matter how wide and general the management responsibility. Personnel specialists must have some specialized skill, and access to some recondite mysteries, if they are to succeed in joining the general hurly-burly of management without being trodden underfoot and becoming superfluous.

In our research we identified a continuum similar to the deviant/conformist dichotomy. The two dominant values among personnel managers appear to be employee relations and manpower control, which stand in contrast with each other. One is concerned with maintaining good working relationships, clear agreements, consistency of management behaviour and frank dialogue on the assumption that this will lead to organizational as well as individual benefits. The other concentrates on understanding the manpower costs, controlling the establishment figures and running a tight ship. They do not necessarily conflict, but they are seldom found in equal proportions.

Review topic 1.2

Are you more of a deviant or conformist innovator? Would you like to alter emphasis in your present activities?

The personnel function of management

So far this chapter has been devoted to considering the personnel specialist, but the personnel function of management as a whole is equally important. Each manager has inescapable responsibilities and duties of a personnel type, so that personnel management is not only of interest to specialists but to all managers. The degree and nature of the involvement differs, but the need for a philosophy or set of beliefs to underpin one's actions remains the same.

Many organizations do not have personnel specialists at all. The existence of a specialized personnel function is clearly related to size, and the increasing number of small businesses do not need, or cannot afford, this type of specialism. They may use consultants, they may use the advisory resources of university departments, they may use their bank's computer to process the payroll, but there is still a personnel dimension to their management activities. Some experienced personnel professionals (for example, Lyons 1985) argue that their main purpose is to work themselves out of a job. They have a message to convey to sensitize their management colleagues to personnel issues. When everyone is their own personnel manager, then the specialist can fade away, or become chief executive. This, however, is becoming a rare point of view, because it implies that personnel management consists of little more than having the right ideas. It under-rates the extensive knowledge and practical management methods that have to be put into operation constantly to get the personnel work of the organization done.

A philosophy of personnel management

The philosophy of personnel management that is the basis of this book has been only slightly modified since it was first put forward in 1979 (Torrington and Chapman 1979, p. 4). Despite all the changes in the labour market and in the government approach to the economy, this seems to be the most realistic and constructive approach, based on the earlier ideas of Enid Mumford (1972) and McCarthy and Ellis (1973). Our proposition is:

> Personnel management is a series of activities which: first enable working people and their employing organizations to agree about the objectives and nature of their working relationship and, secondly, ensures that the agreement is fulfilled.

Only by satisfying the needs of the individual employee will the employer obtain the commitment to organizational objectives that is needed for organizational success, and only by contributing to organizational success will employees be able to satisfy their personal employment needs. It is when employer and employee accept that mutuality and reciprocal dependence that personnel management is exciting, centre-stage and productive of business success. Where the employer is concerned with employees only as factors of production or human resources, personnel management is boring and a cost that will always be trimmed. Where employees have no trust in their employer and adopt an entirely instrumental orientation to their work, they will be fed up and will make ineffectual the work of any personnel function.

Personnel managers are great grumblers, and some will react to the last paragraph by saying that they do not get the support they deserve. Personnel decisions are always taken last, never get proper resources and so forth. Sometimes this is correct, but all too often it is a self-fulfilling prophecy, because the personnel people are pursuing the wrong objectives, or carefully keeping out of the way when things get really tough; which was exactly Harry Callaghan's point. Personnel managers are like managers in every other part of the business. They have to make things happen rather than wait for things to happen, and to make things happen they not only have to have the right approach: they also have to know their stuff. Read on!

Summary propositions

1.1 To understand personnel management, one starts from considering what it is for before considering what it is.

1.2 The complex of contemporary personnel management work is made up of six facets, which have been dominant at various times during the evolution of personnel management ideas.

1.3 Personnel management is the work of personnel specialists; the personnel function of management is an aspect of the work of all managers.

1.4 The philosophy of personnel management in this book is that it is a series of activities which first enable working people and their employing organizations to agree about the nature and objectives of the working relationship between them and, secondly, ensures that the agreement is fulfilled.

References

Fayol, H. (1949), *General and Industrial Management*, London: Pitman.

Legge, K. (1978), *Power, Innovation, and Problem-solving in Personnel Management*, London: McGraw-Hill.

Lyons, T. P. (1985), *Personnel Function in a Changing Environment* (2nd edition), London: Pitman.

Mayo, E. (1933), *The Human Problems of an Industrial Civilization*, New York: Macmillan.

McCarthy, W. E. J. and Ellis, N. D. (1973), *Management by Agreement*, London: Hutchinson.

Message, M. C. (1974), 'Manpower planning'. In D. P. Torrington (ed.), *Encyclopaedia of Personnel Management*, Aldershot: Gower.

Mumford, E. (1972), 'Job satisfaction: a method of analysis', *Personnel Review*, vol. 1, no. 3.

Pocock, P. (1989), 'Is business ethics a contradiction in terms?' *Personnel Management*, vol. 21, no. 11, December.

Taylor, F. W. (1911), *Scientific Management*, New York: Harper & Row.

Torrington, D. P. and Chapman, J. B. (1979), *Personnel Management*, Hemel Hempstead: Prentice Hall.

Worman, D. (1990), 'The forgotten carers', *Personnel Management*, vol. 22, no. 1.

2

The personnel role in the organization

Arthur Hill is thirty-six years old and has been personnel manager in his company for eight years. His comfortable demeanour and friendly personality help him to be well known and respected by all the company employees, to whom he has a strong sense of personal loyalty. He 'walks the floor' constantly and has a keen judgement of which problems will blow over 'by dinner', which need a bit of thinking about, and which will produce a crisis if not tackled immediately and positively. His managerial colleagues have a high regard for his ability to deal with problems and to get things done, once they have decided the policy, as he is a 100 per cent company man.

Charles Hanson is thirty-two years old and has been personnel manager with his company for three years. During that time he has introduced considerable change, streamlining the procedures, clarifying the roles and duties of the personnel staff, introducing more systematic training and developing ideas on how manning can be more efficient and responsive to changes in the product market. He spends most of his time in his office or with other managers, not wishing to appear to be snooping by walking round the factory too often, and keen not to interfere with line managers' responsibilities. He does not see himself necessarily as a career personnel specialist. His keen analytical approach is appreciated by his managerial colleagues, who see him as a man who will go far.

These two thumbnail sketches describe two very different personnel managers, both of whom hold the IPM qualification and who are paid almost identical salaries. We include the descriptions here because they also represent the contrasted tendencies discernible within personnel management today. In the last chapter we suggested that personnel managers tended to emphasize either employee relations or manpower control as dominant features of their work and interests. We can now stretch that out a bit further to suggest that personnel functions are engaged in both personnel management and – increasingly – in human resources management.

Personnel or human resources management?

There has been some tendency for the term 'human resources' to be adopted as an alternative to 'personnel' simply for a change, or to move away from an image that has been associated with previous eras. It has also been adopted by some to avoid the word 'manpower', seen as sexist in phrases like 'manpower planning' and 'manpower administration'. Also, personnel managers seem constantly to suffer from paranoia about their lack of influence and are ready to snatch at anything – like a change in title – that might enhance their status.

There is a more substantive difference that needs to be explored, even though the nature and degree of the difference remain largely matters of opinion rather than fact, and the similarities are much greater than the differences.

Personnel management is *workforce-centred*, directed mainly at the organization's employees; finding and training them, arranging for them to be paid, explaining management's expectations, justifying management's actions, satisfying employees' work-related needs, dealing with their problems and seeking to modify management action that could produce unwelcome employee response. The people who work in the organization are the starting point, and they are a resource that is relatively inflexible in comparison with other resources like cash and materials.

Although indisputably a management function, personnel is never totally identified with management interests, as it becomes ineffective when not able to understand and articulate the aspirations and views of the workforce, just as sales representatives have to understand and articulate the aspirations of the customers. There is always some degree of being in between the management and the employees, mediating the needs of each to the other. Thomason quotes from both Miller and Spates to express this idea:

> Miller argues that the personnel management role is 'different from other staff jobs in that it has to serve not only the employer, but also act in the interests of employees as individual human beings, and by extension, the interests of society' (Miller 1975). Similarly, Spates finds a conception of the personnel management role which provides a place for the goals and aspirations of workers. . . . For him, the function of personnel administration is concerned with 'organizing and treating individuals at work so that they will get the greatest possible realization of their intrinsic abilities, thus attaining maximum efficiency for themselves and their group and thereby giving to the concern of which they are a part its determining competitive advantage and its optimum results'. (Thomason 1981, p. 38)

Human resources management is resource-centred, directed mainly at management needs for human resources (not necessarily employees) to be provided and deployed. Demand rather than supply is emphasized. There is greater emphasis on planning, monitoring and control, rather than mediation. Problem-solving is with other members of management on human resource issues rather than directly with employees or their representatives. It is totally identified with management interests, being a general management activity, and is relatively distant from the workforce as a whole, as employee interests can only be enhanced through effective overall management.

Underpinning personnel management are the twin ideas that people have a right to proper treatment as dignified human beings while at work, that they are only effective as employees when their job-related personal needs are met, and that this will not happen without personnel management intervention in the everyday manager/subordinate relationships. Personnel managers are involved in a more direct way in the relationship between other managers and their subordinates, because the personnel aspects of management are often perceived by line managers as not central to their role.

Underpinning human resources management is the idea that management of human resources is much the same as any other aspect of management and an integral part of it and cannot be separated out for specialists to handle. People have a right to proper treatment as dignified human beings while at work, and they will be effective when their personal career and competence needs are met within a context of efficient management and a mutually respectful working relationship. The specialist role is directed towards getting the deployment of right numbers and skills at the right price, supporting other managers in their people management and contributing to major strategic change.

This is how we interpret the distinction between personnel management and human resources management, but the distinction is one over which there is much debate and uncertainty (see, for example, Torrington 1988; Guest 1989; Legge 1989; Sisson 1989). Legge provides the most scrupulous analysis and concludes that there is very little difference in fact between the two, but there are some differences that are important; first, that human resources management concentrates more on what is done to managers rather than on what is done by managers to other employees; second, that there is a more proactive role for line managers; and third, that there is a top management responsibility for managing culture. We return to all these matters later in the book.

It would be inaccurate to suggest that one approach has taken over from the other, just as it would be wrong to suggest that one is modern and the other old-fashioned, or that one is right and the other wrong. Both are usually present in one organization; sometimes in one person. This can cause tension and ambiguity. As an emphasis for the work of personnel specialists there is a tendency for human resources management to increase at the expense of personnel management, and we suggest the following reasons for this change:

1. The devolution of personnel duties to line managers means that more of the mediation and reconciliation of needs associated with personnel

management is being undertaken by line managers. Managers of all sorts are increasingly their own personnel managers as part of a tendency for all managers to become more general ('all-singing, all-dancing') than specialized in their responsibilities.

2. With widespread unemployment, much temporary and part-time working, a gradual reduction in normal working hours and a shortening of the working lifetime, the workplace is not quite as significant as a source of personal self-esteem and as an arena for achieving personal objectives, as it was 10–15 years ago. When full-time employment is an experience shared by all for most of their adult lives, then it is the source of most opportunities and the means of self-actualization. Now it is an experience which a significant minority do not share at all and a further significant minority only experience in the 'peripheral workforce' (see Chapter 10). Even those employed full-time in 'proper jobs' probably spend no more than 20 per cent of their time for half their lifetime at work. In this situation the meeting of personal goals at work is a prospect denied to many and an instrumental orientation to work becomes more common.

3. Personnel specialists have long sought organizational power, as we saw from Legge's analysis in Chapter 1. What she described as conformist innovation has been one of the main ways in which this has been achieved: close identification with central management interests. Human resources management theoretically provides a repositioning of the personnel function to make it more influential.

4. There is an ever-increasing range of mini-expertise needed within the personnel area. In the opening chapter we showed how the range of activities covered by the function has tended to expand and that range of activities requires a wide variety of specialist knowledge. The law is the most obvious of these additions, including the areas of concern that have a dimension based on law, such as equal opportunity, but there has also been growing involvement with organizational change, pensions, statutory and occupational sick pay, more sophisticated approaches to payment, the Youth Training Scheme, and the application of the computer. This leads to an increasing use of external resources, reinforcing the tendency for personnel managers to become deployers of resources and knowledgeable about sources, rather than just deployers of skills and knowledgeable about people.

5. The reduced assertiveness of most trade unions has made industrial action less likely. At the same time there has been some tendency to develop alternative modes of deploying human resources, as described in Chapters 4 and 5.

6. The economic recession of the late 1970s and early 1980s stimulated management concern with immediate survival at the expense of longer-term development. As the recession eased there was a tendency for new companies to grow very quickly, again emphasizing the benefits of

Table 2.1 Responses from 350 questionnaire respondents to the question; 'Which of the following manpower costs are regularly calculated and considered?'

Item	Number of mentions
Remuneration (pay, pensions, etc.)	325
Training costs	250
Support costs (canteens, welfare, etc.)	206
Recruitment costs	193
Personnel administration costs	173
Relocation costs	172
Leaving costs	74

working at the here-and-now rather than contemplating the future. This has usually been accompanied by a narrow human resource management approach with a greater emphasis on the present and avoidance of long-term commitments other than to key personnel.

7. The emphasis of employment legislation has shifted away from employee rights towards union containment, so lessening the degree of management anxiety about this 'frightener'.

8. There is an increasing need for personnel activities to be justified in cost terms, as, for instance, in the direct charging for internal training events, so that the training function operates in the same way as an external supplier, with the same need constantly to justify its activities. The gradual advance in the application of computerization makes it easier for costs, or notional costs, to be attached to an increasing range of activities that were previously part of general overheads.

Review topic 2.1

List the attractions and drawbacks to you personally of holding a personnel management job and a human resources job.

	Personnel	Human resources
Attractions	_____	_____
	_____	_____
	_____	_____
	_____	_____
	_____	_____
Drawbacks	_____	_____
	_____	_____
	_____	_____
	_____	_____

We deliberately place this comment last out of eight, as 20 per cent of our research respondents stated that it was not desirable to cost out the activities of the personnel function, 34 per cent said it was not feasible, and only 37 per cent said it was actually done. Table 2.1 shows the items that were regularly calculated.

Professionalism

Related to the personnel/human resources emphasis is the question of professionalism. Can personnel management be described as a profession?

What constitutes professionalism for personnel specialists? Some people seem to think that professionalism is a synonym for efficiency or skill, but it is most fully described by Geoffrey Millerson (1964), who examined the lists of characteristics suggested by over twenty different commentators to produce the six features that are mentioned more than any others:

1. A profession involves a skill based on theoretical knowledge.
2. The skill requires training and education.
3. The professional must demonstrate competence by passing a test.
4. Integrity is maintained by adherence to a code of conduct.
5. The service is for the public good.
6. The profession is organized.

These characteristics are demonstrated in such occupations as law, medicine and the Church, and their possession gives their holder a degree of independence and standing in society, which is much envied. Other occupations demonstrate some, but not all, of these characteristics. Social workers, nurses and schoolteachers, for instance, are sometimes referred to as semi-professionals or – even worse – quasi-professionals.

What is the position of personnel managers? They meet most of these criteria, and many individuals would claim strongly that they meet criterion 5, but there is no generally accepted and enforced code of conduct. If we follow through the personnel/human resources distinction, we can suggest that personnel management potentially can have the independence and authority of a profession, but human resources management cannot, as it is inevitably an integral part of general management and the job holder becomes a manager first and a personnel specialist second. We found many of our research respondents had achieved recognition at the highest levels of management, but the penalty for this recognition was a disassociation from the personnel function: many of our respondents were undoubtedly managers first and personnel practitioners second. They were tending to withdraw from being identified as personnel professionals and seeking a closer identification with general management.

They wished to be seen as professional in their approach to the organization but to reduce the emphasis on being members of the personnel function (Torrington and Mackay 1986).

The importance of this question is not to satisfy an academic argument about the precise role of personnel specialists, but to consider the nature of their contribution and of their effectiveness. The expertise of human resources management is the same as that of managers in general. The expertise of personnel management is distinctive and the nature of the personnel position in the organization is different from that of other posts. Furthermore, employees and prospective employees have expectations of personnel management which will not be met by human resources management.

The relationship of personnel to other management functions

If personnel is to maintain a distinctive quality as a management function, it must not only have a distinctive contribution to make, it must also have a working relationship with other functions which enables that contribution to be made.

Personnel specialists, like most members of management, talk solemnly about needing support 'from the top'. They often believe that without the endorsement of the chief executive they have no influence. This is not simple sycophancy, as the affairs of the organization do not of necessity involve them, they are usually looking to make an intervention and are apprehensive about being bypassed. Endorsement from the most powerful person available eases the intervention and makes other people likely to seek it, as they too wish to be looked upon with favour from on high.

The danger of this strategy is that they become over-dependent on the goodwill of an individual and run the risk of antagonizing other colleagues with whom it is necessary to work on an everyday basis. Pratt and Bennett suggest that the staff specialist will often be younger than the line manager, who

> may feel threatened by the younger man's apparent technical expertise, particularly in areas where the line manager is not thoroughly acquainted with recent developments. . . . The specialist is considered to have the ear of senior management and is thus somebody to be handled with greater circumspection than normally justified by his status. (Pratt and Bennett 1985, p. 10)

Personnel people are also often seen as imposers of administrative burdens, asking for information, requiring procedures to be followed and inventing time-consuming activities like performance appraisal, or promulgating soft and distracting issues like equal opportunity or job redesign.

This type of problem has been exacerbated by the traditional split of the organization's managers into two categories: line managers with 'real' responsibilities for getting things done, like marketing, manufacturing and invoicing; and staff managers who have 'only' advisory roles, providing assistance to the line managers without actually being subordinate to them. That distinction is getting more and more blurred as all managers become progressively more general in the range of their responsibilities and more specialized in the nature of their expertise.

The personnel manager is always dependent on expertise and has to earn the ready co-operation of all employees because of that expertise. This is invaluable in a conventional bureaucracy and essential in the more flexible, 'modern' organizations that are beginning to emerge (see Chapter 6).

Support from the top is not only an illogical idea, it is an inadequate basis for action.

Staffing and organization of the personnel function

Personnel departments vary considerably in size from one person only up to several hundreds. Table 2.2 shows the distribution of numbers of subordinates reported by our questionnaire respondents, showing that half of them had between one and four direct subordinates and nearly a quarter had more than twenty-five.

Table 2.2 Responses from 350 questionnaire respondents to the questions: 'How many subordinates report directly to you?' and 'How many report to your subordinates?'

	Directly to you		To your subordinates	
	%	No.	%	No.
None	8.3	29.0	39.7	139.0
1–4	52.3	153.0	10.6	37.0
5–9	30.0	105.0	9.4	33.0
10–24	5.4	19.0	15.1	53.0
25+	0.6	2.0	22.0	77.0
Not given	3.4	12.0	3.1	11.0
Mean		3.4		4.0

We examined forty-two organization charts of the personnel function in different establishments and found that in every case jobs were defined on a functional basis (employee relations manager, recruitment officer, management development adviser, and so forth) or as general responsibilities, such as personnel manager, factory personnel officer, group personnel manager, or manager, human resources. The most significant influence on the organization of the personnel function seems to be either the degree of centralization or the degree of attenuation.

The degree of centralization is an issue affecting only larger organizations. Sisson and Scullion (1985) reported on research in the largest 100 companies in the United Kingdom to show that some companies have very large corporate personnel departments, others have a small head office team, others have a single executive, and others have no corporate personnel activity at all. They explain this in terms of whether or not the management at the centre have retained responsibility for a number of aspects of operating management that are critical as well as discharging responsibility for strategic management. If personnel is a critical function in which a common approach is needed because of the organization being in a single business, like Marks & Spencer or Ford, then there will be a strong corporate personnel function. In the multidivisional corporation, there is not the same logical need for strong centralization.

The degree of attenuation is a more localized issue stemming from making the business leaner and fitter. The organization retains a senior personnel manager with significant rank and responsibility but little specialist support at middle to senior management levels and a personnel administration manager keeping excellent records and dealing with a host of routine matters. The degree of attenuation varies, but the greater it is the fewer specialist roles there will be. Though there are no standard forms of organization, three samples are shown in Figures 2.1, 2.2 and 2.3.

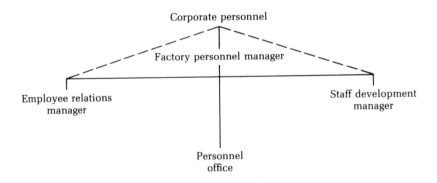

Figure 2.1 *Sample structure of the personnel function in an establishment that is part of an organization with a strong corporate personnel department*

Figure 2.1 shows the situation of a personnel department in a subsidiary of an organization with a strong corporate personnel function determining most policy questions and maintaining consistency of practice across a number of different establishments. Figure 2.2 is in an establishment of similar size, but

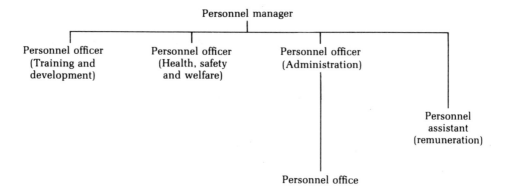

Figure 2.2 *Sample structure of the personnel function in an autonomous establishment*

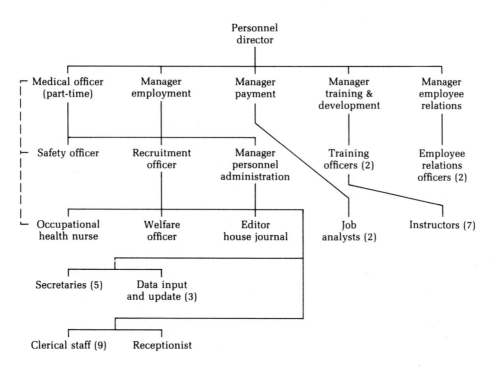

Figure 2.3 *Sample structure of the personnel function in a large, integrated organization*

without the significant central direction. Figure 2.3 is a well-developed, independent function in a large, integrated organization. Notice the dotted lines in Figure 2.1, indicating split accountability between the local manager and head office.

Review topic 2.2

Sketch a rough organization chart of the personnel function in your establishment. Consider the degree of attenuation and centralization of personnel activities in the organization. What effect do they have on the roles and distribution of responsibility among members of the personnel function? How would roles and distribution of responsibility change with a change in the degree of attenuation or centralization?

Most job holders within the personnel function carry several responsibilities. The following are some of the most common job titles and the duties attaching to them.

Personnel Manager/Director This is the general manager in charge of the personnel function, who acts as its figurehead and main spokesperson, representing personnel issues in all senior management discussions and policy-making. There are usually one or more specialist responsibilities attaching to the post, with employee relations being the most common. In Figure 2.2, for instance, the personnel manager is responsible for employee relations and all pay matters. This is the role, together with most of those that follow, for which the Institute of Personnel Management's membership examinations provide the most appropriate and widely regarded qualification.

Personnel Officer In most establishments this is the title of the person who deals with all personnel issues, being a second type of generalist role. In larger establishments it is a general title with a specific explanatory responsibility following in brackets. Figure 2.2 again provides an example.

Employee Relations Manager The most common specialist role is that dealing with the collective relationship between management and employees, especially where this is formalized through union recognition and procedure agreements. This role is one where formal qualifications, such as degrees and diplomas in industrial relations, may be appropriate as an addition to IPM qualifications.

Training and Development Manager   Another strong tradition is to specialize responsibility for training and employee development, although there is an increasing tendency to emphasize one aspect by having a training department with training officers reporting to a management development manager, who will deal with development matters by heavy reliance on outside facilities, such as consultants.

Training Officers   Training officers have similar responsibilities to personnel officers in that they may be single trainers with general training duties in an establishment, or they may be charged with specific training tasks, like operator training. Formal qualifications in organizational or occupational psychology are often held by training specialists, and IPM stage 2 qualifications devote one third of the total syllabus to this area, as well as providing specialist options.

Recruitment and Selection Managers/Officers   These are not as widespread as they were and usually these duties are the regular part-time responsibility of several people in a personnel department, yet the work remains highly skilled and many large organizations still retain specialist personnel, usually with an occupational psychology background expertise.

Human Resource Planner   This is a much less clear job title with many variations, like 'manpower analyst', which is used to describe someone whose expertise is basically in manpower planning and statistics, and who will do much of the preliminary work on personnel planning and strategy.

Organization Development Consultant   This role specializes in enabling the organization to adapt to its changing environment and its members to develop their roles to meet the new challenges and opportunities that are emerging. It is a job with few administrative features and is usually held by someone with an independent, roving commission.

Safety Officer/Welfare Officer   The area of health, safety and welfare is one where there are strong legal constraints on employer action. Of our 350 questionnaire respondents, 289 were in establishments where there was someone with specific responsibility for health and safety, but only 154 of them were part of the personnel function: a surprisingly low proportion. Eighty-five respondents (a surprisingly high proportion) had someone whose sole responsibility was welfare.

Personnel Administration Manager   The final role in this sample list is a long-standing one, which is changing direction. There is some tendency for personnel administration to increase, and a part of the expanding numbers in personnel departments is in the clerical/administrative/keyboard area, with the demands of such tasks as statutory sick pay and the need to maintain a personnel database on the computer. This part of the operation is run by someone who used to be called 'office manager', but who is now more to be described as 'personnel administration manager'.

Differential emphasis in personnel work

In our questionnaire we asked a series of questions to find out how our respondents distributed their time between different areas of personnel work, the amount of discretion they enjoyed, the importance, and the changes in importance, of these activities. Table 2.3 shows these four indicators side by side and enables us to draw several conclusions. First, employee relations is clearly pre-eminent, and recruitment and selection and training both figure promi- nently as these are terms widely used to define areas of specialist expertise. Secondly, there is a tendency for respondents to indicate high discretion in activities that are not high on importance, and low discretion on activities that are important.

Table 2.3 Ranking of personnel activities against four criteria

	Discretion (a)	Time spent (b)	Importance (c)	Increase in importance (d)
Employee relations	1	1	1	3
Recruitment/selection	2	2	2	10
Training	3	3	3	2
Discipline/grievance	4	6	5	9
Health/safety/welfare	5	9	11	11
Appraisal	6	2	9	8
Redundancy/dismissal	7	10	8	7
Job evaluation	8	13	12	11
Organization/management	9	4	7	4
Payment administration	10	5	10	13
Manpower planning	11	8	4	1
Changes in work organization	12	7	6	6
New technology	13	11	13	5
Fringe benefits	14	14	14	14

1 = highest, 14 = lowest

Three hundred and fifty questionnaire respondents were asked four questions:

1. How much discretion would you say the personnel function has over settling matters concerned with the following?
2. Approximately what percentage of your time is spent on the following matters?
3. How would you rank the activities in terms of their importance in the

contribution made by the personnel function to organizational objectives in the last three years?

4. To what extent has this importance changed in the last three years?

Evaluation and future of the personnel function

The members of any personnel function need to evaluate their activities regularly to ensure that they are achieving what they wish to achieve and fulfilling expectations held of them. The appendix to this chapter suggests a way of conducting a regular personnel audit.

How the personnel function will change in the future is a subject that has produced regular prognostications, like those of Chapter 1, for many years. We conclude this chapter by suggesting, not how it may change, but some of the main issues that personnel specialists will be facing.

The quality of working life

In the early 1980s there was great interest in improving the quality of working life and it was a salient personnel activity. This emphasis faded in face of the twin pressures of providing work rather than improving its quality, and developing greater organizational efficiency rather than 'looking after people'. The short-term emphasis of what some called 'macho' management has not found many adherents, and there is renewed concern to provide terms and conditions of employment that will constitute a salient feature of a corporate culture which delivers employee commitment. It is not quite clear what quality people will expect in their working lives in the future, nor what quality will engender the working performance that organizational needs for efficiency will require.

The development of skill

We receive apocalyptic warnings about skill shortages as often as we hear that the ozone layer is damaged:

> The general perception that Britain has lagged behind competitors in this area has led to concern that, in the long term, British firms will become increasingly unable to compete with overseas rivals, particularly where competition turns on non-price factors such as reliability of delivery and product quality and design. Training and education are now seen as one of the main structural problems that underlie the relative weakness of the British economy. (Keep 1989, p. 198)

The late 1980s saw great excitement about a possible sea-change in management education to base it on competences rather than knowledge. But how will personnel management respond to the general and continuing problem that we seem unable to develop the skills, capacities and competences that are needed, not only to make us nationally competitive, but also to provide meaning and worth to the jobs people do?

The agency possibility

The increasing use of consultants and external sources raises the possibility of a human resources agency, like an advertising agency. Businesses use advertising agencies instead of employing their own specialists so that they can choose between alternatives, knowing that the agency will develop expertise through servicing a number of different, non-competing clients. It is also possible to demonstrate or infer a connection between expenditure and results. For some time employment agencies have provided a specialist service based on a partial cornering of the market in certain types of transferable skill. Management selection consultants can provide a level of technical expertise and experience in selection that few companies can match because the companies can never collect the volume of psychological test results, for instance, to produce occupational norms. Training and management development are activities that can at least partly be contracted out on the basis that an external body has greater expertise. It is difficult to see how a personnel agency could work, but we are seeing the development of various agencies to meet a part of an organization's human resources requirements.

Internationalization

Personnel management has remained one of the most culturally constrained management activities, with British practice being applicable within a framework of British law, traditions and social conventions. As the continent of Europe gradually reduces barriers between countries, so the degree of cultural constraint becomes less. Not only will personnel managers have to adapt practice and procedure to meet new (Europe-wide) legal requirements, they will also have to develop practices to deal with a wider range of nationalities seeking employment in British companies in Britain.

Summary propositions

2.1 As an emphasis for the work of personnel specialists there is a tendency for human resources management to increase and for personnel management to decline.

2.2 The expertise of human resources management is similar to that of managers in general. The expertise of personnel management is distinctive and the nature of the personnel position in organizations is different from other management posts.

2.3 The most significant influences on the organization of personnel functions are the degrees of centralization and attenuation.

2.4 Personnel specialists tend to enjoy high discretion on matters of moderate importance and low discretion on matters of increasing importance.

2.5 Among the main issues facing personnel specialists in the future are the quality of working life, the development of skill, the agency possibility and internationalization.

References

Guest, D.E. (1989), 'Personnel and HRM – Can you tell the difference?' *Personnel Management*, vol. 21, no. 1, January.

Keep, E. (1989), 'A training scandal?' In K. Sisson (ed.), *Personnel Management in Britain*, Oxford: Basil Blackwell.

Legge, K. (1989), 'Human resource management: a critical analysis.' In J. Storey (ed.) *New Perspectives on Human Resource Management*, London: Routledge.

Millerson, G. (1964), *The Qualifying Associations*, London: Routledge & Kegan Paul.

Pratt, K. J. and Bennett, S. G. (1989). *Elements of Personnel Management* (revised 2nd edition), Wokingham: Van Nostrand Reinhold.

Sisson, K. (1989), 'Personnel management in perspective' and 'Personnel management in transition', in *Personnel Management in Britain*, Oxford: Basil Blackwell, pp. 3–40.

Sisson, K. and Scullion, H. (1985), 'Putting the corporate personnel department in its place', *Personnel Management*, December.

Thomason, G. (1981), *A Textbook of Personnel Management* (4th edition), London: Institute of Personnel Management.

Torrington, D. P. (1989), 'How does human resources management change the personnel function?' *Personnel Review*, vol. 17, no. 6.

Torrington, D. P. and Mackay, L. E. (1986), 'Will consultants take over the personnel function?' *Personnel Management*, February.

Appendix: The personnel audit

Personnel policy

1. Is there a general personnel policy that is endorsed, understood, implemented and up-to-date?

2. Are there policies in all the appropriate specific areas of personnel activity that are endorsed, understood, implemented and up-to-date?
3. Is there a need for any of these policies to be more widely endorsed or distributed?
4. Are any new policies needed?

Organization

1. Is the overall structure of the organization appropriate to the current position of the business?
2. Is any change needed in any division or department of the business to align it more accurately to the rest of the business or to some recent change in circumstances?
3. Do structure and culture match?
4. Are there any problems of size, age or setting of the organizational units?
5. Are there any problems of individual job definition, operating procedures, span of control, decision-making complexes or integration?
6. Are there managers who are successfully managing the task, but not successfully managing the people?

Communication

1. Are any improvements needed in the formal systems of communications through the business?
2. Can the informal systems of communication be made more effective or used more constructively?
3. Is the general level of political activity within the organization satisfactory?
4. Can the balance between face-to-face and distance communication (paper and electronic) be improved?

Manpower administration

1. Is the current situation in the various labour markets understood?
2. Is there a manpower plan to provide a basis for personnel strategy that is related to the corporate plan, that is implemented and under constant review?
3. Are there alternative forms of employment contract available to ensure flexibility of staffing?
4. Is job analysis used to produce the different types of job description and other job analysis derivatives needed for various applications?

5. Does the recruitment procedure provide satisfactory control of establishment numbers, recruitment costs, speed and effectiveness?
6. Do any of the selection methods used need alteration?
7. Is the safety policy implemented and producing a satisfactory safety record?
8. Does the record of employee sickness absence suggest that there is any organizational factor contributing to this absence that could be overcome?
9. Are the procedures for ensuring equality of opportunity within the organization operating satisfactorily?
10. Does monitoring of the equal opportunity procedures show that they are being effective?
11. Are the procedures for grievance and discipline operating satisfactorily?
12. Is the organization adequately protected against possible tribunal claims of unfair dismissal?

Training and development

1. Are the principles of learning understood within the training function, and is there knowledge about the full range of training methods and resources currently available that might meet the organization's needs?
2. Is training effectiveness evaluated?
3. Is access to training facilities by individual employees adequate?
4. Is performance appraisal used to enhance current performance?
5. Is promotion geared to performance?
6. Is training and development providing the personnel at all levels the organization needs, and is it preparing the personnel the organization will need in the future?

Employee relations

1. Is the present position on trade union recognition satisfactory?
2. Are the present arrangements for employee participation in management decision-making satisfactory?
3. Are the facilities for employee representatives satisfactory?
4. Are the union agreements up-to-date or in need of renegotiation?

Pay

1. Are the wage payment systems and structures satisfactory?
2. Are the systems of salary structure and administration satisfactory?
3. Is there a need for the extension, alteration or reduction of job evaluation?
4. Is the cost of sickness payment adequately controlled?

5. Are pension arrangements satisfactory and satisfactorily administered?
6. Are the arrangements for benefits and incentives worth the money spent on them and satisfactorily administered?

Miscellaneous

1. How much general influence does personnel have in the organization?
2. How much administrative control does personnel have?
3. Is the best use being made of consultants and other external resources?
4. Is the best use being made of the computer and its modelling facility?
5. How socially responsible is the organization?
6. What are the three most important initiatives you have taken in the last twelve months? Have they been successful?
7. What are the three most important initiatives you will take in the next twelve months? Why will you take them? Will they be successful?

Personnel policy and strategy

The word 'policy' causes more confusion than clarity among managers as it means so many different things to different people, and any discussion of the issues lying behind policy formulation requires careful definition of terms. There is also need for close attention to implementation, as many declarations of policy seldom get beyond the stage of being agreed in principle.

In this chapter we first consider the nature of policy and the reasons for having it. We then examine the nature of personnel policies, how they are formulated, how they fit with other features, such as strategy and planning, and how they are made to work.

The nature of policy and its value

Our definition of policy is *a declared mode of action for the future*. In everyday conversation we hear people state that honesty is the best policy, or we ask politicians to state their policy on nuclear disarmament or law and order, or we note the claim of an organization to be an equal opportunity employer. Features of policy we find in business organizations include decisions on whether to manufacture or buy in, whether or not to enter a new market or introduce a new product. There are policy discussions about the timing of a share issue, the recognition of trade unions, trading in South Africa or manufacturing under licence from the Japanese.

The main aspect of all these policy discussions is the concern with the future rather than the past. The objective is to set a framework within which action can be taken, it is not to analyze what has gone wrong in the past – though that may be a preliminary to the policy formulation. Often people in an organization await a policy statement before they can make progress with day-to-day matters, so that the policy is a framework within which other people operate, using their own discretion and making their own decisions. It is not the same as an instruction, which is much more precise, allowing scant discretion.

There is not much point in determining a policy as a framework for action by others if the policy is not known to the others, so the other part of our definition is that the policy is declared. Once the policy is known, it is likely to be criticized, and may be undermined by opponents, so managers may be reluctant to make statements of policy on certain matters – like trade union recognition – in order to avoid the arguments and problems that the statement could cause.

Personnel policy and strategy

Although this chapter is mainly concerned with personnel policy, it would not be complete without a reference to *personnel strategy*. The distinction between strategy and policy is seldom clear, although strategy is usually related to planning what is to be achieved, and policy is the framework within which the plans to implement the strategy will be put into operation.

Stoner and Wankel provide contrasted definitions:

> [Strategy is] . . . the broad program for defining and achieving an organization's objectives; the organization's response to its environment over time. (Stoner and Wankel 1986, p. 695)

> A policy is a general guideline for decision-making. It sets up boundaries around decisions, including those that can be made and shutting out those that cannot. In this way it channels the thinking of organization members so that it is consistent with organizational objectives. Some policies deal with very important matters, like those requiring strict sanitary conditions where food or drugs are produced or packaged. Others may be concerned with relatively minor issues, such as the way the employees dress. (Stoner and Wankel 1986, p. 91)

A further dimension to the strategy idea is provided by Miller:

> strategy is a market-oriented concept: it is fundamentally concerned with products and competitive advantage. Furthermore it is a stratified concept: it is found at different levels in the organization. Thus we may expect to find a *business level* strategy, or perhaps a *functional* level strategy, linked to and dependent on the corporate strategy. (Miller 1989, p. 49)

There are many advantages of a strategic approach to planning, as is described in the next chapter. There is a clear sense of direction and focus on where the business is going. From that clear sense of direction can stem specific objectives, the collation of necessary information, the anticipation of problems and the assessment of strengths, weaknesses and opportunities. Because of the emphasis on analysis and precision there is a tendency for strategists to concentrate on economic data and overlook the way in which people and their values can influence the implementation – or failure to implement – a chosen strategy: 'corporate strategy is . . . concerned with what people want organizations to do . . . the aspirations, expectations, attitudes and personal philosophies which people hold' (Johnson and Scholes 1984, p. 116).

With the increasing number of pressure groups expressing various types of social concern, there are many issues of management strategy that come under public scrutiny, from the dumping of nuclear waste and the use of ozone-friendly materials to the methods of selling timeshare apartments. As those working in organizations become more selective in their employment, management approaches to strategy have to be highly sensitive to matters of public concern, not just to meet customer expectations, but also to avoid offending those of their own employees who may well be members of the pressure groups scrutinizing the organization's strategy.

Inside the business the values to constrain strategy are manifested in trade union organization, in professional groupings and in coalitions of interest which develop, particularly in response to perceived threat. The interest in organizational culture is partly an attempt to get a closer fit between the values of the various stakeholders in the business and the objectives of that business. Strategy is one expression of how that fit is achieved; policy is another.

In today's changing business environment, there is an increasing need for personnel specialists to stop focusing on short-term, tactical 'fire-fighting' and to direct their efforts towards long-term, strategic planning. As Georgiades explains: 'The focus shifts from throwing lifebelts to drowning people, to walking upstream and finding out who is throwing them off the bridge and why' (Georgiades 1990, p. 44). His organizational model emphasizes a move on the part of personnel specialists towards organizational interventions, focusing on issues of leadership, human resorce management strategy and organizational culture. Such a move is seen as enhancing personnel's ability to contribute directly to corporate goals. Examples of such interventions can be found in Yeandle and Clark (1989) and Carolin and Evans (1988).

A framework for management action

There is no clear-cut distinction between policy and other parts of the management process, so we need to set policy-making in a framework of management action, shown in Figure 3.1.

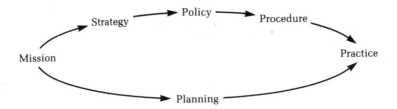

Figure 3.1   *A framework for management action*

- *Mission*: What is the organization for? Where is it going? The general mission of the business is a matter on which the members of the organization will talk for hours and seldom come to a conclusion, but it is the precursor of policy and depends on an appreciation of both the expertise within the business and the nature of customer or client needs that could be met. It is general and visionary.

  At one time the mission of British American Tobacco was to manufacture and distribute tobacco products, but that has now broadened and later narrowed once more. Newspaper barons broaden their mission to encompass television interests, and railroad businesses declare themselves to be in transportation. A business may modify its purpose to include manufacturing as well as marketing, or it may drop manufacture to concentrate on marketing.
- *Strategy*: The overriding mission is then continuously implemented by developing a programme of initiatives to define and achieve the organization's objectives.
- *Policy*: The overall mission and strategy are guided by a series of policies to channel decision and action, shaping the organization and providing the direction that is needed.
- *Procedures*: Procedures are more familiar to personnel managers than to most management specialists as they form the substance of much industrial relations activity, but in our action framework they have the more general meaning of being the drills that implement the policy, so that a policy decision to advertise all vacancies within the organization before external advertising begins is implemented by a procedure to specify who does what, in what order, when and with what authorization or other trigger to action.
- *Planning*: Strategy, policy and procedures can all be co-ordinated and moved into action by planning. Not only does each stage benefit from planning, but a planning approach can ensure that all three are thought through and put into operation together.
- *Practice*: The final element is what actually happens. No organization has a procedure for everything, and no procedure is so comprehensive as to rule

out the need for interpretation and judgement. Practice is a mixture of implemented procedure, *ad hoc* decision, reaction to policy, and the ebb and flow of interaction between the organization and its environment. The effectiveness of policy can only be determined by the practice that ensues. We shall never know how good was Lord Raglan's policy for the Battle of Balaklava because he made a mess of it by sending inaccurate instructions to his troops, who undertook the suicidal Charge of the Light Brigade. The proof of the pudding . . .

These six elements have very blurred edges between them. Sometimes there is policy that bears no relationship to mission, sometimes there is a procedure that has been devised without a policy to inform it, and frequently there is practice without procedure, but by identifying these discrete elements we can see more clearly the nature of the policy step.

The reasons for having policies

Statements of policy produce problems for the policy-maker. If your policy does not work very well, you are criticized for incompetence. If your policy is disliked, you become unpopular and your enemies try to undermine your policy initiative. If your policy is accepted by others, you have very little scope for changing it or trying to forget it. Why do managers bother with policy statements? Would it not be simpler just to make decisions on matters as they arise, 'treating each case on its merits', rather than being bound by the straitjacket of a declared position? Here are six reasons why managers try to use statements of policy.

Clarification

There are always managers who want to make things clear to their colleagues. A manager wishing to get senior colleagues to agree an increased departmental budget will have to set out the policy that the budget increase will be used to implement. A wish to spend £50,000 for new equipment will only be supported if there is a convincing case made of policy for its use.

A manager wanting to increase the amount of responsibility assumed by subordinates will only achieve this if there are clear guidelines for the delegation of that responsibility. Clarification of policy is one means of making that delegation possible.

Reducing dependence on individuals

The development of a strong (but not inflexible) policy framework makes an organization less dependent on the knowledge and judgement of individuals. Most readers will have heard something like one of the following:

> 'If there's anything you want to know about recruitment, ask Charlie. He's got it all at his finger tips.'

> 'We can't make a move on this until we've got the all-clear from the boss.'

> 'Mary really is marvellous at controlling the debtors. She keeps it all in her head and we'd be lost without her.'

Splendid individuals are no substitute for sound policies.

Producing consistent managerial behaviour

Policies can also provide a useful discipline for managers, as they have to behave in a consistent way, avoiding capricious changes of direction and bewildering their colleagues. It is important to distinguish between policy and precedent. Personnel managers are nearly as keen on precedents as are trade union officials, but this is using as a framework for action what has happened in the past instead of what should happen in the future. Imaginative and realistic policy-making is a way of breaking out from the cage of doing things tomorrow in the same way as they were done yesterday, because that is the only security available. Precedents look back: policies look forward.

At first some managers carp about the need to behave consistently, but they soon find that the policy framework's limitation on their own whimsicality prevents them wasting energy thinking up new strategies for problems they have already solved and builds a progressively more positive response from their colleagues.

Specialists seeking power

When a new recruit to the management pantheon is trying to establish a power-base, the ability to form policy is the ideal support. First, because policy-making is the management activity carrying the greatest status; and second, because policy usually delimits the power of others. If you need organizational power to be effective, a stake in policy-making is an essential prerequisite.

Knowing 'where we stand'

There is a growing expectation among members of organizations to be supplied with information. Much of this relates to security of employment and management intentions. Without statements of management policy, employees will assume adherence to management precedent. Whenever there is a new development, managers want to know where they stand as their individual policy platform will have been affected and they will quickly want to know what repairs and redevelopments are needed.

Responding to legal and other external pressures

Finally, there is the organizational response to changes in the law and similar external influences. When a new piece of legislation appears on the statute book, managers wait for policy guidance on its influence. An example is the 1984 Data Protection Act. This had received extensive media coverage for years prior to its enactment and thousands of managers must have attended one-day conferences about its implications, but for each organization there was the need for working out a policy to ensure consistent compliance with its provisions.

Review topic 3.1

What is the purpose of your organization? Is there any value in policy statements that are vague, for example: 'It is our policy to provide attractive terms and conditions of employment for all employees'? Is it necessary for a policy to be written down?

The nature of personnel policy

When we come to consider personnel policy as part of the total policy framework, there is again a problem about definition. We have found the following phrases, which seem to be used to mean the same thing: personnel policy, manpower policy, employment policy, human resources policy, employee relations policy, industrial relations policy.

Workshops of personnel directors at the Henley Centre for Employment Policy Studies have produced this definition:

> An overall employment strategy which integrates the organization's various personnel policies and manpower plans. It should enable it to meet and absorb the changing requirements of technology and markets in the foreseeable future. (Rothwell 1984, p. 30)

There we see a distinction between employment policy, which is a statement of overall strategy, and personnel policies to deal with specific matters. We are not sure about that two-step approach, as we have collected several dozen policy statements in the course of our research and find very few that incorporate an overarching statement that is more than just a ringing phrase. There is, however, a risk of separate policies, which are not compatible or out of date:

> Too often what companies talk of as their employment policy is in reality a set of free-floating personnel policies, often developed in the '60s and '70s, most of which continue regardless, unconnected with each other or the business plan. For example, ruthless redundancies may take place (when a long-term gradual reduction in line with business needs might have been implemented relatively painlessly) while benefit policies encouraging long service remain in existence. (*ibid.*, p. 31)

We find the most helpful definition of personnel policy to be a development of our earlier definition of policy. If policy is a declared mode of action for the future, then personnel policy can be defined as *a series of such declarations about management objectives in relation to employment within the organization*. There will be both the general and the specific, with considerable diversity. A policy about employee involvement will, for instance, be very different from a policy on youth training. Hawkins provides this summary of the theory of policy:

> The main purpose of a policy is to define the industrial relations objectives of the organization. Thus one test of the effectiveness of policy is the extent to which it provides managers who are responsible for industrial relations with a framework of general principles which they regard as helpful and within which they are able to act decisively on day-to-day problems. Without guidelines of some kind, managers may find it difficult to make decisions which are broadly consistent with each other, unless, of course, they are tightly controlled from the top. In many organizations, however, rigid centralization would be both structurally impracticable and, given the general preference for workplace autonomy, politically impossible. (Hawkins 1978, p. 72)

Personnel policies vary considerably from one organization to another, depending on the age of the organization, its size, the nature of the workforce and the position regarding union recognition, but here are the main policy areas:

- *Principles*: This is a statement about the general view by the management of employment in the organization. It is likely to carry ringing phrases about teamwork, fairness, innovation and opportunity, but may also include a declaration about the degree and method of employee involvement and the security of employment in different parts of the workforce. A helpful way of ensuring consistency is to include a brief summary of each personnel policy area that follows.
- *Staffing and development*: Here will be the specific undertakings to employees and the management strategies to be followed in appointing the most appropriate people, providing the opportunities for career growth and ensuring that employees develop their skills and capacities in line with the growth of the business. The main features of this policy area are how vacancies will be determined, where applicants will be sought and how decisions will be made in selection. There will be further sections on how promotions are made, training opportunities and requirements, as well as the use of performance appraisal and assessment centres.
- *Employee relations*: Policies in the area of employee relations will depend on the union recognition situation, but typical features are arrangements about recognition, bargaining units and union membership agreements, agreements relating to negotiation, consultation, shop steward representation, membership of joint committees, safety matters and points of reference, such as following national engineering agreements on the number of days' annual holiday.
- *Mutual control*: Several features of policy and related procedure deal with the working relationship between the organization and the employee or employees. These are mainly to deal with the approach to matters of grievance and discipline, but also the availability of information and methods of dealing with problems like possible redundancy.
- *Terms and conditions*: Policies relating to the individual contract of employment are surprisingly few, but are increasing. Traditionally, this has been an area where managements have been uninterested in policy because of the concern about *force majeure* and the constraint of precedent. Most terms and conditions of employment are still determined by collective bargaining or by statute, so that employers have seen the pressures from outside the organization on terms and conditions as being all directed towards pushing manpower costs up, so that the job of management was to resist: not to create the future, but to prevent it for as long as possible! Gradually, however, policies are being evolved to introduce greater variety into contractual arrangements in attempts to improve manpower utilization at the same time as providing more scope for individual employees to have some flexibility in their personal working arrangements.

    Aspects of terms and conditions policies are approaches to determining differentials in payment, levels of sick pay, pension provision, holidays, study leave and hours of work.

- *Equality of opportunity*: A different type of personnel policy is that relating to equality of opportunity. Theoretically, equalizing opportunity should be subsumed in all the other areas, but legislation and pressure groups have tended to identify this as an area needing separate treatment.

Devising policies

The two most common methods of devising personnel policies are both inadequate. One is to use the policy of another organization as a model; the other is to start with a blank piece of paper to produce something that sounds good. Copying from elsewhere usually means that the policy will be at best very vague and at worst inappropriate through having first been devised for a different situation. The inadequacy of starting with a blank piece of paper is that the writing is likely to reflect the values and prejudices of the author rather than the needs of the organization and its employees.

As a policy is only as good as the practice it produces, we offer a three-part rule for policy formulation:

1. Policy does not translate into effective practice without a commitment to both the policy and the measures needed to make it work.
2. Commitment is more likely when the policy develops out of issues in the organization itself, and
3. Where the policy is devised, and later sustained, by the involvement of all those affected by it.

If a policy is adopted independently of issues relevant to the organization, and not seen as relevant by members of the organization, then commitment is unlikely and the policy will probably not work. Personnel specialists could use the following procedure to devise policies:

- *Identify the topic*: Individual topics on which policy clarification is needed have to be identified and worked on when the time is ripe. One push will be changes in the law, like the Data Protection Act mentioned earlier; another will be a management initiative in some other policy framework, like an intention to double production, or introduce shiftwork, or to use performance appraisal to inform promotion decisions. Other pushes towards policy statements are questions from employees or other managers about where they stand, uncertainties about the future, unexpected change, review of the mission and strategic objectives of the business, or the many organizational muddles.

  In identifying the topic, one has to be sure that it is correctly identified and that a policy statement will be timely. Taking the Data Protection example again, it is little use developing a policy before the legislative details are clear or at a time when other people are saying that the matter lacks urgency.

- *Selling the idea*: Closely related to identifying the topic is getting support for the idea of a policy on that topic. This requires at least an expanded headline to show what should be achieved, and then provisional support for the idea is won through preliminary consultation and testing of reaction. This is the beginning of making sure that there will be commitment. The policy deviser will pick with care those to be consulted, mixing together those with political influence in the organization, so that their support will help produce the necessary political will for the policy to succeed, and those with expertise, so that there is an early input of constructive suggestions.

- *Determine the key features*: After the general idea has been accepted and shaped, there will be the key features of the policy to be determined. In the area of trade union recognition, the idea to be sold is whether or not to recognize. If the idea of recognition is accepted, the key features to be determined will be to decide which union to recognize and for what the union will be recognized – individual grievances only, terms and conditions of employment, manning levels or what?

  This stage is also dependent on effective consultation, so that the commitment is not lost and so that the personnel specialist develops the policy in a way that is relevant to real issues in the organization itself. The person promulgating the policy must at this stage have the nerve to abort the whole exercise or to make a completely fresh start, if general support cannot be sustained.

- *Agree the details*: The last stage is to agree the precise details of the policy statement, with all the implications for later interpretation and implementation. If the key features have been previously determined, then the detailed considerations can be carried through without the risk of jeopardizing what the policy is intended to achieve, but the importance of the details should not be ignored. During the 1984/5 British miners' strike there were several occasions when potential agreement on ending the strike foundered because of the inability of the two parties to agree on 'a form of words' about pit closures.

This simple, outline procedure begs two questions: Who does the drafting? With whom does that person consult? The first question has a straightforward answer. Devising a policy is a job to be centred on one person, who cannot only remain faithful to the original vision, but can also ensure a single style and coherence in the drafting, no matter how many different suggestions and points of view are eventually accommodated. That one person needs to 'own' the drafting of the policy, being seen by all observers as the owner, protecting it from the perils of committee writing when the clarity of the message and the thrust of the policy itself can be lost through the incorporation of unedited chunks from various sources seeking to guard a sectional interest.

Whom one should consult obviously depends on the subject of the policy, but we repeat that the involvement of those affected by the policy will improve its chances of translation into practice.

Implementing policies

There are four steps in putting the final policy into operation.

Publicity

If a policy is to work it must be known to, understood and accepted by those affected. Much of this will have been ensured by devising it properly, but those consultations will mainly have been with representatives of interests only, so there will still be individuals needing to understand and seek answers to their questions. Obviously it is not sufficient simply to send a copy to all concerned; briefing will be needed and possibly training sessions.

Some features of the policy will be unwelcome to some people, as it will involve changing aspects of current practice, so that the publicity, briefing and training need to win commitment, just as the stages of devising the policy in the first place have had that objective. Brewster and Richbell describe the difficulty personnel people face:

> Sometimes it seems as though a great many very talented personnel specialists are wasting an awful lot of time . . . they develop sensible, well thought-out policies that would make their company one of the most progressive and highly respected of employers. And then they see their efforts continually frustrated and subverted by a management team that seems determined to ignore most of what the personnel department does. (Brewster and Richbell 1982, p. 38)

Procedures

The procedures needed to implement the policy must be ready and correct. Procedural method is dealt with in Chapter 7. Seldom can a policy operate without some drill to help it along, like a form to be completed to log personal information held on computer, or a notification of who is empowered to halt a production process because of a health risk. If a policy is being accepted unwillingly, the procedure needs to be as simple and clear as possible to avoid making it even less popular.

Monitoring

Any policy initiative will drift away from the original intention unless its implementation is monitored. First, it has to be monitored for deliberate or accidental breaches. No matter how extensive the consultation and briefing, some managers will forget what they are supposed to do and some may try to avoid it. Secondly, there may be problems about the policy that had not been foreseen, and the first uncertainty will wing its way at high speed back to the person who took the policy initiative. If this type of issue can be spotted and dealt with quickly, the policy will be sustained and strengthened. If the breach is overlooked, there will be many more. If the problems are not resolved by the initiator, *ad hoc* and inconsistent strategies will evolve, thereby destroying one of the main intentions of policy formulation.

Increasingly, policy effectiveness can be assessed by quantitative means. The Commission for Racial Equality has been advocating for some time that organizations should monitor the racial and ethnic mix of employees to assess the effect of any equal opportunity policy that may be introduced. Although not a popular proposal, it is gradually being adopted and is best done through computerizing personnel records. Quantitative assessment is not, however, enough: 'while analytical and quantitative techniques are essential to the development of company employment policies, a qualitative, creative dimension is equally necessary to shape direction and purpose' (Rothwell 1984, p. 30).

Policy effectiveness has to be monitored by discussion, seeing and evaluating the number and type of problems that occur, and by 'walking the job'. We have constantly noticed in our research that the most satisfied, and perhaps the most effective, of the personnel managers with whom we have spoken place great emphasis on getting out of the office for informal walkabouts and chats with people. The computer terminal is no substitute for seeing for oneself.

Modifying

The point of monitoring policy is not just to be sure it is right, but also to modify it where it seems wrong. Though an obvious enough statement, policy modification is not simple. Those who initiate policy are often very reluctant to change it, because of the implied inadequacy of their original formulation. Also, modification requires even more consultation than formulation, as it is not only representatives with whom one must consult, but all those affected.

A further aspect of modifying is that policies become out-of-date, so that policy modification is not only correcting errors, it is also ongoing development of policy to suit changing situations and to create fresh opportunities.

Review topic 3.2

Devise a policy for the allocation of reserved parking places on your organization's premises. With whom would you consult? How would you publicize? What procedures would be needed to implement the policy?

Policy, formality and change

The earlier review topic in this chapter raised the question about whether or not policies need to be written down. The value of writing is the ease of implementation, the support for consistency and the basis for consultation. The problem about writing is that it involves the management in declaring a position that it may not wish to publicize, like a policy decision *not* to recognize trade unions. Also, there is the problem of change. A written, published policy is much harder to change than the informal understanding or strategy, and often that which is written differs from what is practised. Brewster and Richbell (1982) distinguish between policies that are 'espoused', being officially endorsed and often written, and 'operational' policies, which are the strategies that managers actually follow. The latter may deviate slightly or substantially from the former.

In many organizations, the personnel policies are all enshrined in agreements with trade unions. This is probably excellent for producing commitment, but written agreements can be very difficult indeed to change.

If policy is to be a viable framework for action in the future and not simply a confirmation of precedents from the past, it must deliver not only commitment to the status quo but also a commitment to changing that status quo.

Summary propositions

3.1 Policy is a declared mode of action for the future. Personnel policy is a series of such statements about management objectives in relation to employment within the organization.

3.2 Policy is part of a framework for management action to translate mission into practice via strategy, policy and procedures – all integrated by planning.

3.3 The reasons for having policy are clarification, reducing dependence on individuals, producing consistent managerial behaviour, specialists seeking power, knowing 'where we stand' and responding to legal and other external pressures.

3.4 The main areas of personnel policy are principles, staffing and development, employee relations, mutual control, terms and conditions and equality of opportunity.

3.5 A three-part rule for policy formulation is: (1) policy does not translate into effective practice without a commitment to both the policy and the measures needed to make it work; (2) commitment is more likely when the policy develops out of issues in the organization itself; and (3) where the policy is devised, and later sustained, by the involvement of all those affected by it.

3.6 A procedure for devising policy is: identifying the topic, selling the idea, determining the key features, agreeing the details.

3.7 The four steps to put policy into operation are publicity, procedures, monitoring and modifying.

3.8 Strategy is linked to planning what to do, while policy is the framework for carrying forward everyday affairs.

References

Brewster, C. J., Gill, C. G. and Richbell, S. (1981), 'Developing an analytical approach to industrial relations policy', *Personnel Review*, vol. 10, no. 2.

Brewster, C. J. and Richbell, S. (1982), 'Getting managers to implement personnel policies', *Personnel Management*, December.

Carolin, B and Evans, E. (1988), 'Computers as a strategic management tool', *Personnel Management*, July.

Fowler, A. (1983), 'Proving the personnel department earns its salt', *Personnel Management*, May.

Georgiades, N. (1990), 'A strategic future for personnel?' *Personnel Management*, February.

Hawkins, K. (1978), *The Management of Industrial Relations*, London: Pelican.

Johnson, G. and Scholes, K. (1984), *Exploring Corporate Strategy*, Hemel Hempstead: Prentice Hall.

Miller, P. (1989), 'Strategic HRM: what it is and what it isn't', *Personnel Management*, February.

Rothwell, S. (1984), 'Integrating the elements of a company employment policy', *Personnel Management*, November.

Stoner, J. A. F. and Wankel, C. (1986), *Management* (3rd edition), Englewood Cliffs, NJ: Prentice Hall.

Torrington, D. P., Hitner, T. J. and Knights, D. (1982), *Management and the Multi Racial Workforce*, Aldershot: Gower.

Tyson, S. and Fell, A. (1986), *Evaluating the Personnel Function*: London: Hutchinson.

Yeandle, D. and Clark, J. (1989), 'Personnel strategy for an automated plant', *Personnel Management*, June.

4

Human resource planning

Human resource planning is fundamental in developing and implementing the organization's human resource strategy, which in turn enables the organization to meet its goals. The essence of human resource planning is the integration of all human resource activities within a central philosophy of the way that people in the organization should be managed. The result of this should be that human resource activities are coherent, consistent and mutually supportive, and can drive the organization's strategic objectives.

In this chapter we first explore current developments in human resource planning and the use of terminology. We move on to look at the purpose, context feasibility and importance of human resources planning, and its relationship with corporate planning. The chapter concludes with a review of the changing roles in human resource planning and an overview of the activities involved.

Recent developments in human resource planning

The 1980s saw an increased use of the terms 'human resource planning', 'human resource management' and 'human resourcing'. In Chapter 2 (pages 15–18) we explored the differences between human resources management and personnel management, and from our definition of human resource management we can derive the key themes of human resource planning, which are that it:

- Is concerned with all factors that influence the way that people are managed in the organization. This would include culture, informal and formal organizations and systems.

48

- Requires an integrated view of all human resource activities carried out both by specialists and line managers (including senior management).
- Is closely linked with business planning, and that the strategies and policies resulting from it are closely linked into business strategy.

Human resource planning, which translates human resources strategy into day-to-day activities and operations, needs to be concerned with all factors that influence the way that people in the organization are managed and not only the numbers of people and the balance of skills. In this book we shall, therefore, interpret human resource planning to include both planning to reshape the organizational culture (values, beliefs and behaviours) and planning to ensure the organization has the right numbers of the right people in the right place at the right time.

Terminology

Human resource planning is an area where terminology is inconsistent and this is not helpful in persuading the organization of its vital nature, as Manzini (1984) comments. These confusions are partly a result of the rapid development of ideas and practice in the area, but also because different organizations, researchers and writers have very different views on what is the heart of the activity.

Some authors draw a clear distinction between manpower planning (being concerned with numbers and statistical techniques) and human resource planning (reshaping the culture). Bramham, for example supports this view while acknowledging areas of overlap:

> There is a big difference between human resource planning and manpower planning. There are particularly important differences in terms of process and purpose. In human resource planning the manager is concerned with motivating people – a process in which costs, numbers, control and systems interact to play a part. In manpower planning the manager is concerned with the numerical elements of forecasting, supply–demand matching and control, in which people are a part. There are therefore important areas of overlap and interconnection but there is a fundamental difference in underlying approach. (Bramham 1989, p. 147)

A number of other writers simply use the term 'manpower planning' to refer to numbers planning without any recognition of other aspects such as working to ensure a consistent approach to the management of people in the organization (involving appraisal, management development and succession planning) and working to ensure the behaviour of employees meets business priorities like quality or customer service initiatives. And some even more confusingly use the term 'human resource planning' to refer only to numbers and skills planning (as in Burack 1985). This is more often the case in US literature, perhaps due to the earlier use of the words 'human resourcing'.

Some authors retain the term 'manpower planning' (which has a longer history in the United Kingdom than human resource planning) and give to this a new definition, as does Fyfe:

> Usually one thinks of manpower planning as being synonymous with the introduction or use of some kind of numbers game. However, as I hope to demonstrate, manpower planning is far more than that if it is properly related to real people and their development in the organization. (Fyfe 1986, p. 65)

Other authors (for example, Lockwood 1986) regard the terms as interchangeable.

Faced with such an array of definitions we have adopted a position similar to Smith (1983), and as outlined on page 51, which includes in human resource planning all points of the spectrum of human resource issues which may affect the future of the organization.

Human resource planning: purpose and context

In Chapter 1 we looked at what personnel management was for, before looking at what it is. In the same way, before we grapple with the finer points of supply and demand forecasts or discuss current themes in organizational change initiatives, we need to know why we are doing this. What are we hoping to achieve? In broad terms, the purpose of human resource planning is to develop schemes for the acquisition, management, organization and use of the people in the organization so that they contribute as effectively as possible towards the achievement of organizational goals, as with any other valued resource. While the activities and methods of human resource planning will vary with the context in which it is carried out (and we have seen much of this of late), its purpose remains unchanged.

The context of human resource planning can be described from two distinct, but not independent, angles:

1. *The nature of organizational goals*: Most human resource planning literature realistically assumes that the prime objective of the organization is to increase profit in order to ensure a long-term and successful future. However, organizations increasingly recognize a second set of goals,

which concentrate on the needs of employees. These include providing satisfying jobs and careers and individual development. These two sets of goals are mutually supportive. For example, where innovation and creativity are critical success factors, these are supported by encouraging motivation and commitment via appropriately designed jobs and opportunities for personal growth and development.

An example of a UK founded company which recognizes both people and profit growth as key strategic objectives is ICI Pharmaceuticals. These are derived from a statement of organizational purpose which is to 'contribute to human health by providing worthwhile products which enable our business to grow and the people within it to prosper and lead fulfilling lives'. The nature of corporate goals clearly affects the approach to human resource planning, the methods and decisions made.

2. *Environment: local, national and international*: These can affect both organizational goals and planning activities. In the late 1960s and early 1970s activities reflected the prevailing climate of growth. Retaining and recruiting employees was critical. In the early 1980s the economic environment was resulting in plant closures and downsizing so that the spotlight was on redundancies, early retirements, transfers, skills matching and retraining. In the current climate the concerns of the demographic downturn, increasing concerns about competitiveness and increasing environmental uncertainty dominate activities. Human resource planning, therefore, is increasingly concentrating on plans to shape the values and behaviour of employees in line with the changing directions of the organization, and on recruiting and retaining, and on developing staff to a much fuller extent.

The context of human resource planning can, therefore, affect the approach, activities and methods that are used, but not the reason for human resource planning. A good definition of human resource planning, which sums up its essential purpose, is:

> To maintain and improve the ability of the organization to achieve corporate objectives, through the development of strategies designed to enhance the contribution of employees at all times in the foreseeable future. (adapted from Stainer 1971)

Achieving this purpose leads to the employment of people whose skills are fully utilized, and who are provided with challenging work in the context of controlled costs. It avoids the problems of overtime being worked when it is not really needed, people being allocated to jobs for which they have not been adequately trained and employee behaviour bearing no relationship to the organizational goals. This assists the company in being able to compete effectively and, increasingly, being able to survive.

The nature of the human resource

In his book on corporate planning, Hussey (1982) comments that the two fundamental resources of any business are people and money, and that the most complex of these is the people resource for the following reasons:

1. People are different from each other, in physical characteristics, personality, educational level, abilities, and so on. An organization does not have a need for people in general but for specific people who are able to fulfil specific functions. Managers and labourers, for example, are not interchangeable. Money, from wherever it comes, looks the same as other money, and one £5 note has the same value as another £5 note.
2. The resource of people is always needed in a specific place, but it is difficult to move around. Finance is easier to move around.
3. When there is a surplus of the people resource it becomes a drain on profits. Too many people are an unnecessary expense. If there is a surplus of money there is always a way that it can be utilized.
4. Because they are human beings, the people resource should not be treated casually. People cannot be switched on and off like a light. Since the effectiveness of the organization depends on getting the right balance of people, human resource planning must assume some importance.

We would also add that the people resource is more complex because:

5. It has a will of its own. The people resource is dynamic and unpredictable. People can act of their own accord; they may refuse or be unable to meet the requirements of their jobs; they may not understand what is expected of them; they may not co-operate with change and they may decide to leave the organization.

At the same time, the people resource has the advantage of being able to think, to be creative and to improve itself. It may be the most complex resource, but it is also the most valuable. Because the human resource is human, the organization needs to exercise a greater responsibility by involving people in the changes that will be affecting them. This means that they are aware of the implications for themselves and the organization of the planned changes and of alternative courses of action. Where appropriate, employees may be involved in decision-making regarding changes affecting themselves, but at the very least, changes need to be discussed and debated at length with employees in order to secure commitment.

Feasibility and importance of human resource planning

The difficulty of predicting both internal and external events, coupled with the unpredictability of the human resource, may make human resource planning seem an almost impossible task. Interest rate changes, new competitor products, changes in the exchange rate, success of products in development, possible acquisitions and mergers may all be very uncertain. Plans are therefore more profitably seen as preparations for contingencies that may arise, rather than a fixed track to follow. This means that a range of possibilities for human resources are produced. Manzini (1984) comments that 'a plan, imperfect though it may be, will generally get us closer to the target than if we had not planned'.

Neither should planning be seen as an isolated event, but rather something that has to be continuously monitored, refined and updated. Bell (1989) argues that while there may be an annual cycle of planning, this should represent a review activity that goes on throughout the year; and that each cycle should feed into the next.

In spite of the limitations and problematic nature of human resource planning, it is central to both the effectiveness of personnel function and of the business as a whole. Our recent research indicates that planning is one of the most important personnel activities and is the activity that has increased in importance to the greatest extent. Yet despite this the same survey shows that only 66 per cent of establishments said that there was a manpower plan covering the establishment. Greer *et al.* (1989) demonstrate a significant increase in the perceived importance of human resource planning since the late 1970s. However, many organizations still fail to plan for human resources. Burack (1985) found that less than 60 per cent of his survey respondents explicitly carried out human resource planning. Where it does exist, the state of the art is a long way from the state of application, and this is partly due, as Ulrich (1987) comments, to the recency of the discipline, and also to the lack of a common body of knowledge, as noted by Manzini (1984).

Review topic 4.1

What do you think are the reasons for the discrepancy between the acknowledged importance of human resource planning and its apparent lack of application and sophistication?

Organizational and human resource planning and the role of personnel

The definition of human resource planning, which we use on page 49, leaves no room for doubt that human resource planning and corporate planning should be closely integrated activities. Other writers support this close relationship, for example, Bennison (1987); and Handy *et al.* (1989) comment that this integration is vital to the essence of strategic human resource management. There is an abundance of journal papers which consider the extent to which organizational and human resources planning are integrated, and how to achieve this. Ulrich (1987) argues that integration is achieved by ensuring that human resource plans build in competitive advantage and this means that the plans have to cover a wide range of human resource issues; remain simple; offer choices; identify specific human resource activities, which can be used to accomplish business strategy; rely on business rationale and language and raise questions. In general, there is perceived to be insufficient integration at present, and an extreme case of this is exemplified by a respondent from our research:

> There is not a formal link to tie in management training with the corporate strategy of each company. That's becoming an issue. For example, the personal credit side was one region and has become three regions, which compete with each other, and each wants to forge an identity and innovate. I need to know what future demands there are, and about change in structure and need to know the predicted demand for training. (Training manager, commercial sector)

Baird *et al.* take the lack of integration one step further, suggesting that: 'Human resources can not be regarded as a separate element to be integrated into the organisation strategy, because there is no organisation strategy without the inclusion of human resources' (Baird *et al.* 1983, p. 19).

The extent to which human resource planning is a part of organizational planning varies considerably, and Burack (1985) in his research found evidence of much confusion. He found that two-thirds of the human resource specialists in his survey felt that human resources were included in organizational planning, but only one half of the business planners (in the same organizations!) thought this to be the case. There continues to be much scepticism about the value of incorporating a human resource dimension into the corporate planning process. This scepticism results from such issues as the low status of the human resource function and its connection with maintenance functions, the failure of personnel people to understand corporate issues and a lack of acceptable performance criteria to demonstrate the value of human resource planning.

However, the picture is not all gloom. There is evidence that the incorporation of human resource planning is increasing and that the roles of personnel specialists in this area are changing. The increasing remit that is now perceived for human resource planning enables a much more powerful contribution to the organization in the management of strategic change. Developing plans to reshape the culture of the organization to increase flexibility, innovation, quality, goal-directed behaviour, etc., means that human resource specialists are working at the heart of the organization, especially if this is also combined with numbers and skills planning.

Greer *et al.* (1989) discovered not only a greater perceived importance of human resouce planning in their research but also an increased acceptance and use of many human resource planning techniques. They argue very convincingly that this is associated with human resource planning adapting to the environment and also becoming a line management process. This adaptation is reflected in, for example, an increased use of simpler and qualitative techniques rather than sophisticated statistical analyses in supply forecasting (e.g. more use of succession planning charts rather than Markov chains). The value of human resource data-bases is not in question here. Research shows that the quality of data-bases has increased and that they are critical to effective human resource planning. The question is what you do with the data and how you present them to line management.

The other key adaptation is the involvement of line managers in human resource planning. Craft (1988) makes the case that for human resource planning to be implemented successfully, line managers need to be persuaded that it meets a business need. Thus greater line involvement (as demonstrated by Greer *et al.*) is the key to greater acceptance of human resource planning and its full integration with corporate planning. This has implications for the personnel role moving from co-ordinator and controller of human resource planning to an equal partnership with the line and shared responsibility (see, for example, Ulrich 1987). Greer *et al.* (1989) predict that in the 1990s personnel specialists will have less direct involvement in human resource planning, but that their indirect responsibilities will expand. Tichy (1988) sees that personnel specialists will be key change agents in this area. A major input by personnel specialists will be to challenge the line on human resource planning issues and to sensitize line managers to environmental and internal trends which affect the human resource.

Human resource planning activities

We have referred a number of times to the wide range of activities that may be involved in human resource planning from numbers planning to reshaping of the corporate culture. In order to facilitate description we shall look at the 'hard' aspects of human resource planning separately from the 'soft'. It is, however, important to recognize that there is overlap between these two areas and that in many organizations a mixture of hard and soft approaches will be practised and these may or may not be integrated or co-ordinated, or even recognized as human resource planning. Integration between these two approaches is one of the key challenges for the personnel function in the 1990s.

Soft human resources planning

Activities in the realm of soft planning can be divided into four broad areas: defining where the organization wants to be in the future; defining where the organization is at the moment; analyzing environmental influences and trends; and the formulation of plans to effect the desired changes and to ease transition. These activities will involve continuous feedback from one to the other. A diagrammatic interpretation of the relationship between the four areas is shown in Figure 4.1.

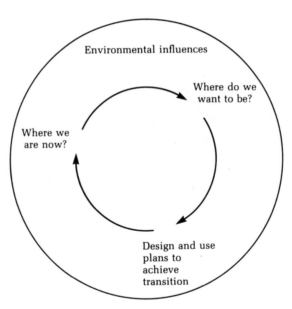

Figure 4.1   *The four areas of soft planning*

In order to plan human resources in a strategic and integrated way an organization needs to have a clear vision of where it wants to be in the future (3–5 years perhaps). This vision may be expressed in terms of, and/or derived from, the mission and strategic objectives of the organization and needs to spell out the implications for human resources. From organizational goals emphasizing areas of competitive advantage, differentiation, profit growth, downsizing, product life-cycle stage, people development, etc., specific human resources goals may be derived. These goals may relate to innovation, effectiveness, efficiency, behaviour, quality, customer service, flexibility, business goal orientation, individual/team performance, and so on, as needs to be generated by the people resource. An example of a specific human resources goal is:

> To introduce a performance management approach to people, which links objective setting, performance review, individual development, and reward.

Environmental scanning is a vital activity, as through this human resource specialists and senior managers can identify other influences and trends which will affect the achievement of the identified business objective(s), and the human resource plans that are designed to meet feasible objectives. Environmental scanning involves collecting both quantitative and qualitative data, and may include information on social/political/industrial/legislative and technological trends and competitor information. The changing expectations of employees and potential employees are key here. A major issue in this area is the effect that the Unification of Europe (1992) will have on both employment legislation and employee expectations and choices.

Before plans can be made for the organization to reach its overall human resource objectives it is essential to identify the current situation in the organization. Data, therefore, need to be collected about, for example, customer service, flexibility, managerial behaviour, or whatever is seen as key for the future. The formal/informal systems and processes, and the culture of the organization, may all need to be analyzed, together with the effects and implications of these.

When data in these three areas are collected, analyzed and fed back, managers are in a better position to make some decisions about the best way forward, and to begin formulating some plans. These plans may cover areas such as organization structure, recruitment/selection, appraisal, rewards, training/development and communication.

Hard human resources planning

What activities need to be carried out to make sure that the level of human resources in the organization is and will be right? How do we find out at an early stage the number and type of employees that will be needed and make plans to ensure they will be available? Hard human resource planning activities centre on:

- Forecast of future demand for human resources.
- Consideration of changes in human resource utilization and the effect of this on demand.
- Analysis of current human resources.
- Forecast of the internal human resource supply.

- Forecast of external human resource supply.
- Reconciliation of forecasts and feedback.
- Decisions and plans.

Figure 4.2 shows these activities and their primary relationships. The demand for human resources can be forecast using information from corporate plans or business plans. Such plans often include an expression of the organization's activity in such terms as production figures, sales figures, number of patients treated, levels of service, and so on. In other words, how many and what types of employee will we need if we are to produce x amount over the next year. A number of techniques can be used to translate production figures into numbers and types of employees. These include managerial judgement, use of statistical techniques and use of work study figures.

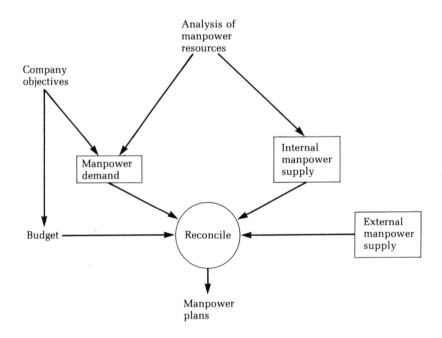

Figure 4.2   *Hard human resource planning*
Source: Bell (1974). Published with permission of Pitman Publishing Ltd, London.

Human resource utilization is an important factor which can affect the demand for people. The way that human resources are used affects, among other things, the number and type of employees required. The way that people are used can be changed in a number of ways, such as:

- The actual tasks performed, as these may be altered, deleted or added to.
- The time spent on each task.
- The level at which the tasks are carried out; that is, in whose job description the task is located.

There are various reasons why human resource utilization may be changed. Changes in utilization are often seen as synonymous with improvements in people utilization in order to increase productivity. While this is perhaps the most common of reasons, it is certainly not the only one. The reasons for changes may be due to:

- Conscious attempts to increase productivity (this can be more product per employee hour, or a product or service of better quality).
- The introduction of new materials or equipment, especially new technology.
- Changes in legislation, for example, health and safety legislation.
- Attempts to provide more satisfying jobs, to improve motivation, commitment, morale, and so on.

Changes in employee utilization often involve negotiation, or at least consultation with trade unions, or other employee representatives. It would be naive to assume that management could decide on the most efficient way to utilize employees and implement this directly. Changes in utilization are also difficult to implement as they require lengthy planning, and also create a certain amount of upheaval before, during and after implementation, just as with soft human resources planning. It is, therefore, more realistic to see employee utilization as an area that management should be primarily aware of and improved where possible.

Review topic 4.2

Think of a specific example of each of the four reasons for changes in employee utilization. For each example what are the implications for:

1. The jobs of the employees directly involved?
2. The jobs of employees indirectly involved?
3. The organization as a whole?

Having forecast the demand for human resources, taking into account any changes in the way people are to be utilized, the next step is to analyze the current supply. Current employees can be analyzed in overall terms, such as numbers of people in each occupation, or by age, or sex. Analysis of individual assets is also important here. The analysis of current human resources is essential as it provides a base from which to forecast the future internal human resources supply. It is also important for the formulation of career, succession and redundancy plans.

Internal human resources supply forecasts attempt to predict future internal resources based on trends of what has happened to employees in the past. Human resource planners are concerned with trends of employees leaving the organization, sometimes called wastage or turnover; but also with trends of internal employee movements. Trends from the past are projected into the future to simulate what will happen to the current human resources in, say, one or two years' time. This is the area of human resource planning where statistical techniques are most advanced, and the forecasting of internal human resources supply is often looked at in statistical terms. There is, however, some interest in increased use of simple statistics and of the behavioural aspects of supply, for example, consideration of the reasons for wastage.

A forecast of external human resources supply is needed if internal human resources supply is unlikely to meet demand in any occupational areas. External human resources supply is, of course, particularly critical if a new plant or office is to be opened. External factors may also have an effect on current employee wastage rates and the expectations of employees may be affected if a company offering similar employment at higher wages locates itself close by.

The supply and demand forecasts need to be balanced or reconciled, and this process necessitates feedback into previous stages of the process. Feedback, in fact, needs to be occurring throughout the whole process, and not just at this stage. Hard human resource planning activities have been described here, for the sake of clarity, as a series of stages. In reality these activities are not carried out in a predetermined order, but to some extent at the same time so that information generated from each activity can be used continuously to inform the others. This feedback is vital if hard human resources planning is to have any practical value. For example, corporate objectives may need to be reconsidered if the analysis and forecast of human resources supply cannot meet the demand that has been derived from these objectives. Alternatively, the type of people employed or the utilization of people may be reconsidered to see if the objectives may be met in another way.

Human resources decisions based on the manpower forecasts and their eventual balancing result in the production of human resource plans which are action plans covering such areas as recruitment/selection, training, productivity. These are discussed in the following chapter.

Summary propositions

4.1 Human resource planning is fundamental in developing and implementing the organization's human resources strategy, which in turn enables the organization to meet its goals.

4.2 The use of terminology in this area is inconsistent.

4.3 Human resource planning covers the whole spectrum of human resource issues, which may affect the future of the organization.

4.4 One of the key challenges for the personnel function is to integrate the hard and soft approaches to human resource planning.

4.5 Human resource planning activities are interdependent, and need to be carried out to some extent in parallel with each other.

4.6 Human resource planning needs to be a continuous process.

4.7 The role of personnel specialists in human resource planning is changing from co-ordinator to partner.

References

Baird, L., Meshoulam, I. and De Give, G. (1983), 'Meshing human resources planning with strategic business planning: a model approach', *Personnel*, vol. 60, pt 5, pp. 14–25.

Bell, D. (1989), 'Why manpower planning is back in vogue', *Personnel Management*, July.

Bennison, M. (1987), 'Manpower planning and corporate policy: making the connection', *Manpower Policy and Practice*, Autumn.

Bramham, J. (1989), *Human Resource Planning*, London: Institute of Personnel Management.

Burack, E. H. (1985), 'Linking corporate business and human resource planning: strategic issues and concerns', *Human Resource Planning*, vol. 8, pt. 2, pp. 133–45.

Craft, J. A. (1988), 'Human resources planning and strategy'. In L. Dyer, *Human Resources Management: Evolving Roles and Responsibility*, Washington DC: Bureau of National Affairs, pp. 47–87.

Fyfe, J. (1986), 'Putting people back into manpower equations', *Personnel Management*, October.

Greer, R., Jackson, D. L. and Fiorito, J. (1989), 'Adapting human resources planning in a changing business environment', *Human Resources Management*, vol. 28, pt. 1, pp. 37–56.

Handy, L., Barnham, K., Panter, S. and Winhard, A. (1989), 'Beyond the personnel function', *Journal of European Industrial Training*, vol, 13, no, 1, pp. 13–18.

Hussey, D. (1982), *Corporate Planning: Theory and Practice*, (2nd edition), Oxford: Pergamon Press.

Lockwood, P. A. (1986), 'Human resource planning: The role of the practitioner', *Health Services Manpower Review*, vol. 12, no. 2, August.

Manzini, A. O. (1984), 'Human resource planning: observations on the state of the art and the state of practice', *Human Resource Planning*, vol. 7, pt. 2, pp. 105–10.

Schuler, R. S. and Jackson, S. E. (1987) 'Linking corporate strategies with human resource management practices', *Academy of Management Executive*, vol. 1, no. 3.

Smith, E. C. (1983), 'How to tie human resource planning to strategic business planning', *Managerial Planning*, vol. 32, pt. 2, pp. 29–34.

Stainer, G. (1971), *Manpower Planning*, London: Heinemann.

Tichy, N. M. (1988), Foreword: 'Setting the global human resources management agenda for the 1990's', *Human Resources Management*, vol. 27, pp. 1–18.

Ulrich, D., (1986), 'Human resource planning as a competitive edge', *Human Resource Planning*, vol. 9, pt. 2, pp. 41–50.

Ulrich, D. (1987), 'Strategic human resource planning: why and how?', *Human Resource Planning*, vol. 10, pt. 1, pp. 37–56.

Part
II

Personnel
Management and
Organization

5

Human resource planning in practice

Human resource planning methods vary from the most sophisticated statistical analyzes to organizational diagnosis tools which help to structure opinions and views based on data from inside and outside the organization. The methods used depend on the issues and needs of the organization, and also on the skills of the human resource planners and managers.

In Chapter 4 we introduced human resource planning as vital to the organization, but underutilized. In this chapter we explore the different human resource planning methods which turn into reality the exhortations that human resource planning is a priority. We look at hard and soft human resource planning methods separately, and then look at forming and implementing human resource plans. We sometimes refer to the example of a hypothetical hotel to illustrate how some of the methods can be used. A description of the hotel and all references from the text are found in the appendix to this chapter.

Soft human resource planning methods

Methods for identifying the future in human resource terms

There is little specific literature on the methods used to translate the strategic objectives of the organization and environmental influences into human resource goals. In general terms, they can be summed up as the use of managerial judgement. If the activity is seen as vital to the organization, then senior managers will be involved in the processes. Brainstorming, combined with the use of structured checklists or matrices, can encourage a more thorough analysis. Organization change literature and corporate planning literature are helpful as a source of ideas in this area. Three simple techniques are a human

Corporate goal	Human resource implications in respect of: New tasks? For whom? What competencies needed? Relative importance of team/individual behaviour? Deleted tasks? How will managers need to manage?	Methods of Achieving this

Figure 5.1   *The beginnings of a human resource implications checklist*

Managers write a corporate goal in the centre and brainstorm changes that need to take place in each of the four areas, one area at a time

Figure 5.2   *Strategic brainstorming exercise*

resource implications checklist (see Figure 5.1), a strategic brainstorming exercise (Figure 5.2) and a behavioural expectation chart (Appendix, note 1).

Analyzing the environment

Data on relevant trends can be collected from current literature, company annual reports, conferences/courses and from contacts and networking. Table 5.1 gives examples of the many possible sources against each major area. In this chapter we refer to the environment broadly as the context of the organization.

Having acquired and constantly updated data on the environment, one of the most common ways of analyzing this is to produce a map of the environment, represented as a wheel. The map represents a time in the future, say three years out. In the centre of the wheel can be written the objective(s) of the organization as it relates to people and the objective of human resource planning as a contribution to this. Each spoke of the wheel can then be filled in to represent a

Table 5.1 Sources of information on environment trends

Trend area	Possible sources
Social	Census information IPM journals News media *Social Trends* *General Household Survey* *Employment Gazette*
Political and legislative	News media Proceedings of European Parliament Proceedings of British Parliament *Hansard* *Industrial Relations Review and Report* *Industrial Law Journal* *IDS Brief*
Industrial and technological	*Employment Digest* Journals specifically for the industry *Financial Times* Employers' association Trade association
Competitors	Annual reports Talk to them!

factor of the environment, for example, current employees, potential employees, a specific local competitor, competitors generally, regulatory bodies, customers, government. From all the spokes the six or seven regarded as most important need to be selected. These can then be worked further by asking what demands each will make of the organization, and how the organization will need to respond in order to achieve its goals. From these responses can be derived the implications for human resource activities. For example, the demands of present employees may be predicted as:

- We need a career not just a job.
- We need flexibility to help with childrearing.
- We want to be treated as people and not machines.
- We need a picture of what the organization has in store for us.
- We want to be better trained.
  And so on.

Managers then consider what the organization would need to offer to meet these needs. This analysis can then be fed back into identifying the future vision in human resource terms. Figure 5.3. gives an outline for the whole process; for a worked example see Appendix, note 2.

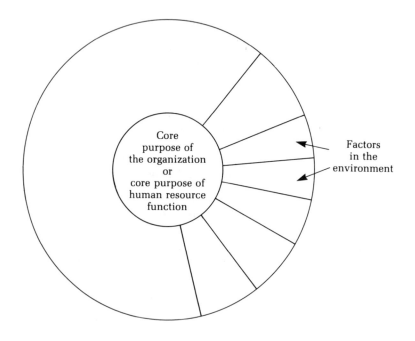

Individual factor in the environment	
Demands from the factor	Responses from the organization

Figure 5.3   *Mapping the environment*

Review topic 5.1

Draw a map of the environment for your organization for three to five years out. Individually or as a group, brainstorm all the spokes in the wheel and select the six most important ones. Draw up a demands and responses list for each. Write a one-side of A4 summary of what you think your organization's priorities should be in the people area over the next three to five years.

Analyzing the current situation

It is in this area that more choice of techniques is available, and the possibilities include use of questionnaires to staff (Appendix, note 3), interviews with staff, managerial judgement, turnover figures, performance data, recruitment and promotion trends and characteristics of employees. These analyses can be conducted to provide information on, for example:

- Motivation of employees.
- Job satisfaction.
- Organizational culture.
- The way that people are managed.
- Attitude to women and equality of opportunity.
- Commitment to the organization and reasons for this.
- Clarity of business objectives.
- Goal-focused and other behaviour.

Data relating to current formal and informal systems, together with data on the structure of the organization, also need to be collected, and the effectiveness, efficiency and other implications of these need to be carefully considered.

Most data will be collected from within the organization, but data may also be collected from significant others, such as customers, who may be part of the environment.

Hard human resource planning methods

Methods for forecasting employee demand

These can be divided into two groups: objective and subjective.

Objective methods I: statistical methods

These methods depend on the assumption that the future situation will display some continuity from the past. Past trends are projected into the future to simulate or 'model' what would happen if they continued.

Models based on the extrapolation of employee number trends
These models are based on the change in people demand, but do not consider the factors that influence this demand. Probably the best-known example would be the extrapolation of the relationship between demand and time, sometimes called time trends or time series, as shown in Figure 5.4. (See Appendix, note 4.) These models are best used only for short- or medium-term forecasts, and they have two major limitations. First, historical figures of people employed do not

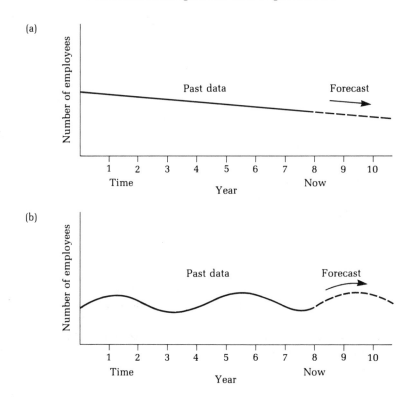

Figure 5.4 *Manpower supply forecasting models based on extrapolation of manpower trends: (a) trend in the number of employees over time; (b) the cyclical nature of the number of employed over time*

necessarily indicate historical people demand; and secondly, these models make no allowances for internal or external changes which may affect demand.

Models based on the extrapolated trends of number employed are most profitably used to stimulate discussion.

Models relating employee number demand to organizational and environmental circumstances

These models are used to calculate people demand as a result of, usually, organizational activities. Models can take account of determining factors, such as production, sales, passenger miles, level of service. These factors can be used separately or in combination with other determining factors. A simple model might relate people demand to production, using a constant relationship, without making any assumptions about economies of scale. In this model if output is to be doubled, then employees would also need to be doubled. (See Appendix, note 5.) More complicated equations can be formulated, which describe the way that a combination of independent factors have affected the dependent employee demand.

By inserting new values of the independent factors, such as new projected sales figures, then the demand for employees can be worked out from the equation. The equations can also be represented as graphs making the relationships clear to see. These models can be adapted to take account of projected changes in utilization, due to factors such as the introduction of new technology.

Objective methods II: work study

This method is based on time study and a thorough analysis of the work done to arrive at the person-hours needed per unit of output. Standards are developed for the numbers and levels of employees that are needed to do the work tasks. These standards may be developed within the organization or elsewhere and are most useful when studying production work. It is important that the standards are checked regularly to make sure they are still appropriate. Work study is usually classified as an objective measure, but Verhoeven (1982) argues that since the development of standards and the grouping of tasks is partly dependent on human judgement, it should be considered as a subjective method.

Subjective methods I: managerial judgement

Sometimes called executive judgement, managerial opinion or inductive method, it can also include the judgements of other operational and technical staff, as well as all levels of managers. This method is based on managers' estimates of manpower demand based on past experience and on corporate plans. Managerial judgements can be collected from the 'bottom up' with lower-level managers providing estimates to go up the hierarchy for discussion and redrafting. Alternatively, a 'top-down' approach can be used with estimates made by the highest level of management to go down the hierarchy for discussion and redrafting. Using this method it is difficult to cope with changes that are very different from past experiences. It is also less precise than statistical methods, but it is more comprehensive. Managerial judgement is a simple method, which can be applied fairly quickly and is not restricted by lack of data, particularly historical data, as are statistical techniques. Stainer makes the point that managerial judgement is important even when statistical techniques are used when he says:

> The aim in employing statistical techniques is to simplify the problem to the extent that the human mind can cope with it efficiently, rather than to eliminate subjective judgement altogether. (Stainer 1971)

(See Appendix, note 6.)

Subjective methods II: Delphi technique

This is a specialized procedure for the collection of managerial opinions based on the idea of the oracle at Delphi. A group of managers anonymously and independently answer questions about anticipated manpower demand. A compilation of the answers is fed back to each individual, and the process is repeated until all the answers converge. Empirical data suggest that this technique is little used at present, although it is often referred to as a common method.

Methods for changing employee utilization

The emphasis on employee utilization varies considerably between different authors – some see it as the most critical issue, whereas others give it only passing attention. There is a vast range of ways to change the way that employees are used:

1. Introducing new materials or equipment, particularly new technology.
2. Introducing changes in work organization, such as:
   (a) quality circles,
   (b) job rotation,
   (c) job enlargement,
   (d) job enrichment,
   (e) autonomous work-groups,
   (f) participation.
3. Organization development.
4. Introducing changes in organization structure, such as:
   (a) centralization/decentralization,
   (b) new departmental boundaries,
   (c) relocation of parts of the organization.
5. Introducing productivity schemes, bonus schemes or other incentive schemes.
6. Encouraging greater staff flexibility and work interchangeability.
7. Enabling unnecessary overtime to be reduced.
8. Altering times and periods of work.
9. Training and appraisal of staff.
10. Developing managers and use of management by objectives techniques.

Some of these methods are interrelated or overlap and would therefore be used in combination. (See Appendix, note 7.) Interconnections between some of these areas and soft human resources planning are also apparent.

Analysis of current employee supply

Current employee supply can be analyzed in both individual and overall statistical terms.

Statistical analysis

Analysis may be made for any of the following factors, either singly or in combination: number of employees classified by function, department, occupation/job title, skills, qualifications, training, age, length of service, performance appraisal results. (See Appendix, note 8.)

Individual analysis

Similar information to the above can be collected on an individual basis to facilitate succession, career, redundancy and relocation planning.

Methods for forecasting internal employee supply

Forecasting of employee supply is concerned with predicting how the current supply of manpower will change over time, primarily in respect of how many will leave, but also how many will be internally promoted or transferred. These changes are forecast by analyzing what has happened in the past, in terms of staff retention and/or movement, and projecting this into the future to see what would happen if the same trends continued. Bell (1974) provides an extremely thorough coverage of possible analyses, on which this section is based. However, although statistical analyses are most well developed for the forecasting of employee supply, behavioural aspects are also important (see Timperley 1980). These include investigating the reasons why staff leave and criteria that affect promotions and transfers. Changes in working conditions and in personnel policy would be relevant here. Statistical techniques fall broadly into two categories: analyses of staff leaving the organization, and analyses of internal movements.

Analyses of staff leaving the organization

Annual labour turnover index This is sometimes called the percentage wastage rate, the conventional turnover index or the BIM turnover index. This is the simplest formula for wastage and looks at the number of staff leaving during the year as a percentage of the total number employed who could have left.

$$\frac{\text{Leavers in year}}{\text{Average number of staff in post during year}} \times 100 = \text{per cent wastage rate}$$

(see Appendix, note 9).

This measure has been criticized because it only gives a limited amount of information. If, for example, there were twenty-five leavers over the year, it would not be possible to determine whether twenty-five different jobs had been left by twenty-five different people, or whether twenty-five different people had tried and left the same job. Length of service is not taken into account with this measure, yet length of service has been shown to have a considerable influence on leaving patterns – such as the high number of leavers at the time of induction.

Stability index   This index is based on the number of staff who could have stayed throughout the period. Usually, staff with a full year's service are expressed as a percentage of staff in post one year ago.

$$\frac{\text{Number of staff with one year's service at date}}{\text{Number of staff employed exactly one year before}} \times 100 = \text{per cent stability}$$

This index however ignores joiners throughout the year and takes little account of length of service. (See Appendix, note 10.)

Bowey's Stability Index   Bowey's Index (Bowey 1974) attempts to take account of the length of service of employees. It looks at the length of service of current employees added together over a certain period. This is converted into a percentage of the total service that these staff would have if they had been employed for the full period. The period usually used is two years, and service is expressed in months:

$$\frac{\text{Length of service in months over two-year period of all staff added together}}{\text{Length of service in months over two-year period of a full complement of staff added together}} \times 100 = \text{per cent stability}$$

(Not illustrated in Appendix.)

Cohort analysis   A cohort is defined as a homogeneous group of people. Cohort analysis involves the tracking of what happens, in terms of leavers, to a group of people with very similar characteristics who join the company at the same time. Graduates are an appropriate group for this type of analysis. A graph can be produced to show what happens to the group. The graph can be in the form of a survival curve or a log normal wastage curve, which can be plotted as a straight line and can be used to make predictions. The disadvantage of this method of analysis is that it cannot be used for groups other than the specific type of group for which it was originally prepared. The information has also to be collected over a long time-period, which gives rise to problems of availability of data and their validity.

Half-life   This is a figure which expresses the time taken for half the cohort to leave the organization. The figure does not give as much information as a survival curve, but it is useful as a summary and as a method of comparing different groups.

Census method   The census method is an analysis of leavers over a reasonably short period of time – often over a year. The length of completed service of leavers is summarized by using a histogram, as shown in Figure 5.5. (See Appendix, note 11.)

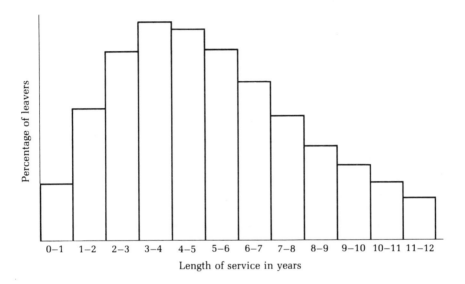

Figure 5.5   *Census analysis: percentage of leavers with differing lengths of service*

Retention profile   Staff retained, that is those who remain with the organization, are allocated groups depending on the year they joined. The number in each year group is translated into a percentage of the total number of individuals who joined during that year.

Analyses of internal movements

These techniques tend to be more sophisticated than those dealing with the analysis of wastage.

Age and length of service distributions   These analyses indicate problems that may arise in the future, such as promotion blocks. They need to be used in conjunction with an analysis of previous promotion patterns in the organization. (See Appendix, note 11.)

Markov chain   This is a method of identifying promotion patterns by looking at past promotions. This analysis gives the probability of staff moving from one grade to another in the organization, and what time periods are involved.

Renewal model   This model describes how promotion probabilities change over time.

Stationary population models   This is an actuarial technique, which is useful for an organization where career development is well defined. Joiners from each year, or group of years, are described in terms of the numbers still employed and their present level of employment. This is a quick and simple method of analysis.

Salary progression curve   A salary progression curve shows corrected salary in relation to age, and can be used to predict future salaries and, from this, future grades.

Review topic 5.2

1. For what reasons do employees leave organizations?
2. What are the determinants of promotion in your organization? Are they made explicit? Do staff understand what the determinants are?
3. What would be your criteria for promotion in your organization?

Methods for forecasting external human resources supply

Information from the local area is usually of primary importance, however sometimes regional, national and international human resources supply information is relevant. Some local factors, which affect the forecast of external human resources supply, are:

- Closures/opening of other workplaces in the area.
- Housing developments.
- Transport developments and travel-to-work patterns.
- Local unemployment levels.
- Previous experience of skills, difficult or easy to recruit.
- Output from the local educational system.
- Facilities for Government Training Schemes, for example YT.

(See Appendix, note 13.)

Reconciliation, decisions and plans

We have already said that, in reality, there is a process of continuous feedback between the different stages of human resource planning activities, as they are all interdependent. In soft human resources planning there is a dynamic relationship between the future vision, environmental trends and the current position. Key factors to take into account during reconciliation and deciding on action plans are the acceptability of the plans to both senior managers and other employees, the priority of each plan, key players who will need to be influenced, and the factors that will encourage or be a barrier to successful implementation. Piercy (1989), in relation to strategic planning generally, offers a series of tools to help managers work through these issues.

Within hard human resources planning feasibility may centre on the situation where the supply forecast is less than the demand forecast. Here, the possibilities are to:

1. Alter the demand forecast by considering the effect of changes in the utilization of manpower, such as training and productivity deals.
2. Alter the demand forecast by considering using different types of employees to meet the corporate objectives, such as employing a smaller number of staff with higher level skills, or employing staff with insufficient skills and training them immediately.
3. Change the company objectives, as lack of manpower will prevent them from being achieved in any case. Realistic objectives may need to be based on the manpower that is, and is forecast to be, available.

When the demand forecast is less than the internal supply forecast in some areas, the possibilities are to:

1. Consider and calculate the costs of overmanning over various timespans.
2. Consider the methods and cost of losing staff.
3. Consider changes in utilization: work out the feasibility and costs of retraining, redeployment, and so on.
4. Consider whether it is possible for the company objectives to be changed. Could the company diversify, move into new markets, etc.?

Once all alternatives have been considered and feasible solutions decided upon, specific action plans can be designed covering all appropriate areas of human resource management activity. For example:

- *Human resource supply plans*: Plans may need to be made concerning the timing and approach to recruitment or de-manning. For example, it may have been decided that in order to recruit sufficient staff, a public relations campaign is needed to promote a particular company image. Promotion, transfer and redeployment and redundancy plans would also be relevant here.

- *Organization and structure plans*: These plans may concern departmental existence, remit and structure and the relationships between departments. They may also be concerned with the layers of hierarchy within departments and the level at which tasks are done. Changes to organization and structure will usually result in changes in employee utilization.
- *Employee utilization plans*: Any changes in utilization that affect human resource demand will need to be planned. Some changes will result in a sudden difference in the tasks that employees do and the numbers needed; others will result in a gradual movement over time. Managers need to work out new tasks to be done, old ones to be dropped and the timescale by which they need the right number of people fully operational. There are implications for communications plans as the employees involved will need to be consulted about the changes and be prepared and trained for what will happen. There will be interconnections with supply plans here, for example, if fewer employees will be needed, what criteria will be used to determine who should be made redundant and who should be redeployed and retrained, and in which areas.
- *Training and management development plans*: There will be training implications from both the manpower supply and manpower utilization plans. The timing of the training can be a critical aspect. For example, training for specific new technology skills loses most of its impact if it is done six months before the equipment arrives. If the organization wishes to increase recruitment by promoting the excellent development and training that it provides for employees, then clear programmes of what will be offered need to be finalized and resourced so that these can then be used to entice candidates into the organization. If the organization is stressing customer service, then appropriate training will need to be developed to enable employees to achieve this.
- *Communications plans*: The way that planned changes are communicated to employees is critical. Plans need to include methods for not only informing employees what managers expect of them, but also methods to enable employees to express their concerns and needs for successful implementation. Communications plans will also be important if, for example, managers wish to generate greater employee commitment by keeping employees better informed about the progress of the organization.
- *Appraisal plans*: The organization needs to make sure that it is assessing the things that are important to it. If customer service is paramount then employees need to be assessed on aspects of customer service relevant to their job, in addition to other factors. This serves the purpose of reinforcing the importance of customer service, and also provides a mechanism for

improving performance in this area, and rewarding this where appraisal is to be linked to pay.

- *Pay plans*: It is often said that what gets rewarded gets done, and it is key that rewards reflect what the organization sees as important. For example, if quantity of output is most important production workers, bonuses may relate to number of items produced. If quality is most important, then bonuses may reflect reject rate, or customer complaint rate. If managers are only rewarded for meeting their individual objectives there may be problems if the organization is heavily dependent on team work.

Once the plans have been made and put into action, the manpower planning process still continues. It is important that the plans be monitored to see if they are being achieved and if they are producing the expected results. Plans will also need to be reconsidered on a continuing basis in order to cope with changing circumstances.

Summary propositions

5.1 Human resource planning activities are all interdependent.
5.2 Human resource planning methods range from sophisticated statistical techniques to simple diagnostic tools to analyze judgemental data.
5.3 As human resource planning deals with people, planners need to plan for what is acceptable as well as what is feasible.
5.4 Manpower planning is a continuous process rather than a one-off activity.
5.5 Human resource plans cover areas such as people supply, communications, training/development, appraisal, organization and pay.

References

Bell, D. J. (1974), *Planning Corporate Manpower*, London: Longman.
Bowey, A. (1974), *A Guide to Manpower Planning*, London: Macmillan.
Piercy, N. (1989), 'Diagnosing and solving implementation problems in strategic planning', *Journal of General Management*, vol. 15, no. 1, pp. 19–38.
Smith, A. R. (ed.) (1980), *Corporate Manpower Planning: a personnel review*, Review Monograph, Aldershot: Gower.
Stainer, G. (1971), *Manpower Planning*, London: Heinemann.
Timperley, S. R. (1980), 'Towards a behavioural view of manpower planning'. In A. R. Smith (ed.), *Corporate Manpower Planning*, Aldershot: Gower.
Verhoeven, C. T. (1982), *Techniques in Corporate Manpower Planning*, Boston/The Hague/London: Kluwer/Nijhoff.

Appendix

The City Hotel is located in the middle of a medium-sized city. It caters mainly for business trade during the week and for holiday trade during the weekends and in the summer. In the summer and at weekends there is, therefore, a greater demand for catering and waiting staff as there is a greater demand for lunches. During the same periods there is a lesser demand for housekeeping staff as the customers are mostly longer-stay. The hotel has been gradually improved and refurbished over the past five years, and trade, although reasonably good to begin with, has also gradually improved over the period. There are plans to open an extension with a further twenty bedrooms next year.

Note 1

The management of the City Hotel decided that one of their key objectives over the next three years was to become known for excellence in customer service. This was seen as a key tool to compete with adjacent hotels. Managers used brainstorming to identify the staff behaviours that they wanted to see in place, and summarized their ideas in the format in Table A5.1.

Table A5.1   Behavioural expectations chart: Organization goal – excellence in customer service

Behaviours needed	How to create or reinforce
Address customers by name	A customer service training course to be developed.
Smile at customer	A group incentive bonus to be paid on basis of customer feedback. Customer service meetings to be held in company time once per week
Respond to requests, e.g. room change in positive manner	
Ask customers if everything is to their satisfaction	
Answer calls from rooms within four rings And so on.	

In addition to this a suggestion scheme was instigated to collect ideas for improvement in customer service. A payment of £50 to be made for each successful suggestion.

Note 2

Having mapped the environment, the hotel management looked at the demands and responses for each priority area. For 'customers' the beginnings of the list are shown in Table A5.2.

Table A5.2 Demands and responses for the 'customer' factor

Customer demands	Responses
Polite staff	Our staff pride themselves on being courteous
Staff understand that we are busy people	We will make procedures quick and simple, and staff will respond to needs immediately
Sometimes we need facilities we have not arranged in advance	We will be flexible and enthusiastic in our response
And so on.	

Note 3

Managers of the City Hotel assessed the levels of customer service at present by collecting questionnaire data from both staff and customers and conducting a series of interviews with staff. They also asked in what areas service could be improved and asked staff how this might be achieved. As well as specific targets for improvement, they found many examples of systems and organization that did not help staff give the best customer service. Staff understood that getting the paperwork right was more important than service to the customer in checking out and in. The paperwork systems were over-complex and could be simplified. Also, shift-change times were found to correspond with busy checkout times. Plans were developed to improve systems, organization and communication.

Note 4

In the City Hotel the following relationship between manpower demand and time has been plotted (Figure A5.1). If this trend continued a further one full-time equivalent staff would be needed in the following year.

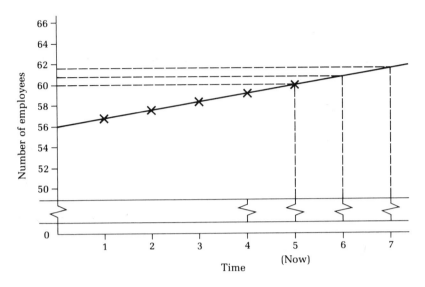

Figure A5.1   *The relationship between manpower and time in the City Hotel*

Note 5

The City Hotel management has plans to open a further twenty bedrooms in a new extension during the coming year. On the basis of this simple model the additional staff required could be worked out as follows:

- Fifty-five bedrooms requires 60 staff.
- The ratio of staff to bedrooms is therefore 1.09 staff per bedroom.
- If the same relationship were maintained (i.e. without any economies of scale) the additional number of staff needed would be: 20 bedrooms × 1.09 staff = 21.8 extra staff needed. Thus total staff needed would = 81.2 full-time equivalent staff.

Note 6

The managerial staff at the City Hotel exercised judgements on the following human resource planning matters:

1. Management considered the probable reasons for the relationship between people demand and time. It was felt that this was most probably due to the

gradual improvement in the hotel over the last five years. Since this improvement had virtually reached its potential it was felt that the relationship between employee demand and time would change.

2. Judgements had to be made on whether the occupancy of the new wing would immediately justify all the additional staff to be appointed.

3. The management considered that since the weather had been very poor in the preceding summer, the bookings for the following summer period might be slightly down on the last year and this shortfall might not be made up by increasing business trade.

4. Judgements were made as to whether staff could be better utilized, with the effect that the additional numbers of staff projected might not be so great.

Note 7

The managers of the City Hotel decided to encourage greater staff flexibility and interchangeability. This interchangeability would be particularly useful between waiting duties and chamber duties. At the present time waiting duties are greatest at the weekend and least during weekdays, whereas chamber duties are the other way around. The effect of this is that waiting staff and chamber staff both have a number of hours of enforced idle time, and the feeling was that there was some overstaffing. By securing flexibility from staff (by paying a flexibility bonus) it was felt that the smooth running and efficiency of the hotel would be considerably increased. It was calculated that the nine chamber posts and eight waiting posts could be covered by sixteen combined posts (all FTEs).

Note 8

The statistical analysis of staff (Table A5.3) was aimed at occupation, age and full-time equivalent posts. This analysis was used primarily for three main purposes:

1. Full-time equivalents needed to be worked out so that this figure could be used in other manpower planning calculations.

2. To consider the occupational balance of staff and to give information which would be useful from the point of view of staff interchangeability.

3. To plan for future retirements and, in consequence, look at recruitment plans and promotion plans.

Table A5.3   Staff by occupation, number and age

Broad occupational group	FTE	Actual number of staff	Ages
General managers and department heads	4 + 5	4 + 5	(45, 43, 30, 21) (51, 47, 45, 35, 32)
Reception/accounts/ clerical	7	8	(55, 24, 24, 23, 21, 21, 21, 18)
Chamber staff	9	12	(52, 51, 35, 35, 34, 33, 31, 31, 30, 29, 20, 19)
Porters	3	3	(64, 51, 20)
Chefs	8	8	(49, 47, 41, 40, 39, 24, 23, 21)
Other kitchen staff	12	16	(59, 59, 57, 52, 51, 31, 29, 28, 27, 27, 24, 24, 24, 23, 19, 18)
Bar/waiting staff	10	14	(51, 45, 35, 35, 33, 32, 30, 29, 26, 26, 25, 25, 20, 21)
Handyperson/gardener	2	2	(64, 63)
Total	60	72	

Note 9

At the City Hotel eighteen staff had left during the preceding year. The annual labour turnover index was therefore worked out to be:

$$\frac{18}{70^*} \times 100 = 25.7 \text{ per cent}$$

(* The average number of staff employed over the year is different from the maximum number of staff that have been employed and were desired to be employed.)

Note 10

At the City Hotel, of the eighteen staff that had been recruited over the year, three of these had been replacements for the same kitchen assistant's job, and two had been replacements for another kitchen assistant's job. The stability index was therefore worked out as:

$$\frac{54}{69^*} \times 100 = 78.26 \text{ per cent stability}$$

(* At exactly one year before there were only 69 of the desired 72 staff in post.)

Note 11

A histogram (Figure A5.2) was plotted of leavers over the past year from the City Hotel. It shows how the majority of leavers had shorter lengths of service, with periods of employment of less than six months being most common.

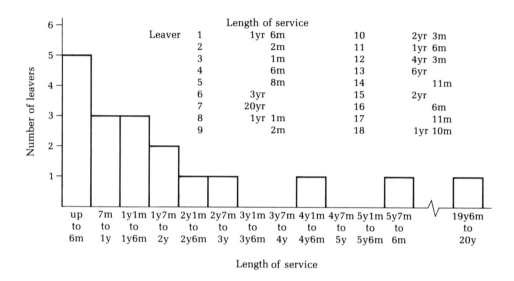

Figure A5.2 shows the following Length of service data:

Leaver	Length of service	Leaver	Length of service
1	1yr 6m	10	2yr 3m
2	2m	11	1yr 6m
3	1m	12	4yr 3m
4	6m	13	6yr
5	8m	14	11m
6	3yr	15	2yr
7	20yr	16	6m
8	1yr 1m	17	11m
9	2m	18	1yr 10m

Figure A5.2 *A histogram of the lengths of service of the eighteen employees leaving during the previous year in the City Hotel*

Note 12

Analysis of the age distribution (Table A5.3) indicates that there may be some difficulties with promotions. In particular, a problem was identified for management promotions. There are four general managers, the youngest being twenty-one. In the past such a junior manager would have been promoted after two years' service, which they had just completed. The ages of the other managers indicate that there will be no retirements in the immediate future and management staff turnover has, in the past few years, been low. In view of this it was thought likely that the junior manager would leave shortly. This was not desired since they were particularly able, so ways of dealing with this promotion block were considered, such as creating of a new post, which might retain the junior manager's services until a promotion became available.

Note 13

There has been a particular problem in recruiting kitchen assistants, waiting and bar staff. This is partly due to local competition, but also to the fact that late starting and early finishing times make travel very difficult. Often there are no buses at these times and taxis are the only available transport. One or two hotels in the area have begun a hotel transport system, and the City Hotel management have decided to investigate this idea in order to attract a higher number of better quality applicants. A second problem has been identified as the lack of availability of chefs and receptionists of the required level of skill. It is felt that the local colleges are not producing potential staff with sufficient skills, and therefore the management of the City Hotel have decided to consider:

1. A training scheme, either run internally or in conjunction with other hotels.
2. Better wages to attract the better trained staff from other employers.
3. Investigation of other localities and the possibility of providing more staff accommodation.

6

Organization structure

To most people the idea of designing an organization is similar to the act of creation recorded in the book of Genesis. It is indeed a beguiling analogy. We read that God created:

> the heaven and the earth. And the earth was without form, and void.
> . . . And God said, Let there be light: and there was light. . . . And
> God said, Let the earth bring forth the living creature after his kind,
> cattle, and creeping thing, and beast of the earth. . . . And God said,
> Let us make man in our image, after our likeness: and let him have
> dominion over . . . all the earth and over every creeping thing that
> creepeth upon the earth. (Authorized Version of the Bible, Genesis 1:
> 1, 3, 4, 26)

We can then reinterpret this as the founder bringing into being a board of directors on the one hand, a company on the other, with the company needing shape and personnel. Enlightenment on how to proceed comes from the contemporary priesthood of consultants and academic philosophers, but then some workers are recruited, with a group of managers to keep the beasts in order and enjoying a special relationship with the founder, following his advice and direction in the hope of eventually joining the board of directors in eternal bliss.

The design of organizations is seen as an act of creation, deploying power and wisdom to put people in a constructive working relationship with each other. It is also seen as a single act: the moment comes and the organization is created in an instantaneous big bang.

Sometimes organizations are brought into being in almost that way. The entrepreneur Richard Branson apparently worked out a complete organization structure for his Virgin Atlantic airline as a preliminary to setting up the company and then recruiting the 102 people needed to fit in all the positions of the organization chart. When a film is made, the form of organization and interrelationships of personnel is well tried and the producer can largely staff the organization in one operation, although the filling of all the vacancies can take months. Other examples of 'big bang' organization design are the opening of a new hospital or a new school.

However attractive this idea may be, it is the minority of managers who find themselves in that situation. For most people the organization is in a steady state of being not right: a pattern of working relationships bedevilled by inefficiency, frustration and obsolescence. For them, organization design is a process of tinkering, pushing and shoving, getting bits and pieces of improvement where possible and occasionally coping with a cataclysm – like a need to shed half the workforce – that seems to leave the worst possible combination of human resources in its wake.

This is likely to be the experience of personnel officers especially. Our research has shown personnel specialists to be involved usually only at the margin of significant changes in work organization. It is interesting that a large proportion of the IPM Employee Resourcing course for the Institute's professional examinations is devoted to this sort of question, yet the questions posed are seldom chosen by students sitting the paper. Alastair Evans and Alan Cowling found that personnel directors rarely had the responsibility for initiating organizational change:

> Most personnel executives in British organizations may be described as having a 'team' role rather than a 'leadership' role in the field of organizational restructuring . . . they are not in most cases initiators of major organizational change nor do they generally have a major role in advising on the forms that new structures might take. (Evans and Cowling 1985)

Whether one is creating the single grand design or coping with the steady state, it is necessary first to understand the process of organizing, and the alternative main forms of organization, before proceeding to consider methods of intervention and the significance of culture.

The fundamentals of the organizing process

Organizing requires both *differentiation* and *integration*. The process of differentiation is setting up the arrangements for an individual job or task to be undertaken effectively, while integration is co-ordinating the output of the individual tasks so that the whole task is completed satisfactorily. There is no one best way of doing either. The organizing of the individual job will vary according to the degree of predictability in what has to be done, so that the organizing of manufacturing jobs tends to emphasize obedience to authority, clearly defined tasks and much specialization. Jobs that have constantly fresh problems and unpredictable requirements, like marketing and social work, produce frequent redefinition of job boundaries, a tendency to flexible networks of working relationships rather than a clear hierarchy, and a greater degree of individual autonomy. Explanations of this process are in Burns and Stalker (1961) and Van de Ven *et al.* (1976).

The integrating process will be influenced by the degree of differentiation. The greater the differentiation, the harder the task of co-ordination. Also Lawrence and Lorsch (1967), in probably the most influential work on organization ever written, have demonstrated that the nature of the integration problem varies with the rate at which new products are being introduced. Galbraith (1977) has further shown that the variations in the level of predictability that require different forms of organization depend on the capacity of the organization to process information about events that cannot be predicted in advance. As the level of uncertainty increases, more information has to be processed with organization being needed to provide the processing capacity.

We can now see how differentiation and integration are put into action in face of uncertainty to produce a working organization. There are three fundamentals:

Task identity and job definition

A job holder or task performer has a label or title which provides the basic identity of tasks the job holder performs, the job content and boundaries. Some of the titles are explicit and understood well enough to meet most organizational requirements. Hearing that someone's job is marketing director, office cleaner, commissionaire, plumber, photographic model or postman provides you with a good initial understanding of that person's role in the organization. Other titles are imprecise or confusing. A single issue of a national newspaper includes the following among the advertised vacancies: clerical assistant, jazz assistant administrator, plastic executive, administrator, information specialist, third party products manager, sub titler, editorial services controller and (most intriguing of all) best boy. Some of these are general titles, which are widely used to cover jobs without highly specific content, others probably are precisely understood by those with experience in a particular industry, and others may be full of meaning for those in a particular business, even though they puzzle those of us without that insider knowledge. However informative the job title, there are still many questions to be answered so that other members of the organization, and those outside, can understand the job holder's status, power, expertise, scope of responsibility and reliability. These questions are especially important where jobs adjoin each other. Where does A's responsibility finish and B's begin? Do areas of responsibility overlap? Are there matters for which no one appears to be responsible?

Review topic 6.1

Write down job titles in your organization that you do not understand, or which you regard as confusing. How would you change
them so that they become more effective labels? How many job titles
are there that have words like 'senior', 'principal' or 'manager' in
them which have no significance other than to confer a spurious
status on the job holder?

The standard device for clarifying task identity and job definition is the job
description, but this is frequently seen as the epitome of stifling, irrelevant
bureaucracy, as well as being lost in a filing cabinet. As we shall see in Chapter 16,
the job description is as central to the work of the personnel specialist as are case
notes to a doctor, but in matters of organization it is a problem. It is an essential
device for allocating people to jobs and tasks to people in a way that can be
understood and to avoid gaps and duplication, but there is always the risk that it
becomes a straitjacket rather than a framework. In our research we found that
only one respondent in four used job analysis for any aspects of organizational
work, compared with one in two using job analysis for recruitment and
selection, two in three for payment arrangements, and one in five for training.
Remembering the significance we have already seen of unpredictability as a key
variable in organizing, there is a further emphasis to the difficulty of using job
descriptions. Here are some typical objections:

> 'I couldn't possibly write down what I do. There is always something
> new.'

> 'If all my staff had job descriptions, I would have even less authority
> than I've got already. They would refuse to do anything unless it was
> specified in the job description.'

> 'Issuing job descriptions is inviting pay claims. As soon as new duties
> come along they are seen as justifying more money.'

> 'A job description ties you down and makes you anonymous. I want a
> job that I can put my own imprint on, making it distinctively my
> individual performance. I'm not a machine.'

In stable organizations the job description is probably an acceptable mechanism
for clarifying the boundaries and content of jobs. In organizations where
uncertainty is the only thing that is certain, the job description will be less
acceptable and appropriate, but identifying the task and defining the job remain
a fundamental of the organizing process.

Structure

People work together, even though the extent to which jobs interlock will vary, so the organization designer has to decide how identified tasks should be grouped together. There are four common bases for such groupings. First is grouping according to *function*, so that the sales personnel are put together in one group, public relations in another group, research in another, and so on. The logic here is that the group members share an expertise and can therefore understand each other, offering valid criticism, leadership and mutual support. This form of grouping is practised more widely than any other and provides an admirable mechanism for deploying within the organization a depth of expertise and specialized skills. The drawback can be the tendency for employees to identify with their function, and its rivalry with other functions, at the expense of the needs of the business.

A second grouping principle is to put people together on the basis of *territory*, with employees of different and complementary skills being co-ordinated by one manager or management in a particular locality. This is usually where there is a satellite separated geographically from the main body of the organization, like the Glasgow office of a nationwide business having a handful of people based in Glasgow covering duties such as sales, service and maintenance, warehousing, invoicing and stock control. The best-known example is the department store or the high street branch of a national bank. This grouping principle reduces the likelihood of misdirected inter-group rivalry by placing the employees close to the customer, but it also reduces the scope for developing depth of expertise.

A third alternative is to group on the basis of *product*, so that varied skills and expertise are again brought together with a common objective; not this time a group of customers in a particular territory, but a product that depends on the interplay of skill variety. John Child gives the example of the hospital, where personnel with medical, nursing, clerical and technical skills are deployed in groups specializing with such 'products' or activities as maternity, paediatrics and accidents. He then explains the difference between the functional and product logics:

> The product-based logic of tasks recognizes how the contributions of different specialists need to be integrated within one complete cycle of work. . . . The product logic is primarily technological, envisaging a flow of work laterally across functional areas. The functional logic is primarily hierarchical, drawing attention to the vertical grouping of people in depth within the boundaries of separate, specialized sections of the company. (Child 1984, p. 87)

The fourth alternative grouping logic is by *time-period*, a form that is dictated by operating circumstances. Where a limited number of people work together at unusual times, like a night shift, then that time-period will be the group boundary for organizational purposes and group members would probably identify first with the group and may feel estranged from the rest of the organization.

When groups are formed, their activities are then linked with those of other groups to aid the necessary co-ordination of activities. This will partly be achieved through the hierarchy with its formal allocation of authority at the various 'cross-over' points so that departments are connected and differences of view between them can sometimes be resolved by this means. Another device is planning, whereby an elaborate plan of interconnecting activities is developed with detailed consultation and agreement, so that different groups are committed to an overall design of their activities over a future period. If each group then goes off and meets that set of objectives, theoretically the output of each fits together according to the prearranged plan and the organization is a corporate success. The cynical laugh you probably produced in reading those last few lines illustrates the shortcomings of the planning approach. There are few examples of corporate plans that succeed in fitting together the activities of disparate groups, and sometimes obsession and conflict about the plan become more important than monitoring the progress of the business. However, some plan is better than no plan at all, and a few plans are very successful. Furthermore, the desire to control some aspects of the future is such a deep-rooted human drive that we shall undoubtedly continue trying to improve our planning methods and the relative autonomy that they provide.

A third way of linking the work of different groups and departments is by meetings. If our reference to planning produced a cynical cough, this reference to meetings probably produced a hollow groan. Managers dislike meetings and tend to disparage those of their colleagues who seem to enjoy them (without actually admitting to enjoyment). That distaste is usually for the routine, dry-as-dust meeting where Jones always goes on and on, Robinson tries to be too damned clever, Smith hasn't read the papers, and as for Blenkinsop . . .! Meetings frequently deteriorate to that stereotyped nightmare, but lack of meetings leads to mistrust of colleagues whose motives are misinterpreted, as well as to simple ignorance about what is happening. Meetings that are properly conceived and well run improve understanding of other people's problems, provide the opportunity of helping to solve those problems, and help to produce decisions and plans of action to which individual members of the organization are committed.

Decision-making complexes

Organizational affairs are pushed along by decisions being made, some by individuals and some by collectives. The scope of decisions to be made by individuals is usually determined by their labelling or by their position in the hierarchy. Some matters, however, are reserved for collective decision. The strategies that emerge from the boardroom have to have majority support among those taking part in the discussion, even if one person may dominate the discussion through ownership influence or personal status. Decisions about the corporate plan, overall marketing strategy, policy on acquisitions are other examples that usually emanate from discussion. The organization designer is interested in determining the nature of the groups that make these decisions and in resolving which matters should be decided in this way.

We use the term decision-making complexes, as the decision is made on the basis of much more than the face-to-face discussion in the meeting which produces the decision. In large undertakings a decision-making group is surrounded by working parties, aides, personal assistants, special advisers and secretaries, who provide position papers, draft reports, mediate between factions and prepare the ground. All these preliminaries partly shape the decision that is eventually made. The increasing number of personnel directors who have effective control of management manning levels are well placed to influence this aspect of organization design by judging which of the endless requests from their colleagues for more staff could put this decision-making process out of balance by increasing the assistance available to one decision-maker at the expense of others.

Alternative forms of organization structure

Charles Handy (1985) drew on earlier work by Roger Harrison (1972) to produce a four-fold classification of organizations according to their basic culture which has caught the imagination of most managers who have read it. Here we present a slightly different explanation, but we acknowledge the source of the main ideas.

There is no single organizational form, no single best way of doing things:

> Organizations are as different and varied as the nations and societies of the world. They have differing cultures – sets of values and norms and beliefs – reflected in different structures and systems. And the cultures are affected by the events of the past and by the climate of the present, by the technology of the type of work, by their aims and the kind of people that work in them. (Handy 1985, p. 9)

Despite this variety there are three broad types of structure found most often and a fourth type that is becoming more common.

The entrepreneurial form

The entrepreneurial form emphasizes central power. It is like the spider's web, with one person or group so dominant that all power stems from the centre, all decisions are made and all behaviour reflects expectations of the centre (Figure 6.1).

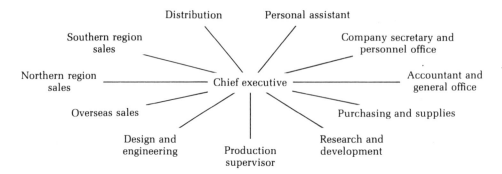

Figure 6.1 *Entrepreneurial organization structure*

There are few collective decisions, much reliance on individuals, and with actions stemming from obtaining the approval of key figures. It is frequently found in organizations where matters have to be decided quickly and with flair and judgement rather than careful deliberation. Newspaper editing has entrepreneurial form in its organization and most of the performing arts have strong centralized direction.

This type of structure is the form of most small and growing organizations as they owe their existence to the expertise or initiative of one or two people, and it is only by reflecting accurately that originality that the business can survive. As the organization grows larger this type of structure can become unwieldy because so many peripheral decisions cannot be made without approval from the centre, which then becomes over-loaded. It is also difficult to maintain if the spider leaves the centre. A successor may not have the same degree of dominance. In some instances the problem of increasing size has been dealt with by maintaining entrepreneurial structure at the core of the enterprise and giving considerable independence to satellite organizations, providing that overall performance targets are met.

The bureaucratic form

The bureaucratic form emphasizes the distribution of power and responsibility rather than its centralization. It has been the conventional means of enabling an organization to grow beyond the entrepreneurial form to establish an existence that is not dependent on a single person or group of founders (Figure 6.2). Through emphasizing role rather than flair, operational processes become more predictable and consistent, with procedure and committee replacing individual judgement.

Responsibility is devolved through the structure and it is a method of organization well suited to stable situations, making possible economies of scale

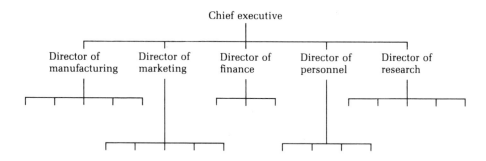

Figure 6.2 *Typical bureaucratic organization structure*

and the benefits of specialization. There is seldom the flexibility to deal with a volatile environment and a tendency to be self-sufficient:

> The bureaucratic approach is intended to provide organizational control through ensuring a high degree of predictability in people's behaviour. It is also a means of trying to ensure that different clients or employees are treated fairiy through the application of general rules and procedures. The problem is that rules are inflexible instruments of administration which enshrine experience of past rather than present conditions, which cannot be readily adapted to suit individual needs, and which can become barriers behind which it is tempting for the administrator to hide. (Child 1984, p. 8)

Bureaucracy has been the standard form of structure for large organizations for thousands of years and remains the dominant form today. It has, however, come under criticism recently because of its inappropriateness in times of change and a tendency to frustrate personal initiative.

The matrix form

The matrix form emphasizes the co-ordination of expertise into project-oriented groups of people with individual responsibility. It has been developed to overcome some of the difficulties of the enterpreneurial and bureaucratic forms (Figure 6.3). It was first developed in the United States during the 1960s as a means of satisfying the government on the progress of orders placed with contractors for the supply of defence material. Much of the material had to be designed and developed before manufacture and delivery, so that officials of government agencies frequently wished to check on progress. This proved very difficult with a bureaucracy, so it was made a condition of contracts that the contractor should appoint a project manager with responsibility for meeting the delivery commitments and keeping the project within budget. In this way the

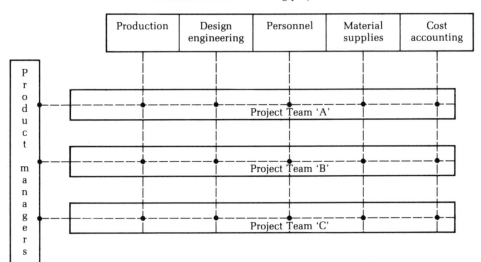

Figure 6.3 *Typical matrix organization structure*

government was able to deal with a single representative rather than with a number of people with only partial responsibility. The contractors then had to realign their organization so that the project manager could actually exercise the degree of control necessary to make the responsibility effective. This is done either by appointing a product manager with considerable status and power, or by creating product teams with specialists seconded from each functional area. The first method leaves the weight of authority with the functional hierarchy, while the product managers have a mainly co-ordinating, progress-chasing role as lone specialists. The second method shifts power towards the product managers, who then have their own teams of experts, with the functional areas being seen as a resource rather than the centre of action and decision. A third, but less common, situation is a permanent overlay of one set of hierarchical connections laid horizontally over a pre-existing conventional, vertical hierarchy. This brings the relative power distribution into approximate balance, but can also make decision-making very slow as a result of that equilibrium.

The matrix is the form that appeals to most managers as a theoretical method of organization as it is based on expertise and provides scope for people at relatively humble levels of the organization to deploy their skills and carry responsibility. It has, however, recently lost favour because it can generate expensive support systems for product managers needing additional secretaries, assistants and all the panoply of office, as well as the unwieldy administration referred to above.

One of the ways in which matrix might find a new lease of life is in the increasing internationalization of business, where the impracticability of bureaucracy will be most obvious:

> Operations which cross national boundaries will almost inevitably run with matrix structures, whether or not they are called that. Dotted lines; more than one boss; activity-based working groups whose members have a primary reporting relationship in many different parts of the organization; more time spent consulting and agreeing and building consensus than in issuing or receiving command-type instructions. (Vineall 1988, p. 47)

The independence form

The independence form emphasizes the individual and is almost a form of non-organization. The other three are all methods of putting together the contributions of a number of people so that the sum is greater than the parts, results being achieved by the co-ordination of effort. The independence form is a method of providing a support system so that individuals can perform, with the co-ordination of individual effort being either subsidiary or absent (Figure 6.4).

Barristers' chambers and doctors' clinics work in this way and it is a form of organization attractive to those of independent mind who are confident of their ability to be individually successful. Some firms of consultants and craft workshops operate similarly, with a background organization to enable the specialists to operate independently. It has been regarded as unsuitable for most types of undertaking because of the lack of co-ordination and control, but it is attractive to many people and there is growing interest in it with the increasing emphasis on individual responsibility in business and a tendency to focus on professional skill rather than expertise.

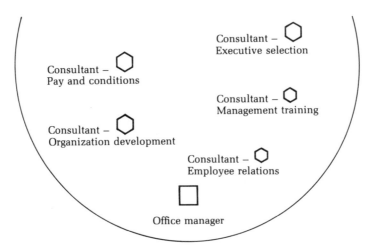

Figure 6.4 *The independence form of organization*

Review topic 6.2

Which of the four forms of organization would you regard as most important for the following:

1. The operating theatre of a hospital.
2. A kibbutz.
3. A library.
4. A university department.
5. A department store.
6. A primary school.
7. A psychiatric ward.
8. A hotel.
9. A fashion house.
10. A trade union.

Differentiated structures

This four-fold classification is a means of analysis rather than a description of four distinct types of organization with any undertaking being clearly one of the four (Figure 6.5). Bureaucracies will typically have matrix features at some points and few entrepreneurial structures are quite as 'pure' as described here. Probably any organization you could name could be classified as having one of these four features dominant and in some there is one form dominant in one section of the business and another form dominant elsewhere. Large banks, for example, are bureaucratic in their retailing operations as consistency is of paramount importance

Form	Conditions
Entrepreneurial	Dominance of single person or group at centre, due to ownership, expertise or the need of the operation for a strong controlling figure. Modest size, simple technology and single, dominant technical expertise. Uncertain or rapidly changing environment.
Bureaucratic	Complex organization with devolved power and expertise. Large size, complex technology and varied technical expertise. Stable environment.
Matrix	Complex organization with bureaucratic features and need to devolve responsibility and enhance responsiveness to clients.
Independence	Simple organization form to support independent activities of specialists, with little co-ordination. Professional, rather than management, orientation among specialists.

Figure 6.5 *Conditions favouring different organizational forms*

and any changes need to be put into operation simultaneously by a large number of people while being comprehensible to a large number of customers. The same banks will, however, tend to an entrepreneurial emphasis in their merchant banking activities and to independence in currency dealings.

A new form of structure?

All these four have some shortcomings, even though bureaucracy seems to have more than the others. There is much discussion about the new forms of organization that will be needed in the future, based on an assessment of current and evolving activities that could make a new form of organization viable. The following are some of the reasons for this view:

- *Big is no longer always beautiful*: Most organizational structures are based on an implicit assumption that the business will expand, but this is no longer seen as the sole form of growth: diversification and change are equally interesting, and sometimes wiser, alternatives.
- *Business is not necessarily directed towards permanence*: Until quite recently enterprises were established with the objective of continuing indefinitely, often with a semi-dynastic objective – 'All this will be yours one day my lad.' There is now greater emphasis on terms like project and venture, setting up an enterprise that will run for a time and then closed or sold on.
- *The customer is king*: There is increased emphasis on the importance of the customer and meeting the customer's needs, so that gradually preoccupation with internal affairs and organizational politics becomes less and the people of the organization become less inward-looking, with issues of hierarchical status having less importance.
- *The proliferation of expertise*: Running a business requires an increasing variety of skills and diverse expertise, so that management relies on people knowing what to do and being required to get on with it. Seldom is a single business big enough to employ all the experts it requires, so many skills have to be bought in on a temporary basis from consultants or contractors.
- *The arrival of information technology*: Gradually, computerized management information systems are able to produce the quality of control data that can depersonalize the management process to a greater extent. Objectives for individuals and sections have a greater degree of quantification and performance is measurable.

Human resource management is partly a response to these factors and ever-growing interest in performance appraisal and performance management is another manifestation. Drucker (1988) suggests the need for a considerable reduction in the number of layers in the management hierarchy, with the idea that the organization of the future will be like a symphony orchestra, with a range of highly skilled experts, who know exactly what to do, provided that a conductor provides co-ordination and brio. That superb metaphor is slightly weakened, as he concedes, by the fact that a business does not have the main co-ordinating mechanism of the symphony orchestra: the score to read from.

We believe that the key to finding a new organizational form lies in reviewing the notion of hierarchy. The analyses of some economists (notably Marglin 1974; Williamson 1975) give us a different angle on working relationships within organizations, as they look for a rational basis. The entrepreneurial, bureaucratic and matrix forms all take hierarchy as a given, and the guiding principle is 'to whom are you accountable?', just as the law sees employees as servants of a master – the employer – and the legal basis on which most of us work is a contract of *employment*. If you start without the hierarchical assumption, it is just as feasible to construe working relationships as transactions. This produces a choice, as the working relationship can either be set in a market, where one buys services from another, or it can be set in a hierarchy, where one obtains work from another. Pinchot (1985) has advocated the idea of 'intrapreneuring' as a way of making members of a hierarchy more entrepreneurial in their approach to dealing with each other and with their responsibilities.

Tentatively, we describe the new form of organization as *professional*. It has many features of the independence form and some of matrix. Fundamental to its operation is the core/periphery type split, which is described in our chapter on labour markets. The core contains all those activities which will be carried out by employees, while the periphery contains activities that will be put out to tender by contractors. The crucial decisions relate to which activities should be in which area. The core should contain those skills that are specialized to the business, rare or secret. Logically, all the other activities are put in the periphery, but suppose there is an unexpected shortage of people to provide peripheral skills? In approaching privatization, several British water authorities reduced their employment of civil engineers, because they were expensive and the work could be done on an occasional basis by consultants. Gradually, however, there developed a shortage of civil engineers in the consultancy firms, so that the simple rules of the market-place ceased to operate. The consultants were normally too small to carry trainees in the same way that the water authorities had done. Should water authorities now employ more core civil engineers?

The approach to the core employees is to give them a strong sense of identification with the business and its success, usually through developing a corporate culture, in the way described in the next chapter, with shared values and reinforced, consistent behaviours. Those on the periphery have a close specification of what is required from them and their continued engagement depends on meeting the terms of the contract.

At first sight there is one way in which this form of organization is unattractive to most people, namely the lack of secure employment. Kanter (1989, p. 358) believes there is no escape from this, and that security in the future will come from *continued employability* rather than continuity of employment. There will be no safe havens for those who can no longer keep up. This seemingly harsh message may nevertheless be the way of overcoming the greatest weaknesses of bureaucracy, as the safe havens are usually in senior posts!

The lessons of the last twenty years for the organization designer are that tinkering with the structure will be fruitless without thinking through the purpose of the organization, the nature of the demands being placed on it from outside, the types of operation which are to be organized, and the people available. Efficient bureaucrats may not make good entrepreneurs, independence is clearly inappropriate if the operation is one with closely interlocking tasks, and moving to a matrix may not be the best way of dealing with a dramatic change in the product market.

Weber (1947) remains the best possible reference for understanding the nature of bureaucracy, although Blau (1966) is useful to read in conjunction with Weber. Davis and Lawrence (1977) is the standard source on matrix structures. Apart from Child (1984) and Handy (1985), the best comprehensive treatment of different approaches to organization is undoubtedly Mintzberg (1979). Peters (1989) and Kanter (1989) are both stimulating in describing the forms of organization of the future.

Review topic 6.3

If you were running an airport, which of the following activities would you locate in the core and which on the periphery of your business:

1. Baggage handling?
2. The fire service?
3. Catering?
4. Newsagency?
5. Airport information?
6. Car park attendance?
7. Maintenance of premises and services?
8. Cleaning?

The alternative inputs to decision-making complexes

The third fundamental of the organizing process is the range of decision-making complexes, which are both a product of differentiation and a means of integration. An attractive notion from management folklore is that decisions made by committees are cautious, slow and ineffectual, while decisions made by individuals are imaginative, swift and creative. As organizational life becomes more complicated, we have to contrast that traditional view with the warning of Toffler:

> Too many decisions, too fast, about too many strange and unfamiliar problems – not some imagined 'lack of leadership' – explain the gross incompetence of political and governmental decisions today. Our institutions are reeling from a decisional implosion. (Toffler 1980, p. 421)

Some decisions are best taken slowly, so that they are based on a thorough analysis of all the factors, and many of the decisions to be taken slowly also need to be taken collectively. Most decisions are still taken by individuals, even though they may seek endorsement from their colleagues, but we have identified five types of decision best made by a decision-making complex (DMC).

1. *Simple structuring*: This is where a relatively simple decision has to be made between alternatives, but the advantages and disadvantages have to be carefully weighed before the decision is made – probably by one person. In order that this person can weigh the alternatives wisely much detailed analysis and calculation is needed. If the problem is remitted to a group like a think tank, the members can prepare the matter for decision by structuring the arguments for and against, leaving the decision-maker to choose between them.
2. *Complex structuring*: This is similar, except that the decision is not simply between two alternatives. The problem is remitted to the group without the lines of action being clear, so that the DMC is finding possible answers to the question as well as preparing the arguments for and against. Now the members of the DMC have greater scope and greater power as their deliberations will determine the options between which a choice is to be made rather than simply preparing the arguments where the choices have already been determined.
3. *Simple consensus*: Simple consensus is the type of decision where the choice is clear between two alternatives, but where the outcome needs to carry the support of those concerned. The difference in practice between this mode and simple structuring is that the membership of the DMC would probably be larger and representative of different interests.
4. *Complex consensus*: Again, a consensus is needed, but the alternatives are not clear before the DMC begins its deliberations.
5. *Development*: This is a quite different type of decision-making from the other four as the reason for remitting the decision to a DMC is either to develop the skills and capacities of the group members or to develop the cohesion of the organization. The decision itself is not as important as the

process of making the decision, which will either develop more effective members of the organization by involving in decision-making those who would otherwise lack that experience, or it will help integrate the different parts of the organization by involving representatives of each in making decisions which affect them all, so keeping their activities in step.

The DMCs appropriate for these various types of decision will also vary. Simple structuring decisions will usually be undertaken by a small group of one or two aides to a person of considerable personal authority. Complex structuring is likely to be by a larger group of people to cope with the complexity as well as the political sensitivity of the task. Either type could go to a semi-permanent DMC, like a think tank, but is more often passed to an *ad hoc* working party. The important feature of the DMCs for consensus decisions will be their representative character and their status. Representation is needed to produce consensus and status may be needed to give recommendations authority so that they are implemented rather than ignored. Sometimes there will be a working party brought into existence for this sole purpose, but we are now moving into the area of permanent committees, many of which do not simply formulate a decision but make the decision itself. This type of DMC is the most powerful nexus in organizational structure. Development decision-making, where the objective is to develop the capacity of subordinates, is usually of the junior board type, but DMCs to integrate the different parts of the organization are rather more influential. We distinguish between them and complex consensus because we see the main purpose as the process of integration and not the substantive decisions, so the DMCs usually have names like co-ordinating group, liaison committee or joint advisory panel.

Organization design and the personnel manager

Of the four fundamentals of the organizing process introduced at the opening of this chapter, we have dealt with structures and decision-making complexes. The others – task identity and operating procedures – are considered in more detail in later chapters. Another aspect – organization development – is referred to in the chapter on management development. For personnel managers to make an effective contribution to implementing their personnel philosophy a stake in organizational design is essential. Some find it too impersonal and political, preferring to concentrate on more individual and specific issues, like training or employee relations, yet the inadequacies of organization design can make impractical many of the other initiatives which personnel managers seek to get underway and the professional expertise of personnel managers makes them better equipped than any of their colleagues to take on this responsibility:

> If the human, social and structural characteristics of the organization are . . . inextricably linked, it follows that personnel managers will not develop the full potential of their function unless they are as proficient in organizational analysis as they are in diagnosing human and social needs. (Fowler 1985, p. 27)

Summary propositions

6.1 Organization design is occasionally a process of creating an entire organization from scratch, but for most people it is modifying bits of an existing organization.

6.2 Personnel officers rarely play a significant role in organization design.

6.3 The four fundamentals of organization design are task identity and job definition, structure, decision-making complexes and operating procedures.

6.4 Alternative forms of structure are entrepreneurial, bureaucratic, matrix and independence. A new form of professional organization can also be seen.

6.5 Alternative forms of decision-making are simple structuring, complex structuring, simple consensus, complex consensus and development.

References

Blau, P. (1966), *The Dynamics of Bureaucracy*, Chicago: University of Chicago Press.

Burns, T. and Stalker, G. M. (1961), *The Management of Innovation*, London: Tavistock.

Child, J. (1984), *Organization: A guide to problems and practice* (2nd edition), London: Harper & Row.

Davis, S. M. and Lawrence, P. R. (1977), *Matrix*, Wokingham: Addison Wesley.

Drucker, P. F. (1988), 'The coming of the new organization', *Harvard Business Review*, vol. 66, no. 1, January–February.

Evans, A. and Cowling, A. (1985), 'Personnel's part in organization restructuring.' *Personnel Management*, January.

Fowler, A. (1985), 'Getting in on organization restructuring', *Personnel Management*, February.

Galbraith, J. R. (1977), *Organization Design*, Wokingham: Addison–Wesley.

Handy, C. B. (1985), *Understanding Organizations* (3rd edition), Harmondsworth: Penguin Books.

Harrison, R. (1972), 'How to describe your organization', *Harvard Business Review*, September/October.

Kanter, R. M. (1989), *When Giants Learn to Dance*, New York: Simon & Schuster.

Lawrence, P. R. and Lorsch, J. W. (1967), *Organization and Environment*, Cambridge, MA: Harvard University Press.

Marglin, S. (1974), 'What do bosses do?' In A. Gorz (ed.), *Division of Labour*, Brighton: Harvester Press.

Mintzberg, H. (1979), *The Structuring of Organizations*, Englewood Cliffs, NJ: Prentice Hall.

Peters, T. (1989), *Thriving on Chaos*, London: Pan Books.

Pinchot, G. (1985), *Intrapreneuring: why you don't have to leave the organization to become an intrapreneur*, New York: Harper & Row.

Toffler, A. (1980), *The Third Wave*, London: Pan Books.

Van de Ven, A. H., Delbecq, A. L. and Koenig, R. (1976), 'Determinants of coordination modes within organizations', *American Sociological Review*, April.

Vineall, T. (1988), 'Creating a multinational management team, *Personnel Management*, October.

Weber, M. (1947), *The Theory of Social and Economic Organizations*, New York: Free Press.

Williamson, O. E. (1975), *Markets and Hierarchies: Analysis and antitrust implications*, New York: Free Press.

7

Organizations and culture

Organizational culture is the characteristic spirit and belief of an organization, demonstrated, for example, in the norms and values that are generally held about how people should behave and treat each other, the nature of working relationships that should be developed and attitudes to change. These norms are deep, taken-for-granted, assumptions, which are not always expressed and are often known without being understood.

The history and traditions of an organization reveal something of its culture because the cultural norms develop over a relatively long period, with layers and layers of practice both modifying and consolidating the norms and providing the framework of ritual and convention in which people feel secure, once they have internalized its elements.

Although it sounds strange to attribute human qualities to organizations, they do have distinctive identities. Wally Olins (1989) cites the example of the world's great chemical companies, which superficially seem similar and produce virtually identical products selling at the same price. Yet they each have strong identities, and in culture are as different as individual human beings.

Corporate culture

Corporate culture is a more self-conscious expression of specific types of objective in relation to behaviour and values. This entices customers to buy; and it entices prospective employees to seek jobs and causes them to feel commitment to the organization:

> research demonstrates that a good organization which is well known
> is admired more and liked better than an equally good company

which is not so well known. It will attract more and better people to work for it, can more readily make acquisitions and more effectively launch new products: it will perform better. (Olins 1989, p. 53)

This identity can be expressed and reinforced in various forms, such as a formal statement from the chief executive, or in such comments as: 'We don't do things that way here'. There is the logo, the stationery, the uniform. In one way or another it is an attempt to ensure commitment. Through all employing organizations there is inevitably some withholding of co-operation by staff, even where they accept the authority of managers and their right to manage. This is, in part, because managers have an unrealistic expectation about co-operation and in part because of the limited extent to which the authority of position can be exercised. Corporate culture can get round this problem.

Schools provide an interesting model for commercial corporations, as they are organizations with a tradition of developing an ethos (which is the same as corporate culture) with skill and great effect. They have, however, had some difficulty in adapting to social change.

Traditionally, the culture in schools was one of high consensus, often centred on strong loyalty to a headteacher who was expected to symbolize and expound the culture of the school, rather like a monarch, through such ritual devices as social distance, taking school assembly, wearing a gown, having a veto on major decisions and running staff meetings in a magisterial way.

In the mid-1970s doubts crept in as the aims for schools became more diverse and the organization more complex. In some cases this led to increased managerialism, an interest in management for its own sake rather than as a means to an end. If a school culture is long-established and widely accepted by staff, the authority of position may be effective. Once change becomes necessary the authority of position becomes insecure unless the person in authority is a charismatic polymath.

Schools have had to cope with a great deal of change in the last decade, but much of that change has involved teachers working in different ways, especially working more closely with each other and across the boundaries of disciplines. Not only has it made great demands on individual teachers, it has also made inoperable a culture of consensus based solely on loyalty to the head. Debate increases as a necessary prelude to action, uncertainty becomes more commonplace, the nature of individual autonomy is being reconstructed (Torrington and Weightman 1989, pp. 17–55).

It is important that those employed in an organization should try to understand the culture they share. Managers in general, and personnel managers in particular, have to understand the extent to which culture can be changed and how the changes can be made, even if the changes may be much harder and slower to make than most managers believe and most circumstances allow.

As we have already said, culture is often not expressed and may be known without being understood. It is none the less real and powerful, so that the enthusiasts who unwittingly work counter-culturally will find that there is a metaphorical but solid brick wall against which they are beating their heads. Enthusiasts who pause to work out the nature of the culture in which they are operating can at least begin the process of change and influence the direction of the cultural evolution, because culture can never be like a brick wall. It is living, growing and vital, able to strengthen and support the efforts of those who use it, as surely as it will frustrate the efforts of those who ignore it.

A further important aspect of organizational cultures is the extent to which they are typically dominated by traditional male values of rationality, logic, competition and independence, rather than the traditional female values of emotional expression, intuition, caring and interdependence (Marshall 1985). Is it necessary that organizational cultures should be so biased? Is that the only way to prosper? Perhaps not, but it seems that an organization has to be set up from scratch by women if it is to develop a different culture:

> Women . . . may not be properly represented at important levels of big corporations, but they are now doing remarkably well in the firms they have set up themselves. Here, they don't have to play the male game according to male rules. They are free to make up their own rules, make relationships rather than play games, run their businesses more on a basis of trust than of fear, co-operation rather than rivalry. (Moir and Jessell 1989, p. 167.

Goffee and Scase (1985) studied women executives and found abundant evidence of women being very successful when able to operate outside a male-dominated culture. Indeed, the cause of equality for women at work may well be jeopardized rather than helped by the argument that the only non-genital differences between men and women are socially determined (Tiger 1970).

Review topic 7.1

Is your organization dominated by male characteristics? Where are there signs of female values? How could the female values spread further in the organization? What would be the effect on the success of the organization?

Culture in national context

No organization is an island, so attempts to foster or alter corporate culture must take account not only of the intentions of those in charge and the expectations of those employed, but also of developments in the surrounding society, both nationally and internationally.

In Britain the idea of an enterprise culture in the 1980s was more than the platform of a political party, it was the articulation of an idea whose time had come. There was a sudden upsurge of new businesses, mostly small and specialized, but there was also an associated change in values and expectations among many working people, especially the young, which was to increase interest in careers, mentoring, customized pay arrangements, networking and others. Whatever business you were in, you had to take on board this change of cultural emphasis. Through the 1980s, the enterprise emphasis has lost some of its momentum, although people remain more willing to take risks in order to get what they want out of life.

Concern for the environment has developed rapidly into the early 1990s, so that the expression of environmental responsibility is becoming necessary in the product market, but it is also necessary as a feature of the corporate culture to which employees will respond. It is becoming more difficult to get people to commit themselves to projects that they regard as unworthy. They may do it for the money, but will not offer commitment. Increasingly, people look to their workplace for their personal opportunities to do what is worthwhile. The extraordinary success of such television spectaculars as Bandaid and Children in Need has been mainly built on money raised by groups of people operating in, or from, their place of work. Marketing specialist Elizabeth Nelson reports the result of consumer surveys:

> Throughout the political spectrum there is a growing awareness that the State should be made more efficient, via competition. Individual responsibility plus collective efficiency is a model for the next twenty years. Our surveys show that there is a strong majority even among the very rich prepared to pay more in tax to alleviate poverty. (Nelson 1989, p. 296)

Concern for the environment is growing apace at the national political level. At the local level there is not only concern about the ozone layer and greenhouse effect, but noise, dirt, smells and inconvenience to fellow citizens. Corporate culture has to assimilate these concerns.

Review topic 7.2

- How could your organization be more protective of the environment?
- What would be the costs of the changes you describe?
- What would be the benefits of the changes you describe?

Culture in international context

As business becomes increasingly international, personnel managers have to become international as well, although not at quite the same speed as their marketing colleagues. International cultural issues are a puzzle. Some things that are apparently nationalistic seem to be understood and welcomed in almost all cultures: pizza, Coca-Cola, chop suey, Rolls-Royce, *Dallas* and *Dynasty*, Scotch wool and the British Royal Family being a few examples. At the same time there are strong cultural differences in language and its use. The French have developed their language as a precision tool for analysis and conceptualization. For the Japanese, language is an emollient for creating an atmosphere conducive to harmonious interaction. And the Americans use their version of English as a store of snappy neologisms to excite, distract and motivate.

The Frenchman Philippe Poirson explains the differences of cultural emphasis in management between the Americans, Japanese and French by pointing to the continuing dominance of the Protestant work ethic:

> belief in the redemptive virtue of work has built a system of values for many founders and directors of American business organizations . . . profit is legitimate, success in business evaluable, 'work ethics' highly developed. (Poirson 1989, p. 6)

In contrast, the Japanese are oriented to human efficiency rather than human functioning because of their quite different heritage. The idea of individual autonomy is a relatively recent development of European/US influences. To a great extent the Japanese continue to espouse the values of an agricultural, feudal nation, living in an introverted manner by developing specific sociability: 'the group's superiority over the individual remains a fundamental particularity of Japanese sociability. However, the new role of firms seems slowly to replace the one traditionally held by the house and the village' (*ibid.*, p. 7). He suggests that the French have a social pact which differs from the American in the approach to the 'book of rules'. For the Americans this is sacrosanct, and liberty is the ability to spread one's own sovereignty – even if it impedes others – providing it is done within the rules. In France, however, there is 'a duty of moderation in acts susceptible to hinder the situation of others. This attitude of moderation is not explicitly codified, neither is it codifiable, but it indicates a certain tendency in French culture' (*ibid.*, p. 7).

The history of the European Community in attempting to establish a supra-national institution is one of constant, but reluctant recognition of the stubbornness of national differences and the accentuation of regional differences among, for instance, the Basques and the Flemish. Nationality is important to personnel management because of its effect on human behaviour and the consequent constraints on management action.

Identity

Nationality is a root source of our individual identity, with all its affiliations and allegiances. An affection for cricket is widespread in England and some countries of the Commonwealth, but not all: something funny about the Canadians. Arabs have a tradition of hospitality to guests that can cause them to be deeply offended when invitations are declined. The Japanese have great difficulty about losing face, and the Germans have made efficiency and attention to detail a national characteristic. There is also the difficulty that we tend to associate certain characteristics unthinkingly with certain nationalities, yet not all Spaniards are hot-tempered and not all Scots are mean.

When national identity is threatened, the members of a nation can quickly demonstrate remarkable solidarity and hostility to the source of the threat. The British resentment of the Argentinian invasion of the Falkland Islands was not just an example of newspaper hype, and it took a long time for the obvious quality of Japanese motor cars to overcome European sales resistance.

Conditioning

Family conventions, religious traditions and forms of education differ markedly between countries, and every adult is partly a product of these features of conditioning, with the attendant values, imperatives and beliefs that shape behaviour and expectation. American children are taught very early the values of individuality and doing your own thing; Japanese children are taught to conform, to work within a group and to develop team spirit. Alan Barratt is a US management development specialist who has extensive dealings with the Arab world and comments:

> The Arab executive is likely to try to avoid conflict . . . on an issue favoured by subordinates but opposed by the executive, he is likely to let the matter drop without taking action. . . . He values loyalty over efficiency. Many executives tend to look on their employees as family and will allow them to by-pass the hierarchy in order to meet them. (Barratt 1989, p. 29)

Political and legal system

Different nations are distinct political units, so that the political institutions and the ways in which they are used are different. This is not just the formal but also the informal political realities that are resistant to change. The laws and the systems of law differ, so that some countries, like Australia and the United States, have legally binding arbitration as a way of resolving industrial disputes.

Not only is this a practice unknown in Britain, it also means that the status of the contract of employment is different.

Geert Hofstede (1980) analyzed no fewer than 116,000 questionnaires administered to employees in forty different countries and concluded that national cultures could be explained by four key factors:

1. *Individualism*: This is the extent to which people expect to look after themselves and their family only. The opposite is collectivism, which has a tight social framework and in which people expect to have a wider social responsibility to discharge because others in the group will support them. Those of a collectivist persuasion believe they owe absolute loyalty to their group.
2. *Power distance*: This factor measures the extent to which the less powerful members of the society accept the unequal distribution of power. In organizations this is the degree of centralization of authority and the exercise of autocratic leadership.
3. *Uncertainty avoidance*: The future is always unknown, but some societies socialize their members to accept this and take risks, while members of other societies have been socialized to be made anxious about this and seek the security of law, religion or technology.
4. *Masculinity*: The division of roles between the sexes varies from one society to another. Where men are assertive and have dominant roles these values permeate the whole of society and the organizations that make them up, so there is an emphasis on showing off, performing, making money and achieving something visible. Where there is a larger role for women who are more service-oriented with caring roles, the values move towards concern for the environment and the quality of life, putting the quality of relationships before the making of money and not showing off.

Hofstede found some clear national cultural differences between nationalities. A sample of scores on the four criteria are given in Table 7.1.

An earlier and less well-known piece of US research (Ronen and Kraut 1977) surveyed work attitudes and expectations in thirty countries and were able to group some of these into clusters indicating broadly similar values and attitudes among employees. Representative countries in the five clusters were:

1. *Anglo-American*: Australia, Canada, Great Britain, New Zealand, United States.
2. *Central European*: Austria, Germany, Switzerland.
3. *Latin American*: Argentina, Chile, Mexico, Peru.
4. *Latin European*: France, Italy, Spain.
5. *Nordic*: Denmark, Norway, Sweden.

It might seem that the language common to most of these groups is the overwhelming reason for the similarity, but the cultural differences between,

Table 7.1 Cultural differences between nations

Criterion	High	Low
Power distance	Mexico	Austria
	Philippines	Denmark
	Venezuela	Israel
	Yugoslavia	New Zealand
Uncertainty avoidance	Belgium	Denmark
	Greece	Hong Kong
	Japan	Singapore
	Portugal	Sweden
Individualism	Australia	Colombia
	Canada	Pakistan
	Great Britain	Peru
	United States	Venezuela
Masculinity	Austria	Denmark
	Italy	Norway
	Japan	Sweden
	Venezuela	Yugoslavia

say, the British and the Americans are reasonably apparent to those nationalities and the cultural differences between the French and the Germans may well be obscured to British perceptions because of not sharing the same linguistic heritage.

Developing organizational culture

The most penetrating analysis of organizational culture is by Schein (1985), who distinguishes between the ways in which an organization needs to develop a culture which enables it to adapt to its changing environment (pp. 52–65) and, at the same time, build and maintain itself through processes of internal integration (pp. 65–83).

How do cultures change? How do they become consolidated? The general comment of Schein is that there are primary and secondary mechanisms. The primary mechanisms are:

1. What leaders pay most attention to.
2. How leaders react to crises and critical incidents.
3. Role modelling, teaching and coaching by leaders.
4. Criteria for allocating rewards and determining status.
   and
5. Criteria for selection, promotion and termination (Schein 1985, pp. 224–37).

This places great emphasis on example-setting by those in leadership roles. If the manager walks round a construction site without a hard hat, then it unlikely that other people will regard such headgear as important. The comment about how leaders react to crises and critical incidents is interesting. At one level this is to do with reactions like calmness or urgency, but it is also a question of what is identified by leaders as crises and critical incidents. If there is great attention paid by managers to punctuality and less to quality, then punctuality receives greater emphasis in the eyes of everyone.

The comment about coaching and teaching by leaders indicates the degree of social integration there needs to be between the opinion formers and those holding the opinions and producing the behaviour that those opinions shape. Research on how people learn demonstrates quite clearly that attitude formation is developed effectively by social interaction and scarcely at all by other methods. Exhortation and written instructions or assurances are likely to do little to change the culture of an organization: working closely with people can.

There is an important connection here with soft human resource planning described in Chapter 4. Personnel managers can produce the most wonderful plans, but there will be no progress unless there is commitment to the plans and commensurate behaviour by leaders and opinion-formers.

The most significant reinforcement of attitudes and beliefs comes from that which is tangible and visible. What do people need to do to get a pay rise? What do you have to do to get promoted? What can lead to people being fired?

Those working in and around organizations usually want the first two and try to avoid the third. If loyalty is rewarded you will get loyalty, but may not get performance. If performance is rewarded, people will at least try to deliver performance.

This line of argument by Schein presents two difficulties. First, such emphasis on 'leadership' can imply dependence on one Great Person to whom everyone else responds. Second, it is too easy to confuse cultural leadership with position leadership; those who are most effective in setting the tone may not be those in the most senior posts even though they are well placed for this.

Focusing on the Great Person also emphasizes hierarchical principles of organization. There are limits to what can be achieved by hierarchical means, as we have already seen, and some radical views of organizations, such as Hyman (1987), criticize all hierarchical forms of organization as preventing their members giving of their best. Organizational culture is the concern of all members, and change in a culture is effective and swift only when there is wide agreement and ownership concerning the change to be sought. Wide agreement about important aspects of culture seems to be best obtained, paradoxically, through a recognition and toleration of a legitimate plurality of views and styles on less central matters. Differences will not be resolved by the Great Person exercising 'the right to manage', but through discussion among all parties concerned. This also affects the planning process as planners need to devote considerable time and energy to generate commitment to their plans at the same time as avoiding those that will not be acceptable.

Review topic 7.3

Think of an organization, of which you are or have been a member, that had a strong leader. This may not necessarily have been an employing organization, but a school, youth club, operatic society, political association, etc.

1. Did the leader shape the culture?
2. Did the culture resist the leader?
3. How did the shaping or resistance manifest itself?

An elevated position in a hierarchy, though possibly helpful, is not a guarantee of effectivenesss in the pursuit of, or opposition to, cultural change.

A third difficulty is an assumption, in much of the theory, that the stamp of its culture leaves an identical mark across all of an organization. We referred above to a 'legitimate plurality of views and styles' as a counterweight to the Great Person. In fact, we have to go further because all organizations, especially professional organizations, contain groupings each with a distinctive culture, depending on its members' views, the nature of its expertise or tasks, its history, and so on. A visitor walking round the premises of any organization notices different cultures in different areas; when this variety is respected, the culture of the organization as a whole will be quite different from that in an organization where such variety is suppressed.

Schein's secondary mechanisms for the articulation and reinforcement of culture are:

1. The organizational structure.
2. Systems and procedures.
3. Space, buildings and façades.
4. Stories and legends about important events and people.
5. Formal statements of philosophy and policy (Schein 1985, pp. 237–42).

This introduces a wider range of possible actions, but notice what comes last! So often we find in practice that attempts to develop aspects of culture actually begin with formal statements of policy, or that cultural inertia is attributed to the lack of such statements. The connection with structure cannot be emphasized enough, as a bureaucratic structure will, for instance, be the biggest single impediment to introducing a corporate culture emphasizing risk-taking and personal initiative. The use of space, façades and stories appeals to the romance that is in all of us. The company logo now assumes extraordinary significance in providing a symbol of corporate identity, which everyone can see, understand and share. The stories that go round the grapevine may be those of management incompetence or greed. On the other hand, they may be stories of initiative or dedication to duty. There may be stories only about managers in key positions or there may be stories about how X saved the day by ordinary initiative and Y got a letter from the overseas visitor who had appreciated a small act of kindness. These are the things that shape culture, and managers can influence all of them, for it is the cultural leaders who will make all of these things happen.

Without a central sense of unity, organizations are no more than a collection of people who would rather be somewhere else, because they lack effectiveness and conviction in what they are doing. The effective organization has a few central ideals about which there is a high degree of consensus, and those ideals are supported and put into operation by simple rules and clear procedures. The organization that depends principally on rules for its cohesion is in the process of decay.

Rosabeth Moss Kanter (1989, pp. 361–5) believes that the demands of the future will require seven particular qualities from managers. First, the ability *to operate without relying on the might of hierarchy* behind them. Managers will have to rely on their personal capacities to achieve results rather than depending on the authority of their position.

Second will be a need *to compete in a way that enhances rather than undercuts co-operation*. This is a tall order, but the argument is that the nature of competitive striving must be to stimulate those with whom one has a working relationship, instead of trying to win the fight.

Her third quality is a *high standard of ethics*. Her reasoning follows closely from the previous point and is very similar to the old-fashioned British idea of 'a gentleman's word is his bond'. Collaborations, joint ventures and similar alliances make it necessary for people to be candid and to reveal information, but also being able to rely on partners not to violate that trust. This sounds optimistic, but the logic is clear enough.

The fourth requirement is *humility, as there will always be new things to learn.*

Fifth is *the need to develop a process focus.* How things are done will be just as important as what is to be done. There may be problems to solve that present intriguing intellectual challenges, but success lies not in being able to decide what should be done, but in being able to implement the decision: to make it happen.

The sixth suggestion is the need to be *multifaceted and ambidextrous*:

> able to work across functions and business units to find synergies that multiply value, able to form alliances when opportune but to cut ties when necessary, able to swim effectively in the mainstream and in newstreams. (*ibid.*, p. 364)

To some extent this 'all-singing, all-dancing' approach makes a nonsense of the idea of functional expertise, which is the basic premise of a book like this. On the other hand, personnel expertise is one of the key areas of skill for the business athlete Dr Kanter is describing.

Her final suggestion is that it is necessary to *gain satisfaction from results*. A shift of emphasis from status to contribution and from attainment of position to attainment of results.

Review topic 7.4

- How many of these seven qualities have you got?
- How appropriate are these qualities for where you are in your organization now?
- How necessary do you think each of these qualities will be in your future career?

Summary propositions

7.1 The culture of an organization is the characteristic spirit and belief of its members, demonstrated by the behavioural norms and values held by them in common.

7.2 Corporate culture is a culture that those directing the organization seek to create and foster in the interests of the organization achieving its objectives.

7.3 The most significant reinforcement of attitudes and beliefs comes from that which is tangible and visible, rather than what is urged upon people as values they should adopt.

7.4 No organization is an island, so attempts to foster or alter corporate culture must take account not only of the intentions and expectations of those within the organization, but also of developments in the surrounding society, both nationally and internationally.

7.5 The most significant differences in work values and attitudes between cultures can be measured on the four criteria of power distance, uncertainty avoidance, individualism and masculinity.

References

Barratt, A. (1989), 'Doing business in a different culture', *Journal of European Industrial Training*, vol. 13, no. 4, pp. 28–31.

Goffee, R. and Scase, R. (1985), *Women in Charge*, London: Allen & Unwin.

Hofstede, G. (1980), *Culture's Consequences*, Beverly Hills, California: Sage.

Hyman, R. (1987), 'Strategy or structure? Capital, labour and control', *Work Employment and Society*, vol. 1, no. 1, March.

Kanter, R. M. (1989), *When Giants Learn to Dance*, London: Simon & Schuster.

Marshall, J. (1985), 'Paths of personal and professional development for women managers', *Management Education and Development*, vol. 16, pp. 169–79.

Moir, A. and Jessel, D. (1989), *Brain Sex*, London, Michael Joseph.

Nelson, E. (1989), 'Marketing in 1992 and beyond', *Royal Society of Arts Journal*, vol. cxxxvi, no. 5393, April, pp. 292–304.

Olins, W. (1989), *Corporate Identity*, London: Thames & Hudson.

Poirson, P. (1989), *Personnel Policies and the Management of Men* (Trans. Thierry Devisse), Ecole Supérieure de Commerce de Lyon, France.

Ronen, S. and Kraut, A. I. (1977), 'Similarities among countries based on employee work values and attitudes', *Columbia Journal of World Business*, Summer.

Schein, E. H. (1985), *Organizational Culture and Leadership*, San Francisco: Jossey-Bass.

Tiger, L. (1970), 'The biological origins of sexual discrimination', *The Impact of Science on Society*, vol. 20, no. 1.

Torrington, D. P. and Weightman, J. B. (1989), *The Reality of School Management*, Oxford: Basil Blackwell.

8

Authority, leadership and management

Every type of management job involves the exercise of authority and some element of leadership. Personnel managers not only have these features in their own jobs, they also need to engender them in the jobs of all their managerial and professional colleagues. When dealing with questions of organization design they are developing a structure within which leadership and management can be undertaken. Unless they understand what aspects of organization bestow authority on individuals and the differences between managerial jobs, their efforts in organizational design will not succeed. Personnel managers also need to know what they are seeking when they recruit managers and how the requisite qualities and skills can be developed in their colleagues. Understanding authority is a basis for operating grievance and disciplinary procedures that work rather than procedures that are ignored.

The personnel specialist who has a good grasp of authority, leadership and management will find that this illuminates almost all areas of personnel work, so that initiatives are more apt and reactions of colleagues better understood. Shelagh Fallows tried very hard to get her management colleagues to follow the agreed disciplinary procedure in her company, but was constantly frustrated as other managers forgot to put warnings in writing when she asked them to, ignored essential steps in procedure, sometimes expected her to take extreme action over minor offences and frequentiy waived final warnings in more serious cases. Memoranda and exhortation had little effect. So she took advice and realized that the authority of her expertise was not consistent with the authority of her office, that most of the managers had great difficulty in maintaining their day-to-day authority at the same time as coping with the formality of the procedural method, and managerial authority was not clear in the organizational structure. This did not solve her problem, but enabled her to see what the problems were that she had to tackle.

Power and authority in the organization

Man creates organizations as power systems, and the individuals who become employees of the organization surrender a segment of their personal autonomy to become relatively weaker, making the organization inordinately stronger. The benevolence of the organization cannot be guaranteed, so individuals seek to delimit its power in relation to themselves.

Usually, the authority to be exercised in an organization is impersonalized by the use of *role* in order to make it more effective. New recruits to the armed services have an early lesson from their drill sergeant, who points out to them a young and unimpressive officer in the distance with colourful, disparaging remarks about him as a *man* before the sergeant calls the recruits to attention and presents an immaculate salute to the *uniform* of the officer. Quality assurance staff in factories (who are no longer called quality *controllers*) are likely to wear white coats and send unfavourable reports in writing so as to deploy the authority of their role rather than test the authority of their own selves.

Dependence on role is not always welcome to those in managerial positions, who are fond of using phrases like 'I can handle the workers', 'I understand my chaps' and 'I have a loyal staff'. Partly this may be due to their perception of their role as being to persuade the reluctant and command the respect of the unwilling by the use of personal charismatic qualities because there is no other source of authority in their position; therefore there is no other source of self-confidence.

The Milgram experiments with obedience

Obedience is the reaction expected of people by those in authority positions, who prescribe actions which otherwise may not necessarily have been carried out. Stanley Milgram (1974) conducted a series of experiments to investigate obedience to authority and highlighted the significance of obedience and the power of authority in our everyday lives.

Subjects were led to believe that a study of memory and learning was being carried out which involved giving progressively more severe electric shocks to a learner when incorrect answers were given. If the subject questioned the procedure a standard response was received from the authority figure conducting the experiment, such as:

1. 'Please continue' or 'Please go on'.
2. 'The experiment requires that you continue'.
3. 'It is absolutely essential that you continue'.
4. 'You have no other choice: you must go on'.

These responses were given sequentially: (2) only after (1) had failed, (3) after (2), and so on.

The 'learner' was not actually receiving shocks, but was a member of the experimental team simulating progressively greater distress as the shocks were made stronger. Eighteen different experiments were conducted with over 1,000 subjects, with the circumstances varying between each experiment. No matter how the variables were altered the subjects showed an astonishing compliance with authority even when receiving 'shocks' of 450 volts. Up to 65 per cent of subjects continued to obey throughout the experiment in the presence of a clear authority figure and as many as 20 per cent continued to obey when the authority figure was absent.

Milgram has been extensively criticized for this study, largely because of questions about the ethics of requiring subjects to behave in such a distressing way, but we cannot evade the fact that he induced a high level of obedience from a large number of people who otherwise considered their actions to be wrong. Understandably, the reaction of Milgram to his own results was of dismay that:

> With numbing regularity good people were seen to knuckle under to the demands of authority and perform actions that were callous and severe. Men who are in everyday life responsible and decent were seduced by the trappings of authority, by the control of their perceptions, and by the uncritical acceptance of the experimenter's definition of the situation into performing harsh acts. (1974, p. 123)

Our interest in Milgram's work is simply to demonstrate that individuals have a predilection to obey instructions from authority figures, even if they do not want to.

Milgram explains the phenomenon of obedience for us by an argument which he summarized thus:

> (1) organized social life provides survival benefits to the individuals who are part of it, and to the group; (2) whatever behavioural and psychological features have been necessary to produce the capacity for *organized* social life have been shaped by evolutionary forces; (3) from the standpoint of cybernetics, the most general need in bringing self-regulating automata into a co-ordinated hierarchy is to suppress individual direction and control in favour of control from higher level components; (4) more generally, hierarchies can function only when internal modification occurs in the elements of which they are composed; (5) functional hierarchies in social life are characterised by each of these features, and (6) the individuals who enter into such hierarchies are, of necessity, modified in their functioning. (*ibid.*, p. 132)

He then points out that the act of entering a hierarchical system causes individuals to see themselves acting as agents for carrying out the wishes of another person, and this results in these people being in a different state, described as the *agentic state*. This is the opposite to the state of *autonomy* when individuals see themselves as acting on their own. Milgram then sets out the factors that lay the groundwork for obedience to authority.

1. *Family*: Parental regulation inculcates a respect for adult authority. Parental injunctions form the basis for moral imperatives as commands to children have a dual function. 'Don't tell lies' is a moral injunction carrying a further implicit instruction 'And obey me!'. It is the implicit demand for obedience that remains the only consistent element across a range of explicit instructions.
2. *Institutional setting*: Children emerge from the family into an institutional system of authority: the school. Here they learn how to function in an organization. They are regulated by teachers, but can see that the teachers themselves are regulated by headmaster, local authority and central government. Throughout this period they are in a subordinate position. When, as adults, they go to work it may be found that a certain level of dissent is allowable, but the overall situation is one in which they are to do a job prescribed by someone else.
3. *Rewards*: Compliance with authority is generally rewarded, while disobedience is frequently punished. Most significantly, promotion within the hierarchy not only rewards the individual but ensures the continuity of the hierarchy.
4. *Perception of authority*: Authority is normatively supported: there is a shared expectation among people that certain institutions do, ordinarily, have a socially controlling figure. Also, the authority of the controlling figure is limited to the situation. The usher in a cinema wields authority which vanishes on leaving the premises. As authority is expected it does not have to be *asserted*, merely presented.
5. *Entry into the authority system*: Having perceived an authority figure, this figure must then be defined as relevant to the subject. The individual does not only take the voluntary step of deciding which authority system to join (at least in most of employment), but also defines which authority is relevant to which event. The firefighter may expect instant obedience when calling for everybody to evacuate the building, but not if asking employees to use a different accounting system.
6. *The overarching ideology*: The legitimacy of the social situation relates to a justifying ideology. Science and education formed the background to the experiments Milgram conducted and therefore provided a justification for actions carried out in their name. Most employment is in realms of activity regarded as legitimate, justified by the values and needs of society. This is vital if individuals are to provide willing obedience, as it enables them to see their behaviour as serving a desirable end.

Legitimizing authority

All our discussion in the last few pages leads us to the assertion that employees are predisposed to obey rather than defy instructions from authority, providing that there are certain conditions like a hierarchical setting, identification of authority figures, a voluntary entry to the system and a justifying ideology. We can now look at some aspects of organizational life that can be developed in order to support the effective exercise of authority.

Sources of power

The willingness of people to obey those who are in authority is greatly enhanced if the person is also an authority, with some element of expertise which makes their instructions both welcome and convincing. French and Raven (1959) suggest that there are five main bases or sources of power to influence others.

First there is the situation where A (the person wanting to exercise power) is able to control the *rewards* of B (the person to be influenced). Managers are an important source of praise – a considerable reward – and influence promotions as well as pay rises and some aspects of fringe benefits. Personnel managers are in a position to influence all of these.

The second basis is where A is able to *coerce* B as a result of being able to provide punishments. Managers are able to do this by withholding praise, by blocking promotions, producing unenthusiastic performance appraisals, assigning boring duties to B, rebuking, and perhaps eventually dismissing, B.

A may have *legitimate* influence due to his role. Just as police officers have a right to act towards ordinary citizens at times that other people do not have, so most managers have duties that give them a legitimate power in relation to their colleagues, like the auditor who can look at the books or the quality assurance official who can examine work done by other people.

Where B wishes to identify with A, A then has *referent* power. Managers with attractive personalities and an aura of confident success often have a degree of referent power.

Finally, A has power when in possession of *expertise* that B recognizes and wants to use. The importance of this power base is that it does not depend on the relative 'height' of the hierarchical position of A. To rework an old shopfloor saying: 'It's what you know, not who you know, that counts.' The one person who has the expertise to make the central heating work when everyone is shivering, or who can de-bug the computer when it has crashed, is a person of supreme expertise power.

Review topic 8.1

The signs of being *in* authority include job title, position in the organization, being a signatory for necessary authorizations and being asked to chair meetings. What are the signs of being *an* authority?

The general willingness of people to do as they are told is something of which managers need frequent reassurance, but that alone is not sufficient for the manager to produce a performance from 'the managed'. Milgram's volunteers mainly complied with the instructions they received, but a substantial minority disobeyed. Furthermore, they were being asked to do a straightforward task requiring blind obedience. It is unlikely that the Milgram method would have been effective in producing a performance requiring imagination, enthusiasm or creativity. In most working situations the manager has to build something on top of the general predilection of subordinates to comply with instructions from a superior. The manager also has to exercise leadership.

Leadership

The notion of leadership implies that there is a combination of skills and personal qualities, which enables some people to draw forth from their subordinates a much more effective performance than can be achieved by other managers in a similar situation. To balance this view we need to consider not only the qualities of the leader but also the needs of the led. Social science investigation over the last thirty years has produced many explanations of the leadership phenomenon and we have chosen three pieces of work that provide us with a convincing and practical way of using leadership ideas.

Fiedler (1967) has developed a *contingency model of leadership effectiveness* in which he argues that any leadership style may be effective, depending on the situation, so that the leader has to be *adaptive*. He also appreciates that it is very difficult for individuals to change their style of leadership as these styles are relatively inflexible: the autocrat will remain autocratic and the freewheeling *laissez-faire* advocate will remain freewheeling. As no single style is appropriate for all situations, effectiveness can be achieved either by changing the manager to fit the situation or by altering the situation to suit the manager. Three factors will determine the leader's effectiveness:

1. *Leader–member relations*: How well is the leader accepted by the subordinates?
2. *Task structure*: Are the jobs of subordinates routine and precise or vague and undefined?
3. *Position power*: What formal authority does the leader's position confer?

Fiedler then devised a novel device for measuring leadership style. It was a scale that indicated *the degree to which an individual described favourably or unfavourably the least preferred co-worker* (LPC):

> a person who describes his least preferred co-workers in a relatively favourable manner tends to be permissive, human relations oriented and considerate of the feelings of his men. But a person who describes his least preferred co-worker in an unfavourable manner – who has what we have come to call a low LPC rating – tends to be managing, task-controlling and less concerned with the human relations aspects of the job. (Fiedler 1967, p. 261)

Fiedler then argues that high LPC managers will want to have close ties with their subordinates and regard these as an important contributor to their effectiveness, while low LPC managers will be much more concerned with getting the job done and less interested in the reactions of subordinates. It is then possible to combine all these elements to show how the style of leadership that is effective varies with the situation in which it is exercised. Figure 8.1 shows the result of 800 studies which Fiedler carried out, using eight categories of leadership situation and two types of leader.

Condition	Leader-member relations	Task structure	Position power	
1	Good	High	Strong	Low LPC leader more effective
2	Good	High	Weak	Low LPC leader more effective
3	Good	Low	Strong	Low LPC leader more effective
4	Good	Low	Weak	High LPC leader more effective
5	Poor	High	Strong	High LPC leader more effective
6	Poor	High	Weak	Similar effectiveness
7	Poor	Low	Strong	Low LPC leader more effective
8	Poor	Low	Weak	Low LPC leader more effective

Figure 8.1 *Leadership performance in different conditions*
Source: Fiedler (1976, p. 11).

- *High LPC leaders* tend to be permissive, human relations-oriented and considerate.
- *Low LPC leaders* tend to be concerned with getting the job done and less interested in the reactions of subordinates.

High LPC leaders were likely to be most effective in situations where relations with subordinates are good but task structure is low and position power weak. They do reasonably well when they have poor relationships with their subordinates but there is high task structure and strong position power. Both of these are moderately favourable combinations of circumstance. Low LPC leaders are more effective at the ends of the spectrum, when they have either a favourable combination or an unfavourable combination of factors in the situation.

The value of Fiedler's work is that it concentrates on *effectiveness* as its yardstick and demonstrates the fallacy of believing that there is a single best way to lead in all situations. It is interesting that the majority of situations he describes appear to call for a generally less attractive type of person as leader, but he was examining a range of situations for the purpose of explanation, and situations at the extremes of his continuum may not be very frequent in organizational life. Although this remains the most widely accepted analysis of the leadership process, some people have found rather depressing Fiedler's accompanying argument that individual leaders have little chance of adopting a style that is more appropriate to their situation, so that it is more important to match available managers to a situation than to try changing the individual manager's style. An alternative is to tinker with the situation: modifying the task structure, varying the formal authority or changing the subordinates. The last is the most drastic and is usually only possible to any significant extent in very few situations. It could, however, transform condition 8 to condition 4.

Hersey and Blanchard (1977) have produced the *life-cycle theory of leadership* with the basic concept that the leader's strategies and behaviour should be situational, but in particular should take account of the maturity or immaturity of those who are led.

Maturity is the capacity of people to set their own targets for performance, which are both demanding and attainable. This stems from a combination of education, training and experience, and should be considered by the leader in relation to the task to be performed.

Task behaviour is the degree to which the leader organizes and defines exactly what it is that the subordinates are to do and how jobs are to be done.

Relationship behaviour describes the personal contact and relationship between the leader and the subordinates; how much support is provided and how close the contacts are. Figure 8.2 shows the relationship between the variables, suggesting that the style of the leader should change with the maturity of the subordinates. The figure can be used by first determining the maturity level of the subordinates on the lowest horizontal line and then plotting a vertical until it reaches the curved line. The point of intersection determines which of the four basic leadership styles is most appropriate in the situation:

- Quadrant 1   High task and low relationship.
- Quadrant 2   High task and high relationship.
- Quadrant 3   High relationship and low task.
- Quadrant 4   Low relationship and low task.

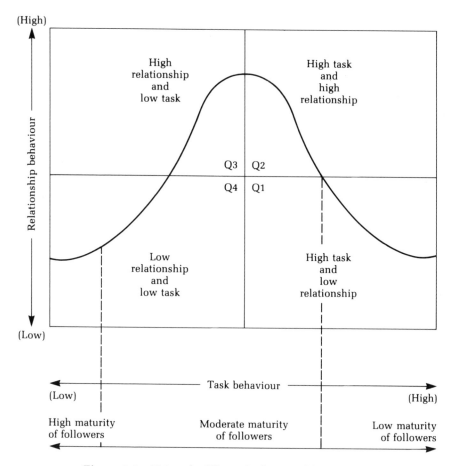

Figure 8.2 *Using the life-cycle theory of leadership*

The authors use the example of parents and children to illustrate their argument, pointing out that children need much greater direction and control when young than when they are older. It is important to remember, however, that the theory states that leadership behaviour has to be considered in relation to a specific task: general maturity of subordinates is not enough.

The British writers Wright and Taylor (1984) point out that this type of analysis can be no more than generally informative if there is no emphasis on the job of leadership being done *skilfully*. Concentrating on the individual leader coming to terms with improving the working performance of a subordinate they have produced the checklist shown in Table 8.1.

This type of approach makes the issue of leadership practical and puts methods of improvement at the disposal of the individual manager.

Table 8.1   A checklist for improving work performance

1. What is the problem in behavioural terms? What precisely is the individual doing or not doing which is adversely influencing his or her performance?
2. Is the problem really serious enough to spend time and effort on?
3. What reasons might there be for the performance problem? (See column 1)
4. What actions might be taken to improve the situation? (See column 2)

Possible reasons for performance problem	Possible solutions
Goal clarity: Is the person fully aware of the job requirements?	Give guidance concerning expected goals and standards. Set targets. M60.
Ability: Does the person have the capacity to do the job well?	Provide formal training, on the job coaching, practice, secondment, etc.
Task difficulty: Does the person find the task too demanding?	Simplify task, reduce work load, reduce time pressures, etc.
Intrinsic motivation: Does the person find the task rewarding in itself?	Redesign job to match job holder's needs.
Extrinsic motivation: Is good performance rewarded by others?	Arrange positive consequences for good performance and zero or negative consequences for poor performance.
Feedback: Does the person receive adequate feedback about his/her performance?	Provide or arrange feedback.
Resources: Does the person have adequate resources and delegated for satisfactory task performance?	Provide staff, equipment, raw materials as appropriate.
Working conditions: Do working conditions, physical or social, interfere with performance?	Improve light, noise, heat, layout, remove distractions, etc., as appropriate.

5. Do you have sufficient information to select the most appropriate solutions? If not, collect the information required, e.g. consult records, observe work behaviour, talk to person concerned.
6. Select most appropriate solution(s).
7. Is the solution worthwhile in cost-benefit terms?
   (a) If so, implement it.
   (b) If not, work through the checklist again, or relocate the individual or reorganize the department/organization, or live with the problem.
8. Could you have handled the problem better? If so, review own performance. If not, and the problem is solved, reward yourself and tackle next problem.

Source: Wright and Taylor (1984, p. 13).

Using these three approaches enables the personnel manager first to understand the type of sectional organization and the type of manager likely to be needed in a range of situations within the organization. Secondly, it is possible to discuss with managers general aspects of their style that could help them modify their approach to subordinates using the life-cycle explanation of subordinates' response. In specific situations where managers have subordinates whose performance is unsatisfactory, the skills approach of Wright and Taylor provides a framework for dealing with that type of problem.

Management

Management is the role that members of the organization take on in order to exercise formal authority and leadership. In most organizations it is the role carrying the greatest status and rewards, although there has recently been a tendency to emphasize the term 'professional' as a noun rather than as an adjective preceding 'manager'. In analyzing the responses to our research questionnaires we were interested to see the following breakdown of reports by respondents of the manpower distribution in their organizations:

Manual unskilled and semi-skilled	36.1 per cent
Manual skilled and technical	13.4 per cent
Clerical/secretarial	17.2 per cent
Supervisory	7.1 per cent
Middle management/administrative	3.8 per cent
Technical/professional specialists	21.1 per cent
Senior management	1.0 per cent

The term 'administrative' may have disconcerted some respondents, but it is still interesting to see the large proportion of technical and professional specialists. It is important to distinguish between the various levels of management job. Rosemary Stewart (1976) was so dissatisfied with the conventional terms of 'senior', 'middle', and so forth that she coined a new set of descriptions after detailed analysis of the demands made by 252 management jobs. This is shown in Figure 8.3.

Hub jobs have necessary contact with subordinates, superiors, peers and others above and below them in the hierarchy. This was the most common type of job among the managers studied and had a dominant man-management component (116 jobs)

Peer dependent jobs were those where there was less 'vertical' demand and much dependence on winning the co-operation of peers. They were much found at the boundaries of the organization (63 jobs)

Man-management jobs were those concerned primarily with the vertical type of working relationship, having contact mainly with superiors and subordinates (52 jobs)

Solo jobs were those of managers who spent a large proportion of their time working alone on assignments (22 jobs)

Figure 8.3 *The Stewart method of classifying jobs*
Source: Stewart (1976, pp. 15–16).

Despite the thoroughness of Dr Stewart's research (which received a special award for excellence in management literature) its practical value has not been greatly used in management circles, where categorization by level remains commonplace.

In practice, the duties undertaken by people at different levels vary significantly, and one of the effects of microtechnology applications in business has been to make senior management less dependent on those in the middle. This is one of several factors leading to a 'middle management problem'. Middle management cannot be seen simply as a training ground for more senior positions; it is now a whole career for most of the people in that category. One very large, and expanding, company produced data in 1981 to show that the average age at which managers reached the grade in which they eventually retired was between 43 and 48 for middle managers and between 46 and 53 for senior managers, so that the career development escalator stops earlier for middle managers. That was in an *expanding* company: in most the situation is one of fewer promotion opportunities.

Technological advance means that many middle managers find their technical skills obsolete and there are several studies showing growing dissatisfaction in their ranks (Cooper *et al*. 1980). White (1981) conducted a participant observation study in an electrical company on the south coast and explained middle management's resistance to change by the facts that they are structurally dissociated from the satisfaction of ownership, technically dissociated from the technique of production and socially dissociated from the workforce.

One mistake that is frequently made by managers in general, and middle managers in particular, is to neglect their technical skills. When moving into a managerial position they may not keep up-to-date the technical skills they acquired at the beginning of their careers. Moving into management, they look to acquire new managerial skills to replace the technical skill which they now regard as less important. Research suggests (Torrington and Weightman 1982) that managers actually undermine their own authority of expertise when they do this, and are likely to become less effective and less satisfied with their jobs. Although this is important for all managers to appreciate, it is especially important for personnel managers, as their activities are very close to the general running of the business and they can easily become general managers rather than personnel managers. In the short term that may be a boost in status and salary, but they must maintain a distinctive technical expertise in personnel work if they are to remain influential and effective (Torrington and Mackay 1986). As was discussed in Chapter 2, personnel management is more than mere management.

Review topic 8.2

What are the most significant aspects of personnel management expertise that you would classify as technical skill?

Summary propositions

8.1 The authority of managers is underpinned by a general predilection of people to obey commands from those holding higher rank in the hierarchy of which they are members.

8.2 Effective leadership depends on the situation in which it is exercised, the maturity of the subordinates in relation to the task to be undertaken, and the skill of the leader.

8.3 Managers in general, and personnel managers in particular, need to preserve technical skills and not rely simply on the acquisition of management skills for effectiveness and personal satisfaction.

References

Cooper, M. R., Gelford, P. A. and Foley, P. M. (1980), 'Early warning signs: growing discontent among managers', *Business*, January/February.

Fiedler, F. E. (1967), *A Theory of Leadership Effectiveness*, New York: McGraw-Hill.

Fiedler, F. E. (1976), 'The leadership game: matching the man to the situation', *Organizational Dynamics*, Winter.

French, W. L. and Raven, S. (1959), 'The bases of social power'. In D. Cartwright (ed.), *Studies in Social Power*, Michigan: University of Michigan.

Hersey, P. and Blanchard, K. H. (1977), *Management of Organization Behavior*, Englewood Cliffs, NJ: Prentice Hall.

Milgram, S. (1974), *Obedience to Authority*, London: Tavistock.

Stewart, R. (1976), *Contrasts in Management*, Maidenhead: McGraw-Hill.

Torrington, D. P. and Mackay, L. E. (1986), 'Consultants: friend or foe of the personnel function?' *Personnel Management*, February.

Torrington, D. P. and Weightman, J. B. (1982), 'Technical atrophy in middle management', *Journal of General Management*, vol. 7, no. 4.

White, C. (1981), 'Why won't managers co-operate?' *Industrial Relations Journal*, March/April.

Wright, P. L. and Taylor, D. S. (1984), *Improving Leadership Performance*, Hemel Hempstead: Prentice Hall.

9

Organizational communication

Without communication an organization would not survive. People spend a lot of time communicating in organizations, but much of the communication is ineffective and inefficient. In this chapter we look first at what communicating means, ways of looking at it and its importance. We then consider in more detail the process of communicating and the barriers to communication, before considering the many different ways of communicating within organizations.

Communicating in organizations

Meaning of communication

Communication involves both the giving out of messages from one person and the receiving and understanding of those messages by another or others. If a message has been given out by one person but not received or understood by another, then communication has not taken place. The methods of communicating in organizations include speech, non-verbal communication, writing, audio-visual and electronic means. These methods are considered in greater detail later on in the chapter. The method used will depend on the precise message that needs to be passed on. In general, messages may contain factual information, opinion and emotion. In organizations a wide variety of messages will need to be communicated, and may include the following:

1. Information on how to fill out expenses claims forms in a memo from the accounts department.
2. Comments from a boss to a subordinate that continued lateness is not acceptable.

3. Employment details given to a new employee in the contract of employment from the personnel department.
4. Information on sales figures from the sales manager to the chief executive.
5. Information and persuasion on safe working practices in a safety training film.
6. Status information indicated by size of desk.
7. Comment from subordinate to boss during a performance appraisal that he/she would welcome a transfer.
8. A welcome smile and a handshake given by the boss to a new employee.
9. Personnel manager informing the finance manager of new salary structures.
10. Development plans passed on from top to middle management for comment.
11. Request from an employee to a co-worker to perform certain work tasks when the former will be absent the following day.
12. Comment from an employee to a co-worker that she/he knows from informed sources that half the workforce is going to be made redundant.
13. Company financial details as laid out in the annual report.
14. Statement from the trade union to management that there will be a strike unless the pay negotiations are successfully concluded within the week.
15. Information of the company's new technology policy and planned acquisition of equipment given out in a circular.

Scope of communication in organizations

We can draw some conclusions about organizational communication and what it is *generally* seen to include:

1. Organizations are dependent on communication.
2. Organizational communication includes not only communications from management to workers, but also from management to other levels of management.
3. Some authors have defined organizational communication as the transfer of information that was deliberately intended to be communicated and is backed up by an explicit system of communication.

From the above examples it is clear that we have taken a broader view of organizational communication, to include any communication that impinges on the operation of the organization. We do, however, acknowledge the difference between the explicit organized communications and other communications in organizations:

1. Some organizational communication is between managers of the organization and trade unions rather than to individual members of the organization.

2. Organizational communication can include information that is intended to be used as persuasion to change attitudes and/or behaviour. Information for the purpose of manipulation is not included, the difference being that manipulation:

> usually involves lies or tricks to gain acceptance of a point of view whereas persuasion relies on the weight of logic and fact supported by a relationship of trust between the communicator and the audience. (Ginsberg and Reilly 1957, p. 49)

3. There is communication within the organization and communication between the organization and the outside world. Company newspapers, for example, are often directed partly at informing employees of what is going on in the company but also seen as a way to present an image to the outside world. While this chapter concentrates on communication within the organization, some parts also apply to communication between the organization and the outside world. The following chapter on interpersonal communication applies equally to internal and external communication as this is relevant both to, say, internal disciplinary interviews and the interviewing of external applicants for jobs.

4. Within any organization there are both formal and informal channels of communication. The formal channels are those that are officially acknowledged and approved, such as circulars, meetings, posters, and so on. Informal channels of communication can either facilitate or inhibit communication through official channels (Glen 1975). Foy (1983) argues that in order to improve corporate communication the grapevine should not be eliminated, but an effort should be made to ensure that official communication channels match the informal ones. The informal channels of communication are not officially acknowledged, but are, however, often privately acknowledged and approved and sometimes deliberately used: government 'leaks' are a good example. In other organizations the same type of leak may be used from time to time to see what the reaction would be to a proposed management initiative, so that the initiative can be modified before being made official. It is a form of consultation that can save face by avoiding a formal espousal of a strategy that is shown to be unsatisfactory.

5. Within organizations the existence of such informal channels of communication often encourages managers to communicate officially, as the information will in any case be passed on. On these grounds it may be assumed that an increase in official communication would result in a decrease in the unofficial informal communication. Interestingly, this has been shown not to be the case and that increasing official communication results in increasing informal communication. Effectiveness in communication usually requires a careful blend of both formal and informal channels, with formal statements of fact and reasons, supported by informal explanations and interpretations.

6. Information is not only communicated downwards, but also upwards and laterally. Downwards communication receives more attention and seems more in evidence in organizations than upwards or lateral communication, and there are more explicit communication systems to support this type of communication. Horizontal or lateral communication is often a neglected aspect of communication and is least well served by explicit systems. Lack of lateral communication can be demonstrated by hostility between different departments in an organization because they fail to understand each other's problems and points of view.

Review topic 9.1

In your organization:

1. What formal channels of lateral communication are there?
2. How effective are these? Why?
3. Suggest ways in which lateral communication could be improved.

The importance of communication

Downwards communication is important for the following reasons:

1. It enables decisions taken by managers to result in action by employees.
2. It ensures that this action is consistent and co-ordinated.
3. Costs should be reduced because fewer mistakes are made.
4. It may stimulate a greater commitment from employees and from this result in a better service to customers (Parsloe 1980).
5. From all of these should stem greater effectiveness and profitability.

Upwards communication is important for the following reasons:

1. It helps managers to understand employees' business and personal concerns.
2. It helps managers to keep more in touch with employees' attitudes and values.
3. It can alert managers to potential problems.
4. It can provide managers with workable solutions to problems.
5. It can provide managers with the information that they need for decision-making.
6. It helps employees to feel that they are participating and contributing and can encourage motivation.
7. It provides some feedback on the effectiveness of downwards communication, and ideas on how it may be improved.

McClelland (1988) suggests that the following factors, among others, are important for successful upwards communication: access to senior managers, sufficient business understanding, an atmosphere of trust with no fear of reprisals, and sufficient feedback.

Lateral communication is important, among other reasons, for ensuring co-ordination of activities and goals.

The process of communicating: the telecommunications analogy

A convenient and well-established method of approaching and understanding communication is to draw the analogy with telecommunications. Here one examines the human process by comparing it with the electronic process. Figure 9.1 shows how the communication process begins with some abstract idea or thought in the mind of the person seeking to convey information. The first step in the communication process is for the central nervous system of that person to translate the abstractions through the vocal organs into speech patterns or into some form of written or other visual message. If the channel of communication is speech, then the patterns of speech travel through the air as sound waves to be received by the ears and conveyed as nervous impulses to the brain. If the channel of communication is visual, as in written communications, the message is either manually, mechanically or electronically transferred and is received by the eyes and conveyed again by nervous impulses to the brain.

The message is unscrambled in the central nervous system of the receiver, which then instructs the listener to understand; the final stage comes when there is registration and the receiver understands.

Through these various stages of translation from the mind of one to the mind of the other there is a number of points at which error is possible, and even likely. It is almost impossible to know whether the abstract idea in the mind of one person has transferred itself accurately to the mind of the other. One essential element in the whole process is feedback. This completes the circuit so that there is some indication from the listener that the message has been received and understood. It is probable that the feedback response will give some indication to the transmitter of the quality of the message that has been received. If the transmitter expects a reaction of pleasure and the feedback received is a frown, then it is immediately known that there is an inaccuracy in the picture that has been planted in the mind of the receiver, and the opportunity arises to identify the inaccuracy and correct it.

A further element in the communication process is that of 'noise'. This is used as a generic term to describe anything that interferes in the transmission process: inaudibility, inattention, physical noise, and so forth. The degree to which some

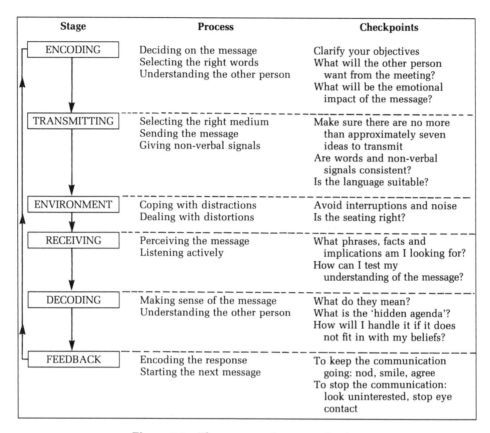

Stage	Process	Checkpoints

ENCODING	Deciding on the message
	Selecting the right words
	Understanding the other person
		Clarify your objectives
		What will the other person
		  want from the meeting?
		What will be the emotional
		  impact of the message?

TRANSMITTING	Selecting the right medium
	Sending the message
	Giving non-verbal signals
		Make sure there are no more
		  than approximately seven
		  ideas to transmit
		Are words and non-verbal
		  signals consistent?
		Is the language suitable?

ENVIRONMENT	Coping with distractions Dealing with distortions	Avoid interruptions and noise Is the seating right?

RECEIVING	Perceiving the message
	Listening actively
		What phrases, facts and
		  implications am I looking for?
		How can I test my
		  understanding of the message?

DECODING	Making sense of the message Understanding the other person	What do they mean? What is the 'hidden agenda'? How will I handle it if it does not fit in with my beliefs?

FEEDBACK	Encoding the response
	Starting the next message
		To keep the communication
		  going: nod, smile, agree
		To stop the communication:
		  look uninterested, stop eye
		  contact

Figure 9.1   *The process of communication*
Source: Torrington *et al.* (1985). Used with permission of
the Institute of Personnel Management.

noise element is present will impair the quality of both transmission and feedback.

A further development of this simple idea is enshrined in the so-called ten commandments of good communication, which were set out as guidelines by the American Management Association in 1955 (in Megginson 1972):

1. Seek to clarify your ideas before communicating.
2. Examine the true purpose of each communication.
3. Consider the total physical and human setting whenever you communicate.
4. Consult with others, wherever appropriate in planning communications.
5. Be mindful, while you communicate, of the overtones as well as the basic content of your message.
6. Take the opportunity, when it arises, to convey something of help or value to the receiver.

7. Follow up your communication.
8. Communicate for tomorrow as well as for today.
9. Be sure your actions support your communications.
10. Last, but by no means least: seek not only to be understood but to understand – be a good listener.

It is unlikely that a body like the AMA would produce commandments to managers of quite that flavour today, because they are essentially unitary in the way in which the communication activity is perceived. Since that time we have come to realize that communication cannot be much improved only by the process of managers thinking carefully about what they are doing and concentrating on doing it better. More recent analysis of the communication process has led to a greater understanding of the setting in which communication takes place, so that now perhaps we focus more on understanding the process and the activity of receiving and interpreting information than we do on the activities involved in transmitting information. Shoveller (1987) lists no fewer than twenty-four reasons why communications in organizations may fail. These range from people failing to accept the responsibility to communicate to lack of interest on behalf of the recipient.

Peter Drucker (1970) has described the four fundamentals of communication as: (1) perception, (2) expectation, (3) involvement, (4) not information. Here Drucker is emphasizing that it is the recipient who communicates. The traditional communicator only 'utters'. Unless somebody hears, there is no communication, only noise. The utterer does not communicate, but only makes it possible or difficult for the recipient to perceive.

Barriers to communication

It is the listener or reader who will determine the extent to which the message is understood. What we hear, see or understand is shaped very largely by our own experience and background, so for example, instead of hearing what people tell us, we hear what our minds tell us they have said – and the two may be different. There are various ways in which expectation determines communication content and a number of these ways of determination can impair the accuracy of message transmission. They act as 'noise', interfering both with transmission and feedback. We will look at some of the principal difficulties.

The frame of reference

Few of us change our opinions alone. We are likely to be influenced by the opinions developed within the group with which we identify ourselves: the reference group. If a particular group of people hold certain values in common, individual members of that group will not easily modify their values unless and until there is a value shift through the group as a whole. This is perhaps most apparent in the relative intractability of opinions relating to political party allegiance. There are certain clearly identifiable social class groupings who tend to affiliate to particular political parties; and a change in that affiliation by an individual is rare and difficult. Managers frequently direct to an individual a message, request, instruction or rebuke which would find a more likely response if it were mediated through a representative of the group of employees rather than being directed at an individual. An interesting example of this is the way in which safety campaigns (Strauss and Sayles 1972) are mounted, where the attempt is usually by the use of slogans and posters in order to persuade individual employees about the importance of safe working practices and similar aspects of behaviour rather than negotiating a change of behaviour through group representatives.

Whenever a matter is being discussed, the people among whom it is being considered will view it from their particular personal frame of reference. Where the frames of reference of transmitter and receiver differ widely, there may be substantial difficulties in accurate transmission of messages and even greater difficulties in ensuring that the response of the receiver is that which the transmitter intended.

The stereotype

An extreme form of letting expectation determine communication content is stereotyping, where we expect a particular type of statement or particular type of attitude from a stereotype of a person. It is, for instance, quite common for the English to expect certain types of behaviour and intention from the Irish ('Never stop talking and always ready for a fight'). Equally, there is a stereotype expectation about the Scots, that they will be mean or at least extremely careful with their money. People also have stereotypes of certain office holders. There is a widespread stereotype of shop stewards which shows them as being militant, politically extreme in one, and only one, direction, unreasonable, unintelligent and obstructive. Equally, there are widespread stereotypes of different types of manager and for some people there is a stereotype of managers as a whole. One of the greatest difficulties in achieving equal opportunities at work is the challenging of deeply-held stereotypes about men and women. Stereotypes about women include the view that they are unwilling to be away from home due to family commitments, that they do not want to rise too high in the hierarchy and that they will invariably leave to have children. Men, on the other hand, are often seen as career-driven and intent on promotion. There are also stereotypes relating to age, such as an older person being seen as unable to stand the pace, no longer able to think quickly and unwilling to change.

The effect of these stereotypes in communication matters is that the person who encounters someone for whom they have a stereotype will begin hearing what the person says in the light of the stereotype held. If somebody has stereotyped pictures in their mind of the Irish and shop stewards, and if they then meet a shop steward with an Irish accent they will begin hearing what that person says and evaluating it in the context of their expectations. It will be some time before their listening, understanding and evaluation will adjust to the actual performance they are witnessing in contrast to that which they expected.

Cognitive dissonance

Another area of difficulty, which has been explored extensively by Festinger (1957) and others, is the extent to which people will cope successfully with information inputs that they find irreconcilable in some particular way. If someone receives information that is consistent with what they already believe, they are likely to understand it, believe it, remember it and take action upon it. If, however, they receive information that is inconsistent with their established beliefs, then they will have genuine difficulty in understanding, remembering and taking action.

A middle-aged married man was spending a night in a hotel and about nine in the evening there was a knock on the door. When he opened the door he found standing in the corridor the sort of vision that peoples the erotic fantasies of middle-aged men. When the vision spoke and indicated that her idea of an appropriate way to spend the next few hours was to join him inside his bedroom with the door firmly closed behind her, the middle-aged man had a cognitive dissonance difficulty! Hard experience for the previous thirty years had convinced him that young women looking like the vision in the corridor never ever expressed that sort of intention as far as he was concerned. He found it difficult to understand and impossible to take action appropriate to the situation! That type of problem is one that can be found in less beguiling forms time and time again in working situations. It has an additional dimension to it. Not only do recipients of information find it difficult to understand, remember and take action, they will also grapple with the dissonance that the problematical new information presents. One of the ways in which they do this is to distort the message so that what they hear is what they want to hear, what they expect to hear and can easily understand rather than the difficult, challenging information that is being put to them.

The halo or horns effect

A slightly different aspect of expectation determining communication content is the halo or horns effect, which causes the reaction of receivers of information to move to extremes of either acceptance or rejection. When we are listening to somebody in whom we have confidence and who has earned our trust we may be predisposed to agree with what they say because we have placed an imaginary halo around their head. Because of our experience of their trustworthiness and reliability we have an expectation that what they say will be trustworthy and reliable. On the other hand, if we have learned to distrust someone, then what we hear them say will be either ignored or treated with considerable caution. Perhaps the most common example of this is the reaction that people have to the leaders of political parties when they appear on television.

Semantics and jargon

One difficulty about transferring ideas from one person to another is that ideas cannot be transferred because meaning cannot be transferred – all the communicators can use as their vehicle is words or symbols, but unfortunately the same symbols may suggest different meanings to different people. The meanings are in the hearers rather than the speakers and certainly not in the words themselves. A simple example of this is 'quite ill' which could have a variety of weightings according to how it was heard and the circumstances in which the comment was made.

The problem of jargon is where a word or a phrase has a specialized meaning that is immediately understandable by the cognoscenti, but meaningless or misleading to those who do not share the specialized knowledge. The Maslovian hierarchy of human needs is by now quite well known in management circles. On one occasion a lecturer was describing the ideas that were implicit in this notion and was rather surprised some months later in an examination paper to see that one of the students had heard not 'hierarchy' but 'high Iraqui'. The unfamiliarity of the word 'hierarchy' had been completely misinterpreted by that particular receiver, who had imposed her own meaning on what she heard because of the need to make sense of what it was that she received.

Another interesting example was in a school of motoring, where for many years trainee drivers were given the instruction 'clutch out' or 'clutch in', which nearly always confused the trainee. Later the standard instruction was altered to 'clutch down' or 'clutch up'.

Not paying attention and forgetting

The final combination of problems to consider here is first the extent to which people do not pay attention to what is being said or to what they see. There is a human predilection to be selective in attention. There are many examples of this, perhaps the most common being the way in which a listener can focus attention on a comment being made by one person in a general babble of sound by a group of people. This is complicated by the problem of noise, which we have already considered, but it has the effect of the listener trying very hard to suppress all signals other than the particular one that they are trying to pick up.

The rate at which we forget what we hear is considerable. We have probably forgotten half the substance of what we hear within a few hours of hearing it, and no more than 10 per cent will remain after two or three days. Figure 9.2 provides a summary of the main phases in communication and the barriers to effectiveness.

	Sender	Recipient	Social/environmental
Barriers in sending a message	Unaware message needed Inadequate information in message Pre-judgements about message Pre-judgements about recipient		
Barriers to reception		Needs and anxieties Beliefs and values Attitudes and opinions Expectations Pre-judgements Attention to stimuli	Effects of other environmental stimuli
Barriers to understanding	Semantics and jargon Communication skills Length of communication Communication channel	Semantic problems Concentration Listening abilities Knowledge Pre-judgements Receptivity to new ideas	
Barriers to acceptance	Personal characteristics Dissonant behaviour Attitudes and opinions Beliefs and values	Attitudes, opinions and prejudices Beliefs and values Receptivity to new ideas Frame of reference Personal characteristics	Interpersonal conflict Emotional clashes Status differences Group frame of reference Previous experience of similar interactions
Barriers to action	Memory and retention Level of acceptance	Memory and attention Level of acceptance Flexibility for change of attitudes, behaviour, etc. Personal characteristics	

Figure 9.2 *The main barriers to effective communication*

> **Review topic 9.2**
>
> When a computer system is designed in-house, analysts from the computer services department will liaise with members of the user department.
>
> Why is the computer system that results from this rarely what the user department wanted?

Ways of communicating in organizations

As discussed at the beginning of this chapter, there is a number of communication media: speech, non-verbal communication, writing, audio-visual and electronic means. Using each medium there is a variety of methods of communication which can be employed in organizations. A summary of communication media and the main methods of organizational communication are found in Figure 9.3. Some methods are appropriate only for downwards communication, such as films and posters, other methods are suitable for upwards communication only, such as suggestion schemes. Many methods, however, are suitable for both downwards and upwards communication as well as for lateral communication. The choice of communication method will depend not only on the direction of the communication but also on the specific nature of the message to be communicated. An initial comment from a manager to a subordinate about unsatisfactory work would not be communicated appropriately by means of an official memo. Many messages, however, are best transmitted by the use of more than one communication medium. Company rules, for example, might most effectively be communicated verbally; communication on an induction course supported by a written summary for employees to take away as a reminder. Company performance may well be written about in the company newspaper, but may also be displayed diagrammatically via a poster or on the notice board. As a general rule, messages are more successfully communicated if more than one communication medium is used. Another factor to consider when choosing a communication medium is cost. Films, videos and some tape-slides are particularly expensive, and a decision has to be made as to whether the message could be conveyed equally effectively for less money. Variety is another important factor when choosing a communication method. If any particular channel of communication is overloaded, this may result in escape, queueing, loss of quality, delegation or prioritizing. If, for example, a company tries to communicate too many messages by means of posters, then employees may escape by ceasing to read any posters, or not read them properly, and so

Communication medium	Communication methods	Used mainly for communication:		
		Downwards	Upwards	Laterally
Written	Official paperwork	*	*	*
	Info. bulletins	*		
	Newsletters	*	*	
	Company newspapers	*	*	
	Company reports	*		
	Employee reports	*		
	Notice boards	*		
	Manuals	*		*
	Training handouts	*		
	Suggestion scheme		*	
	Attitude survey		*	
Speech	Mass meetings	*		
	Meetings of reps.	*		*
	Departmental meetings	*	*	*
	Interdepartmental meetings	*		*
	Briefing groups	*	*	
	One-to-one exchanges	*	*	*
	Formal presentations	*	*	*
	Grapevine	*	*	*
	Lectures	*		*
	'Open door' policy		*	
Audio visual	Slides	*		
	Tape-slides	*		
	Film strips	*		
	Film	*		
	Television/video	*		
	Audio tape	*		
	Company radio	*		
	Posters/flip chart/blackboard	*		
Electronic	Electronic mail	*	*	*
	CBT	*		
Non-verbal	Present during any communication via speech and some audio visual communications			

Figure 9.3 *Different methods of communicating within organizations*

on. If a communication channel is overused it becomes less effective. For a full description of all the different methods of communication, see Bland (1980).

We do not have the space here to review all the different methods of communication within the work organization, but we will briefly discuss team briefing which has now become quite well established, and then discuss interpersonal communication in some depth, in the following chapter.

Team briefing

Team briefing is a method of face-to-face communication in groups of about 10–20 employees. The leader of the group provides up-to-date organizational information, with explanation and rationale, and the group members are given an opportunity to ask questions. Townley (1989) suggests team briefing is probably the most systematic method of providing top-down information to employees. It is a method of communication pioneered by the Industrial Society, particularly John Garnett, and has been encouraged in some form since the mid-1960s.

In 1975 a BIM survey established that 51 per cent of firms regularly used team briefing, and higher percentages have since been reported, such as 62 per cent in the Second Workplace Industrial Relations Survey (Millward and Stevens 1986). Team briefing is adopted to improve communications with the workforce and to gain the advantages of upwards and downwards communication (page 135). The Industrial Relations Review and Report comments that organizations introduce team briefing: 'as a means of communicating with their employees, improving employee attitudes and increasing their involvement at work' (Industrial Relations Review and Report, 4 February 1986, p. 2).

Team briefing is often seen as a way of encouraging employee commitment to the organization, particularly to major organizational change, by providing the reasons behind intended changes and an opportunity for employees to ask questions. Marchington (1987) also suggests other reasons behind the growth of team briefing: employers' desire to avoid industrial action by trade unions by channelling conflict; increasing expectations of employees to have more influence over their lives at work; and legislation requiring employers to develop employee involvement, such as the 1982 Employment Act, are all mentioned.

Team briefing also provides other potential advantages, which include the strengthening of the supervisor's role and the discouragement of reliance on shop stewards and informal networks. This is because in the team briefing system the shopfloor workers will be briefed as a group by their supervisor. In particular, Marchington suggests, it enhances the supervisors' reputation as the providers of information and reinforces their role as being accountable for team performance.

The type of information that is transmitted in briefing groups includes management information, sales figures, progress made, policies, and the implications of all these for the workers involved. It is critical that the information passed on is made relevant to those who will hear it.

The team briefing system works from the top downwards in gradual stages: it is suggested that these stages do not exceed four. The system starts with a board meeting, or meeting of executives, and this is followed by briefing groups being held at the next level down, using as their base briefing notes issued by the first meeting, but adding any other information that may be relevant at this level. The last level of briefing group is the level of the supervisor or first line manager briefing the shopfloor workers. Briefing notes from the next level of briefing group are used here, together with local information. It is usually suggested that those who are 'briefers' and lead the briefing group should, between meetings, make notes of any items of importance that should be included in the next meeting. Meetings are held at intervals varying from fortnightly to quarterly, depending on the circumstances, but it is important that meetings are arranged well in advance so that they are clearly seen as part of the structure. Many organizations have a regular interval between meetings.

Training is important for all those who take part in briefing groups, and particularly for those who will act as briefers, as they may be unused to dealing with groups as opposed to individuals. The success of team briefing is heavily dependent on the skills of the briefer.

Briefing groups are not intended to replace other channels of communication but to supplement them, and urgent matters should of course be dealt with immediately and not saved for the next team briefing session (Industrial Relations Review and Report 1986). However, the potential importance of briefing groups in the whole communications structure is exemplified by a comment from Mike Judge of Talbot Motors (in Romano 1984): 'Team briefing is the cornerstone of our communications policy.' Some guidelines on team briefing are found in Figure 9.4.

There can be difficulties, however, in establishing a team briefing system. Marchington notes that team briefing is 'managerial in tone' and is concerned with reinforcing 'managerial prerogative', and can therefore be seen by the trade unions as a way of weakening their power. He goes on to comment that team

Team briefings should be:	How team briefing works
Held at regular intervals and not just at times of crisis	1. The briefer collects information relating to progress, people, policy and points for action in preparation for the meeting
Brief, ideally lasting no longer than 30 minutes	2. A few days before the meeting, he prepares a local brief which is checked by his manager
Led by the immediate foreman or supervisor of the work group	3. Following a board meeting, for example, three or four relevant items are typed and sent to briefers at the next level
Face-to-face and not reduced to a series of circulars and memos	4. Directors meet with their teams and any questions which cannot be answered immediately are noted and answered within 48 hours. In addition to local information, the brief will have explained the items passed down from the board

Structured to cover
  progress: how are we doing?
  people: who is coming and going?
  policy: any changes affecting the team?
  points: for further action?
	5. This process continues down the line, ensuring there is a local brief and that management points have been included

Monitored to assess their success or failure	6. The majority of people should be briefed at the same time and the number of levels through which information passes should be no more than four
	7. After meetings, breifers should find and feed back answers to unanswered questions. Absentees should be briefed on their return

Figure 9.4 *Guidelines for team briefing*
Source: Romano (1984, p. 40).

briefing stands most chance of success either where there is little or no union organization, or where the union is well established and supported by the company with good channels of communication. The prognosis is not good where there has been previous union conflict or mistrust.

Review topic 9.3

What do you think would be the most effective way(s) of communicating the following in a non-unionized organization with 3,000 employees:

1. Instructions from the computer services department on how to use the new computer system.
2. Sales targets for the forthcoming year.
3. Plans to relocate to a new plant 5 miles away.
4. New absence and holiday reporting procedures.

Summary propositions

9.1 Communication is the flow of information through the organization structure that can produce understanding and action, but may produce mistrust and inefficiency.
9.2 Formal communication is supported by informal communication, and managerial use of both systems has to be kept in balance.
9.3 Effective communication is multilateral and 'bottom-up' not simply 'top-down'.
9.4 Barriers to communication include the frame of reference, stereotyping, cognitive dissonance, the halo or horns effect, semantics, jargon and not paying attention or forgetting.

References

Bland, M. (1980), *Employee Communication in the 1980's: A personnel manager's guide*, London: Kogan Page.

Drucker, P. (1970), 'What communication means', *Management Today*, March.

Festinger, L. (1957), *A Theory of Cognitive Dissonance*, Stanford, Calif: Stanford University Press.

Foy, N. (1983), 'Networkers of the world unite', *Personnel Management*, March.

Ginsberg, E. and Reilley, E. H. (1957), *Effecting Change in Large Organizations*, New York: Columbia University Press, p. 49.

Glen, F. (1975) *The Social Psychology of Organizations*, Essential Psychology Series, London: Methuen.

Industrial Relations Review and Report (1986), *Team Briefing: Practical steps in employee communications*, IRRR, 4 February.

Marchington, M. (1987), 'Employee participation'. In B. Towers (ed.), *A Handbook of Industrial Relations Practice*, London: Kogan Page.

McClelland, V. A. (1988), 'Communication: Upward communication: Is anyone listening?' *Personnel Journal*, June.

Megginson, L. C. (1972), *Personnel: A behavioural approach to administration*, Homewood, Ill.: Irwin, p. 609.

Millward, N. and Stevens, M. (1986), *The Second Workplace Industrial Relations Survey, 1980-1984*, Aldershot: Gower.

Parsloe, E. (1980), 'Why bother? Overcoming the attitudes barrier'. In M. Bland, *Employee Communications in the 1980's*, London: Kogan Page.

Romano, S. (1984), 'Shopfloor briefing: Talbot proves its value', *Works Management*, April.

Shoveller, S. E. (1987), 'A problem of communications', *Work Study*, June.

Sisson, K. (1989), *Personnel Management in Britain*, Oxford: Basil Blackwell.

Strauss, G. and Sayles, L. R. (1972), *Personnel: The human problems of management*, Englewood Cliffs, NJ: Prentice Hall.

Torrington, D. P., Weightman, J. B. and Johns, K. (1985), *Management Methods*, London: Institute of Personnel Management.

Towers, B. (ed.) (1987), *A Handbook of Industrial Relations Practice*, London: Kogan Page.

Townley, B. (1989), 'Employee communication programmes, in K. Sisson, *Personnel Management in Britain*, Oxford: Basil Blackwell.

10

Interpersonal communication

The significance of interpersonal communication cannot be doubted in managerial life. In her study of how managers spent their time, Rosemary Stewart (1970) found that the mean for discussion with one other person was 32 per cent of working hours and for discussion with two or more people it was 34 per cent. Later Mintzberg (1973) showed a mean of 78 per cent of working hours and 67 per cent of working activities being devoted to interpersonal communication.

In this chapter we shall first look at the performance element of interpersonal communication, and then at non-verbal communication, followed by interactive incidents and communication ploys. We shall conclude with a summary of interpersonal communication and the personnel manager.

The elements of performance

Interpersonal interactions provide conundrums for those who participate, because all participants are performing rather than being their true selves. We present a self to the observer and the listener which is an idealization: how we wish to be seen and evaluated; not what we are. Constantly, people will display understanding to disguise unacceptable incomprehension, will conceal dislike by appearing friendly, and will agree with what they inwardly reject.

Clarion calls to people to be 'open' and 'honest' will have only marginal effect. Man is a dissembler, particularly when social mobility is involved.

> Commonly we find that upward mobility involves the presentation of proper performances and that efforts to move upwards and efforts to keep from moving downward are expressed in terms of sacrifices made for the maintenance of front. Once the proper sign equipment

has been obtained and familiarity gained in the management of it, then this equipment can be used to embellish and illumine one's daily performances with a favourable social style. (Goffman 1972, p. 45)

In describing the way in which people express themselves, Goffman draws a distinction between the expression that people *give* and the expression that they *give off*. The first involves what the person says or other direct attempts to communicate and to inform. The expression that the individual gives off is more involuntary and covers a range of actions and signs by which people give clues to their real feelings about the situation as they attempt to sustain the performance they are presenting. We appear generally to be more able to learn how to interpret the involuntary impression given off by those with whom we are conferring than we are able to manipulate and control our own expressions. Although the human in communication is a dissembler, there are two types of such dissembling. To some extent we express an artificial self to others quite deliberately and we are aware of the truth at the same time as we express the image. There is also, however, an extent to which we delude ourselves about the reality. In presenting a performance, we come to believe that the performance is the reality. Therefore, the interactive performer is by no means being cynical. We will delude ourselves as often as we mislead our interlocutor.

Non-verbal communication

In recent years there has been great interest in the extent to which communication takes place in addition to communication through articulated language. This has been particularly due to the work of Argyle (1972, 1973) in the United Kingdom and Berne (1966) in the United States, with the area becoming popular following the writings of Julius Fast (1971). A somewhat different approach is in the writings of Desmond Morris (1977), who has brought the eye of the zoologist to this type of study. More recently, interest in neuro-linguistic programming has developed, partly on the basis of using non-verbal signals to develop rapport more quickly and in the case of sales representatives, for example, to increase sales orders. The foundation of NLP is the conscious copying of the non-verbal signals of others so as so keep in tune and pace with them.

While communication is taking place, there are various other things going on, as well as speech. We can usually see the person with whom we are interacting and this itself adds a major dimension. Even if interaction is solely by letter or telex, where the exchanges appear to depend almost exclusively on language, there are still influential factors such as delay in answering, length of message and other subtleties to consider.

Bodily contact

It is relatively uncommon for people to communicate via bodily contact in working situations in Great Britain. Such communication is much more common in Mediterranean and African countries, where the embrace is more familiar and there is more widespread use of kissing on both cheeks at welcome and parting.

In Britain bodily contact as communication is limited almost exclusively to the handshake. There is a mysterious folklore attached to the handshake which decrees that somebody shaking hands with a palm that is dry and a grip that is firm indicates that he has a strong and a reliable personality, while somebody whose handshake is relatively limp and moist is indicating a personality of low quality and generally not to be trusted. This folklore applies to men only, as it is only recently that handshaking has developed among women and we lack the comforting, though misleading, stereotypes. Despite the ease with which a handshake can be manipulated in the direction of firm dryness, the folklore continues and is powerful for men.

There is a number of variations about the handshake. First of all there is the duration; some people seek to sustain the grip on the other party for a relatively long period, while with other conjunctions it is quite brief. One variation is what is sometimes known as the 'Methodist' handshake, where the left hand is added to the right in order to indicate a greater degree of warmth and feeling and to convey a sense of comfort and security. A further variation is 'jollying', which is usually used to encourage or to demonstrate friendship or sympathy, either to the person at the other end of the handshake or to an audience watching. The technique is to place the left hand on the forearm or elbow of the other person. More extravagant forms have the left hand on the shoulder of the other person or even between the shoulder blades.

Proximity and critical space

We take up a position in relation to the other person which will enable us to feel comfortable. This, of course, only applies when the two or more parties to an encounter have freedom of control over their relative positioning, and the lack of such freedom is one of the many contributors to the feeling of uncertainty and discomfort which is experienced by candidates for formal interview.

We tend to get slightly closer to those people whom we like and in whom we have confidence, and to move slightly away from those people whom we suspect or distrust. If our suspicions are allayed, then we may move nearer again. There are many situations in which people experience an acutely uncomfortable degree of proximity. The most familiar is travelling in a lift, which produces proximity so unnatural as to cause discomfort to most people making the journey.

Gesture

Gesture can be looked at in two ways. First of all, it can be used to emphasize and underline speech, so that the speaker who can control her gestures can use them directly as a manipulator. Alternatively and frequently, gestures derive from an emotional state and may involuntarily indicate that emotional state to a keen observer.

Examples of the first aspect of gesture would be the stabbing forefinger of the orator who is seeking to compel the attention of the audience or the melodramatic banging of his shoe on the table, which Khrushchev produced at a meeting of the United Nations. Very common examples of gesture to emphasize speech are beckoning, waving, nodding and shaking the head.

Krout (1954) conducted some experiments in the United States which suggested a link between certain types of involuntary gesture and specific attitudes:

- Steepled fingers indicate suspicion.
- Hand to nose indicates fear.
- Fingers to lips indicate shame.
- Clenched fists indicate aggression.
- Open hand dangling between the legs indicate frustration.

Posture

Height tends to make one person dominate another, due to childhood conditioning when parents are always taller than their children during the formative years. Frequently, height is emphasized by artificial devices such as the rostrum for the public speaker, or high-heeled shoes. Relative shortness is seen as an interpersonal disadvantage and frequently short people try to compensate by emphasizing other dominating characteristics such as aggressiveness. Some short people feel they interact more effectively when sitting, which reduces the height differential. Conversely, tall people deliberately seek dominance by standing.

Furthermore, posture can be an indicator of emotional state, somewhere between the very tense and completely relaxed. At one extreme there is the 'open' posture. The person leans back comfortably, perhaps with hands behind the head, legs apart and muscles relaxed. At the opposite extreme there is the 'closed' posture, where the legs are crossed or pressed tightly together, feet sometimes off the floor, looped, hunched or coiled like a spring. The closed posture stems from ancient behaviour in preparing to be attacked and can be compared with the stance of a boxer.

We cannot, however, take these extremes simply on their face value, as it is necessary to interpret the degree of tenseness for each individual. The naturally tense person may perhaps be very thin, and will exhibit an open posture less often than the normally more tranquil person, who may be pleasantly plump.

Foot wagging may indicate nervousness, but some people wag their feet, like cats purring, as an indication of pleasure.

Gaze

The influence of gaze and its direction has been investigated principally by Argyle (1973). One person influences her interaction with another in an important way by looking at him. In the main we look at other people to obtain information and also to obtain feedback, and we look at the other approximately twice as much while listening as while talking.

Another aspect of gaze is that long periods of looking can be interpreted as a desire to be friendly and we tend to look at the other more when we are further apart, to compensate for the separation, while looking is almost taboo when people are very close. This is something that the public speaker will be familiar with. It is relatively easy to maintain eye contact with one member of a large audience for a sustained period, while such eye contact would not be sustained so comfortably if the person were closer.

Shifts of gaze can also be used to synchronize speech between people, so that a speaker will usually give a prolonged look at the other before ending a statement to indicate that it is becoming time for the other person to speak.

Looking too long or too intently can disconcert and there are many instances of people expressing concern or discomfort about the basilisk stare of another person.

Review topic 10.1

For the next three meetings that you attend make a log on the non-verbal behaviour of all participants (including yourself), covering the aspects outlined above.

1. What behaviours were helpful, and in what circumstances?
2. What behaviours were unhelpful, and in what circumstances?

Interactive incidents and communication ploys

Running through the majority of interviews and other types of discussion with which managers are concerned are certain standard aspects of behaviour, and in this section we consider these.

Rapport

The situation in which effective social interaction between the interviewer and the respondent takes place

Every encounter has to begin, and the opening is likely to be characterized by a degree of skirmishing as each party assesses the other. While this is going on both interviewer and respondent are tuning into each other and establishing some sort of relationship, which will enable the subsequent interview or meeting to be effective. This is one of the most common types of human behaviour, which most people undertake quite instinctively dozens of times a day. In the working situation interview, however, there is a greater degree of formality and ritual about this stage of the encounter because the interview is of greater significance potentially than most casual encounters.

The standard methods, which are likely to be used in establishing rapport by both parties, but particularly by the interviewer, who will be seen as appropriately controlling the encounter, are the following:

1. A *friendly, easy manner*: This, of course, is easier to advocate than to produce. Many people aspire to have an open manner with others that is friendly and easy, but the experience of every individual is that not many of those encountered are successful at it.
2. *Attentiveness*: The interviewer needs to pay careful attention to what the respondent is saying, and to demonstrate that he is paying this attention. This focuses the thinking and the responsiveness on the respondent.
3. *Easy and non-controversial opening topic*: It has long been a music-hall joke that the British discuss the weather when they meet. What is happening in that discussion is that the participants are using a neutral topic like the weather as a vehicle for their preliminary exchanges while they adjust to the other's tone and volume, and assess the opposing personality. This, of course, is only a matter of seconds or minutes of ritual exchange rather than laborious drawn-out preliminaries to the conversation.
4. *Calmness*: The interviewer who is able to project a feeling of peacefulness and quiet will elicit a response from the other party more quickly and more constructively than the interviewer who consciously or unconsciously conveys a great air of business and preoccupation – the 'I have managed to fit you in but we only have ten minutes' syndrome. The busy and preoccupied atmosphere will delay the start of frank discussion and may in fact prevent it altogether.
5. *Smile and eye contact*: We all respond when someone smiles at us, even though in some circumstances our response will be circumscribed by suspicion. The interviewer who smiles will warm the atmosphere between

herself and the respondent, and if she is able to maintain a degree of eye contact which will focus the attention of the two parties without being overbearing and relentless, then there is a speeding up of the process of establishing rapport.

All this presupposes that the interviewer begins in a situation of social advantage in relation to the respondent, and that the opening shots, as it were, from the interviewer are to equalize the social position between them.

Reward

Sustaining the interaction with the respondent

The establishment of rapport is something that essentially takes place at the opening of an interview. After a very short period of such exchanges the interview will move round to the substance that the two people have come together to discuss. It is important that interviewers do not leave behind the warm and affiliative behaviour that was displayed at the beginning. If they do this, then their good behaviour appears to the respondent overtly manipulative in a calculating and worrying way. The interviewer is trying at the beginning not to establish a false sense of relaxation and security but an accurate and constructive sense of such security. This therefore needs to be maintained while the interview proceeds. There are various ways in which it is conventionally done:

1. *Interest*: The interviewer continues to display interest in what it is that the respondent is saying. If she can also indicate agreement with what the respondent is saying she will reinforce the other's responses.
2. *Eye behaviour*: Individually we influence the behaviour of other people or seek to influence the behaviour, extensively by the use of our eyes. Gaze has already been referred to and there are other ways in which each individual develops a repertoire of signals which her eyes convey, such as encouragement, surprise, understanding, etc. If interviewers deploy these in an interactive situation they are able to sustain the interaction of the other without actually speaking while the other is seeking to speak.
3. *Noises*: Conversation contains a variety of noises, which are ways of rewarding the other party. Unfortunately, they are almost impossible to reproduce on paper for the sake of explanation, but they form a part of conversation that is inarticulate yet meaningful. In conjunction with eye behaviour, nods, etc., they serve the purpose of keeping things going by encouraging the other without interrupting.

Closed questions

Questions seeking precise, terse information

Basic, factual information is usually elicited from a respondent in small packages and the method of eliciting is the closed question, which does not invite anything more than a terse response:

'What time is it?'
'How much holiday do I get each year?'
'Who is in charge?'

An interview that proceeds along the lines of many closed questions from the interviewer is more of an interrogation than a conversation, and the information offered by the respondent is closely prescribed and strictly *factual*. But facts are of limited value in interactions. People come face to face because of a need to share or exchange opinions, attitudes and ideas. That type of exchange is dependent on a contrasting type of question.

Open-ended questions

Questions avoiding terse replies and inviting the respondent to open up on a topic

Evidence of opinions, attitudes and ideas is elicited by enabling the respondent to speak rather than prescribing his answers. The open-ended question does little more than mention a topic or area and invite comment:

'How are you getting on?'
'Could you give me an outline of what is involved in your present post?'
'What's happening with the current project?'

This style of questioning is almost an extension of rapport in that it makes things easy for the respondent, who has latitude to decide what to talk about and is helped to relax and get going by beginning to talk, hearing themselves talk and developing their poise. To ensure direction of the interview the interviewer will need to focus replies.

Follow-up questions

Methods of developing and focusing the answer to an open-ended question

Once the interviewer begins to get response this can be built upon. In this way the interviewer is developing what the respondent has been able to start, steadily enlarging the picture in his mind. To illustrate the follow-up method, let us assume that a school-leaver, applying for a first job, has been posed the following conventional open-ended question: 'Can you tell me something of what you did at school, and your examination achievements?'

Depending on the response the interviewer might follow-up in one of three ways:

1. The respondent has replied to only part of the question and has not said anything about examinations, so there is a reminder follow-up: 'And what about your examinations. . .?'
2. The respondent has replied with evidence that would have additional weight if further evaluated. This calls for the forced-choice follow-up: 'Which was your stronger subject – French or maths?'
3. The reply has given a cue to a potentially useful additional area of discussion, requiring the very common second-step follow-up: 'So what was the main benefit from being captain of cricket?'

Direct questions

Questions demanding both a reply and precision

With the direct question the interviewer is asserting authority in the interactive situation and the 'right to know'. It is using the prescriptive style of the closed question, yet seeking the more informative response that the open-ended question is designed to obtain. It is most likely to be used where it is anticipated that the reply will be evasive:

'Why did you leave that job?'
'Did you take the money?'
'When will you let me know?'

Summary and re-run

Drawing together in summary various points from the respondent and obtaining their confirmation

As the interview progresses the respondent will produce lots of information, from which the interviewer will be selecting what is important to retain and understand. Periodically, she will interject a summary sentence or two with an interrogative inflection:

'So the new MD did not see eye-to-eye with you and you felt the time had come to widen your experience with a move, but in retrospect you regret your decision?'

'You did take his wallet out of his locker, then. But this was because he had asked you to fetch it for him on your way back from the canteen because he owed Susan a fiver?'

This tactic serves several useful purposes. It indicates that the interviewer is listening and gives the respondent the chance to correct a false impression. Also, it can be a useful control device by drawing a phase of the interview to a close. After the respondent has assented to the summary and re-run, it is natural and easy to move on to a fresh topic.

Probes

Questioning to obtain information that the respondent is reluctant to divulge

The tactics described so far rest on the comfortable assumption that the interviewer is always and necessarily encouraging, supportive and permissive in style, with the implication that this is what is required to conduct an effective interview. For most phases of most interviews we would argue that this is the appropriate mode, and that the most usual overall strategy will be to build a sympathetic, trusting relationship.

Any interview may still have phases in which the interviewer realizes that information is being deliberately withheld by the respondent. When this happens interviewers have to make an important, and probably difficult, decision: Do they respect the respondent's unwillingness and let the matter rest, or do they persist with the enquiry? They will persist if they feel it important to find out what they were seeking.

Reluctance by respondents is quite common in disciplinary interviews for obvious reasons, and in grievance interviews because the employee grievance usually implies a criticism of some other employee, like a supervisor. In selection interviews there is often some aspect of the applicant's employment history that he or she feels would be best glossed over.

If the interviewer decides to probe, this sequence may help:

1. *Direct questions*: Open-ended questions are quite inappropriate as they give too much latitude to the respondent. The phrasing needs to be careful so as to avoid a defensive reply if possible.
2. *Supplementaries*: The first direct question may produce the required information. If it produces only an opaque or evasive response, then a supplementary question will be needed, rephrasing or reiterating the first.

   If this is not likely to produce what is required there is a rather nasty alternative, a device sometimes used by television policemen, that is:
3. *Overstatement*: If a question is put to the respondent that implies a reason for the respondent's reluctance which is more grave than the real reason,

then the respondent will rush to correct the false impression; now being happy to replace the appalling with the disquieting as being the lesser of two evils:

> Q. 'There appears to be a gap in the record at the beginning of last year. You weren't in prison or anything were you?'
> A. 'Oh no, I was having treatment for . . . er . . . well, for alcoholism, actually.'

Crude and rather nasty, but effective. The probe stands the best chance of working if it is used at the point in the interview when the rapport between the parties is at its peak. Also, a probe needs to be closed with care. If the respondent finally declares something she has been trying to conceal, it is not the time for a pregnant silence or a gleeful 'Ah-ha'. Either of these would destroy rapport and demoralize the respondent, putting her one-down beyond redemption. There is a need for:

4. *Face-saving close*: The interviewer makes the disclosed information seem much less worrying than the respondent had feared, so that the interview can proceed with reasonable confidence. For example:
   'Yes, well, you must be glad to have that behind you.'

Braking

Slowing the rate of response from the respondent

Encouraging and permissive interviewers may nod and smile their way to a situation in which the respondent is talking too much, having been relaxed to the point of talking on and on . . . and on. To re-establish control the interviewer may be tempted to become peevish and silence the respondent in a curt irritable manner. We are, however, naturally inhibited from such candour and the following hierarchy of less drastic techniques could achieve the same objective. Probably no more than one or two will be needed in sequence, but a longer list is provided for the really tough cases.

1. *Closed questions*: We have already seen that the closed question invites a terse response. One or two closed, specific, data-seeking questions may stem the tide.
2. *The furrowed brow*: In contrast to the bland, reassuring behaviours of reward, the interviewer furrows his brow to indicate mild disagreement, lack of understanding or professional anxiety.
3. *Glazed abstraction*: We are all familiar with the look about the eyes of a person who has stopped listening. It is in two stages. First, they maintain the other signals, like the nods and the smiles, but alter their eyes and the other components of their expression from 'Yes, that's interesting' to 'Now

let me have a turn'. The second stage is when they give up and just wait for the torrent to end, while their eyes speak of last night's film on television or the trip to the caravan planned for the forthcoming week-end. This is a pretty severe signal and can be particularly effective in decelerating a respondent because the behaviour is in such stark contrast to that which came earlier.

4. *Looking away*: If two people are conversing and one of them looks at his watch it implies that the other had better stop talking as they are over-running their time. In interviews there is a very strong constraint on this signal. Others not quite so punitive are looking for matches, looking at the aircraft making rather a noise outside the window or looking (again) at the application form.

5. *Interruption*: The simplest method of all, but the one which most people avoid at all costs.

Disengagement

Closing the interview without 'losing' the respondent

Books about interviewing are replete with advice about starting interviews but seldom mention how to finish them. Closing an interview is as difficult a social task as beginning it. Interviewers seem to have problems about how to close and get rid of the respondent and many respondents become agitated about over-running their time and look for a signal that will release them. A significant minority of interviews end with the respondent feeling aggrieved or put down, usually because it was clumsily closed by the interviewer. Yet the close is important because it is the phase where future action is clarified or confirmed. The difficulty is surprising when one considers that there is a simple, short sequence that can hardly fail:

> *Closing signal – verbal plus papers*: The interviewer indicates that she believes the interview to be approaching its conclusion. In case the respondent has stopped listening, the interviewer adds to the words an underlining action by gathering papers together and tapping them square on the table top before putting them down in a neat pile:
> 'Well now, I think we have covered the ground, don't you?'
> 'I don't think there is anything else I need to ask you. Is there anything further you want from me?'
> This is not only giving a closing signal; it is also obtaining the respondent's confirmation of the impending closure. A final statement can also include reaffirmation of what will happen next in the process.

Review topic 10.2

- Which interpersonal skills would you consider to be critical when counselling another person? Why?
- How would you structure a counselling interview?

Interpersonal communication and the personnel manager

It almost goes without saying that interpersonal skills are critical for the successful personnel manager. Not only do they have a people management responsibility within their own function, they also use these skills in personnel activities throughout the organization such as recruitment and selection. They also need to deploy these skills professionally and effectively in order to act as a role model for line managers. Interpersonal skills are essential to the credibility of the personnel manager, particularly if part of their role is in coaching senior management, or playing any part in management and supervisory training. Increasingly, the role of personnel managers requires them to influence management at all levels in the organization. Some general points can be made regarding interpersonal effectiveness which have particular importance for personnel managers:

1. *Asking good questions is key*: Lewis (1989) suggests that we are not very good at this for four reasons: inadequate technique, cultural reluctance, too much interest in self rather than the other, and the threat to psychological comfort of receiving emotional responses to difficult questions.
2. *The importance of listening cannot be overrated*: In most interviews the balance between interviewer and respondent needs to be around 70:30 with interviewers restricting their contribution to 30 per cent.
3. *Using problem-centred and solution-centred conversation at the appropriate time*: Margerison (1988) argues that too often we fall into solution-centred conversation before we really understand what the problem is. This results in defensive reactions, rejection of ideas and failure to solve the problem. Problem-centred conversation includes asking for more information and helping to diagnose the problem. Solution-centred conversation includes directing people to what they should or must do, suggesting and proposing ideas.
4. *Giving feedback constructively is an important part of the personnel role*: This involves concentrating on:
   (a) specific incidents and recounting them,

(b) the behaviour displayed and not the person,
(c) things that can be changed,
(d) the positive as well as the negative,
(e) facts not inferences.

Further guidance on handling feedback can be found in Wood and Scott (1989) and Kirk and Macdonald (1989).

Summary propositions

10.1 Interpersonal communication is the major activity of managers, taking more time than any other.
10.2 Interpersonal communication skills are particularly important in enhancing the credibility and effectiveness of the personnel manager.
10.3 Asking good questions is dependent on good questioning technique, and also on feeling comfortable doing this, being interested in the answers and being prepared to cope with difficult reponses.

References

Argyle, M. (1972), *The Psychology of Interpersonal Behaviour*, Harmondsworth: Penguin Books.

Argyle, M. (1973), *Social Interaction*, London: Tavistock.

Berne, E. (1966), *Games People Play*, London: Deutsch.

Fast, J. (1971), *Body Language*, London: Pan.

Goffman, E. (1972), *The Presentation of Self in Everyday Life*, Harmondsworth: Pelican.

Kirk, P. and Macdonald, I. (1989), 'The role of feedback in management learning', *Management Education and Development*, vol. 20, pt. 1, pp. 9–19.

Krout, M. H. (1954), 'An experimental attempt to determine the significance of unconscious manual symbolic movements', *Journal of General Psychology*.

Lewis, P. (1989), 'Learning to ask good questions', *Journal of European Industrial Training*, vol. 13, no 3.

Margerison, C. (1988), 'Interpersonal skills – some new approaches', *Journal of European Industrial Training*, vol. 12, no. 6.

Mintzberg, H. (1973), *The Nature of Managerial Work*, London: Harper & Row.

Morris, D. (1977), *Manwatching*, London: Jonathan Cape.

Stewart, R. (1970), *Managers and their Jobs*, London: Pan Piper.

Wood, B. and Scott, A. (1989), 'The gentle art of feedback', *Personnel Management*, April.

11

Procedures for administrative action and mutual control

Procedures for administrative action are the means whereby things get done in organizations. They are the link between decisions and practice; between ideas and their implementation. Managers typically take little interest in procedures because they are dull and curb individuality, yet they are fundamental to organizational success.

Procedures for mutual control are used to regulate the employment relationship, clarifying the steps to be taken if an employee feels that there is a legitimate grievance about what the management is doing, or if the management is dissatisfied with the employee. These procedures have been mostly developed through the processes of collective bargaining as the parties to collective agreements have sought means to limit the freedom of action of each other.

The first type of procedure is important to the personnel manager in the same way as it is important to all managers, as a way of getting things done. The second type is a much more specialized interest of personnel managers as this is an area where they claim particular expertise, with collective procedures being acknowledged as part of their managerial domain. In both types the personnel manager has the opportunity of increasing organizational influence by deploying the authority of office. There is still the need for expertise, as we saw in the case of Shelagh Fallows in Chapter 8, but procedures can only be used as a source of influence provided that the person developing the procedures is seen as having the authority to do so and is then able to ensure that others follow the procedural rules that have been established.

Personnel managers who develop effective procedures for such activities as selection, performance appraisal, transfer, pay review and promotion can then ensure that these personnel activities are carried out consistently and with an appropriate input of personnel expertise, with the personnel manager controlling the activity. If the procedure is not effective, through being too fussy or insensitive to the interests of managerial colleagues, then personnel managers will not only have great problems in administering the activity, but will also find the general authority of the personnel function being undermined. They will experience a similar loss of influence if the procedure is too slow, if it has flaws in its system or if it is not enforced. The personnel manager needs the authority of office to introduce the procedures, but will find that the consistent enforcement of those procedures will reinforce that official authority.

Mutual control procedures also depend on the authority of office, as here the personnel manager is representing the management as a whole in dealings with employees, both collectively and individually, so that the effective procedure depends on the personnel manager having the authority to represent the management in that way, and effective use of procedures reinforces that authority.

Procedures for administrative action

A familiar procedure is fire drill. There is an implicit management decision: 'If fire breaks out, we do not want the employees to burn to death', and the drill is a procedure to translate the good intention into action. It will specify a sequence of things people in the premises should do if they smell smoke or if they hear the fire alarm. Some of these will be a reiteration of common sense, like leaving the building as quickly as possible; but others will need greater emphasis as the reason may not be apparent, like assembling in a specified place so that possible missing persons can be identified. Less familiar procedures are getting someone on the payroll, terminating an employee's employment, or arranging the annual sales conference. All depend on a series of sequential steps to turn an idea into practice:

> Procedures . . . establish a customary method of handling future activities. They are truly guides to action, rather than to thinking, and they detail the exact manner in which a certain activity must be accomplished. Their essence is chronological sequence of required actions. (Koontz, O'Donnell and Weihrich 1980, p. 166)

The purpose of administrative procedures

Using procedures *reduces the need for future decisions*. It is like a cookery recipe. A chef does not decide how to cook lobster by trial and error, nor even from first principles. He uses a recipe, a routine that has worked before and will work again. The personnel officer needing to fill a vacancy will similarly use a 'recipe' or standard operating procedure. This is speedy because the decision-making has been done before and it is efficient through previous use and modification, and the smooth procedure can be operated with ease by those with less skill than the procedure inventor, just as a million cooks can use a classic recipe.

The second value of procedure is *consistency*. Most operations that are repeated benefit from being repeated in the same way, particularly when other people have to respond to the operation. Customers gradually become familiar with an organization's procedures and practices, so that they waste less time if all organization members treat them consistently. Employees become accustomed to a routine of departmental practice and are able to develop smooth interaction and swift handling if the method remains the same. Here we see one of the problems, as well as an advantage, of procedures. They are very difficult to alter and those who use them will abandon them only under duress (Cyert and March 1963, p. 101).

Thirdly, procedures provide *autonomy* for organization members. Subordinates are less dependent on superiors as they do not have to be told how things are to be done as well as what has to be done. Procedure authorizes and informs, providing scope for individual action and initiative that lack of procedure inhibits. Clever procedure provides the information and authority that is needed, while allowing freedom of action to make judgements in interpreting the rules for particular situations.

Procedure is also a means towards *management control of operations*. The delegation implicit in providing the autonomy mentioned above enables the manager to turn to other things, confident in the procedure and those operating it. There will be fewer requests for information and guidance, fewer complaints and fewer errors. At the same time as providing freedom from control for the individual, procedure provides effective management control of the overall operation.

Problems with administrative procedures

Procedures are *dull*: 'managers often fail to obtain the interest and support of top managers in the tedious and unromantic planning and control of procedures'. (Koontz *et al.* 1980, p. 769). There is seldom a commitment to other people's procedures, which seem like a yoke one has to bear, and the initiator of the procedure is often irritated by the grumbles of colleagues, who cannot remember what the stages of procedure are and who grumble about the discipline of having to follow the steps. If, however, the personnel manager has the authority to insist on the procedure being followed, and if the procedure genuinely provides an efficient way of getting things done, then the dullness can become an advantage as few people will be sufficiently interested to make an issue out of it: they will grumble and do as they are told.

Procedure can be too *rigid*. The standard way of doing things may be regarded by some as the only way of doing things. When organizational change is needed the rigidity of procedure can prove too much for the enthusiasm of those pursuing the changes.

The *complexity* of procedures can produce procedural steps, which are intended to eliminate all discretion. Such procedures are difficult to remember and understand, so that they can work only when the employee literally goes 'by the book'. They also form a challenge to the ingenuity of those who resent the limitation of personal judgement and interpretation that is involved. Safe working procedures, for example, are often ignored by those with the skill and knowledge to do safely what for others would be extremely dangerous.

Procedures can also *inhibit change*. When everyone has learned the procedural rules, they become a comfortable, secure routine and thus an aspect of organizational life with which people feel familiar and which they do not want to change, as they would lose an anchor in the organizational turmoil. There is always the risk that useful administrative procedure becomes immutable custom and practice.

Overlapping and duplication are a possible problem when each section of the organization has a set of procedures, which does not conveniently coincide at the boundaries with other sections. Purchasing have procedures that do not quite coincide with those of Accounts and are quite different from those of Design and Development. The differences come from the fact that accountants have different interests from buyers and designers. The problems come from disconnections between the drills of different departments.

A more serious problem is when procedures are used to deal with matters that require a *policy solution*. Just as procedures are needed to put policy into practice, policies are needed for procedures to be effective. The personnel manager in a small textile company was anxious to eradicate racial discrimination within the organization and made a number of procedural adjustments. Wording to be used in job advertisements was standardized, telephonists were told how to handle telephone enquiries, shortlisting arrangements in the personnel office were altered and other methods of preventing unfair discrimination were introduced. The manager failed, however, to explain these moves to anyone outside the department and was accused of high-handedness and deviousness by his colleagues. The procedural devices did not work: checks on advertisement wording were overlooked, departmental managers disagreed with shortlists and there was a formal complaint to the Commission for Racial Equality. This was due to a lack of policy decision and commitment. The policy decision was made only in the personnel manager's mind, being neither discussed with, nor communicated to, anyone else. The telephonists and personnel staff did not fully understand the reasons for the changes they had been asked to make and other managers did not know what was being done. Once the policy was clear and accepted, the procedure worked well. Procedure can only deal with problems for which a procedural solution is appropriate.

To overcome these difficulties procedures should always be *simple*, so that they can be understood by those who operate them and who are affected by them, allowing scope for interpretation to suit particular circumstances. Procedures should also be as few as possible, so that there is less to remember and so as to limit overlapping and duplication. A new procedure should be introduced only when really necessary. To be necessary there has to be a series of future events requiring some thought-out decisions in advance. Producing a procedure to deal with a situation that occurs seldom but with similar results is useful. Producing a procedure to deal with a situation that occurs seldom and with very varied results is pointless.

Procedures should be tested to see if they meet their objectives. A hospital was receiving a number of complaints from patients' relatives, so a complaints procedure was set up. This had the unfortunate effect of lengthening the time taken to deal with complaints and increasing their number. Procedures need not only an internal logic, they must also do what they are set up to do.

Procedures must have the *before and after* stages of policy and communication. There must be a policy for the procedure to implement, even if it is only the implicit policy of established practice, and all affected must know what the procedure is.

Monitoring can prevent procedures becoming obsolete and inefficient. Monitoring checks that they are being worked properly without any unintended effects that should be smoothed out before too much damage is done.

Review topic 11.1

Think of two procedures with which you are familiar, one which you find comfortable to work with and one which you find irksome. (They may be at work or other situations, like student registration or sending in football pools.)

1. Why is one comfortable to work with while the other is irksome?
2. How would you modify the irksome procedure in line with the suggestions above?

Procedures for mutual control

Although having many of the same features as procedures for administrative action, such as the objective of consistency and the danger of complexity, those for mutual control provide one of the main ways of regulating the employment relationship. Some rules of this relationship derive from statute, some from unilateral employer decision, some from custom and practice, and some come from procedure. They provide a framework within which the parties can engage each other in discussion, problem-solving and negotiation at the same time as exercising some degree of control over each other by specifying what the other party will and will not do in certain specified circumstances. The procedural structure *prescribes* certain actions by the actors in the arena (that, for instance, employees initially take grievances to their first-line supervisors) and *proscribes* others (like changing a payment scheme without prior consultation).

The purposes of mutual control procedures

Procedures bring under public examination a greater degree of the activities by the parties, so that those involved *know more clearly* what is going on and what will happen in certain future eventualities. During the 1960s there was extensive productivity bargaining, which usually had some procedural element:

> Prior to productivity bargaining, decisions were made in terms of precedent, customary practice or the dictates of stewards and foremen. Such a control system could be characterized as haphazard and personal. By contrast, under productivity bargaining, the control system becomes much more deliberate, rational and professional. It remains just as much a product of joint influence, but the process of joint regulation has been placed on a much more systematic and impersonal basis. (McKersie and Hunter 1973, p. 287)

In reducing the degree of irrationality in actions, procedures can also contribute to a *fairer working situation* at the workplace, making nepotism or overbearing supervision less likely and ensuring that all employees discharge the obligation of their contracts.

Through the inherent monitoring facility procedures tend to ensure *managerial consistency*. Not only does this help towards the fairness already mentioned, it also acts as a safeguard against legal repercussions, as consistency in treatment is one of the cardinal criteria of the tribunals in examining a case presented to them.

Problems with mutual control procedures

As we have already seen procedures will not be readily abandoned, as those who have created them will cling to them for the security they offer. The industrial relations actors have working lives of considerable uncertainty and tend to be very anxious to sustain procedures. As they have the effect of freezing the action at the time they were devised, they can *inhibit change* by becoming sacrosanct.

This can be a particular frustration for managers seeking a swift change of working arrangements to cope with a shift in the company's affairs. Part of the tradition of procedures is that they are a means whereby employees reduce the extent to which they are the sole element in managerial flexibility to meet changing circumstances, so procedural discussion becomes a way of buying time in the face of endangered job security.

Some would regard the view of McKersie and Hunter, quoted earlier, as naively optimistic; the claim that the control system becomes 'much more deliberate, rational and professional' is seen as more shadowy than substantial. Employees may not welcome the procedural restraints on their individuality and the real control of the workplace lies in the sense that people have of convention and tradition in the workplace – *custom and practice* – which produces rules having a greater cogency. Just as managers may not like to get involved in procedures because they lose freedom of action, employees may circumvent procedures for the same reason:

> The workers may not like the new rules, or at least may consider they can be improved. Secondly, workers may be more prepared to challenge formal plant-level rules than they were to challenge the same understandings in a C & P form. This preparedness is tied up with . . . a feeling of loss of personal control over their working lives. Thirdly, where these conditions apply, and the workers are in a position to put pressure on foremen, this tactic will be the most logical and likely one for them to apply. Fourthly, the likely outcome of such low-level negotiations will be informal rules and understandings. (Terry 1977, p. 87)

So collective procedures are one element in the structure of relationships and they provide positive benefits so long as the expectations of the actors do not exceed what the procedures themselves can offer:

> the procedure ought to be closely related to the actual behavioural process, but just how formal it is, along what dimensions, and how closely it should be followed are key issues in contingency analysis. In essence we would argue that informality has increasing disadvantages with increasing conflict and a deteriorating attitudinal climate. It is also important to note that a conflict relationship can change in degree and kind so that the procedures for resolution become out of date. (Thomson and Murray 1976, p. 124)

Forms of mutual control procedure

The Industrial Relations Code of Practice gives a useful summary to provide a starting point in the discussion of what procedures are in practice. Procedural provisions should lay down the constitution of any joint negotiating body or specify the parties to the procedure. They should also cover:

1. The matters to be bargained about and the levels at which bargaining should take place.
2. Arrangements for negotiating terms and conditions of employment and the circumstances in which either party can give notice of their wish to renegotiate them.
3. Facilities for trade union activities in the establishment and the appointment, status and functions of shop stewards.
4. Procedures for settling collective disputes and individual grievances and for dealing with disciplinary matters.
5. The constitution and scope of any consultative committees.

(Industrial Relations Code of Practice 1972, p. 21)

If an organization recognizes a trade union, such recognition brings with it a need to establish a way of working. If the parties are to negotiate and consult on a range of matters, they need to agree the mechanisms. This will usually be in a *negotiating procedure*. A prerequisite is a constitution, which will usually specify some central committee or body to act as the focus for negotiation. This will provide the main piece of machinery for differing employer/employee interests to be resolved in relation to all the bargaining units affected. The membership of the committee will be agreed by the parties, but will, of course, be joint. The constitution will also spell out the scope of the committee, specifying which groups of employees are covered by its deliberations, what the matters are that come within its orbit and – often more significant – which do not.

The range of coverage will normally have been settled at the recognition stage, but there can be a number of complications. For instance, if the committee is negotiating on behalf of the members of more than one union, then it may be that the topics to be negotiated about will vary from one union to another. Also, there may be an agreement that supervisors will be excluded from the outcome of certain aspects of negotiation, as newly negotiated rules might produce role conflict for them but not for other union members.

If the organization is a large one the central committee may spawn sub-committees as replications of itself to deal with similar matters on a smaller scale, often with an increasing degree of informality. The naming of these groups as *negotiating* committees describes them as committees set up to resolve differences of interest, where there is a basic conflict or divergence between that which is in the *employer* interest and that which is in the *employee* interest. This does not call for a particular operational procedure, although we consider later in this book the question of negotiating skill. Singleton makes the comment:

> There has to be a way in which negotiations are carried out which constitutes the negotiating procedure, however simple, however lacking in explicit formulation. In time, however, with the repetition

of previous practice, with the adoption of methods for handling new problems as they are encountered, even the least sophisticated negotiating arrangements take on the character of an established procedure, the accepted method of conducting negotiation. (Singleton 1975, p. 16)

Because of its individual focus, and because of the legal requirement, *grievance procedure* exists in many organizations where there is no trade union recognized. In such a situation it will be devised unilaterally by the management, even though they may take advice on how to frame it.

The grievance of an individual can, nevertheless, have collective implications of the 'there but for the grace of God go I' type, quite apart from the fact that the grievance expressed by one person may actually be aggrieving others at the same time. For this reason there is customarily an extension of grievance procedure, where trade unions are recognized, to allow for collective endorsement of a grievance with which an individual employee has not been successful. At that time it has turned itself into a collective dispute. But dispute can also arise from a failure to agree within the negotiating procedure, so we need to consider the processing of grievances as a separate issue from disputes procedure even though one may develop into the other.

One very helpful discussion of British procedures is by Thomson and Murray (1976), which enables us to understand the operation of procedure more clearly. They succeeded in interviewing 268 managers in thirty-five plants about their views on grievance procedure and their experience with it, and they present their analysis of this fieldwork in a wider perspective to develop both a composite view of the process and a contingency-based approach to procedural structure. The book is also very agreeable to read. One invaluable chapter in it (pp. 134–63) deals with the practical issues in development of procedures, describing five main areas:

1. *Basic structure*: The number of steps; the final stage; time limits; recording of grievances; written or oral presentation and answers; co-operation clause.
2. *Roles of participants*: Line management; staff management; employers' association representatives; shop stewards; senior shop stewards; full-time union officials; grievance committee; the individual grievant.
3. *Scope of procedure*.
4. *Procedural differentiation*.
5. *Impact of procedure*: Formalization of procedural usage; status of the grievance decision; no-strike clause; sanctions; external impact; procedural review.

They also present six alternative organizational scenarios, suggesting the type of procedural element appropriate for each.

The original 1972 Code of Practice had one of its most comprehensive sections devoted to *disciplinary procedures*, specifying the following key elements: rules, offences, penalties, procedural steps, location of responsibility:

> A disciplinary procedure is in many ways the converse of a grievance procedure. In a grievance procedure an employee is concerned with something unsatisfactory in the employer's performance or at least within the employer's power to alter; in a disciplinary procedure the employer is concerned with something unsatisfactory in the employee's performance. (Singleton 1975, p. 23)

The complementary nature of grievance handling and discipline is explored further in Chapter 30, dealing with those processes of mutual control. Employees collectively may wish to agree to or modify the arrangements whereby disciplinary matters will be dealt with by the management. It is very rare for them to share the task of enforcing discipline, but quite common for them to participate in preparing an acceptable judicial framework of procedure, which will constrain the activities of individual managers and help to underpin the employment rights of the individual. It can also have the effect of legitimizing dismissal decisions by management as it provides some guidelines for managers in disciplinary situations involving individuals, who are judged according to principles agreed with the majority:

> group 'indiscipline' normally results from a widespread rejection of a working arrangement or rule and the resolution of any conflict lies in the negotiation of new work standards, individual indiscipline indicates merely a personal deviation from standards generally accepted by other employees. (Department of Employment 1973, p. 2)

Review topic 11.2

Apart from the applications mentioned above, are there any other aspects of organizational life that you think would be made more efficient by developing procedures for mutual control?

Procedural methods

There are four methods of producing procedures:

1. *Task logic*: Task logic is the method of work study and associated techniques, where the logic of the task dictates a sequence of actions or activities to be carried out in task performance. This method is not dealt with in this book.

2. *The checklist method*: This involves setting up a series of check questions as a basis of formulating the procedure.
3. *Modelling*: This is a method much used with mutual control procedures. A typical procedural system is devised as a model that could be modified to suit a wide variety of similar situations.
4. *Flowcharting*: The most sophisticated method is flowcharting, which is a simplified form of systems analysis. This is appropriate for those procedures that comprise a lengthy system of interrelated activities, possibly involving several different departments and certainly involving a number of different people.

It is dangerous to regard procedures as dull and not requiring managerial time and attention. The organization without satisfactory procedures can rarely operate effectively unless it is in an unusually favourable business situation. Any organization can be hamstrung if its procedures get out of control. The need for managerial initiative and creativity has to be balanced against the need for swift action and consistent decision-making.

Summary propositions

11.1 Although managers take little interest in procedures, they are vital to organizational success.
11.2 Procedures for administrative action get things done in organizations: procedures for mutual control regulate the employment relationship.
11.3 The value of administrative procedures is that they reduce the need for future decisions, provide consistency and autonomy, and improve management control.
11.4 Mutual control procedures produce clarity, fairness and managerial consistency.
11.5 The four main methods of producing procedures are task logic, modelling, checklist and flowcharting.

References

Cyert, R. M. and March, J. G. (1963), *A Behavioural Theory of the Firm*, Englewood Cliffs, NJ: Prentice Hall.
Department of Employment (1973), *In Working Order*, Manpower Paper no. 6, London: HMSO.
Industrial Relations Code of Practice (1972), London: HMSO.

Koontz, H., O'Donnell, C. and Weihrich, H. (1980), *Management* (7th edition), Tokyo: McGraw-Hill.

McKersie, R. B. and Hunter, L. C. (1973), *Pay, Productivity and Collective Bargaining*, London: Macmillan.

Singleton, N. (1975), *Industrial Relations Procedures*, Department of Employment Manpower Paper no. 14, London: HMSO.

Terry, M. (1977), 'The inevitable growth of informality', *British Journal of Industrial Relations*, March.

Thomson, A. W. J. and Murray, V. V. (1976), *Grievance Procedures*, London: Saxon House.

12

Computers in personnel work

The past decade has seen a rapid increase in the number of personnel departments using computing facilities. In July 1990 Richards-Carpenter reported that 91 per cent of the personnel departments responding to a survey by the IMS were using computers in some way for personnel work.

In this chapter we first look at the development of personnel computer usage and discuss in more detail why computers are used. We then consider software and its development, the facilities that the computer has to offer and the areas of personnel management for which the computer is most used.

We conclude by looking at confidentiality, privacy, security and the Data Protection Act.

Development of computer usage

In mid-1983, at a seminar on using computers in the personnel department, one of the delegates commented to the effect:

> Well as far as I'm concerned it's all a waste of time. We spend hours filling out forms to send to the computer department, but we get very little back. If we request information from the computer department it can take weeks, sometimes months, to get it back, and then it's very often wrong and has to be redone. The information's always out of date anyway.

The equipment being demonstrated at the seminar was a microcomputer to show how information could be directly input or changed. Information could be directly accessed and interrogated, the computer's response to queries being

175

almost immediate. Computing was certainly coming out of the dark ages of batch processing, illustrated by the delegate's comment.

The development of cheap but powerful microcomputers and of adequate on-line and real-time access to a mainframe or minicomputer have provided the essential basis for a personnel system which uses, in part, constantly changing information. On the software side, the development of data-base management techniques and of specific personnel 'packages' have enabled flexible and imaginative use of the stored data. The computer can now meet the needs of the personnel department where the traditional 'computational' systems of the past could not. Software has been developed which increasingly takes account of the user's needs and abilities, and systems are often described as 'user-friendly'. Indeed personnel managers are now being encouraged to become 'computer-friendly'.

All this development underlies the increasing use of computers for personnel work, particularly in smaller organizations, and computing skills are now generally seen as essential to and compatible with personnel work. However high figures of computer usage (Richards-Carpenter 1990), and articles (for example, see Ive 1982) and conference papers (see Page 1982–90) describing sophisticated and comprehensive systems, belie the fact that we are not yet completely out of the dark ages. Many personnel departments still have computer systems that are inadequate for their needs. Most personnel departments use their computing facilities only to a very modest extent. A number of systems that are used were designed to meet the strategic needs of headquarters personnel and general management, and have been largely imposed on operating units. The result of this is that although operating units are required to put a lot of effort into the computer, they are not able to use the system to meet many operational needs as it was not designed with these needs in mind.

The computer is used in many different ways in personnel departments, and the lack of common computer terminology hinders the effective description of the ways it is used. Such basic questions as, 'What is the difference between a computerized personnel information system and personnel computing?', and 'What is an integrated system?' have not been sufficiently answered.

In a book such as this there is not the space to discuss computer hardware – how it works and how to use it – or screen design and layout. For further information on these areas, refer to Gallagher (1986); Wille and Hammond (1981); Rowan (1982); Norman and Edwards (1984); and Bramham and Cox (1983).

Why use the computer?

What has prompted thousands of personnel managers with little computer knowledge to tear themselves away from their day-to-day management activities and spend long hours planning and organizing a computer system? There is a variety of reasons.

It is a well-rehearsed idea that using computers will enable a personnel department to provide speedier and more accurate information, and most systems eventually live up to this expectation. Computer systems are often introduced because manual systems are messy and time-consuming to update, and the inevitable duplication of information results in inaccuracies (Fell 1983). The difficulty or impossibility of obtaining summary statistics from manual records has prompted many organizations to use the computer. As one personnel manager commented: 'I was making decisions by the seat of my pants on the basis of information on one side of A4.'

Some organizations adopt computer use with the aim of reducing staff numbers and therefore costs. Organizations setting out to do this seem to achieve their aim with no real problems. Computer use can reduce staffing – if this is a requirement. But are staffing reductions generally required? Is it wise to make them a requirement? An Urwick Nexos report on 'Office Automation for Personnel Managers' puts forward the following view:

> Any application of new technology which involves significant invest-ment must be cost justified. The most obvious and frequently used justification is the cost substitution equation – the price of the equipment is outweighed by savings on other resources, particularly staff. New technology enables the same (and more) work to be carried out by fewer people. This is an important but essentially defensive aim. A complementary positive justification is to identify value added improvements promoted by the new technology – the opportunities for improving policy formulation and management decision making, opening up new product markets and client services, other ways of deploying the technology to extend corporate activities. (Urwick Nexos 1982)

We have frequently been told by personnel managers that justifying the use of a computer in advance is an extremely difficult thing to do. However, we identify below a number of value-added improvements, in addition to the speed and accuracy of information produced, which may be promoted by using computers within the personnel department:

1. The decision to use a computer can spark off a review of personnel records: What information is kept? What is needed? In what format? What do we want to do with it? And so on. In other words, rather than replicating previous manual records on the computer, there is the opportunity to redefine the needs, format and uses of personnel information. A good example of this is given by Fell (1983) when he describes how his organization replaced their manual absence record system with a com-puterized time-loss analysis system. Reasons for absence were redefined

in thirty-five different categories, and periods of absence were recorded by the hour instead of full or half-days as in the past. This information could then be analyzed to identify problem areas, and trends, which had not been possible with the manual records.

2. Using the computer can enable a much more flexible combination of information. This allows previously identified needs to be fulfilled, and new ways of doing things can generate new ideas. There is a greater opportunity for the personnel department to be proactive. For example, a large company making a promotion decision may wish to take into account present post, job and salary history, appraisals, training, foreign languages spoken and absence record. Identifying possible candidates from a variety of manual recording systems would not be easy. Using an appropriate computer system, the operation could be fairly simple and quick.

3. The facilities that the computer provides, encourages more creative use of information. This applies in particular to modelling facilities. Using these facilities for, say, human resource planning or salary negotiations allows a much wider range of possibilities to be considered than trial and error and informed guesswork.

4. Better management decisions can be made not only on more information, but on information that is more appropriate, more accurate and available when needed. It is of limited use for the personnel department to work out the exact financial implications of a pay settlement three weeks after the settlement has been agreed.

5. Computer usage can give the personnel department the opportunity to play a greater part in the corporate planning process, through having more to offer in terms of information and skills. If, for example, the corporate plan includes an intended 20 per cent increase in production, the personnel department can demonstrate, rapidly and accurately, the implications that this will have for manpower resources.

6. Using the computer may enable the personnel department to provide a better service to line management. For example, more effective and appropriate storage of absence data will provide line managers more readily with the information that they need. Also, the improved quality and quantity of information can enable the personnel department to monitor activities more effectively, providing better guidelines and more appropriate advice for line managers.

7. The personnel department may be able to respond more quickly to trade unions in some matters if a computer is used. This could apply both during negotiations and in regard to *ad hoc* requests or grievances, for example, pressure for an extra half-day's holiday or regrading of some groups of staff.

8. Overall there is the possibility that computer usage will improve the credibility and image of the personnel department. The personnel department can be more professional.

There are thus some impressive reasons why personnel managers might feel that computer usage will enhance the work of the department. However, a general awareness of the possible advantages outlined above is not sufficient as a basis for adopting a system. Many authors recommend a detailed consideration of the needs that the computer is intended to meet, and the setting of specific requirements and objectives.

Review topic 12.1

- If you do not use a computer in the personnel department, how could a computer be used to meet the needs of the personnel department? What specific objectives would you set for a computer system?
- If you do use a computer in the personnel department, how is the computer used to meet the needs of the personnel department? What needs are not being met? Why not? What specific objectives would you set for a new or improved system?

Recent research has, however, indicated that computers are often admitted into the personnel department for reasons other than their potential usefulness to the business of personnel management (Hall and Torrington 1986). Sometimes, computers were adopted because most other departments in the organization were using them and the personnel department did not want to be left behind. Occasionally, it was felt that the personnel department should use computers so that they would be seen as 'suffering' along with the others, and also be able to demonstrate that it was possible for staff to accept computers. Many personnel managers felt that there was a growing pressure on all managers to use computers. This pressure can be seen in the many advertising campaigns seeking to persuade personnel managers that unless they adopt the 'system' they will not be running an effective department. The pressure becomes stronger as more and more personnel departments adopt computer usage.

Types of computer system

There is an infinite variety of ways in which personnel managers can organize their use of computer facilities. The methods selected will to some extent reflect the status and power of personnel management in the organization and the priority that it is given; the structure and needs of the organization and the personnel department; and the ideas, goals and skills of the personnel manager. Computer systems used by the personnel department can be grouped into three broad categories: systems owned by other departments; systems owned by the personnel department; and interdepartmental systems.

Using another department's computer system

In most organizations the personnel department's first experiences of computer use began with some form of payroll system. Most personnel departments continue to use the system in a very limited way, but in a few cases it has been extended in an attempt to meet other personnel needs. Common patterns of use are:

1. Payroll send the personnel department regular (often monthly) computer reports giving standard information from the system, which is useful for the personnel department. An example of this would be a list of staff in post with current salary grouped by department.
2. In addition to the above, the personnel department may be able to request *ad hoc* reports as the need arises. These may be received the following day or may take weeks, or even months, depending on the nature of the request, and the system.
3. Additional items of personnel information may be put onto the payroll system – although the same limitations in accessing the information remain as above.
4. In a minority of circumstances the personnel department may acquire an on-line terminal whereby they can directly access some of the payroll system's information. However, the personnel department are not responsible for inputting information and have no real control over the system.

These types of computer usage have been grouped together because in all cases the personnel department is using a system which does not belong to it; a system which was not designed to meet its needs; a system over which it has no control and which it can very rarely use directly.

Using personnel computer systems

Personnel computer systems cover a wide range. They differ from the first group in that they were designed or bought to meet the needs of the personnel department. Personnel staff will have been involved to some extent from the very beginning in defining their requirements and either contributing to the development of an in-house system or exercising choice of the package to be purchased. The main distinctions in this group of systems are between comprehensive computerized personnel information systems, computerized personnel tools, knowledge-based systems and human resource networks.

Comprehensive computerized personnel information systems

These are comprehensive systems containing, or with the potential to contain, information relating to individual employees for all or most areas of personnel work. The key feature of the system is the individual employee record, and such systems substantially replace the manually-held personal file. These are sometimes referred to as integrated systems (Ive 1982) as they combine different areas of essential employee information into a whole system. However, the term 'integrated systems' is also used to refer to those that integrate personnel information with information from other departments, which we discuss later on. To avoid confusion we will use the term 'comprehensive computerized personnel information system' (CCPIS) for a system that attempts to cover all or most areas of employee information. The areas of employee information which could be computerized include:

- Basic personal and contract details.
- Training/development/education details.
- Appraisal details/career progression.
- Payment and pension details.
- Fringe benefits.
- Discipline/grievance details.
- Termination/redundancy/dismissal details.
- Health/safety/welfare details.
- Absence details.

Information relating to these areas may be stored in varying amounts of depth depending on the needs of the particular department, as illustrated in Figure 12.1.

➤Increasing depth of information ————————————————————➤

Devinition of level of depth	Level 1	Level 2	Level 3	Level 4
Example of how definition relates to an area of personnel information; educational qualifications	Highest educational qualification	Highest educational qualification, date and subject	All educational qualifications since leaving school with dates and subjects	All educational qualifications, with dates and subject for those after leaving school
Individual example	HND	HND Business Studies 1974	ONC Business Studies 1972 HND Business Studies 1974	5 'O' Levels 1 'A' Level ONC Business Studies 1972 HND Business Studies 1974

Figure 12.1　*Individual information stored in a CCPIS: an example showing various levels of information that may be stored*

Some areas of stored information will remain unchanged over time, for example, date of birth and national insurance number. In other areas there is space for adding to the original information. For example, as an individual gains a new professional qualification this may be put on a new line, the original information remaining where it is. Other pieces of information will be replaced as more up-to-date information becomes available. For example, current job title and current salary will be replaced as the individual moves to another job and/or is awarded a salary increase. The original information, however, need not be lost, and can be transferred to a history screen with all the relevant dates of when the changes took place. Long salary histories are often built up extremely rapidly in this way. Where a record of history is not seen as important the original information is lost when it has been updated.

Increasingly, CCPISs are providing facilities for storing establishment information and linking this to individual employees. Items of information may include:

- Post number, title, grade.
- Reporting relationships.
- Job evaluation details.
- Full job description.

The overriding advantage of a CCPIS is that since all the personnel information is stored within the one system, any combination of information can be drawn from that system. Further information on the way that the system can be used will be found below (pages 185–188).

Computerized tools

These are systems or applications that cover one or a very small number of personnel tasks and are not intended for expansion into a CCPIS. These tools, however, sometimes link into a CCPIS, if the department uses one. Data can be received from the CCPIS and the computerized tool can be used to manipulate these. If the computerized tool is used to collect individual information it can feéd this directly into the CCPIS. There is a vast range of imaginative computerized tools in use. Some tools are used to store individual information, for example, a system to record and analyze absences, a succession planning system, or a system concerned with individual allocation of company cars. Other examples include systems for administering the allocation of safety equipment, or accident recording and analysis systems. One final example would be a system for storing the names and details of individuals waiting to go on training courses together with course information and availability of places, so that the individuals and the courses could be matched.

Other types of computerized tools, such as employee number modelling, or labour cost modelling or shift rostering systems are not used as a way of storing individual information. Establishment or overall statistical information is put on to the computer as and when that particular application needs to be run. These types of application may be built into a very sophisticated CCPIS. This is not common, however, and most organizations have found it simpler, so far, to keep these types of application separate, but often linked to a CCPIS, if there is one.

Expert systems

A whole new generation of personnel computerized tools are now becoming available. These are the 'expert' or 'knowledge-based systems'. These systems have a totally different approach from the CCPISs and computerized tools discussed above. An expert system has a built-in knowledge base that contains judgemental and qualitative knowledge, and can only be used interactively. Such systems were originally developed in other professional areas, like helping doctors with diagnosis. The computer was programmed to ask the doctor certain questions depending on the doctor's reply to a previous question. Systems in personnel management concentrate on areas such as the job analysis process, and on recruitment/promotion decisions using assessment centre data.

Human resource networks

These systems are similar to 'Prestel' and 'Teletext' and contain factual, textual information. Human resource networks are now marketed in the United States, although they have yet to appear in the United Kingdom. The networks are organized and kept up-to-date by the supplier, and organizations pay to 'link in' to the system. The type of information included is pay survey data, current employment legislation and so on.

Interdepartmental integrated systems

Systems that are shared by two or more departments are sometimes referred to as integrated systems because the data from more than one department are combined and located in one system. The most usual form, which many personnel managers have considered but which few have adopted, is the integrated payroll and personnel system. Another option is to integrate payroll, personnel and pensions. This type of computer use is of a different nature from personnel's use of the payroll system, because an integrated system is intended to serve the needs of all user departments from the beginning. Integration of systems carries the ultimate possibility of a totally integrated organizational system. However, personnel's use of integrated systems has so far had mixed success.

Problems of an integrated payroll and personnel system

1. There is a lack of good appropriate software.
2. Payroll is seen as the priority and personnel's needs may be affected by being in second place.
3. Any adaptations to the system which personnel may need may be more difficult to achieve because of payroll's use of the system.

Advantages of an integrated payroll and personnel system

1. Duplication of records is avoided.
2. The two departments are using data that are consistent.
3. The personnel department can more effectively carry out cost budgeting and labour cost applications.

The decision to use an integrated computer system often results in a redefinition of the relationship between the two departments. Sometimes the personnel department will ultimately report to the finance department. Most often payroll will report to personnel.

Links with other systems

Links with other systems are increasingly common. They can facilitate a more flexible approach to computing and can expand the use made of the computer. There is a variety of ways in which personnel systems may link into other systems or with each other. The possibilities include:

1. The personnel system may be linked to the payroll system so as to feed the payroll system automatically with appropriate data. This is sometimes referred to as 'personnel driving payroll'. Instead of forms and letters being sent from the personnel department to the payroll department when an employee is promoted, the information is transmitted via the computer systems.
2. Electronically-stored 'clocking-in information' may be fed automatically into a CCPIS or integrated system to update records on lateness and absence, and to facilitate analysis.
3. Information from a CCPIS or integrated system run on a mainframe may be dumped onto a micro in order to run a specific application, as a computerized tool. Manpower modelling and pay modelling are often done in this way with up-to-date information from the mainframe being put onto the micro just in advance of pay negotiations so that it is readily available to use for 'what if . . .' questions in preparation and during negotiations.
4. Local systems can be linked into head office systems. For example, if networked micros were used in all locations, or if micros were used in local

sites and a mainframe in head office. Instead of having to contact all locations for up-to-date manpower statistics, awaiting replies and then collating all the information, head office could just key their request into the computer.

5. A feed into the Banks Automated Clearing System (BACS) can be useful for the payment of those staff with bank accounts.

Personal computing

Increasingly, personal computing is being introduced into all types of department in line with the organizational policy on computer facilities. A number of personnel departments receive this type of facility before they have a CCPIS. The advantages of this are:

1. Individuals can have personal space on the computer to use as they wish.
2. There is often an electronic mail facility for individuals to use.
3. Other packages such as word processing, spreadsheet and general modelling packages may be available on the computer.
4. Often, computerized tools can be quickly developed.

Output: nature and extent of computer use

Whichever type of computer system is used, the most critical element is what comes out of the computer and whether this meets the needs of the personnel department. The most basic function of the computer is the storage and updating of individual records – the computer instead of files of paper being used as a reference point.

Some personnel departments have not yet progressed beyond using the computer as a substitute manual filing system. A number of others have developed more ambitious ways to use the computer's facilities, including listing reports, statistical reports, *ad hoc* reports, modelling, automatic letter production, diarizing, automatic computational facilities and automatic updating.

Listing reports

As the name suggests, these reports contain lists of individuals from the system. The order of the lists can vary, for example, alphabetical order, clock number order, grade order, or grouped by department and then in alphabetical order. The reports can be for all employees or just selected groups such as an alphabetical list of part-time staff.

Other items of information can be added to the list. For example, an alphabetical list of male employees giving age, job title, number of years employed and membership of the pension scheme. Listing reports are often used for the production of internal telephone directories, or for individuals on SSP (Fell 1983).

Statistical reports

Statistical reports are those that summarize information relating to all or sub-groups of employees. The concern here is with an overall picture rather than individual employee information. An example of such a report would be the number of days lost in each department due to sickness in a particular month. Another would be number of days lost through accidents at work in each year for each plant in an organization. This type of summary information would be presented in the form of a matrix, as shown in Figure 12.2. Information from statistical reports can also be produced in the form of line graphs, pie charts and bar charts by using the appropriate software.

Department: 050026		Plant engineering				Total employees = 4	
	Salaried		Hourly paid				
Absence reason	Male	Female	Male	Female	Total hours	As % of hours paid	Cost of hours
01 Annual holiday	00.00	00.00	28.00	00.00	28.00	4.17	84.560
03 Certified sick	00.00	00.00	24.00	00.00	24.00	3.57	64.080
06 Works accident/disease	00.00	00.00	16.00	00.00	16.00	2.38	42.720
Recorded paid hours lost	00.00	00.00	68.00	00.00	68.00	10.12	191.360
Public holidays	00.00	00.00	64.00	00.00	64.00	9.52	172.560
Company holidays	00.00	00.00	00.00	00.00	00.00	00.00	00.000
Fix annual holidays	00.00	00.00	00.00	00.00	00.00	00.00	00.000
Less attendance on co./ pub. hols.	00.00	00.00	00.00	00.00	00.00	00.00	00.000
Total paid hours lost	00.00	00.00	132.00	00.00	132.00	19.64	363.920
Total paid hours worked	00.00	00.00	540.00	00.00	540.00	80.36	1.447.960
Total hours paid	00.00	00.00	672.00	00.00	672.00	100.00	1.811.880
Unpaid leave hours	00.00	00.00	00.00	00.00	00.00		
Total hours available	00.00	00.00	672.00	00.00	672.00		

1. All hours refer to the basic contractual hours for each employee
2. Total employees refers to the number of employees who have contributed to the organization during the month
3. The report reflects internal movements within the reporting organization as well as starters and leavers
4. Cost of hours is calculated as the basic hourly remuneration per employee

Figure 12.2 *May and Baker Ltd: Time loss summary by department, May 1982*
Source: Fell (1983). Used with permission of the Institute of Personnel Management.

Ad hoc reports

These are sometimes called random reports. The facility that enables these to be produced is often termed a 'random report generator'. This facility is generally available with recently developed systems.

The reports produced in this way are no different in nature from the listing and statistical reports described above. The difference between an *ad hoc* report and a standard report is that standard reports have have to be 'built in' to the programme, and therefore have to be defined as the system is being developed. The random or *ad hoc* report facility enables previously unthought of reports to be defined and requested at any time after the system is in operation. These reports can be defined by the user and can be stored in the computer's memory. Once stored they can be called up quickly if needed again, in the same way as a standard report.

Modelling

Modelling is a form of simulation: 'What would happen if we did . . .?', 'What if . . .?'. Simulation has been used in pilot training for a long time. The obvious disadvantages of allowing a trainee to pilot a plane 5 miles off the ground to discover what would happen if he decided to pull a lever were avoided by keeping trainees firmly on the ground in a plane which has been programmed to simulate the effects of the trainee's decisions. The same logic applies to management. There are better ways of finding out the results of a certain course of action than actually taking that course of action and suffering the consequences. A personnel manager might wish to know the total annual cost of giving all employees a 5 per cent pay rise. She may also wish to know the total cost of giving some groups 3 per cent, some 4 per cent and some 6 per cent; or the cost of giving all employees 3 per cent now and an additional 3 per cent in six months' time; and so on for other scenarios.

These questions can become increasingly complicated when there are a number of different unions involved, each settling for different groups at different times of the year. This information can aid management decision-making, replacing the few scribbled figures on the back of an envelope. Further information on pay modelling can be found in Thompson (1983). In a similar way the modelling facility can be used as an aid to manpower planning (Mandl 1983) or as an aid to shift rostering (Hall 1983; Lepping 1983).

Automatic letter production

This facility is most useful when a large number of letters of a standard format are required. Using the appropriate software and a letter quality printer, names and other individual details that are stored in the system can be linked with standard letters also stored in the system in order to print letters automatically. The only action that the user needs to take is to type in the relevant names and codes of the appropriate letters in one short operation. This is much quicker than using a word processor, which would require the user to type in the individual details as each standard letter came up on the screen. The computer can also be programmed to update the individual's record with an entry indicating the type of letter sent out and the date. This facility is very useful for recruitment administration (see Ive 1982).

Automatic computational facilities

These facilities enable automatic calculations to be performed on items of information that already exist in the system. If date of birth was recorded for each individual, the system could be asked to calculate the ages of individuals if required. The user could ask the system to print out the names and ages of all those employees over a particular age.

Diarizing

Diarizing facilities enable the user to ask the computer to give a reminder once a certain time-period has elapsed in relation to an item of information in the system. This alerts the user that a decision or further action needs to be taken. This may be useful in conjunction with SSP procedures, probationary employees, grievance and disciplinary procedures, and so on.

Bulk updating

This facility enables all or some employee records to be updated by one input from the user. For example, if all salaries had been increased by 4 per cent, one input from the user would cause all relevant details to be updated. This is an improvement on the lengthy process of updating each employee's file individually.

Extent of computer use

Our recent research has shown that the use of these facilities varied greatly. Record storage was predictably used to the greatest extent with analysis, including both listing and statistical reports, a close second. The more sophisticated and visible facilities such as modelling and automatic letter production were used to a much lesser extent. The areas of personnel management for which the computer was most used so far are payment administration, individual employee records, fringe benefits, absence and training. The computer is hardly used at all for health, safety and welfare, discipline and grievance matters and employee relations. Further details are shown in Table 12.1.

Table 12.1   Nature and extent of personnel computer use and computer facilities used: survey results of 238 respondents who used a computer in some way for personnel work

Area of work	Computer activities undertaken					
	a	b	c	d	e	Total
Payment administration	192*	150	41	121	30	534
Individual employee records	157	122	20	95	13	407
Absence	105	96	13	61	8	283
Fringe benefits	87	63	15	43	9	217
Training	84	52	6	29	11	182
Recruitment/selection	70	49	9	29	21	178
Redundancy/dismissal	46	32	5	20	7	110
Appraisal	46	30	4	25	4	109
Job evaluation	46	29	6	14	5	100
Management development	40	37	6	20	3	106
Health, safety, welfare	26	21	0	7	1	55
Discipline/grievance	22	13	1	10	2	48
Employee relations	12	9	2	5	2	30
Total	933	703	128	479	116	2,359

Notes:
Computer activities:
(a) Records stored on the computer.
(b) Computer used to analyze as well as record those data.
(c) 'Modelling facility' that is used ('what if . . .' questions).
(d) When information is input: automatic updating of all the records that the new information would affect.
(e) Updating of an employee's record causing any relevant letters to be automatically produced.

*   The figures in the table represent the number of mentions for each activity.

Review topic 12.2

You are the personnel manager in a manufacturing plant with a total of 1,500 employees. It is necessary, due to financial problems, to lose 15 per cent of the total wage bill. You have an excellent computer system to assist you in dealing with this problem. How would you use it?

Implications of computer use

As can be seen, the extent and nature of computer use varies considerably between different organizations. Further research by the authors (Hall and Torrington 1989) confirms that the full potential of the computer is rarely exploited. Where there was thoughtful and sophisticated use, the computer had a significant impact on the shape and effectiveness of the personnel function, and in particular on its credibility and professional image. Support was provided for:

1. The development of a human resources approach to personnel work, as a fuller and better quantified view of personnel issues is attainable which assists identification with business objectives.
2. An emerging role as an information centre, where the personnel function controls more information, although they may well be less involved in the day-to-day data input and extraction.
3. Development of an internal consultancy role, as the personnel department is seen as having a better overview of the organization from a business perspective.
4. Development of a change agent role in the introduction of new technology.

In parallel with these personnel managers were more actively seeking staff with computer skills, fewer clerical staff were employed and the role of computer guru was emerging.

Review topic 12.3

What do you think are the barriers to exploitation of the full potential of the computer in the personnel function? How would you overcome these?

Confidentiality, privacy and security

Concerns about confidentiality, privacy and security of personal information have always been present but have been highlighted by the growing use of computers.

Confidentiality

Confidentiality relates to information sought, obtained or held by an organization, the disclosure of which might be detrimental to that organization or to the third party that supplied it. The guarantee to the reference writer that everything he says will be treated in the strictest confidence is to protect the reference writer rather than the person about whom the reference is written.

Privacy

This relates to information sought, obtained or held by an organization about a past, present or prospective employee, the use of which might be detrimental to that employee. A Home Office document on computers and privacy suggests that there are three areas of potential danger to privacy:

1. Inaccurate, incomplete or irrelevant information.
2. The possibility of access to information by people who should not need to have it.
3. The use of information in a context or for a purpose other than that for which it was obtained.

The Data Protection Act 1984

The Data Protection Act attempts to regulate the above dangers. It is the result of various studies on the need for standards in the computer processing of personal information. In 1972 the Yourger Committee produced a report, and in 1978 a report was produced by the Data Protection Committee headed by Sir Norman Lindop. There was also pressure from Europe partly in the form of the Convention for the Protection of Individuals with regard to the Automatic Processing of Personal Data, which was prepared by the Council of Europe in 1981.

When does the Data Protection Act apply

The Act applies to organizations holding personal data. Personal data has been defined as:

> data which relates to a living individual who can be identified from the information including an expression of opinion about an individual but not any indication of the intentions of the data user in respect of that individual. (Data Protection Act, sect. 1(3))

All organizations using a computerized personnel information system have to be registered giving the sources and purposes of the information that is held.

Each purpose must be registered. Information that is held manually is not covered by the Act, only data that can be processed by automatic equipment. Although the Act was passed in 1984 most of the provisions did not come into force immediately. A Data Protection Registrar was appointed in 1985, and data users could register from November 1985 and were required to have done so by May 1986. Users of personal data have an obligation to follow the data protection principles outlined in the Act.

Eight data protection principles

Very briefly these are:

1. Personal data shall be obtained and processed fairly and lawfully.
2. Personal data shall be held only for specified purposes.
3. Personal data shall not be used or disclosed in a manner incompatible with the specified purposes.
4. Personal data shall be adequate, relevant and not excessive in relation to purpose.
5. Personal data shall be accurate and where relevant kept up to date.
6. Personal data shall not be kept for longer than necessary.
7. An individual is entitled to be informed where data are held about him or her and is entitled to access to the data and where appropriate to have the data corrected or erased.
8. Appropriate security measures should be taken against unauthorized access, alteration, disclosure or destruction, and against accidental loss or destruction.

Implications for personnel managers

In our recent research we found one organization that had used a CPIS, but had ceased to do so, partly due to worries about the Data Protection Act. Most organizations, however, felt that the Data Protection Act was going to have little effect on the way that they handled personal data. Bell comments that:

> The most significant part of the legislation for personnel managers concerns the seventh principle – the right of access to personal data by the 'data subject', in this case the employee or the applicant for a job, if details are kept on a computer or word processor. (Bell 1984)

It is in this area that personnel managers expressed most concern. Most, though, were happy for individuals to see data about themselves, and in many cases these data had been directly supplied by the individual. There was, however, a distinct tendency not to keep sensitive information on the computer. A few employers expressed concern about occupational health data, as there were occasions, for example, where an employee had a terminal illness, but for good reasons was not told of his condition. If such data were kept on computer, there would be no way to shield the employee from this information. A number commented that appraisal data were deliberately not kept on the system, partly due to the Data Protection Act, but also because it was already their policy to send an individual's computerized details to them each year for checking. Personnel managers often pointed to a locked drawer in their desk as the place where assessment of performance and potential data and career planning data were kept. The Data Protection Act gives individuals the right to see any expression of opinion about themselves, but not any indication of the intentions of the data user regarding themselves. Although in many organizations appraisal records are 'open', employers are usually less keen to reveal career planning and employee potential information. There is concern that some information regarding employee potential may be classified as an expression of opinion, and therefore, if kept on the computer, may be viewed by the individual employee. Top executives were omitted from the system in most cases.

Security

Appropriate security is necessary in order to protect both the individual, as outlined in the Act, and to protect the employer. The most common methods are the use of passwords to gain access to the data, careful positioning of VDUs and printers, regular back-up copies and the use of audit trails to log the day's transactions.

Review topic 12.4

John Angel says that the Data Protection Act just reinforces good personnel practice. How would you specify good personnel practice in relation to the Act?

Summary propositions

12.1 As personnel information is constantly changing, the most effective way to use the computer is direct use of an on-line system.

12.2 Although computers are sometimes adopted in order to reduce staff numbers, it is more useful to use them for value-added improvements. These include: speedier and more accurate information, more flexible and creative use of information, better management decisions, better personnel service to the rest of the organization, and improved image of personnel.

12.3 Some personnel departments use information from the payroll computer. Others use a personnel system for just small areas of personnel management – computerized tools. The most effective way to use a computer is to use a comprehensive computerized personnel information system (CCPIS), or an integrated system which combines this with payroll information.

12.4 The computer facilities that are particularly useful for the personnel department include: listing reports, statistical reports, modelling, automatic letter production, diarizing, automatic computational facilities and bulk updating facilities.

Glossary

Ad hoc **reports** Reports available immediately which have not been specified in advance and have not been previously programmed into the system.

Audit trails A log of all the transactions which have taken place on the computer, including details about information that has been input or changed, and who has done this.

Back-up copies Copies of the data that are stored on the computer, usually on tape. This is often done as part of a nightly routine and is stored in a safe place to be used in the event of loss of data in the computer.

Batch-processing The computer processes input and requests for information on a block basis, often overnight, but sometimes weekly or monthly. Users will therefore have to wait for files to be updated and reports to be produced until processing time, even though the information has already been keyed in.

Electronic mail Messages can be sent from one person to another via their computer terminals. This can be done within a building, or over long distances such as between here and the United States (as does the Wellcome Foundation).

On-line A direct link to the computer via a keyboard.

Real-time Information is processed by the computer immediately that it is keyed in. The opposite to batch processing.

Package A set of computer programs that can be purchased ready for immediate use.

Spreadsheet Like an accountant's spreadsheet, which is a matrix with variables across the top and down one side. At the intersection of each variable with another figures are filled in and there are totals along the bottom and down the opposite side. This can be used for basic modelling by changing the values in the variables. A number of spreadsheet packages are available, for example, Lotus 1–2–3.

References

Bell, D. (1984), 'Practical implications of the Data Protection Act', *Personnel Management*, June.

Bramham, J. and Cox, D. (1983), *Personnel Administration made Simple. Forms, cards and computers*, London: Institute of Personnel Management.

Fell, A. (1983), 'Time loss analysis and management'. In T. Page (ed.), *Towards the Personnel Office of the. Future*, London: Institute of Personnel Management and Institute of Management Studies.

Gallagher, M. (1986), *Computers and Personnel Management*, London: Heinemann.

Hall, L. A. and Torrington, D. P. (1986), 'Why not use the computer? The use and lack of computers in personnel'. *Personnel Review*, vol. 15, no. 8.

Hall L. A. and Torrington, D. P. (1989), 'How personnel managers come to terms with the computer', *Personnel Review*, vol. 18, no. 6.

Hall, G. (1983), 'Manpower scheduling in the British Airports Authority'. In T. Page (ed.), *Towards the Personnel Office of the Future*, London: Institute of Personnel Management and Institute of Management Studies.

Ive, T. (1982), 'Ready made package or sharing the mainframe?' *Personnel Management*, July.

Lepping, R. (1983), 'A strategy for reducing the cost of manpower and equipment utilization'. In T. Page (ed.), *Towards the Personnel Office of the Future*, London: Institute of Personnel Management and Institute of Management Studies.

Mandl, F. (1983), 'Applying computers to manpower planning', In T. Page (ed.), *Towards the Personnel Office of the Future*, London: Institute of Personnel Management and Institute of Management Studies.

Norman, M. and Edwards, T. (1984), *Microcomputers in Personnel*, London: Institute of Personnel Management.

Page, T. (ed.) (1982), *Computers in Personnel*, Papers of the National Conference and Exhibition of Computers in Personnel, 22–24 June 1982, London: Institute of Personnel Management and Institute of Management Studies.

Page, T. (ed.) (1983), *Towards the Personnel Office of the Future*, Papers of the Second National Conference and Exhibition on Computers in Personnel, July 1983, London: Institute of Personnel Management and Institute of Management Studies.

Page, T. (ed.) (1984), *Making Manpower Profitable*, Papers of the Third National Conference and Exhibition on Computers in Personnel, 26–28 June 1984, London: Institute of Personnel Management and Institute of Management Studies.

Page, T. (ed.) (1985), *Computers in Personnel. Today's decisions – tomorrow's opportunities*. Published in association with the Fourth National Conference and Exhibition on Computers in Personnel, 9–11 July 1985, London: Institute of Personnel Management and Institute for Management Studies.

Page, T. (ed.) (1986), *Computers in Personnel: From potential to performance*, London: Institute of Personnel Management and Institute of Management Studies.

Page, T. (ed.) (1987), *Computers in Personnel: Achieving practical solutions*, London: Institute of Personnel Management and Institute of Management Studies.

Page, T. (ed.) (1988), *Computers in Personnel: A generation on*. The CIP 88 Conference Book, London: Institute of Personnel Management and Institute of Management Studies.

Page, T. (ed.) (1989), *Computers in Personnel: Managing the technology*, London: Institute of Personnel Management and Institute of Management Studies.

Page, T. (ed.) (1990) *Computers in Personnel: Your system – develop or die*, IMS Report No. 195, Institute of Manpower Studies, Falmer, Sussex.

Richards-Carpenter, C. (1990), 'The personnel power plant has arrived', *Personnel Management*, July.

Rowan, T. (1982), *Managing with Computers*, London: Pan Books in association with Heinemann.

Thompson, N. (1983), 'Using the micro for pay structuring and negotiation'. In T. Page (ed.), *Towards the Personnel Office of the Future*, London: Institute of Personnel Management.

Torrington, D. P. and Hall, L. A. (1985), 'Computers in personnel: slow progress', *Industrial Management and Data Systems*, November/December.

Urwick Nexos (1982), *Managing Office Automation: Office automation for personnel managers*, Report Series 6, London: Urwick Nexos.

Wille, E. and Hammond, V. (1981), *The Computer in Personnel Work*, London: Institute of Personnel Management.

13

Consultancy and consultants

The Preying Mantis

'Of all the businesses, by far,
Consultancy's the most bizarre.
For, to the penetrating eye,
There's no apparent reason why,
With no more assets than a pen,
This group of personable men
Can sell to clients more than twice
The same ridiculous advice,
Or find, in such a rich profusion,
Problems to fit their own solution.

The strategy that they pursue –
To give advice instead of do –
Keeps their fingers on the pulses
Without recourse to stomach ulcers,
And brings them monetary gain,
Without a modicum of pain.
The wretched object of their quest,
Reduced to cardiac arrest,
Is left alone to implement
The asinine report they've sent.
Meanwhile the analysts have gone
Back to client number one,
Who desperately needs their aid
To tidy up the mess they made.
And on and on – ad infinitum –

197

The masochistic clients invite 'em.
Until the merciful reliever
Invokes the company receiver.

No one really seems to know
The rate at which consultants grow,
By some amoeba-like division?
Or chemo-biologic fission?
They clone themselves without an end
Along their exponential trend.

The paradox is each adviser,
If he makes his client wiser,
Inadvertently destroys
The basis of his future joys.
So does anybody know
Where latter-day consultants go?

Ralph Windle, 1981

That *Bertie Ramsbottom Ballad* incorporates nearly all the nightmares about consultants. Although the ballad is directed at external consultants, whose services are bought in, many of the reservations also apply to much personnel work, which is advisory and seeking to bring about change in the attitudes and practices of managerial colleagues.

Scepticism about consultants probably reached its apogee when organizational development was at its most popular and the organizational world was knee-deep in change agents and OD consultants. Although many managers now regard organization development as a luxury that only other people can afford, a consultancy mode of operating by personnel specialists is now widely adopted by personnel specialists, who are themselves using external consultancy services increasingly. The consultancy style of the personnel specialist has to be geared to meet all the reservations expressed in the ballad, as herein lies one of the keys to organizational effectiveness and authority. The personnel manager who cannot perform the consultancy role skilfully is in danger of having only a peripheral role in organizational affairs. The personnel manager who cannot make shrewd selections of external expertise that managerial colleagues will respect is in danger of losing even a peripheral role.

In this chapter we consider first the use of external consultants and advisers, then the question of how to be an effective consultant. Finally, there are comments about specific consultancy methods. A general introduction to the state of the art in consultancy is to be found in the article by Turner (1982), and a helpful *vade mecum* on most aspects of using consultants is the guide commissioned by the International Labour Organization (Kubr 1976).

The use of external consultants

In our research we found that the use of consultants had been increasing among our respondents, and was expected to continue to increase rather than to decrease, as shown in Table 13.1. This, however, actually understates the true position as more detailed analysis of questionnaire results showed that the use of consultants for training and management selection was often not included. Although there was greater use in the private sector than in the public, use in the public sector was increasing more rapidly. Statistical analysis of the data showed that consultants were less often used in situations where employment costs were high in relation to total costs and where trade union membership was high.

Table 13.1 The use, and expected use, of consultants in 350 organizations

'Has the use of consultants in this establishment increased, decreased or stayed the same in the last three years?'

	Increased (%)	Decreased (%)	Stayed the same (%)
Private sector	46.3	12.4	41.3
Public sector	54.5	6.5	38.6

'Do you expect the use of consultants to increase, decrease or stay the same in the next three years?'

	Will increase (%)	Will decrease (%)	Will stay the same (%)
Private sector	18.8	14.8	66.4
Public sector	25.0	22.7	52.3

Table 13.2 shows the areas in which personnel consultants were used in the search for external expertise to complement the skills available internally. Training, recruitment and management development head the list.

Although heeding the comments of Bertie Ramsbottom at the beginning of this chapter, there are some activities that are undoubtedly best undertaken by consultants. An example is the use of psychological tests in selection. These have been available for many years as a means of making selection more systematic and objective, yet their use remains limited. This is partly because only the largest organizations have a scale of recruitment for similar posts that produces a large enough set of results for analysis to be fruitful. The selection of

Table 13.2   Areas in which consultants had been used in the previous three years by 350 questionnaire respondents

Activity	Percentage of all respondents (N = 350)	Percentage of respondents using consultants (N = 159)
Training	23.4	51.6
Recruitment and selection	8.9	41.5
Management development	16.6	36.5
Computers	14.9	32.7
Job evaluation	12.6	27.7
Organizational structure	11.1	24.5
Communications	11.1	24.5
Employee relations	8.0	17.6
Pay	7.4	16.3
Management style	7.1	15.7
Manpower planning	6.6	14.5
Appraisal	6.3	13.8
Discipline and grievance	3.7	8.2
Health and safety	3.7	8.2
Fringe benefits	3.7	8.2
Redundancy	3.4	7.5
Job design	2.0	4.4
Harmonization	0.9	1.9
Welfare	0.6	1.3

trainee pilots by the Royal Air Force can be based around a battery of psychological and physiological tests that have had their effectiveness proven and developed over many years. The Royal Air Force has a wealth of evidence, from tests and subsequent performance, enabling the ability to fly an aircraft successfully to be predicted with reasonable accuracy from test results only. Few employers can accumulate the volume of data needed to make comparable predictions, but consultants who specialize in selection can establish large banks of test result data acquired from applicants to a wide range of organizations. Although applying to different organizations, the people completing the tests are often applying for similar jobs, so consultants can, at least theoretically, produce occupational norms to provide useful performance predictors from test results.

Duncan Wood (1985) has calculated that there are about 1,000 people in the United Kingdom who can be described as personnel consultants, of whom half are genuine specialists with expertise concentrated in one area, such as recruitment, pay or communications, while the remainder offer more general services. He asked senior representatives of fourteen well-established consultancies to rank seven reasons for their use in personnel work and the result was:

First.   To provide specialist expertise and wider knowledge not available within the client organization

Second.	To provide an independent view
Third.	To act as a catalyst
Fourth.	To provide extra resources to meet temporary requirements
Fifth.	To help develop a consensus when there are divided views about proposed personnel changes
Sixth.	To demonstrate to employees the impartiality/objectivity of personnel changes or decisions
Seventh.	To justify potentially unpleasant decisions.

(Wood 1983, p. 41)

In our enquiry we found that the reason given by the personnel specialists themselves was overwhelmingly the need for external expertise. The interview phase of our research probed practitioners' views of consultants more thoroughly. This is reported fully elsewhere (Torrington and Mackay, 1986), and is summarized in Figure 13.1. Confident and competent personnel managers can call on the services of outside experts without fear of jeopardizing their own position and can specify closely what they require. Where the personnel function is under-resourced, or where the personnel manager lacks professional expertise, then consultants will be used reluctantly, with a poor specification of requirements and the likelihood of an unsatisfactory outcome for both client and consultant.

Review topic 13.1

What personnel problems currently facing your organization do you think might best be approached by using outside consultants? Why? How would you specify the requirements? What personnel problems currently facing your organization would you not remit to outside consultants? Why not?

In deciding whether or not outside consultants should be used for a specific assignment we suggest the following approach:

Describe the problem

What is the matter about which you might seek external advice? This may not be obvious, as worrying away at an issue can show that the real matter needing to be addressed is not what is immediately apparent. If, for example, the marketing manager leaves abruptly – as they often seem to do – the immediate problem will present itself as: 'We must find a replacement.' So you begin to think of ringing up the executive search consultant you used when you needed someone for the Middle East in a hurry. Working at finding a correct description of the problem could suggest that the presenting cause is easy to deal with because young X has been waiting for just such an opportunity for months and all the signals suggest that X would be ideal. The 'real' problem may turn out to be what caused the marketing manager to leave, or whether there is a string of other 'young Xs' waiting in the wings. It could require attention to succession planning, remuneration strategy, management development, organization structure or many more alternative possibilities.

Formulate an approach

The next step is to rough out an approach to the problem, with the emphasis here on 'rough'. If you knew the answer you would not need any further advice; if you have no idea of the answer you cannot brief a consultant (but you might give him a blank cheque!). What is needed is a clear but not inflexible strategy so that you can go through the remaining stages of making up your mind without putting the consultant, and yourself, in the wrong framework. If you decide that the problem behind the departure of the marketing manager is a combination of succession planning and remuneration policy, the approach you would then formulate would be based on ideas about how those two issues could be tackled, without an absolute commitment to a single method or technique.

Work out how you could do it in-house

Later in this chapter is reference to the '5 W-H' method, which could be used at this stage, as you decide how it could be tackled by using your own existing resources, how much it would cost, how long it would take and what the repercussions would be, such as stopping work on something else.

Find out how it could be done by consultants

Provided you have done the first two steps satisfactorily, it should be possible to brief one or more potential outside suppliers of expertise, so that they can bid for the business. If the problem is not correctly described there may be bids for the wrong things, and if the approach is not accurately formulated, the consultant will be obliged to carry out a preliminary study, at your expense, to formulate an approach for you. When this happens you are beginning to lose control of the operation. Even if consultants are not as rapacious and asinine as Bertie Ramsbottom suggests, they too have a business to run and will not welcome failure through an assignment being misconceived, so they will guard against the risk. The main questions to ask of the consultants are again how would it be done, how much would it cost and how long would it take.

Decide between the alternatives

A set of alternatives from which to choose gives you the opportunity to compare relative costs, times and likely outputs, as well as implications. In making the final decision the comments in Figure 13.1 are helpful, but the most important point to remember is that the responsibility is inescapably yours. If the consultant can produce the 'best' outcome, have you the resources to implement it? Can you wait? If you can save £10,000 by relying on your own staff and time, will you produce an outcome that adequately meets the needs of your rough-cut approach? The eventual outcome is all that matters.

A. Favourable views
   1. The personnel manager knows what to do, but proposals are more likely to be implemented if endorsed by outside experts.
   2. The outsider can often clarify the personnel manager's understanding of an issue.
   3. Specialist expertise is sometimes needed.
   4. The personnel manager has insufficient time to deal with a particular matter on which a consultant could work full-time.
   5. The consultant is independent.
   6. Using consultants can be cheaper than employing your own full-time, permanent specialists.

B. Less favourable views
   1. The personnel function should contain all the necessary expertise.
   2. In-house personnel specialists know what is best for the company.
   3. Other members of the organization are prejudiced against the use of outside advisers.
   4. Using consultants can jeopardize the position of the personnel specialists and reduce their influence.

Figure 13.1   *Categorization of views from sixty-two respondents about outside consultants*

Being a consultant

The personnel specialist has many activities which require the consultancy approach – providing advice and services to other managers. Indeed, the concept of the personnel function as an internal consultancy activity appears to be gaining support, particularly in the public sector. A review of two such schemes currently operating within local authorities can be found in Griffiths (1989).

It would appear that there is an increasing requirement for personnel specialists to develop expertise in the consultancy process. How do you become an effective management consultant?

Leavitt's Alcoholics Anonymous analogy

Harold Leavitt makes an interesting comparison between management consulting and the approach of Alcoholics Anonymous (AA). He first summarizes the AA approach:

> One finds no threat, no command, no surreptitiousness in the process. The alcoholic stops drinking; he is not stopped. He is helped to change himself. He is helped by being shown alternative means, substitute behaviours, new sources of faith – by anything that will fit his needs. This is a predominantly augmentative, supportive process in which responsibility never actually leaves the changee. (Leavitt 1972, p. 159)

Leavitt goes on to point out the obvious differences between that process and management consulting. The consultant cannot usually wait until people feel disposed to change what they are doing; it is not usually possible for managers to solve their own problems in their own way, there has to be some conformity to organizational norms and time constraints. Finally, there is the risk of there being no control by the changer over the changee. The personnel manager acting in a consultancy mode cannot simply allow people to do things differently if they feel like it.

While displaying the limitations of this method in the management situation, Leavitt suggests a general set of conditions for effecting behaviour change in continuing relationships at work. A is the consultant, B is the person who has to do things differently:

1. A perceives a problem. A will not be able to wait for B to see the problem, so it will have to be pointed out, either by a simple statement or by producing persuasive evidence. A must not, however, suggest that B is the problem, nor should B perceive A as the problem!
2. B takes responsibility for finding solutions to the problem, but realizes that A could be a useful source of ideas.
3. A and B evaluate alternatives and their implications. As B now sees A as a potential source of help, the alternatives can be evaluated to make sure that a change is likely to be an improvement, rather than simply different.
4. B decides on an alternative that A can accept. The responsibility for making and implementing the decision remains with B, even though it will need to be *acceptable* to A; it does not have to be *ideal*.

> This is a little like collective bargaining but even more like a discussion between husband and wife about where they shall take their vacation. If a location can be found that is entirely acceptable to both, all to the good. If the location is only a satisfactory compromise to each, that is still pretty good. If no compromise is possible, then A, if in a position of authority, can always revert to the simple use of the veto (Leavitt 1972, p. 168).

5. B tries the changed method and A provides support, help and reassurance. The early stages will be the time of greatest difficulty for B and the time for a positive contribution from A. It is not helpful if A disclaims responsibility or joins the critics.
6. B either consolidates the change in behaviour or abandons it in favour of another. A may also be abandoned if seen as the source of unhelpful advice.

This sequence can be a useful framework for those personnel activities that are close to coaching and acting as a personal assistant. It assumes a close, personal working relationship between two people with time for that relationship to develop a high degree of trust and mutual respect, with A being seen as a counsellor rather than a consultant.

The Blake and Mouton consultation approach

The inventors of the famous managerial grid also produced an interesting, if rather difficult, analysis of the consultation process. This suggests a range of five alternative forms of contract between the consultant and client (Blake and Mouton 1976):

1. The acceptant contract is one of the classic helping approaches of psycho-therapeutic counselling. The emphasis is on listening, being supportive and not evaluative of the client's behaviour:

   > Acceptant consultation attempts to aid a client through sympathetic listening and empathic support. it might seem that any good friend of the client can do this just as well – but some clients have no good friends and, in any case, the consultant avoids certain actions that friends might take. For example, the consultant does not adopt a partisan point of view and help the person justify the reasonableness of his or her own positions and feelings – the client's behaviour cycle must be broken not perpetuated. (Blake and Mouton 1976, pp. 14–15)

   This is very similar to the approach Leavitt describes.
2. The catalytic contract is similar to the process in chemistry where a reaction is speeded up by adding a catalytic agent to other substances. The consultant aids the process of change by providing new information and assisting in problem-diagnosis. To do this it is necessary to get inside the frame of reference of the client, so that the assistance is provided to solve the problem the client has already identified. The consultant does not provide answers, only information, interpretation and diagnosis.
3. The confrontation contract is a much more direct challenge to the validity of what a client is doing, where expressed values contrast starkly with

actual behaviour. The consultant brings the client's underlying values into focus and shows how values influence behaviour, so that the expressed belief – in a policy statement – that there is equal employment opportunity for all may be a sham in practice if the values of an individual manager produce behaviour that invalidates the policy. By demonstrating the dissonance between belief and behaviour, the consultant may induce some change in belief which leads to a change in behaviour.

4. Prescriptive contracts are the most obvious as they are where the consultant explicitly tells the client what to do, deploying an authority to which the client's compliance is expected. There may be occasions for this approach in modifying behaviour, but the simpler examples for personnel managers are in advising people of the works rules, which have to be obeyed, or the procedural mechanisms, which have to be followed. An inescapable precondition is that the consultant has some specialist expertise that is not available to the client.

5. Theory/principles contracts are very similar to prescriptive contracts in that they rest on the consultant teaching the client theories or principles that the client will then apply to problems being experienced. The difference is that prescription says, 'Do this and you will be able to . . .' while the theories/principles consultant says, 'Learn this and you will be able to work out how to . . .'

Review topic 13.2

Identify an area of personnel managers' duties for each of the five approaches categorized by Blake and Mouton. Why would the approach be suitable for the area you have identified?

Taylor and Singer's skills for change agents

Finally, in this section of the chapter we consider the skills of the change agent summarized by Taylor and Singer, who say that change agents need the ability to:

1. Identify and isolate problems.
2. Discriminate between fact and fiction.
3. Systematize data.
4. Listen – as opposed to hearing only.
5. Ask the right question at the right time.
6. Summarize a discussion.
7. Remain silent.
8. Make verbal presentations.

9. Write persuasively.
10. Help individuals and groups to acquire confidence.

(Taylor and Singer 1983, p. 93)

They make no reference to being able to walk on water, but perhaps this was an oversight.

Methods for consultants

To conclude this chapter we consider some aspects of practical method that personnel specialists may find helpful in their consulting activities.

Problem identification

Whether one is specifying a brief for an outside consultant or coming to terms oneself with a problem that has been presented, there is a need for some device to describe the problem as a preliminary to formulating an approach to solving it. Priestley and his colleagues (1978, p. 28) suggest a simple '5 W-H' method which is What? Who? Where? When? Why? and How? A typical problem could be approached thus:

What is the problem?   Communications in the office are poor.
Who is involved?   Everyone, but most problems are at the level of first-line supervision.
Where is it worst?   In Accounts and in the Print Room.
When is it worst?   At the end of the week and at the end of the month.
Why does it happen?   Because of an erratic flow of work between the two departments, which is worst at those times.
How could it be tackled?   By getting the first-line supervisors to tackle it, smooth out the flow of work, helping them to appreciate the effect of their work flows on the other departments, etc.

This is a very simple problem, with a minimal number of questions serving to do no more than illustrate the method. Each question would probably have dozens of supplementaries in order to fill out the details of a complex problem.

The main value of the consultant at this stage is the ability to raise questions that those close to the matter have not thought about. This is not because consultants are cleverer, but because they have a different pattern of experience and take for granted different things from those who are looking at the presenting problem every day.

Information gathering

There is much material in this book about *interviewing*, particularly in Chapter 10, and personnel specialists tend to be both more skilled and more experienced at this task than most of their managerial colleagues, but they may not think of themselves as interviewers when they are consulting. Priestley, writing for a non-personnel audience, has three simple suggestions:

> 1. Listen to what the person being interviewed is saying. . . . Listening also implies not talking too much. In assessment the interviewer should not be talking for more than 10 per cent of the time.
> 2. Be courteous. . . . One good way of doing this is to treat interviewees as though they were slightly more intelligent, slightly older, possibly of the opposite sex, and of slightly higher status than yourself . . . unless, of course, you encounter someone who actually fulfils all these conditions: the best thing to do in those circumstances is to try to treat such a person as an equal.
> 3. Be confident. You are not on show and are just doing your job to the best of your ability. (Priestley *et al.* 1978, p. 181)

Kubr (1976, pp. 353–60) contains a section on person-to-person communication in consulting which takes a more detailed look at this process.

Although interviewing is the most common method of gathering data that consultants use, they will also analyze documents and observe their surroundings. There are two forms of observation that may be deployed.

Non-participant observation is where the consultant is acquiring information through observing what is happening in the place where the consultation is being carried out. The poet and novelist Christopher Isherwood expressed it thus: 'I am a camera with its shutter open, quite passive, recording, not thinking.' Much understanding of organizational dynamics and working relationships comes from this process of noting the small incidents and tensions, the modes of dress and address and the various minutiae of behaviour that in some way provide explanations of what has to be understood. Isherwood's comment about not thinking is important. This is similar to the point about not rushing to judgement in selection interviews on the basis of first impressions. Consultants do not make snap judgements about organizational problems on the basis of the graffiti in the lavatories, but they do collect data which may subsequently aid their understanding.

Structured observation is a more specialized and difficult technique, which records for subsequent analysis the working behaviour and activities of people: 'unlike interviewing, it allows the researcher to record behaviour as it occurs and thus free him from dependence on the respondent's ability or willingness to describe his actions' (Scott 1965, p. 286). This is very common in efficiency and productivity studies, but has also been used in studies of management work (for example, Mintzberg 1970) and as a preliminary to improving time management, where the observer records the frequency of changes in activity. The difficulties are the uncertainty of knowing the extent to which the observation alters the normal behaviour of the person observed and the likelihood that those willing to be observed are not typical of all those in the category whose work is to be reviewed (Hensen and Barlow 1976, p. 99).

Questionnaires are sometimes used by consultants to collect information that is precise and factual or dealing with clear preferences, like whether people would prefer to implement a one-hour reduction of the working week by finishing twelve minutes earlier each day or one hour earlier on one day. Questionnaire design is not difficult but requires great care. The main points are these:

1. How can the subject be presented to respondents to achieve a high response? In-company investigations have fewer problems with response rate than those conducted among the public at large, but even a small proportion of refusals can reduce the reliability of the results.
2. What is the best order in which to introduce topics? It is helpful to begin with questions that are easy for respondents to understand and reply to accurately, as well as getting them 'on the wavelength' of the inquiry before proceeding to more complex questions.
3. What wording of questions will produce precise data? There is a need to use words that are not only unequivocal, but also where the meaning is not likely to drift with the respondent. Another consideration is the distinction between questions to obtain facts and questions to seek opinion. These are best separated.
4. How long can the questionnaire be? The need to know has to be balanced with the ability of the respondent to reply. Some respondents will not be willing to spend long periods working through a questionnaire, others will have difficulty in maintaining concentration and others will have much more to say than the questionnaire provides for.
5. What is the best layout of the survey forms?

Problem analysis

When the data are gathered, they have to be assembled and analyzed in order that alternative courses of action can be developed. Methods of analysis vary greatly, according to the nature of the study and the discipline within which it is set. Whatever method is used, satisfactory analysis depends on effective organization of the raw data. Ideas for grouping and categorizing material will be suggested by the type of information gathered and by the previous experience of the consultant. One of the hardest aspects of consultancy is making sense of an amorphous mass of material so that the argument develops logically and convincingly.

It is important to start writing early and to write often. This cannot be emphasized too strongly. Part of the skill that is developed in consultancy is the organization and compression of material into succinct summary and analysis. This requires considerable reworking of the material to make it clearer and clearer.

When problems have proved to be intractable there is usually a need to generate more alternative solutions than anyone so far has been able to think of. One method of generating alternatives was devised by Kepner and Tregoe in 1965 and has since been represented (1982). A more popular method is Edward de Bono's lateral thinking (1982), which aims both to enable people to find new solutions to problems and to escape from old solutions to which they may have become attached. De Bono provides an illustration:

> In a singles knock-out tennis tournament, there are 111 entrants. What is the minimum number of matches that must be played? It is easy enough to start at the beginning and to work out how many first round matches there must be, and how many byes. But this takes time. . . . Instead of considering the players trying to win, consider the losers after they have lost. There is one winner and 110 losers. Each loser can lose only once. So there must be 110 matches. (de Bono 1982, p. 7)

When working with a group of other people, rather than with individuals, the brainstorming technique can be used to generate a large number of fresh ideas, some of which may be worth further development. A drill for conducting a brainstorming session is shown in Figure 13.2.

---

1. Decide the purpose of the session.
2. Appoint a note-taker (someone who can write large and fast).
3. Ask group members to call out any idea that comes into their head.
4. Note-taker writes all ideas on blackboard or large sheet of paper that all can see.
5. Encourage group members to develop the ideas of others ('hitch-hiking') as well as 'sparking' in different directions.
6. Stop judgements by anyone. All ideas are valid, however bizarre, even if they seem to be repeating what has already been said.
7. Keep the group going.
8. Stop after no more than 30 minutes; probably 20.
9. Classify the ideas into five or six groups.
10. Rank the ideas in each group.
11. Decide how to follow up any of the ideas that are worth further consideration.

Figure 13.2 *A drill for brainstorming*

Implementation

> The implementation is the most important step in the process and is the area where consultants are the weakest . . . it is no use to present a brilliant solution to a problem and not be able to implement it throughout the organization. (Chickillo and Kleiner 1989, p. 29)

The decision to adopt a change must be the client's decision, as it is the client who has to live with it and make it happen, even though the consultant may provide an initial shove. The consultant can explain alternatives and ask the client to pick between them, or can recommend a course of action, but it is still essential for the client to believe in the rightness of that course of action. The consultant may well develop detailed action steps of what the client should do to implement the solutions, but ownership must pass to the client.

Summary propositions

13.1 The personnel manager is both a consultant and a user of consultancy services.

13.2 The use of outside consultants for personnel activities is rising.

13.3 In deciding between outside and in-house resources the stages are to describe the problem, formulate an approach, work out how to do it in-house, find out how it could be done by consultants and then decide between the alternatives.

13.4 Leavitt's Alcoholics Anonymous analogy can provide a model for those consultancy situations where there is a close and continuing working relationship between consultant and client.

13.5 The Blake and Mouton consultation approach suggests a range of five alternative approaches to the consulting relationship: acceptant, catalytic, confrontation, prescriptive and theory/principles.

13.6 Among the methods of problem identification and analysis for consultants are the 5 W-H method and lateral thinking.

13.7 Personnel specialists may need to modify their customary interviewing expertise for their consultancy activities.

References

Adams, M. and Meadows, P. (1985), 'The changing graduate labour market', *Department of Employment Gazette*, September.

Blake, R. R. and Mouton, J. S. (1976), *Consultation*, Reading, Mass.: Addison-Wesley.

Chickillo, G. P. and Kleiner, B. H. (1989), 'Skills and roles of consultants', *Journal of European Industrial Training*, vol. 14, no. 1, pp. 26–30.

de Bono, E. (1982), *Lateral Thinking for Management*, Harmondsworth: Penguin Books.

Griffiths, W. (1989), 'Fees for "house" work – the personnel department as consultancy', *Personnel Management*, January, pp. 36–9.

Hensen, M. and Barlow, D. H. (1976), *Single Case Experimental Designs: Strategies for studying behaviour change*, Oxford: Pergamon.

Kepner, C. H. and Tregoe, B. B. (1982), *The Rational Manager: A systematic approach to problem-solving and decision-making*, Maidenhead: McGraw-Hill.

Kubr, J. (ed.) (1976), *Management Consulting: A guide to the profession*, Geneva: International Labour Office.

Leavitt, H. J. (1972), *Managerial Psychology* (3rd edition), Chicago: University of Chicago Press.

Mintzberg, H. (1970), 'Structured observation as a method to study managerial work', *Journal of Management Studies*, vol. 7, pp. 87–104.

Priestley, P., McGuire, J., Flegg, D., Hemsley, V. and Welham, D. (1978), *Social Skills and Personal Problem Solving*, London: Tavistock.

Scott, W. R. (1965), 'Field methods in the study of organizations'. In J. G. March (ed.), *Handbook of Organizations*, Chicago: Rand McNally.

Taylor, D. E. and Singer, E. J. (1983), *New Organizations from Old*, London: Institute of Personnel Management.

Torrington, D. P. and Mackay, L. E. (1986), 'Will consultants take over the personnel function?' *Personnel Management*, February, pp. 34–7.

Turner, A. N. (1982), 'Consulting is more than giving advice', *Harvard Business Review*, September/October.

Windle, R. (1985), *The Bottom Line*, London: Century-Hutchinson.

Wood, D. (1985), 'Uses and abuses of personnel consultants', *Personnel Management*, October, pp. 40–7.

Part
III

Employee
resourcing

14

Labour markets

One of the most basic tasks to be undertaken by the personnel function in an organization is to fill vacancies. These are the identified gaps in the manpower resources that an organization requires. This probably sounds like a cumbersome way of saying 'people', but it is necessary, first, to determine manpower needs; and secondly, to decide how those needs can be met. It may be by recruiting a person, by recruiting a lot of people, by contracting for a slice of a person's time or by subcontracting the requirement to another organization. This aspect of personnel strategy and policy is mainly dealt with in the chapters on human resource planning, but a preliminary to that is to consider some features of labour market theory. This is how economists explain the way supply and demand works between those who offer employment and those who offer their labour, with the emphasis on the economic aspects of the options open to the parties:

> Theory suggests that job choice is determined by the bundle of wage
> and non-wage conditions attached to different jobs. Current earn-
> ings, employment prospects, probable future earnings, the nature
> and conditions of work and similar factors are all evaluated by the
> person seeking work, whose ultimate decision between alternative
> job openings depends on the balance of net advantages. (Mackay *et
> al*. 1971, p. 16)

Our consideration in this book will necessarily be superficial and limited to those features of labour market data and analysis that impinge on the vacancy filling problems of organizations.

Definitions

Labour market   A general geographical and/or occupational area of labour supply and demand.

Local labour market   This is both the geographical area containing those actual or potential members of the labour force that a firm might induce to enter its employ under certain conditions, and the other employers with which the firm is in constant flux as firms expand and contract, as transport facilities and housing change or educational and training provisions alter (Robinson 1970, p. 29).

Internal labour market   A term used to describe the single employing organization, within which employees can move from one position to another.

Dualism   In the labour market this is used to describe the hypothesis that supply and demand factors are distorted by the coexistence of primary and secondary labour markets; the first for those of high skill and high potential earnings due to the scarcity and value of their skills; the second for those with less bargaining power due to lack of skill or mobility and union organization (such as some women and those from racial minorities).

Within these broad definitions there is a number of practical variations and special cases. The labour market for accountants is different from that for chemists, with quite different modes of dealing and other conventions. There is a growing interest in the world labour market, as organizations not only choose the country in which it is most cost-effective to locate their manufacturing, but also increasingly 'import' and 'export' large numbers of temporary workers.

Although in this chapter we are considering aspects of labour markets, it is unrealistic to view these operations as separate from the workings of product markets. The terms and conditions that employers offer will be greatly influenced by the state of their order book and their business prospects. Drawing mainly on Australian evidence, Brown and his colleagues made the following comment:

> It is unrealistic to divorce labour market processes from those of the product market. Where competition in the product market leaves employers with little latitude to do otherwise, what wage drift they permit will reflect the pressures of the labour market, or the comparability arguments of their better organised employees. But when their position in the product market gives them more room to manoeuvre, they may use the leeway to make additional payments to cope with problems particular to their own establishment rather than in response to competitive labour market pressures from outside.'
> (Brown *et al.* 1984, p. 175)

Labour market mechanics and data

It is clearly unrealistic to think of the labour market as a single entity, for people enter some markets but not others. Even the great leveller of unemployment operates on the assumption that some people will be sorted and classified as professional and executive while others will not.

For managers the importance of these differences lies in being sure of the conventions of the particular market-place they wish to enter. They need to know the convention on *the mode of dealing and the going rate.* It would be ludicrous to suggest that employees and employers always behave in a rational economic way in making mutual selections and terminations. However, the employer needs to know the going rate as accurately as possible in order to make the right offer in the market-place.

Modes of dealing vary greatly. For some jobs the convention is to begin with face-to-face transactions of a very perfunctory nature in which the prospective employee canvasses employers door to door. In other cases the convention is to deal through intermediaries like employment agencies or consultants, while in others the way of making contact is through newspaper advertising or some other means.

The level of the labour market will vary with the type of work to be done. Graduates seeking a first post are typically likely to come from a wide area, so that the market is nationwide. The same applies to senior and many professional and middle management posts as the balance of net advantages could be sufficient to justify a move over several hundred miles. At the other extreme the market for word processor operators, telephonists, semi-skilled personnel and clerical staff tends to be a local one, with the majority of prospective employees seeking employment only within a limited geographical area. There is then a number of intermediate levels so that the catchment area of 5–10 miles for the clerk may become a 50-mile radius for the area sales manager. For highly specialized employment, like technologists in mineral exploration, the market is international, and in any organization apart from the smallest, there is also an internal labour market.

In understanding the operations of labour markets, we have already said that it is unrealistic to expect employers and employees to behave in a completely rational way. Everyone may have their price, but there is a host of differences in terms and conditions of payment between various jobs that cannot be explained in purely financial terms. The labour economist talks of factors that put 'added structure' into labour markets. In other words, factors that prevent an explanation of labour market behaviour in straightforward terms of supply and demand. Clark Kerr (1954) has listed some of these.

First, there are the preferences of individual workers, who may persist in jobs that pay less than could be earned with a competitor, for reasons of sentiment, familiarity, convenience or inertia. Employees with new skills may be younger and therefore more interested in moving around than their older colleagues, so that their rates of pay become rather higher. A second factor is the preferences of individual employers, who also do not always behave with ruthless logic. Some will strive to develop loyalty and attachment to the organization, while others will prefer a higher level of turnover to ensure the constant input of fresh ideas and enthusiasm.

Actions of trade unions can have major effects, although this is less marked than it used to be. The nationally agreed terms and conditions of employment for a trade or occupation shift the basis of competition between employers for scarce employees to the fringe considerations like starting times or parking space. In some cases the employer may actually consider redesigning the job! To a small extent employers' associations put added structure into the labour market in the same way as unions, but their influence has probably declined more sharply than that of trade unions in this area. The final factor is actions by the government. The overwhelming influence, which we have not seen since the mid-1970s, is incomes policy when labour market flexibility is deliberately restrained in an attempt to reduce inflation by preventing employers outbidding each other. It may well be that we shall see the return of incomes policy at some time, but we shall certainly continue seeing the effect on labour markets of other aspects of government policy, such as strategy on regional development and the letting of contracts by government departments.

Review topic 14.1

In which type of labour market would you seek the following types of employee, and what would be the mode of dealing:

1. A bricklayer
2. A graduate trainee manager
3. A comedian for the company Christmas party
4. The first officer on an oil tanker
5. A personnel director
6. A nurse qualified in occupational health
7. A team of people to build a hospital in the Middle East?

The main source of labour market data is the monthly *Gazette*, produced by the Department of Employment. This includes articles on labour market issues as well as comprehensive statistics, some of which are published every month and some at different periods through the year. The main monthly indicators of interest to personnel managers are the figures on employment, vacancies and earnings, which are analyzed by occupation, industrial sector and region. Another source is the *New Earnings Survey*, also published by the Department of

Employment. This gives much more comprehensive data, but is published less often. It is still useful in providing a scale of relativities against which the organization's pay arrangements can be compared. Table 14.1 comprises extracts from the 1981 and 1989 *New Earnings Surveys*, giving gross weekly earnings for various occupations. Although the cash figures are soon out of date, they can be used as index numbers against which to compare what you are paying for the various occupations in which you have an interest.

There is also a number of commercial agencies that supply labour market information and most of the professional journals include regular comment on going rates in their particular sector of the labour market. For the more specialized data about terms and conditions in overseas countries, the main source is Employment Conditions Abroad, of 13 Devonshire Street, London W1N 1FS.

Table 14.1 Full-time earnings by occupation for April 1981 (men) and 1989 (men and women)

	Average gross weekly earnings (£)		
	1981 (men)	1989 (men)	1989 (women)
Professional and related management and administration	189	403	300
Professional and related in science, engineering and technology	169	322	219
Managerial	163	315	216
Clerical and related	119	210	162
Selling	125	238	139
Materials processing, excluding metal	124	211	131
Processing, making and repairing, metal and electical	130	216	123
Painting, repetitive assembling, product inspection	117	203	133
Transport operating	120	205	142
Total for all manual	122	212	129
Total for all non-manual	163	321	192
Total for all occupations	140	263	178

Source: Summarized from Department of Employment (1981 and 1989), *New Earnings Survey*, Table 86.

Review topic 14.2

Look at the various lists in Table 14.2 and identify key indicators for the organization where you work. Have you got the necessary in-house information to make useful comparisons?

Table 14.2   Monthly labour market data on employment, vacancies and earnings published in the Department of Employment Gazette

Employment
1.1	Working population
1.2	Employees in employment: industry
1.3	Employees in employment: index of production and construction industries
1.4	Employees in employment
1.7	Manpower in the local authorities
1.8	Indices of output, employment and production
1.11	Overtime and short-time operatives in manufacturing industries
1.12	Hours of work: operatives: manufacturing industries

Vacancies
3.6	Regions: occupations

Earnings
5.1	Average earnings index: all employees: main industrial sectors
5.3	Average earnings index: all employees: by industry
5.4	Average earnings and hours: manual workers: by industry
5.5	Index of average earnings: non-manual workers
5.6	Average weekly and hourly earnings and hours: manual and non-manual employees
5.7	Labour costs: all employees: main industrial sectors and selected industries

Labour market issues for personnel managers

Core and peripheral workforces: the flexible firm

Atkinson is one of a number of commentators who has described the way in which firms are developing flexibility in their approach to employment and therefore inducing changes in labour market mechanisms:

> firms have found themselves under pressure to find more flexible ways of manning. . . . They have put a premium on achieving a workforce which can respond quickly, easily and cheaply to unforeseen changes, which may need to contract as smoothly as it expands, in which worked time precisely matches job requirements, and in which unit labour costs can be held down. (Atkinson 1984, p. 37)

The flexible firm in this analysis has a variety of ways of meeting the need for human resources. First are *core* employees who form the primary labour market. They are highly regarded by the employer, well paid and involved in those activities that are unique to the firm or give it a distinctive character. These employees have improved career prospects and offer the type of flexibility to the employer that is so prized in the skilled craftsworker who does not adhere rigidly to customary protective working practices.

There are then two *peripheral groups* – first, those who have skills that are needed but not specific to the particular firm, like typing and word processing. The strategy for these posts is to rely on the external labour market to a much greater extent, to specify a narrow range of tasks without career prospects, so that the employee has a job but not a career. This is a further development of the labour process described by Braverman (1974). Some employees may be able to transfer to core posts, but generally limited scope is likely to maintain a fairly high turnover, so that adjustments to the vagaries of the product market are eased.

The second peripheral group is made up of those enjoying even less security, as they have contracts of employment that are limited, either to a short-term or to a part-time attachment. There may also be a few job sharers and many participants in the Youth Training Scheme or the Community Programme find themselves in this category. An alternative or additional means towards this flexibility is to contract out the work that has to be done, either by employing temporary personnel from agencies or by subcontracting the entire operation, as has happened so extensively in office cleaning and catering.

It is difficult to see how far this tendency has developed and it is almost certainly more common in newer companies and industries. To most people it may be an unwelcome development as it provides few safe havens for people seeking security. For others, however, it provides the attraction of being one's own boss, having a variety of work experiences and being able to organize one's life to accommodate, for instance, periods of several months away from work to take a long holiday, renovate the house, update skills or simply to have a break. Posts in the peripheral group of jobs appear more suitable for, and maybe more attractive to, married women, many of whom adopt a lifestyle that has been called 'portfolio living', maintaining a mix of activities without the single-minded preoccupation with one job that is more common among men. The recent increase in the number of part-time jobs have been almost entirely filled by women. Whether this is providing them with the sorts of opportunity they are seeking, or exploiting the workforce as a whole by providing the sorts of job that only women will accept because of their limited employment opportunities is a matter of opinion.

As we saw in the chapter on organization structure, a slightly different version of the peripheral workforce is the way in which the organization boundary may be adjusted by redefining what is to be done in-house and what is to be contracted out to various suppliers. This produces less emphasis on peripheral workers being in precarious work:

> There is no overwhelming evidence of a significant expansion in this type of employment in the 1980s. The only employment forms for which the evidence of expansion is unambiguous are self-employment and part-time employment. The latter is in any case primarily both permanent and direct employment. . . . Temporary

and contract work, homeworking and black economy work . . . are
the employment forms where expansion appears to have been at best
modest. (Rubery 1988, pp. 56-7)

Changes in the external labour market

There are four major issues facing employers in the 1990s in relation to the
external labour market.

Labour shortages

In 1971 there were around 900,000 live births in the United Kingdom. By 1977, it
was less than 700,000 and has since failed to reach 800,000 per annum. Thus,
although the workforce is still growing, the extra numbers are in the middle and
older age groups rather than among the young. Thus, the 1990s are likely to be
characterized by labour shortages, in the same way as the 1980s were characterized by labour surplus. The joker in the pack on this question may well be the
effect of the single European market. If some recent forecasts are proved correct
(for example, Rajan 1990), the United Kingdom could suffer substantial job
losses in the early years of the single market.

Age composition

By the year 2000 there will be about 2.3 million more people aged between 25
and 64 in the labour force than there are now, and about 1.3 million fewer aged
under 25. The result is a growing workforce of which a higher proportion is
older than now. Employers who rely on young people in certain jobs, or as
trainees for specific career plans, will experience particular problems. However
it is likely that the majority of employers wil be forced to review policy as regards
the preferred age of new recruits.

Sex composition

Due to the decline in population growth, employers will have to rely more on
increasing the readiness of individuals to work. Current civilian activity rates
(the proportion of the population in or seeking work) are expected to continue
their trend of recent years, which means that while male activity rates decline,
female rates will continue to increase. So marked are these effects that almost all
(90 per cent) of the expected increase in labour supply to 2000 is among women.
By 2000, women will comprise 44 per cent of the labour force. The ability of

employers to attract female recruits may well depend on provision of facilities such as crèches, training for returners and career breaks.

Skill shortage

Demand for labour in manual and unskilled jobs is expected to continue to contract during the 1990s. The growth in demand for labour will therefore be concentrated among the higher skilled occupations, and in particular among professional, scientific and technical occupations (Table 14.3).

Table 14.3   Occupational change to 1995

	Expected change in employment 1987–95	
	000s	%
Managers	324	+10.3
Professional	1,028	+18.9
Clerical/secretarial	219	+ 6.1
Sales/service	240	+ 5.1
Craft/skilled	258	+ 8.0
Operatives	−353	− 7.8

Source: Atkinson (1989, p. 21).

University graduates are the main source of supply for these higher skilled occupations, but higher education is also influenced by demographic factors and the need to compete with employers anxious to recruit 'A' level school-leavers. While demand for graduates generally is up, there is a particular need for two specific types: the technologist, required by the electronic, electrical engineering and computing sectors, and the high flyer, increasingly sought to meet the long-term needs of senior management. Many employers are attempting to solve their problems by broadening the entry requirements, so that now nearly half the vacancies currently advertised are open to all graduates.

There is some evidence to suggest that so far as these highly qualified staff and new graduates are concerned, implementation of the single European market in 1992 will produce a net worsening of supply in the United Kingdom as more potential recruits seek employment overseas (Pearson and Pike 1989).

A planned response to demographic change

Overall, these demographic and labour supply factors are certain to cause a tightening of labour markets in all parts of the country. However, what may well exacerbate the situation is the failure of employers to devise and implement suitable responses. John Atkinson has suggested a sequential response by firms to the predicted demographic downturn (Figure 14.1):

> This shows the most likely types of response and the sequence in which they will be introduced. It suggests that we will see a progression from the tactical towards more strategic responses, and towards an external labour market (supply side) perspective, back to an internal one (demand side). It suggests that firms will progress from doing little or nothing, through competing for available labour, to identifying substitutes for it, ending with the improved deployment and performance of the existing workforce. (Atkinson 1989, p. 22)

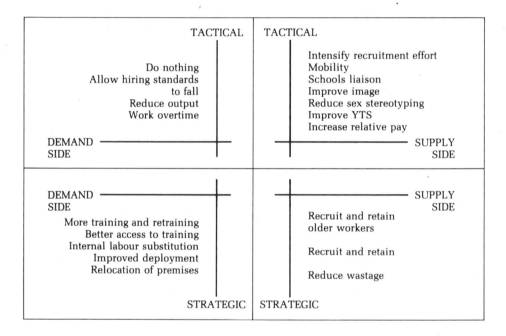

Figure 14.1 *Employer's response to shortages*
Source: Atkinson (1989, p. 23).

Despite extensive publicity regarding the so-called demographic 'time bomb' of the 1990s, research suggests that the majority of employers have taken little or no action to resolve the problem. While the labour shortages themselves may be no more serious than those experienced in the mid-1970s, what may exacerbate the problem is the complacency of employers and their failure to take appropriate action. Various recommendations for overcoming the predicted shortages can be found in Poole (1989) and Fairchild (1989).

The single European market

Few topics have attracted so much attention in recent years as the single European market, which is due to come into existence in 1992. This initiative has galvanized the European Community after an uncertain period in the early 1980s when it sometimes seemed that the EC would disintegrate.

The overall objective is to remove the barriers to trade between member states in Europe in the hope that this will stimulate economic growth and raise the general level of international competitiveness and prosperity. The programme has been given additional momentum by the social and political changes in Eastern Europe.

The economic development is accompanied by a social programme intended to harmonize working conditions and terms of employment across the community, removing the apparent inflexibilities and assisting free movement across national boundaries. Sample inflexibilities are a German law preventing the non-EC spouse of an EC national being allowed to practise medicine, non-Italians being barred from working as frogmen in Italy, and permanent employment as nurses in French public hospitals being limited to French nationals.

A specific objective is to achieve the free movement of EC nationals to work wherever they wish in the Community. There are long histories of migration between countries, with movement from the Irish Republic to the United Kingdom being one of the prominent patterns, but there has been a general movement from the less developed to the more developed countries and a further pattern suggesting cultural affiliation. France receives four times as many Spaniards as Italians, while Germany receives twice as many Italians as France. Furthermore, for most EC countries the number of non-EC nationals is greater than the number of EC nationals among the employed foreigners in the country – 43 per cent in France and the United Kingdom, 31 per cent in Greece.

Some of these traditional migration patterns have changed in recent years as the demand for unskilled labour in manufacturing industries has abated or been moved to the Pacific Rim. A different pattern is emerging of skilled Europeans moving between Community states, usually remaining with the same employer. Organizations become more international in their operations and develop a cadre of skilled personnel who are needed to run the business, and they may be needed in any one of several countries:

> 'transnationals are compensating for shortcomings in the Community labour market, such as the lack of free movement of workers or skill shortages in specific regions, by developing their own EC-wide internal labour markets. The significant point to grasp about this form of cross-national labour mobility is that it surmounts the various cultural and practical barriers associated with traditional forms of migration. (Teague 1989, p. 18)

The world labour market

A phenomenon that is only just beginning to receive attention is the world labour market. There has long been a concern about the so-called brain drain, whereby well-qualified people are attracted to go to work in foreign countries where greater prosperity means better levels of material reward and often generally better prospects. For some years the British textile trade has suffered from competition in the Far East, where labour costs are lower than those in the West. Migrant workers from less developed countries moved to Europe in large numbers during the 1950s and 1960s when over-full employment produced difficulties in recruiting people for the lower-paid jobs.

Recently, migration has increased around the world more generally with some governments encouraging employers to recruit in the countries for overseas destinations. One of the strange sights for the international air traveller is to see squads of Thai, Filipino, Korean or Indonesian workers sitting forlornly in departure lounges waiting to be shipped off as a job lot to work on some particular assignment. Among the worst affected victims of the Iraq/Kuwait conflict of 1990/1 were the very large numbers of migrant workers who were stranded in Kuwait after their employers had fled or been dispossessed.

There has also been a growth in the distribution of work to where the workers are, with parts of a British washing machine, for instance, being manufactured in Seoul and Manila before final assembly in Britain. This type of movement reduces the selling price of the finished article but also upsets the operations of the labour markets both by removing jobs from one country to another and by altering the pay rates in countries. Migrant workers may escape the poverty of their home country to find work in a new country at what initially appears to be a very attractive rate of pay, but it will usually be at the bottom of the pay scale in the host country and with scant security. Fluctuations of the product market make these workers yet another aspect of 'flexibility', as they become expendable at the onset of economic recession. If they are illegal immigrants they are particularly vulnerable and will nearly always be resented by the indigenous workers. Gerhardt and his colleagues (1985) point out how the international labour market tends to destabilize domestic labour markets by the example of youth unemployment. One of the main exporters of cheap labour is Sri Lanka, and the main reason for this is a youth unemployment rate of 30 per cent. At the same time the UK youth unemployment rate has reached 23 per cent (Gerhardt *et al.* 1985, p. 49).

Personnel managers have tended not to consider labour market implications for their recruitment and manning strategies in the past, but current developments make an understanding of labour market operations more important to the whole process of meeting manpower requirements. It is also important as an aspect of meeting the social obligations of companies. These themes are developed further in the next two chapters, and aspects of the dual labour market are considered in Chapter 21.

Summary propositions

14.1 Personnel managers need to understand the range of labour markets as well as the going rates and modes of dealing in each.

14.2 Labour market changes are influenced by product market changes.

14.3 The behaviour of employers and employees in the labour markets is not completely rational.

14.4 Demographic changes in the 1990s will lead to an overall shortage of labour, and the need for employers to re-examine their recruitment strategies.

14.5 Increasingly, manpower requirements can be met by developing a range of different types of employment contract, as well as sub-contracting work to outside suppliers.

References

Atkinson, J. (1984), 'Manpower strategies for flexible organizations', *Personnel Management*, August, pp. 28–31.

Atkinson, J. (1989), 'Four stages of adjustment to the demographic downturn', *Personnel Management*, August, pp. 20–4.

Braverman, H. (1974), *Labor and Monopoly Capital*, New York: Monthly Review Press.

Brown, W., Hayles, J., Hughes, B. and Rowe, L. (1984), 'Product and labour markets in wage determination: some Australian evidence', *British Journal of Industrial Relations*, Vol. 22, no. 2, pp. 169–76.

Fairchild, P. (1989), 'A planned response to demographic change', *Personnel Management*, September, p. 99.

Kerr, C. (1954), 'The Balkanization of labour markets'. Re-printed in B. Barrett, *et al.*, *Industrial Relations and the Wider Society*, London: Macmillan.

Gerhardt, P., Howard, S. and Parmar, P. (1985), *The People Trade*, London: International Broadcasting Trust.

Mackay, D. I., Boddy, D., Brack, J., Diack, J. A. and Jones, N. (1971), *Labour Markets under Different Employment Conditions*, London: Allen & Unwin.

Pearson, R. and Pike, G. (1989), *The Graduate Labour Market in the 1990s*, Falmer, Sussex: Institute of Manpower Studies.

Poole, M. (1989), 'Time to tackle the labour supply problem', *Personnel Management*, July, p. 79

Rajan, A. (1990), *1992: A zero sum game*, Birmingham: The Industrial Society.

Robinson, D. (ed.) (1970), *Local Labour Markets and Wage Structures*, Aldershot: Gower.

Rubery J. (1989), 'Precarious forms of work in the UK'. In. G. and J. Rogers (eds.), *Precarious Jobs in Labour Market Regulation: The growth of a typical employment in Western Europe*, Geneva: International Institute of Labour Studies.

Teague, P. (1989), *The European Community: The social dimension*, London: Kogan Page.

15

Forms of employment and the contract of employment

It has been conventional to think of employment as full-time employment, but gradually a range of alternative forms is emerging. In this chapter we first review those alternatives, as well as various forms of full-time employment, and then consider the contract of employment itself.

Since the development of the factory system employees have always been required to attend work at predetermined times in rigid blocks of time, with some variation available through the use of overtime. The logic of this was not seriously questioned until 1968 when the concept of flexible working hours developed in West Germany. Although the majority of people still work some version of '9 to 5', there is a growing range of different practices, which have been evolving since the idea of flexible working hours broke the mould.

By the 1980s there was considerable interest in finding variations so as to introduce greater flexibility in the manning of business and providing individual employees with the scope to match working requirements with personal and domestic preferences. This interest is reflected in a number of reports and publications, such as BIM (1985), CBI (1981) and Clutterbuck (1985).

The development of working patterns

By 1850 the normal working week in Britain had been established as 60 hours spread over 6 days of 10 hours each. Bienefeld (1972) analyzes how normal weekly hours fell at four distinct periods:

Period	Weekly hours' reduction	Percentage fall
1850–75	60–54	(10%)
1896–1920	54–48	(11%)
Late 1940s	48–44	(8%)
Early 1960s	44–40	(9%)

Since then there has been a further drop of 2 hours or (6 per cent). Bienefeld argues that these reductions in working hours all came at a time when economic conditions were favourable, unemployment was low and union bargaining power high, and that the reason for unions seeking the reductions was in anticipation of future unemployment when the trade cycle moved from relative prosperity to relative recession:

> The four periods during which there were reductions in hours were marked by a configuration of economic factors that distinguished them from other periods. They were periods of particularly rapid rises in money wages; they were periods of great prosperity, hence low unemployment, and hence great union bargaining power; finally, they were periods when unemployment was felt to be a serious threat. (Bienefeld 1972, p. 224)

There has always been an obvious tension between unions seeking a reduction in the working week without a loss of earnings while employers have needed to be convinced that reductions in hours will not reduce productivity. When hours were very long there was a convincing argument based on fatigue. More recently, moves have been based on a bargain: a reduction in hours in exchange for some major union concession, such as a change in working practices, that gives the management greater control of operations.

It is interesting that during industrial action by electricity power workers in the early 1970s, the government introduced a three-day week to save fuel. In most instances production remained as high, or nearly as high, as it had been during the previous five-day week.

Shift working can be traced back to the dawn of human history, with many examples for soldiers and sailors, for instance. In industry split shifts were operated as early as 1694 in glassmaking, and there was a 1785 experiment in the largest ironworks in south Wales of three eight-hour shifts as an alternative to the norm of two twelve-hour shifts. Recently, there has been an extension of shift working patterns and an increase in the number of people working shifts. Atkinson (1982, p. 2) calculated that by 1980 one manual worker in four worked on shifts in the manufacturing sector and that 22 per cent of all industrial workers were employed in this way.

There have been various attempts to stagger working hours, initially to ease public transport problems and more recently to ease problems of internal organization. The retail store, for example, may find this a useful way of staffing the store throughout the day while individual employees are present for only a part of the day.

Part-time working was relatively unusual until recently and was scarcely economic for the employer as the national insurance costs of the part-time employee were disproportionate to those of the full-timer. The part-time contract was one regarded as an indulgence for the employee and only a second-best alternative to the employment of someone full-time. This view was endorsed by lower rates of pay, little or no security of employment and exclusion from such benefits as sick pay, holiday pay and pension entitlement.

In the last twenty-five years, however, the proportion of the workforce on part-time contracts has increased dramatically and had reached 21 per cent of total employees by 1981. This rise is interrelated with the increased proportion of women in the workforce: 90 per cent of the recent rise in part-time working has been female. This has coincided with campaigns to enhance the employment opportunities of women, with the Equal Opportunities Commission advocating the development of job sharing, a specialized form of part-time working where two people split a full-time job between them so that the employer has a full-time service and the employees have only a half-time commitment. Although increasing, and probably continuing to do so, part-time still lacks the status of full-time employment.

Flexible working hours were initially seen as a way of overcoming travel-to-work problems and as an inducement to prospective employees to join a company that offered this type of flexibility. By the 1980s there was a lessening of interest in this type of scheme, but it is now returning to employer favour, both to provide flexibility and as a means of achieving better management control of employee working hours (IDS 1983). Union resistance has reduced, but there is still fear that overtime opportunities may be reduced and attention distracted from the need to reduce working hours (Lee 1983).

Compressed hours is a method of reducing the working week by extending the working day so that people work the same number of hours but on fewer days. An alternative method is to make the working day more concentrated by reducing the length of the midday meal-break. The now commonplace four-night week on the night shift in engineering was introduced in Coventry as a result of absenteeism on the fifth night being so high that it was uneconomic to operate.

Other more unusual variations include the idea of annual hours contracts, whereby the employee contracts to provide the employer with a specified number of hours' work per year and then enjoys considerable latitude in deciding when to work those hours. The academic idea of the sabbatical, whereby an employee has a period of several months away from normal duties for specialized study, travel or some other work-related activity is also beginning to emerge elsewhere. Clutterbuck (1985) quotes the example of the plan operated by the John Lewis Partnership since 1978 under which employees satisfying certain conditions can qualify for up to six months' leave of absence with full pay.

Although there has not been a revolution yet, there are already considerable changes in working patterns and further extension of variations seems likely. The advantage to the employer is flexibility, not only to cope with the commercial ebb and flow but also to maintain a level of manning for a period of organizational operation that is now almost always longer than a standard working week for an individual employee. The appeal to the employee is more diverse. For some there is the attraction of working only part-time, for others there is a more comfortable interface between work and non-work, and for yet others there is the opportunity of combining more than one form of employment.

Review topic 15.1

What types of job would you regard as most appropriate for the following variations for the conventional '9 to 5' working pattern?

1. Shift working.
2. Part-time working.
3. Job sharing.
4. Flexible hours.
5. Compressed hours.
6. Annual hours.

What types of job would not be suitable for each of these?

Shift working

There are situations where there is no alternative to working shifts or at least abnormal hours. In the continuous process industries like steel-making and glass manufacture, the need for employees to be in attendance at all hours is dictated by the impracticality of interrupting the manufacturing cycle. In other circumstances there is the overwhelming imperative of customer demand, so that commuter trains are used more out of normal working hours than within them, and morning newspapers have to be prepared in the middle of the night.

The operation of shifts carries an implicit assumption that it is unattractive to the individual employee: it carries a premium payment all of its own and recently the drafters of incomes policies have introduced the notion of special treatment for those who work 'unsocial hours'. Such a generalization may make sound industrial relations sense, but is no more accurate a statement about individuals than the statement that gentlemen prefer blondes. Wedderburn gives examples of the range of reactions he discovered in interviewing 500 shiftworkers:

> One young couple work the same shift so that they can use their spare time together working on their old house; another couple work opposing shifts, so that they can manage a handicapped child between them. One young father loves shiftwork because he sees more of his infant children; another feels he is losing contact with his time-locked school children. One can fish all day in uncrowded waters; another gave up fishing because weekend shiftwork meant that he missed crucial competitions. One foreman enjoys the total responsibility that shiftwork gives him; another fears that he has missed his chances of promotion, isolated on shiftwork. (Wedderburn, 1975)

For most people the prospect of working shifts may well be appalling, but for a substantial minority it provides a welcome element of flexibility in the employment contract at a time in their lives when it is perhaps very convenient for them to spend a period working unusual hours – for a higher rate of pay.

There are various patterns of working shifts, each of which brings with it a slightly different set of problems and opportunities.

The part-timer shift

Here a group of people are employed for a few hours daily at the beginning or end of normal working hours. The most common group are the office cleaners, who may work from 6 a.m. to 9 a.m. or for a similar period in the evening. Also there are some shifts for four or five hours in the evening to provide a small amount of extra output. Usually these shift-workers are married women, who welcome the hours because they fit in with their domestic routine. For this reason they are often known as 'housewives' shifts', even though this must be no more than a sobriquet.

The advantages to employers are that they are making use of relatively small units of time that would be insufficient for a full-time employee, but they are getting more use out of the plant, whether it be manufacturing plant or the computer, and it is a very convenient working arrangement for a fairly large number of people. The snags are that the employees are permanently operating outside normal hours so they are never integrated into the main working community. Also, those working such shifts are usually looking upon it as a temporary pattern of work, out of which they will move as soon as their circumstances change. Where the employer is seeking a short spell of additional work from people who require little training (either because the work is straightforward or because the skills are generally available) the part-timer shift may be an ideal arrangement. It is less satisfactory as a permanent feature.

The permanent night shift

The permanent night shift is another arrangement which creates a special category of employee who is set apart (or cut off) from everyone else. They are working full-time, but have no contact with the rest of the organization's members, who leave before they arrive and return after they have left. Apart from the specialized applications like national newspapers, this form is usually used either to undertake cleaning and maintenance of plant while it is idle or to increase output on a rather more permanent basis than can be achieved through part-timer shifts. A further development is to run a permanent night shift as a means of increasing output without disturbing the normal day pattern of the bulk of the employees.

The attraction of this arrangement is that it makes use of plant at times when it would otherwise be idle and, if it is used for maintenance, it avoids maintenance interrupting production. It also avoids the upheaval of the existing workforce that would be involved by introducing double-day shifts.

The drawbacks can be considerable. As with part-timer shifts, employees are operating permanently outside normal working hours, and as they are full-time employees that may be even more critical than it is with part-timers. There is an inevitable 'apartheid' for the regular night worker, who is out of touch with the mainstream of union and company activities. A further problem is the provision of services, like catering, medical and routine personnel services. For the evening worker these are either unnecessary or can be provided relatively cheaply by a few daily employees working occasional overtime. For night workers the services are both more difficult to provide and more costly. Night working is the form that is likely to be most difficult for employees to sustain as most human beings are diurnal rather than nocturnal creatures. A small minority seem genuinely to prefer working regular nights and maintain this rhythm for their working lives over many years, but for most it will be undertaken either reluctantly or for relatively short periods.

Alternating day and night shifts

If night working is being used to increase output rather than for cleaning and maintenance, then alternation is another possibility. It mitigates many of the difficulties of regular night working, but does present employees with the problem of regular, drastic changes in their daily rhythms.

Double-day shift

The double-day shift variation is surprisingly unpopular. Instead of working a normal day shift, employees work either 6 till 2 or 2 till 10. This means that plant is in use for sixteen hours, all employees are present for a large part of the 'normal' day, there is no night working and the rotation between the early and late shift enables a variety of leisure activities to be followed.

One of the reasons for resisting the method is that overtime is usually no longer possible, so that employees do not have that additional flexibility in their hours and earnings under their own control. Another problem is the fact that it may be the first experience of shifts for the bulk of employees, if it is introduced in place of a system of regular days or regular days and nights. There may be difficulties about transport in the early morning and all the inconvenience of eating at unfamiliar times.

Three-shift working

Three-shift working represents a further development and the most widespread pattern: 6 till 2, 2 till 10 and 10 till 6. The 24-hour cycle is covered so that there is continuous operation. There is a further subdivision: *discontinuous* three-shift working is where the plant is running but stops for the weekend, and *continuous* shift-working is an extension into the weekend whereby the plant never stops. Here we have the inescapable night shift and, with continuous working, the final loss of overtime and the sacrosanct weekend. If shifts are run on the traditional pattern of changing every week the shift workers have the unattractive feature of the 'dead fortnight' of two weeks when normal evening social activities are not possible because of late return home after a 2 till 10 shift or early departure for a 10 till 6 shift. The most common solution to this is to accelerate the rotation with a 'continental' shift pattern. Below is a typical arrangement for a four-week cycle of four shifts:

Week 1	Week 2	Week 3	Week 4	
MTWTFSS	MTWTFSS	MTWTFSS	MTWTFSS	
AABBCCC	DDAABBB	CCDDAAA	BBCCDDD	6 a.m.–2 p.m.
DDAABBB	CCDDAAA	BBCCDDD	AABBCCC	2 p.m.–10 p.m.
CCDDAAA	BBCCDDD	DDAABBB	CCDDAAA	10 p.m.–6 a.m.

Reductions in the number of hours in the basic working week have induced a range of variations in shiftworking pattern that were not necessary until the 40-hour barrier was broken. Useful examples of such variations have been described by IDS (1985).

Table 15.1 Working patterns of a sample of employees in the north of England

Working pattern	Total employed	Male	Female	Total (%)
Normal days	118,460	74,046	44,414	70.8
Double days	739	396	343	0.4
Alternating days/nights	11,323	10,222	1,101	6.8
Three shifts	19,661	18,743	918	11.7
Permanent nights	1,441	1,440	1	0.9
Evening shift	802	165	637	0.5
Other arrangements	14,999	14,613	386	8.9
Total	167,425	119,625	47,880	100.0

Source: Based on Dobson (1986).

Part-time working

For many practical purposes anyone who works less than the normal hours is a part-timer, but for legal purposes it is only the person working less than sixteen hours a week who does not have the same employment rights as a full-time counterpart. It is unrealistic to regard part-time employees as second-class citizens in comparison with full-time employees. They cannot necessarily be used (some would use the word 'exploited') simply as a convenience to deal with short-term problems or jobs that others will not tackle, if such use means regarding them as having no entitlement to those other benefits of employment, apart from salary, that full-time workers enjoy. Part-time workers acquire entitlement to holidays and holiday pay, sickness pay, maternity rights, pension contributions and so forth if they are employed for more than sixteen hours a week.

Recent changes in the labour market, together with the predicted labour shortages of the 1990s have led to an increasing number of organizations turning to part-time employment as a means of attracting new recruits. This form of flexible working is particularly appealing to women, mothers returning to work, students seeking vacation work, pensioners, etc.

One of the largest recruitment drives for part-timers was carried out by Lowndes Queensway (Crofts 1989). A nationwide advertising campaign to recruit 1,700 part-time sales people was launched, aimed directly at 'Students, mums, grandparents and pensioners'. Increasingly, customers expected stores to be open in the evenings and at weekends. By switching to a largely part-time salesforce the company could meet these requirements more effectively.

In a similar vein, the Alliance and Leicester Building Society, faced with local labour shortages, introduced term-time working for parents of school-age children in an attempt to make themselves more attractive to potential employees. The target group was mothers of children at school. The scheme allows them to continue a career while bringing up a young family and also opened up new recruitment sources for employers (Spencer 1990).

Part-timing is predominantly a female occupation, because so many women either wish to work only part-time or because their share of domestic responsibilities only allows them to work in this way. Many of them will be working short shifts and sometimes two will share a full working day between them. Others will be in positions for which only a few hours within the normal day are required or a few hours at particular times of the week. As described, retailing is an occupation that has considerable scope for the part-timer, as there is obviously a greater need for counter personnel on Saturday mornings than on Monday mornings. Also many shops are now open for longer periods than would be normal hours for a full-time employee, so that the part-timer helps to fill the gaps and provide the extra manning at peak periods. Catering is another example, as are market research interviewing, office cleaning, typing and some posts in education. Another aspect of the increasing number of women returning to part-time employment is the provision of funded crêche facilities for children (Falconer 1990). As labour shortages become more acute, this issue is likely to become of greater importance to both employers and potential employees.

A specialized form of part-time work is that which is a kind of overtime, in which a person works extra time for a second employer in order to increase earnings. Known as *moonlighting*, this includes such jobs as taxi-driving and bartending as well as the more specialized tasks like dealing with other people's income tax claims. The second employer gains considerable benefit, obtaining the services of perhaps a skilled and experienced employee without having to invest in that person's training or future career.

Syrett (1983) gives a comprehensive guide to the employment of part-timers and job sharers, including an analysis of the costs of employing part-timers. The national insurance contribution is zero where earnings are below a specified minimum and earnings have to reach a relatively high point before the joint national insurance contribution is greater than that for one full time employee.

Flexible working hours

Flexible working hours can be defined as:

> An arrangement whereby, within set limits, employees may begin and end work at times of their own choice, provided that they are all present at certain 'core-time' periods of the day and that, within a 'settlement period' – usually a week or a month – they work the total number of hours agreed. Not surprisingly, there are wide variations in the degree of flexibility different schemes allow. (Sloane 1975, p. 3)

A typical arrangement is where the organization abandons a fixed starting and finishing time for the working day. Instead employees start work at a predetermined time in the period between 8.00 a.m. and 10.00 a.m. and finish between 4.00 p.m. and 6.00 p.m. They are obliged to be present during the *core time* of 10 till 4, but can use the *flexible time* at the beginning and end of the working day to produce a pattern of working hours that fits in with their personal needs and preferences. The main advantage of this scheme is that it enables people to avoid peak travel times and the awkward rigidity of the inflexible starting time. From the organization's point of view it can eliminate the tendency towards a frozen period at the beginning and end of the day when nothing happens – for the first twenty minutes everyone is looking at the paper or making coffee, and for the last twenty minutes everyone is preparing to go home. If the process of individual start-up and slow-down is spread over a longer period the organization is operational for longer.

The scheme described above assumes that the necessary number of hours will be worked each day. The variations on the theme increase flexibility by allowing a longer *settlement period*, so that employees can work varying lengths of time on different days, provided that they complete the quota appropriate for the week or month or whatever other settlement period is agreed. This means that someone can take a half day off for shopping or a full day off for a long weekend as long as the quota is made up within a prescribed period.

As most organizations depend on a high degree of interaction between staff members for their operations to be viable, all are required to be in attendance for the core time period of the day, although this is waived in schemes where people are allowed to take half or whole days off. A further control is on the *bandwidth*, which is the time between the earliest feasible starting time and the latest possible finishing time. If this becomes too great the working day attenuates in a rather costly way.

Reactions to the schemes from employers and employees have generally been favourable. Employers feel that the arrangement creates a more satisfactory working atmosphere with heightened morale:

> Flexible working hours raise morale and job satisfaction, create a better working climate, all but eliminate time lost through lateness and the need for petty discipline this can entail, and lead to a greater degree of self-regulation and responsibility on the part of employees, with work started more quickly on arrival and jobs in hand more often finished before departure. (Sloane 1975, p. 11)

One feature of flexible hours which is often resented by employees is the way in which their *attendance is registered*, as there has been a tendency to reintroduce time clocks or the more sophisticated elapsed time recorders as a way of controlling the attendance of the individual. While it is conventional for employees to 'fight' mechanical time recording because of its rigidity, there is also the feeling that it is at least fair. There can be no suspicion that some people are not putting in their full complement of hours, nor that some have bluer eyes than others.

In many areas of white-collar employment time-keeping is a matter of mutual trust rather than control. In this type of situation there might be strong resistance to mechanical time recording, largely because the motives for its introduction would be suspect. Management will also have reservations about installing expensive time-recording equipment that has not previously been necessary.

The most detailed and extensive evaluation has been carried out in various parts of the public sector of employment, and one of the studies (Drye 1975) found the following results from a questionnaire asking the employees to state the main advantage of flexible hours:

		Percentage of staff
1.	The ability to adjust lunch breaks	73
2.	The ability to finish earlier	69
3.	A better balance between work and domestic commitments	62
4.	The ability to build up a half-day off	55
5.	Better travel	45

Working Time Analysts (1984) describe five forms of monitoring employee attendance in FWH systems. The first is *trust* where there is no control other than the conscience of the employee. Secondly, there are *manual systems* where employees keep a written record which is checked by their supervisors. *Clocking systems* employ the traditional clock and card method, while *mechanical/electrical* systems are more sophisticated versions using a personal card or key to activate the clock. A further refinement is the *computer system* where hours are registered by entering a personal code.

Annual hours

New working patterns offer the opportunity to reduce costs and improve performance. Organizations need a better match between employee working hours and the operating profile of the business in order to improve customer response time and increase productivity.

The 'annual hours' approach has proved to be an effective method of tackling the problem. Central to each annual hours agreement is the fact that the period of time within which full-time employees must work their contractual hours is defined over a whole year. All normal working hours contracts can be converted to annual hours; for example, an average 38 hour week becomes 1,732 annual hours, assuming five weeks' holiday entitlement. The principal advantage of annual hours in manufacturing sectors which need to maximize the utilization of expensive assets, comes from the ability to separate employee working time from the operating hours of the plant and equipment. Thus we have seen the growth of five-crew systems, in particular in the continuous process industries. Such systems are capable of delivering 168 hours of production a week. All holidays can be rostered into 'off' weeks, and fifty or more weeks of production can be planned in any one year without resorting to overtime.

Of course, there are many sectors of industry which do not have an operational need to work 168 hours a week and yet they wish to improve productivity. Lynch provides an example:

> a company that is operating a three shift system on a $37\frac{1}{2}$ hour week (Monday to Friday) may currently use weekend hours at premium rates to meet extra production, this being the only flexible option available. A move to six-day working (i.e. from 112 operating hours to 144) would increase production by 28%. A move to seven-day working would increase production by 50%. (Lynch 1988, p.37)

The move to annual hours is an important step for a company to take and should not be undertaken without careful consideration and planning. Managers need to be sure of all the consequences. The tangible savings include all those things that are not only measurable but are capable of being measured before the scheme is put in. Some savings such as reduced absenteeism are measurable only after the scheme has been running and therefore cannot be counted as part of the cost justification.

Distance working

In the quest for greater flexibility many employers are beginning to explore new ways of getting work done which do not involve individuals working full-time on their premises.

Working overseas, selling in the field and home-working are the most obvious types of distance working. Other types of distance employment include teleworking, working on far-flung sites, or off-site as subcontractors and consultants. Contractually 'distant' or 'peripheral' working can include anything that is different from the traditional full-time contract even though employees may be geographically present for part or all of the time; for example, part-time and job sharing, temporary and short-term working, on-site subcontracting and consultancy. Rothwell (1987) has identified several issues relating to the employment of distance workers. These are considered next.

Finding the right people

A major problem facing organizations contemplating the possibility of employing distance workers is finding the right people. One source may be existing staff who would prefer more flexible working arrangements. Similarly, staff who have left employment for family reasons, travel, redundancy or early retirement could be another valuable source. Some employers already maintain lists of people who can be contacted at short notice and have often found them to be cheaper and more effective than agency or contract workers. This is certainly the case in the NHS where most large hospitals have an agency bank of nurses available to provide cover at short notice.

Subcontractors whose businesses have been set up as a result of company hive-offs or buy-outs are another potential source. Information regarding the relevant public and private agencies, subcontractors and consultants may well be something which more managers need to acquire. More effective relationships can be established by taking time to classify needs and developing longer-term arrangements with public/private agencies and with subcontractors. In the public sector subcontracting may be open to tender. This requires careful planning and background knowledge of the contractors.

Job specification and selection

Job specification is important in all selection processes but is critical in most forms of geographically and contractually distant working, particularly in subcontracted work. It is important to set out clearly defined parameters of action, criteria for decision and issues which need reference back. Person specifications are also crucial since in much distance working there is less scope for employees to be trained or socialized on-the-job. In addition, 'small business' skills are likely to be needed by teleworkers, networkers, consultants and subcontractors.

Communication and control

Attention needs to be given to the initial stages of settling in these distance workers. Those off-site need to know the pattern of regular links and contacts to be followed. Those newly recruited to the company need the same induction information as regular employees. In fact those working independently with less supervision may need additional material, particularly on health and safety. Heightened team building skills will also be needed to encompass staff who are working on a variety of different contracts and at different locations.

Pay and performance

A key aspect of the employment of distance workers is the close link between pay and performance. Managers must be able to specify job targets and requirements accurately and to clarify and agree these with the employees or contractors concerned. Where a fee rather than a salary is paid, the onus is on the manager to ensure that the work has been completed satisfactorily. Others (consultants, teleworkers, networkers) may be paid on the basis of time, and it is down to the supervisor to ensure the right level and quality of output for that payment.

It is doubtful whether pay levels of peripheral staff can be related to existing job-evaluated systems or salary structures. Indeed one great advantage of extending the variety of peripheral workers is the ability to move outside those constraints, which may no longer be appropriate. Concepts of the total compensation package may need to be examined more closely in deciding how much should be paid; if normal perks such as canteens, sports facilities, etc., become less relevant to distance workers, will financial services (e.g. low interest loans) and provision of home computers become more important?

Examples of distance working schemes currently in operation can be found in Stanworth and Stanworth (1989).

The contract of employment

Employees who work sixteen hours a week or more have the same legal rights as full-timers, but those who work between eight and sixteen hours only acquire these rights when they have been in continuous service with the employer for five years. Employers are not legally obliged to pay the same rates to those working part-time as to those working full-time, but they are bound by the Equal Pay Act, so that part-timers could have a claim for equal pay if they can identify a full-time worker of the opposite sex carrying out similar work. Useful guidance on the Contract of Employment can be found in Employing People (ACAS 1985) and in Written Statement of Main Terms and Conditions of Employment (DoE 1979).

Expiry or performance of contract may be the most normal form of termination for most contracts, consultants or short-term workers. Termination of part-timers will be likely to follow the same legal and contractual procedures as for other staff, depending on their length of service, notice of period of terms and conditions agreed with unions and incorporated into their contracts. Where dismissal is for reasons of redundancy, selection only of part-timers or of other peripheral groups could constitute unlawful 'indirect' discrimination if these were mainly of one sex; proportionate percentage selection of part-time and full-time employees might be more appropriate unless the work was only performed by one group and no suitable alternative offers at all could be made.

Termination of peripheral workers' contracts or disciplinary dismissal may call for legal advice, given the complexity of the position of many categories of flexi-workers.

Table 15.2   Checklist for preparing a contract of employment

1.   Name of employer; name of employee.
2.   Date on which employment began.
3.   Job title.
4.   Rate of pay, period, and method of payment.
5.   Normal hours of work and related conditions, such as meal-breaks.
6.   Arrangements for holidays and holiday pay, including means whereby both can be calculated precisely.
7.   Terms and conditions relating to sickness, injury and sick pay.
8.   Terms and conditions of pension arrangements, including a note about whether or not the employment is contracted out under the provisions of the Social Security Pensions Act 1975.
9.   Length of notice due to and from employee.
10. Disciplinary rules and procedure.
11. Arrangements for handling employee grievances.
12. (Where applicable) Conditions of employment relating to trade union membership.

Review topic 15.2

Consider either the organization where you work or an organization where you have a fair idea of what is involved in a number of different jobs, like a hospital or a television company. Which jobs would it be most suitable, from a management point of view, to staff on the following bases?

Compressed hours	1	3
	2	4
Annual hours	1	3
	2	4
Short-term contracts	1	3
	2	4
Consultancy	1	3
	2	4

Summary propositions

15.1 Patterns of employment are changing in order to give the employer greater flexibility in manning the organization and to give the employee greater autonomy.

15.2 Significant reductions in working hours usually come in times of relative prosperity.

15.3 The use of shift working is increasing.

15.4 The use of part-time working (particularly by women) has increased considerably in recent years.

15.5 The use of flexible working hours is now well established. The logical development of this principle – annual hours – is gaining increased application.

References

ACAS (1985), *Employing People*, London: Advisory Conciliation and Arbitration Service.

Atkinson, J. (1982), *Shiftworking*, IMS Report no. 45, London: Institute of Manpower Studies.

Bienefeld, M. A. (1972), *Working Hours in British Industry: An economic history*, London: Weidenfeld & Nicolson.

British Institute of Management (1985), *Managing New Patterns of Work*, London: British Institute of Management Foundation.

Confederation of British Industry (1981), *Working Time: Guidelines for managers*, London: Confederation of British Industry.

Clutterbuck, D. (1985), *New Patterns of Work*, Aldershot: Gower.

Crofts, P. (1989), 'What's in store for part-timers?' *Personnel Management July*, p. 19

Department of Employment (1979), *Written Statement of Main Terms and Conditions of Employment*, London: HMSO.

Dobson, G. (1986), *Working Patterns in the North of England*, London: BIM.

Drye, E. S. (1975), 'Flexible hours in DHSS local offices', *Management Services in Government*, February.

Falconer, H. (1990), 'Children at work', *Personnel Today*, April, p. 14

Incomes Data Services (1983), *Flexible Working Hours*, IDS Study 301, London: Incomes Data Services Ltd.

Incomes Data Services (1985), *Improving Productivity*, IDS Study 331, London: Incomes Data Services Ltd.

Lee, R.A. (1983), 'Hours of work – who controls and how?' *Industrial Relations Journal*, vol. 14, no. 4.

Lynch, P. (1988), 'Matching worked hours to business needs', *Personnel Management*, June, pp. 36–9.

Rothwell, S. (1987), 'How to manage from a distance', *Personnel Management*, September, pp. 22–6.

Sloane, P.J. (1975), *Changing Patterns of Working Hours*, Department of Employment Manpower Paper no. 13, London: Department of Employment.

Spencer, L. (1990), 'Parent Power', *Personnel Today*, April, p. 32–3.

Stanworth, J. and Stanworth, C. (1989), 'Home truths about teleworking', *Personnel Management*, November, pp. 48–52.

Syrett, M. (1983), *Employing Jobsharers, Part-timers and Temporary Staff*, London: Institute of Personnel Management.

Wedderburn, A. (1975), 'Waking up to shiftwork', *Personnel Management*, vol. 7, no. 2.

Working Time Analysts (1984), *Flexible Working Hours Theory and Practice*, London: Working Time Analysts Ltd.

Job Analysis

Job analysis is a central technique which is the basis for many personnel management activities. However, this effective management tool is not always used to the full extent of its potential.

In this chapter we first look at the nature of job analysis and its objectives and uses. We then consider the process of job analysis by looking at the information to be collected, who does job analysis, the role of personnel management, sources of information, and methods of collecting and analyzing the information. We conclude by discussing information collation and the writing of job descriptions and personnel specifications.

The nature of job analysis, its objectives and uses

Nature and objectives

Job analysis is the process of collecting and analyzing information about the tasks, responsibilities and the context of jobs. The objective of job analysis is to report this information in the form of a written job description, and sometimes, additionally, in the form of a person specification.

The job description encapsulates the business role of the job incumbent and should tell the reader why the job exists, and the contribution to the organization for which the job holder will be held accountable.

Definitions

At this stage it is useful to define some of the terms of job analysis that we shall use in this chapter:

Task A piece of work which can be identified in terms of its end results or objectives.

Job A number of tasks that are sufficiently alike to be grouped together and allocated to an individual.

Position The individual's place in the organization. Some jobs require only one person to do a particular group of tasks. Other jobs may require a number of positions to be filled. Thus ten employees could fill ten different positions, but all doing the same job.

Job description A summary report of information relating to a particular job. This may be a very individual job, which has just one position, or a job, that has a number of different positions. The report will vary in nature and length with the nature of the job, the job analysis procedures used and the purpose for which the job was analyzed.

Person specification A statement, derived from the job analysis process and the job description, of the characteristics that an individual would need to possess in order to fulfil the requirements of a job. Sometimes referred to as the personnel, worker or job specification.

Occupation A group of similar jobs.

Uses of job analysis

The uses of the information derived from job analysis can be grouped according to whether the purpose is in dealing primarily with individuals; in dealing with overall organizational needs; in dealing with legislative requirements; or in dealing with industrial relations issues. The uses of job analysis are summarized in Table 16.1. Job analysis has benefits both for individuals and for the organization.

In dealing primarily with individuals

Job analysis information is used frequently in the process of recruiting and selecting individuals for jobs. There are benefits for individuals in knowing details about the job for which they may apply, and for the organization in making the individuals aware of job demands and in defining the individual characteristics that are required. Job analysis can therefore considerably assist the effectiveness of the process of matching individuals to jobs. Similarly, job analysis is important when employees are transferred or promoted, and for career counselling within organizations. Job analysis is also a critical basis for the appraisal process. It is difficult to imagine how job performance can be accurately appraised unless the job to be performed has been clearly defined. For individuals it is important to know the tasks on which they will be appraised and the performance standards that are expected. Training and development needs cannot be sensibly determined unless related to the job that has to be

Table 16.1 The various uses of job analysis and a way of grouping them

In dealing primarily with individuals	In dealing with organizational needs	Legislative requirements	Industrial relations
Selection	Organizational analysis	Health and safety	New machinery
Induction	Restructuring	Equal opportunities	New technology
Promotions	Organizational development		Productivity bargaining
Transfers	Job design and development		New working arrangements
Career counselling	Human resource planning		
Appraisal	Salary administration		
Training			
Development Salary progression Grievance Discipline			

done. An excellent guide to job analysis for training purposes has been written by Campbell (1989). Organizations using individual and merit pay increases related to job performance will find this difficult without a clear definition of job and performance standards. Job descriptions based on job analysis can help individuals who feel they have a grievance and for managers who are considering dismissing an individual for incapacity. A good job description not only ensures fairness but can also play a large part in demonstrating to an industrial tribunal that a dismissal was fair. Walton (1989) points out that the job description can become a contractual document between the employer and the individual.

In dealing with organizational needs

The definition of jobs is a critical factor in organization design as expressed in Chapter 6. Schneider talks about:

> The essentially organizational nature of tasks and jobs; they do not just exist, they exist in organizations. Because organizations create them, jobs are in fact very explicit statements by organizations of what they have determined as the most appropriate means for accomplishing their goals. (Schneider 1976, p. 23)

Attempts to change the way that organizations are designed in terms of restructuring, organizational development and job design and development are all dependent on an initial review of the jobs being done and a consideration of the way that they could be done. Job analysis is an important basis for human resource planning, in assisting decisions regarding the utilization of people, work study, the evaluation of various options for people demand, and in the planning of recruitment campaigns. Payment administration, for example, in the development of wage and salary structures, and grading and incremental systems, is dependent on adequate job descriptions derived from job analysis. Similar criteria apply to the development and maintenance of job evaluation systems.

Legislative requirements

Job analysis is also important in meeting legislative requirements, in such areas as health and safety, and equal opportunities.

Industrial relations

Issues such as the introduction of new machinery and new technology, productivity bargaining and new working arrangements can benefit from the use of job analysis.

Our research shows that job analysis is most used for salary administration and job evaluation purposes, followed some way behind by recruitment and selection needs.

Review topic 16.1

- For what purposes is job analysis used in your organization?
- How would you explain the reasons for this?
- For what other purposes would job analysis be particularly helpful at present?

The information to be collected

While the information to be collected to some extent depends on the purpose of the job analysis, the following categories of basic information are useful:

1. *Job identification data*: Job title, department, division, company name, location.

2. *Relationships with others*: Reporting relationships, supervisory relation-ships, liaison with others, co-ordinating relationships.
3. *Job content*: Actual tasks or duties of the job, level of responsibility for tasks, importance of tasks, how often performed.
4. *Working conditions*: Physical environment, such as heat, noise, light, accident and health risks; social environment, such as whether working alone or in a group, unusual times of work; economic environment, such as salary and benefits.
5. *Performance standards/objectives*: These can either be for the job as a whole or for specific tasks. They can either be expressed in quantitative terms such as amount of output or sales, budgets or time-limits to meet; or in qualitative terms, such as maintaining group cohesiveness.
6. *Other relevant information*
7. *Human requirements*: The physical and psychological characteristics of the individual who could fulfil the demands of the job. Sometimes this information is given in more detail, separately, in the person specification.

Who does job analysis?: The role of personnel management

The purpose of job analysis and the analytical techniques that are required, together with the resources of the organization, determine who should perform the job analysis. For many applications the appropriate skills, such as defining questions, interviewing and assessing, are found in the personnel department, although further training may be required to develop these. If the use of specialized techniques is needed, job analysts or work study practitioners may have to be employed, although for some techniques personnel staff may be able to develop the appropriate skills. When job analysis is seen as a continuing activity, specialist staff would normally need to be employed as the work would be too time-consuming to be taken on by the personnel department. For some purposes the use of external job analysts may seem the most appropriate solution. For example, it can be useful for an analysis of job evaluation to be carried out by people who are detached from the situation. The main disadvan-tage of using external expertise, apart from the cost, is their lack of familiarity with the organization both in the process of collecting information and in the analysis. One way around this is to use external specialists in conjunction with employees.

Another possibility is that of the job analysis being carried out by the job holder. This is different from the idea of the job holder being involved in job analysis as a source of information by being interviewed or filling out question-naires. Ungerson (1983) suggests that job holders should marshal the information about their jobs sufficiently to write the job description themselves, or at least draft it out for discussion with a supervisor and/or the personnel manager. The extent to which the job holder could be involved would depend on their ability, and sometimes the job description would need to be prepared in conjunction with a supervisor. This approach to the analyzing of jobs and the writing of job descriptions would necessitate the training of a large number of people. There would also still be the problem of inconsistency, in style, format and content, between different job descriptions. For this reason, and because of the possibility of bias, it would be difficult to use such job descriptions for purposes which required comparisons between jobs, such as payment administration and job evaluation. The advantage of this approach is that less information is lost between job incumbent and written job description.

Our research has identified that immediate managers or supervisors most frequently perform job analysis, followed closely by the personnel officer and, some way behind, the job holder.

Review topic 16.2

- Why do you think that supervisors so often carry out job analysis?
- What are the advantages and disadvantages of this?

Even if the personnel department did not carry out the job analysis it will usually assume a role in co-ordinating and maintaining the process.

Sources of information

Whoever carries out the analysis will have to collect the job-related information from a source. The job holder is the most usual source, but other individuals can also be important, particularly the immediate manager, as can written sources of information. As a general rule the more sources used, the more valid and complete the information collected (Ghiselli and Brown 1955). The various sources of information, based on a categorization by Torrington and Chapman (1983), are as follows.

The job incumbent

The job incumbent has the most detailed knowledge of the job being done and is therefore a key source of information. This information, though, will be biased to some extent, depending on the way that the individual him- or herself sees his job. Eliciting information from the job incumbent is partly dependent on the individual's co-operation, which is affected by how the individual sees the purpose of job analysis. Job analysis is sometimes associated with time-and-motion studies, which are seen as attempts to get more work out of the individual (Jewell 1985). Such associations obviously decrease the individual's co-operation.

The immediate manager/supervisor

Although often used as a source of information, the supervisor sometimes has only a superficial knowledge of the job being done at present. The supervisor is, however, in the best position to determine the job that needs to be done in order to meet team/group/departmental objectives. The major problem with collecting information from supervisors is that defensive reactions may lead them consciously or unconsciously to give misleading information.

Other members of the role set

Peers and subordinates can provide job-related information from a different angle. These sources could not provide sufficient information for job analysis, but might be useful in conjunction with other sources.

Technical experts

Experts who are aware of the tasks that organizational systems and processes require job holders to carry out may also be a useful source of information.

Existing written records

This source of information, again, could not be used alone, but it can be a valuable addition to information from other sources. Such records can include:

1. Company records, for example, those relating to the original design of the job.
2. Blueprints of equipment, work layout, etc.
3. Existing job descriptions and personnel specifications.
4. *The Dictionary of Occupational Titles* (DOT), which lists thousands of titles, together with a narrative description of each (US Department of Labor 1977). DOT's standard job definitions state in each case what gets done, how it is done and why it is done (see Jewell 1985).

5. Relevant statistics. These might include performance and output figures, quality control figures, and consumption and waste of materials.
6. Organizational analysis.

Methods of collecting and analyzing the information

Although most of the various methods of collecting information are suitable for use on their own, analysis is more reliable if more than one method is used.

Self-report or supervisor led

Using self-report the individual job incumbent collates the information about their job, and reports it in the form of a job description, as referred to in the section on 'Who Does Job Analysis?'. A further advantage of this method is that it provides an appropriate time for the individual to raise problems that decrease their work effectiveness, with which they cannot deal themselves. Ungerson also suggests that:

> It is undesirable that job descriptions should be imposed upon the job holder by a manager or other senior person. In this process, as in all management situations participation is likely to make the process and the final product more acceptable to all concerned. (Ungerson 1983, p. 14)

This method of collecting job information would be most appropriate for purposes such as improving the way that the job is structured, altering work tasks, training and appraisal processes. It can be particularly useful for setting general job objectives and performance standards. Immediate job objectives, say over the next year, can be incorporated if there is continuous job analysis providing an opportunity for a review of work and a new job description on an annual basis. The role of the supervisor can be variable in this, depending on the needs of the organization. If the information is to be used for job evaluation purposes, for example, the supervisor would take a clear and strong lead, perhaps just testing it out with the individual concerned.

Individual interviews

An interview with the job incumbent is usually of most value; interviews with supervisors, peers and subordinates can provide additional information. The interview may be totally unstructured, semi-structured or fully structured. The choice would depend upon the type and level of job being studied, but the most usual type for job analysis would be semi-structured. Thus the interviewer would have formulated a set of questions to which they required answers, but would also be prepared to digress and follow up additional areas that suggested themselves during the interview. One variation of this is the critical incident technique developed by Flanagan (1954) where individuals are asked to recount critical incidents related to successful performance of the job, and those related to failure. This is a particularly suitable method for training purposes, but the disadvantage of the technique is that more mundane and routine activities may be overlooked. There are also some standard interview systems, such as functional job analysis, developed by the United States Training and Employment Service (USTES) where the information is analyzed on the basis of three dimensions: data, people and things. 'On the job' interviews may be carried out while the individual actually performs the job. Interviewing is the most usual method of obtaining job-related information, but it does require high level skills from the interviewer to help avoid loss and misinterpretation of information. Individual interviews, as with self-report, are very much dependent for their success upon the co-operation of the individual. Even with full co-operation the interviewee may forget to mention some job details, especially tasks that are not carried out very often. Individual interviews are a costly and time-consuming method of collecting information, but if well done are an excellent method of getting a complete picture of the job.

Methods of collecting information	Sources of information				
	Job holder	Supervisor	Other members of role set	Technical experts	Job analyst
Self-report	*				
Individual interviews	*	*	*		
Other individual methods Checklists Questionnaires Work diaries	 * * *	 * *	 * *		
Group methods Group interviews Technical conference Mixed conference	 * *	 *		 * *	
Observation	*				
Participation					*
Existing records					*

Figure 16.1 *Summary of the methods of collecting job-related information, and sources of information*
Source: Adapted from Torrington and Chapman (1983, p. 374).

Other individual methods

Checklists

These are very highly structured lists of items relating to work. The individual checking the list, usually the job incumbent or perhaps supervisor, is required to check off whether or not each item applies to the job in question. Scales are sometimes used so that the frequency, importance or time spent on each item can be indicated. Checklists are useful because they are easy for the individual to respond to, but the adequacy of the information collected very much depends on the quality and appropriateness of the list. Such lists require a great amount of preparation and development, and generally fail to provide an integrated picture of the job (for an example, see Tiffin and McCormick 1971).

Questionnaires

Internally produced questionnaires may be used, or standard instruments that have been produced elsewhere. Questionnaires can be highly structured as with checklists, or can be less specific, asking the respondent to give narrative accounts in response to more general questions. The adequacy of this approach depends on the proper wording of questions, and more errors are likely to go undetected than with interview methods (Ghiselli and Brown 1955). Question-naires are often used when there is a large number of people doing the same job. Standard instruments, such as the Position Analysis Questionnaire, which contains 194 questions in six groups (information input, mental processes, work output, relationships, job content, other job characteristics), are particularly useful for job evaluation or other job comparison purposes.

Work diaries

Work diaries or log books can be used to form a daily record of the individual's work activities and the amount of time spent on them. These are particularly useful for higher-level jobs, such as management and scientific positions, as a great deal of information can be systematically collected. The chief problem with this method is that it is very time-consuming for the job incumbent who fills out the diary and it requires a great deal of commitment. Well-designed diary report forms will help to reduce the extent to which diary writing interferes with normal job duties.

Critical incidents

This technique, developed by Flanagan (1954), is based on diaries or interviews involving the job incumbent or supervisor. Respondents are often asked to recall critical incidents related to the successful performance of their job and those related to failure. The problem with this process is that more routine and mundane behaviours may be overlooked.

Group methods

Interviews can be held on a group basis with either job incumbents alone or together with supervisors. This method is useful in that it is time-saving and can lead to the collection of more thorough information if there is a group of individuals in different positions doing the same job. It can be a particularly appropriate method to use for the identification of training needs of individuals doing the same job but based at separate locations. Sometimes a group of technical experts is brought together to discuss a job, in the form of a 'technical conference'. Alternatively there may be a 'mixed conference' of technical experts and job incumbents (Torrington and Chapman 1983).

Observation

Observation can either be direct or recorded. Direct observation is the process of making notes of job-related information. Alternatively, what is seen may be recorded by means of photography, film, instrument recording and taped commentary. Observation is often regarded as the best method of collecting information, and is particularly useful when combined with individual interviews. Observation, however, is time-consuming, and the information may be biased as a result of the Hawthorne effect (Jewell 1985). Observation is often used for work study and other human resource utilization purposes.

Participation

Participation, or participant observation, involves the job analyst in doing the job themselves in order to collect information. Hugh Beynon, for a slightly different purpose, in his book *Working for Ford* (1973), demonstrates that this can be a clearly effective method. It is, however, a very time-consuming method. There is a danger, especially if the participation is for an insufficient length of time, that information on certain aspects of the job may be lost since the participant observer is not skilled at the job, and will in any case have a different view of the job than a skilled job incumbent.

Existing records

Information can be collected from existing records, as discussed in the section on sources of information.

Collating job-related information and writing a job description

When the job-related information has been collected and analyzed it needs to be presented in some form of job description. The form of job description can vary considerably in length, detail and the balance of qualitative and quantitative information, depending on the original purpose for the job analysis and the nature of the information. Most job descriptions consist of a narrative description of the job (see Figure 16.2). Below are some guidelines for writing a narrative job description.

Content

It is useful to have a checklist of information items that are to be included in the job description, and how these are to be organized. The two checklists in Figure 16.3 show how job information can be organized differently for different purposes.

Style

Style is particularly important when writing a job description, and it is advisable to:

1. Describe tasks or duties by a sentence starting with an action verb, and using the present tense. For example, 'Sorts incoming mail by department'.
2. Be concise, keep words to a minimum and avoid duplication.
3. Distinguish between the tasks the individual actually carries out and those that he has to see that others carry out, thus distinguishing between direct responsibility and managerial responsibility.
4. Express performance standards using as much quantitative information as possible, for example 'Introduce at least three new customers per calendar month'.

Problems with job descriptions

The production of job descriptions is not without problems. These problems do not make job descriptions invalid, but it is important to be aware of them.

Job title: Senior Sales Assistant

Context: The job is in one of the thirteen high technology shops owned by 'Computext'
Location – Leeds
Supervised by, and reports directly to the Shop Manager
Responsible for one direct subordinate – a Sales Assistant

Job summary: To assist and advise customers in the selection of computer hardware and software, and to arrange delivery and finance where appropriate.
Objective is to sell as much as possible, and for customer and potential customers to see 'Computext' staff as helpful and efficient.

Job content: *Most frequent duties in order of importance*
1. Advise customers about hardware and software
2. Demonstrate the equipment and software
3. Organize delivery of equipment by liaising with distribution department
4. Answer all after-sales queries from customers
5. Contact each customer two weeks after delivery to see if they need help
6. Advise customers about the variety of payment methods
7. Develop and keep up to date a computerized stock control system
Occasional duties in order of importance
1. Arrange for faulty equipment to be replaced
2. Complete deferred payment forms and send to Head Office
Responsibility for others
1. Check that junior sales assistant carried out all duties in job description
2. Monitor performance of junior sales assistant as defined in job description
3. Advise and guide, train and assess junior sales assistant where necessary

Working conditions: Pleasant 'business-like' environment in new purpose-built shop premises in the city centre. There are two other members of staff and regular contact is also required with the Delivery Department and Head Office. Salary is £12,000 p.a. plus a twice yearly bonus depending on sales. Five weeks' holiday per year plus statutory holidays. A six-day week is worked.

Other information: There is the eventual possibility of promotion to shop manager in another location depending on performance and opportunities.

Performance standards: There are two critically important areas
1. *Sales volume* Minimum sales to the value of £400,000 over each six-month accounting period
2. *Relations with customers* • Customers' queries answered immediately
   • Customers always given a demonstration when they request this
   • Delivery times arranged to meet both customer and delivery dept's needs
   • Complaints investigated immediately
   • Customers assured that problem resolved as soon as possible
   • Customers never blamed
   • Problems that cannot be dealt with referred immediately to Manager

Note: This job description relates to the person specification found in Figure 18.1.

Figure 16.2 *Job description for senior sales assistant*

Part of job analysis checklist for use in job evaluation

1 Job title ....

2 General statement of duties ....

3 Level of education required
  (a) Basic secondary ☐   (b) 4–6 GCE 'O' levels ☐
  (c) 2 GCE 'A' levels ☐   (d) Degree in .... ☐
  (e) Postgraduate/professional ☐
       qualification

4 Amount of previous similar or related work experience necessary for a person starting this job
  (a) None ☐   (b) Less than 3 months ☐
  (c) 3 months to 1 year ☐   (d) 1 to 3 years ☐

5 How much supervision does the job require?
  (a) Frequent ☐   (b) Several times daily ☐
  (c) Occasional ☐   (d) Limited ☐
  (e) Little or none ☐

6 Number of people supervised by job holder
  (a) None ☐   (b) 1 ☐
  (c) 2–5 ☐   (d) 6–20 ☐
  (e) 21–50 ☐   (f) 51 + ☐

7 Cost to organization of errors made by job holder
  (a) Under £25 ☐   (b) £25–£100 ☐
  (c) £100–£500 ☐   (d) £500–£5,000 ☐
  (e) More than £5,000 ☐

8 How often is the possibility of such errors checked?
  (a) Daily ☐   (b) Weekly ☐
  (c) Monthly ☐   (d) Quarterly ☐
  (e) Annually ☐   (f) Not regularly checked ☐

9 Contacts with other people, *initiated by job holder*

	Constantly	Often	Occasionally	Never
In own dept				
In other depts				
With suppliers				
With customers				
With civic authorities				
Other				

10 Aspects of the job involving confidentiality/security
....

11 Disagreeable/dangerous aspects of job
....

12 Resourcefulness or initiative required
....

A job analysis checklist for use in selection

- Job title and identification

- Organizational context: company name
  department
  location
  supervision
  reporting relationships
  direct subordinates

- Job summary: purpose and objectives of job

- Job content: tasks/duties
  frequency
  relative importance
  equipment/methods used
  scope of responsibility

- Working conditions: physical conditions, hours and holidays
  social conditions
  economic conditions

- Other information: promotion opportunities
  possible transfers
  training/development opportunities
  scope for developing the job

- Performance standards: specific objectives
  expectations
  assessment standards

- Individual requirements: physical and psychological characteristics required for an
  individual to do the job

Figure 16.3 *Comparisons of two job analysis checklists: one for selection purposes,*
one for job evaluation purposes
Source: Torrington *et al.* (1985, p. 142).

Sources of error

If the job analysis information were collected from an insufficient number of sources, it might be incomplete or biased. The job analyst may also be unintentionally biased in their interpretation of the information that has been collected. The environment of job analysis may lead to errors in the analysis. Such factors as time pressures which cause the collection and interpretation of information to be rushed; lack of interest/commitment on the part of managers, supervisors and job incumbents; and distracting physical or environmental conditions would be relevant here.

Appropriateness of job descriptions

Ungerson (1983) identifies a further set of problems relating to the appropriateness of job descriptions:

1. Job descriptions are often seen as not appropriate for top management as these people should be free to map out their own territory and use their initiative.
2. Job descriptions are inflexible and they can be a hindrance to the development of organizations that are growing rapidly or changing technologically.
3. Job descriptions become out of date very quickly as there is always a drift in job content.

Ungerson meets these criticisms by arguing that flexibility can be built into the structure and wording of job descriptions, and that there should be plans for the regular updating of job descriptions on an ongoing basis.

Purposes served by job descriptions

It is usually considered that a job description designed for one purpose is not suitable for another purpose. This problem can be approached by:

1. Being aware of a number of possible purposes when writing the job description, while giving priority to the primary purpose.
2. Where this approach is not possible or is inadequate it is often feasible to return to the collected job analysis information, if this is sufficiently good, and use this to develop a new job description for a different purpose. The job, therefore, need not necessarily be reanalyzed.

Writing a person specification

This is the specification of a job in terms of the human characteristics required in order to do the job. The person specification is derived from the demands of the job specification. This person specification is sometimes referred to as the 'human specification' or, rather confusingly, as the 'job specification'. The person specification is most widely used in the recruitment and selection process, but it is also used for promotion, transfer, training and human resource planning purposes. A number of different frameworks have been suggested for preparing person specifications. The two most often used are Alec Rodger's Seven Point Plan and John Munro Fraser's Five Fold Framework (see Table 19.3, page 326). There are three important points to bear in mind when preparing a person specification:

1. Avoid overestimating the characteristics of the person required to do the job. This can sometimes happen if the job description was derived from critical incident analysis where there is less attention paid to the routine and mundane parts of the job. An overestimation of the characteristics

required to do the job can have two consequences. First, it restricts the number of people who can be considered for the position; and secondly, it may result in the appointment of someone who is overqualified.

2. Consider the importance of potential when preparing the person specification. The potential to be able to learn a task may be an acceptable substitute for a person who has already obtained those skills, if suitable training is available or can be arranged.

3. In order not to be unnecessarily restrictive it is important to distinguish which characteristics are essential and which are preferred.

A sample person specification is found in Figure 18.1 (page 286).

Review topic 16.3

Write a job description and person specification for your own job.

Summary propositions

16.1 Job analysis is a process which is fundamental to many personnel activities

16.2 The more sources of information and methods of collecting the information that are used, the more reliable will be the job analysis.

16.3 Sometimes specialist techniques are used to analyze the information collected, but very often this is done on a commonsense basis.

16.4 The end-product of job analysis is a job description. The form, length and content of a job description may vary considerably depending on its purpose, however narrative job descriptions of 1–3 pages are most widely used.

16.5 Human characteristics required to do the job are sometimes included in the job description, but very often a person specification is prepared. It is important not to overestimate the individual characteristics that are required.

References

Beynon, H. (1973), *Working for Ford*, London: EP Publishing.

Blum, M. L. and Naylor, J. C. (1956), *Industrial Psychology*, New York: Harper & Row.

Campbell C. P. (1989), *Job Analysis for Industrial Training*, Bradford: MCB, University Press.

Dictionary of Occupational Titles (1977), Washington DC: US Department of Labor.

Employment and Training Administration (1977), *Dictionary of Occupational Titles* (4th edition), Washington DC: US Department of Labor.

Flanagan, J. C. (1954), 'The critical incident technique', *Psychological Bulletin*, vol. 51, pp. 327–58.

Fraser, J. M. (1966), *Employment Interviewing*, London: MacDonald & Evans.

Ghiselli, E. E. and Brown, C. W. (1955), *Personnel and Industrial Psychology* (2nd edition), New York: McGraw-Hill.

Jewell, L. N. (1985), *Contemporary Industrial/Organizational Psychology*, St Paul, Minnesota: West Publishing Co.

Rodger, A. (1952), *The Seven Point Plan*, London: NIIP.

Schneider, B. (1976), *Staffing Organizations*, Glenview, Ill.: Scott Foresman.

Tiffin, J. and McCormick, E. J. (1971), *Industrial Psychology* (2nd edition), London: George Allen & Unwin.

Torrington, D. P. and Chapman, J. (1983), *Personnel Management* (2nd edition), Hemel Hempstead: Prentice Hall.

Torrington, D. P., Weightman, J. B. and Johns, K. (1985), *Management Methods*, London: Institute of Personnel Management.

Ungerson, B. (1983), *How to Write a Job Description*, London: Institute of Personnel Management.

Walton, F. (1989), 'The importance of the job description', *Employment Bulletin*, vol. 5, pt 2, pp. 5–7.

17

Recruitment strategy and employment documentation

> Recruitment is the biggest single challenge facing personnel managers in the 1990's. Current skill shortages and forecasts of a huge drop in the number of young people available for work in the coming decade point to rapidly deteriorating recruitment prospects . . . the situation looks bleak for those employers who fail to change their ways and are slow to look to non-traditional methods of recruitment, as well as more innovative forms of employment (Curnow 1989)

This is the conclusion reached in a survey of over 1,000 personnel professionals carried out by *Personnel Management* (November 1989) with the assistance of MSL International. Over 54 per cent of the respondents confirmed that the proportion of their time spent on recruitment had increased over the last two years; 41 per cent indicating that it now accounted for between 25 per cent and 100 per cent of their total time.

The recruitment shortages facing employers in the 1990s are in marked contrast to the buoyant labour market of the 1980s, when high unemployment and the economic recession led to something of a buyers' market for labour. This turnaround in the labour market will necessitate a reformulation of recruitment strategy by employers. The position calls for a new breed of professional recruiter working closely with other branches of personnel (training, remuneration, etc.) to market employing organizations effectively to a decreasing number or potential recruits in an increasingly competitive market-place.

In this chapter we shall consider various aspects of an employer's recruitment strategy; determining the appointment, the range of recruitment methods available, recruitment advertising, and several features of recruitment method, including employee documentation and shortlisting.

Determining the vacancy

Is there a vacancy? Is it to be filled by a newly recruited employee? These are the first questions to be answered in recruitment. Potential vacancies occur either through someone leaving or as a result of expansion. When a person leaves, there is no more than a *prima facie* case for filling the vacancy thus caused. There may be other ways of filling the gap. Vacancies caused by expansion may be real or imagined. The desparately pressing need of an executive for an assistant may be a plea more for recognition than for assistance. The creation of a new post to deal with a specialist activity may be more appropriately handled by contracting that activity out to a supplier. Recruiting a new employee may be the most obvious tactic when a vacancy occurs, but it is not necessarily the most appropriate. Listed below are some of the options.

- *Reorganize the work*: Jobs may be rearranged so that the total amount of work to be done in a section is done by the remaining employees without replacement of the leaver. One clue to the likelihood of this being the right move lies in the reasons for leaving. If the person has left because there was not enough to do, or because the other employees formed a tight-knit group that was difficult to break into, then there may be grounds for considering this strategy. It can also work between departments, with people redundant in one area being redeployed elsewhere.
- *Use overtime*: Extra output can be achieved by using overtime, although there is always the possibility that the work to be done is simply expanded to fill the greater amount of time available for its completion. The number of operatives working overtime in manufacturing industries moved up from 29.5 per cent in 1980 to 36.4 per cent in 1985. Few personnel managers like the extensive use of overtime, and it lacks logic at a time of high unemployment, but it may be the best way of dealing with a short-term problem where, for instance, one employee leaves a month before another is due back from maternity leave.
- *Mechanize the work*: There are all sorts of ways in which the work of a departing member of staff can be mechanized, though it is seldom feasible to mechanize, or automate or robotize on the basis of a single, casual vacancy. However, the non-replacement of a departing member of staff is often used to justify the expense of introducing a computer or word-processor.
- *Stagger the hours*: As we saw in Chapter 15, there can be manpower economies in introducing shifts, staggering hours or trying flexible working hours methods. It is again rarely practicable to take these steps when there is a single vacancy, although sometimes a staggering of hours can work in that sort of situation.

- *Make the job part-time*: Replacing full-time jobs with part-time jobs has obviously become a widespread practice and has the attraction of making marginal reductions more possible at the same time as providing the possibility of marginally increasing the amount of staff time available in the future by redefining the job as full-time. It also provides potential flexibility by making it possible to turn one full-time job into two part-time posts located in two separate places.
- *Subcontract the work*: By this means the employer avoids ongoing costs and obligations of employing people by transferring those obligations to another employer. It is simpler to do this when the work can be easily moved elsewhere, like some features of computer programming, than when the work has to be done on your own premises, with the comparisons of terms and conditions that inevitably take place. Also the advantages of avoiding employment costs and obligations have to be offset against the disadvantages of less direct control and probably higher overall costs in the medium term.
- *Use an agency*: A similar strategy is to use an agency to provide temporary personnel, who again do not come onto the company payroll.

Cannon (1979, pp. 77–82) provides suggestions for quantifying some of these decisions, although they may well be taken in practice without careful preliminary evaluation.

Review topic 17.1

Can you think of further ways of avoiding filling a vacancy by recruiting a new employee? What are the advantages and disadvantages of the methods you have thought of? For what types of job with which you are familiar would each of your methods, and those listed above, be most appropriate?

If your decision is that you are going to recruit, there are then four questions to determine the vacancy:

1. What does the job consist of?
2. In what way is it to be different from the job done by the previous incumbent?
3. What are the aspects of the job that specify the type of candidate?
4. What are the key aspects of the job that the ideal candidate wants to know before deciding to apply?

The conventional personnel approach to these questions is to produce job descriptions and personnel specifications, as described in the last chapter. We have found, however, that less than half of personnel departments use job analysis and its products for recruitment and selection. While we obviously would urge it upon readers, we must recognize that it is not universally adopted and our set of four questions is offered as an alternative.

Methods of recruitment

Once an employer has decided that external recruitment is necessary, a cost-effective and appropriate method of recruitment must be selected. Figure 17.1 shows the methods used by over 1,000 personnel professionals questioned in a recent IPM survey (Curnow 1989).

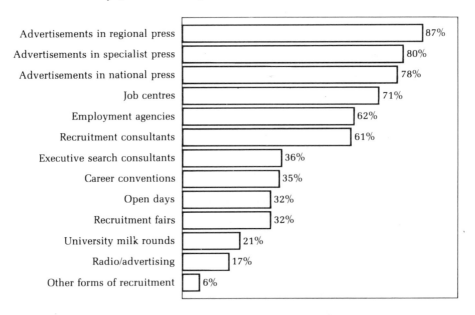

Figure 17.1 *From what source do companies attract their staff?*

Respondents were asked whether they were using these methods more, the same or less than previously. Their responses were broken down into three categories: the use of media (Figure 17.2), the use of external consultancies/agencies (Figure 17.3), and the use of open days, conventions, etc. (Figure 17.4).

Figure 17.2 shows the increased use of regional press and the decreased use of

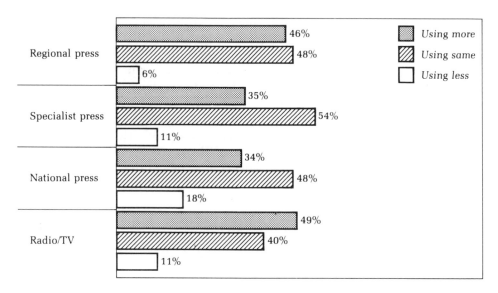

Figure 17.2   *Trends in the use of media*

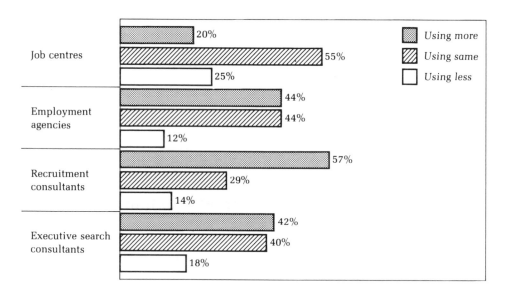

Figure 17.3   *Trends in the use of external consultancies/agencies*

national press. These indicators reflect the growing problem of job mobility, and support responses elsewhere in the survey which suggest that housing, location and cost of living in an area are significant constraints on recruitment. Figure 17.3 shows a high increase in the use of recruitment consultancies and smaller increases in the use of employment agencies and executive search consultants. Employers are obviously turning to outside professional help to assist in their recruitment plans. It is also worth noting that job centres suffered the largest fall in use of 25 per cent. Finally, Figure 17.4 shows an overall increase in the use of open days, conventions and recruitment fairs. This can be seen as part of a more proactive recruitment strategy by employers in a competitive market-place.

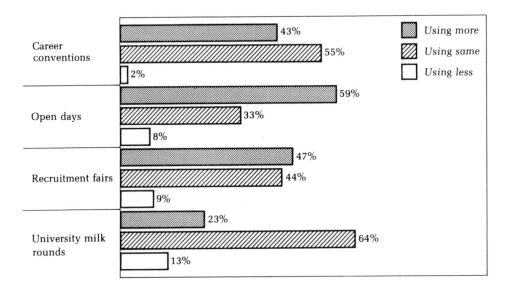

Figure 17.4   *Trends in the use of open days, conventions, etc.*

The recruitment methods compared

The various methods of recruitment all have benefits and drawbacks, and the choice of a method has to be made in relation to the particular vacancy and the type of labour market in which the job falls. A general review of advantages and drawbacks is given in Figure 17.5.

Job Centres and Professional and Executive Recruitment
Advantages: (a) Applicants can be selected from nationwide sources with convenient, local availability of computer-based data.
(b) Socially responsible and secure.
(c) Can produce applicants very quickly.
Drawbacks: (a) Registers are mainly of the unemployed rather than of the employed seeking a change.

Commercial employment agencies
Advantages: (a) Established as the normal method for filling certain vacancies, e.g. secretaries in London.
(b) Little administrative chore for the employer.
Drawbacks: (a) Can produce staff who are likely to stay only a short time.
(b) Widely distrusted by employers (Knollys 1983, p. 234).

Management selection consultants
Advantages: (a) Opportunity to elicit applicants anonymously.
(b) Opportunity to use expertise of consultant in an area where employer will not be regularly in the market.
Drawbacks: (a) Internal applicants may feel, or be, excluded.
(b) Cost.

Executive search consultants ('headhunters')
Advantages: (a) Known individuals can be approached directly.
(b) Useful if employer has no previous experience in specialist field.
(c) Recruiting from, or for, an overseas location.
Drawbacks: (a) Cost.
(b) Potential candidates outside the headhunter's network are excluded.
(c) The recruit may remain on the consultant's list and be hunted again.

Visiting universities ('The milk round')
Advantages: (a) The main source of new graduates from universities.
(b) Inexpensive and administratively convenient through using the free services of the University Appointments Service.
Drawbacks: (a) Interviewees are often enquirers rather than applicants.
(b) Interviewing schedules can be fatiguing.

Schools and the careers service
Advantages: (a) Can produce a regular annual flow of interested enquirers.
(b) Very appropriate for the recruitment of school-leavers, who seldom look further than the immediate locality for their first employment.
Drawback: (b) Schools and the advisers are more interested in occupations than organizations.

Youth Training (colloquially known as YTS)
Advantages: (a) The government subsidy provides a 'free trial offer' of the prospective employee.
(b) The employee should be properly prepared and trained, requiring limited further induction.
Drawbacks: (a) Some young peole regard YTS as a route to employment that they try to avoid.
(b) YTS schemes do not necessarily attract the most able young people.

Figure 17.5 *The advantages and drawbacks of various forms of recruitment*

Review topic 17.2

We have seen the significance of informal methods of recruitment whereby new employees come as a result of hearing about a vacancy from friends, or putting their names down for consideration when a vacancy occurs. Employees starting employment in this way present the employer with certain advantages as they come knowing that they were not wooed by the employer: the initiative was theirs. Also they will probably have some contacts in the company already that will help them to settle and cope with the induction crisis. What are the drawbacks of this type of arrangement?

Recruitment advertising

Apart from using recruitment consultants, most employers will deal with an advertising agency to help with drafting the advertisements and placing them in suitable media. The basic service such an agency will provide is considerable:

> only one copy of the text need be supplied no matter how many publications are to be used; the agency will book space; prepare the layout and typography; read and correct proofs; verify that the right advertisement has appeared in the right publications at the right time; and only one cheque has to be raised to settle the agency's monthly account. (Plumbley 1985, p. 55)

These basic technical services are of great value to the personnel manager and are 'free' in that the agency derives its income from the commission paid by the journals on the value of the advertising space sold. The personnel manager placing, say, £50,000 of business annually with an agency will appreciate that the agency's income from that will be between £5,000 and £7,500, and will expect a good standard of service. The important questions relate to the experience of the agency in dealing with recruitment, as compared with other types of advertising, the quality of the advice they can offer about media choice, and the quality of response that their advertisements produce.

Well-known agencies can provide another benefit to the employer wishing to advertise anonymously, as the advertisement can appear under the agency's masthead. This can be more productive than using a box number in those few situations where it is prudent to conceal the company's identity in the early stages.

Internal advertisement

Advantages: (a) Maximum information to all employees, who might then act as recruiters.

              (b) Opportunity for all internal pretenders to apply.

              (c) If an internal candidate is appointed there is a shorter induction period.

              (d) Speed.

              (e) Cost.

Drawbacks: (a) Limit to number of applicants.

              (b) Internal candidates not matched against those from outside.

              (c) May be unlawful if indirect discrimination. See Chapter 21.

Vacancy lists outside premises

Advantages: (a) Economical way of advertising, particularly if premises are near a busy thoroughfare.

Drawbacks: (a) Vacancy list likely to be seen by few people.

              (b) Usually possible to put only barest information, like the job title, or even just 'Vacancies'.

Advertising in the national press

Advantages: (a) Advertisement reaches large numbers.

              (b) Some national newspapers are the accepted medium for search by those seeking particular posts.

Drawbacks: (a) Cost.

              (b) Much of the cost 'wasted' in reaching inappropriate people.

Advertising in the local press

Advantages: (a) Recruitment advertisements more likely to be read by those seeking local employment.

              (b) Little 'wasted' circulation.

Drawbacks: (a) Local newspapers appear not to be used by professional and technical people seeking vacancies.

Advertising in technical press

Advantages: (a) Reaches a specific population with minimum waste.

              (b) A minimum standard of applicant can be guaranteed.

Drawbacks: (a) Relatively infrequent publication may require advertising copy six weeks before appearance of advertisement.

              (b) Inappropriate where a non-specialist is needed, or where the specialism has a choice of professional publications.

Figure 17.6   *The advantages and drawbacks of various methods of job advertising*

Advertising media

Choosing the appropriate medium for your advertisement will be a subject for advice from your advertising agency, but remembering the basis of their income you may want to take an independent view as well. The best source of information on what to choose will be previous experience. If three column centimetres of classified advertising in your local weekly free-sheet have always produced an adequate number of prospective sales representatives before, why change? Many posts, however, do not recur often enough to provide that background data. Also, the labour market is changing constantly and last year's experience may be this year's irrelevance.

The key pieces of information are circulation and readership, as these tell you both how wide the readership is and how much of that will be wasted. Table 17.1 shows the circulation and percentage share of the main daily and Sunday newspapers in the last quarter of 1981 and the last quarter of 1984, indicating a decline in the sale of quality dailies over that period. To this must be added the information about who constitutes the readership. The National Readership Survey, which is commissioned annually by the media owners, gives figures based on occupations, showing, for instance, that 61,000 accountants read the *Daily Telegraph* and 73,000 graduate engineers read the *Daily Express*, suggesting that you advertise for accountants in one paper and for engineers in the other. The more general classification that is used by media sellers is a peculiar mystique of social classification. This was developed on the basis that advertisers sell their products in this way, and the operating assumption is that

Table 17.1 Circulation of market shares of national newspapers

	Readership (millions)	
	1971	1988
Popular dailies	38.8	33.3
Sun	8.5	11.3
Daily Mirror	13.8	8.7
Daily Express	9.7	4.3
Daily Mail	4.8	4.3
Daily Star		3.3
Today		1.5
Quality dailies	6.5	7.0
Daily Telegraph	3.6	2.7
Guardian	1.1	1.3
The Times	1.1	1.1
Independent		1.1
Financial Times	0.7	0.8
Popular Sundays	53.1	40.9
News of the World	15.8	13.2
Sunday Mirror	13.5	8.9
Sunday People	13.4	7.8
Sunday Express	10.4	5.7
Mail on Sunday		5.3
Quality Sundays	8.2	8.2
Sunday Times	3.7	3.8
Observer	2.4	2.1
Sunday Telegraph	2.1	2.3

Source: Based on *Social Trends 20* (1990, p. 157).

potential job holders also fit into these classifications, so that the recruiter will advertise certain jobs in the *Sunday Times* confident that 45 per cent of men in social class A and 28 per cent of men in social class B read that journal, compared with a mere 9 and 10 per cent respectively that read the *Guardian*. The meanings of the classifications are given in Table 17.2.

Table 17.2   Social status classifications

Social status	Head of household's occupation
A Upper middle class	Higher managerial, administrative, professional
B Middle class	Intermediate managerial, administrative, professional
C1 Lower middle class	Supervisory or clerical, junior managerial, administrative, professional
C2 Skilled working class	Skilled manual worker
D Working class	Semi- and unskilled manual worker
E Lowest level of subsistence	State pensioners or widows; casual or lowest grade workers

The 'Recruitment Report' section of *Personnel Management* reports monthly on the distribution of recruitment advertising in quality newspapers, but the main source of detailed information about the readership of newspapers and journals is *British Rate and Data*, which includes advertising rates, dates by which advertisements have to be received, and occasional additional information by the publisher, for example:

> *Accountancy Age*, Britain's only weekly newspaper for accountants, is received by over 72,000 qualified accountants in industry, commerce, public practice, the City and both national and local government. It has the highest circulation and the highest readership among qualified accountants of any publication in the UK. (BRAD 1984, p. 237)

Drafting the advertisement

The decision on what to include in a recruitment advertisement is important because of the high cost of space and the need to attract attention; both factors will encourage the use of the fewest number of words. The agency placing it will be able to advise on this, as they will on the way the advertisement should be worded, but the following is a short checklist of items that must be included.

Name and brief details of the employing organization

The recruiter seeking anonymity will usually eschew press advertising in favour of some other medium. The advertisement that conceals the identity of the advertiser will be suspected by readers, not least for fear that they might be applying to their present organization. If the advertisement conceals the name but gives clues to the identity of the organization ('our expanding high-precision engineering company in the pleasant suburbs of . . .') then there is the danger that the reader will guess . . . wrongly.

The brief details will fill in some of the uncertainty about what exactly the organization is and does. The better known the employer the less important the details.

Job and duties

The potential applicant will want to know what the job is. The title will give some idea, including a subjective assessment of its status, but rarely will this be sufficient. Particularly for knowledge workers some detail of duties will be sought.

Key points of the personnel specification

If you really believe that the only candidates that will be considered are those aged between 24 and 29, then this may be included in the advertisement. Not only do you preclude other applicants who would be wasting your time and theirs, you also bring the vacancy into sharper focus for those you are seeking. Other typical key points are qualifications and experience, as long as these can be expressed clearly. 'Highly qualified' and 'considerable experience' are value-less in an advertisement.

Salary

Many employers are coy about declaring the salary that will accompany the advertised post. Sometimes this is reasonable as the salary scales are well-known and inflexible, as in much public sector employment. Elsewhere the coyness is due either to the fact that the employer has a general secrecy policy about salaries and does not want to publicize the salary of a position to be filled for fear of dissatisfying holders of other posts, or does not know what to offer and is waiting to see 'what the mail brings'.

Whatever the reasons, the effect of this concealment is to reduce the number of applicants. The most cursory examination of advertisements shows that there is a wide discrepancy in the salaries attaching to apparently similar posts. If the salary is not declared in the advertisement it is inevitable that some of the applicants will be disqualified because of the salary they are currently receiving, and many others will not apply for fear of wasting their time.

What to do

Finally, the advertisement tells potential applicants what to do. This will vary according to the nature of the post. It is conventional for manual employees to call at the personnel department, while managerial employees will be more disposed to write. Applicants who obey the instruction 'write with full details to . . .' will be understandably discouraged if the response to their letter is an application form to be completed, giving roughly the same information in a different way. Application forms are now generally accepted, but applicants not only feel it is unnecessary to be asked for the same information twice, they also develop reservations about the administrative efficiency of the organization that they had been thinking of joining.

Advertising control

The personnel manager needs to monitor the effectiveness of advertising and all other methods of recruitment, first to ensure value for money and secondly to ensure that the pool of applicants produced by the various methods is suitable. Jenkins (1983, p. 259) provides a useful example of monitoring the effectiveness of advertising for management trainees in retailing (Table 17.3).

Table 17.3   Monitoring the effectiveness of advertising for management trainees in retailing

Medium	National press
Size of advertisement	60 column cm
Initial response	370
Booklet and application form sent out to	321
Application form returned from	127
Selection board attended by	95
Job offered to	23
Jobs accepted by	19
Employment actually started by	15
Total cost	£1,440
Cost per starter	£96

Source: Jenkins (1983, p. 259).

Table 17.3 shows a number of interesting points, the first being that employment decisions are mainly taken by applicants rather than by employers. Of the 370 originally expressing interest, over half eliminated themselves by not returning the application form. Of the twenty-three to whom jobs were offered over a third did not take up the offer. An important part of the whole employment process is making sure that inappropriate people eliminate themselves from consideration, and they can only do this when given sufficient information to make that decision. The table also provides the information on approximately what number of initial applications are needed to produce a specific number of accepting candidates and what it costs to fill the vacancies by this means. We would suggest this type of simple, clear recording of developments is the most useful way of building up a stock of control data on which to develop a recruitment advertising strategy.

Employment documentation

Table 17.3 shows the importance of one type of documentation – the booklet sent out to applicants – as a means of focusing the minds of recruits on whether the job will suit them or not. We must also remember the significance of informal recruitment and the need to have information available to the casual enquirer, as well as documents for reference, like the works rules or details of the pension scheme. We shall review some of the key documents.

The job description

As we saw in the last chapter, the job description is a basic element in providing information to applicants so that they can confirm or withdraw their application.

The advertisement

A copy of the advertisement will not only be needed for internal purposes (see Tables 17.1, 17.4 and 17.5) and for the advertising agent, it can also form the basic information to the job centre and to casual inquirers.

The 'glossy'

Larger organizations tend to produce recruitment literature for general use or to target specific potential employees, like graduates. These publications are usually described as 'glossies', indicating some suspicion about their contents.

A study by Cooksey examining student attitudes towards recruitment brochures found that 'the company brochure was the single most important influence on students' decisions to apply to a particular company' (Cooksey 1988, p. 75).

However, the influencing factors lie not in the glossy presentation but in the *content* of the brochure – information about the company, training, promotion prospects, etc.

> ## Review topic 17.3
>
> Recruiters are interested in the job to be done, so that they concentrate on how the vacancy fits into the overall structure of the organization and on the type of person to be sought. Applicants are interested in the work to be done, as they want to know what they will be doing and what the work will offer to them. Think of your own job and list both types of feature.
>
> | The job to be done | The work that is offered |
> |---|---|
> | 1 .... | .... |
> | 2 .... | .... |
> | 3 .... | .... |
> | 4 .... | .... |
> | 4 .... | .... |
> | 5 .... | .... |
>
> How does your listing of features on the right-hand side alter the wording of advertisements and other employment documentation?

Internal control documentation

It is essential to have some method of tracking recruitment, either manually or by computer, so that an immediate and helpful response can be given to applicants enquiring about the stage their applications have reached

Correspondence

It is also necessary to ensure that all applicants are informed about the outcome of their application. This will first of all reduce the number of enquiries that have to be handled, but it is also an important aspect of public relations, as the organization dealing with job applicants may also be dealing with prospective customers. Very many people have the experience of applying for a post and then not hearing anything at all. Particularly when the application is unsolicited, personnel managers may feel that there is no obligation to reply, but this could be bad business as well as disconcerting for the applicant. Standard letters ('I regret to inform you that there were many applications and yours was not successful . . .') are better than nothing, but letters containing actual information ('out of the seventy-two applications, we included yours in our first shortlist of fifteen, but not in our final shortlist of eight') are better. Best of all are the letters that make practical suggestions, such as applying again in six months' time, asking if the applicant would like to be considered for another post elsewhere in the organization, or pointing out the difficulty of applying for a post that calls for greater experience or qualifications than the applicant at that stage is able to present.

Miscellaneous information

Among the items of peripheral value in the employment process are works rules, general terms and conditions of employment, publicity material about products, the annual report, house magazines, etc.

Perhaps the most important source of information is people. Do telephonists and receptionists know how to handle the tentative employment enquiry? Is it made simple for enquirers to check key points by telephone or personal visit? Is there an unnecessary emphasis on written applications before anything at all can be done?

Shortlisting

Shortlisting of candidates for some posts has become problematic for personnel managers in some instances because of small numbers of applicants. In other instances advertisements produce extremely large numbers of applicants. This can occasionally be attributed to inadequate specification of the criteria. For example:

> One advertisement that was placed in 1983, seeking management trainers and offering a salary in excess of £20,000, asked only for applicants to be of graduate level with some managerial or consulting experience. It appeared in the national press and gave very little additional information. Needless to say, it produced a huge response, as a large number of people, attracted by the salary, would meet the rather vague criteria. (Lewis 1985, p. 123)

There are, however, many instances when a job is attractive and widely understood as being similar to many others (like headteacher, sales representative or management trainee) where an inconspicuous advertisement can produce large numbers of applicants. The conventional method of handling these is to compare key points on the application form with the personnel specification, but large numbers sometimes induce a further stage of arbitrary pre-selection on the basis of some additional, whimsical criterion. Methods we heard about in the last two years include ruling out:

- Applicants over 45.
- Married women.
- Handwritten applications.
- Typewritten applications.

- Applicants who have been on a YTS scheme.
- Applicants with poor hand-writing.

No doubt there are other arbitrary criteria being adopted by managers appalled at making sense of 100 or so application forms and assorted *curricula vitae*. Apart from those that are unlawful, these criteria are grossly unfair to applicants if not mentioned in the advertisement, and are a thoroughly unsatisfactory way of recruiting the most appropriate person. In addition, an increasing number of employers who fail to apply fair and objective selection and promotion procedures can expect to be given a tough time in the courts (Aikin, 1988).

Care with shortlisting improves the prospects of being fair to all candidates and lessens the likelihood of calling inappropriate people for interview. Where selection is to be made by a panel, it also provides panel members with practice at working together and can clarify differences in attitude and expectation between them. The following outline procedure has been developed for use in that most difficult of situations: selection by a heterogeneous panel with a long list of applicants:

Stage 1   Agree essential criteria for those to be placed on the shortlist.
Stage 2   Using those criteria, selectors individually produce personal lists of, say, ten candidates. An operating principle throughout is to concentrate on who can be included rather than who can be excluded, so that the process is positive, looking for strengths rather than shortcomings.
Stage 3   Selectors reveal their lists and find their consensus. If stages 1 and 2 have been done properly the degree of consensus should be quite high and probably sufficient to constitute a shortlist for interview. If it is still not clear, they continue to:
Stage 4   Discuss those candidates preferred by some but not all in order to clarify and reduce the areas of disagreement. A possible tactic is to classify candidates as 'strong', 'possible' or 'maverick'.
Stage 5   Selectors produce a final shortlist by discussion, guarding against including compromise candidates: not strong, but offensive to no one.

Summary propositions

17.1 Current skill shortages and the predicted reduction in the number of young people available for work has necessitated a revision of recruitment strategy by employers, with the emphasis on a more proactive approach to recruitment.
17.2 Alternatives to filling a vacancy include reorganizing the work; using overtime; mechanizing the work; staggering the hours; making the job part-time; subcontracting the work; using an employment agency.

17.3 Recent trends indicate a greater use by employers of recruitment agencies and executive consultants, open days, recruitment fairs, etc. Relocation constraints have also prompted a move towards the use of regional as opposed to national recruitment advertising.

17.4 Advertising agencies and specialist publications provide a wealth of information to ensure that advertisements reach the appropriate readership.

17.5 Recruiters need to think not only of the job that has to be done, but also of the work that is offered.

17.6 Increasing the amount of information provided to potential applicants reduces the number of inappropriate applications.

17.7 Care with shortlisting increases the chances of being fair to all applicants and lessens the likelihood of calling inappropriate people for interview.

References

Aikin, O. (1988) 'Subjective criteria in selection', *Personnel Management*, September, p. 59.

British Rate and Data (1984), vol. 31, no. 12, London: BRAD.

Cannon, J. (1979), *Cost Effective Personnel Decisions*, London: Institute of Personnel Management.

Central Statistical Office (1990), *Social Trends 20*, London HMSO.

Cooksey, L. (1988), 'Recruitment brochures – are students getting the message?' *Personnel Management*, p. 75.

Curnow, B. (1989), 'Recruit, retrain, retain; personnel management and the three R's', *Personnel Management* November, pp. 40–7.

Jenkins, J. F. (1983), 'Management trainees in retailing', In B. Ungerson, (Ed.), *Recruitment Handbook* (3rd edition), Aldershot: Gower.

Knollys, J. G. (1983), 'Sales staff'. In B. Ungerson, (Ed.), *Recruitment Handbook*, Aldershot: Gower.

Lewis, C. (1985), *Employee Selection*, London: Hutchinson.

Plumbley, P. R. (1985), *Recruitment and Selection* (4th edition), London: Institute of Personnel Management.

18

Selection methods

While the search for the perfect method of selection continues, in its absence personnel managers continue to use a variety of imperfect methods to aid the task of predicting which applicant will be most successful in meeting the demands of the job. Selection is increasingly important as more attention is paid to the costs of poor selection, and as reduced job mobility means that selection errors are likely to stay with the organization for longer.

Legislation promoting equality of opportunity has underlined the importance of using well-validated selection procedures and there is increasing emphasis on ensuring that the selection process discriminates fairly, and not unfairly, between applicants.

In this chapter we first consider the role of personnel management in selection, and selection as a two-way process. Next we look at selection criteria and choosing appropriate selection methods. Various selection methods are then considered, including application forms, testing, interviews, group selection and assessment centres, references, use of consultants, and some less traditional methods such as graphology. We conclude by looking at the validation of selection procedures, and selection and the law.

The role of personnel management in selection

Personnel managers play a large part in the selection process, and in our recent research we found that recruitment and selection was an area of high importance in which personnel managers spent almost the most time and exercised almost the greatest discretion. The personnel manager has a particular role to play in the construction of selection procedures and their administrative control, and is additionally involved in shortlisting, interviewing and selection validation procedures.

Construction of selection procedures and administrative control

Personnel managers are able to draw on their expertise to recommend the most effective selection methods for each particular job or group of jobs. They are also in a position to encourage the development and use of personnel specifications as an aid to selection. The personnel manager will normally be the organization's expert on test use, and in an organization where tests are particularly appropriate selection methods, they will be qualified to administer tests and advise managers on the most suitable tests to use. In a more general sense personnel managers can act as an advice centre on selection methods for other managers, and are usually involved in the formal and informal training in selection skills, particularly interviewing skills. The personnel department will normally be responsible for the smooth running of the administrative procedures used in connection with the selection of staff.

Shortlisting for interview

Members of the personnel department often shortlist applicants for interview in conjunction with the line manager. On some occasions this shortlist may be compiled by personnel alone.

Interviewing

For many positions, particularly manual workers, the line manager will interview alone. For managerial and some higher graded white-collar jobs the line manager will interview together with a member of the personnel department, or there may be two separate interviews. The role of the member of personnel in interviews will depend on the position being filled for and the role of personnel in that organization. It can range from a commanding role to pure provider of conditions of service information. Occasionally, interviews will be carried out by the personnel department alone, for example, with secretarial trainees, where the individuals will not be directly employed, initially, by any specific department.

Validation procedures

The personnel department will have a key role in collecting the appropriate information and conducting validation procedures, as outlined later in this chapter in the section 'Validation of Selection Procedures'.

Selection as a two-way process

The various stages of the selection process provide information for decisions by both the employer and potential employee. This is not, however, a traditional view as employment decisions have long been regarded as a management prerogative and are still widely regarded in this way. With the exception of French (1974), many of the main US texts on personnel management (Megginson 1972; Jucius 1974; Pigors and Myers 1981; Glueck 1985) emphasize the management decision and describe the process in terms of hurdles over which prospective employees have to try to leap to avoid rejection. This view is likely to persist for various reasons:

1. It is attractive to managers because it underlines their authority, and they frequently feel that the ability to choose their subordinates is a key to their own effectiveness.
2 It is supported by much academic research. Psychologists have studied individual differences, intelligence and motivation extensively and have produced a number of prescriptions for those managing selection procedures on how to make sound judgements about candidates.
3. Candidates are convinced of their helplessness in selection, which they see as being absolutely controlled by the recruiting organization.

Despite these features of the situation, we continue to advocate a more reciprocal approach to employment decision-making which is increasingly being accepted (Lewis 1985), in the belief that managers will be more effective in staffing their organizations if they can bring about some shift of stance in that direction. We must be concerned not only with the job to be done, but also with the work that is offered.

Throughout the selection process applicants choose between organizations by evaluating the developing relationship between themselves and the prospect. This takes place in the correspondence from potential employers; in their experience of the selection methods used by the employer; and in the information they gain on interview. Applicants will decide not to pursue some applications. Either they will have accepted another offer, or they will find something in their correspondence with the organization that discourages them and they withdraw. Jenkins (1983) gives a specific example of how applicants drop out, which we refer to in more detail Chapter 17. After newspaper advertising 321 booklets and application forms were sent out to 321 applicants: 127 were returned, so 60 per cent withdrew at that point. Dropping out later was only slightly less in percentage terms. Posts were offered to twenty-three candidates and accepted by nineteen of whom only fifteen started. Thirty-five per cent dropped out.

This type of example illustrates that the managers in the organization do not have total control over who is employed and that there are two parties to the bargain. Figures of the type that Jenkins provides can be viewed with pride or alarm. It might be that 194 applicants received the information booklet and were immediately able to make a wise decision that they were not suited to the organization and that time would be wasted by continuing. On the other hand, it might be that potentially admirable recruits were lost because of the way in which information was presented, lack of information, or the interpretation that was put on the 'flavour' of the correspondence.

Herriot (1985) gives a good example of the criteria that graduates use to select potential employers. The frame of reference for the applicant is so different from that of the manager in the organization that the difference is frequently forgotten. It would not be unrealistic to suggest that the majority of applicants have a mental picture of their letter of application being received through the letterbox of the company and immediately being closely scrutinized and discussed by powerful figures. The fact that the application is one element in a varied routine for the recipient is incomprehensible to some and unacceptable to many. The thought that one person's dream is another's routine is something the applicant cannot cope with.

If they have posted an application with high enthusiasm about the fresh prospects that the new job would bring, they are in no mood for delay and they may quickly start convincing themselves that they are not interested, because their initial euphoria has not been sustained. They are also likely to react unfavourably to the mechanical response that appears to have been produced on a duplicating machine that was due for the scrapheap. Again there is a marked dissonance between the paramount importance of the application to the applicant and its apparent unimportance to the organization. The demographic decline has, however, begun to force organizations to view applicants as increasingly important. Some of the points that seem to be useful about correspondence are:

1. Reply, meaningfully, fast. The printed postcard of acknowledgement is not a reply, neither is the personal letter which says nothing more than that the application has been received.
2. Conduct correspondence in terms of what the applicants want to know. How long will they have to wait for an answer? If you ask them in for

interview, how long will it take, what will it involve, do you defray expenses, can they park their car, how do they find you, etc.?

Selection criteria

Lewis (1985) suggests that selection criteria can be understood in terms of three aspects: organizational criteria, departmental or functional criteria and individual job criteria.

Organizational criteria

The organizational criteria are those attributes that an organization considers valuable in its employees and that affect judgements about a candidate's potential to be successful within an organization. For example, the organization may be expanding and innovating and require employees who are particularly flexible and adaptable. These organizational criteria are rarely made explicit and they are often used at an intuitive level. They are made less subjective if a group of selectors join together to share their ideas of what characteristics are required if an individual is to be successful in the organization.

Functional/departmental criteria

Between the generality of the organizational criteria and the preciseness of job criteria there are departmental criteria such as the definition of appropriate interpersonal skills for all members of the personnel department.

Individual job criteria

Individual job criteria contained in job descriptions and person specifications are derived from the process of job analysis as described in Chapter 16. It is these criteria that are most often used in the selection process, and in our research we found that recruitment and selection was the second most important reason for producing job descriptions and person specifications. It is also noteworthy that more than half of the respondent organizations did not produce job descriptions and person specifications for the purposes of recruitment and selection. A sample person specification can be found in Figure 18.1.

Unless the criteria against which applicants will be measured are made explicit, it will be difficult to select the most appropriate selection procedure and

---

Person specification for the job of Senior Sales Assistant

Physical make-up
Essential: Tidy and dressed in a 'business-like' manner.

Attainment
Preferred: GCSE Maths grade A–C; Essential: grade D–E
Preferred: Attendance at a programming course, in or out of school; or demonstrate some self-taught knowledge of programming
Essential: Good keyboard skills

General intelligence
Essential: Above-average and quick to grasp the meaning of problems

Special aptitudes
Essential: Ability to relate to people – to be outgoing and form relationships quickly

Interests
Essential: Interested in both computer hardware and software

Disposition
Essential: Patience

Circumstances
Essential: Circumstances that enable attendance at work every Saturday

---

Note: This person specification relates to the job description for a senior sales assistant in Figure 16.2.

Figure 18.1 *An example of a person specification based on Rodger's seven-point plan*

approach, and it will be difficult to validate the selection process. Increasingly, these criteria are framed in terms of competencies required for the job and can be listed as threshold (needed in order to perform the job competently) and distinguishing (needed for superior performance). A more detailed explanation of competencies is given in Chapter 23. Further information on the validation and evaluation of the selection process is found in the final section of this chapter.

Choosing selection methods

It is unusual for one selection method to be used alone. A combination of two or more methods is generally used, and the choice of these is dependent upon a number of factors:

1. *Selection criteria for the post to be filled:* For example, group selection methods and assessment centre activities would only be useful for certain types of job, such as managerial and supervisory.

2. *Acceptability and appropriateness of the methods*: For the candidates involved, or likely to be involved, in the selection. The use, for example, of intelligence tests may be seen as insulting to applicants already occupying senior posts, and could elicit the following response:

> You should be aware that University examining bodies, which awarded me B.Sc., M.Sc., Ph.D. are quite competent and moreover have the services of some of the country's most eminent people. For a Personnel Officer to presume that he is more fitted for this task may be good for his ego but to me is a repugnant suggestion. (Torrington 1969, p. 36)

3. *Abilities of the staff involved in the selection process*: This applies particularly in the use of tests and assessment centres. Only those staff who are appropriately qualified by academic qualification and/or attendance on a recognized course may administer psychological tests.
4. *Administrative ease*: For administrative purposes it may be much simpler to, say, arrange one or two individual interviews for a prospective candidate rather than organize a panel consisting of four members, each needing to make themselves available at the same time.
5. *Time factors*: Sometimes a position needs to be filled very quickly, and time may be saved by organizing individual interviews rather than group selection methods which would mean waiting for a day when all candidates are available.
6. *Accuracy*: Accuracy in selection generally increases in relation to the number of appropriate selection methods used.
7. *Cost*: The use of tests may cost a lot to set up but once the initial outlay has been made they are reasonably cheap to administer. Assessment centres would involve an even greater outlay and continue to be fairly expensive to administer. Interviews, on the other hand, cost only a moderate amount to set up in terms of interviewer training and are fairly cheap to administer. For the costlier methods great care needs to be taken in deciding whether the improvement in selection decision making would justify such costs.

Selection methods

Application forms

Growing use is being made of the application form as a basis for employment decisions. For a long time it was not really that at all, it was a personal details form, which was intended to act as the nucleus of the personnel record for the individual when they began work. It asked for some information that was difficult to supply, like national insurance number, and some that seemed irrelevant, like the identity of the family doctor and next-of-kin. It was largely disregarded in the employment process, which was based on an informal and unstructured 'chat'. As reservations grew about the validity of interviews for employment purposes, the more productive use of the application form was one of the avenues explored for improving the quality of decisions.

Forms were considered to act as a useful preliminary to employment interviews and decisions, either to present more information that was relevant to such deliberations or to arrange such information in a standard way rather than the inevitably idiosyncratic display found in letters of application. This made sorting of applications and shortlisting easier and enabled interviewers to use the form as the basis for the interview itself, with each piece of information on the form being taken and developed in the interview.

More recently the application form has been extended by some organizations to take a more significant part in the employment process. One form of extension is to ask for very much more, and more detailed, information from the candidate. In this way there is some improved prospect of preparing an employment decision before the interview by garnering the maximum amount of data for analysis before the incalculable element of the face-to-face discussion comes in. This method has limited application, as there are not many posts for which one can expect the applicants to complete lengthy forms. Candidates are not always as distrustful of the interview as are some analysts, and may feel resentment at being denied an interview in which to put their case.

Another extension of application form usage has been in weighting, or biodata. Biodata has been defined by Anderson and Shackleton (1990) as 'historical and verifiable pieces of information about an individual in a selection context usually reported on application forms'. This method is an attempt to relate the characteristics of applicants to characteristics of successful job holders. The method is to take a large population of job holders and categorize them as good, average or poor performers, usually on the evaluation of a supervisor. Common characteristics are sought out among the good and poor performers. The degree of correlation is then translated into a weighting for evaluating that characteristic when it appears on the application form. The obvious drawbacks of this procedure are first the time that is involved and the size of sample needed, so that it is only feasible where there are many job holders in a particular type of position. Secondly, it smacks of witchcraft to the applicants who might find it difficult to believe that success in a position correlates with being, *inter alia*, the first born in one's family. However, Robertson and Makin (1986) report that biodata was used by 8 per cent of major British companies, at the time of their survey.

Generally, application forms are used as a straightforward way of giving a standardized synopsis of the applicant's history. This helps applicants present their case by providing them with a predetermined structure, it speeds the sorting and shortlisting of applications and it guides the interviewers as well as providing the starting-point for personnel records. Here are some points for a checklist:

1. Handwriting is usually larger than typescript. Do the boxes on the form provide enough room for the applicant to complete their information?
2. Forms that take too long to complete run the risk of being completed perfunctorily or not being completed at all, as the prospect decides to ignore the possibility in favour of other applications to other employers. Is the time the form takes to complete appropriate to the information needs of the employment decision?
3. Some questions are illegal, some are offensive, others are unnecessary. Does the form call only for information that is appropriate to employment decision-making?
4. Allan (1990) also suggests that in the age of word processors there is no excuse for failing to produce separate application forms for each vacancy advertised, or for not personalizing forms and making them more user-friendly. One way of increasing user-friendliness is to use introductory paragraphs explaining why the information in each section is being sought.

Among the most useful references on application forms are Miner (1969) and Edwards (1975). An example of an application form that could be used for skilled, unskilled and semi-skilled jobs is found in Figure 18.2.

Review topic 18.1

Design an application form for senior management posts maximizing critical information, but asking only for information that is strictly relevant.

Self-assessment

There is increasing interest in providing more information to applicants concerning the job. This may involve a video, an informal discussion with job holders, or further information sent with the application form. This is often termed as giving the prospective candidate a 'realistic job preview', enabling them to assess their own suitability to a much greater extent. Another way of achieving this is by asking the candidates to do some form of pre-work. This may involve asking them questions regarding their previous work experiences which would relate to the job for which they are applying.

BETA BROTHERS: JOB APPLICATION

JOB APPLIED FOR _____

PERSONAL DETAILS

Surname _____ Christian names _____

Address _____

_____ Tel no. _____

Date of birth _____

JOB DETAILS

Present/last job _____

Employer _____

Date started _____ Date finished _____

Immediately previous job _____

Employer _____

Date started _____ Date finished _____

Immediately previous job _____

Employer _____

Date started _____ Date finished _____

EDUCATION AND TRAINING

Highest educational qualification _____

Training/apprenticeship _____

_____

_____

IS THERE ANYTHING YOU'D LIKE TO ADD? Please write overleaf

WHERE DID YOU HEAR OF THIS JOB? _____

SIGNED _____ Date _____

When you have completed this form, please return it to:
Mrs J. Rank, Personnel Officer, Beta Brothers, Toolmakers, 71 Western Estate, Greater Manchester.

We will let you know of the progress of your application within the next 14 days. If you do not hear from us please telephone 432–1256

Figure 18.2 *A sample application form for skilled, semi-skilled and unskilled jobs*

Telephone screening

Telephone screening can be used instead of an application form if speed is particularly important, as interviews with appropriate candidates can be arranged immediately. This method works best where a checklist of critical questions has been prepared so that each candidate is being asked for standardized information. There are, however, problems with this method. Because the organizational response to prospective employee is immediate the decision can be haphazard unless pre-set standards are agreed in advance. The difficulty with setting standards in advance is that these may turn out to be inappropriate in either selecting too many or too few candidates to interview. The standards can, of course, be changed as enquiries are coming in but the best candidate, who may have called early, might not be invited to interview if the standards were initially too high. Also, since organizational response has to be immediate there is no time for reflection and little opportunity to be flexible.

Testing

The use of tests in employment procedures is surrounded by strong feelings for and against. Those in favour point to the unreliability of the interview as a predictor of performance and the greater potential accuracy and objectivity of test data. Tests can be seen as giving a credibility to selection decisions. Those against either dislike the objectivity that testing implies or have difficulty in incorporating test evidence into the rest of the evidence that is collected. The strongest objections of all are about the objectivity of testing, particularly among candidates, who feel that they can improve their prospects by a good interview 'performance' and that the degree to which they are in control of their own destiny is being reduced by a dispassionate routine. Tests are chosen on the basis that test scores relate, or correlate, with subsequent job performance, so that a high test score would predict high job performance and a low test score would predict low job performance.

Critical features of test use

Validity

There is a number of different types of validity that can be applied to psychological tests. Personnel managers are most concerned with predictive validity, which is the extent to which the test can predict subsequent job performance. Predictive validity is measured by relating the test scores to measures of future performance, such as error rate, production rate, appraisal scores, absence rate, or whatever criteria are important to the organization. If test scores relate highly with future performance then the test is a good predictor.

Reliability

The reliability of a test is the degree to which the test measures consistently whatever it does measure. If a test is highly reliable then it is possible to put greater weight on the scores that individuals receive on the test. However a highly reliable test is of no value in the employment situation unless it also has a high validity (see Tiffin and McCormick 1966).

Use and interpretation

Tests need to be used and interpreted by trained or qualified testers. Test results require very careful interpretation, especially personality tests, as some aspects of personality will be measured that are irrelevant to the job. Wills (1990) reports concerns that tests are carried out by unqualified testers. The British Psychological Society has now introduced a new system (Summer 1990) whereby all testers will have to be qualified by a chartered psychologist before they can use psychometrics.

Context of tests

Test scores need to be evaluated in the context of other information about individuals. Selection decisions need to be made up of a number of different pieces of information. Test results cannot be seen as having a simple relationship with job performance, as, for example, there are many relevant aspects of an individual which a test cannot measure.

Problems with using tests

1. In the last section we commented that a test score that was highly related to performance criteria has good validity. The relationship between test scores and performance criteria is usually expressed as a correlation coefficient (r). If $r = 1$ then test scores and performance would be perfectly related; if $r = 0$ there is no relationship whatsoever. Correlation coefficients of $r = 0.4$ are comparatively good in the testing world and this level of relationship between test scores and performance is generally seen as acceptable. Tests are, therefore, not outstanding predictors of future performance.
2. Validation procedures are very time-consuming, but are essential to the effective use of tests.

3. The criteria that are used to define good job performance in developing the test are often inadequate. They are subjective and may account to some extent for the mediocre correlations of test results and job performance. As Drenth comments: 'All too frequently, subjective classification, arbitrary grades or unreliable performance ratings are gratuitously accepted. One cannot expect to obtain acceptable validities with unreliable criteria' (Drenth 1978, p. 27).

4. Tests are job-specific. If the job for which the test is used changes, then the test can no longer be assumed to relate to job performance in the same way. Also, personality tests only measure how an individual sees themself at a certain point in time and cannot therefore be reliably re-used at a later time point.

5. Tests may not be fair as there may be a social, sexual or racial bias in the questions and scoring system. People from some cultures may, for example, be unused to 'working against the clock'.

Review topic 18.2

In what ways could you measure job performance for:
- A mobile telephone engineer?
- A clerk?
- A foreman?

Where tests are used

The use of different types of test tends to be associated with different levels of staff, as shown in Table 18.1. In our recent research we found that for blue-collar staff tests of trade knowledge devised by the employer were most commonly used, closely followed by mental ability tests. For white-collar staff these were again the most popular types of test, but mental ability tests were used to the

Table 18.1 Types of test used for different types of staff

Type of test	Blue-collar	White-collar	Management
Interest tests	17	16	9
Personality tests	16	40	67
Mental ability tests	70	96	43
Work sampling tests	50	80	8
Trainability tests	48	21	3
Own tests of trade knowledge	92	65	31

greatest extent. Management applicants were most often given personality tests with mental ability tests second in the running. The importance of test results was also viewed differently for the various groups of staff. They were viewed as more important for white-collar and for blue-collar staff than for management staff in organizations where these tests were used. Overall, almost two-thirds of our respondent organizations used tests in some way for selection. Wills reports a similar percentage (58 per cent) of county councils using them in 1990, with a further 31 per cent considering whether they should use them.

Types of test for occupational use

Aptitude tests

People differ in their performance of tasks, and tests of aptitude measure an individual's potential to develop in either specific or general terms. This is in contrast to attainment tests, which measure the skills an individual has already acquired. The words aptitude and ability are often used interchangeably, as, for example, by Ghiselli (1966). However, some authors see them as slightly different things. Lewis (1985) defines ability as being a combination of aptitude and attainment. For the purposes of this chapter we shall use aptitude and ability interchangeably, and as something quite separate from attainment. When considering the results from aptitude tests it is important to remember that there is not a simple relationship between a high level of aptitude and a high level of job performance, as other factors, such as motivation, also contribute to job performance.

Aptitude tests can be grouped into two categories. Those measuring general mental ability or general intelligence, and those measuring specific abilities or aptitudes.

General intelligence tests

Intelligence tests, sometimes called mental ability tests, are designed to give an indication of overall mental capacity. A variety of questions are included in such tests, including, vocabulary, analogies, similarities, opposites, arithmetic, number extension and general information. As Plumbley (1985) indicates, it has been shown that a person's ability to score highly on such tests correlates with the capacity to retain new knowledge, to pass examinations and to succeed at work. However the intelligence test used would still need to be carefully validated in terms of the job for which the candidate was applying. Examples of general intelligence tests are the AH4 (Heim, in Sweetland *et al.* 1983), and the Wechsler Adult Intelligence Scale Revised (Wechsler, in Sweetland *et al.* 1983).

Special aptitude tests

These are tests that measure specific abilities or aptitudes, such as spatial abilities, perceptual abilities, verbal ability, numerical ability, motor ability (manual dexterity), and so on. There is some debate over the way that general intelligence and special abilities are related. In the United Kingdom the design of ability or aptitude tests has been much influenced by Vernon's (1961) model of the structure of abilities. Vernon suggested a hierarchical model of abilities with general intelligence at the top and abilities becoming more specific and finely divided lower down in the hierarchy. Here an individual's potential ability to perform a task is the result of a combination of the specific appropriate ability and general intelligence. In the United States abilities are generally seen as more distinct (Thurstone 1938), and less emphasis is put on general intelligence as a contributing factor. The development of tests of specific aptitudes obviously influenced by the model of intelligence and ability that is used. Tests of special abilities are those such as the Bennett Mechanical Comprehension Test (Bennett, in Sweetland *et al.* 1983).

Trainability tests

These are used to measure a potential employee's ability to be trained, usually for craft-type work. The test consists of the applicants doing a practical task that they have not done before, after having been shown or 'trained' how to do it. The test measures how well they respond to the 'training' and how their performance on the task improves. Because it is performance at a task that is being measured these tests are sometimes confused with attainment tests, however they are more concerned with potential ability to do the task and response to training.

Attainment tests

Whereas aptitude tests measure an individual's potential, attainment or achievement tests measure skills that have already been acquired. There is much less resistance to such tests of skills. Few candidates for a typing post would refuse to take a typing test before interview. The candidates are sufficiently confident of their skills to welcome the opportunity to display them and be approved. Furthermore, they know what they are doing and will know whether they have done well or badly. They are in control, while they feel that the tester is in control of intelligence and personality tests as the candidates do not understand the evaluation rationale. These tests are often devised by the employer.

Personality tests

Swinburne (1985) comments that there are very many articles on training and management development which continue to emphasize the importance of personality for competence in management jobs (Harrison 1979; Hollis 1984; Willis 1984) and yet there is a dearth of papers on the use of personality questionnaires for selection, guidance or development. In our survey less than 20 per cent of organizations used personality tests for management selection, as shown in Table 18.1. Swinburne argues that the lack of papers may well reflect the state of the art, in that although the need for personality assessment is high, few questionnaires lend themselves easily to occupational use. An additional reason is that there is even more resistance to tests of personality than to tests of aptitude, partly because of the reluctance to see personality as in any way measurable.

Personality is itself susceptible to a variety of definitions. In this context we can use the comment of the Jessups:

> personality is that which makes one person different from another and includes all the psychological characteristics of an individual . . . personality is used to describe the non-cognitive or non-intellectual characteristics of an individual. It refers more to the emotional make-up of a person and is reflected in the style of his behaviour rather than the quality of his performance. (Jessup and Jessup 1975)

Theories of human personality vary as much as theories of human intelligence. The psychiatrist Karl Jung was content to divide personalities into extroverts and introverts; more recently Eysenck (1963) regards the factors of neuroticism and extroversion as being sufficient. The most extensive work has been done by Cattell (1965) who has identified sixteen factors:

reserved	outgoing
less intelligent	more intelligent
affected by feelings	emotionally stable
submissive	dominant
serious	happy-go-lucky
expedient	conscientious
timid	venturesome
tough-minded	sensitive
trusting	suspicious
practical	imaginative
forthright	shrewd
self-assured	apprehensive
conservative	experimenting
group dependent	self-sufficient
uncontrolled	controlled

The use of personality tests for employment purposes is dependent on two factors. First, the general policy decision about whether to incorporate this feature in the recruitment/selection process; and second, on whether qualified personnel are available to operate the procedures. Considerations on the first point are similar to those about the weighted application form. There needs to be a large number of employment prospects in identical jobs in order to build up sufficient evidence of successful individuals so that correlations can be derived. It is dangerous to assume that there is a standard profile of 'the ideal employee'. Miller (1975) quotes the example of two establishments in the same organization using the Cattell inventory to produce a profile of systems analysts. Though the work of each group was similar, the factors most associated with success in the two locations were different.

Another problem with the use of personality tests is that they rely on an individual's willingness to be honest, as the socially acceptable answer or the one best in terms of the job are often easy to pick out (Lewis 1985). There is a further problem that some traits measured by the test will not be relevant in terms of performance on the job.

Some examples of personality tests in common use are Cattell's 16PF (Cattell *et al.* 1962) and the OPQ (Saville and Holdsworth Ltd 1984).

Interest tests

Interest tests suffer from the same problems as personality tests, without the literature to support their theoretical usefulness. They may perhaps be useful when selecting school-leavers for a range of possible jobs, but otherwise their occupational use is not usually recommended.

Interviewing

Selection interviewing, the most common method of selection, is dealt with in Chapter 19. See also Chapter 10, which includes a section on interpersonal skills in interviews.

Group selection methods and assessment centres

Group methods

The use of group tasks to select candidates is not new, dating back to the Second World War, but such measures have gained greater attention through their use in assessment centres. Plumbley (1985) describes the purpose of group selection methods as being to provide evidence about the candidate's abilities to:

1. Get on with others.
2. Influence others and the way they do this.

3. Express themselves verbally.
4. Think clearly and logically.
5. Argue from past experience and apply themselves to a new problem.
6. The type of role they play in group situations.

These features are difficult on the whole to identify using other selection methods and one of the particular advantages of group selection methods is that they provide the selector with examples of behaviour on which to select. When future job performance is being considered it is behaviour in the job that is critical, and so selection using group methods can provide direct information on which to select rather than indirect verbal information or test results.

Plumbley (1985) identifies three main types of group task that can be used, each of which would be observed by the selectors:

1. *Leaderless groups*: A group of about six to eight individuals are given a topic of general interest to discuss.
2. *Command or executive exercises*: The members of the group are allocated roles in an extensive brief based on a real-life situation. Each member outlines his/her solution on the basis of their role and defends it to the rest of the group.
3. *Group problem solving*: The group is leaderless and has to organize itself in order to solve, within time-limits, a problem which is relevant to the job to be filled.

Business games and case studies may also be used. There are further details about these techniques as they are used in the training situation in Chapter 25. Participants are observed during the group activities, and the observers note the quality and quantity of social and intellectual skills of each individual.

Group selection methods are most suitable for management and sometimes supervisory posts. One of the difficulties with group selection methods is that it can be difficult to assess an individual's contribution, and some individuals may be unwilling to take part.

Review topic 18.3

To what extent does an individual's behaviour on these group selection tasks accurately reflect behaviour on the job? Why?

Assessment centres

Assessment centres could be described as multiple method group selection (Lewis 1985). The group selection techniques outlined above form a major element of assessment centre selection, and are used in conjunction with other work simulation exercises such as in-basket tasks (described in more detail in Chapter 25), psychological tests and a variety of interviews. Assessment centres are used to assess, in depth, a group of broadly similar applicants. At the end of the procedure the judges have to come to agreement on a cumulative rating for each individual, related to job requirements, taking into account all the selection activities. The procedure as a whole is then validated against job performance rather than each separate activity. The predictive validities from such procedures are not very consistent, but there is a high 'face validity' – there is a feeling that this is a fairer way of selecting people. The chief disadvantages of these selection methods are that it is a costly and time-consuming procedure, the time commitment being extended by the need to give some feedback to candidates who have been through such a long procedure which involves psychological assessment. Fletcher (1986) gives some guidelines on how this feedback can be organized. Time commitment is also high in the development of such activities. Smith and Tarpey (1987) describe how inter-rater reliability can vary in the assessment of in-tray exercises. Reliability was much improved by the quality of assessor training, greater clarity in marking instructions, more time allowed for marking, and a structured approach to marking. All these activities are very time-consuming.

Work sampling

Work sampling of potential candidates for permanent jobs can take place by assessing candidates' work in temporary posts or on the Youth Training Scheme in the same organization. For some jobs, such as photographers and artists, a sample of work in the form of a portfolio is expected to be presented at the time of interview.

References

One way of informing the judgement of managers who have to make employment offers to selected individuals is the use of references. Previous employers or others with appropriate credentials are cited by candidates and then requested by prospective employers to provide information. There are two types: the factual check and the character reference.

The factual check

This is fairly straightforward as it is no more than a confirmation of facts that the candidate has presented. It will normally follow the employment interview and decision to offer a post. It does no more than confirm that the facts are accurate.

The knowledge that such a check will be made – or may be made – will help focus the mind of candidates so that they resist the temptation to embroider their story.

The character reference

This is a very different matter. Here the prospective employer asks for an opinion about the candidate before the interview so that the information gained can be used in the decision-making phases. The logic of this strategy is impeccable: who knows the working performance of the candidate better than the previous employer? The wisdom of the strategy is less sound, as it depends on the writers of references being excellent judges of working performance, faultless communicators and – most difficult of all – disinterested. The potential inaccuracies of decisions influenced by character references begin when the candidate decides who to cite. They will have some freedom of choice and will clearly choose someone from whom they expect favourable comment, perhaps massaging the critical faculties with such comments as: 'I think references are going to be very important for this job.' 'You will do your best for me, won't you?'

Cowan and Cowan (1989) ask whether references are worth the paper they are written on, and conclude that they are mostly misused, and that two key questions should be. 'Would you re-employ this person?' and 'Do you know of any reason that we should not employ them?'

Other methods

A number of other less conventional methods such as physiognomy, phrenology, body language, palmistry, graphology and astrology have been suggested as possible selection methods. While these are fascinating to read about there is little evidence to suggest that they could be used effectively. Fowler (1990), however, comments on their greater use in the EC and pressures, therefore, for greater use in the United Kingdom. For further information on graphology, see Lynch and Wilson (1985), and for graphology and other methods, see Mackenzie Davey (1982) and Mackenzie Davey and Harris (1982).

Using consultants

Consultants are increasingly involved in the recruitment and selection process and will in some cases directly apply a variety of the selection methods outlined above, although it is very rare that they would make the final selection decision.

The difficulty with using consultants is that organizations may have difficulty in communicating their exact requirements to the consultants and that some criteria, for example, ability to fit into the organization and be successful in it, are best judged directly by the personnel manager rather than by an intermediary. For a further discussion of the consultant's role in this and other areas see Chapter 13.

Validation of selection procedures

We have already mentioned how test scores may be validated against eventual job performance for each individual in order to discover whether the test score is a good predictor of success in the job. In this way we can decide whether the test should be used as part of the selection procedure. The same idea can be applied to the use of other individual or combined selection methods.

The critical information that is important for determining validity is the selection criteria used, the selection processes used, an evaluation of the individual at the time of selection and current performance of the individual.

Selection criteria

The selection criteria will be those derived from the job description, and from any departmental and organizational requirements which have been combined in the personnel specification.

The processes used

The processes used include the selection methods that are chosen, together with any weightings that were applied. For example, test scores may have contributed 25 per cent to the final selection decision and interview assessment have contributed 75 per cent. The weighting of the various selection methods used will depend on the requirements of the person specification and must be decided in advance of the selection procedures taking place.

Evaluation of individuals at the time of selection

If a group of individuals are selected at the same time, for example, graduate trainees, it will be unlikely that they were all rated equally highly in spite of the fact that they were all considered employable. It is useful for validation purposes if selected individuals are graded according to how well they performed in the selection procedure. Some sophisticated systems will enable a percentage score to be produced, but the activity need not be arduous, and a simple grading system may suffice, for example:

A = Exceeds all selection criteria
B = Meets all selection criteria, and exceeds some
C = Meets all selection criteria
D = Meets most selection criteria

There is a variety of simple grading systems that could be used, and the method adopted will depend on the nature of the job, the selection criteria and the selection methods used. When more than one selection method is used the grading system may have to be more complex to cope with the amalgamation of results from each selection method.

Current performance

Current performance includes measures derived from the job description, together with additional performance measures:

1. *Measures from the job description*: Quantitative measures such as volume of sales, accuracy, number of complaints, and so on may be used, or qualitative measures like relations with customers and quality of reports produced.
2. *Other measures*: These may include appraisal results, problems identified, absence data and, of course, termination.

Current performance is often assessed in an intuitive, subjective way, and while this may sometimes be useful it is no substitute for objective assessment.

Validation

Selection ratings for each individual can be compared with eventual performance over a variety of time-periods. Large discrepancies between selection and performance ratings point to further investigation of the selection methods used, the weightings of each method the selectors used, and the appropriateness of the selection criteria. The comparison of selection rating and performance rating can also be used to compare different selection criteria.

There is a number of other approaches to the validation of selection procedures, some more sophisticated than the one that we have outlined. We suggest the above system on the basis that investment in a simple system is better than investment in no system at all.

Selection, the law and equality of opportunity

The law puts pressure on employers to select employees in a non-discriminating way in terms of sex and race. There is also some less effective pressure on employers not to discriminate in terms of age and disability (except for positive discrimination). These issues are dealt with in more detail in Chapter 21:

Summary propositions

18.1 Selection is a two-way process. The potential employer and the potential employee both make selection decisions.

18.2 A combination of selection methods is usually chosen, based upon the job, appropriateness, acceptability, time, administrative ease, cost, accuracy, and the abilities of the selection staff.

18.3 The application form as a selection method is frequently under-used or misused.

18.4 Testing gives the appearance of accuracy but correlations with job performance are not particularly high and they are therefore not effective predictors.

18.5 Assessment centres have the advantage of providing a full range of selection methods, but they have not been able to claim consistently high predictive validities with job performance.

18.6 Selection methods should be validated. A simple system is better than no system at all.

References

Allan, J. (1990), 'How to recruit the best people', *Management Accounting*, February.

Anderson, N. and Shackleton, V. (1990) 'Staff selection decision making into the 1990s', *Management Decision*, vol. 28, no. 1.

Cattell, R. B. (1965), *The Scientific Analysis of Personality*, Harmondsworth: Penguin Books.

Cattell, R. B., Eber, H. W. and Tatsuoka, M. M. (1962), *Handbook for the Sixteen Personality Factor Questionnaire (16PF)*, London: NEFR Publishing.

Cowan, N. and Cowan, R. (1989) 'Are references worth the paper they're written on?', *Personnel Management*, December.

Drenth, P. (1978) 'Principles of selection', In P. B. Warr, (Ed.), *Psychology at Work*, Harmondsworth: Penguin Books.

Edwards, B. J. (1975), 'Application forms'. In B. Ungerson, (Ed.), *Recruitment Handbook* (2nd edition), Aldershot: Gower.

Eysenck, H. J. and S. B. G. (1963), *The Eysenck Personality Inventory*, London: University of London Press.

Fletcher, C. (1986), 'Should the test score be kept a secret?' *Personnel Management*, April.

Fowler, A. (1990), 'The writing on the wall', *Local Government Chronicle*, 26 January, pp. 20–8.

French, W. L. (1974), *The Personnel Management Process* (3rd edition), Boston: Houghton Mifflin.

Ghiselli, E. E. (1966), *The Validity of Occupational Aptitude Tests*, Chichester: John Wiley.

Glueck, W. F. (1985), *Personnel: A diagnostic approach* (4th edition), Dallas, Texas: Business Publications.

Harrison, R. G. (1979), 'New personnel practice: life goals planning and interpersonal skill development: a programme for middle managers in the British Civil Service', *Personnel Review*, vol. 8, no. 1.

Herriot, P. (1985), 'Give and take in graduate selection', *Personnel Management*, May.

Hollis, W. P. (1984), 'Developing managers for social change', *Journal of Management Development*, vol. 3, no. 1.

Jenkins, J. F. (1983), 'Management trainees in retailing', In B. Ungerson, (Ed.), *Recruitment Handbook* (3rd edition), Aldershot: Gower.

Jessup, G. and Jessup, H. (1975), *Selection and Assessment at Work*, London: Methuen.

Jucius, M. J. (1974), *Personnel Management* (7th edition), Homewood, Ill.: Irwin.

Lewis, C. (1985), *Employee Selection*, London: Hutchinson.

Lynch, B. and Wilson, R. (1985), 'Graphology – towards a hand-picked workforce', *Personnel Management*, March.

Mackenzie Davey, D. (1982), 'Arts and crafts of the selection process', *Personnel Management*, August.

Mackenzie Davey, D. and Harris, M. (1982), *Judging People*, Maidenhead: McGraw Hill.

Megginson, L. C. (1972), *Personnel: a behavioural approach to administration*, Homewood, Ill.: Irwin.

Miller, K. M. (1975), 'Personality assessment', In B. Ungerson, (Ed.), *Recruitment Handbook* (2nd edition), Aldershot: Gower.

Miner, J. B. (1969), *Personnel Psychology*, Basingstoke: Macmillan.

Pigors, P. and Myers, C. S. (1981), *Personnel Administration* (9th edition), New York: McGraw Hill.

Plumbley, P. R. (1985), *Recruitment and Selection* (4th edition), London: Institute of Personnel Management.

Robertson, I. T. and Makin, P. J., (1986) 'Management Selection in Britain; A Survey and Critique', *Journal of Occupational Psychology*, vol. 59, pp. 45–57.

Saville and Holdsworth Ltd (1984), *Manual of the Occupational Personality Questionnaire*.

Smith, D. and Tarpey, T. (1987), 'In-tray exercises and assessment centres; the issue of reliability', *Personnel Review*, vol. 16, no. 3, pp. 24–8.

Sweetland, R. C., Keyser, D. J. and O'Connor, W. A. (1983), *Tests*, Kansas City: Test Corporation of America.

Swinburne, P. (1985), 'A comparison of the OPQ and 16PF in relation to their occupational application', *Personnel Review*, vol. 14, no. 4.

Thurstone, L. L. (1938), 'Primary mental abilities', *Psychometric Monographs*, no. 1, Chicago: University of Chicago Press.

Tiffin, J. and McCormick, E. J. (1966), *Industrial Psychology* (3rd edition), London: George Allen & Unwin Ltd.

Torrington, D. P. (1969), *Successful Personnel Management*, p. 36. Staples Press.

Vernon, P. (1961), *The Structure of Human Abilities* (2nd edition), London: Methuen.

Willis, Q. (1984), 'Managerial research and management development', *Journal of Management Development*, vol. 3, no. 1.

Wills, J. (1990), 'Cracking the nut', *Local Government Chronicle*, 26 January, pp. 22–3.

19

Employment interviewing and decision-making

We now discuss one of the most familiar and forbidding encounters of organizational life – the employment interview. Most people have had at least one experience of being interviewed as a preliminary to employment and few reflect with pleasure on the experience. Usually, this is because the interviewer seems more concerned with finding fault than with being helpful. Personnel departments have a critical role in selection interviewing. This role involves them in carrying out many of the interviews and also in encouraging good interviewing practice in others by example, support and training.

In this chapter we begin by looking at a definition of and varieties of employment interviewing. We then consider the criticism that has been made of the selection interview, and in spite of its importance as a selection tool. Interview strategy and the number of interviews and interviewers are then considered. Interview preparation, structure and conduct are then dealt with. The chapter concludes with a section on employment decision making.

Varieties of interview

There is a wide variety of practice in employment interviewing. At one extreme we read of men seeking work in the docks of Victorian London and generally being treated as if they were in a cattle market. In sharp contrast is the attitude of Sherlock Holmes to a prospective employer:

> I can only say, madam, that I shall be happy to devote the same care to your case as I did to that of your friend. As to reward, my profession is its reward; but you are at liberty to defray whatever

expenses I may be put to, at the time which suits you best. (Conan Doyle 1966)

There is a neat spectrum of employee participation in the employment process which correlates with social class and type of work. While the London docks situation of the 1890s is not found today, there are working situations where the degree of discussion between the parties is limited to perfunctory exchanges about trade union membership, hours of work and rates of pay: labourers on building sites and extras on film sets being two examples. In most manual employment the emphasis of the interview is largely on the representative of the organization questioning the applicant to judge their prospective competence. As interviews move up the organizational hierarchy there is growing equilibrium with the interviewer becoming more courteous and responsive to questions from the applicant, who will probably be described as a 'candidate' or 'someone who might be interested in the position'. For the most senior positions it is unlikely that people will be invited to respond to vacancies advertised in the press. Individuals will be approached, either directly or through consultants, and there will be an elaborate pavane in which each party seeks to persuade the other to declare an interest first. Chairmen of large organizations, retired prime ministers and those of comparable stature apparently just wait for offers.

Another indication of the variety of employment practice is in the titles used. The humblest of applicants seek 'jobs' or 'vacancies', while the more ambitious are looking for 'places', 'posts', 'positions', 'openings' or 'opportunities'. The really high-flyers seem to need somewhere to sit down, as they are offered 'seats on the board', 'professorial chairs' or 'places on the front bench'.

Definition and purpose of a selection interview

An interview is a controlled conversation with a purpose. In an interview there is a higher number of exchanges in a shorter period of time related to a specific purpose than in an ordinary conversation. In the selection interview the purposes are:

1. To collect information in order to predict how successfully the individual would perform in the job for which they have applied, by measuring them against predetermined criteria.
2. To provide the candidate with full details of the job and organization to facilitate their decision-making.
3. As Plumbley (1985) suggests, to conduct the interview in such a manner that candidates feel that they have been given a fair hearing.

Criticism of the interview

The interview has been extensively criticized as being unreliable, invalid and subjective. There has been much criticism of it as a means of managerial selection of candidates rather than as a ritual in the employment process. In his helpful review of recent research, Morgan comments:

> The bald conclusion from all the empirical evidence is that the interview as typically used is not much good as a selection device. Indeed, one might wonder, thinking rationally, why the interview was not long ago 'retired' from selection procedures. (Morgan 1973, p. 5)

This opinion is echoed by Sidney and Brown:

> Some of the results of attempts to assess the value of the interview have been so depressing that people have argued that it should be replaced wherever possible by more objective procedures, such as intelligence and personality tests. (Sidney and Brown 1966, p. 186)

Lopez (1975) maintains that interview results should be treated with great caution until further research and refinement indicate that they can be used with greater confidence.

It is difficult to justify the interview as an accurate way of predicting working performance, and there is disturbing evidence of the inability of different interviewers to agree in the evaluation of the same candidates (for example, Wagner 1949).

The most perceptive criticism is contained in the work of Webster (1964) summarizing extensive research. The main conclusions were:

1. Interviewers decided to accept or reject a candidate within the first three or four minutes of the interview and then spent the remainder of the interview time seeking evidence to confirm that their first impression was right.
2. Interviews seldom altered the tentative opinion formed by the interviewer seeing the application form and the appearance of the candidate.
3. Interviewers place more weight on evidence that is unfavourable than on evidence that is favourable.
4. When interviewers have made up their minds very early in the interview, their behaviour betrays their decision to the candidate.

However much this criticism is justified, it does not solve the problem, it only identifies it. Lopez points to the fact that all the complaints and denunciations boil down to the argument that it is the interviewer and not the interview that is at the heart of the problem (Lopez 1975, p. 5). The critical feature, then, is how the interview is handled. Some guidance in dealing with interviews and other interpersonal encounters is found in Chapter 10 and additional information specifically relating to the selection interview is found further on in this chapter. Also, in spite of the limitations of the interview, it can provide a number of important advantages which cannot be provided by any other means.

Review topic 19.1

In what ways might a personnel manager work to improve managers' interviewing skills?

Importance of the interview

There is a number of areas in which the potential of the interview cannot be surpassed by other selection methods. These areas are the collecting and giving out of information and the human and ritual aspects of the interview.

The potential for collecting information

The interview is a very flexible and speedy means for gathering information. If carried out well it can be a very inclusive method as it can take into account a broader range of factors than can be tested. Furthermore, it is a logical conclusion to the employment process, as information from a variety of sources – such as application forms, tests and references – can be discussed together.

The potential for giving information

The employer is given the opportunity to sell the company and explain job details in depth. The employee has the chance to ask questions about the job and the company in order to satisfy the information requirements for his selection decision.

Human aspects

In an interview some assessment can be made of matters that cannot be approached any other way, like the potential compatibility of two people who will have to work together. Both parties need to meet each other before the contract begins to 'tune in' to each other and begin the process of induction. The interview is therefore acceptable to both potential employee and potential employer. As Lopez suggests, it gives interviewees the feeling that they matter as another person is devoting time to them and they are not being considered by a computer. Also, since it gives the applicants a chance to ask questions, they feel that they are making the decision. It not only provides a means of giving a candidate a fair hearing, it also demonstrates to candidates that they are being given a fair hearing.

Ritual aspects

The interview is important as ritual behaviour. It is necessary for the outsider to present himself and display certain performances before the representatives of the organization as an initiation ceremony. The significance of the ritual is illustrated by the experience of one of the authors who gives a lecture on the interview each year to third-year undergraduates as part of a programme run by the University Careers and Appointments Service. The size of the audience (300–400) is larger than that for any other lecture in the programme, showing the anxiety of those entering the labour market about this feature of their entry. Also, the questions asked are usually about behaviour in the ritual: whether or not to shake hands, what to wear, whether to smoke, when to stand up, how formal to be, how to address the interviewer, and so forth. There is a clear conviction that there is a set of insider rules, knowledge of which will lead to success.

No matter what other means of making employment decisions there may be, the interview is crucial, and when worries are expressed about its reliability, this is not a reason for doing away with it: it is a reason for conducting it properly.

Interview strategy

Interview strategy can vary considerably. Those strategies relevant to the selection interview can be categorized in the following ways.

Frank and friendly strategy

This type of interview has been suggested by Hackett (1978). Here the interviewer is concerned to establish and maintain the rapport, which is described in greater detail in Chapter 10. This is done partly in the belief that if interviewees do not feel threatened, and are relaxed, they will be more forthcoming in the information that they offer. This approach also has the potential advantage that the interviewees will leave feeling reassured and with a favourable impression of the company.

Problem solving strategy

A variation of the frank and friendly strategy is the problem-solving approach. It is the method of presenting the candidate with a hypothetical problem and evaluating his or her answer, like the king in the fairy tale who offered the hand of the princess in marriage to the first suitor who could answer three riddles.

These interviews are sometimes called situational interviews. The questions asked are derived from the job description and candidates are required to imagine themselves as the job holder and describe what they would do in a variety of hypothetical situations.

This method is most applicable to testing elementary knowledge, like the colour coding of wires in electric cables or maximum dosages of specified drugs. It is less effective to test understanding and ability, like the following intriguing poser put to a candidate for the position of security officer at a large department store:

> If you were alone in the building and decided to inspect the roof, what would you do if the only door out on to the roof banged itself shut behind you and the building caught fire?

The retired police superintendent to whom that question was posed asked, very earnestly and politely, for six pieces of additional information, like the location of telephones, time of day, height of building, fire escapes. The replies become progressively more uncertain and the interviewer hastily shifted the ground of the interview to something else. Even if that pitfall can be avoided and the candidate produces an answer that can be assessed, there is no guarantee that he would do what he says he would. The quick thinker will score at the expense of the person who can take action more effectively than they can answer riddles.

Behavioural event strategy

This method is similar to the problem-solving strategy, but the questions are about real situations and events in which the candidate has been involved. The focus is therefore on past behaviour and performance, which is a more reliable way of predicting future performance than asking the interviewee what they would do in a certain situation. Examples of questions used in this type of interview are given by Jenks and Zevnik (1989). Candidates are requested to describe the background to a situation and explain what they did and why; what their options were; how they decided what to do; and the anticipated and real results of their action. The success of this method is critically dependent on in-depth job analysis, and preferably competency analysis in order to frame the best questions.

Patterned Behaviour Description strategy

This approach is a slightly different method of using past behaviour to predict the future. With the Patterned Behaviour Description interview major life-event changes are explored with the interviewee. From this the interviewer aims to achieve an understanding of the candidate's reasoning in moving from one thing to the next.

Stress strategy

The stress approach is where the interviewer becomes aggressive, disparages the candidate, puts him or her on the defensive or disconcerts them by strange behaviour. The Office of Strategic Services in the United States used this method in the Second World War to select men for espionage work, and subsequently the idea was used by some business organizations on the premise that executive life was stressful, so a simulation of the stress would determine whether or not the candidate could cope.

   The advantage of the method is that it may demonstrate a necessary strength or a disqualifying weakness that would not be apparent through other methods. The disadvantages are that evaluating the behaviour under stress is problematical, and those who are not selected will think badly of the employer.

   The likely value of stress interviewing is so limited that it is hardly worth mentioning, except that it has such spurious appeal to many managers, who are attracted by the idea of injecting at least some stress into the interview 'to see what they are made of', 'to put them on their mettle' or some similar jingoism. Most candidates feel that the procedures are stressful enough, without adding to them. In addition, Sidney and Brown comment:

> There is seldom any reason for assuming that the stress of dealing
> with a hostile . . . potential . . . employer . . . resembles the kind of
> stress the applicant would be asked to face if he were appointed . . .
> the [stress] interview yields possible evidence on only one aspect of
> personality . . . and perforce omits much else that should be relevant.
> (Sidney and Brown 1961, pp. 164–5)

Sweet and sour strategy

The sweet and sour strategy has been described by Hackett (1978) and is similar to the frank and friendly approach being based on the idea that when the interviewee is relaxed they will be more forthcoming. It differs from the frank and friendly interview in that it presupposes that they are most likely to feel relaxed if this relaxation follows a period of pressure. The candidate is interviewed by a team of two interviewers. The first interviews in a hard, stressful manner and then the second takes a turn, apologizes for his or her colleague and appears sympathetic, which is theoretically designed to encourage the interviewee to tell all. This approach is less damaging to the public image than a stress interview, but has little else to commend it.

Screening interview

The screening interview is styled on the frank and friendly basis, but differs in that it is seen as an initial rather than a full interview, and is therefore briefer and more superficial.

Number of interviews and interviewers

There are two broad traditions governing the number of interviewers. One tradition says that effective, frank discussion can only take place on a one-to-one basis, so candidates meet one interviewer, or several interviewers, one at a time. The other tradition is that fair play must be demonstrated and nepotism prevented so the interview must be carried out, and the decision made, by a panel of interviewers. Within this dichotomy there are various options.

The individual interview

This method gives the greatest chance of establishing rapport, developing mutual trust and the most efficient deployment of time in the face-to-face encounter, as each participant has to compete with only one other speaker. It is usually also the most satisfactory method for the candidate, who has to tune in only to one other person instead of needing constantly to adjust their antennae to different interlocutors. They can more readily ask questions, as it is difficult to ask a panel of six people to explain the workings of the pension scheme, and it is the least formal.

The disadvantages lie in the dependence the organization places on the judgement of one of its representatives – although this can be mitigated by a series of individual interviews – and the ritual element is largely missing. Candidates may not feel they have been 'done' properly. Our recent research indicates that a sole interview with the line manager is very popular in the selection of blue-collar staff, being used in over one third of cases. It is much less popular for white-collar and management staff. Table 19.1 shows how different numbers of interviews and interviewers are used for the different groups of staff.

Table 19.1   Number of interviews and interviewers used for blue-collar, white-collar and managerial staff

Number of interviews and interviewers	Percentage of survey replies		
	Blue-collar	White-collar	Managerial
Line interview only	38.3	10.9	6.0
Line interview and personnel interview	39.6	45.0	10.4
More than two interviews	2.0	7.7	32.1
Panel interview	13.8	25.7	38.7
Other	2.7	2.4	3.6
Combinations	3.7	8.3	9.2
Total[a]	100.1	100.0	100.0

a, Totals do not necessarily add up to 100 due to the effects of rounding.

Review topic 19.2

Table 19.1 shows that a representative of the personnel function often takes part in selection interviews. What variety of roles might the personnel manager play in selection interviews?

Sequential interviews

This is a series of individual interviews. Our recent research indicates that the series most often consists of just two interviews for blue- and white-collar staff, but more than two for managerial staff. The most frequent combination is an interview with the line manager and an interview with a representative of the personnel department. For managerial posts this will be extended to interviews with other departmental managers, top managers and significant prospective colleagues. These extended interviews are often used for academic posts where five or six interviews may take place with professors, lecturers and researchers, most of whom will be working in the same or similar fields. In academic circles, of course, this series would be followed by a panel interview for the most promising candidates. Sequential interviews are useful as they can give the employer a broader picture of the candidate and they also allow the applicant to have contact with a greater number of potential bosses and colleagues. However, the advantages of sequential interviews need to be based on effective organization and interviews all on the same day. Lopez (1975) argues that it is important that all interviewers meet beforehand to agree on the requirements of the post and decide how each will contribute to the overall theme. Immediately following the interviews a further meeting needs to take place so that the candidates can be jointly evaluated. One disadvantage of the method is the organization and time that it takes from both the employer's and the candidate's point of view. It requires considerable commitment from the candidate who may have to keep repeating similar information and whose performance may deteriorate throughout the interviews due to fatigue.

Interviews in tandem

These interviews have the advantage of providing evaluation from two interviewers while only organizing the one interview. They are less formidable than a panel interview, which consists of more than two interviewers, but it is still more difficult to develop rapport than in the individual interview. Interviews in tandem are most likely to be carried out by the departmental head and a representative from the personnel department.

Panel interviews

This method has the specious appeal of sharing judgement and may appear to be a way of saving time in interviewing as all panel members are operating at once. It is also possible to legitimize a quick decision – always popular with candidates – and there can be no doubt about the ritual requirements being satisfied. Muir (1988) also argues that panel interviews are less influenced by personal bias, ensure the candidate is more acceptable to the whole organization, and allow the candidate to get a better feel for the whole organization.

The drawbacks lie in the tribunal nature of the panel. They are not having a conversation with the candidate; they are sitting in judgement upon them and assessing the evidence they are able to present in response to their requests. Careful jockeying ensures that candidates commit themselves before the interview, as a standard opening question is: 'Are you still a candidate for this position?' There is little prospect of building rapport and developing discussion, and there is likely to be as much interplay between members of the panel as there is between the panel and the candidate. Alec Rodger makes the observation:

> The usefulness of the board interview may depend a good deal on the competence of the chairman, and on the good sense of board members.
>
> A promising board interview can easily be ruined by a member who does not appreciate the line of questioning being pursued by one of his fellow-members and who interrupts with irrelevancies. (Rodger 1975)

Panel interviews tend to over-rigidity and give ironic point to the phrase 'it is only a formality'. Ritualistically they are superb, but as a useful preliminary to employment they are questionable.

In this context it is interesting to note Argyle's comment on the social skills that candidates should display:

> Interviewers seem to prefer candidates who are well-washed and quietly dressed, who are politely attentive, submissive and keen, and they are likely to reject candidates who are rude, over-dominant, not interested or irritating in other ways. There seems to be a definite 'role of the candidate' – he is expected to be nicely behaved and submissive – although he may not be expected to be quite like that if he gets the job.
>
> There are certain subtleties about being a good candidate – it is necessary for the candidate to draw attention to his good qualities while remaining modest and submissive. He may need to show what a decisive and forceful person he is – but without using these powers on the selection board. (Argyle 1972)

However, the benefits of the panel interview can be gained, and the disadvantages minimized, if the interviewers are well trained and the interview well organized, thoroughly planned and is part of a structured interviewing process, as, for example, described by Campion, Pursell and Brown (1988).

Group interviews

These interviews are not generally common, or applicable, but may be used for certain types of job, particularly in sales. It is a method where a group of candidates are interviewed simultaneously by one or more interviewers. The interviewers can monitor the interviewees in a competitive situation and can make some assessment of their self-confidence, aggressiveness and sociability. From the point of view of the candidate, however, the process is somewhat daunting, especially the first time that it is encountered.

Review topic 19.3

In your organization how many interviews and interviewers are used?
How effective is this approach and why?
In what ways could the approach be improved?

Interview preparation

Preparation for all aspects of the interview is critical to its effectiveness.

Interviewer briefing

We assume that the preliminaries of job analysis, recruitment and shortlisting are complete and the interview is now to take place. The first step in preparation is for the interviewer to brief themselves. They will collect and study:

- Job description for the post to be filled.
- Personnel specification/competencies.
- Application forms.

They will now have refreshed their memory about the post and the candidates, as well as the specification of the ideal candidate. This will enable them to make their pre-interview notes in line with the requirements of the encounter, and to plan the structure of the interview(s). Structure is dealt with more detail on pages 319–23.

Timetable

If there are several people to be interviewed the interview period needs greater planning than it usually receives. The time required for each interview can only approximately be determined beforehand. A rigid timetable will weigh heavily on both parties, who will feel frustrated if the interview is closed arbitrarily at a predetermined time and uncomfortable if an interview that has 'finished' is drawn out to complete its allotted span. However, the disadvantages of keeping people waiting are considerable and under-rated.

Conventional thinking seems to be that candidates are supplicants, waiting on interviewers' pleasure, they have no competing calls on their time and a short period of waiting demonstrates who is in charge. There is a number of flaws in this reasoning. At least some candidates will have competing calls on their time, as they will have taken time off without pay to attend. Some may have other interviews to go to. An open-ended waiting period can be worrying, enervating and a poor preliminary to an interview. If the dentist keeps you waiting you may get distressed, but when the waiting is over you are simply a passive participant and the dentist does not have the success of his operation jeopardized. The interview candidate has, in a real sense, to perform when the period of waiting is over and the success of the interaction could well be jeopardized.

The most satisfactory timetable is the one what guarantees a break after all but the most voluble candidates. If candidates are asked to attend at hourly intervals, for example, this would be consistent with interviews lasting between 40 and 60 minutes. This would mean that each interview began at the scheduled time and that the interviewer had the opportunity to review and update their notes in the intervals.

Reception

The candidate arrives on the premises of their prospective employer on the look out for every scrap of evidence they can obtain about the organization – what it looks like what the people look like, and what people say. Although no research has been carried out on the subject, it is reasonable to suppose that candidates make judgements as quickly as interviewers, and we have already seen that at least one study (Webster 1964) found interviewers making their decisions within a few minutes and then using the rest of the time to confirm it. A candidate is likely to meet at least one and possibly two people before they meet the interviewer. First will be the commissionaire or receptionist. There is frequently also an emissary from the personnel department to shepherd them from the gate to the waiting-room. Both are valuable sources of information, and interviewers may wish to prime such people so that they can see their role in the employment process and can be cheerful, informative and helpful.

The candidate will most want to meet the interviewer, the unknown but powerful figure on whom so much depends. Interviewers easily forget that they know much more about the candidates than the candidates know about them, because the candidates have provided a personal profile in the application form.

Interviewers do not reciprocate. To bridge this gap it can be very useful for interviewers to introduce themselves to the candidate in the waiting-room, so that contact is made quickly, unexpectedly and on neutral territory and the rapport stage of the interview when it begins later is made easier.

Waiting

Candidates wait to be interviewed. Although there are snags about extended open-ended waiting periods, some time is inevitable and necessary to enable the candidate to compose themself. It is a useful time to deal with travelling expenses and provide some relevant background reading about the employing organization.

Setting

The appropriate setting for an interview has to be considered both from the point of view of what is right for the ritual and from the point of view of what will enable a full and frank exchange of information. It is difficult to combine the two.

Many of the interview horror stories relate to the setting in which it took place, like the candidate for a post as Deputy Clerk of Works who was interviewed on a stage while the panel of seventeen sat in the front row of the stalls. The author observed an educational panel in operation on one occasion when a candidate came in and actually moved the chair on which he was to sit. He only moved it two or three inches because the sun was in his eyes, but there was an audible frisson and sharp intake of breath from the members of the panel.

Remaining with our model of the individual interviewer, there is a series of simple suggestions about the setting.

1. The room should be suitable for a private conversation.
2. If the interview takes place across a desk, as is common, the interviewer may wish to reduce the extent to which the desk acts as a barrier, emphasizing the distance between the parties and therefore inhibiting free flow of communication.
3. Visitors and telephone calls will not simply interrupt: they will intrude and impede the likelihood of frankness.
4. It should be clear to the candidate where they are to sit.

Interview structure

There is a number of important reasons why the employment interview should be structured:

1. The candidate expects the proceedings to be decided and controlled by the interviewer and will anticipate a structure within which to operate.
2. It helps the interviewer to make sure that they cover all relevant areas and avoid irrelevant ones.
3. It looks professional. Structure can be used to guide the interview and make it make sense.
4. It assists the interviewer in using the time available in the most effective way.
5. It can be used as a memory aid when making notes directly after the interview.
6. It can make it easier to compare candidates.

The interview can be structured in a number of different ways. Among the helpful outlines developed in recent years is the WASP method of Sidney, Brown and Argyle (1973), where the interaction is set in the four stages of Welcome, Acquiring information, Supplying information and Parting.

A structure that we would recommend is set out in Table 19.2. This structure divides activities and objectives into three interview stages: beginning, middle and end. While there are few, if any, alternative satisfactory ways for conducting the beginning and the end of the interview, the middle can be approached from a number of different angles, depending on the circumstances. The various approaches are discussed in more detail in the following section on conducting the interview.

The interviewer needs to work systematically through the structure that has been planned, but the structure does not have to be adhered to rigidly. As Sidney and Brown (1961) suggest, interviewers should abandon their own route wherever the candidate chooses one that seems more promising.

Table 19.2 Interview structure: a recommended pattern

Interview stage	Objectives	Activities
Beginning	Put the candidate at ease Develop rapport and set the scene	Greet candidate by name Introduce self Neutral chat Agree interview purpose Outline how purpose will be achieved
Middle	To collect and give information, maintain rapport	Asking questions within a structure. Structure might be biographical, in chronological order or backwards; or based on areas of information, such as work, education, training, or based on competencies identified for the job Listening Asking questions Answering questions
End	Close the interview and confirm future action	Summarize interview Check candidate has no more questions Indicate what happens next and when

Conducting the interview

The interview process

Beginning

The opening of the encounter is the time for mutual preliminary assessment and tuning in to each other. Rapport is discussed later in this chapter, but one or two specific points about it in this context can be added.

A useful feature of this phase is for the interviewer to sketch out the plan or procedure for the encounter and how it fits in with the total employment decision process. It is also likely that the application form will provide an easy, non-controversial topic for these opening behaviours.

One objective is for the two parties to exchange words so that they can adjust their receiving mechanism in order to be mutually intelligible. It also provides an opportunity for both to feel comfortable in the presence of the other. If the interviewer is able to achieve these two objectives they may then succeed in developing a relationship in which the candidate trusts the interviewer's ability and motives so that they will speak openly and fully.

The interviewer's effectiveness will greatly depend on their skill with rapport. Bayne regards a prerequisite as being a 'calm-alert' state of consciousness that can be sustained throughout the interview:

> At times the good interviewer is sharp and in focus, specific and rational; at other times intuitive, picking up nuances and rationaliza-tions; at others stepping back to see the whole interaction, fitting things together and taking note of the amount of time left and the areas to cover . . . the interviewer's calmness helps the candidate to relax and his or her clear perception allows productive silences and the easy asking of questions. The state also counteracts habituation to interviews, when the interviewer is calm but bored. And it allows intuitive processes as well as the usual thinking, evaluating ones. (Bayne 1977)

Middle

The biographical approach is the most straightforward. It works on the basis that the candidate at the time of the interview is a product of everything in their life that has gone before. To understand the candidate the interviewer must understand the past and they will question the candidate, or talk to the candidate, about the episodes of his or her earlier life – education, previous employment, etc.

The advantage of this is that the objectives are clear to both interviewer and interviewee, there is no deviousness or 'magic'. Furthermore, the development can be logical and so aid the candidate's recall of events. Candidates who reply to inquiries about their choice of 'A' level subjects will be subconsciously triggering their recollection of contemporaneous events, like the university course they took, which are likely to come next in the interview. The biographi-cal approach is the simplest for the inexperienced interviewer to use as discussion can develop from the information provided by the candidate on their application form.

One American author has produced an interview structure, which suggests the interviewer begin with questions about the employment history of the candidate and then goes through their educational record, early home background and present social adjustment (Fear 1958). This has the advantage that it begins with what the candidate is best able to handle and later moves to those areas that are not so easy to recall.

Some authorities counsel a more detailed approach by prescribing a checklist of questions to be asked. A form designed by Dodd (1970) includes a series of boxes at every stage in which the interviewer is asked to check 'acceptable or unacceptable'. This highly structured method does, of course, turn the interview into an interrogation rather than a conversation, making it very difficult to unearth opinions and attitudes, as well as closing certain avenues of enquiry that might appear as the interview proceeds. Furthermore, it inhibits the candidate from initiating their own topics for discussion.

Some version of sequential categories like employment, education and training, etc., seems the most generally useful, but it will need to have the addition of at least two other categories: the work offered and the organizational context in which it is to be done. The middle of the interview can be structured by systematically working through items of the job description as Green (1983) describes, or the person specification. Increasingly, where competencies have been identified for the job, these are used as the basis of the structure.

In the preparatory stage of briefing the interviewer will also prepare notes on two elements to incorporate in their plan: key issues and check-points.

Key issues will be the main two or three issues that stand out from the application form for clarification or elaboration. This might be the nature of the responsibilities carried in a particular earlier post, the content of a training course, the reaction to a period of employment in a significant industry, or whatever else strikes the interviewer as being productive of useful additional evidence.

Check-points are matters of detail that require further information: grades in an examination, dates of an appointment, rates of pay, and so forth.

End

The standard drill for disengagement can be used, but the explanation of the next step needs especial attention. The result of the interview is of great importance to the candidates and they will await the outcome with anxiety. Even if they do not want the position they will probably hope to have it offered. This may strengthen their hand in dealings with another prospective employer – or their present employer – and will certainly be a boost to their morale. The great merit of convention in the public sector is that the chosen candidate is told before the contenders disperse: the great demerit is that they are asked to say yes or no to the offer at once.

In the private sector it is unusual for an employment offer to be made at the time of the interview, so there is a delay during which the candidates will chafe. Their frustration will be greater if the delay is longer than expected and they may start to tell themselves that they are not going to receive an offer, in which case they will also start convincing themselves that they did not want the job either! It is important for the interviewer to say as precisely as possible when the offer will be made, but ensuring that the candidates hear earlier rather than later than they expect, if there is to be any deviation.

Interview purpose and method

Purpose

The substance of the interview is the exchange of data between the participants. Remembering again Webster's structure, we must declare that the purpose of this is to exchange data for the basis of judgements later. Judgement has to be deferred as long as possible in the interview, preferably until it is over. The interviewer's task is to elicit evidence as a preliminary to judgement and to provide it as required by the candidate for his decision-making.

The purpose of the interview can be summarized as an activity through which:

1. The interviewer gets to know the candidate.
2. The candidate gets to know the work being offered.
3. The candidate gets to know the organization in which the work is done.

The knowledge is not complete at the end of the interview, but it has to be sufficient for two decisions: the interviewer has to decide whether the candidate as the interviewer now knows him or her is the appropriate person for the vacant position, and the candidate has to decide whether the position is the one he or she wants to fill.

Method

To handle the interview the interviewer will need to call into play the tactics discussed in Chapter 10. There are five aspects of method.

Observation
Some data can be collected by simple observation of the candidate. Notes can be made about dress, appearance, voice, height and weight, if these are going to be relevant, and the interviewer can also gauge the candidate's mood and the appropriate response to it by the non-verbal cues that are provided.

Listening
The remainder of the interviewer's evidence will come from listening to what is said, so they have to be very attentive throughout. Not only are they listening to the answers to questions, they are listening for changes in inflection and pace, nuances and overtones that provide clues on what to pursue further. The amount of time that the two spend talking is important as an imbalance in one

direction or the other will mean that either the candidate or the interviewer is not having enough opportunity to hear information.

During these first two stages we must remember the danger of making yes/no decisions too quickly.

Questioning

In order to have something to hear the interviewer will have to direct the candidate. This, of course, is done by questioning, encouraging and enabling the candidate to talk, so that the interviewer can learn. The art of doing this depends on the personality and style of the interviewer who will develop their personal technique through a sensitive awareness of what is taking place in the interviews they conduct. Edgar Anstey has described this as the highest stage of interviewing skill:

> Once rapport has been established, the actual questions matter less and less. The candidate senses what one is getting at, without worrying about the form of words, becomes increasingly at ease and responds more spontaneously. This is the ideal . . . (Anstey 1977)

Of the ploys described in Chapter 10, those most appropriate to the employment interview are:

- Reward.
- Open-ended questions.
- Follow-up questions.
- Direct questions.
- Summary and re-run.
- Probes.
- Braking.

Closed questions may be needed to check-points, or as part of braking, but are generally to be discouraged in order to avoid a too interrogative style.

Notes

The best place to make notes is on the application form. In this way they can be joined to information that the candidate has already provided and the peculiar shorthand that people use when making notes during conversations can be deciphered by reference to the form and the data that the note is embellishing. It also means that the review of evidence after the interview has as much information as possible available on one piece of paper. An alternative is to record notes on the interview plan where the structure is based on job specification, person specification or competencies.

Interviewers are strangely inhibited about note-taking, feeling that it in some way impairs the smoothness of the interaction. This apprehension seems ill-founded as candidates are looking for a serious, businesslike discussion, no matter how informal, and note-taking offers no barrier providing that it is done carefully in the form of jottings during the discussion, rather than pointedly writing down particular comments by the candidate which make the interviewer seem like a police officer taking a statement.

Pace and control

Data exchange marks a change of gear in the interview. Rapport is necessarily rather rambling and aimless, but data exchange is purposeful and the interviewer needs to control both the direction and the pace of the exchanges. The candidate will be responsive throughout to the interviewer's control, and the better the rapport the more responsive they will be. The interviewer closes out areas of discussion and opens fresh ones. They head off irrelevant reminiscences and probes where matters have been glossed over. They can never abandon control. Even when the time has come for the candidates to raise all their queries they will do this at the behest of the interviewer and will look to him or her constantly for a renewal of the mandate to enquire by using conversational prefixes like 'Can I ask you another question . . .?', 'If it's not taking up your time, perhaps I could ask . . .?', 'I seem to be asking a lot of questions, but there was just one thing . . .'

Employment decision-making

The judgement of candidates should wait until after the interview. All available information must be gathered together in order to make the employment decision which rests on two bases. The primary concern is to match the individual against the demands of the job as described in the job specification. Secondly, each candidate needs to be compared with the others.

> Typically the line manager or the personnel man (or the two together) look over the application blanks, test results, and interview summaries, and make their decision on the basis of their subjective weighting of these imperfect indices and any other facts (or prejudices) they have at hand. Though this process can be called a clinical approach, often it is pure hunch. But most experienced personnel men feel that only in this way can the various important but unmeasurable intangibles be given proper consideration. (Strauss and Sayles 1972)

More mechanical methods have been devised whereby, for instance, points are awarded for different factors of the candidate specification and candidates are scored on each. The one with the highest score receives the first offer. This method worries many people, who feel that the element of human judgement is too closely proscribed. It can, however, provide useful criteria for judgement, and Green explains a system where points and weightings can used effectively by a panel, based on the elements of the job description.

Schneider (1976) stresses the importance of using an actuarial method to combine information mechanically from *all* validated performance predictors using a carefully thought-out statistical procedure, which allows every item of information to be appropriately weighted. Holman (1975) offers ideas on how to treat a range of factors in order to inform a subsequent decision.

The most familiar and popular method of producing decision criteria is the human attribute classification approach. The best known is the seven-point plan that was developed by Alec Rodger after extensive research in 1939 (Rodger 1951). Later, Fraser developed his five-fold grading (1958). More recently, Isbister (1968) has built on earlier experience with the National Institute of Industrial Psychology to produce his ROGBY scheme. All these provide a basis for consistency and system in making employment decisions.

The use of such systems has a number of advantages:

1. The classification can be used as a basis for the middle part of the interview.
2. It divides information into chunks and so encourages the interviewer to make sure that the information is as complete as possible.
3. It sets out the areas of information that are relevant to the employment decision.
4. It encourages the interviewer to think systematically about an applicant rather than using an unsubstantiated general impression which may be affected to a greater degree by their own biases and prejudices.
5. These systems emphasize facts and help to prevent concentration on subjective feelings.

In our recent research the most well-used systems were those designed by Fraser and Rodger, and these are shown in Table 19.3.

Table 19.3 Two well-used human attribute classification systems: Rodger's seven-point plan and Fraser's five-fold grading

Rodger's seven-point plan	Fraser's five-fold grading
Physical make-up	Impact on others
Attainments	Qualifications or acquired knowledge
General intelligence	Innate abilities
Special aptitudes	Motivation
Interests	Adjustment or emotional balance
Disposition	
Circumstances	

Summary propositions

19.1 Although strongly criticized, the interview is an essential feature of the selection process.

19.2 Most criticism of the interview relates to interviewer performance rather than the interview as a method.

19.3 The interview surpasses other selection methods in its potential for collecting and giving information, and in its human and ritual aspects.

19.4 Interview effectiveness can be improved by training and the use of structure.

19.5 In order to make employment decisions the candidate has to be matched primarily against the demands of the job, and secondarily against other candidates.

References

Anstey, E. (1977), quoted in R. Bayne, 'Can selection interviewing be improved'? The British Psychology Society Annual Occupational Psychology Conference, Sheffield.

Argyle, M. (1972), *The Psychology of Interpersonal Behaviour*, Harmondsworth: Penguin Books.

Bayne, R. (1977), 'Can selection interviewing be improved?' Paper presented to The British Psychological Society Annual Occupational Psychology Conference, Sheffield.

Campion, M. A., Pursell, E. D. and Brown B. K. (1988), 'Structured interviewing: Raising the psychometric properties of the employment interview', *Personnel Psychology*, vol. 41, pp. 25–43.

Conan Doyle, A. (1966), *The Adventures of Sherlock Holmes*, London: John Murray.

Dodd, J. H. B. (1970), 'Personnel selection – interviewing', *Applied Ergonomics*, September.

Fear, R. A. (1958), *The Evaluation Interview*, Maidenhead: McGraw-Hill.

Fletcher, J. (1973), *The Interview, at Work*, London: Duckworth.

Fraser, J. M. (1958), *A Handbook of Employment Interviewing*, London: Macdonald & Evans.

Green, J. (1983), 'Structured sequence interviewing', *Personnel Executive*, April.

Hackett, P. (1978), *Interview Skills Training: role play exercises*, London: Institute of Personnel Management.

Holman, L. J. (1975), In B. Ungerson, *Recruitment Handbook* (2nd edition), Aldershot: Gower.

Isbister, W. L. T. (1968), *Performance and Progress in Working Life*, Oxford: Pergamon.

Jenks, J. M. and Zevnik, L. P. (1989), 'ABCs of job interviewing', *Harvard Business Review*, July-August.

Lewis, C, (1986), *Employee Selection*, London: Hutchinson.

Lopez, F. M. (1975), *Personnel Interviewing* (2nd edition), Maidenhead: McGraw-Hill.

Morgan, T. (1973), 'Recent insights into the selection interview', *Personnel Review*, Winter.

Muir, J. (1988), 'Recruitment and selection', *Management Services*, November.

Plumbley, P, (1985), *Recruitment and Selection* (4th edition), London: Institute of Personnel Management.

Rodger, A. (1951), *The Seven Point Plan*, London: National Institute of Industrial Psychology.

Rodger, A. (1975), 'Interviewing techniques', In B. Ungerson, (Ed.), *Recruitment Handbook* (2nd edition), Aldershot: Gower.

Schneider, B. (1976), *Staffing Organizations*, Glenview, Ill.: Scott Foresman.

Sidney, E. and Brown, M. (1961), *The Skills of Interviewing*, London: Tavistock.

Sidney, E., Brown, M. and Argyle, M. (1973), *Skills with People*, London: Hutchinson.

Strauss, G. and Sayles, L. R. (1972), *Personnel: The human problems of management* (3rd edition), Englewood Cliffs, NJ: Prentice Hall.

Wagner, R. F. (1949), 'The employment interview: a critical appraisal', *Personnel Psychology*, vol. 2, pp. 17–40.

Webster, E. C. (1964), *Decision Making in the Employment Interview*, Industrial Relations Centre, McGill University, Canada.

West, A. (1983), 'Recruitment and selection', In D. Guest, and T. Kenny, (Eds.), *Textbook of Techniques and Strategies in Personnel Management*, London: Institute of Personnel Management.

20

Health, safety and welfare

There is always a conflict between the needs of the employer to push for increased output and efficiency and the needs of the employee to be protected from the hazards of the workplace. In the mid-nineteenth century these tensions centred almost entirely on the long hours and heavy physical demands of the factory system. In the closing years of the twentieth century the tensions are more varied and more subtle, but concern about them remains as great, being expressed by employers, employees, trade unions, government agencies and campaign groups. Some aspects of protection are provided by statute, but most come from the initiatives of managements, employees and their representatives. No matter what the source of the initiative or the nature of the concern, the personnel manager is the focus of whatever action has to be taken.

In this chapter we first consider definitions of health, safety and welfare, and then discuss the development and importance of this area of work and the role of personnel management. Following this we cover legislation relating to health, safety and welfare and then look at the management of health and safety matters. We conclude by discussing some more general aspects of occupational health and welfare.

Definitions of health, safety and welfare

The dictionary defines 'welfare' as 'well-being', so health and safety are strictly aspects of employee welfare, which have been separately identified as being significant areas of welfare provision for some time. Other authors (e.g. Beaumont 1984), have also noted that welfare can be very broadly defined. Using Fox (1966) as an example, he notes that welfare has been defined to encompass not only the early concern with workers' physical working conditions (sanitation, canteens, hours of work, rest pauses, etc.), but also the 'human relations school of thought', due to the achievement of job satisfaction being seen as a way to achieve higher productivity. He also notes the importance attached to counselling by early welfare workers and the human relations school.

There are two primary areas of benefit to the individual from the provision of welfare facilities – physical benefits and emotional/psychological benefits. Physical benefits would stem primarily from measures to improve health and safety, as well as from the provision of paid holidays, reduced working hours, and such like. Emotional welfare stems chiefly from any provisions made to improve mental health, for example, counselling, improved communications, or anything involving the 'human relations' needs of people at work. These benefits are, however, highly interrelated, and most welfare activities would potentially have both physical and emotional benefits. It can also be argued that employers provide for the material and intellectual welfare of their employees, in the material provisions of sick pay and pensions, and in the intellectual benefits that come from the provision of satisfying work and appropriate training and development. However, since these aspects are covered elsewhere in this book, we shall concentrate on physical and emotional welfare in this chapter.

Many provisions are less clearly seen as welfare when, for example, they are long-standing provisions made by many employers, such as canteens and time off for doctor's appointments. Other provisions are less clearly seen as welfare when they are enshrined in the contract of employment and therefore seen as standard. Holiday entitlement would come into this group: however, the amount of holiday is far from standard. In the United Kingdom holiday entitlement generally ranges from three to six weeks a year, which compares very favourably with the two weeks to which many US employees are entitled.

The development and importance of health, safety and welfare provision and the role of personnel management

Development

The development of health, safety and welfare provision is to a large extent interrelated with the development of personnel management itself. As mentioned in Chapter 1, one of the early influences on the development of personnel management was the growth of industrial welfare workers at the turn of the century. Enlightened employers gradually began to improve working conditions for employees and the industrial welfare worker was often concerned in implementing these changes. Much of this work was carried out voluntarily by employers, although not necessarily from altruistic motives alone. Another influence on personnel management was that of the 'human relations school', in particular the work of Elton Mayo at the Hawthorne plant of the Western Electric Company. Here there was an employee counselling programme, which operated from 1936 to 1955. It was found that such a programme was beneficial both for the mental health of the employees and their work. Other aspects of welfare provision, particularly in respect of safety, such as limitations on the hours of work of children, were enshrined in the law from as early as the 1840s and these again have become identified with the personnel function. Our recent research shows that in 53.4 per cent of those firms with a safety officer, this person comes within the ambit of the personnel function. In those firms without a health and safety officer the personnel department had a primary responsibility for health and safety. The activities of the personnel department in relation to health and safety are shown in Table 20.1. As health and safety legislation has become more pervasive, in particular with the Health and Safety at Work Act 1974, and the regulations stemming from it, the personnel department has taken the role of advising managers on the consequences of this, as with the deluge of other employment law at the same period.

However, personnel managers often find their welfare origin a source of embarrassment, feeling that it has contributed to their 'soft' image, and accordingly were not sorry when the emphasis on welfare decreased between the 1950s and the 1970s. There is considerable support for the view that the personnel function can only achieve authority and status in the organization when its activities have moved substantially beyond the welfare function (Fox 1966). More recently Mackay comments:

> Today, the personnel function seeks to be, and often is, a full member of the management team, aiming to participate and contribute to the success and survival of the organization. . . . It is the credibility of personnel management in the eyes of other managers that matters, not their credibility in the eyes of the workforce. (Mackay 1986, p. 3)

Watson (1977) has also noted the need for personnel to distance itself from its welfare image in order to facilitate full acceptance as part of the management team.

During the 1970s, however, there was some attempt to rediscover welfare (Kenny 1975). In the 1980s this renewed interest was maintained; the personnel function still had a role to play in welfare provision. The issues have changed from the early days. There has been a change in emphasis from purely physical to both physical and emotional welfare. In aspects of occupational health related to stress and personal problems, the involvement of line managers (Slaikeu and Frank 1986) and separate occupational counselling services have been advocated. Whatever role personnel managers may play in health, safety and welfare, our research indicates that they do not rate this area of their work very highly in terms of the time that they devote to it and the importance they accord

Table 20.1   Activities of the personnel department in relation to health and safety activities

Activity	Role of personnel department			
	Undertakes wholly	Undertakes in part	Does not undertake	Totals[a]
Formulating policy statement on safety	32	43	25	100
Formulating safety regulations	19	44	37	100
Formulating safe systems of work	9	47	43	99[b]
Formulating accident reporting procedures	41	37	22	100
Recording industrial accidents and notifiable diseases	43	31	26	100
Formulating accident investigation procedures	29	35	34	98[b]
Advising management of health and safety legislation	44	38	18	100
Designing, providing, recording health and safety training	32	44	24	100
Compiling, analyzing health and safety statistics	37	23	40	100
Designing safety publicity, leaflets	18	22	60	100
Liaising with occupational health and other bodies	34	33	33	100
Liaising with inspectorate	33	38	29	100
Monitoring health and safety policy, procedures	35	29	26	100
Advising on provision of protective clothing	26	39	35	100

a. Figures are percentages of 350 potential responses indicating the role of the personnel department in each of the health and safety activity areas.
b. Figures may not total 100 due to rounding.

to it among their other activities. Health, safety and welfare was ranked ninth out of fourteen for time spent, eleventh out of fourteen for importance, and eleventh out of fourteen for degree of increase in importance (Torrington, Mackay and Hall 1985).

Importance

The importance of health, safety and welfare from the employees' point of view is clear – their lives and futures are at risk (see Table 20.2). Health and safety has

Table 20.2 Injuries to employees in Great Britain as a result of work activities, 1983

1. Despite the health and safety laws, the number of accidents continued to rise.
2. New technologies were continually being introduced that created new hazards not covered by existing laws.
3. New diseases caused by working conditions began to be detected.
4. Over six million workers in the rapidly growing welfare and state sectors (like schools, hospitals and government services) were not covered by any legislation.
5. Several incidents had also cast doubt on the ability of the factory inspectorate to uphold the law.
6. The early 1970s was a period of pay restraint and the unions were keener at this time to get involved in health and safety.

been given increasing emphasis by the trade unions, especially from the late 1960s. Eva and Oswald (1981), in their book on the trade union approach to health and safety, identify a number of health and safety concerns of the unions in the early 1970s:

1. Despite the health and safety laws, the number of accidents continued to rise.
2. New technologies were continually being introduced that created new hazards not covered by existing laws.
3. New diseases caused by working conditions began to be detected.
4. Over six million workers in the rapidly growing welfare and state sectors (like schools, hospitals and government services) were not covered by any legislation.
5. Several incidents had also cast doubt on the ability of the factory inspectorate to uphold the law.
6. The early 1970s was a period of pay restraint and the unions were keener at this time to get involved in health and safety.

From the point of view of the employer there is a variety of reasons for supporting health, safety and welfare provision, apart from their legal obligations. It would be unfair to say that altruism does not play a part in employers' motives for improving these provisions, but there are other major influencing factors. The number of working days lost due to accidents at work was $10\frac{1}{2}$ million in the year 1981/2 (Health and Safety Executive 1985). If this figure were reduced by only a small percentage, the employer would save a considerable amount of money and trouble. One of the side-effects of employees with personal problems is that the quality of their work is often affected, as indicated by Knox and Fenley 'One of the earliest signs of problem drinking is a detrimental change in attitude, performance and efficiency at work which can be detected by an alert supervisor many years before other serious consequences of alcoholic dependence' (Knox and Fenley 1985, p. 32). There is also a general feeling that employees whose health, safety and welfare needs are well looked after by the employer will be more productive and loyal employees, and may cause fewer industrial relations problems, as indicated by the following quotes from a personnel director: 'It's very difficult for people who have been treated well to take a militant attitude to one per cent one way or the other on a pay deal' (Mackay 1986, p. 13); and a personnel manager: 'Let's be honest. From our point of view, I far prefer to have a contented employee, because he's doing a good job and generating income for the company' (Ibid.).

However, there is a continual conflict between health, safety and welfare considerations and other business priorities, as Beaumont *et al.* comment:

> Many safety officers interviewed suggested that, as a result of the recession, production considerations consistently tended to outweigh health and safety matters as a priority in management calculations. As one health and safety officer put it, trying to bring about improvements in health and safety now was very much an uphill battle. (Beaumont *et al.* 1982, p. 38)

Health, safety and welfare legislation

In the area of health and safety legislative intervention has existed continuously for well over 100 years, longer than for any other matter we consider. The principal current statutes are:

- The Factories Act 1961.
- The Offices Shops and Railway Premises Act 1963.
- The Fire Precautions Act 1971.
- The Health and Safety at Work Act 1974.
- The Control of Substances Hazardous to Heath Regulations 1988 (COSHH).

The first three Acts have all been brought up to date by the Health and Safety at Work Act. The above list is extended by a host of regulations, especially in relation to the Health and Safety at Work Act, to expand specific areas of the legislation, the most significant of which is COSHH. Increasingly, regulations have been based on EC directives, such as noise control and the manual handling of heavy loads. Regulations are also supplemented by an increasing number of Codes of Practice which are not legally enforceable.

The Factories Act 1961

This statute applies to all factories where two or more persons are employed in manual labour by way of trade or for the purpose of gain in a range of operations. This list is very wide and includes, for instance, building sites, dry docks, gas holders of over 5000 cubic feet and the production of films.

The Act sets out to ensure that minimum standards are maintained in factories on cleanliness, space for people to work in, temperature and ventilation, lighting, conveniences, clothing, accommodation and first-aid facilities. Many of the standards are fairly obvious, like keeping factories clear of the effluvia from drains, but some of them provide very precise levels that have to be met. Workshops must be so organized that every person employed has a minimum of 410 cubic feet of space excluding any air space more than 14 feet from the floor. That means that employees must have at least 29 square feet of space to work in, or more if the ceiling is less than 14 feet from the floor.

Another very specific figure is for working temperature, which must be at least 60° Fahrenheit (15.5° Centigrade) after the first hour, if a substantial proportion of the work of employees in a workroom is to be done sitting and does not involve serious physical effort. Lavatories must be provided in the proportion of at least one for every twenty-five men and one for every twenty-five women, and first-aid boxes must be provided on the scale of one for every 150 employees. If a factory employs more than fifty people, there must be at least one person trained in first-aid.

There are further requirements relating to general safety, fire precautions and various statutory registers and reports that have to be kept on things like reportable accidents and industrial diseases. Although there are excellent guides to the legislation available from Her Majesty's Stationery Office, these only deal with the main points in the Act (Health and Safety Executive 1977). In every factory there needs to be readily available the standard work of reference, originally produced by Redgrave (Fife and Machin 1976). Part of the enforcement machinery is the Factory Inspector, whose authority was reinforced under the Health and Safety at Work Act.

The Offices, Shops and Railway Premises Act 1963

The Offices, Shops and Railway Premises Act was introduced to extend to these buildings protection similar to that provided for factories. The legislation covers the type of premises described, but does not include offices in which fewer than 21 person-hours are worked in a week or moveable offices in which people will work for less than six months.

The general provisions are very similar to those of the Factories Act, and deal with cleanliness, lighting, ventilation and so on. There is a difference in the minimum space provision for employees. This is set at at least 40 square feet of floor space for each person employed, or 400 cubic feet for each person if the ceiling height is less than 10 feet. The temperature requirement is slightly higher than for factories: 61° Fahrenheit (16.0° Centigrade) after the first hour.

The Fire Precautions Act 1971

The Fire Precautions Act lists designated premises for which a fire certificate is required, and this list includes premises being used as a place of work. When issuing a fire certificate a fire authority can impose requirements on the certificate holder. These may concern such things as:

- The means of escape from the building.
- Instruction and training for employees on what to do in the case of a fire.
- Limits to the number of people on the premises.

The Health and Safety at Work Act 1974

The Health and Safety at Work Act 1974 is an attempt to provide a comprehensive system of law, covering the health and safety of people at work:

> The objectives of the Act, which are very ambitious, include both raising the standards of safety and health for all persons at work, and protection of the public, whose safety and health may be put at risk by the activities of persons at work. Because it is of general application, it brings within statutory protection many classes of persons who were previously unprotected. (Howells and Barrett 1982, p. 1)

The Act is an enabling Act and, as Howells and Barrett (1982) comment, for this reason its provisions are of necessity wide, and remain somewhat vague, except where they have been interpreted by the courts or augmented by regulations produced under the Act by the Secretary of State. By September 1985, 147 regulations had been issued under the Act (Health and Safety Executive 1985), although some of these are modifications or repeals of existing health and safety laws. The Act imposes, for the first time, criminal liability to comply with its provisions. The legislation is based largely on the recommendations of the Robens Committee (1970–2) and creates various new bodies and reinforces the authority of others as detailed below.

The Health and Safety Commission

The Health and Safety Commission was formed under the Act and has a chairman and between six and nine other members appointed by the Secretary of State to represent employers, employees and local authorities. The commission is responsible for carrying out the policy of the Act and providing advice to local authorities and others to enable them to discharge the responsibilities imposed upon them by the Act. It issues codes of practice and regulations, as well as having the power to make investigations and inquiries.

The Health and Safety Executive

The Commission, together with the Secretary of State, appoints three people to form the Health and Safety Executive whose duty it is to make adequate provision for the enforcement of the Health and Safety at Work Act, and to undertake the daily administration of affairs. There can also be other enforcement bodies as well as the Executive, for example local authorities.

The Factory Inspectorate

Factory inspectors had been employed for some time prior to the 1974 Act, and we have previously mentioned them regarding the enforcement of the 1961 Factories Act. As the enforcing authority of the Health and Safety at Work Act, the Executive is given the power to appoint inspectors. The role of the Inspectorate was strengthened by the 1974 Act as they were given the power to issue improvement and prohibition notices to appropriate employers. In general, inspectors have the right to enter employers' premises; carry out examinations/investigations; take measurements, photographs and recordings; take equipment and materials and examine books and documents. Initially, the number of inspectors was increased, from 681 in 1973 to 986 in 1980. However, by 1985 the number had fallen to 823. See Davis (1979) for further coverage of this aspect.

The Employment Medical Advisory Service

The Employment Medical Advisory Service was set up in 1972 to provide general advice to the government on industrial medicine matters and a corps of employment medical advisors to carry out medical examinations of employees whose health may have been endangered by their work. Responsibility for this service is now delegated by the Secretary of State to the Health and Safety Commission.

Enforcement of the Health and Safety at Work Act

Employer health and safety policy

Every employer is required to prepare a written statement of their general policy on health and safety, and the organization and arrangements for carrying out that policy which are in force at the time. All employees must be advised of what the policy is. It is perhaps inevitable that many employers have regarded this as a statutory chore and have gone through the motions of articulating a policy in terms of the bare minimum that is possible, rather than thinking out a policy statement that will have genuine impact on safe working. The report of the inspectorate for 1976 is very critical of companies where this happens, especially where the policy is a hollow statement without action to implement the declared intentions. Other specific criticisms were the lack of information in policy statements about particular hazards and how they could be dealt with, and a failure to stress management responsibility for safety as strongly as those of safety representatives (Health and Safety Commission 1978).

Booth (1985) makes similar criticisms based on research carried under the auspices of the PPITB. He comments that of the 121 policy documents investigated, most expressed a clear commitment to health and safety, but few contained appropriate details of the necessary arrangements for implementing the policy.

Another requirement of the Act is updating: 'it is the duty of every employer to prepare, and as often as may be appropriate revise, a written statement of general policy with respect to the health and safety at work of his employees' (Health and Safety at Work Act 1974, sect. 2(3)). If a safety policy is produced as something then to be filed away and forgotten, there is little chance that arrangements for coping with new hazards or changed working conditions will be made. The need for safety policy statements to be specific to the circumstances makes it difficult to offer models, but a useful starting point is provided by Armstrong:

> The general policy statement should be a declaration of the intention of the employer to safeguard the health and safety of his employees. It should emphasize four fundamental points: first, that the safety of employees and the public is of paramount importance; second, that safety will take precedence over expediency; third, that every effort will be made to involve all managers, supervisors and employees in the development and implementation of health and safety procedures; and fourth, that health and safety legislation will be complied with in the spirit as well as the letter of the law. (Armstrong 1977, p. 337)

Review topic 20.1

Devise a health and safety policy for your organization. Include information about:

1. General policy on health and safety.
2. Specific hazards and how they are to be dealt with.
3. Management responsibility for safety.
4. How the policy is to be implemented.

Managerial responsibility

The management of the organization carry the prime responsibility for implementing the policy they have laid down, and they also have a responsibility under the Act for operating the plant and equipment in the premises safely and meeting all the Act's requirements whether these are specified in the policy statement or not. In the case of negligence, proceedings can be taken against an individual, responsible manager as well as against the employing organization. The appointment of a safety officer can be one way of meeting this obligation. The officer does not become automatically responsible for all managerial failures in the safety field, but does become an in-house factory inspector.

Employee responsibility

For the first time in health and safety legislation a duty is placed on employees while they are at work to take reasonable care for the safety of themselves and others, as well as their health, which appears a more difficult type of responsibility for the individual to exercise. The employee is, therefore, legally bound to comply with the safety rules and instructions that the employer promulgates. Rose (1976) reported that nine employees had been prosecuted under this section of the Act.

Employers are also fully empowered to dismiss employees who refuse to obey safety rules on the grounds of misconduct, especially if the possibility of such a dismissal is explicit in the disciplinary procedure. An employee who refused to wear safety goggles for a particular process was warned of possible dismissal because the safety committee had decreed that goggles or similar protection were necessary. His refusal was based on the fact that he had done the job previously without such protection and did not see that it was now necessary. He was dismissed and the tribunal did not allow his claim of unfair dismissal (*Mortimer* v. *V. L. Churchill* 1979).

Safety representatives

To reinforce the employees' role in the care of their own health and safety, provision has been made for the appointment of safety representatives by trade unions. The Safety Representatives and Safety Committees Regulations 1978 set out the functions of safety representatives and provide for various types of inspection and investigation which they may carry out. Safety representatives have a legal duty of consultation with employers and are entitled to paid time off for training to enable them to carry out their function. There is also a Code of Practice for Safety Representatives recommending that they keep themselves informed, encourage co-operation with management and bring matters to their employer's attention (Davis 1979). However, in practice, things do not always work out this well, as Codrington and Henley comment:

> The innovations of [HASWA] can only produce significant improvements in the construction industry's apalling safety record if there are improvements in trade union site organization, for without it safety representatives have very little real power or authority . . . . With a declining membership and increasing fragmentation of employment relationships on site, the construction unions will only have limited resources available to encourage the development of safety representatives' activities. (Codrington and Henley 1981, p. 308)

Safety committees

Although the Act does not specifically instruct employers to set up safety committees, it comes very close:

> it shall be the duty of every employer, if requested to do so by the safety representatives . . . to establish, in accordance with regulations made by the Secretary of State, a safety committee having the function of keeping under review the measures taken to ensure the health and safety at work of his employees and such other functions as may be prescribed. (Health and Safety at Work Act 1974, sect. 2(7))

The safety representatives also have to be consulted about the membership of the committee, and detailed advice on the function and conduct of safety committees is provided in the guidance note on safety representatives (Health and Safety Commission 1976).

Research by Leopold and Coyle (1981) has shown that there has been a great increase in the number of safety committees in operation since the passing of the Act, especially in companies employing fewer than 200 people and in those industries where there was previously a low level of accidents. They also found the effectiveness of such committees to be much dependent on the employment of trained safety officers. This was generally confirmed by the work of Donnelly and Barrett (1981).

Safety training

There is a general requirement in the Act for training to be given, along with information, instruction and supervision, to ensure 'the health and safety at work of his employees'. There is thus fairly wide scope to determine what is appropriate in the differing circumstances of each organization.

We deal more fully with safety training and other methods of persuasion later in this chapter.

Codes of practice

The commission is empowered to follow the growing practice of issuing codes of practice for people to follow in various situations. Codes have been issued covering such aspects as:

- The protection of persons against ionizing radiation.
- Control of lead pollution at work.
- Time off for the training of safety representatives.
- Control of substances hazardous to health (various).

The codes are not legally enforceable, but the use or not of the codes may be interpreted in a legal case as an indication of the employer's efforts in that area of health and safety.

Improvement notices

Inspectors can serve improvement notices on individuals whom they regard as being in breach of the HASWA provisions, or earlier legislation, like the Factories Act 1961. This notice specifies the opinion of the inspector and the reasons for it, as well as requiring the individual to remedy the contravention within a stated period. Most frequently, this will be issued to a member of the management of an organization, depending on which individual the inspector regards as being appropriate, but such a notice could also be issued to an employee who was deliberately and knowingly disobeying a safety instruction.

Prohibition notices

An alternative, or subsequent, power of the inspector is to issue a prohibition notice, where he believes that there is a risk of serious personal injury. This prohibits an operation or activity being continued until specified remedial action has been taken. In 1983, 3,805 prohibition notices were issued compared with 12,268 improvement notices (HSE 1986).

It is possible for employers to appeal against both improvement and prohibition notices. In 1978 an employer appealed successfully against a prohibition notice issued against a hand-operated guillotine that had been used – as had nine similar machines – for eighteen years without accident. Another successful appeal was against an improvement order that was issued requiring safety shoes to be provided free of charge to employees. The tribunal found that the cost of £20,000 in the first year and £10,000 a year thereafter was disproportionate to the risk involved, and that the fact of the shoes being provided free did not make it more likely that they would be worn (IDS 1978).

Control of Substances Hazardous to Health Regulations, 1988

These regulations, which came into force on 1 October 1989, were made under the Health and Safety at Work Act 1974. They comprise nineteen regulations plus four approved codes of practice, and were described by Norman Fowler, Secretary of State, in 1988, as the most far reaching health and safety legislation since the Health and Safety at Work Act (Powley 1989).

The purpose of the legislation is to protect all employees who work with any substances hazardous to their health, by placing a requirement on their employer regarding the way and extent that such substances are handled, used and controlled.

The regulations apply to all workplaces, irrespective of size and nature of work – so, for example, they would apply equally to a hotel as to a chemical plant, and in firms of a handful of employees as well as major PLCs. The regulations not only place a responsibility for good environmental hygiene on the employer, but on employees too. All substances are included, except for asbestos, lead, materials producing ionizing radiations and substances underground, all of which have their own legislation, as explained by Riddell (1989).

The regulations require employers to focus on five major aspects of occupation in respect of hazardous substances. These are:

1. Assessing the risk of substances used, and identifying what precautions are needed. This initial assessment of substances already in use, and those that are intended for use is a major undertaking in terms of both the number of substances used and the competency of the assessor. Cherrie and Faulkner (1989) report that one employer in their survey used over 25,000 different substances! The assessment needs to be systematic, and key questions to ask are contained in the HSE's guide, *Introduction to COSHH*. Assessors may be internal or external consultants or specialists. Should the internal approach be adopted, the assessors require rigorous training and education as at ICI, described by Mountfield (1989).

2. Introducing appropriate measures to control or prevent the risk. These may include:-
   (a) removing the substance, by changing the processes used,
   (b) substituting the substance,
   (c) controlling the substance where this is practical, for example, by totally or partially enclosing the process, or by increasing ventilation or instituting safer systems of work and handling procedures.
   These measures would be designed to undercut Maximum Exposure Limits (MEL) and meet Occupational Exposure Standards (MES). For a fuller explanations of MEL and OES, see Powley (1989).

3. Ensure that control measures are used – that procedures are observed and that equipment involved is regularly maintained. Where necessary, exposure of the substance to employees should be monitored. This would particularly apply where there could be serious health risks if the control

measures were to fail or be sub-optimal. Records of monitoring should be made and retained.

4. Health surveillance. Where there is a known adverse effect of a particular substance, regular surveillance of the employees involved can identify problems at an early stage. When this is carried out, records should be kept and these should be accessible to employees.

5. Employees need to be informed and trained regarding the risks arising from their work and the precautions that they need to take.

Although the legislation has been widely publicized and produced in a clear and appropriate format, as judged, for example, by Foy (1989), there is early survey evidence of the lack of awareness, understanding and training in smaller firms from Cherrie and Faulkner (1989). The authors recommend three major initiatives to prepare this sector of employers better, which are that:

1. A major publicity campaign should be aimed specifically at small firms.
2. Small organizations need better access to professional health and safety advice.
3. The regulations must be enforced effectively.

The management of health, safety and welfare

There is a number of ways in which managerial responsibility can be discharged to implement the policy statement and ensure compliance with legal requirements.

Making the work safe

Making the work safe is mainly in the realm of the designer and production engineer. It is also a more general management responsibility to ensure that any older equipment and machinery that is used is appropriately modified to make it safe, or removed. The provision of necessary safety wear is also a managerial responsibility – for example, making sure goggles and ear protectors are available.

Enabling employees to work safely

Whereas making the work safe is completely a management responsibility, the individual employee may contribute his or her own negligence to work unsafely in a safe situation. The task of the management is two-fold; first, the employee must know what to do; secondly, this knowledge must be translated into action:

the employee must comply with the safe working procedures that are laid down. To meet the first part of the obligation the management need to be scrupulous in communication of drills and instructions and the analysis of working situations to decide what the drills should be. That is a much bigger and more difficult activity than can be implied in a single sentence, but the second part of getting compliance is more difficult and more important. Employee failure to comply with clear drills does not absolve the employer and the management. When an explosion leaves the factory in ruins it is of little value for the factory manager to shake his head and say: 'I told them not to do it.' We examine the way to obtain compliance shortly, under the discussion about training and other methods of persuasion.

The initiative on safe working will be led by the professionals within the management team. They are the safety officer, the medical officer, the nursing staff and the safety representatives. Although there is no legal obligation to appoint a safety officer, more and more organizations are making such appointments. One reason is to provide emphasis and focus for safety matters. The appointment suggests that the management mean business, but the appointment itself is not enough. It has to be fitted into the management structure with lines of reporting and accountability which will enable the safety officer to be effective and which will prevent other members of management becoming uncertain of their own responsibilities – perhaps to the point of thinking that they no longer exist. Ideally, the safety officer will operate on two fronts: making the work safe and ensuring safe working, although this may require an ability to talk constructively on engineering issues with engineers as well as being able to handle training and some industrial relations-type arguments. Gill and Martin (1976) have demonstrated that there is usually a clear dissonance between what is prescribed and what takes place, because the engineering approach produces complex and detailed manuals based on the belief that safety is a technical rather than human problem, whereas the people who do the work tend to produce different working practices based on experience:

> When we came to study the chemical plants we found an apparent paradox. On the one hand there existed a comprehensive body of written safety practices and procedures to cater for every conceivable contingency, and on the other hand actual working practice often differed considerably from the rules specifying safe working practices. Nevertheless the plants ran well and both the frequency of dangerous incidents and accidents were very low by national standards. (Gill and Martin 1976, p. 37)

The medical officer (if one is appointed) will almost certainly be the only medically qualified person and can therefore introduce to the thinking on health and safety discussions a perspective and a range of knowledge that is both unique and relevant. Secondly, a doctor speaks with a rare authority. In the eyes of most employees the medical officer will probably carry more social status than the managers dealing with health and safety matters, and he or she will be detached from the management in their eyes and his or her own. Doctors have their own ethical code, which is different from that of the managers. They are an authoritative adviser to management on making the work safe and can be an authoritative adviser to employees on working safely. They are an invaluable member of the safety committee and a potentially important feature of training programmes.

Occupational nurses also deal directly with working safely and often play a part in safety training, was well as symbolizing care in the face of hazard.

Safety training and other methods of persuasion

Safety training has three major purposes. First, employees should be told about and understand the nature of the hazards at the place of work; secondly, employees need to be made aware of the safety rules and procedures; and thirdly, they need to be persuaded to comply with them. The first of these is the most important, because employees sometimes tend to modify the rules to suit their own convenience. Trainers cannot, of course, condone the short-cut without implying a general flexibility in the rules, but they need to be aware of how employees will probably respond. In some areas the use of short-cuts by skilled employees does not always mean they are working less safely, as Gill and Martin (1976) have demonstrated, but there are many areas where compliance with the rules is critical, for example, the wearing of safety goggles.

Persuading employees to keep to the safety rules is difficult and there often appears to be a general resistance on the part of the employees. A study by Pirani and Reynolds (1976) throws some light on this, as they used the repertory grid technique to obtain from both managers and employees a construct of the safety conscious employee:

> The management sample saw this 'ideal' safety-conscious operative as a half-witted, slow but reliable person who gave little trouble. They saw him as a worker who could be left safely alone but prone to making trivial complaints. He certainly was not depicted as a worker to be respected. The major construct to emerge from the operatives' data alone was that the ideal safety conscious man was rather a 'cissy' and somewhat unsociable. It is important to note, however, that individual operatives did not see him in these terms but felt that this was how the rest of the operatives would view him – a feeling substantiated by a large sample of operatives. (Pirani and Reynolds 1976, p. 26)

Safety training needs to be carried out in three settings: at induction, on the job and in refresher courses. A variety of different training techniques can be employed, including lectures, discussions, films, role-playing and slides. These methods are sometimes supplemented by poster or other safety awareness campaigns and communications, and disciplinary action for breaches in the safety rules. Management example in sticking to the safety rules no matter what the tempo of production needed can also set a good example. A four-stage systematic approach to health and safety training is described by Culliford (1987).

Research by Pirani and Reynolds (1976) indicated that the response to a variety of methods of safety persuasion – poster campaigns, film shows, fear techniques, discussion groups, role-playing and disciplinary action – was very good in the short term (over two weeks) but after four months the initial improvement had virtually disappeared for all methods except role playing. From this it can be concluded that: first, a management initiative on safety will produce gratifying results in the obeying of rules, but a fresh initiative will be needed at regular and frequent intervals to keep it effective. Secondly, the technique of role playing appears to produce results that are longer-lasting.

Also important is external training for managers, supervisors and safety representatives. Following the 1974 Act, a substantial provision for health and safety training and education was introduced in colleges of further education, but in recent years there has been a decline in the take-up of places (Booth 1985).

Review topic 20.2

- Why do you think that there has been a decline in the take-up of places on health and safety courses at colleges?
- What are the implications of this decline? Why?

Job descriptions and the role of the supervisor

Attention can be drawn to the safety aspects of work by inserting a reference to safe working practices in job descriptions. In particular, the supervisor's role in ensuring safe working practices should be made as specific as possible in the supervisor's job description.

Risk assessment

Risk assessment is one of the newer approaches to health and safety which concentrates on accident prediction – as opposed to the more traditional prevention of reoccurrence after the event (Booth 1985). This approach reflects current concerns that expenditure on health and safety matters should be cost-effective, and the Royal Society paper (1983) on the subject discusses risk decision-making based on cost-benefit models.

Occupational health and welfare

Occupational health and welfare is a broad area, which includes both physical and emotional well-being. The medical officer, occupational health nurse and welfare officer all have a contribution to make here. In a broader sense so do the dentist, chiropodist and other professionals when they are employed by the organization. The provision of these broader welfare facilities is often found in large organizations located away from centres of population, especially in industrial plants, where the necessity of at least an occupational health nurse can be clearly seen.

In terms of physical care the sorts of facility that can be provided are:

1. Emergency treatment, beyond immediate first-aid, of injuries sustained at work.
2. Medical, dental and other facilities, which employees can use and which can be more easily fitted into the working day than making appointments with outside professionals.
3. Immediate advice on medical and related matters, especially those connected with work.
4. Monitoring of accidents and illnesses to identify hazards and danger points, and formulating ideas to combat these in conjunction with the safety officer.
5. On-site medicals for those joining the organization.
6. Regular medicals for employees.
7. Input into health and safety training courses.
8. Regular screening services. For example, cervical cancer screening at British Shipbuilders, Leyland Vehicles and United Biscuits.
   (*Personnel Management* 1986)

In terms of emotional welfare (although this cannot necessarily be clearly separated from physical welfare) Slaikeu and Frank (1986) make a convincing case for provision by the employer:

Research shows that marital, family, financial or legal crises are workers' most prevalent problems. Poor resolution of such crises can lead to long-term psychiatric damage resulting in depression, alcoholism, physical illness and even death. Untreated and unresolved crises affect worker productivity and contribute to labour turnover; the annual cost to US business of alcoholism alone is put at five billion. The 'hard' costs of ill and unhappy employees (absence, recruitment, and training expenses) are high enough. Still greater are inefficient and inadequate job performance, discredit to the company and diminished morale engendered among co-workers. The bottom line?

Estimated cost for 'emotional problems' in US business and industry
is $17 billion a year. (in *Management Today*, p. 35)

This, however, only deals with the emotional problems that employees bring
with them to work and the effects that these have on their work. What about
problems that are caused by the work itself, and the interaction between 'home'
and 'work' problems? There is not only a financial argument for the provision of
health and welfare assistance here, but possibly a moral argument as well. It is
very difficult, of course, to ascribe some problems to a definite cause, however
Eva and Oswald (1981) argue that conditions of work, speed of work, how
boring or demanding the job is, and how the job affects family and social life are
all major elements in the causation of stress.

Stress at work is not a new idea, although it was originally viewed in terms of
'executive stress' (for example, Levinson 1964), and seen only to apply to those
in senior management positions. There is a large number of books and articles
on the subject of stress at work (for example, Cooper and Marshall 1980; Palmer
1989; Nykodym and George 1989). Stress is now also seen to apply to those in
manual work (Cooper and Smith 1985) as well. It is the response of individuals
to work pressures, though, that determines whether they display the symptoms
of stress. Different people react to the same pressures in different ways. It has
been shown that the experience of stress is related to 'type A' coronary-prone
behaviour. Stress is a threat to both physical and psychological well-being.
Glowinkowski summarizes the effects of stress:

> While stress can be short-lived it can represent a continuous burden
> leading to short-term outcomes such as tension, increased heart rate,
> or even increased drinking or smoking. In the long term, stress is said
> to cause disorders such as depression, coronary heart disease,
> diabetes melitus and bronchial asthma. . . . Indeed, while stress may
> be a direct causal factor in heart disease, its effects may be indirect.
> Stress may increase smoking and cause overeating, which are also
> high risk factors in coronary artery disease (Glowinkowski 1985, pp.
> 1–2)

In relation to the variety of psychological and physical problems, there is a
number of facilities that the employer can provide to ease the difficulties that
employees may be experiencing.

Someone to talk to/someone to advise

This could be the individual's manager, or the personnel manager, but it is often
more usefully someone who is distinct from the work itself. An occupational
health nurse, welfare officer or specialized counsellor are the sort of people well
placed to deal with this area. There are two benefits that come from this, the first
being advice and practical assistance. This would be relevant, for example, if the

individual had financial problems, and the organization was prepared to offer some temporary assistance. Alternatively, the individual could be advised of alternative sources of help, or referred, with agreement, to the appropriate agency for treatment. The second benefit to be gained is that from someone just listening to the individual's problem without judging it – in other words counselling. De Board (1983) suggests that the types of work-related problems that employees may need to be counselled on are: technical incompetence, underwork, overwork, uncertainty about the future, and relationships at work. Counselling aims to provide a supportive atmosphere to help people to find their own solution to a problem.

Organization of work

This is a preventive measure involving reorganization of those aspects of work that are believed to be affecting the mental health of employees. This may include changes that could be grouped as 'organizational development', such as job rotation and autonomous work-groups. Eva and Oswald (1981) suggest greater control over the speed and intensity of work, an increase in the quality of work and a reduction in unsocial hours. Individually-based training and development programmes would also be relevant here. Specifically for the 'executive', there is growing use of the 'managerial sabbatical'. In the United States, some companies have begun to give a year off after a certain number of years' service in order to prevent 'executive burnout'. In the United Kingdom, the John Lewis Partnership has a programme allowing six months away from work.

Positive health programmes

Positive health programmes display a variety of different approaches aimed at relieving and preventing stress and associated problems. Some approaches are not new and include the use of yoga and meditation. Others, like 'autogenic training', are based on these principles, but are presented in a new guise. Autogenic training is developed through exercises in body awareness and physical relaxation which lead to passive concentration. It is argued that the ability to do this breaks through the vicious circle of excessive stress, and that as well as the many mental benefits, there are benefits to the body including relief of somatic symptoms of anxiety, and the reduction of cardiovascular risk factors (Carruthers 1982). A newer approach is 'chemofeedback', which is geared towards the connection between stress and coronary heart disease, high blood pressure and strokes. Chemofeedback (Positive Health Centre 1985) is designed as an early warning system to pick up signs of unfavourable stress. The signs are picked up from the completion of a computerized questionnaire together with a blood test. This approach is being offered as a 'stress-audit' on a company-wide basis.

Other issues currently in the health and safety arena are passive smoking, alcohol and drug abuse, the control of AIDS and the threat of violence.

Review topic 20.3

We are buying their [the employees'] skills and their energy and industry and commitment. Whilst they are at work we don't feel we've got responsibility to manage their social life, marriages, religious faith or anything else . . . (personnel manager)

How do you think employees see the provision of facilities at work to deal with their personal, emotional problems?

Summary propositions

20.1 Occupational welfare is the 'well-being' of people at work, encompassing occupational health and safety.

20.2 There are four aspects of welfare at work: physical, emotional, intellectual and material.

20.3 The history of personnel management is interrelated with the development of welfare. Many personnel managers find this association a disadvantage when trying to develop the authority and status of personnel management.

20.4 There was a surge in interest in health, safety and welfare in the late 1960s and early 1970s and this culminated in the Health and Safety at Work Act 1974, and its associated regulations.

20.5 By the early 1980s the interest in safety had waned but there is increasing interest in occupational health and welfare, particularly related to stress, alcoholism and counselling.

References

Armstrong, M. (1977), *Handbook of Personnel Management Practice*, London: Kogan Page.

Beaumont, P. B. (1984), 'Personnel management and the welfare role', *Management Decision*, vol. 22, no. 3.

Beaumont, P. B. Leopold, J. W. and Coyle, J. R. (1982), 'The safety officer: an emerging management role?' *Personnel Review*, vol. 11, no. 2.

Booth, R. (1985), 'What's new in health and safety management?' *Personnel Management*, April.

Carruthers, M. (1982), 'Train the mind to calm itself', *General Practitioner*, 16 July.

Central Statistical Office (1985), *Social Trends*, no. 15, London: HMSO, p. 112.

Cherrie, J. and Faulkner, C. (1989), 'Will the COSHH regulations improve occupational health? *Safety Practitioner*, February, pp 6–7.

Codrington, C. and Henley, J. S. (1981), 'The industrial relations of injury and death', *British Journal of Industrial Relations*, November.

Cooper, C. L. and Marshall, J. (1980), *White Collar and Professional Stress*, Chichester: John Wiley.

Cooper, C. L. and Smith, M. J. (Eds.) (1985), *Job Stress and Blue Collar Work*, Chichester: John Wiley.

Culliford, G. (1987), 'Health and safety training', *Safety Practitioner*, July, pp. 10–14.

Davis, K. P. (1979), *Health and Safety*, Wokingham: Van Nostrand Reinhold.

de Board, R. (1983), *Counselling People at Work: An introduction for managers*, Aldershot: Gower.

Donnelly, E. and Barrett, B. (1981), 'Safety training since the Act', *Personnel Management*, June.

Eva, D. and Oswald, R. (1981), *Health and Safety at Work*, London: Pan Books.

Fife, Judge I. and Machin, E. A. (1976), *Redgrave's Health and Safety in Factories*, London: Butterworth.

Fox, A. (1966), 'From welfare to organization', *New Society*, 9 June.

Foy, K. (1989), 'COSHH package appraisal', *Safety Practitioner*, February, pp 18–9.

Gill, J. and Martin, K. (1976), 'Safety management: reconciling rules with reality', *Personnel Management*, June.

Glowinkowski, S. P. (1985), 'Managerial Stress: a longitudinal study', unpublished PhD thesis, UMIST, Manchester.

Health and Safety Commission, (1976), *Safety Representatives and Safety Committees*, London: HMSO.

Health and Safety Commission, (1978), *Health and Safety in Manufacturing and Service Industries (1976)*, London: HMSO.

Health and Safety Executive, (1985), *Statistics for Health and Safety (1981/2)*, London: HMSO.

Health and Safety Executive (1986), *Health and Safety Executive Statistics (1983)*, London: HMSO.

Health and Safety Executive (1988), *Introducing COSHH*, London: HMSO.

Howells, R. and Barrett, B. (1982), *The Health and Safety at Work Act: A guide for managers*, London: Institute of Personnel Management.

Incomes Data Services, (1978), *IDS Brief No. 145*, London: Incomes Data Services.

Kenny, T. (1975), 'Stating the case for welfare', *Personnel Management*, vol. 7, no. 9.

Knox, J. and Fenley, A. (1985), 'Alcohol problems at work: some medical and legal considerations', *Personnel Review*, vol. 14, no. 1.

Leopold, J. and Coyle, R. (1981), 'A healthy trend in safety committees', *Personnel Management*, May.

Levinson, H. (1964), *Executive Stress*, New York: Harper & Row.

Mackay, L. E. (1986), *The Workforce and the Personnel Function*, Unpublished paper, UMIST, Manchester.

Mortimer v. *V. L. Churchill*, (1979), *Personnel Management*, News and notes, March 1986

Mountfield, B. (1989), 'Preparing for COSHH at ICI', *Occupational Health Review*, June/July, pp. 6–7.

Nykodym, N. and George, K. (1989), 'Stress busting on the job', *Personnel*, July, pp. 56–9.

Palmer, S. (1989), 'Occupational stress', *The Safety and Health Practitioner*, August, pp. 16–18.

Pirani, M. and Reynolds, J. (1976), 'Gearing up for safety', *Personnel Management*, February.

Positive Health Centre, (1985), *Chemo Feedback*, London: Positive Health Centre.

Powley, D. (1989), 'Life under the COSHH', *Manufacturing Engineer*, September, pp. 24–31.

Riddell, R. (1989), 'Why COSHH will hit hard on health and safety', *Personnel Management*, September, pp. 46–9.

Rose, P. (1976), 'Surveying the new safety structure', *Personnel Management*, November.

Royal Society, (1983), *Risk Assessment: A study group report*, London: The Royal Society.

Slaikeu, K. and Frank, C. (1986), 'Manning the psychological first aid post', *Management Today*, February.

Torrington, D. P. Mackay, L. E. and Hall, L. A. (1985), 'The changing nature of personnel management', *Employee Relations*, November/December.

Watson, T. J. (1977), *The Personnel Managers*, London: Routledge & Kegan Paul.

Equalizing employment opportunity

We discriminate between people in many aspects of our life and work. The selection process in particular directly discriminates between people in order to offer the reward of a job to one but not the others. Certain forms of discrimination are acceptable but others are not, and have been made unlawful. Facts rather than prejudice, and relevant facts rather than irrelevant facts, are important criteria in determining what type of discrimination is acceptable; but the law expects more from employers than this. It forces employers to exercise some form of social responsibility in the decisions they take in respect of potential and present employees. Discrimination in employment is inextricably linked with discrimination in the rest of society.

Disadvantaged groups and the argument for equal treatment

There are always certain groups in our society that are discriminated against unfavourably due to the prejudices and preconceptions of the people with whom they have to deal. These preconceptions are sometimes verbalized, but often not, and the people holding these preconceptions may well be unaware of the way that they see and judge things and people. However, verbalized or not, these preconceived ideas influence the actions of the people who hold them, and the way they deal with others. The effects of this can be seen in the employment arena. Disadvantaged groups, who have already been identified, are:

- Women.
- People from other racial backgrounds.
- Disabled people.
- Older people.

353

By far the most attention, in terms of public interest and legislation, has been paid to the first two groups. There is, however, some legislation relating to disabled people, and in the United States there is also legislation affecting the employment of people aged over 40.

The types of preconception that affect the employment of these four groups are:

1. Ideas that women should not work because their place is in the home or with children (although this idea has much less support these days); that women do not want too much responsibility at work because of their home commitments; that women are less reliable workers because of their home commitments; that you cannot move a woman to the other end of the country if her husband works at this end.
2. Ideas that Sikhs or Muslims are difficult to employ because of problems with religious holidays and practices; that Indians or Pakistanis overstate their qualifications; that qualifications gained abroad are not as good as those gained in this country; that employees would not want to work for a black supervisor; that the ability to fill out an application form in good English is an indication of an individual's potential to do a manual job.
3. Ideas that a person in a wheelchair will be an embarrassment to other workers; that a person in a wheelchair is in some way mentally disadvantaged/abnormal; that someone who has suffered from mental illness will automatically crack up under the slightest of pressure; that workers would not be able/wish to cope with someone suffering from epilepsy in case they had a seizure at work.
4. Ideas that older people are less adaptable; that they are not interested in coping with new technology; that they work much more slowly and cannot keep up with the pace of things; that they have become less interested in their careers.

All these and many other, unproven, preconceptions can affect the access that these groups have to employment, their level of employment and their occupation, the treatment that they receive at work, and their terms and conditions of employment.

There are two schools of thought concerning the action that should be taken to alleviate the disadvantages that these groups suffer. One school supports legislative action, while the other argues that this will not be effective and that the only way is to change fundamentally the attitudes and preconceptions that are held about these groups. So far there has been an emphasis on legislative action in the hope that this will affect attitudes. Legislation, however, appears to have a poor track-record where social change is involved. There have also been attempts to change attitudes directly, especially concerning disabled people. For example, 1981 was the International Year for the Disabled. So far these actions have only had a limited effect in changing the treatment of these groups, and attitudes are changing only very slowly.

The most pervasive argument against discrimination in employment or anywhere else is the argument based on an appreciation of rights and obligation. From the Universal Declaration of Human Rights and similar statements of principle, those who see themselves at a disadvantage are likely to assert their rights and point out that the discrimination from which they suffer is unjust and probably unlawful. Many of those who do not personally suffer from the effects of discrimination will still support the rights argument, claiming that the more fortunate have an obligation to level up opportunities. Practical arguments are less well known and need stating here.

Work is still central to people's lives as an important means towards personal and material fulfilment. The place of employment is therefore crucial to racial, sexual and other equality. That is where there needs to be a will and belief in the need for change, which goes beyond simply obeying the law. Other provisions like better educational opportunities and certain legal protections against discrimination will have only a marginal effect. The employing organization depends on the surrounding society, not only in the obvious sense as a source of prospective employees, but also in the sense that those employees import attitudes and experiences into their employment from the world outside. A company that discriminates directly or indirectly against women or ethnic minorities will, first, be curtailing the potential of available talent (and employers are not well known for their complaints about the surplus of talent); but secondly, they will be contributing to a situation in which social stability is put at risk and economic growth may be held back.

Employer inaction aggravates discrimination as it is principally through employment that progress can be made. If employers open up employment opportunities for women, then women will acquire the confidence to follow the lead and gradually broaden their social role. If employers open up employment opportunities for black people, then they too will grow in confidence and achieve social integration. The employer cannot necessarily expect gratitude and certainly not immediate short-term miracles, but in the longer run the effectiveness of the organization will improve. With the demographic downturn there is now more pressure on employers to change. The pain of being unable to recruit or retain the employees required by the organization has begun to force employers to reconsider their approach to equal opportunities so that they can benefit from an expanded labour market. Mahon (1989) demonstrates how an equal opportunities policy at Wellcome has shifted from good employment practice to sound business sense, and from personnel policies to business issues.

Women

Women form a large, and increasing, proportion of the working population. In 1971 women formed around 38 per cent of the workforce, in 1987 this had risen to around 42 per cent, and is projected to be around 44 per cent by 1995. A comparison of the employment participation rates of women in 1987 and projected to 2000 is shown in Figure 21.1. Comparisons with other countries indicate that there is a high participation rate in the United Kingdom, although many women work part-time.

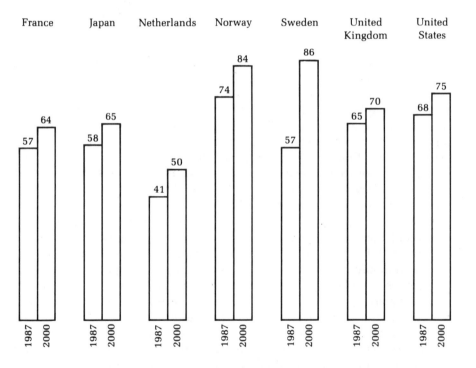

Figure 21.1   *Female participation rates in a selection of OECD countries, 1987–2000*
Source: ICI paper (1987) *Demographic Trends.*

The idea of women working to support the family is not new. Prior to the industrial revolution, women took on a heavy productive burden, albeit doing their work from home. After the advent of the factory system women also worked long hours away from the home in factories, and played a well-acclaimed role in outside employment during the two world wars. Changing attitudes and periods of high male unemployment have been factors, which, combined with others, have in the past eased women away from employment outside the home.

As society became more children-oriented there was a considerable lobby persuading mothers that their place was at home caring for the children. Quality of life was perceived in terms of there being a home-based 'carer' to look after the home environment, provide meals, and so on. Compared with women's lives when working in the factory, there was a certain status in being a 'housewife'. Additionally, in periods of high male employment, particularly after the Second World War, working was made harder for women in an environment of moral indignation about the lack of jobs for those men who had been overseas risking their lives for our safety as they were clearly entitled to some reward for their sacrifices.

Since then there has been a turnaround in attitudes and women are now seen as being equally entitled to a career outside the home on the same terms as men.

Legislation promoting sexual equality

The chief legislation relating to the promotion of sexual equality in employment are:

- The Equal Pay Act 1970.
- The Sex Discrimination Act 1975.
- The Employment Protection (Consolidation) Act 1978.
- The Social Security Act 1989.

The Equal Pay Act 1970

This was the first of the legislation promoting equality at work between men and women. The Act was passed in 1970, came into full force on 29 December 1975, and was amended by the 1983 Equal Pay (Amendment) Regulations Statutory Instrument 1983, No. 1794 and the 1983 Industrial Tribunals (Rules and Procedures) (Equal Value Amendment) Regulations, which came into effect from January 1984. A very good guide, particularly to the amendments, is Gill and Ungerson (1984).

The Act specifies circumstances where a woman's pay should be equal to that of a man. These are:

1. Where the woman can show that she is doing like work to a man – for example, a woman assembly worker sitting next to a male assembly worker, assembling similar items, would clearly be entitled to equal pay. An example of this is *Capper Pass* v. *Lawton* where:

   A woman worked as a cook in a company directors' dining room, providing lunches for between 10 and 20 persons. She sought equal pay with two assistant chefs who worked in the factory canteen and who prepared 350 meals each day. Other differences were that she worked 40 hours per week, and had no one supervising her, whereas the men worked 45 hours per week and were under the supervision of the head chef. The EAT upheld a decision of the Industrial Tribunal that she was entitled to equal pay. The work did not have to be the same; it was sufficient if it was broadly similar and the differences were not of practical importance. (Selwyn 1978, p. 80)

2. Where a woman can show that she is carrying out work rated as equivalent to that of a man, for example, under a job evaluation scheme. In this case the woman may be in a clerical post, but if the organization has an overall job evaluation scheme and her job is given the same points as a different job done by a man, then she can claim pay equal to the man.

3. Since 1984, where a woman can show that her work is of equal value to that of a man's. Equal value is defined in terms of the demands made by the job, and include skill, effort and decision-making. To claim under this rule there need be no job evaluation scheme as demonstrated in the case when a cook at Camel Laird claimed that her work was of equal value to painters and joiners (see Wainwright 1985). The cook was awarded equal pay.

Selection of a comparator
There is a number of limitations on the job holder which the woman may select as a comparator. The comparator needs to be of a different sex, but employed by the same employer and at an establishment covered by the same terms and conditions.

Enforcement of the Act
A woman may claim on an individual basis to a tribunal. Appeal is possible to an Employment Appeal Tribunal, then the Court of Appeal, and finally the House of Lords. Should the job be declared equal the individual applicant may then receive equal pay, which can be backdated to a maximum of two years before the date at which she applied to the tribunal.

Genuine material factors
An employer, however, may admit that a woman's job is equal to a man's in one of the three ways defined above, but that the pay is different and should remain different 'genuinely due to a material factor which is not the difference of sex' ((S1 (3) Amended) Equal Pay Act). A genuinely material factor (GMF) applies in a slightly different way to like work and work rated as equivalent under a job evaluation scheme, from work of equal value cases. In the first the employer may cite a difference of personal factors such as length of service, superior skill or qualifications, higher productivity or red circling. In relation to equal value cases skill shortages and market forces would come into play.

The Sex Discrimination Act 1975

This Act came into force at the same time as the Equal Pay Act: December 1975. The Sex Discrimination Act promotes the equal treatment of women and men in employment and other areas. Equal treatment in employment centres on such activities as selection, the availability of opportunities for training and progression, the provision of benefits and facilities, and dismissal. The Equal Opportunities Commission was established by the Sex Discrimination Act, and its duties are primarily to:

1. Eliminate discrimination on the grounds of sex or married status.
2. Generally promote equal opportunities between men and women.
3. Monitor the implementation of the Sex Discrimination Act and the Equal Pay Act.

The Sex Discrimination Act makes discrimination against women or men, or discrimination on the grounds of marital status, unlawful in the employment sphere. The meaning of both direct and indirect discrimination is clarified in the Act.

Ways of discriminating
1. Direct sex discrimination occurs when a person is treated less favourably due to their sex than a person of the opposite sex would be in similar circumstances. For example, advertising for a man to do a job which could equally well be done by a woman.
2. Direct marriage discrimination occurs when a married person is treated less favourably, due to their married status, than a single person of the same sex would be treated in similar circumstances. This would apply if a married woman was denied promotion because she was married, and it was considered she might leave to follow her husband's job or start a family. The Act makes no mention of discrimination against employees on the basis of their unmarried status, and this is not unlawful.
3. Indirect sex discrimination occurs when a requirement or condition is applied equally to men and women. However, the condition has the effect that in practice it disadvantages a significantly larger proportion of one sex than the other, because they find it harder to fulfil, and it cannot be justified on any grounds other than sex. Indirect sex discrimination has been demonstrated by the age limit of twenty-eight years maximum, for entry into the executive officer grade of the civil service. In the case of *Price* v. *The Civil Service Commission* it was successfully argued that this was considerably disadvantageous to women as they were often raising a family at this time, and that therefore the age limit constituted indirect discrimination (IPM 1978; EOC Sex Discrimination Decisions no. 9).
4. Indirect marriage discrimination occurs when an employer places a requirement or condition on both married and unmarried people, but the practical effect of this is that a significantly smaller proportion of married

people can comply compared with single people of the same sex, and there is no other justification for the condition than their marital status. An employer who offered promotion on the basis that the employee was prepared to be away from home for considerable spells of time, when in reality this was never or rarely required would be indirectly discriminating on the grounds of married status. If the spells away from home were needed in practice then the employer would not be acting unlawfully.

5. Victimization occurs when an employer treats an employee of either sex less favourably than other employees would be treated on the grounds that they have been involved in, or intend to be involved in (or is suspected of either of these), proceedings against the employer under the Sex Discrimination Act or the Equal Pay Act.

Unlawful discrimination

In the employment sphere it is unlawful to discriminate on the basis of sex or married status in relation to potential and present employees:

1. *Potential employees*: It is unlawful to discriminate in recruitment arrangements, for example, in advertising and interviewing; and in the terms and conditions of a job offer, for example, in whether a permanent or temporary position is offered. It is also unlawful to discriminate in the adoption of selection criteria, in selection methods and in other selection matters, for example in refusing or deliberately omitting to offer employment because of a person's sex:

   In *Batisha* v. *Say*, a woman was turned down for a job as a cave guide because 'it is a man's job', and in *Munroe* v. *Allied Supplies* a man was not taken on as a cook because women employees would not work with him. In both cases it was held that an act of discrimination had occurred. (Selwyn 1978, p. 70)

2. *Present employees*: It is unlawful to discriminate in the provision of opportunities for promotion, transfer or training; in the provision of facilities or services such as study leave or company cars; and in unfavourable treatment, like dismissal.

   In *Gubala* v. *Crompton Parkinson*, the choice of a dismissal in a redundancy situation lay between a man and a woman. The woman had longer overall service, but the employers took into account that the man was 58 years old and had a family to support and a mortgage to keep up. The woman was young and married with a husband who was working, and she was dismissed. It was held that this amounted to unlawful discrimination; the tribunal refused to accept the 'breadwinner' criteria as a basis for redundancy selection. (Selwyn 1978, p. 72)

Exceptions to the Sex Discrimination Act
1. *Work outside Great Britain*: The Act does not apply to employees who work wholly or mainly outside Great Britain.
2. *Employment in private households and small firms*: The Act (except for the victimization provisions) does not apply to potential or current employees of private households or small firms employing five or less. Pressure from Europe may mean that these exemptions will be changed in the near future.
3. *Genuine occupational qualifications*: Sex discrimination, but not marriage discrimination or victimization, may be permitted where sex is a genuine occupational qualification (GOQ). This can apply in the recruitment, promotion or transfer to a job or in the training provided. It cannot be applied in dismissal cases. A GOQ cannot be claimed because a job requires physical strength or stamina, but may apply, for example, where a man or woman is needed because of physical form as in modelling or acting, or where a man or woman is required due to decency as in the job of lavatory attendant. A full list of GOQs is described by the Equal Opportunities Commission (1985, pp. 5–6).
4. *Pregnancy, childbirth, retirement or death*: Another area where the Act does not apply is in pregnancy, childbirth, retirement or death, for example, by giving a woman maternity leave but not allowing a man paternity leave.
5. *The armed forces*: The armed forces are not covered by the Act.
6. *Special provisions*: Special provisions are made for the police, prison officers, ministers of religion and competitive sports.
7. *Factories Acts*: The Act does not cover those areas where women's employment is covered by the Factories Acts.
8. *Positive action*: The Act allows for positive action by the employer, if during the previous year a particular type of employment has been done entirely or mainly by members of one sex. The employer may then provide training solely for employees of the other sex. Also, members of that sex only may be encouraged to take up the work. For example, applications from women may be encouraged for, say, sheet metalworking jobs, and men may be encouraged to apply for midwifery jobs. However, the selection process must not discriminate in favour of one sex rather than the other.

Enforcement of the Sex Discrimination Act
There are two aspects to enforcement:

1. The EOC is the only body that can take action about instructions or pressure to discriminate, about discriminatory practices or advertisements, or persistent discrimination.
2. In all other cases any individuals who feel they have suffered as a result of discrimination may make a claim to a Tribunal as described under the Equal Pay Act.

Further details about enforcement may be found in Equal Opportunities: a guide for employers (EOC 1985).

The Employment Protection (Consolidation) Act 1978

The 1980 Employment Act provided the right to paid time off during working hours for ante-natal care. In effect this was done by adding a new section to the Employment Protection (Consolidation) Act 1978. Other rights in addition to those gained under the Employment Protection Act 1975 include the right not to be unfairly dismissed due to pregnancy or a reason connected with pregnancy; the right to six weeks' maternity pay; and the right to return to work after the birth of a child. For a much fuller description of these rights, see the guide produced by Incomes Data Services (1983).

The Social Security Act 1989

From 1 January 1993 it is unlawful for occupational benefit schemes (including health insurance and pensions) to discriminate directly or indirectly on grounds of sex. Areas such as survivors' benefits, optional pensions and pensionable age are, however, not covered by the Act. In-depth explanations of the provisions may be found in *Industrial Relations Review and Report* (1989, no. 384).

Equal opportunity policies

Equal opportunities policies are not required by law but are recommended, and the Equal Opportunities Commission produces a model policy for those employers who wish to adapt this for use in their own organization. A summary of the EOC's model policy is found in Figure 21.2. The IPM strongly recommend the use of such policies: 'They [EO policies] are an essential part of good management. Properly administered and monitored, they can be an effective tool in helping to eliminate unfair discriminatory practices and useful as evidence in cases of alleged discrimination' (IPM 1978, p. 43).

Legislation promoting sexual equality – implications for personnel managers

The legislation has several implications for personnel management:

Advertisements, notes and circulars

Advertisements must not discriminate on the basis of sex or marital status. This means that job titles should either be sexless, as in 'cashier', 'machinist' or 'salesperson', or indicate an acceptability of either sex, as in 'waiter/waitress' or 'manager/manageress'. If a job title is used indicating one sex, such as 'chair-man', this must be accompanied by a statement that both men and women are

1. *Introduction*: Desirability of the policy and that it is required to be strictly adhered to.

2. *Definitions*: Direct and indirect discrimination defined.

3. *General statement of policy*: A commitment to equal treatment and the belief that this is also in the interests of the organization. Staff in the organization should be made aware of the policy and key personnel trained in the policy.

4. *Possible preconceptions*: Examples of preconceptions that may be erroneously held about individuals due to their sex or marital status.

5. *Recruitment and promotion*: Care to be taken that recruitment information has an equal chance of reaching both sexes and does not indicate a preference for one group of applicants. Care that job requirements are justifiable and that interviews conducted on an objective basis. An intention not to discriminate in promotion.

6. *Training*: An intention not to discriminate with some further details.

7. *Terms and conditions of service and facilities*: An intention not to discriminate.

8. *Monitoring*: Nomination of a person responsible for monitoring the effectiveness of the policy and with overall responsibility for implementation. An intention to review the policy and procedures. Intention to rectify any areas where employees/applicants are found not to be receiving equal treatment.

9. *Grievances and victimization*: An intention to deal effectively with grievances and a note of the victimization clauses in the Act.

Figure 21.2 *Summary of the EOC's model Equal Opportunity Policy*
Source: Summarized from EOC (1985), *A Model Equal Opportunities Policy*.

invited to apply. To save any misunderstandings, it may be wise to use this statement in all advertisements. Illustrations used in advertisements and in recruitment literature should depict both men and women.

Other recruitment procedures

Personnel managers also need to consider the implications of other recruitment procedures. For example, in admitting school-children into the organization for a careers visit, care should be taken that the boys are not shown only round the parts of the factory where the traditional male jobs are to be found, while the girls are only shown around the canteen and the offices. Similarly, if local schools are visited, then both boys' and girls' schools should be included.

Selection procedures

Equal opportunities legislation reinforces the need for job analysis and the production of job descriptions and person specifications. In particular, the person specification should be carefully considered to ensure that the person requirements are not unnecessarily restrictive and indirectly discriminate between men and women, making it easier for men to comply. Care should also be taken that any selection tests have been well validated in that they have been demonstrated to predict performance in the job, and that they have been developed using data from both sexes.

The interview

Although interviewers may not be able to banish their prejudices and stereo-types, an awareness of these may at least allow some compensation. Other methods, such as interviewing in a structured and consistent way, can also be used to help limit the effects of preconceptions. Care should also be taken to avoid questions that may indicate an intention to discriminate, even where discrimination is not intended, for example, questioning a woman about her husband and domestic arrangements (although these questions would not in themselves constitute discrimination if they were also put to male interviewees). Similarly, questions about dependants are fair if are asked of both sexes. In fact, discriminating against someone on the grounds of their dependants is not unfair so long as men and women are treated equally in this respect. It would, however, be reasonable to assume that an individual applying for a job will have made or will make suitable arrangements for the care of dependants. Finally, it is always wise to keep notes of an interview and the reason for rejection in the event of a claim for unfair discrimination.

Job evaluation

The equal value amendments may well be a persuasive factor in the introduction of a job evaluation scheme. If a scheme is already in existence it should be reviewed periodically to ensure that it does not discriminate between men and women.

Review topic 20.1

We have suggested five implications for personnel managers of the legislation relating to women. What other major implications are there in your organization? What is the role of the personnel function in monitoring the effects of the legislation?

Effects of the Legislation to promote equal opportunity on the basis of sex

There is some evidence to suggest that women are beginning to enter previously male-dominated occupations, for example, the first woman minister of religion in the Church of England has now been ordained.

Similarly men are beginning to enter some previously female-only occupations, such as midwifery. There are, however, still few women in higher levels of management and not many male secretaries. O'Sullivan (1989) reports that only 8 per cent of the executive workforce are women. Snell, Glucklich and Povall (1981) report that widespread job segregation has continued. Dickens and Colling (1990) explain how continued job segregation in respect of both role and hours/arrangements is one of the influencing factors which results in discriminatory agreements between employers and unions. They also highlight the problem of job evaluation schemes which perpetuate old values and hence encourage rather than discourage equality of pay. Although progress has been made towards equal pay, these factors still remain as barriers to be overcome.

Although women have equal access to pensions schemes under the Sex Discrimination Act, and many other inequalities in schemes are now illegal under the Social Security Act 1989, McGoldrick (1984) notes that pensions schemes still work to women's disadvantage. They are normally organized and administered on the basis of traditional male employment patterns – such as rewarding long, continuous service and based on full-time rather than part-time employment.

There has been a clear removal of overt discrimination, particularly in recruitment advertising, following on quickly from the Acts, but there is much less evidence of changes in training and promotion practices, and no use of the provision enabling positive action in training (Snell *et al.* 1981).

In spite of the EOC's model Equal Opportunity Policy and the IPM's support for such policies, our recent research indicates that such policies are only produced by 60 per cent of organizations, and that on the whole they are not seen as very useful. Indeed, a large number of organizations saw their policy as irrelevant.

The effects of the legislation have been limited. To some extent this was recognized at the outset:

> Nobody believes that legislation by itself can eradicate overnight a whole range of attitudes which are rooted in custom, and are, for that very reason, often unchallenged because unrecognized. But if the law cannot change attitudes overnight, it can, and does effect change slowly. (House of Lords 1972/3, p. 22)

As this comment recognizes, the roots of discrimination go very deep. Simmons (1989) talks about challenging a system of institutional discrimination and anti-female conditioning. In the United States, where equal opportunities legislation has been in force for longer than in the United Kingdom, Dipboye (1975) notes that the misconceptions, e.g. that women work primarily for pin money and women are less concerned with promotion than men, still persist. Schein (1973) found that the adjectives that male middle managers selected to describe successful middle managers were much more highly related to those they selected as applying to men in general than those they selected as applying to women in general. This also demonstrates that most workplaces are built around male cultures where success is related to conforming to the prevailing culture. However, Avery (1979) points out that since there is a considerable overlapping of the distribution of males and females on any trait, statements concerning all or most women are clearly misleading. These stereotypes are not very helpful in assessing candidates for selection or promotion. A more helpful way of understanding the difference between men and women at work is looking at their cultures.

Recognizing that men and women present different cultures at work, and that this diversity needs to be managed, is key to promoting a positive environment of equal opportunity, which goes beyond merely fulfilling the demands of the statutory codes. Masreliez-Steen (1989) explains how men and women have different perceptions, interpretations of reality, languages and ways of solving problems, which, if properly used, can be a benefit to the whole organization as they are complementary. She described women as having a collectivist culture where they form groups, avoid the spotlight, see rank as unimportant and have few but close contacts. Alternatively, men are described as having an individualistic culture, where they form teams, 'develop a profile', enjoy competition and have many superficial contacts. The result of this is that men and women behave in different ways, often fail to understand each other and experience 'culture clash'. However, the difference is about *how* things are done and not *what* is achieved.

The fact that women have a different culture with different strengths and weaknesses means that women need managing and developing in a different way. They need different forms of support and coaching. For example, women more often need help to understand the need for making wider contacts and how to make them. In order to manage such diversity, key management competencies for the future would be: concern with image, process awareness, interpersonal awareness/sensitivity, developing subordinates and gaining commitment.

Another aspect of the management of diversity is that women need different forms of organizational support particularly in terms of flexibility, to enable them successfully to combine a career with parenthood. Such forms of support include career breaks, flexible working hours, annual hours, job sharing and part-time work, childcare facilities and support. Liff (1989) also suggests that non-linear career paths are important and the restructuring of jobs. Progress in these areas is patchy. Field and Paddison (1989) comment that women in the United Kingdom spend less time out of paid employment than women in any other EC country, and that 90 per cent of women are returning to work after having children. However, there is least nursery provision for the under-fives in the United Kingdom than the rest of Europe (Industrial Relations Review and Report 1988). Anecdotal evidence suggests that childcare provision is a difficult need to meet as needs vary so considerably, that it is almost impossible for the employer to win. Some companies have surveyed present and/or potential women employees to help identify some of their support needs, as did Mothercare (Arkin 1990).

Racial minorities

Between the 1950s and early 1970s there was immigration largely of black workers from the New Commonwealth countries, and it was an awareness that this group of people was disadvantaged in employment and other areas that prompted anti-discrimination legislation. The legislation, however, is designed to apply to any racial minority group.

Black workers are particularly at risk because not only are their customs and practices often different from those of our indigenous population, although this decreases over time, but their colour clearly identifies them as being different.

Immigrant labour in the United Kingdom was identified as being heavily concentrated in less desirable, non-skilled, manual jobs, causing Smith (1974) to remark that the composition of the minority workforce was 'markedly different, by type of job, from the total workforce' (in Braham *et al*. 1981). Smith also comments that on the basis of the preliminary results of the 1971 Census, minority groups are almost twice as likely as white people to be unemployed.

Legislation promoting racial equality

There has been legislation since 1968 making it unlawful for employers to discriminate directly on the grounds of race, colour, nationality or ethnic origin. The Race Relations Act 1976 replaces the 1968 Act, and extends it by, for example, making indirect discrimination illegal, using a similar approach to the Sex Discrimination Act. The 1976 Act also set up the Commission for Racial Equality with similar powers to the Equal Opportunities Commission.

The Race Relations Act 1976

The Act identifies ways in which racial minority groups may be discriminated against, and makes these illegal:

1. Direct discrimination occurs if an employer treats an employee, or prospective employee, less favourably than they treat, or would treat other employees, on the grounds of his race. Racial grounds have been defined as colour, race or nationality or ethnic or national origin. Less favourable treatment may occur, for example, in selection for recruitment, promotion, shiftwork, overtime, and so on. Discrimination may also occur in the work environment, for example, in the use of separate canteens.
2. Indirect discrimination is defined in the same way as for the Sex Discrimination Act. An example here would be requiring a good standard of written English for a manual labourer's job:

To insist that applicants for a specified job should be of a certain minimum height may well be discriminatory against Indians unless it can be shown that the requirement is justified. But to insist that workers on a building site should wear steel helmets would not be discriminatory against Sikhs, the condition is capable of being justified irrespective of the race of the person concerned (see *Singh* v. *Lyons Maid*). (Selwyn 1978, p. 87)

3. Victimization provisions give individuals the right of complaint to an industrial tribunal, as with the Sex Discrimination Act, if they feel they have been victimized in their employment because they have been connected with bringing proceedings under the Act.

Exceptions to the Race Relations Act
A number of areas have been identified where discrimination in recruitment, training, promotion or transfers on the grounds of 'genuine occupational qualification' is acceptable. These are:

1. *Entertainment*: If it is necessary to have a person of a particular racial group to achieve an authentic presentation.
2. *Artistic or photographic modelling*: If it is necessary to use a person from a particular racial group to provide authenticity for a work of art, visual image or sequence.
3. *Specialized restaurants*: If it is necessary to have a person from a particular racial group to sustain the special setting of an establishment where food or drink is served to the public, like a Chinese restaurant.
4. *Community social workers*: If a person provides personal services to members of a particular racial group and the services can best be provided by someone of the same racial group.

However, these do not permit discriminatory treatment in the terms and conditions of employment.

Enforcement of the Race Relations Act
The pattern of enforcement is similar to that for the Sex Discrimination Act. Individuals who feels they have been discriminated against can complain to a tribunal, and the Commission for Racial Equality can also bring complaints to a tribunal where there may be direct discriminatory practices, but no particular casualty, or in cases of discriminatory advertisements.

Legislation promoting racial equality – implications for the personnel manager

The implications for the personnel manager run along the same lines as for the Sex Discrimination Act, in particular:

Advertisements

Advertisements should be carefully worded so that there is no indication that people of some racial backgrounds are preferred to others. A statement to this effect, as with the Sex Discrimination Act, may well be the best policy. Illustrations should show a mix of different races. Personnel managers also need to be careful where they place advertisements. An internally-placed advertisement in an organization employing only white people may constitute indirect discrimination against those racial groups who will have less chance to hear about the job from their friends.

Selection procedures

The use of a job description and specification are again very helpful here, and care should be taken not to draw up a specification that is unjustifiably demanding. When considering individuals from different racial groups against this specification it is important to distinguish between attainment and potential. People from disadvantaged groups often have a poor record of attainment by employers' standards, but their potential to do the job may at the same time be very good. Also, as a general rule, application forms require a level of English in excess of job requirements and so selection on that basis may constitute unfair discrimination against those whose mother tongue is not English and yet who may be suitable employees (Runnymede Trust and BPS 1980).

Selection tests

The use of selection tests should be carefully monitored. Many tests discriminate against people from minority backgrounds due to assumptions made when the tests were designed and due to the fact they may have been standardized on, for example, all-white groups of individuals. Also, people from different racial backgrounds may be at a disadvantage because the ethos of testing is more alien to their culture (IPM 1978).

Personnel managers will overcome these difficulties if they scrutinize very carefully, for example, a test that rejects 70 per cent of black applicants but only 30 per cent of white applicants. They must be able to show that this cut-off point is justifiable and that the test is valid in terms of job performance. It is also worthwhile considering whether there are equally valid selection criteria that can be used which have a less adverse impact on disadvantaged groups. If tests are used, personnel managers should try to ensure that these are 'culture-fair' (although it has been argued that this is impossible (Runnymede Trust 1980, p. 23)); that adequate pre-test orientation is given, for example, about the purpose of testing; that pre-test practice is given; and perhaps produce a self-help pamphlet.

Interviewing

One of the common problems with interviewing is the tendency of interviewers to select in their own image (Runnymede Trust 1980). This works against minority groups and also reinforces the current structure of the workforce. Interviewers need to be aware of this problem as well as the others mentioned under the Sex Discrimination Act. Interviewers also need consciously to remember that the way individuals present themselves is partly dependent on their culture and background. Things that are acceptable, or even expected, in one culture may not be acceptable in another.

Effects of the legislation to promote equal opportunity on the grounds of race

Braham, Rhodes and Pearn (1981) argue that by 1980 the Race Relations Act did not appear to have been very successful in eliminating discrimination. The number of successful cases brought before tribunals each year was insignificant compared with the scale of racial discrimination, which research studies have revealed (Runnymede Trust 1979).

As with discrimination on the grounds of sex, employers frequently feel that they should wait until public opinion has changed before they make changes in employment conditions, but with racial discrimination in particular one can argue that it is the place where public opinion is formed. Tom Connelly, the first Chief Executive of the Commission on Racial Equality, put it this way:

> What happens in employment is crucial for the whole issue. A person's job and employment prospects obviously determine his current and material welfare, the well-being of his family and his status in the community. . . . An indispensable condition for fuller acceptance is the breakdown of the association between colour and inferiority. If coloured workers are seen mainly in low status jobs and in poor housing, the association will be sustained and strengthened. The more they are seen in higher status jobs, particularly those which involve the exercise of authority, the weaker the association with inferiority will become. The experience of coloured workers in industry will therefore influence crucially the attitudes and behaviour of the host society. (Connelly 1972, pp. 194–5)

In our survey we asked to what extent personnel managers should be concerned with the 'social responsibility' of their organizations to the wider community and although only 26 per cent answered 'to a great extent', 65 per cent answered 'to some extent' and only 3 per cent answered 'not at all'. Personnel managers, therefore, are not unkeen to see themselves taking a leading role in such social issues as equal opportunity.

In attempts to stimulate progress, two administrative devices have been authoritatively advocated by the CRE (1978). One is the development of equal opportunity policies in companies, and the other is monitoring. Research has not succeeded in showing the introduction of policy 'from the top' as being effective, except in situations where the employment of minority employees has produced major problems that needed to be resolved (Torrington, Hitner and Knights 1982).

The idea of monitoring is that records should be kept of those in racial and ethnic minorities who are employed in the organization. This produces the immediate reaction that it is a discriminatory act in itself. However, the potential dangers are offset by the need to take positive steps to check what the penetration into the more attractive areas of the organization actually is.

The experiences of two organizations in respect of ethnic monitoring is given below.

Mars Ltd

Tony Harbour (1980) reports that managers at Mars have been consciously concerned with being an equal opportunities employer for some time, and decided to use ethnic monitoring, partly to see if their ethnic minorities policy was working, and to identify any problems in recruitment, promotion, transfer, merit and disciplinary practices. Ethnic data were asked for on application forms and were also put onto both personnel and payroll records all of which were accessible for the individual concerned. Equality in recruitment was measured by comparing the racial structure of the workforce at Mars with that in the local area, and the racial groups used were: Caucasian, Latin, Negro, Asian, Arabic and Oriental. Comparisons of the racial structure of different work groups, departments and grades were also made.

London Borough of Hackney

John Carr, Equal Opportunities Officer (1980) argues that there is a wide range of employment activities that need to be monitored and suggests a list of the areas that the London Borough of Hackney intend to cover:

(a) Wording, presentation and media used for advertising.
(b) Responses to advertising.
(c) Shortlisting from returned application forms.
(d) Interviewing.
(e) Offers of employment.
(f) Acceptance of offers of employment.
(g) Reviews of probationary periods.
(h) Job specifications and criteria for employment. (related to (a) to (f)).

(i) Terms and conditions.
(j) Promotions.
(k) Re-grading.
(l) Transfers.
(m) Disciplinary procedures.
(n) Grievance procedure.
(o) Dismissals.
(p) Leavers in employment with the borough.
(q) Reasons for leaving.
(r) Access to and take up of training opportunities.
(s) Existing staff.

(Carr 1980, pp. 20–1)

These monitoring exercises will be used to provide statistical tables reflecting the position of ethnic minorities. Carr suggests that the comparison of the statistics over a period of time is the most vital factor and that the frequency of monitoring needs to be carefully considered. He points to the importance of qualitative as well as quantitative information.

Review topic 21.2

Prepare an equal opportunity policy for racial equality for the organization in which you work.

Disabled people

There were 420,000 people who registered as disabled in 1984. The true figure of disabled people in the workforce must be more than this. Walker (1986) notes that disabled people have always experienced higher levels of unemployment than the workforce as a whole, and once unemployed have greater difficulty in returning to work and therefore often remain unemployed for longer periods. Their choice of job is often restricted and where they do find work it is likely to be in low-paid, less attractive jobs. Periods of high general unemployment exacerbate these problems.

Employers have a wide range of concerns regarding the employment of disabled people. These include worries about general standards of attendance and health, safety at work, eligibility for pension schemes and possible requirements for alterations to premises and equipment.

The legal framework and the Manpower Services Commission

Walker (1986) comments that political and moral pressure to make provision for the war disabled, together with a practical need to reduce labour shortages, resulted in the setting up of the Tomlinson Committee on the rehabilitation and resettlement of disabled persons. The recommendations of this committee resulted in the 1944 Disabled Persons (Employment) Act, which, together with the 1958 Act of the same name, is the main legislation in operation, with some additional regulations coming into force in 1980. The legislation provided for:

1. Assessment of disabled people. This is usually carried out by occupational psychologists at employment rehabilitation centres.
2. Rehabilitation of disabled people. Disabled people usually attend an employment rehabilitation centre for about six weeks.
3. Retraining of disabled people. There are four residential training colleges specifically available for the retraining of disabled people.
4. A register of people with disabilities (see the MSC leaflet entitled the Disabled Persons Register, DPL 1).
5. A quota scheme in respect of registered disabled people, see below.
6. Reserved employment for disabled people, see below.
7. Sheltered employment, for example, Remploy.

The Manpower Services Commission Employment Division (1984) produced a very helpful booklet on employers' obligations regarding disabled people resulting from these Acts. The MSC have also produced a Code of Good Practice on the Employment of Disabled People (1984). At Job Centres there are specialist Disablement Resettlement Officers who specifically assist disabled people in their search for employment and training. They also liaise with employers regarding the employment of disabled people.

The quota scheme

It is in the areas of the quota scheme and reserved occupations that the 1944 Act has most implications for employers. The quota scheme is a method of positive discrimination where every employer of more than twenty people has to employ sufficient disabled people to make up 3 per cent of their total workforce. If firms are under their quota they should not employ another non-disabled person until they are up to quota unless they have obtained a special permit.

There has been much discussion over the future of the quota scheme, but it has been decided to retain it for the time being in spite of its reducing effectiveness. More and more employers are requesting and receiving special permits and the percentage of employers not fulfilling their quota is increasing from around 40 per cent in 1961 to over 60 per cent in 1978 (Manpower Services Commission 1980). Walker (1986) reports that since the scheme began, only ten firms have been prosecuted and Disablement Resettlement Officers have attempted to persuade employers to take on disabled people rather than invoking the law. An MSC working group considering ways of improving the quota scheme has made a number of recommendations including changes in the issue of permits and methods of increasing employers' awareness of the quota scheme (MSC 1985). Walker, however, comments: 'These reforms are no substitute for the establishment of clear rights to employment protection along the lines of other European countries such as West Germany' (Walker 1986, p. 45)

Reserved occupations

In addition, certain jobs are reserved or designated to be filled only by registered disabled people. To date, these jobs are car park and lift attendants. Disabled people employed in reserved occupations cannot be counted towards the 3 per cent quota.

Policy on the employment of disabled people

All employers with 250 or more staff, on average, are obliged to include, in the Directors' Report, a statement of their policy on the employment of disabled people. The Code of Good Practice recommends that this policy should include items about: communication and consultation in the drawing up of the policy; objectives of the policy; the role of managers, employees and their representatives; the advice and help that are planned to be used; good practices and the areas where these are particularly important; and how it is planned to monitor and assess the policy.

The Job Introduction scheme and the Pathway scheme

Both these schemes enable employers to employ disabled workers on a trial basis.

Fit for work awards

About 100 of these awards are made annually to those employers who have done most to assist the employment of disabled people.

Older people

The main protection for the older employee is against redundancy, for which they will be financially compensated, but there is no protection for them in seeking fresh employment, training or promotion (unless they happen to be black!). The problems of unemployment in the 1980s have tended to militate against the employment prospects of those who are older, because the working population appears to be too large for our total employment requirements. People have been under pressure to retire early in many circumstances and find it very difficult to continue working after normal retirement age.

In the United States recent legislation has been introduced to prevent discrimination in employment on the grounds of age. There are no signs of this spreading to the United Kingdom, but we need to consider not only whether citizens' rights are being impaired because of the lack of such legislation, but also – as with other types of anti-discrimination legislation – whether the effectiveness of organizations is being impaired by people suggesting to older employees that they are becoming less effective and that they may be standing in the way of the legitimate career aspirations of others.

Megginson put some of the reasons to favour people over forty years of age:

> greater experience and better judgement in decision-making; more objectivity about personal goals and abilities, as the older men have already satisfied many of their needs for salary and status and are able to concentrate more on job responsibilities; increased social intelligence and the ability to understand and influence others; decreased risk, as the older person's potentialities can be more easily determined from their performance record; reduced training time, as their previous experience is easily transferable, especially into management positions; and proven value as the older workers have proven their abilities. . . (Megginson 1972, pp. 235-6)

Review topic 21.3

The legislation protecting disadvantaged groups in employment has so far only had a limited effect, and attitudes are changing only very slowly.

How would you promote and encourage equal employment opportunity for these groups? How successful do you think this would be?

Why?

Learning, attitudes and equality

Intentional discrimination is based on a set of clearly expressed beliefs about the differences between people. But much discrimination is unintentional and primarily arises from our unconscious learning experiences as individuals and as a society. We are conditioned by our experiences that, for example, women are nurses and men are surgeons, and these form a framework within which we operate and interpret and react to new experiences or the possibility of change. We make inferences from this framework, for example, that women make the best nurses and men make the best surgeons. Frameworks determine our attitudes. Gradually, as more new experiences of a particular type arise, we change our framework to accommodate these. This is not a speedy process and may take many generations. For a long time many people will react defensively to new experiences and will reject or deny them.

Discrimination, therefore, reflects frameworks that have not yet adapted to a new societal view or to changing circumstances. This may be because of very high defences to change or due to a lack of direct experiences to assimilate. Attitudes and frameworks may be changed by a variety of means. Literature can be aimed directly or indirectly at changing attitudes. For example, literature from the Manpower Services Commission and Job Centres is aimed directly at changing attitudes about the employability of disabled people. Other literature, for example, books published by the Women's Press, have a role in indirectly changing women's perceptions of themselves. Research into the opportunities for disadvantaged groups focuses attention and highlights areas of disadvantage and the mechanisms that support this. Much research has been funded or initiated by the Equal Opportunities Commission and the Commission for Racial Equality. Both these bodies also produce large amounts of literature, codes, guidelines, and so on, and their existence in itself acts as a focus for equality of opportunity for women and racial minorities. However, all these activities are providing input at a secondary level rather than a direct level. It is direct experience that has the most powerful impact on the frameworks and attitudes within which people operate.

This is where the law, arguably, has its most important, but least recognized impact. The law attempts to force employers and others to provide opportunities on an equal basis for all groups. From this other advantages accrue. First, the experience of having, say, women senior managers and managing directors in evidence makes this idea less unusual, fearful or laughable, and it gradually becomes acceptable and normal. Secondly, this gives individuals from disadvantaged groups an equal opportunity to show that they, too, can be successful in these areas.

Summary propositions

21.1 The essence of much personnel work is to discriminate between individuals. The essence of equal opportunity is to avoid unfair discriminaton.

21.2 Equalizing employment opportunity is not only meeting legal and social responsibilities, it is also ensuring organizational effectiveness.

21.3 Unfair discrimination often results from people being treated on the basis of limited and prejudiced understanding of the groups to which they belong rather than on the basis of an assessment of them as individuals.

21.4 Legislation can have only a limited effect in reducing the level of unfair discrimination.

21.5 Although employers can usually find ways of avoiding the effects of legislation relating to discrimination, personnel managers generally express a sense of social responsibility on such matters.

21.6 Actual changes in practice relating to equalizing opportunity are taking place very slowly.

References

Anon. (1988), 'Childcare provision 1 – employers head for the nursery', *Industrial Relations Review and Report*, October, no. 425, pp. 2–7.

Anon. (1989), 'Social Security Act 1989, Guidance Note', *Industrial Relations Review and Report*, Legal Information Bulletin, no. 384, pp. 2–8.

Arkin, A. (1990), 'Mothercare makes a play for women returners', *Personnel Management Plus*, July pp. 20–1.

Avery, R. D. (1979), *Fairness in Selecting Employees*, Wokingham: Addison-Wesley.

Braham, P., Rhodes, E. and Pearn, M. (1981), *Discrimination and Disadvantage in Employment*, Milton Keynes: The Open University.

Carr, J. (1980), 'Comments on monitoring'. In *Record Keeping and Monitoring in Education and Employment*, London: Runnymede Trust.

Clark, A. (1984), In D. Gill and B. Ungerson, *The Challenge of Equal Value*, London: Institute of Personnel Management.

Commission for Racial Equality (1978), *Equal Opportunities in Employment and Monitoring on Equal Opportunities Policy*, London: CRE.

Connelly, T. J. (1972), 'Racial integration in employment'. In D. P. Torrington, (Ed.), *A Handbook of Industrial Relations*, Aldershot: Gower.

Dickens, L. and Colling, T. (1990), 'Why equality won't appear on the bargaining agenda', *Personnel Management*, April, pp. 48–53.

Dipboye, R. L. (1975), 'Women as managers and stereotypes and realities', *Survey of Business*, Center for Business and Economic Research, The University of Tennessee, no. 10, May/June, pp. 22–5.

Equal Opportunities Commission. (1985), *A Model Equal Opportunities Policy*, London: Equal Opportunities Commission.

Equal Opportunities Commission, (1985), *Equal Opportunities: A guide for employers to the Sex Discrimination Act 1975*, London: HMSO.

Equal Opportunities Commission, (1985), *Sex Discrimination Decisions no. 9. women and family responsibilities, Price v. Civil Service Commission*, EOC Information Leaflet, London: Equal Opportunities Commission.

Field, S. and Paddison, L. (1989), 'Designing a career break system', *Industrial and Commercial Training*, Jan./Feb., pp. 22–5.

Gill, D. and Ungerson, B. (1984), *The Challenge of Equal Value*, London: Institute of Personnel Management.

Harbour, T. (1980), 'Monitoring: The mass experience'. In *Record Keeping and Monitoring in Education and Employment*, Proceedings of a one-day seminar, London: Runnymede Trust.

Home Office (1985), *Sex Discrimination: A guide to the Sex Discrimination Act 1975*, London: HMSO.

Incomes Data Services, (1983), *Maternity Rights*, Handbook Series no. 26, London: Incomes Data Services.

Institute of Personnel Management, (1978), *Towards Fairer Selection: A code for non-discrimination*, IPM Joint Standing Committee on Discrimination, London: Institute of Personnel Management.

Lawrence, E. (Ed.). (1986), *CSO Annual Abstract of Statistics* (1986 edition), no. 122, London: HMSO.

Liff , S. (1989), 'Assessing equal opportunities policies', *Personnel Review*, vol. 18, no. 1, pp. 27–34.

Mahon, T. (1989), 'When line managers welcome equal opportunities', *Personnel Management*, October, pp. 76–9.

Manpower Services Commission (1980), *The Quota Scheme for the Employment of Disabled People: A discussion document*, Sheffield: Manpower Services Commission.

Manpower Services Commission (1984), *Code of Good Practice on the Employment of Disabled People*, Sheffield: Manpower Services Commission.

Manpower Services Commission Employment Division (1984), *The Disabled Persons Register*, Sheffield: Central Office of Information and Manpower Services Commission.

Manpower Services Commission Employment Division (1984), *The Disabled Persons (Employment) Acts 1944 and 1958: Employers' obligations*, Sheffield: Manpower Services Commission.

Manpower Services Commission (1985), *Working Group Report on Suggestions for Improving the Quota Scheme's Effectiveness*, Sheffield: Manpower Services Commission.

Martin, J. and Roberts, C. (1980), *Women and Employment: A lifetime perspective*, Report of the 1980 DE/OPCS Women and Employment Survey. London: HMSO.

Masreliez-Steen, G. (1989), *Male and Female Management*, Kontura Group, Sweden.

McGoldrick, A. (1984), *Equal Treatment in Occupational Pension Schemes*, Research report, London: Equal Opportunites Commission.

Megginson, L. C. (1972), *Personnel: A behavioral approach to administration*, Homewood, Ill.: Irwin.

O'Sullivan, A. (1989), 'Women in senior management', *MBA Review*, vol. 1, pt 2, pp. 5–7.

Runnymede Trust. (1979), *A Review of the Race Relations Act*, London: Runnymede Trust.

Runnymede Trust and BPS (1980), *Discriminating Fairly: A guide to fair selection*, Report by the Runnymede Trust/BPS Joint Working Party on Employment Assessment and Racial Discrimination, London: Runnymede Trust and BPS.

Schein, V. E. (1973), 'The relationship between sex role stereotypes and requisite management characteristics', *Journal of Applied Psychology*, vol. 57, pp. 95–100.

Schein, V. E. (1975), 'Relationships between sex role stereotypes and requisite management characteristics among female managers', *Journal of Applied Psychology*, vol. 60, pp. 340–4.

Select Committee on the Anti-discrimination Bill (House of Lords) (1972–1973), *Second Special Report from the Select Committee*, London: HMSO.

Selwyn, N. M. (1978), *Law of Employment*, London: Butterworth.

Simmons, M. (1989), 'Making equal opportunities training effective', *Journal of European Industrial Training*, vol. 13, no. 8, 19–24.

Smith, D. J. (1974), *Racial Disadvantage in Employment* (PEP Study of Racial Disadvantage), vol. XL, Broadsheet 544, The Social Science Institute.

Snell, M. W., Glucklich, P. and Povall, M. (1981), *Equal Pay and Opportunities. A study of the implications and effects of the Equal Pay and Sex Discrimination Acts in 26 organizations*, Research Paper no. 2, London: Department of Employment.

Terbourg, J. R. (1977), 'Women in management: a research review', *Journal of Applied Psychology*, vol. 62, pp. 647–64.

Torrington, D. P., Hitner, T. J. and Knights, D. (1982), *Management and the Multiracial Workforce*, Aldershot: Gower.

Wainwright, D. (1985), 'Equal value in action', *Personnel Management*, January.

Walker, A. (1986), 'Disabled workers and technology: quota fails to quote', *Manpower Policy and Practice*, Spring.

22

Termination of the employment contract

Having set up the contract of employment in the first place, the personnel manager monitors the performance of that contract to ensure that both parties are satisfied. Eventually, the contract has to be terminated, either because the mutual satisfaction no longer holds or because the contract has come to its natural conclusion: retirement, the end of a fixed-term contract or a range of other reasons such as emigration, career change or following a spouse to a different part of the country. In this chapter we look mainly at dismissal, with some comment on resignation, retirement and notice.

Dismissal

Although there has been a long-standing employee right to claim wrongful dismissal by an employer, the legal framework of current practice mainly stems from the 1971 Industrial Relations Act, which first established the right of employees to claim unfair dismissal, with recourse to industrial tribunals, via ACAS conciliation, in search of a remedy.

Before the 1971 Act there were approximately three million dismissals according to a Ministry of Labour calculation in 1967 (Ministry of Labour 1976 p. 57). That estimate included dismissals of all types and stated that one third were due to sickness and slightly fewer were due to redundancy. Of less significance were dismissals for unsuitability and misconduct. This was in a situation of untrammelled freedom of action by employers, as well as full employment. No similar authoritative estimate has been made since, but we do have figures of unfair dismissal cases. Since 1979 the number of applications to industrial tribunals has been between 25,000 and 50,000 each year. That is a small proportion of the previously estimated three million, but it is only cases that employees report because they believe they have a chance of compensation. In 1983 and 1989 ACAS dealt with cases as follows:

	1983	1989
Cases received for conciliation	37,123	48,817
Settled by ACAS	15,591	27,749
Withdrawn	9,171	8,927
To tribunal	12,575	8,528

(ACAS 1985, p. 84; 1990, p. 59)

Even if the current level of dismissal is only one million annually, we see that the scale of decisions against the employer is very small indeed.

A survey for the Department of Employment in 1983–4 showed that only 6 per cent of employers were deterred from taking dismissal action because of fears of an application to tribunal, but 65 per cent reported that they now took greater care in deciding on whether or not to dismiss (Evans *et al.* 1985, p. 34).

Wrongful dismissal

There is a long-standing common law right to damages for an employee who has been dismissed *wrongfully*, that is, when the employer has not given proper notice: either the notice period is incorrect or the dismissal has been summary when the behaviour of the employee did not warrant such peremptory treatment. This remains a form of remedy that is used by very few people, but it could be useful to employees who have not sufficient length of service to claim unfair dismissal, so the employer who has learned that it is possible to dismiss people unfairly if they do not have two years' service needs to remember that this does not permit wrongful dismissal. There may also be cases where a very highly paid employee might get higher damages in an ordinary court than the maximum that the tribunal can award.

Unfair dismissal

Every employee who has been with an employer for two years has the right not to be unfairly dismissed; the fairness being determined by the provisions of the Employment Protection (Consolidation) Act 1978, though the main structure of unfair dismissal legislation has remained unaltered since it was first introduced in the Industrial Relations Act 1971. In some areas of employment the legal provisions have made little difference, as the existing personnel policies of the employer have provided a similar or better degree of protection. The protection of the employee is due to a specific set of rules and precedents that have developed in that particular place of work and which are particularly relevant to it.

Obtaining a legal remedy from the tribunal involves a dependence on interpretation of the law and the situation by outsiders, and this may not necessarily be in the best interests of either participant. The tribunal members are concerned with fairness for employment as a whole; not within one industrial concentration. Furthermore, the compensation ordered by tribunals seldom approaches the maximum figures stated in the Acts and, of course, the tribunal can only act when the dismissal is a fact. It cannot prevent in specific instances.

This does not mean that the law can safely be ignored by employers, as the level of complaints to tribunals remains low only as long as practice is ahead of legislation. Even a 'cheap' unfair dismissal could be costly in terms of the unfairness stigma which will influence employee relations generally, can have a damaging public relations effect and could jeopardize the career of the manager to blame. Thus the law determines management practice.

Review topic 22.1

Consider the working activities of some of your colleagues (and perhaps your own working activities). What examples are there of behaviour that you feel justify dismissal? Make a list of your ideas and check them when you have finished this chapter and see how many might be classified as unfair dismissals by a tribunal.

Determining fairness

The novel legal concept of fairness relating to dismissal is determined in two stages – *potentially fair* and *actually fair*.

A dismissal is potentially fair if there is a fair ground for it. Such grounds are:

- *Lack of capability or qualifications*: If an employee lacks the skill, aptitude or physical health to carry out the job, then there is a potentially fair ground for dismissal.
- *Misconduct*: This category covers the range of behaviours that we examine in considering the grievance and discipline processes – disobedience, absence, insubordination and criminal acts. It can also include taking industrial action.
- *Redundancy*: Where an employee's job ceases to exist, it is potentially fair to dismiss the employee for redundancy.

- *Statutory bar*: When employees cannot continue to discharge their duties without breaking the law, they can be fairly dismissed. Almost invariably the operation of this category is for drivers who have been disqualified from driving for a period.
- *Some other substantial reason*: This most intangible category is introduced in order to cater for genuinely fair dismissals that were so diverse that they could not realistically be listed. Examples have been security of commercial information (where an employee's husband set up a rival company) or employee refusal to accept altered working conditions.

Having decided whether or not fair grounds existed, the tribunal then proceeds to consider whether the dismissal is fair in the circumstances. Here there are two questions: Was the decision a *reasonable* one in the circumstances? And was the dismissal carried out in line with the *procedure*? The second is the easier question to answer as procedural actions are straightforward, and the dismissal should be procedurally fair if the procedure has been carefully followed without any short cuts. Here is a cautionary tale:

> A charge nurse in a hospital attacked a hospital official, punched him and broke his glasses. He was dismissed for misconduct. Later he was convicted of assault and causing damage. A tribunal found his dismissal to be unfair because he was not given a chance to state his case and because his right of appeal was not pointed out. (*Amar-Ojok* v. *Surrey AHA* (1975))

In this book we have separated the consideration of discipline from the consideration of dismissal in order to concentrate on the practical aspects of discipline (putting things right) rather than the negative aspects (getting rid of the problem). The two cannot, however, be separated in practice and the question of discipline needs to be reviewed in the light of the material in Chapter 30. The question about decisions that are reasonable in the circumstances is a more nebulous one and the most reliable guide is a commonsense approach to deciding what is fair. It would, for instance, be unreasonable to dismiss someone as incapable if the employee had been denied necessary training; just as it would be unreasonable to dismiss a long-service employee for incapacity on the grounds of sickness unless future incapacity had been carefully and thoroughly determined.

Automatic decisions

Although fairness usually has to be judged, there are some defined situations in which dismissal is automatically fair or unfair.

It is automatically fair to dismiss an employee who refuses to join a trade union designated in a union membership agreement, unless there are genuine grounds of conscience or other deeply-held personal conviction, provided that the union membership agreement meets the requirements of the 1980 Act, described in Chapter 28. It is also fair to dismiss strikers, providing that they are *all* dismissed while the strike is in progress. If only some of the strikers are dismissed, then the reason must be one of the fair grounds listed above. The 1982 Act varies this by allowing the employer to discriminate between those who remain on strike and those who return to work, providing that the employer gives notice of this intention. A dismissal will automatically be adjudged unfair if no reason is given, or if an employee is selected for dismissal or redundancy on the grounds of trade union membership. Selection for redundancy would also be automatically unfair if an employee were selected in breach of a customary arrangement or procedure, as would dismissal on grounds of pregnancy or a spent conviction.

Fair grounds revisited

Having mentioned the potentially fair grounds for dismissal, we can now look again at the first three – incapability, misconduct and redundancy – in more detail.

Lack of capability or qualifications

The first aspect of capability relates to skill or aptitude. Although employers have the right and opportunity to test an applicant's suitability for a particular post before that individual is engaged, or before promotion, the law recognizes that it is possible that mistakes will be made and that dismissal can be an appropriate remedy for the error, if the unsuitability is gross and beyond redemption. Normally there should be warning and the opportunity to improve before the dismissal is implemented, but there are exceptions if the unsuitability of the employee is based on an attitude that the employee expresses as a considered view and not in the heat of the moment. Another exception is where the employee's conduct is of such a nature that continued employment is not in the interests of the business, no matter what the reasons for it might be:

> An employee of a shop-fitting company tended to irritate the customers, lacking 'the aptitude and mental quality to be co-operative with, and helpful to, important clients'. His employer dismissed him and the tribunal accepted the fairness of the ground but not the procedural fairness of the decision. On appeal the tribunal judgement was overturned as specific warnings of the procedure type would not have altered the employee's performance. He had known for some

time that he was at risk because of his difficuity in gettng on with the customers and was not able to change his attitude. (*Dunning* v. *Jacomb* (1973))

Where an employee is going through a period of probation at the time of termination, Lewis suggests that tribunals judge the fairness of a dismissal by soliciting answers to the following questions:

> Has the employer shown that he took reasonable steps to maintain the appraisal of the probationer through the period of probation? Did he give guidance by advice or warning when it would have been useful or fair to do so? Did an appropriate person make an honest effort to determine whether the probationer came up to the required standard, having informed himself of the appraisals made by supervisors and other facts recorded about the probationer? (Lewis 1983, p. 122)

The employer will always need to demonstrate the employee's unsuitability to the satisfaction of the tribunal by producing evidence of that unsuitability. This evidence must not be undermined by, for instance, giving the employee a glowing testimonial at the time of dismissal.

In cases of dismissal for lack of capability the dismissal does not necessarily have to be procedurally fair, if the use of procedure would have made no difference. If warnings will make no difference, then there is no need to give them.

> Mr Lowndes was employed by an engineering company and was deemed incompetent. After making five different serious mistakes, each of which was costly to the employer, he was dismissed. There were no warnings and he was not given an opportunity to state his case. The tribunal accepted the employer's argument that it would have made no difference if procedure had been followed and held that the dismissal was fair. (*Lowndes* v. *Specialist Heavy Engineering Ltd* (1977))

Lack of skill or aptitude is a fair ground when the lack can be demonstrated and where the employer has not contributed to it – by, for instance, ignoring it for a long period – but normally there must be the chance to state a case and/or improve before the dismissal will be procedurally fair.

The second aspect of capability is *qualifications*; the degree, diploma or other paper qualification needed to qualify the individual to do the work for which employed. The simple cases are those of misrepresentation, where an employee claims qualifications he or she does not have. More difficult are the situations where the employee cannot acquire necessary qualifications:

> A Post Office recruited a telegraph officer. In order to guard against dilution the Union of Postal Workers had negotiated an agreement

with the Post Office that all those recruited would have to pass a special aptitude test by a specified date, providing that their practical work was acceptable. They would be allowed three attempts at the test. The officer failed the test three times and was dismissed after five years' service. An Industrial Tribunal and the National Industrial Relations Court both judged the dismissal fair. (*Blackman* v. *Post Office* (1974))

The third aspect of employee capability is health. It is potentially fair to dismiss someone on the grounds of ill-health which renders the employee incapable of discharging the contract of employment. Even the most distressing dismissal can be legally admissible, providing that it is not too hasty and providing that there is consideration of alternative employment. Also, there is no question of diverting the decision to a medical adviser. The medical evidence will be sought by the employer and has to be carefully considered, but the decision to dismiss remains an employer's decision, not a medical decision.

Normally, absences through sickness have to be frequent or prolonged, although absence which seriously interferes with the running of a business may be judged fair even if it is neither frequent nor prolonged, but in all cases the employee must be consulted before being dismissed.

Drawing on the judgment of the EAT in the case of *Egg Stores* v. *Leibovici* in 1977, Selwyn lists nine questions that have to be asked to determine the potential fairness of dismissing someone after long-term sickness:

> (a) how long has the employment lasted (b) how long had it been expected the employment would continue (c) what is the nature of the job (d) what was the nature, effect and length of the illness (e) what is the need of the employer for the work to be done, and to engage a replacement to do it (f) if the employer takes no action, will he incur obligations in respect of redundancy payments or compensation for unfair dismissal (g) are wages continuing to be paid (h) why has the employer dismissed (or failed to do so) and (i) in all the circumstances, could a reasonable employer have been expected to wait any longer? (Selwyn 1985, p. 241)

This case was of frustration of contract, and there is always an emphasis in all tribunal hearings that the decision should be based on the facts of the particular situation of the dismissal that is being considered, rather than on specific precedents. For this reason the nine questions are no more than useful guidelines for personnel managers to consider: they do not constitute 'the law' on the matter.

A different situation is where an employee is frequently absent for short spells, as here the employee can be warned about the likely outcome of the absences being repeated:

The employee . . . can be confronted with his record, told that it must improve, and be given a period of time in which its improvement can be monitored. Indeed, the employer should not overlook the powerful medicinal effect of a final warning, and a failure to give one may mean that the employee is unaware that the situation is causing the employer great concern. The effect of such a warning might be to stimulate the employee into seeking proper medical advice in case there is an underlying cause of the continuous minor ailments, it may deter the employee from taking time off when not truly warranted, and it may even lead the employee to look for other work where such absences could be tolerated. (Selwyn 1985, p. 244)

In the intriguing case of *International Sports Ltd* v. *Thomson* (1980), the employer dismissed an employee who had been frequently absent with a series of minor ailments ranging from althrugia of one knee, anxiety and nerves to bronchitis, cystitis, dizzy spells, dyspepsia and flatulence. All of these were covered by medical notes. (While pondering the medical note for flatulence, you will be interested to know that althrugia is water on the knee.)

The employer issued a series of warnings and the company dismissed the employee after consulting its medical adviser, who saw no reason to examine the employee as the illnesses had no connecting medical theme and were not chronic. The EAT held that this dismissal was fair.

It is appropriate to mention here that dismissal for pregnancy is unfair, unless the employee is unable to carry on doing her job or unless continuing to employ her would be contravening a statute, such as the Ionizing Radiation Regulations.

The first successful claim for unfair dismissal on the grounds of pregnancy, following the provisions of the Employment Protection Act, was in November 1976:

A woman with a poor record of sickness absence was given time off for a gynaecological operation. She was also warned that any further time off in the following six months would lead to dismissal. Two months later she was dismissed after going into hospital where she had a miscarriage. The employer contended that the dismissal was fair because pregnancy was not the principal reason for the dismissal. The tribunal found the dismissal unfair on the grounds that she would not have been dismissed if she had not had a miscarriage, which was a reason connected with pregnancy. (*George* v. *Beecham Group* (1977))

Misconduct

The range of behaviours that can be described as 'misconduct' is so great that we need to consider different broad categories, the first being disobedience. It is implicit in the contract of employment that the employee will obey lawful instructions; but this does not mean blind, unquestioning obedience in all circumstances: the instruction has to be 'reasonable' and the employee's disobedience 'unreasonable' before the dismissal can be fair. The tribunal would seek to establish exactly what the employee was engaged to do and whether the instruction was consistent with the terms of employment:

> A woman was employed on the understanding that she could have leave during her children's holidays. After a period she was informed that it was not feasible to continue her employment on these terms and she was given twelve months' warning of the need to make alternative arrangements. She did not make any such arrangements and was then dismissed for refusing to work during school holidays. The dismissal was found to be fair as the company had shown it needed her services during the holidays, the nature of her work had not changed and she had been unreasonable in rejecting the new terms. We must also note that her trade union had agreed to the change. (*Moreton* v. *Selby* (1974))

In a recent case (*Payne* v. *Spook Erection* (1984)) an employee was asked to rank subordinates each week on a merit table, even though he had very little contact with some of the men whose merit he was assessing. The scheme was used as a basis both for promotion and for possible dismissal. Mr Payne refused to operate this system as he averred that his assessments could often amount to no more than guesswork. Because of his disobedience he was dismissed, but this dismissal was found unfair by the EAT:

> In our judgment, a scheme bearing these characteristics can only be described as obviously and intolerably unfair. . . . To hold that an employer has the right to require the implementation of a scheme such as this would be to strike at the principles of the Employment Protection legislation and the codes of practice of recent years. (*Payne* v. *Spook Erection* (1984))

Although it is generally fair to dismiss the employee for *absence*, including lateness, the degree of the absence will be an issue. Lateness will seldom be seen to justify dismissal, unless it is persistent and after warning. Absence may be appropriate for dismissal if the nature of the work makes absence unsupportable by the employer. It will normally be expected that the employer will take account of an employee's previous record before taking extreme action.

The third area of misconduct is *insubordination* or rudeness:

> words or conduct showing contempt for one's employers – deserved or otherwise, and as distinct from disagreement or criticism – may make it impossible for the employer to exercise the authority which the law regards as his or to assume that the job in hand will be properly done. (Whincup 1976, p. 85)

It is important that the insubordination should be calculated, rather than a single moment of hysteria. The willingness of the employee to apologize can also be important.

> A woman employee with five years of satisfactory service called her manager a 'stupid punk' in a heated moment and in front of other employees. Later she refused to apologize. The tribunal held that the dismissal was unfair as it was based on a single episode in a substantial period of service. The compensation for the employee was, however, reduced to £20 because she would not apologize. (*Rosenthal* v. *Butler* (1972))

Rudeness to customers is more likely to result in dismissal that a tribunal will find fair.

The employer retains the right to dismiss summarily, without notice, if the employee's conduct merits summary termination. Difficulties occur with the interpretation of certain phrases:

> There have been half a dozen cases on the precise meaning of 'fuck off' – apparently a common industrial salutation. In *Futty* v. *Brekkes*, (1974), a foreman in the course of a discussion with a fish filleter on Hull docks said to him, 'If you don't like the job you can fuck off'. He made no bones about it! The filleter took him at his word and then claimed damages for unfair dismissal. The tribunal held that what the foreman actually meant was, 'if you are complaining about the fish you are working on, or the quality of it, or if you do not like what in fact you are doing then you can leave your work, clock off, and you will be paid up to the time when you do so. Then you can come back when you are disposed to start work again the next day.' His remark was therefore no more than 'a general exhortation' whose precise effect the filleter had failed to appreciate. (Whincup 1976, p. 72)

In another case a supervisor was held to have been constructively dismissed when his employer told him to 'fuck off and get some overalls on'. This remark was to be construed as a demotion, repudiating the contract! (*Walker* v. *Humberside Erection Company* (1976)).

Another area of misconduct is *criminal action*. Tribunals are not courts for criminal proceedings, so that they will not try a case of theft or dishonesty, they will merely decide whether or not dismissal was a reasonable action by the employer in the circumstances. If a man is found guilty by court proceedings this does not justify automatically fair dismissal, it must still be procedurally fair and reasonable, so that theft off-duty is not necessarily grounds for dismissal. On the other hand, strong evidence that would not be sufficient to bring a prosecution may be sufficient to sustain a fair dismissal. Clocking-in offences will normally merit dismissal. Convictions for other offences like drug handling or indecency will only justify dismissal if the nature of the offence will have some bearing on the work done by the employee. For someone like an apprentice instructor it might justify summary dismissal, but in other types of employment it would be unfair, just as it would be unfair to dismiss an employee for a driving offence when there was no need for driving in the course of normal duties and there were other means of transport for getting to work.

Examples are first of the college lecturer who was convicted of gross indecency in a public lavatory with another man. His subsequent dismissal by the college was held to be fair as he was responsible for a foundation course for students in their mid-teens (*Gardiner* v. *Newport CBC* (1977)). In the case of *Moore* v. *C&A Modes* (1981) there was another criminal offence. This time it was a store supervisor with over twenty years' service, who was found shoplifting in another store. Although this was a criminal act away from the place of work, the tribunal held that her subsequent dismissal by C&A Modes was fair, because the criminal act was directly relevant to her employment, even though the action had taken place elsewhere:

> The employer must satisfy the three-fold test laid down in *British Home Stores* v. *Burchell*. First, the employer must show that he genuinely believes the employee to be guilty of the misconduct in question; second, he must have reasonable grounds upon which to establish that belief; third, he must have carried out such investigation into the matter as was reasonable in all the circumstances. (Selwyn 1985, p. 187)

Redundancy

Dismissal for redundancy is protected by compensation for unfair redundancy, compensation for genuine redundancy and the right to consultation before the redundancy takes place:

> An employee who is dismissed shall be taken to be dismissed by reason of redundancy if the dismissal is attributable wholly or mainly to:
> (a) the fact that his employer has ceased, or intends to cease, to carry on the business for the purposes of which the employee was employed by him, or has ceased, or intends to cease, to carry on that business in the place where the employee was so employed, or
> (b) the fact that the requirements of that business for employees to carry out work of a particular kind, or for employees to carry out work of a particular kind in the place where he was so employed, have ceased or are expected to cease or diminish. (Employment Protection (Consolidation) Act 1978, Sect. 81)

Apart from certain specialized groups of employee, anyone who has been continuously employed for two years or more is guaranteed a compensation payment from an employer, if dismissed for redundancy. The compensation is assessed on a sliding scale relating to length of service, age and rate of pay per week. If the employer wishes to escape the obligation to compensate, then it is necessary to show that the reason for dismissal was something other than redundancy.

The employer has to consult with the individual employee before dismissal takes place, but there is also a separate legal obligation to consult with recognized trade unions and the Department of Employment. If ten or more employees are to be made redundant, and if those employees are in unions that are recognized by the employer, then the employer must give written notice of intention to the unions concerned and the Department of Employment at least thirty days before the first dismissal. If it is proposed to make more than 100 employees redundant within a three-month period, then ninety days' advance notice must be given. Having done this, the employer has a legal duty to *consult* with the union representing the employees on the redundancies: he is not obliged to negotiate with them, merely to explain, listen to comments and reply with reasons. Employees also have the right to reasonable time off with pay during their redundancy notice so that they can seek other work.

One of the most difficult aspects of redundancy for the employer is the selection of who should go. The convention is that people should leave on the basis of a long-standing convention known as last-in-first-out, or LIFO, as this provides a rough-and-ready justice with which it is difficult to argue. Our researches show, however, that an increasing number of employers are using other criteria, including skill, competence and attendance record. Less than two-thirds of employers have agreements on redundancy, yet these are the most satisfactory means of smoothing the problems that enforced redundancy causes.

Increasingly, employers are trying to avoid enforced redundancy by a range of strategies, such as not replacing people who leave, early retirement and voluntary redundancy.

Part-time employees can be vulnerable as they can be made redundant if their jobs are made full-time, but they are not able to comply with the revised terms.

The large scale of redundancies in recent years has produced a variety of managerial initiatives to mitigate the effects. One of the most constructive has been a redundancy counselling service. Sometimes this is administered by the personnel department through its welfare officers, but many organizations use external services. Giles Burrows (1985) lists fifteen different firms providing redundancy advisory services, and there has been a number of courses arranged for redundant executives to enable them to set up in business on their own account. Burrows cites evidence from a study by Gibbs and Cross (1985) to say:

> a fraction of one per cent of the total market is reached by the nine prominent redundancy counselling organizations that were surveyed. Information gained from 21 large companies which attempted some form of resettlement assistance indicates that only 51 managers out of 7,604 made redundant were sponsored at redundancy counselling organizations. (Burrows 1985, p. 320)

Constructive dismissal

When the behaviour of the management causes the employee to resign, the ex-employee may still be able to claim dismissal on the grounds that the behaviour of the employer constituted a repudiation of the contract, leaving the employee with no alternative but to resign; the employee may then be able to claim that the dismissal was unfair. It is not sufficient for the employer simply to be awkward or whimsical; the employer's conduct must amount to a significant breach, going to the root of the contract, such as physical assault, demotion, reduction in pay, change in location of work or significant change in duties. The breach must, however, be significant, so that a slight lateness in paying wages would not necessarily involve a breach, neither would a temporary change in place of work: 'If an employer, under the stresses of the requirements of his business, directs an employee to transfer to other suitable work on a purely temporary basis and at no diminution in wages, that may, in the ordinary case, not constitute a breach of contract (*Millbrook Furnishing Ltd* v. *McIntosh* (1981)).

There is no scope for the employer to assume an employee has resigned because of having apparently repudiated the employment contract by not turning up. The breach does not exist until the repudiation is accepted by the employer in dismissing the employee. Unless dismissed, the employee still has a binding contract of employment: 'If a worker walks out of his job or commits any other breach of contract, repudiatory or otherwise, but at any time claims that he is entitled to resume work, then his contract of employment is only determined if the employer expressly or impliedly asserts and accepts the repudiation on the part of the worker' (*LTE* v. *Clarke* (1981).

In all matters of dismissal, the personnel manager should follow scrupulously the suggestions regarding disciplinary and grievance handling set out in Chapter 30. Procedural fairness is a significant test in deciding whether a dismissal was actually fair and not just potentially fair; and the consistent, thorough use of procedure and interviewing can frequently make a dismissal unnecessary as all the other possibilities of restoring satisfaction between the parties are explored first.

Compensation for dismissal

Having considered the various ways in which the employee might have some legal redress against an employer when the employment contract is terminated, we now consider the remedies. If an employee believes the dismissal to be unfair, the employee should complain to an industrial tribunal. The office of the tribunal will refer the matter first to ACAS in the hope that an amicable solution between the parties can be reached. As was indicated at the beginning of this chapter, a number of issues are settled in this way. Either the discontented employee realizes that there is no case, or the employer makes an arrangement in view of the likely tribunal finding. If an agreement is not reached, the case will be heard by an industrial tribunal and, if either party is not satisfied with the finding, they can appeal to the Employment Appeal Tribunal.

The tribunal can make two types of award: either they can order that the ex-employee be re-employed or they can award some financial compensation from the ex-employer for the loss that the employee has suffered. The Employment Protection (Consolidation) Act makes re-employment the main remedy, although this was not previously available under earlier legislation. They will not order re-employment unless the dismissed employee wants it and they can choose between *reinstatement* or *re-engagement*. In reinstatement the old job is given back to the employee under the same terms and conditions, plus any increments, etc., to which the individual would have become entitled had the dismissal not occurred, plus any arrears of payment that would have been received. The situation is just as it would have been, including all rights deriving from length of service, if the dismissal had not taken place. The alternative of re-engagement will be that the employee is employed afresh in a job comparable to the last one, but without continuity of employment. The decision as to which of the two to order will depend on assessment of the practicability of the alternatives, the wishes of the unfairly dismissed employee and the natural justice of the award taking account of the ex-employee's behaviour.

If the employer disagrees with the tribunal award of re-employment and refuses to comply, a penalty award of between 13 and 26 weeks' pay will be incurred depending on the circumstances, and if the dismissal was based on discrimination arising from union membership, race or sex, the penalty must be between 26 and 52 weeks' pay, subject to a maximum. In addition to this, the employee would be entitled to a two-tier award as compensation for the dismissal. The first tier is a *basic award* calculated in the same way as redundancy compensation on each full year of service in various brackets: most applicants to tribunal want their old jobs back at the time of making their claim, but want cash compensation instead by the time the hearing takes place. Even those still wanting reinstatement and having it ordered by the tribunal will still probably not be reinstated by their employer, who will prefer enhanced compensation. Only six of Lewis's 343 respondents achieved reinstatement or re-engagement (Lewis 1981).

Later research by Evans, Goodman and Hargreaves (1985, p. 47) showed that 78 per cent of the respondent firms which they investigated would never re-employ a dismissed employee, and only 1 per cent actually had re-employed a dismissed employee.

Review topic 22.2

In what circumstances do you think a dismissed *employee* might welcome reinstatement or re-engagement, and in what circumstances might the *employer* welcome it?

Written statement of reasons

The Employment Protection (Consolidation) Act gives employees the right to obtain from their employer a written statement of the reasons for their dismissal, if they are dismissed after at least twenty-six weeks' service. If asked, the employer must provide the statement within fourteen days. If it is not provided, the employee can complain to an Industrial Tribunal that the statement has been refused and the tribunal will award the employee two weeks' pay if they find the complaint justified. The employee can also complain, and receive the same award, if the employer's reasons are untrue or inadequate – provided, again, that the tribunal agrees.

Such an award is in addition to anything the tribunal may decide about the unfairness of the dismissal, if the employee complains about that. The main purpose of this provision is to enable the employee to test whether there is a reasonable case for an unfair dismissal complaint or not. Although the statement is admissible as evidence in tribunal proceedings, the tribunal will not necessarily limit their considerations to what the statement contains. If the tribunal members were to decide that the reasons for dismissal were other than stated, then the management's case would be jeopardized.

Resignation

In any organization there will be a stream of people leaving to move on to other things, even though tightness of the labour market has recently reduced many streams to a trickle. Even the most serious of these losses actually provides an opportunity, as a new person will come in or there will be some reshuffling among the existing stock of employees, so that individuals will find fresh scope, and new ideas and energies will be deployed. What is important to the personnel manager is to find out and analyze reasons for leaving, as this will provide information that can be used to iron out problems.

Most people simply move on, but some move on because the 'push' factors are stronger than the 'pulls'. By interviewing everyone who leaves, the personnel manager can collect the range of reasons for people resigning in order to see what the pattern is in the decisions. The difficulty is that at that time the employee has not only decided to go, but also has another job to go to, so that the reasons that first caused the employee to look around may have been forgotten in the enthusiasm about the attractions of the new job. Also, the new job must be presented as better, otherwise the leaver looks foolish. With these reservations, the personnel manager can see what features of organizational practice are unsettling people.

An important legal point about resignation is that an employer cannot avoid the possibility of an unfair dismissal by offering the employee the choice between resigning or being dismissed. Resignation under duress is likely to be construed as dismissal. This is not the same as giving an employee the choice between performing the contract and resigning. The employee who resigns in that situation is making a personal choice to resign rather than discharge those duties the employer is legally entitled to expect.

Retirement

The final mode of contract termination is retirement, and this has the advantage for the employer that there is usually plenty of notice, so that succession arrangements can be planned smoothly. It is now rare for people to retire abruptly after working at high pressure to the very end. Some sort of phased withdrawal is much preferred, so that the retiree adjusts gradually to the new state of being out of regular employment and with a lower level of income, while the employing organization is able to prepare a successor to take office.

Another advantage of this arrangement is that there may be 'a life after death' with the retiree continuing to work part-time after retirement, or coming back to help out at peak periods or at holiday times. Many organizations go to great lengths to keep in touch with their retired personnel, often arranging Christmas parties, excursions and other events with people returning year after year.

Early retirement has become a widespread method of slimming payrolls and making opportunities both for some people to retire early and for others to take their place. The nature of the pension arrangements are critical to early retirement strategies, as early retirees are ideally voluntary and the majority of people will accept, or volunteer for, early retirement if the financial terms are acceptable. It is not, of course, possible to draw state retirement pension until the official retirement ages of 60 or 65, but many people will accept an occupational pension and a lump sum in their fifties if they see the possibility of a new lease of life to pursue other interests or to start their own business.

Notice

An employee qualifies for notice of dismissal on completion of four weeks of employment with an employer. At that time the employee is entitled to receive one week's notice. This remains constant until the employee has completed two years' service, after which it increases to two weeks' notice, thereafter increasing on the basis of one week's notice per additional year of service up to a maximum of twelve weeks for twelve years' unbroken service. These are minimum statutory periods. If the employer includes longer periods of notice in the contract, which is quite common with senior employees, then they are bound by the longer period.

The employee is required to give one week's notice after completing four weeks' service and this period does not increase as a statutory obligation. If an employee accepts a contract in which the period of notice to be given is longer, then that is binding, but the employer may have problems of enforcement if an employee is not willing to continue in employment for the longer period.

Neither party can withdraw notice unilaterally. The withdrawal will only be effective if the other party agrees. Therefore, if an employer gives notice to an employee and wishes later to withdraw it, this can only be done if the employee agrees to the contract of employment remaining in existence. Equally, the employee cannot change his mind about resigning unless the employer agrees.

Notice only exists when a date has been specified. The statement 'We're going to wind up the business, so you will have to find another job' is not notice: it is a warning of intention.

Personnel managers and the law

Personnel managers should not be overconcerned with the legalism of the tribunal system, as this is a danger that the legal system itself is regularly trying to avoid. The following is an extract from a recent EAT judgment:

> Industrial tribunals are not required, and should not be invited, to subject the authorities to the same analysis as a court of law searching in a plethora of precedent for binding or persuasive authority. The objective of Parliament when it first framed the right not to be unfairly dismissed and set up a system of industrial tribunals (with a majority of lay members) to administer it, was to banish legalism and in particular to ensure that, wherever possible, parties conducting their own case would be able to face the tribunal with the same ease and confidence as those professionally represented. A preoccupation with guideline authority puts that objective in jeopardy. (IRLR (1984), p. 131)

Summary propositions

22.1 Of the many dismissals that take place in a year, a minority are reported to tribunal and a small minority are found in favour of the ex-employee.

22.2 The grounds on which an employee can be dismissed without the likelihood of an unfair dismissal claim are lack of capability, misconduct, redundancy, statutory bar, or some other substantial reason.

22.3 If an employee is dismissed on one of the above grounds, the dismissal must still be procedurally fair: following the agreed procedure and being fair in the circumstances.

22.4 An employee who resigns as a result of unreasonable behaviour by the employer could still be able to claim unfair dismissal: constructive dismissal.

22.5 Personnel managers will not wish to discourage employees from resigning, but they will need to monitor reasons for leaving.

22.6 When employees retire from an organization, a phased withdrawal rather than abrupt termination is likely to be a better arrangement for both employer and employee.

22.7 When contemplating the potential fairness of a dismissal, personnel managers should concentrate on the statute and the facts of the situation rather than examining tribunal precedent.

References

ACAS (1985), *Annual Report 1984*, London: Advisory, Conciliation and Arbitration Service.

ACAS, (1990), *Annual Report 1989*, London: Advisory, Conciliation and Arbitration Service.

Amar-Ojok v. *Surrey AHA* [1975] IRLR 252.

Blackman v. *Post Office* [1974] ICR 151, [1974] IRLR 46.

Burrows, G. (1985), *Redundancy Counselling for Managers*, London: Institute of Personnel Management.

Cant v. *James Edwards (Chester) Ltd* (1981).

Dunning & Sons Ltd v. *Jacomb* [1973] ICR 448, [1973] IRLR 206, 15 KIR 9.

East Lindsay District Council v. *Daubney* [1977] ICR 566, [1977] IRLR 181, 12 ITR 359.

Evans, S., Goodman, J. and Hargreaves, L. (1985), *Unfair Dismissal Law and Employment Practice in the 1980s*, DoE Research Paper no. 53, London: Department of Employment.

Flutty v. *D. & D. Brekkes Ltd* [1974] IRLR 130.

Gardiner v. *Newport County Borough Council* [1974] IRLR 262.

George v. *Beecham Group Ltd* [1977].IRLR 43.

Gibbs, A. and Cross, M. (1985), *A Study of Managerial Resettlement*, London: Manpower Services Commission.

International Sports Co. Ltd v. *Thomson* [1980] IRLR 340.

Lewis, D. (1983), *Essentials of Employment Law* London: Institute of Personnel Management.

Lewis, P. (1981) 'Why legislation failed to provide employment protection for unfairly dismissed employees', *British Journal of Industrial Relations*, November, pp. 316–26.

London Transport Executive v. *Clarke* [1981] ICR 355, [1981] IRLR 166.

Lowndes v. *Specialist Heavy Engineering Ltd* [1977] ICRI, [1976] IRLR 24, 11 ITR 253.

Millbrook Furnishing Industries Ltd v. *McIntosh* [1981] IRLR 309.

Ministry of Labour (1976), *Dismissal Procedures*, London: HMSO.

Moore v. *C&A Modes* [1981] IRLR 71.

Moreton v. *Selby* [1974] IRLR 239.

Payne v. *Spook Erection Ltd* [1984] IRLR 221.

Rosenthal v. *Louis Butler Ltd* [1972] IRLR 39.

Selwyn, N. (1985), *Law of Employment* (5th edition), London: Butterworth.

Walker v. *Humberside Erection Company* [1976] IRLR 105.

Whincup, M. (1976), *Modern Employment Law*, London: Heinemann.

Part
IV

Training and Development

23

The training framework

A recent report on industrial training included the following statements:

> Britain's future international competitiveness and economic perform-
> ance will be significantly influenced by the speed with which substantial
> improvements can be made in the scale and effectiveness of training
> by British companies.
>
> Few employers think training sufficiently central to their business
> for it to be a main component in their corporate strategy; the great
> majority did not see it as an issue of major importance – a few openly
> stated as much. (MSC/NEDO 1985, p. 4)

This theme of a great need for more and better training, at the same time as a
great reluctance by employers to provide it, has been echoed in various recent
diagnoses (NEDO 1984; Mackay and Torrington 1986), as well as being a theme
that has worried politicians for the last thirty years. The end of the 1980s has
seen some increase in training, especially as a response to product market
competition, skills shortages and technological change. Nevertheless, the reports
on underprovision of training continue. One of the most telling was by Rajan
and Fryatt (1988) about the situation in the City of London. By 1987 this mélange
of financial institutions was employing 275,000. The stock market crash of Black
Monday at the end of that year led to a loss of 4,000 jobs, but 1,750 others were
created and there was the potential to create 37,000 more in five years. Despite
this rapid growth, training provision remained low and skill shortages were
tackled by hiking salaries and poaching from other industries.

It has also been suggested that the most significant feature of an employment
package offered by recruiters to new graduates is the extent of training and
development that is 'promised' in the offer. There is an obvious need to offer
training in order to recruit the next people and this will become more acute as
the effect of the single European market develops.

In 1964 an Industrial Training Act was passed through parliament with the objective of stimulating training in companies. This Act included the provision of a company levy to fund training initiatives, with individual companies being required to pay an annual sum of as much as 2½ per cent of payroll to the industrial training board for their industry, with the board then making a grant in recognition of the training the company organized. This approach was widely regarded as a tax on industry and had the drawback that it did not ensure training took place. A company that was not interested in training could simply pay the levy and ignore the possibility of obtaining a grant. Also, it was based on industrial sectors, such as engineering and glass, which was not the most appropriate way to develop training in skills to be used in a number of different sectors. The system of industrial training boards and levy/grant has been steadily wound down, but the problem remains.

There is a widespread acceptance of the argument that more training needs to be provided, but a lack of enthusiasm to make the provision. The significance of this for personnel managers is substantial. Training and development is a major feature of the personnel function, and makes up one third of the course for professional membership of the Institute of Personnel Management, yet apathy towards training by other managers causes personnel specialists themselves to lose interest and to advocate the need for training with insufficient vigour.

The training function

In our research we found that half of our respondents had a training department, a further 16 per cent had a training officer, but nearly one in three had neither. Twenty-eight per cent of respondents also reported that training provision in their establishments had decreased over the previous three years (Mackay and Torrington, 1986, p. 11).

The training department or training officer is almost always a part of the personnel function. In the late 1960s (just after the Industrial Training Act) some trainers were set up as entities separate from personnel on the basis that personnel was an activity of routine matters, but training was important, and a bright-eyed, bushy-tailed young training officer could not be expected to be subordinate to the solid but status-lacking personnel officer. That did not last long as the frighteners of employment law and 1970s-style trade union activity came along to enhance the status of personnel management and training became the poor relation. There is also the logic of the close interrelationship between training and many other personnel activities such as recruitment, selection, performance appraisal and equal opportunity.

Training is not, however, a separate activity that can be limited to the training school. It must be closely connected with the workplaces of those that are to be trained:

> with the increasing range both of areas in which training is needed and of ways in which this training can be provided, specialists have a major role to play. However, they are unlikely to be playing that role effectively if they are operating in isolation from the line managers of those trained. (Open University 1986, p. 3)

The company training officer also has to maintain contacts with potential external providers of training. Training is the area of personnel work in which there is the greatest use of consultants and other external providers. These range from colleges, universities, commercial consultants, government agencies to suppliers of do-it-yourself training facilities, like computer-based training. Figure 23.1 shows the training officer's basic network of contacts.

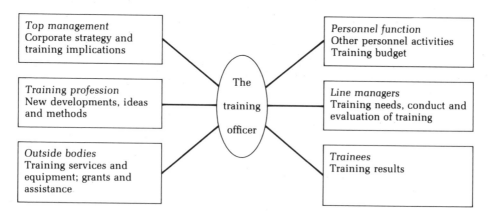

Figure 23.1 *The training officer's network*

There is a number of advantages to drawing on outside sources for training, as it provides a range of skills that very few organizations can maintain in-house and means that the commissioner of the training need only think of what is needed to provide good training, without any concern about keeping trainers occupied. It also provides the opportunity of saving in costs overall as there are not the continuing, month-by-month employment costs of training personnel. On the other hand, the organization needs an expert to choose the appropriate supplier and the appropriate product, as well as negotiating for the supply of exactly what is needed rather than what happens to be available. Furthermore, there is a tendency for the external supplier to provide nothing but courses, even though the training need might be better served by some other strategy, and an external supplier will be tempted to diagnose a problem that needs a training solution rather than a different type of solution, as is considered later in this chapter. The best combination is for the organization to maintain a strong but lean training operation in-house, while using a substantial proportion of its training budget to deploy external expertise for specific assignments, but this is only possible in the large undertaking that can afford both. Referring back to the discussion in Chapter 2, training is a personnel activity that can perhaps benefit more than most from strong centralization.

Review topic 23.1

Refer back to Chapter 2 and the distinction between human resources management and personnel management. Now write a 100-word definition of training with a human resources emphasis, and a 100-word definition with a personnel management emphasis.

Why training suffers

The opening of this chapter illustrated that few employers put into training the investment that common sense seems to suggest, and it is important for us to try to understand why this should be.

The problem of results

The first reason is that it is difficult to identify and demonstrate the results that training produces. When economic conditions are difficult, a normal management reaction is to concentrate on those activities that will produce immediate results because of the need to make enough money to pay next week's bills. Training seldom produces quick results with a tangible pay-off. Training that is most likely to produce useful skills is that associated with long-term preparation, like craft apprenticeship and management development, yet this requires a relatively stable situation in which it is possible to think of the future. We thus have the irony that training is most likely to be supported at times of company prosperity, rather than at times of greatest need.

Even prosperous companies do not necessarily invest in training, however, as there remains the question about what training produces. A selector fills vacancies, an industrial relations officer concludes an agreement with a trade union, a pay expert introduces a revised system of payment, but the trainer has to rely only on secondary indicators of achievement, like courses completed and vague feelings of satisfaction. If the trainer defines training objectives, the satisfaction of these in behaviour change can be observed and demonstrate results, but how many trainers define objectives so precisely, especially in the area of most expensive training such as management development? Where training is thoroughly evaluated, before and after the training itself, then the direct effects could be demonstrated more clearly, but this is a cumbersome process requiring a great deal of support from others and it may be that most trainers are much more interested in input than output. Training appears to be something you have to believe in and faith is a powerful driving force in those who have it, but what is there to drive those without it?

The lack of external controls

Two external influences are less potent than in the 1970s: training boards and labour turnover. In our research we found that the majority of respondents regretted the passing of the training boards. Although the levy/grant system had been unpopular, the other activities of the boards were seen to have given status to training that had been absent beforehand and declining since. The fact that the boards have been mostly wound up is in some ways more unfortunate than if they had never been established, as abolition carries the overtone of undesirability or obsolescence of the boards' activities as well as of their administrative operations.

The drop in labour turnover has had an even more direct effect, particularly at shopfloor level. The organization that had an annual turnover of 40 per cent and a workforce of 1,000 will have a drastically reduced initial training and induction need if its turnover is now 15 per cent with a workforce of 600: an annual intake of 400 potential trainees has dropped to 90.

Personnel managers' values

It would be inaccurate to suggest that disinterest in training is limited to those outside the personnel function. Our respondents were asked to identify the activity that they regarded as most central to the personnel function: only 11 per cent of respondents picked training. Interviewees generally were half-hearted about the value of training, although this usually only emerged after careful and persistent probing. Although emphasis on training has increased in the 1990s, not all personnel managers have the thoroughgoing commitment to it that their public statements indicate, especially when it is training and development outside the area of management development. This may well be because of the lack of interest by other managers, yet it has the effect that training is not always defended forcefully or promoted vigorously.

The vigorous minority

Although there are problems about support for training, there are large numbers of organizations in which training provision is expanding and being driven as a key element in plans for organizational growth and development.

In some organizations this is further development of a well-established function, and in others it is because of the presence of key figures who possess the necessary belief in training, but there is also a significant influence from two relatively new areas: financial services and retailing.

Financial services, such as banking and insurance, have stepped up their training activities considerably. This has been partly due to business expansion in an activity that has a degree of labour intensivity, but also due to a keener competitive edge within the industry and the resultant concern to ensure a high standard of capability among employees.

Financial services share with retailing an urgent sense of needing to satisfy the customer, and that urgency has been transmitted to their training activities, with much of the training being directed to ensuring customer satisfaction with the treatment they receive from staff. In related fields, both British Airways and British Rail have run extensive training programmes for all their employees to develop greater customer awareness and concern. Many companies have increased their quality training because of the need for products to meet a high standard in customer satisfaction.

The general shift towards a marketing orientation in companies has partly replaced the external stimulus that was previously provided by training boards, but that type of stimulus carries with it the inevitable concern with the immediate and short term, and only a limited range of training objectives can be quickly satisfied. Furthermore, an increase in training is usually the fruit of success rather than its cause, although continued training may be seen as essential to sustaining that success:

> High performance businesses are twice as likely to train, and train twice as many employees as low performance businesses, and high performance businesses have increased their training by 25 per cent over the past five years, with low performers reducing their training by 20 per cent. (MSC/NEDO 1985, p. 26)

A further positive indication is that training is becoming – in the successful companies – more carefully undertaken, with training needs identified closely, methods carefully selected and the whole training process monitored with costs and requirements judiciously evaluated.

Review topic 23.2

We have suggested some of the reasons why training may be cut back in organizations. Which of these reasons do *not* apply where you work? Can you think of other reasons? How would you justify increased investment in training within your organization?

Identification of training needs

Identifying training needs (ITN) is a key stage in training administration. What actually is the training need? The reason for care with the question is to ensure that the training is needed as well as being correctly undertaken. It is easy to assume that an operating problem can be solved by a training initiative, when a quite different solution is needed. Training supervisors in skills of interpersonal communication will have limited value if there is an underlying problem of communication or organization structure which will remain no matter how skilful in communication the supervisors become. Stephen Robbins (1978, p. 143) suggests that correct identification of training needs is achieved through asking four questions:

1. What are the organization's goals?
2. What tasks must be completed to achieve these goals?
3. What behaviours are necessary for each job holder to complete his or her assigned tasks?
4. What deficiencies, if any, do job holders have in the knowledge, skills or attitudes required to perform the necessary behaviours?

Those questions obviously echo questions that are asked in manpower planning and recruitment and selection, showing the interdependence of all such activities, and the outcome is a training gap; showing the need for a training initiative to deal with the identified deficiencies.

The crucial question is the fourth, and the starting point in finding an answer is to look at indicators – mainly indicators of unsatisfactory productivity, especially where there are valid comparators like higher levels of output by staff doing similar work in another department or lower manning levels in a rival company. Other indicators are levels of scrap, accidents, customer complaints, absence, punctuality and employee grievances. Looking at the indicators is, however, only the starting point in finding the answer as any one of the indicators may be indicating a problem different from a training need. What looks like a training deficiency may in fact be a lack of proper equipment, or poor pay rates or low morale. The information from the indicators has to be interpreted by discussion with line managers, work study officers and the people doing the jobs. The trainer will distil the essence from this mass of information and assess it in the light of his own training expertise and experience to produce a plan of what can be done, what the likely pay-off would be and how much it would cost, guarding against the danger of the £5,000 solution to the £1,000 problem.

Robbins' questions introduce another set of initials from the trainer's basic vocabulary: KSA, standing for knowledge, skills and attitudes to categorize the aspects of the deficiencies that may be identified. *Knowledge* is what the employee needs to know in order to achieve the goals the job specifies, like the learner driver needing to know the highway code. *Skills* are what the employee has to possess in order to be able to do the job, like the ability to keep the proper balance between clutch and accelerator. *Attitudes* are what the employee needs to display in connection with achieving the tasks, like respect for other road users.

We must avoid the trap of considering ITN in a limited way of assessing only what is there and palpably needing to be done. Good trainers always construe their role as being partly to bring about necessary change by helping employees to be able to accept and welcome change. This is where attention to the 'A' of KSA is important. Two examples are equality of opportunity, and health and safety. Equality of opportunity will be furthered by policies and procedures, by monitoring and by determined managerial action, but some of the most significant advances will come through training, which can enable people to understand equal opportunity issues more clearly and to welcome rather than resist management initiatives in that area. Safe working practices similarly are only partly achieved through supervisory vigilance and management invest-ment in better equipment. The employee who believes in working safely, who is aware of the hazards and who develops an attitude of placing priority on safe working will be much more safe in working habits – permanently.

At this point we need to refer to *competencies* as this is an idea that has taken the world of management training and development by storm, as well as camouflaging some extremely woolly thinking. The basic idea of competency-based training is that it should be *criterion-related*, directed at developing the ability of trainees to perform specific tasks directly related to the job they are in or for which they are preparing, expressed in terms of performance outcomes and specific indicators. It is a reaction against the confetti-scattering approach to training as being a good thing in its own right, concerned with the general education of people dealing with general matters.

The key piece of research on competencies is by Richard Boyatsis, who carried out a large-scale intensive study of 2,000 managers, holding 41 different jobs in 12 organizations. He defines a competency as: 'an underlying characteristic of a person which results in effective and/or superior performance in a job' (Boyatsis 1982, p. 21).

It may be a *trait*, which is a characteristic or quality that a person has, like *efficacy*, which is the trait of believing you are in control of your future and fate.

When you encounter a problem you then take an initiative to resolve the problem, rather than wait for someone else to do it.

It may be a *motive*, which is a drive or thought related to a particular goal, like *achievement*, which is a need to improve and compete against a standard of excellence.

It may be a *skill*, which is the ability to demonstrate a sequence of behaviour that is functionally related to attaining a performance goal. Being able to tune and diagnose faults in a car engine is a skill, because it requires the ability to identify a sequence of actions, which will accomplish a specific objective. It also involves being able to identify potential obstacles and sources of help in overcoming them. The skill can be applied to a range of different situations. The ability to change the sparking plugs is an ability only to perform that action.

It may be a person's *self-image*, which is the understanding we have of ourselves and an assessment of where we stand in the context of values held by others in our environment. For example: 'I am creative and innovative. I am expressive and I care about others.' In a job requiring routine work and self-discipline, that might modify to: 'I am creative and innovative. I am too expressive. I care about others and lack a degree of self-discipline.'

It may be a person's *social role*, which is a perception of the social norms and behaviours that are acceptable and the behaviours that the person then adopts in order to fit in.

It may be a *body of knowledge*.

If these are the elements of competency, some of them can be developed, some can be modified and some can be measured, but not all.

Boyatsis makes a further distinction of the *threshold competency*, which is: 'A person's generic knowledge, motive, trait, self-image, social role, or skill which is essential to performing a job, but is not causally related to *superior* job performance' like being able to speak the native tongue of one's subordinates. Figure 23.2 summarizes these.

Threshold competencies
Use of unilateral power: Using forms of influence to obtain compliance.
Accurate self-assessment: Having a realistic or grounded view of oneself, seeing personal strengths and weaknesses and knowing one's limitations.
Positive regard: Having a basic belief in others; that people are good; being optimistic and causing others to feel valued.
Spontaneity: Being able to express oneself freely or easily, sometimes making quick or snap decisions.
Logical thought: Placing events in causal sequence; being orderly and systematic.
Specialized knowledge: Having usable facts, theories, frameworks or models.
Developing others: Helping others to do their jobs, adopting the role of coach and using feedback skills in facilitating self-development of others.

Figure 23.2 *The seven threshold competencies identified by Richard Boyatsis*

Competencies are required for *superior* performance and are grouped in clusters, shown in Figure 23.3.

The *goal and action management cluster* relates to the requirement to make things happen towards a goal or consistent with a plan.

The *leadership* cluster relates to activating people by communicating goals, plans and rationale and stimulating interest and involvement.

The *human resource management* cluster relates to managing the co-ordination of groups of people working together towards the organization's goals.

Management competency clusters

The **goal and action management cluster**:

Concern with impact: Being concerned with symbols of power to have impact on others, concerned about status and reputation.

Diagnostic use of concepts: Identifying and recognizing patterns from an assortment of information, by bringing a concept to the situation and attempting to interpret events through that concept.

Efficiency orientation: Being concerned to do something better.

Proactivity: Being a disposition toward taking action to achieve something.

The **leadership cluster**:

Conceptualization: Developing a concept that describes a pattern or structure perceived in a set of facts: the concept emerges from the information.

Self-confidence: Having decisiveness or presence; knowing what you are doing and feeling you are doing it well.

Use of oral presentations: Making effective verbal presentations in situations ranging from one-to-one to several hundred people.
(Plus threshold competency of logical thought)

The **human resource management cluster**:

Use of socialized power: Using forms of influence to build alliances, networks, coalitions and teams.

Managing group process: Stimulating others to work effectively in group settings.
(Plus threshold competencies of accurate self-assessment and positive regard)

The **focus on others cluster**:

Perceptual objectivity: Being able to be relatively objective, avoiding bias or prejudice.

Self-control: Being able to inhibit personal needs or desires in service of organizational needs.

Stamina and adaptability: Being able to sustain long hours of work and have the flexibility and orientation to adapt to changes in life and the organizational environment.

The **directing subordinates cluster**:

(Threshold competencies of developing others, spontaneity and use of unilateral power)

Figure 23.3 *The five clusters of management competencies identified by Richard Boyatsis*

The *focus on others* cluster relates to maturity and taking a balanced view of events and people.

The *directing subordinates* cluster relates to providing subordinates with information on performance, interpreting what the information means to the subordinates and placing positive or negative values on the interpretation.

The basically useful idea of competency-based training is being applied to training nationally by the National Council for Vocational Qualifications, but the identification of the appropriate competencies is undertaken by a 'lead body' which represents those who have to employ and deploy the people who are trained. This inevitably leads to lists of competencies which are a consensus of good (or inoffensive) ideas, but all too often they represent a lowest common denominator of narrowness. In management development there is the risk identified by Tony Berry, of the Manchester Business School:

> there seems to be a drift towards a training agenda in management education, such that students are technically equipped to take up a task but intellectually incapable of addressing the ideas that have shaped the creation of that task. (Berry 1990)

Evaluation of training

One of the most nebulous and unsatisfactory aspects of the training job is evaluating its effectiveness, yet it is becoming more necessary to demonstrate value for money. Evaluation is straightforward when the output of the training is clear to see, like reducing the number of dispatch errors in a warehouse or increasing someone's typing speed. It is more difficult to evaluate the success of a management training course or a programme of social skills development, but the fact that it is difficult is not enough to prevent it being done.

A familiar method of evaluation is the post-course questionnaire, which course members complete on the final day by answering vague questions that amount to little more than 'good, very good or outstanding'. The drawbacks with these are, first, that there is a powerful halo effect, as the course will have been, at the very least, a welcome break from routine and there will probably have been some attractive fringe benefits like staying in a comfortable hotel and enjoying rich food. Secondly, the questionnaire tends to evaluate the course and not the learning, so that the person attending the course is assessing the quality of the tutors and the visual aids, instead of being directed to examine what has been learnt. Easterby-Smith and Tanton surveyed evaluation of training in fifteen organizations to conclude:

> All but one of the 15 organizations conducted some form of evaluation on a regular basis, and invariably this consisted of an end-of-course

questionnaire. . . . The impression gained from training managers was that this was regarded largely as part of the ritual of course closure; they commented that completed questionnaires were normally filed away – the data thus produced was rarely used in decisions about training . . . if a negative comment is voiced by one individual, that criticism is often seen to reflect poorly on the individual rather than on the course. (Easterby-Smith and Tanton 1985, p. 25)

The authors then advocate the simple strategy of asking participants and their bosses to complete short questionnaires at the beginning of the course to focus their minds on what they hope to get from it. At the end of the course there is a further questionnaire focusing on learning and what could be applied back on the job. Later, they complete further questionnaires to review the effects of the course on the subsequent working performance. This overcomes the problem of the learning remaining a detached experience inducing nostalgic reflection but no action, but it also encourages the course participant to concentrate on what he or she is learning and not assessing objectively the quality of the service.

Taking the broader issue of evaluating training in general rather than the experience of trainees, researchers at Warwick University concluded:

Evaluation is notoriously difficult, but our research indicates that those firms which have the most positive attitudes (and carry out the most training) typically employ 'soft' criteria relating to broad human resource goals (recruitment and retention, career management etc.), and tend to be sceptical about 'hard' cost-benefit evaluation, related to bottom-line outcomes. (Pettigrew, Sparrow and Hendry 1988, p. 31)

Training for different groups of employee

Training provision by organizations is largely focused on the development of managerial talent, but there are a number of other categories that seldom receive the attention they need.

Shopfloor

General shopfloor or manual jobs are usually specific to one employer or one type of process, so that storekeeping in one organization can be very different from a job in another organization carrying the same title. Skills may be limited and the recent deskilling of jobs may make training superfluous apart from a short period of 'being shown how'. Comprehensive training can, however, produce a higher level of performance more quickly from a more satisfied employee. Shortening training times reduces manpower costs and can reduce staff turnover. This argument is sustained by the examination of the learning curve for a particular job. A recent example is a study by James (1984).

The training may be provided by an instructor if there is a large throughput of recruits; otherwise the supervisor can be trained in instructional techniques. Half of all training is carried out on the job itself (Sloman 1989)

Clerical and administrative

Clerical and administrative jobs are much more likely to have a common core of knowledge or skill, partly dictated by equipment. The skills of typing and word processing are determined by the model of typewriter or PCW, rather than the type of organization, although there will be many aspects of organizational routine and procedure that new recruits have to acquire.

The further education service is helpful as courses in office skills and computer operation are generally available, so that organizationally-specific training is normally limited to induction.

Technical training

Another area that is based on widely used skills is the training of technicians and technologists. Craft apprenticeships assume the acquisition of generally useful capacities and there is attendance at college to provide the necessary element of theoretical knowledge and some manual skills.

There have been many attempts to make the training in craft skills more varied so that people become multi-skilled and their deployment more flexible.

Professional engineers achieve membership of one of the constituent bodies of the Council of Engineering Institutions, when they can show a high level of academic attainment, together with appropriate working experience. The employing organization will have to provide that working experience as well as making provision for college attendance to reach the necessary academic level.

Youth training

The Youth Training Scheme (YTS), organized by the Manpower Services Commission during the 1980s, must be one of the largest and most expensive training programmes ever devised, and it was a unique experiment in occupational preparation. Our research showed that one third of our respondents were acting as managing agents and another third were providing work experience under the scheme. The overwhelming reason for being involved with the scheme was to meet social obligations. Only nine respondents saw it as a means of meeting organizational *training needs*, although 165 identified YTS as a means of *recruitment*.

In January 1986 YTS was relaunched as a two-year programme instead of a twelve-month programme and this initiative was not widely welcomed. There was a renewal of the complaints about the shortage of 'real' jobs compared with jobs on schemes, and questions about whether YTS was providing an occupational preparation or merely a staging-post between school and (possibly) employment. There have also been a number of complaints from employers, particularly managing agents, about costs and bureaucratic controls. Keith Lathrope of IPM poses the following question:

> Ask the question: 'Should I (or my organization) join in?' If the answer is 'No' check that it's not just an easy way out, that the problems, difficult as many are, are not just an excuse. If the answer is 'Yes' then there is a crusade to undertake but more on strategic than tactical issues. . . . How will YTS be transformed into a genuinely work-based, employer-led scheme? And, perhaps most crucial of all, how do we provide better opportunities for trainees to be employees? (Lathrope 1986, p. 31)

In 1989 there was a further change in government strategy as responsibility for YTS (now called Youth Training) is transferred to new Training and Enterprise Councils (TECs), which are local bodies, led by people with industrial and commercial expertise, and able to direct training towards actual skill shortages and meet real employment growth prospects. TECs are not intended merely to take over responsibility for Youth Training, but to develop training that is appropriate for all levels in the local area.

Induction

New employees are most likely to leave the organization in the early weeks of employment: a period often described as the *induction crisis* before the period of settled connection begins. The approach by managers to this problem is to attempt initiatives that will lead quickly and surely to a settled connection rather than just waiting to see what happens. The costs of unproductive appointments are high and the clinching of the employment decision by integrating the new employee into the organization is a vital element of the employment process. Induction has been defined as:

> Arrangements made by or on behalf of the management to familiarize the new employee with the working organization, welfare and safety

matters, general conditions of employment and the work of the department in which he is to be employed. It is a continuous process starting from the first contact with the employer. (DoE 1971)

It is thus different from instruction in that it is concerned not with the specific content of the work to be done, but with the context in which it was carried out. Pigors and Myers (1977) provide a checklist of steps in an induction programme, which is abbreviated below.

- The organization – history, development, management and activity.
- Personnel policies.
- Terms of employment – including disciplinary rules and union arrangements.
- Employee benefits and services.
- Physical facilities.
- General nature of the work to be done.
- The supervisor.
- Departmental rules and safety measures.
- Relation of new job to others.
- Detailed description of job.
- Introduction to fellow workers.
- Follow-up after several weeks.

Although this is comprehensive, it is not likely to turn into an effective programme unless worked out in careful detail about timing, pace and the essence of social adjustment. Some new recruits may be easy to integrate because they have experience of frequent job changes, but others change employment less often and everyone has to start at some time. The induction of school-leavers and graduates has different dimensions because they are entering the world of work for the very first time and will be quite unfamiliar with the myriad of conventions that are common knowledge among all those who have some experience. Another group who may have special problems are married woman returners, who may have lost confidence in their own abilities after a prolonged period of absence. There can also be considerable difficulties for those beginning work again after a prolonged period of unemployment. Gomersall and Myers (1966) describe an interesting scheme at Texas Instruments where experimentation was carried out under controlled conditions. An experimental group was given an additional period of six hours' social orientation with four elements:

1. Detailed factual explanations of how long it took to achieve various levels of competence.
2. Advice to ignore comments that they would hear from existing employees about the difficulty of achieving standards.
3. Instruction to take the initiative in asking for help from the supervisor.
4. Detailed description of the sort of person the supervisor was.

The sponsors of the scheme report that training time was halved and training costs reduced by two-thirds as a result of this approach, as it focused on the actual anxieties and reservations of the new employees, instead of concentrating on what it was thought appropriate for them to be told. The key to successful induction is enabling the new employee to be confident in the new situation. However important information about the history of the organization might be, it is something that is easily deferred until the induction crisis is over. It is doubtful that an individual would leave a new job due to lack of information regarding the history of the company.

Training costs

> The Manpower Services Commission survey calculated that with a total training expenditure of £2 billion per year, this works out at £200 per employee and represents only 0.15% of the average firm's turnover. This lack of investment is not only foolhardy but considerably below that of others: in fact only one seventh of the American figure and one fourteenth of the best in West Germany. (Open University 1986, p. 5)

Two years later the Manpower Services Commisison had become the Training Commission and had conducted a further survey reported by Sloman (1989). This reached the conclusion that in 1986/7 British employers spent £14.4 billion on the provision of training for their workforce, which worked out at £800 per employee. Despite the wildly differing conclusions about how much is actually spent, they at least demonstrate that we do not spend as much on training as other countries, but not widespread agreement on who should pay more.

An analysis by the Industrial Society (1985) at least shows how companies in different areas distribute their training budget and what proportion it is of turnover. In answer to a questionnaire with 134 useable responses, 64.6 per cent of responding organizations said that they spent less than 0.5 per cent of their annual turnover on training their employees, including all twelve of the public service respondents. Only seven respondents spend more than 1.5 per cent. The items comprising the training budget were staff education schemes, equipment costs, training centres and consultants. The survey does not reveal whether salary costs for training staff are included, but 77 per cent of firms include trainees' expenses and only 35 per cent include trainees' salaries.

Summary propositions

23.1 The level of training provision in companies is lower than is needed for international competitiveness, economic performance and the reasonable expectations of employees.

23.2 Effective company training cannot come from the training officer or department alone. It must involve both the workplace and the line manager of the trainee.

23.3 Training is one of the first casualties of financial economies in organizations because of the problem of results, the lack of external controls and lack of advocacy by personnel managers.

23.4 A greater interest in marketing has provided some stimulus to training in more efficient companies.

23.5 Training is not only responding to requirements; it is also seeking out training needs before they become obvious and anticipating ways in which training could make a contribution to business growth.

23.6 Evaluation of training is more effective when directed at trainees' behaviour and how this has changed than when directed at their opinions.

23.7 Training costs constitute a lower proportion of company turnover than in West Germany and the United States.

References

Berry, A. J. (1990), 'Masters or subjects?', *British Academy of Management Newsletter*, no. 5, February.

Boyatsis, R. E. (1982), *The Competent Manager*, New York: John Wiley.

Department of Employment (1971), *Glossary of Training Terms*, London: HMSO.

Easterby-Smith, M. and Tanton, M. (1985), 'Turning course evaluation from an end to a means', *Personnel Management*, April.

Gomersall, E. R. and Myers, M. S. (1966), 'Breakthrough in on-the-job training', *Harvard Business Review*, July/August, pp. 62–71.

Industrial Society (1985), *Survey of Training Costs*, London: The Industrial Society.

James, R. (1984), 'The use of learning curves', *Journal of European Industrial Training*, vol. 8, no. 7.

Lathrope, K. quoted in Milton, R. (1986), 'Double, double, toil and trouble: YTS in the melting pot', *Personnel Management*. April.

Mackay, L. E. and Torrington, D. P. (1986), 'Training in the UK: down but not out', *Journal of European Industrial Training*, vol. 10, no. 1.

MSC/NEDO (1986), *A Challenge to Complacency: Changing attitudes to training*, Sheffield: Manpower Services Commission.

NEDO (1984), *Competence and Competition*, London: National Economic Development Office.

Open University (1986), *Managing People: 2*, Milton Keynes: The Open University Press.

Pettigrew, A. M., Sparrow, P. and Hendry, C. (1988), 'The forces that trigger training', *Personnel Management*, December, pp. 28–32.

Pigors, P. and Myers, C. S. (1977), *Personnel Administration* (8th edition), New York: McGraw-Hill.

Rajan, A. and Fryatt, J. (1988), *Create or Abdicate: The City's human resource choice for the 90s*, London: Witherby.

Robbins, S. P. (1978), *Personnel: The management of human resources*, Englewood Cliffs, NJ: Prentice Hall.

Sloman, M. (1989), 'On-the-job training: A costly poor relation', *Personnel Management*, vol. 21, no. 2, February.

24

Work design and motivation

It is important that training and development are soundly based on job analysis, which we described in Chapter 16. However, jobs cannot be analyzed until it has been decided exactly what tasks should constitute each job, and how they relate to other tasks and other jobs. It is this process of work design which we now consider. In 1985, Robertson and Smith wrote:

> A decade ago, judging by the reports in the serious press and the informal talk among professionals in the field, it might have seemed that redesigning jobs to improve their motivational content was of the highest importance. Since that time the theoretical basis of the job redesign movement has come under criticism and some negative feelings have emerged. Nevertheless by today's more sceptical standards redesigning jobs to bring about higher levels of employee motivation is an important management strategy which can produce valuable results and make life satisfying. (Robertson and Smith 1985, p. 93)

In this chapter we look at what work design is and the link between work design, motivation, job satisfaction and job performance. We then review some theories of motivation and consider the work characteristics which motivate. Various types of job design are considered, a process for introducing job design suggested and the role of personnel management discussed. We conclude with an evaluation of job design.

What is work design?

Work design has been variously referred to in the literature as job design, job redesign and work redesign – all being used to indicate very much the same process. In this chapter we will use the terms interchangeably. Job design is essentially a process of allocating task functions among organizational roles (Cooper 1974). However, the terminology is increasingly used to indicate the frame of reference of the job designer. In this context a good definition of the meaning of job design as it is often currently used is found in Davis:

> Job design is concerned with the specification of the contents, methods and relationships of jobs in order to satisfy technological and organizational requirements, as well as the social and personal requirements of the job holder. (Davis 1966)

Earlier in this century job design had traditionally been interpreted in a much narrower fashion and the criteria used in job design were largely based on the principle of minimum cost. A US study in 1955, quoted in Robertson and Smith (1985, p. 3), demonstrated that the three major criteria used in job design were:

1. Maximum specialization through the limitation of both the number of component tasks in a job and variations in the tasks.
2. Maximum repetitiveness.
3. Minimum training time.

This ties in with classical economic theory which emphasized the improvement of the utilization of resources through the subdivision of tasks and the specialization of skills. It is also in line with the view that people have a purely instrumental attitude to work, and Taylor's ideas of the rationalization of work.

Since then there has been a considerable change in our attitudes about work, and this is reflected in more recent approaches to the design of work. Greater affluence, education, mobility and awareness, and the erosion of traditional patterns of authority and other changes have led to greater expectations of work than purely the satisfaction of financial need. As Robertson and Smith (1985, p. 5) argue: 'We are beginning to ask much more from our organizations; instead of simply serving them, we want to know how they can contribute to the quality of our work experience and personal development.'

Employers, too, have taken note of developments in the behavioural sciences. In addition to requiring high performance from their employees, they have begun to recognize that another important outcome of work is the satisfaction that an individual worker experiences. Individuals are no longer seen as working for financial rewards alone, but for the satisfaction that can be achieved through actually doing the job; that is, the intrinsic (internal) content of the job, as well as from the external (extrinsic) factors such as pay and conditions.

All these factors have influenced our concepts of job design, making them far more inclusive than traditional concepts, and in line with the quotation from

Table 24.1 Reasons for introducing job changes

Reason Source	Birchall and Wild		Reif and Schoderbek	Wilkinson	Total
	Blue-collar	White-collar	Blue- and white-collar	Blue- and white-collar	Blue- and white-collar
1. System output					
to improve productivity	12	9		11	32
to reduce costs	5	3	21		29
to improve quality	7	5	13		25
to reduce downtime	1				1
to reduce inventories	1				1
to make better use of skills	2	2			4
to increase flexibility	3	3			6
to reduce specialization			14		14
commercial factors				4	4
2. System changes					
introduction of automated equipment	2	1			3
introduction of new plant	3	2			5
introduction of new productivity agreement	2				2
3. Personnel problems					
to reduce labour turnover	6	5		6	17
to reduce absenteeism	4	1			5
to attract labour	1				1
to improve labour relations	2	2			4
4. Concern for employee					
to improve worker 'morale'	10	7	15		32
to give 'meaning', etc., to work	4	4			8
to reduce monotony			11		11
to eliminate social problems				11	11
5. Changing supervisory role					
concern about the role of first-line supervision	2			8	10
6. Others	8	3	11		22
Total	75	47	85	40	247

Source: Adapted from Birchall (1975, p. 31).

Davis (1966, p. 420 above). Employers, of course, have not, in their enthusiasm to satisfy the needs of their workers, jettisoned their desire for an effective, efficient organization that meets its goals. Indeed, in many cases employers see job design as a way to achieve those goals.

Table 24.1 shows how the reasons that employers redesign jobs are a mix of providing satisfying work for employees, reducing organizational problems and improving productivity. Job design is just one approach to improving individual performance. Others include training, personal development, performance appraisal, clear roles, standards and expectations, and reinforcement of desired behaviour – such as making pay and promotion contingent upon productivity, and the manager giving praise where this is appropriate.

The link between work design, motivation, job performance and job satisfaction

The theory of work design can make sense only when one understands the relationship between motivation, job satisfaction and job performance. Motivation is a psychological concept related to the strength and direction of behaviour. People who are highly motivated towards passing their exams will display this in their behaviour – by studying notes and reading for considerable periods of time. A less well-motivated person would display less of this behaviour, and more alternative forms of behaviour like going out for a drink. Each individual has a different pattern of motivation, but until very recently job design theory has been based on the assumption that a general pattern of motivation can be identified.

We shall discuss some theories of motivation in the next section, but in summary these theories suggest that individuals are increasingly motivated by a need to fulfil their potential and continue their self-development. Factors intrinsic to the content of the job, such as experiencing a sense of achievement, recognition and responsibility at work, are those that motivate employees. Motivation theory suggests that an individual's behaviour at work will be directed towards satisfying these needs. If a job is designed so that these needs can be fulfilled, then the employee will perform to a high standard because he is satisfying personal as well as organizational requirements. A simplification of these concepts is shown in Figure 24.1. Most job design schemes have been based on these concepts, but there is a number of problems with these ideas, and reality, of course, is far more complex than Figure 24.1. These problems and constraints are dealt with at the end of this chapter in the section on evaluation of job design.

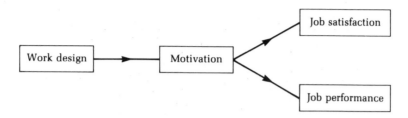

Figure 24.1 *The link between work design, motivation, job satisfaction and job performance*

Theories of motivation

Maslow's hierarchy of needs

Maslow (1943) suggested that human motivation was dependent on the desire to satisfy various levels of needs. He argued that people are motivated to conduct themselves in a way that they feel is a means of fulfilling their needs. Maslow saw these needs as being organized in a hierarchy, as shown in Figure 24.2, with basic physiological needs at the bottom ranging up through safety, social and esteem needs to self-actualization needs at the top. As the lowest need becomes satisfied then an individual is motivated to satisfy the need that is next in the hierarchy, so higher needs can only become operative once a lower need has been satisfied. Once a need has been satisfied then it ceases to motivate an individual, although the higher needs of esteem and self-actualization are more powerful and self-sustaining, and so satisfaction of these needs motivates a person towards further satisfaction of these needs. In a work context this would mean that employees who are so underpaid they can hardly afford to eat properly (as perhaps in the sweat-shops of India) will be more concerned with earning money in order to eat than they will be in the development of their true potential in their jobs. It would also mean that once employees are reasonably paid and have sufficient job security in a context where their social needs are satisfied, then they are less interested in the pay and conditions of their work than they are in 'doing a good job' being respected for this and developing their abilities to the full.

Although intuitively attractive, Maslow's theory is difficult to define and test in operational terms. There are also problems which make it difficult to use as a basis for job design. First, higher order needs may not be satisfied at work, but outside of work, and secondly, satisfaction is seen as the outcome, and no

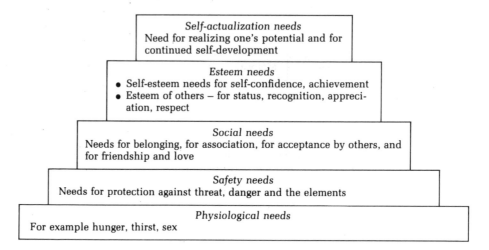

Figure 24.2   *Maslow's hierarchy of needs*

attention is given to performance outcomes. A study by Hall and Nougaim (1968) does provide some modest support for the theory, but there is little consistent support (Wahba and Bridwell 1979).

Review topic 24.1

We have suggested several problems about Maslow's theory of motivation. Think of three different people you know doing quite different jobs and note any other ways in which you feel Maslow's theory provides an inadequate explanation of motivation at work.

Alderfer's need hierarchy

The need hierarchy suggested by Alderfer (1969) is similar in some respects to Maslow's, but it has only three levels:

1. *Existence*: Material and physiological desires.
2. *Relatedness*: For example, social contact, friendships and other bonds.
3. *Growth*: Using skills and abilities and developing potential.

The satisfaction of lower needs is not a prerequisite for the emergence of higher needs, and this may well be a more useful concept for current theories of job design.

Herzberg's two-factor theory of motivation

Like Maslow, Herzberg expressed his theory of motivation in terms of satisfaction rather than productivity outcomes. The theory assumes that a satisfied employee will be a productive employee. Herzberg's (1968) theory was developed from an interview investigation of 203 accountants and engineers. They were asked what job events had occurred in their work that had led to extreme satisfaction or extreme dissatisfaction on their part. The responses were broken down into positive job events (leading to satisfaction) and negative job events (leading to dissatisfaction), as shown in Figure 24.3. In positive experiences, intrinsic sources, such as achievement, recognition, the work itself, responsibility, advancement and growth, were mentioned almost four times as often as extrinsic sources. In negative experiences, extrinsic sources, such as company administration, supervision, relationships with supervisor, peers and subordinates, personal life, status and security, were mentioned nearly twice as often as intrinsic sources. This prompted Herzberg to argue that the factors which provide satisfaction for people at work are different from the factors which can result in dissatisfaction. He called the extrinsic factors, which can only dissatisfy, 'hygiene' factors, and the intrinsic factors, which are capable of producing satisfaction, he called 'motivators'. The implications of these findings are clear – if the intrinsic factors are properly manipulated in the design of jobs, then this will result in feelings of satisfaction for those doing the job. Manipulation of extrinsic factors will not lead to satisfaction, but merely to the absence of dissatisfaction. According to the theory high pay will never make an employee feel satisfaction from his job, but giving him a challenge so he can feel a sense of achievement on completion of a task will lead to feelings of satisfaction.

Herzberg does not describe specific means in jobs that lead to satisfaction, but refers to the process, such as achievement or recognition that will result from work behaviour (Cooper 1974). Critics of Herzberg's theory argue that the results he obtained are artificial and reflect an inherent weakness in the method he used to collect the data. People will naturally ascribe unfavourable events to causes outside themselves, and favourable events to something from within. Two factors will also emerge, one for satisfaction outcomes and one for dissatisfaction outcomes, because the questions were structured by this dichotomy.

These motivation theories tend to assume that people are all alike. Other theories, such as expectancy/valence/instrumentality theories, take into account that people have different needs, and that they make decisions about their behaviour at work.

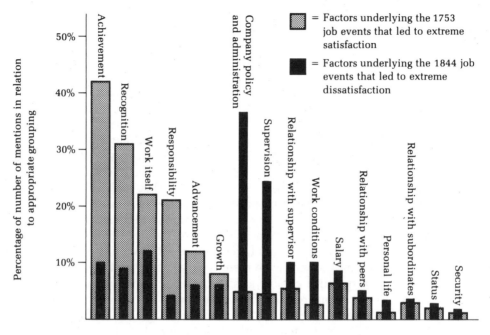

Figure 24.3   *Factors contributing to job satisfaction and dissatisfaction*
Source: Adapted from Herzberg (1968, p. 57).

Expectancy/valence/instrumentality theories

Expectancy/valence/instrumentality theories are based on concepts identified by Vroom (1964) and Lawler and Porter (1968). The theories of motivation we have discussed previously have assumed that people will behave in order to meet the goals that they value and thereby satisfy their needs. Expectancy theory states that the relationship between behaviour and goals is not so simple. First, each individual will have different goals; and secondly, people will only act to achieve their goals if they feel there is a reasonable expectation that their action will lead to the desired goals. Goals can be seen in two ways – the first is the direct goal of increased performance, and the second is indirect goals which are seen to result from achievement of the direct goal. Such an indirect goal may, for example, be promotion. The value, or valency, of the goal will also affect motivation and behaviour.

Perceiving that action will result in performance (expectancy)

To illustrate this we shall compare two hypothetical employees. The first is given a productivity target to meet at work, but knowing the likelihood that the machine he is using will break down he decides this will probably prevent him from reaching the target so he does not aim for it. The second employee has a sales target to meet and thinks that if she makes five extra calls each day for the next five days, that these additional calls will result in sufficient additional sales for her to reach the target. She decides that it is worth the effort. The first employee does not work any harder because he expects that this will not help him reach his target, whereas the second employee does work harder because she expects that this will enable her to reach her target.

Perceiving that performance will lead to other desired goals (instrumentality)

If an employee has goals that stem from good performance, such as recognition, promotion or salary increases, then the employee will also evaluate whether high performance will lead to the desired results. For example, Lawler and Porter (1967) report a study of managers in industrial and government organizations. They compared the performance of a group of managers who felt that pay was a probable outcome of performance, with another group who felt that there was little relation between performance and pay. Rated performance was significantly higher for the former group. This is one of the foundation stones for any pay for performance systems, including performance management which is being introduced increasingly at present and is discussed further in Chapters 27 and 35.

Valence

The value of the goal will also affect behaviour. If the salesperson referred to above was about to begin a new job in a different company the following month, and had a lot of preparation to do for this, the goal of meeting the sales target may seem less important, and she may decide not to spend the extra time needed to make the extra calls to achieve this goal.

Expectancy/valence/instrumentality theories suggest implications for the improvement of motivation and performance. There are implications for both managers and organizations. (See Robertson and Smith (1985) for an excellent summary of this.) Organizational implications include the design of pay and benefit systems and also for the design of tasks and jobs to enable people to satisfy their needs through work. The theories allow for people having different needs, and that some may want autonomy and responsibility at work, whereas others may not. Motivation theory has clearly moved its ground to accommodate individual differences. Further recognition of these is demonstrated in recent initiatives to help individuals understand their self motivation and to harness this power for personal growth and achievement. In this context, Bentley (1989) discusses 'personal motivation coaching'. Turner and Lawrence (1987), in a guide to personal success, consider the development of positive self motivation as one of the keys to successful goal achievement.

> **Review topic 24.2**
>
> Think of your own job. What tasks are you motivated to do well, and what tasks are you not motivated to do well? Can you account for this?

Translating factors that motivate into work characteristics that motivate

Based on motivation theory, characteristics of jobs have been examined to identify those which satisfy higher order needs, such as self-development and the fulfilling of potential, and which provide opportunities for satisfaction from the intrinsic content of the job, such as autonomy and recognition. Several authors have suggested lists of characteristics which correspond with each other fairly well. Some of the best known are those devised by Cooper (1973), Turner and Lawrence (1965) and Hackman and Oldham (1976).

Cooper suggested four intrinsic job characteristics which would increase motivation. These are variety in tasks, surroundings and people available for interaction; discretion in choosing the means and tools of one's work, and selecting the appropriate knowledge to solve problems; goals which are very clear and of sufficient difficulty; and being able to make a visible contribution so that workers can identify the constructive change they have made which contributes to the end-product or service. The six task attributes which can act as motivators in jobs, identified by Turner and Lawrence, are not dissimilar from Cooper's job characteristics. They include variety, autonomy in determining methods of work, required interactions with others necessary for task performance, optional interactions, knowledge and skill, and responsibility for problem-solving and other decisions.

Ford (1969), when writing on the Bell Telephone System's experience with job design, suggested that job/task characteristics needed to combine in order to motivate employees. Hackman and Oldham developed a model that combines task characteristics and is based on a set of job characteristics which they felt should be key factors when designing jobs. These five core job dimensions are task identity, skill variety, task significance, autonomy and feedback. This model is different from the other two as it attempts to link these factors with motivation and performance via critical psychological states as shown in Figure 24.4. This model is also different in that it allows for the fact that people differ in their levels of 'growth need' (similar to self-actualization as defined by Maslow). Those people with a high growth need strength (GNS) are more likely to

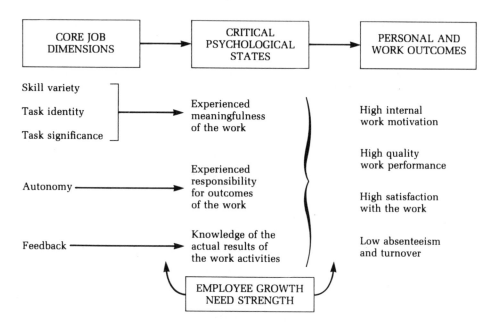

Figure 24.4 *Job characteristics model*
Source: Hackman and Oldham (1976). Published with the permission of Academic Press.

experience changes in critical psychological states when core job dimensions are improved.

We can derive from the above theories a number of job characteristics that have motivational properties and that could fruitfully be emphasized in the design of jobs. We can also derive an understanding of why individuals will react differently to such changes in their jobs. Job characteristics that have motivational properties are:

1. *Variety*: In tasks, tools/machinery used, location and people available for interaction. Cooper, however, argues that the value of this characteristic is only limited to repetitive jobs where it could reduce feelings of boredom.
2. *Autonomy*: In determining methods and tools of work. Sometimes referred to as means discretion.
3. *Responsibility*: For example, in making decisions about how to solve a problem.
4. *Challenge*: Choice of appropriate knowledge in the solution of problems and leading to a sense of achievement on completion of a task. Sometimes called skill discretion.
5. *Interaction*: Necessary contact with others for the performance of the job and optional opportunities for contact.

6. *Task significance*: Including task identity and contribution, which allow for recognition of work done and a sense of achievement.
7. *Goals and feedback*: Clearly stated goals, which are sufficiently challenging and clear, and direct information about performance effectiveness. It is also important that job holders accept the goals that they are expected to meet, and it is particularly useful if they participate in setting them.

Practical job design

Practical job design utilizes motivation theory, imperfect though this is, and the work characteristics that have been identified as increasing motivation. Most job design studies attempt to improve both work satisfaction and performance. The majority of studies have been carried out on the assumption that employees will all be motivated by an increase in the types of job characteristic we discussed in the last section, as it is only recently that much emphasis has been placed on individual differences. In retrospect, some commentators have sought to explain the lack of clear, positive results from many job design studies by pointing to the lack of consideration of individual differences.

Practical job design is not solely directed by the use of motivation theory and work characteristics that motivate. Other factors have to be considered and these may limit the way that jobs can be redesigned. Such factors as technology (see, for example, Woodward 1965); level of mechanization, due to the cost of providing additional equipment that may be required; union and employee attitudes, for example inter-job demarcations; and management values and style, all effect the way that jobs can be redesigned.

The terminology of job design is used in a rather less consistent way; sometimes job enrichment is used to encompass all forms of job design, rather than one particular form, and very often the distinction between job enlargement and job enrichment is very hazy (Aldag and Brief 1979). We shall, however, follow Herzberg (1968) and distinguish between three common forms of job design – job rotation, job enlargement and job enrichment – and then discuss a fourth form which is autonomous working groups.

Job rotation

Job rotation is probably the simplest form of job design to organize, and it is perhaps because of this that it was the most popular form of job design that had been implemented by the respondents to our recent survey. Job rotation involves the movement of workers between different tasks. Although the tasks will be different they will probably be of a similar nature. This rotation may be completely directed by management or may be voluntarily organized by the workers involved. An example of a voluntary scheme was that experienced by one of the authors in a yogurt-making factory. Three workers manned a conveyor belt – one job (easy, sitting) was to place trays on the belt, a second was to collect the pots as they moved past and place them on the tray (standing, tiring and relatively difficult), and a third was to turn the trays around when full for packaging (standing, easy). Most workers perceived the jobs as different in degree of difficulty, although there were seen to be attractions and detractions of each job. Each team of three organized their own form of job rotation so that workers moved from one task to another according to the scheme that they had devised.

From the workers' point of view, job rotation provides variety and also enables them more effectively to cope with jobs that would be a strain on their bodies if done all day long. There are advantages for management too. First, this form of job design rarely involves any major additional costs in the form of additional machinery and tools, and requires little restructuring of work. Also job rotation results in a more flexible workforce, which may be useful at holiday time or when employees are off sick, particularly when the jobs are more complex than described in the above example. There are, however, a number of problems and disadvantages. Workers may resist job rotation if it is enforced by management as it may interfere with group development, and some workers may prefer to be 'super-skilled' at one job rather than moving around. It may also be difficult to trace mistakes if tasks are organized in this way, and training, where tasks are more complex, will have to be more extensive and hence more expensive. Job rotation can also create problems for workers at change-over time, for example, when the workstation has been left in a mess or the task left unfinished. Also the amount of change for workers is very limited. Birchall (1975) argues that job rotation has limited value with regard to improving the motivational content of jobs as workers soon become familiar with each type of work and the actual work done remains unchanged and is still repetitive. Cooper (1974) argues that variety is not a true motivator.

In spite of the numerous disadvantages, however, Miller *et al.* (1973) conclude that job rotation had increased the productivity of a group of assembly workers and Birchall (1975) reports that Volvo workers in Sweden expressed themselves in a positive way about job rotation. Job rotation is most often seen as a method of job design most suitable for unskilled or maybe semi-skilled jobs. Our recent research, however, indicates that it is also a well-used method of job design for white-collar jobs. Twelve per cent of organizations had used job rotation for blue-collar jobs, and 16 per cent had used it for white-collar jobs.

Job enlargement

Job enlargement involves widening a job from a central task to include one or more related tasks, usually of the same type as the original task. Because one individual is carrying out a wider range of tasks it lowers the individual's dependence on others and therefore reduces the extent to which the individual's work is paced by others. As the variety of tasks assigned to an individual increases there is less specialization in that job. A pre-enlarged clerical job may consist of typing personnel documents, filing these and updating personnel information on the computer (at a time of day when the salaries department were not doing their updating). The enlarged job may consist of typing personnel and salaries documents, filing these and updating personnel and salary information on the computer. The greatest advantage of the enlarged job is that the clerk has greater control over the time of day when they use the computer, which was not possible before. Although the additional tasks are separate from the original ones they are of a very similar nature. Critics of job enlargement often argue that the enlarged job is usually only composed of multiples of the original task and that nothing is added that will increase job satisfaction or motivation (Birchall 1975). Herzberg (1968) talks of job enlargement as merely adding to the meaninglessness of the job.

Problems from management's point of view may be that, especially for blue-collar jobs, additional tools, machines and space may be required, together with additional training. There may, therefore, be considerable costs in introducing job enlargement which can only be weighed against uncertain benefits. From the workers' point of view any motivational effect of the increased variety of tasks may wear off once the tasks are familiar. Also, the research evidence concerning worker behaviour and attitudes in relation to repetitive jobs is conflicting. Some workers may prefer repetitive jobs as they give a sense of security and this may even be a source of satisfaction. Enlarging a repetitive job may also prevent workers from socializing or daydreaming, and this may be an attractive part of the job.

The results of job enlargement are conflicting. Hackman and Lawler (1971) reported that workers in jobs with more variety were generally more satisfied with their jobs, and performed better in some respects than those with less variety. Kilbridge (1960), however, found that following the enlargement of some industrial jobs, workers preferred the pre-enlarged jobs.

Job enrichment

Job enrichment has been divided into vertical job enrichment and horizontal job enrichment. Horizontal job enrichment is very much the same as job enlargement and has more limited value. In this section we shall concentrate on vertical job enrichment, which is a method of giving the employee a greater opportunity for achievement and recognition and, as Birchall (1975) comments, is aimed at increasing the worker's involvement in the organization and/or the job. Employees are allowed to complete a whole, or a much larger part of a job and there is some degree of 'task closure' – that is a clear end-point of a task. The tasks that are added are of a different nature from the tasks that are already performed, and this is the critical difference between job enrichment and job enlargement. Very often the job is enriched to include functions that were previously considered to be supervisory or managerial. Siegal and Ruh (1973) have commented on a relationship between job satisfaction and decision-making.

There is a number of studies of job enrichment for blue-collar jobs, for example, Birchall (1975) reports the redesign of some low-skilled operative jobs in textile manufacturing. The work previously consisted of a limited set of standardized tasks and workers were told which machine to work on and the time allowed for the job. In the revised job the operatives were subjected to less detailed control, they were given the opportunity to plan and organize their own work, plan meal-breaks and organize cover. They were given additional training to carry out certain inspection procedures and make machinery checks. At the same time, consultative machinery was set up, which gave the operatives a greater opportunity to participate in decision-making. Production improved and staff turnover fell, but absenteeism rose.

The problem with many blue-collar jobs is that job enrichment may lead to the abandonment of the conveyor-belt system and other traditional equipment, all of which still form highly efficient methods of production, where it has not been feasible to introduce newer technology. Also the cost of development of alternative methods of working may be high.

Job enrichment can also be carried out for white-collar and management jobs. In our recent research, job enrichment had been carried out for white-collar jobs in 14 per cent of organizations, for blue-collar jobs in 10 per cent, and for management jobs in 11 per cent. Job enrichment for managers will clearly link into organization design and structure (see Chapter 6), and implications for other jobs in the hierarchy will clearly be an issue here. Herzberg (1968) gives a good example of job enrichment applied to clerical jobs. He selected a group of stock-holder correspondents employed by a very large corporation. Performance and job attitudes were low. Herzberg redesigned these jobs so that they gave greater responsibility and a sense of personal achievement and recognition together with feelings of growth and advancement. The actual changes to the jobs are shown in Table 24.2, together with the appropriate job enrichment principle and the motivators involved.

Hertzberg also selected a control group and monitored its performance in order to identify any changes due to the Hawthorne effect. After three months, the performance of those in the job enrichment group dropped considerably below those in the control group, but after six months their performance was significantly higher. Herzberg also measured changes in attitudes towards tasks for both groups. The attitudes of the job enrichment group were clearly more positive.

Table 24.2 Enrichment of correspondents' tasks showing job enrichment principles used and motivators involved

Tasks	Job enrichment principles	Motivators involved
Subject matter experts were appointed within each unit for other members to consult with before seeking supervisory help. (The supervisor had been answering all specialized and difficult questions.)	Assigning individuals specific or specialized tasks, enabling them to become experts	Responsibility, growth, and advancement
Correspondents signed their own names on letters. (The supervisor had been signing all letters.)	Increasing the accountability of individuals for own work	Responsibility and recognition
The work of the more experienced correspondents was proof-read less frequently by supervisors and was done at the correspondents' desks, dropping verification from 100% to 10%. (Previously, all correspondents' letters had been checked by the supervisor.)	Removing some controls while retaining accountability	Responsibility and personal achievement
Production was discussed, but only in terms such as 'a full day's work is expected.' As time went on, this was no longer mentioned. (Before, the group had been constantly reminded of the number of letters that needed to be answered.)	Granting additional authority to an employee in his activity; job freedom	Responsibility, achievement, and recognition
Outgoing mail went directly to the mailroom without going over supervisors' desks. (The letters had always been routed through the supervisors.)	Removing some controls while retaining accountability	Responsibility and personal achievement
Correspondents were encouraged to answer letters in a more personalized way. (Reliance on the form-letter approach had been standard practice.)	Giving a person a complete natural unit of work (module, division, area, and so on)	Responsibility, achievement, and recognition
Each correspondent was held personally responsible for the quality and accuracy of letters. (This responsibility had been the province of the supervisor and the verifier.)	Making periodic reports directly available to the worker himself rather than to the supervisor	Internal recognition
	Increasing the accountability of individuals for own work	Responsibility and recognition

Source: Adapted from Herzberg (1968, pp. 59–60).

Autonomous working groups

Birchall (1975) comments that the primary operational purpose of the formal work-group is the efficient subdivision of work which is beyond the capacity of one person alone, for example, the team used to carry out surgical operations, where different but interdependent skills have to be brought together in order to achieve the task. In most organizations, however, work-groups are created on the basis of administrative convenience, and the best way to use available space and equipment.

In contrast, the formation of autonomous working groups aims to achieve the individual advantages of job enrichment as well as a number of broader advantages. Individuals' social needs can be taken into account with this approach, and individuals can be given greater flexibility, so that a work-group might decide to use job rotation for most members, but make other provisions for those who did not want this variety. Birchall (1975) also argues that a group task, because of its greater content and complexity, is more likely to provide a suitable base for the development of responsibility and discretion than more limited individual tasks.

The facility for self-organization and self-regulation in work-groups encourages autonomy. Emery (1959) also comments that group tasks have more potential to motivate than individual tasks. Within a work-group, employees not only have the opportunity of using a greater range of skills, but can also take over responsibility for basic management activities such as deciding upon methods of work, and the allocating and planning of work.

One example is at Saab-Scania in Sweden (reported by Norstedt and Anguren, 1973). This vehicle manufacturer organized groups so that the group had discretion over the quality of their work and could move between different tasks. Though these changes were small they apparently contributed to improved performance as measured by a decrease in stoppages on the line and improved quality.

Birchall (1975) reports a job design experiment for assemblers of office equipment. Prior to job design the cycle time was 3 minutes. Each line was divided into five main sections and manned by approximately sixty-five workers. The sections at the beginning of the line had the more complex tasks. The jobs were changed so that the cycle time was 20 minutes and the layout of the line rearranged to facilitate greater interpersonal contact. Groups were given the responsibility for checking quality and for fault rectification. They arranged their own meal-breaks among themselves and were free to rearrange the work methods if they so desired. Improvements were reported to include a 35 per cent increase in output.

Autonomous working groups often emphasize self-supervision, and as such the role of the supervisor is affected. Careful thought needs to be given to the new role of the supervisor, to avoid supervisors either holding on to tasks that have been reallocated to the working groups, or being left with an empty job. Wall (1984) suggests that the supervisor's job can be widened to encompass more managerial tasks or the supervisor's role may in some cases be removed.

Review topic 24.3

Describe a job in your organization and suggest how this may be
redesigned to improve its motivational content.

The process of redesigning jobs and the role of personnel managers

A number of authors (see Cooper 1974; Robertson and Smith 1985) state that job
design needs to be seen as a method of organizational change. Its success will
depend on the quality and extent of planning and preparation and its integration
with other organizational structures. A suggested plan of action for job design,
based on a framework suggested by Aldag and Brief (1979), is as follows:

1. Identification of the need to redesign jobs. Such indices as absence or
   performance levels may be useful, although it is important to consider that
   there may be other solutions to these problems such as training or
   reviewing selection methods. Information from surveys of job attitudes
   and/or motivation may be helpful. For a full discussion on such surveys,
   see Robertson and Smith (1985, pp. 69–92).
2. Identification of a target group of jobs and the consideration of whether
   they are suitable for job redesign. Satisfaction and motivation information
   needs to be collected from job holders, and jobs considered as to whether
   increased motivation would make a difference in performance.
3. Set up a job design group to have responsibility for the project. Some
   authors argue that the team should be solely composed of management
   (see Herzberg 1968), and that participation by employees would contaminate
   the results of the job design. Other authors such as Aldag and Brief (1979)
   support the inclusion of employees. For a good summary of the arguments
   for and against see Maitland (in Cooper 1974, pp. 103–12).
4. Detailed data concerning the tasks, duties, relationships and context of the
   jobs need to be collected, preferably using some form of job analysis.
5. The activities of the jobs should then be considered as to the extent to
   which they provide any job characteristics which motivate. Activities that
   would improve these characteristics then need to be identified. There are
   several ways of doing this. One method is by using the brainstorming
   technique (see, for example, Summers and White 1976). Alternatively,
   target job holders could be asked such questions as: 'How much discretion
   do you have?', and 'What could be done to improve your discretion?'
   (Aldag and Brief 1979). The questions being phrased in accordance with

the type of job and job holder. From this information a redesign plan needs to be formulated, considering characteristics one at a time. Aldag and Brief (1979) suggest four important essentials of successful job design, which are to ensure that:

(a) It is technologically feasible to place the activity in the target jobs.
(b) The incumbents of the target jobs are willing and able to perform that activity, and to be trained if needed.
(c) The previous performers of the activity are willing to relinquish it and have it replaced.
(d) There is a high likelihood of making the activity dependent upon some level of performance to increase the effort and results of the job incumbents.

6. Try out the job design for a reasonable period. Note that in Herzberg's (1968) study there was a 'settling in' period of three months where performance deteriorated before it improved.
7. Evaluate the job redesign in terms of a variety of criteria which have been identified as being important to the organization, such as absence level, termination level, attitudes, motivation, satisfaction, job performance in quantitative and qualitative terms.

If the job design project meets its criteria for success, the next step is to spread the process to other appropriate groups of staff.

Review topic 24.4

What are the practical problems of designing jobs in organizations?

Evaluation of work design

A large number of job design studies have been reported which have been successful in terms of improved job satisfaction and performance, however there are a number of problems with the job design work which has been done so far. These problems concern the motivation theory on which the design studies have been based and also the conduct and reporting of the studies themselves.

1. There is a lack of precision in the motivation theories. It is difficult to test Maslow's theory and there are methodological criticisms of Herzberg's study.

2. There is not such a simple relationship between motivation and job performance as is assumed in the theories and studies. Other factors moderate this relationship including ability, acquired skills, equipment used and, of course, the degree to which it is expected that effort will lead to results.

3. Much motivation theory is more concerned with job satisfaction than job performance and the relationship between the two is unclear. It is, however, often assumed that increased job satisfaction will lead to increased job performance. This assumption is questionable. An individual may be well motivated to do a job and may feel job satisfaction, but at the same time might not be performing well, due, perhaps, to lack of the appropriate skills. There is also some evidence to suggest that the relationship may work the other way around and that increased job performance may lead to increased job satisfaction.

4. There has been, until recently, a lack of attention to individual differences both in motivation theory and in job design projects. People are different both in the needs that they have and in the strength of their desire for those needs to be fulfilled. For example, Hulin and Blood (1968) argue the concept of alienation from work. They claim that some groups of individuals do not want satisfaction from the intrinsic aspects of their work and are motivated by other norms. Job design studies have tended to ignore the fact that people may satisfy their needs in contexts other than the work context.

5. Some job design studies have failed to take extrinsic factors into account and failed to note the way these have moderated the relationship between motivation and performance. Weed (1971) reported on a job design study at Texas Instruments. Following these changes performance was reported to have increased due to job design. In a review of this study some time later, Fein (1979) found that during the same period as the job design study, pay had increased by 46 per cent, there were better conditions of employment and working conditions, and as a consequence it had been possible to recruit better employees. Similarly, but in a slightly broader sense, there has been a lack of attention to work context factors which may be related to motivation and job performance. Robertson and Smith (1985) suggest:
(a) Supervisory and management practices.
(b) Organizational reward system.
(c) Supervisory/management style.
(d) Organizational climate.
(e) Technology and the physical environment.
(f) Organizational structure.
(g) Social/group factors.

Steers (1979) suggests four major work context factors which may affect individual performance:

(a) Managerial policies and practices.

(b) Organizational structure.

(c) Technology.

(d) External environment.

6. In many studies the possible results of the Hawthorne effect have been ignored.

7. Job design is a never-ending process, as Herzberg himself admits. The effects of design changes on motivation and performance seem to wear off (although this may not apply to all types of job) and new design initiatives are needed.

8. There is a danger that the results of studies have been exaggerated as those who have been involved have put so much effort into the project and have much to gain from success and little from failure.

9. There is little written about the studies that have failed, as individuals are not keen to write about failures and journals not keen to publish articles about them. The results of job design have therefore been reported selectively only.

Summary propositions

24.1 Employers have become interested in redesigning jobs in order to provide satisfying work for employees and to improve job performance.

24.2 Job design theory is based on motivation theory: the assumption of a causal link between increased motivation and increased job satisfaction and performance.

24.3 Factors that motivate have been translated into task attributes/job characteristics that motivate and jobs have been redesigned to include more of these.

24.4 Although many job design studies have been successful in terms of increased job satisfaction and performance, there is a number of problems with the theory, practice and reporting of job design studies.

24.5 The relationship between motivation and performance is not clear-cut. Personal factors and the organizational context also influence job performance.

24.6 People are different – not everybody wants a redesigned job that offers satisfaction from intrinsic job content.

24.7 In spite of a more critical and cautious approach to job design it is still seen as a useful management initiative which can produce valuable results and make jobs more satisfying.

References

Aldag, R. J. and Brief, A. P. (1979), *Task Design and Employee Motivation*, Glenview, Ill.: Scott Foresman.

Alderfer, C. P. (1969), 'An empirical test of a new theory of human needs', *Organisational Behaviour and Human Performance*, vol. 4, pp. 142–75.

Bentley, T. J. (1989), 'Personal motivation coaching', *Training Officer*, March.

Birchall, D. (1975), *Job Design: A planning and implementation guide for managers*, Aldershot: Gower.

Cooper, R. (1973), 'Task characteristics and intrinsic motivation', *Human Relations*, vol. 26, pp. 387–413.

Cooper, R. (1974), *Job Motivation and Job Design*, London: Institute of Personnel Management.

Davis, L. E. (1966), 'The design of jobs', *Industrial Relations*, vol. 6, pp. 21–5.

Emery, F. E. (1959), *Characteristics of Socio-technical Systems*, London: Tavistock/Institute of Human Relations.

Fein, M. (1979), 'Job enrichment: a re-evaluation'. In R. M. Steers and L. M. Porter, *Motivation and Work Behaviour* (2nd edition), New York: McGraw Hill.

Ford, R. N. (1969), *Motivation Through Work Itself*, New York: American Management Association.

Hackman, J. R. and Lawler, E. E. (1971), 'Employee reactions to job characteristics', *Journal of Applied Psychology*, vol. 55, pp. 259–86.

Hackman, J. R. and Oldham, G. R. (1976), 'Motivation through the design of work: test of a theory', *Organisational Behaviour and Human Performance*, vol. 16, pp. 250–79.

Hall, D. T. and Nougaim, K. E. (1968), 'An examination of Maslow's need hierarchy in an organisational setting', *Organisational Behaviour and Human Performance*, vol. 3, pp. 12–35.

Herzberg, F. (1968), 'One more time: how do you motivate employees?' *Harvard Business Review*, vol. 46, pp. 53–62.

Hulin, C. L. and Blood, M. R. (1968), 'Job enlargement, individual differences and worker responses', *Psychological Bulletin*, vol. 69, pp. 41–55.

Kilbridge, M. D. (1960), 'Deduced costs through job enlargement: a case', *Journal of Business*, vol. 33, pp. 357–62.

Lawler, E. E. and Porter, L. W. (1967), 'Antecedent attitudes of effective managerial performance', *Organisational Behaviour*, vol. 2, pp. 122–42.

Lawler, E. E. and Porter, L. W. (1968), *Managerial Attitudes and Performance*, Chicago: Irwin Dorsey.

Lawrence, T. C. and Kleiner, B. H. (1987) 'The keys to successful goal achievement', *Journal of Management Development*, vol. 6, pt. 5, pp. 39–48.

Maitland, R. (1974), 'Sources of proposals for job redesign', In R. Cooper, *Job Motivation and Job Design*, London: Institute of Personnel Management.

Maslow, A. H. (1943), 'A theory of human motivation', *Psychological Review*, vol. 50, pp. 370–96.

Miller, R. G., Dhaliwal, T. S. and Magas, L. J. (1973), 'Job rotation raises productivity', *Industrial Engineering*, vol. 5, no. 6, pp. 24–6.

Norstedt, J. P. and Anguren, S. (1973), *The Saab-Scania Report*, Stockholm: Swedish Employers' Confederation.

Robertson, I. T. and Smith, M. (1985), *Motivation and Job Design: Theory, research and practice*, London: Institute of Personnel Management.

Siegel, A. L. and Ruh, R. A. (1973), 'Job involvement, participation in decision-making, person backgound and job behaviour', *Organisational Behaviour and Human Performance*, vol. 9, pp. 318–27.

Steers, R. M. (1979), 'Work environment and individual behaviour', In R. M. Steers and L. W. Porter, *Motivation and Work Behaviour*, New York: McGraw-Hill.

Summers, I. and White, D. E. (1976), 'Creativity techniques: towards improvements in the decision process', *Academy of Management Review*, April, pp. 99–107.

Turner, A. N. and Lawrence, P. R. (1965), *Industrial Jobs and the Worker: An investigation of response to task attributes*, Boston, Mass.: Harvard University Graduate School of Business Administration.

Vroom, V. H. (1964), *Work and Motivation*, Chichester: John Wiley.

Wahba, M. A. and Bridwell, L. G. (1979), 'Maslow reconsidered: a review of research on the need hierarchy theory'. In R. M. Steers and L. W. Porter, *Motivation and Work Behaviour*, New York: McGraw-Hill.

Wall, T. (1984), 'What's new in job design?' *Personnel Management*, April.

Wall, T. D., Clegg, C. W. and Jackson, P. R. (1978), 'An evaluation of the job characteristics model', *Journal of Occupational Psychology*, vol. 51, pp. 183–96.

Weed, E. O. (1971), 'Job enrichment "cleans up" at Texas Instruments'. In J. R. Maher (ed.), *New Perspectives in Job Enrichment*, New York: Van Nostrand Reinhold.

Woodward, J. (1965), *Industrial Organization: Theory and practice*, Oxford: Oxford University Press.

25

Learning principles and training skills

Harry Plant had a rare spring in his step as he walked the half mile to the textile factory. After no luck at all for months he had finally landed a job as a trainee machinist, nearly a year after leaving school. First day today.

An hour later Harry wasn't so sure. The foreman had started by saying that he hoped he was better than the last one before giving him a long and bewildering explanation of how the machine worked, including all sort of strange words that Harry had never heard before. He then gave a quick and polished demonstration of what to do, turned to Harry and said, 'There you are, lad. Easy as shelling peas. You have a go while I sort out the job cards with May. Fred'll keep an eye on you.'

Harry's foreman did not have any knowledge of training skills or learning principles and showed a strange attitude to a new recruit. You can guess that Harry fared badly. The next day he did not go in to work at all, and the foreman explained to May and Fred that these young people were all the same . . . didn't really want to work at all.

In this chapter we shall deal in turn with all the factors that trainers need to take into account when designing and conducting training. We first take a look at learning and then consider the identification of training needs and the formulation of learning objectives. Next we consider the characteristics of the trainees and then training resources with particular reference to the tools of training. The design of training programmes is then discussed and the variety of training methods that may be used. We conclude with some brief comments on the evaluation of training.

Learning

Although some of our behaviour is based on reflex and instinctive reactions, most of our behaviour is learned. At home we learn how to talk, how to dress ourselves correctly, how to cross the road safely, how to respond politely to 'grown ups'. At school we learn how to write things down, how to work out numbers according to a set of rules, how to solve problems using ideas and concepts. In a social context teenagers (and the rest of us) learn what's 'in' and what's 'out', how to respond and react to people and situations and how to fit in with others. We don't stop learning because we go to work. We learn from family, friends, teachers, bosses, books, television, and so on. Sometimes we learn in a formal way as in a classroom, sometimes in an informal way when a workmate says, 'If you send it to the typing pool it will take three days to get it back. I always type short notes myself.'

Learning is a major tool in adapting to our environment. It has been defined in a variety of ways, but a widely accepted definition, based on Kimble (1961), is:

> Learning is a relatively permanent change in behavior or in behavioral potentiality that results from experience and cannot be attributed to temporary body states such as those induced by illness, fatigue or drugs. (Hergenhahn 1982, p. 8)

The trainer needs an understanding of learning characteristics, learning theories and learning principles as these will guide many of the decisions that need to be made in the design of training.

Learning characteristics

The behavioural changes that result from learning experiences can be quantified and plotted on a graph and presented in the form of a learning curve. The curve can be plotted either for an individual or for a group by using averages. The curve usually shows cumulative changes in behaviour that take place over time. Behaviour would be defined according to indicators appropriate for the particular task being learned and may be time taken to complete a task, error rate, number of items completed in a day, and so on. The shape of the curve will depend on the task in question and the particular criterion chosen to measure behaviour. Learning curves can be useful in the evaluation of trainer effectiveness and in the evaluation of individual performance. These would be achieved by the comparison of appropriate curves.

Within any learning curve there very often occurs a learning plateau, which is the flattening-off of the curve after a significant improvement in performance has already taken place. Following the plateau, performance normally increases again and the curve begins to incline again. There are two implications here for the trainer. First is that trainees may need reassurance, when their performance stops increasing, that this is a normal part of the learning process. Secondly, this plateau may be shortened by a change in instructional method, so it is a cue for the trainer to consider alternative training methods. This is a very simple model of the way that people learn, and in reality learning is more complex. This is particularly important to understand in learning interpersonal skills, for example, influencing others or negotiating. Inductive learning of these skills does not produce a smooth curve, but 'trainees' experience a series of learning loops, gradually improving their skills as they pass around the loops, as shown in Figure 25.1.

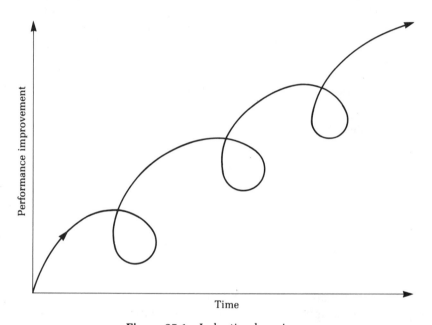

Figure 25.1 *Inductive learning*

A further characteristic of learning is forgetting. People will forget learned material over time if it is not used or added to by more learning. From the trainer's point of view, this may well point to the value of refresher courses. Relearning material usually takes less time than the original learning.

Theories of learning

There is a large number of learning theories, each attempting to explain comprehensively how learning occurs. The vast majority of these can be divided into two schools of thought – the stimulus–response school and the cognitive school. There are also two other areas of theory which may be utilized by trainers, and these are social learning theory and facilitation.

Theories in the stimulus–response school may also be termed behaviourist, associationist or connectionist, and included are those put forward by Watson (1930), Thorndike (1913), Hull (1943), Pavlov (1941), and Skinner (1953). All these theories treat learning as the development of links between a stimulus and a response. The theorists were interested, for example, in demonstrating how links can be encouraged, how long they take to develop, and the ways in which the experience of other stimuli can change these bonds. Many experiments were done with animals, and principles derived from these experiments were then applied to human learning. Skinner demonstrated the role of reinforcement when he put hungry rats into cages where there was a variety of levers to press. The rats eventually began to explore the levers and found that one of them caused a pellet of food to be dropped. This particular lever was pressed more and more in order to obtain food, and eventually the rats became conditioned to pressing it. The food reinforced the lever-pressing activity. As the link between the stimulus (seeing the lever) and the response (pressing the lever) became well established there was less need to reinforce the bond by providing reinforcement (food) every time. This has led to the role of reinforcement being considered in the human learning situation in the form of perhaps a nod, smile or comment which is rewarding for the trainee.

Cognitive theorists, for example, Piaget (1928) and the Gestalt psychologists, place greater emphasis on the functioning of the brain, and the role of perception, insight and the development of understanding. Gestalt psychologists emphasize the importance of the 'whole', and that in order to promote learning, 'parts' should be meaningful units and always related to the 'whole'. This, of course, has implications for the design of courses and the organization of training sessions.

Social learning theory (for example, see Bandura *et al.* 1963) looks at the importance of social interaction and initiation in the learning process. Bandura argues that anything that can be learned from direct experience can also be learned from observation, and that we model our behaviour on the behaviour that we see others display. This theory has implications for the use of training media, particularly the use of film and video, which will be discussed later in this chapter in the behaviour modelling method of training.

Carl Rogers (1969) presents a different theory of learning which emphasizes the learner's involvement in the process. Rogers sees the learners themselves as rich resources, who should be encouraged to participate in their own learning and that of others. Trainers are seen as facilitators of this process rather than a stimulator or controller (Laird 1978). Again, this theory has implications for the choice of method of training, and provides a theoretical background for the often heard comment: 'Well the conference papers weren't so good, but I learned so much from talking to the others who were there.'

Gagne (1965) effectively put learning theories in their place when he said: 'I do not think learning is a phenomenon which can be explained by simple theories, despite the admitted intellectual appeal such theories have.' Although none of the theories comprehensively explains the learning process, they are useful in that they each provide clues about different aspects of learning. These can be collated to form a group of learning principles which can be used to guide the organization of learning experiences.

Learning principles

Direction/guidance

Employees who are being trained need direction, especially at the beginning of training. This reduces the need for trial and error learning, which not only costs money but can make the trainee feel anxious if he does not know what to do or is consistently doing the wrong thing. Mumford (1971) comments that individuals need to learn through the experience of success and not through the experience of failure.

Standards of performance and knowledge of results

As people learn best when they are aware of what they are aiming for (Mumford 1971), it is important that employees, in an off-the-job or on-the-job training situation, know what standard of performance is expected of them. These standards of performance need to be related to an employee's personal objectives, as Kolb *et al.* (1984) argue that unless personal objectives are clear, the process of learning will be erratic and inefficient. Trainers need to make sure that individuals have sufficient feedback so that they know how appropriate their performance is. Feedback is most effective if it is specific and immediate.

Reward and reinforcement

Learning will be more effective if correct or improved performance is reinforced by the trainer and manager. The reward may be in the form of praise, a promotion or a salary increase, or whatever else may be appropriate.

Motivation

Extrinsic motivation may be increased by the use of rewards, as described above. Intrinsic motivation may be encouraged by relating the training to work experiences and by taking account of the goals of the trainees. Mumford (1971) comments that individuals can often be motivated by an awareness of their present performance and also of their potential which implies a working situation where there is continuous feedback. Mumford also suggests that it implies the learners' involvement in the definition of their learning needs.

Transfer

If learning takes place off-the-job, it is important that what is learned can be transferred back to the work situation. This process is assisted if there are a lot of similarities between the training and the work situations and if there is the immediate opportunity to use what has been learned, and if managers discuss progress with individuals. In our recent research we spoke to two organizations where large numbers of staff had been sent on computer training courses in anticipation of the imminent arrival of their computer system. In both cases the 'imminent' arrival was significantly delayed. Six months later, when the computer system did eventually arrive, the staff had forgotten all they had learned and had to re-attend the training course.

In the 1950s and 1960s there was a lot of interest in the timing of the presentation of training material and in the timing of practice. Since this time, research on management development and training has prompted a move from this very technical way of specifying the principles underlying the most effective learning to a more qualitative approach.

Different learning theories have value in different contexts

Burgoyne and Stuart (1978) derive eight schools of thought about learning theory from the literature and indicate that different approaches to the process of learning are useful for different learning activities and contexts. The job of the trainer is, therefore, to select the appropriate learning process for the identified training needs and select the right teaching or facilitation strategy which reflects this.

The individual process of learning

Kolb *et al.* (1984) concentrate on the role of the individual learner when they argue that it is useful to combine the characteristics of learning, which is usually regarded as passive, with the characteristics of problem-solving, which is usually regarded as active. From this combination Kolb develops a four-stage learning cycle:

- Concrete experiences.
- Observation and reflections.
- Formation of abstract concepts and generalizations.
- Testing of implications of concepts in new situations.

Within this context he proposes that individuals can, if asked the right questions, work out their own learning style which indicates their strengths and weaknesses. Kolb argues that no particular profile is best, but that the ability to learn is the ability to be competent in each mode when this is appropriate. Knowledge of their own learning style helps individuals to select the most appropriate learning opportunities for themselves in different contexts, and gives them a basis for developing those styles which they find most difficult. Honey and Mumford's *Manual of Learning Opportunities* (1989) is helpful in this respect. Stuart (1984) extends these concepts to show how, in the self-development of managers, this learning cycle can be applied to the idea of using others to learn. Sims (1989) also suggests that trainers must adapt their methods and their individual styles to suit the different learning styles of trainees.

Identification of training needs

When and where training needs should be investigated

We argued in Chapter 23 that although operating problems may well indicate the existence of a training need, they may well indicate other remedies such as work redesign or a review of communication structures. It may be clear that the employees in question do have the knowledge and skills to perform their jobs as the organization requires, and therefore some other remedy is more appropriate than training. If attitudes are clearly a problem, it could still be that changes other than direct training are the best remedy. However, the appropriateness of other solutions is not always clear before training needs are investigated in depth. There are four levels of information which the training manager can use to indicate where training needs should be investigated in depth. As with the development of selection criteria, training needs should be identified at the organizational level, the department level and the job level. Training needs should also be identified at the individual level.

1. *The organizational level*: The pointers that would suggest further investigation here would be changes in organizational strategy and/or goals, changes in organizational structure, the introduction of new processes or technologies, human resource plans, and productivity and reputation with competitors. Information from attitude surveys and changes in the law may also suggest that training needs should be identified.
2. *The department level*: At this level pointers may come from the analysis of personnel statistics such as absence levels, turnover levels, production levels and customer complaints. Attention at this level would be focused on the differences in these measures between different departments. Information from exit interviews may also be useful at this level, as would training requests from management. Changes in departmental role will also indicate that training needs should be investigated.
3. *The job level*: Similar analyses to those used for the department level can be used in order to compare the differences between jobs or groups of jobs.
4. *The individual level*: At this level information from appraisals may be useful, as may assessment centre ratings and individual or manager requests for further training.

Methods used to identify training needs

In Chapter 23 we refer to Stephen Robbins' suggested approach to the identification of training needs. This begins with the identification of organizational goals. These are not always clearly stated, but if the organization has a corporate or strategic plan, this should be a profitable source of information. Following this, the key method of identifying training needs is job analysis which is more fully described in Chapter 16. A variety of methods of job analysis are suitable for the identification of training needs, particularly interviews, questionnaires, group methods and the critical incident technique. In Chapter 16 we mentioned the importance of including performance standards in the job description which results from job analysis. This is of critical importance in identifying training needs. Only if these standards are clearly defined can any deficiencies in meeting them be identified.

For the purposes of identifying training needs, performance achieved also needs to be considered. The difference between the performance standards that are required and the performance achieved indicates a potential training need. Where performance cannot be considered because individuals are new to the job, then account needs to be taken of their abilities and experience as so far assessed.

Review topic 25.1

What would be the most appropriate methods of identifying training needs for the following:

1. Fifty clerks working in different departments in a head office building.
2. A newly appointed sales manager in a small company.
3. Three hundred assembly workers organized in recently designed autonomous work groups.

A more structured approach would be to use the job description as a basis for analyzing the tasks that comprise the job and to derive from these the knowledge and skills that any person would need to carry out these tasks to the required standard. The current level of knowledge and skills of the person in post are then analyzed, and the difference between these and those required for the job would indicate a training need.

Whichever method of job analysis is used, employees can also be asked about areas where they feel their performance is inadequate, areas where they have problems, and any deficiencies in their knowledge and skills. This approach would only be feasible where employees have fully understood the performance standards expected of them. The great benefit of this method is that the

A group of regionally-based managers, having the same job title and performing the same or very similar duties had, at various times, expressed difficulties in carrying out their jobs. As there was no other obvious cause of the problems they faced it was decided to investigate their training needs.

As the officers were geographically widely spread, a short questionnaire, which they could fill in at their place of work coupled with a half-day training needs seminar for the whole group, was felt to be an appropriate method of identifying training needs. The training officer believed that completion of the questionnaires would enable the officers to focus their minds on the relevant issues before these were discussed as a group. It also had the advantage of giving the managers time to consider their responses as they completed the questionnaire – an advantage over the interview method. The completed questionnaires were returned to the training officer prior to the training needs seminar.

In the questionnaire the managers were asked to write a description of their job, in a guided format, and their performance objectives. They were asked about areas where they experienced difficulties and problems and where they felt they weren't meeting their performance objectives. They were asked their opinion of what caused these things, and how they might be overcome. In particular they were asked:

- Is there anything you need to know?
- How might this knowledge be gained?
- Is there anything you need to be able to do?
- How might you learn how to do this?
- Is there anything you need to experience?
- How might you experience this?

When the managers met as a group they were asked to identify the same issues. Their previous preparation and the benefits of working as a group produced even more ideas. The trainer then joined the group and went through their ideas to ensure a full understanding of what was meant, to ensure that appropriate solutions were adopted, and to ensure commitment to the training initiative which was to follow.

After the group meeting they collated all the ideas and information in a structured format using the following headings:

- The group's definition of what they need to know.
- The groups suggestions as to how they might gain this knowledge.
- Did the group directly identify a training need?
- What are the implications for the Training Officer?

This format was gone through for each knowledge need, then each skill and experience need. Using this information the training officer derived training objectives and designed a training programme for the nine managers.

Figure 25.2　*Identification of training needs: a practical example*

employees become more committed to any learning experiences that are provided to rectify these deficiencies. Job incumbents can also be asked what they think would be the most appropriate methods for rectifying these deficiencies. This increases commitment to a greater extent. Figure 25.2 gives an example of job analysis by questionnaire and group methods, in which one of the authors was involved, where employees were encouraged to participate fully in identifying their own training needs. One disadvantage of reliance on information from job holders is that they cannot be expected to identify areas where their own attitudes are the problem.

The choice of job analysis method will depend on such factors as time and money available, type of job to be analyzed, experience and numbers of job incumbents, and the experience of the training officer. Whichever method is chosen, it is important to talk to the manager of the employees whose needs are being investigated. As Laird (1978) comments, two of the most useful questions here will probably be: 'What are your people doing that they shouldn't be doing?' And: 'What are your people not doing that they should be doing?'

Development of training objectives

Once training needs have been identified they need to be translated into training objectives. Objectives will be more specific than needs, indicating what is to be achieved at the end of the training period. Laird (1978, p. 101) comments that the thesis of Mager's book (1962) was that: 'If you're not sure where you're going, you're liable to end up someplace else – and not even know it.'

Laird (1978) suggests that learning objectives should contain three types of information. First, the behaviour to be achieved, for example, type a letter, replace a tyre, give a presentation or lay bricks. Second, there should be some information about the criteria for performing the behaviour. These criteria need to be measurable and may be expressed in the form of how many, how often, how long it takes, how many mistakes are acceptable, and so on. So an objective may be expressed as 'type a letter with no more than one mistake', or 'lay bricks that are straight when measured both horizontally and vertically by a spirit level'. The final part of the objective gives any information about the conditions of performance. Thus an objective may read: always be polite and helpful when taking telephone calls.

In translating a need into an objective a good way to start outlining the objective is by 'the employee will be able to . . . [use a verb] . . .', taking account of the requirements of the organization, the ability of the trainees, and what is reasonable in the circumstances. Figure 25.3 gives some examples of how training needs may be translated into training objectives.

Training objectives link the identification of training needs with the content, methods and technology of training, and they are useful for the trainees, the trainer and the trainees' manager. For a further development of some of these points and advice on how to write learning objectives, see Laird (1978).

Review topic 25.2
Identify your own training needs and translate these into learning objectives.

Training needs	Learning objectives
To know more about the Data Protection Act	The employee will be able to answer four out of every five queries about the Data Protection Act without having to search for the details.
To establish a better rapport with customers	The employee will immediately attend to a customer unless already engaged with another customer.
	The employee will greet each customer, using the customer's name where known.
	The employee will apologize to every customer who has had to wait to be attended to.
To assemble clocks more quickly	The employee will be able to correctly assemble each clock within thirty minutes.

Figure 25.3 *Some examples of translating training needs into learning objectives*

Understanding the trainees

The design and methods of training need to be based on an understanding of the potential trainees, in particular their experiences of learning, their ability, attitudes, age and their level in the organization (Walters 1983). Previous work experience is also a factor that needs to be taken into account.

Previous learning experiences can have a positive or negative effect on current willingness and ability to learn. New graduates usually find it easy to concentrate on and accept lecture-type training sessions as this is what they have used successfully in the past. Sixteen-year-old recruits direct from school may not have found lecture-type sessions such a rewarding experience, feeling that they have come to work in order to work, and not to be lectured at again. Similarly, older workers who have had little formal education may find the lecture situation belittling and intimidating.

Previous work experience is also critical. The greater the work experience that trainees have had, the greater is their potential to use that experience, for the benefit of all the trainees, and participate in the learning process. If the trainees have a similar level of ability then pacing and spacing of training can be geared to meet their needs so that they will be neither bored nor overwhelmed. On the other hand, if trainees are of very mixed ability then self-paced learning may be more appropriate. Self-paced 'discovery learning' may also be more successful with older employees (Belbin and Belbin 1972).

Trainees' attitudes to training also influence training design. If the attitudes are negative then some attempt to encourage more positive attitudes should be incorporated into the training. If training is seen as irrelevant, it is useful to include a lot of early participation, getting trainees to talk about their jobs and how they feel they could do better. Variety of training methods and resources can also help to stimulate employees. If employees are anxious, then a lot of simple tasks at the beginning, providing the opportunity to experience success, can ease the anxiety. Above all trainees need to be treated as individuals.

Training resources

The training resources that are available will depend on how much money is available for the training function. This will in turn depend on the profitability of the organization and the attitudes of the most senior managers and directors to training. The two key resources are the tools of training, now more popularly termed training media or training technology; and human resources available for training. Other important resources, though, include space and time. Figure 25.4 sets out the human and media resources and matches them against the methods of training in which they are principally used.

Training Resources	On-the-job	Field	Lecture	Demonstration	Simulation	Behaviour modelling	Group methods	Self-paced
Trainer	*	*	**	**	**	**	*	*
Other trainees						*	**	
Other employees	**	**						
Manager/supervisor	**			**				
Blackboard			**					
Print	*		**				**	**
Slides/overheads			**	**				
Video/film				**		**		**
Television			**					**
Radop								**
Computer					**		**	**
Interactive video								**
Audio tapes								**
Real tools/ equipment	**	*		**				*
Simulated tools/ equipment					**			

Figure 25.4   *Chief methods of training and their principal utilization of training resource*

Human resources

The trainer is usually seen as the chief human resource put into training. However, others such as supervisors/managers in particular, other trainees and other employees may make significant contributions or be the primary or only human resource that is used.

Physical training media

Kearsley (1984) divides 'hard' technology into static media, dynamic media and interactive media. Static media include the age-old blackboard and chalk, and the printed word on paper, now often seen as out of date. It would still be impossible to imagine how training departments and universities could function without huge quantities of printed paper used directly to facilitate learning. Slides and overhead projector transparencies are now generally preferred and can be particularly effective if well thought out and prepared. These static media tend to be associated with the traditional lecture. One of the chief disadvantages of these static media is that they encourage a passive role for the learner. Flip charts can be used, of course, as static media, prepared in advance, or can be used in a more dynamic way on the event.

Dynamic media include radio, television, audio tape, film and video tape. These often attract more attention and have greater potential for learner involvement and stimulation which result in more effective learning. Film, and especially video because of its greater ease of use, are particularly flexible as they can be stopped at any point for the trainer to bring in some discussion of what is happening, or to stress a point. Difficult parts can be re-run so that trainees have the opportunity to see what they may have missed the first time. Video also has the advantage that it can be used in self-paced learning either in conjunction with learning as a class or as a method of distance learning. A further advantage of video is that trainers can use it to record role play and other exercises for trainees to review and learn from. Trainers can also make semi-professional videos to demonstrate particular behaviours to trainees.

Interactive training media include computers, simulators and interactive video. Computers have successfully been used for some time to provide instruction for self-paced learning. Programmes have been devised that can provide material and then ask check questions so the trainee is given the opportunity to demonstrate whether he has understood what has gone before. Depending on how the trainee answers a question, another question may follow, or some further material. Computers are also increasingly being used as a resource for group training activities such as in-depth case studies. Simulators are interactive media as they are built to represent the real equipment or machinery, and to respond to actions taken by the trainee in a way that represents what would happen in reality. Trainees then respond to the machine's response, and so on. Simulators are generally computer-driven. The ultimate so far in the combination of technologies is interactive video, sometimes referred to as video disc. Here video sequences can be interspersed with the presentation of text and the use of questions. The same flexibility applies here as with computers. Depending on the trainee's response to a question either text, video or another question will be presented. The trainee also has the capacity to go to various parts of the disc in order to re-run sequences when needed. The programme can be designed to record learning time, errors, and so on. Interactive video has the great advantage that it is possible for trainers to put together the programmes themselves. However, the production of even a short session can often take many hours of preparation.

Training methods

We shall not go into a detailed evaluation of the different methods. We shall consider the scope of each method and its primary benefits, with particular emphasis on recent developments. For a more detailed treatment of training methods see, for example, Walters (1983) or Rae (1983). The selection of training methods needs to be based on identified training needs, training objectives, an understanding of the trainees, the resources available and an awareness of learning principles.

On-the-job training

On-the-job training is sometimes referred to as informal training as there is usually a lack of structure to the learning experiences that take place. Walters (1983) identifies three different forms that on-the-job learning can take. The first is where there is a complete lack of structure and the employee is 'thrown in at the deep end to sink or swim', that is, the employee will learn by trial and error – if he stays in the job. The process can be very disheartening for the trainee and wasteful of time and materials. Secondly, a variation of on-the-job training is 'sitting next to Nellie', where Nellie the experienced worker shows the trainee what to do. This is a far more positive approach, but much depends on Nellie's skill as a worker, and her ability and willingness to train others. Nellie won't be too keen if she's on a payment-by-results system. Thirdly, a more sophisticated method of on-the-job training is coaching, where trainees learn by guided on-the-job instruction. This is similar to the way in which tennis players, swimmers, athletes, and so on learn skilled performance. One-to-one coaching on this basis may often be impractical in the workplace. A similar approach to this is 'mentoring', which is a form of on-the-job training for managers and will be discussed in more detail in the following chapter on management development.

The great advantage of on-the-job training is that its relevance and applicability to the work that has to be done is quite clear.

Job rotation, traineeships and field training

Job rotation is often used as a method of training for 'high fliers', the object being that when the individual reaches the top of the organization he will be able to draw on a vast range of experiences from different parts of the organization. The time spent in each of the various jobs is usually between one to three years. A variant on this is graduate or 'A' level traineeships where the trainees spend shorter periods in either a variety of sections in the same department or in a variety of departments. Walters (1983) identifies four less job-related forms of training in the field. These range from observational visits through to consultancy exercises where the trainees tackle and hopefully solve a real problem. The value of these experiences very much depends on the way that they are structured, and often trainees become frustrated as they want to get on with a real job. Work shadowing, where the trainee spends a period of time accompanying an experienced person in post, could also be included here.

Simulation

Undoubtedly, the most familiar example of simulation training is in the training of pilots. Although costly to set up, simulation is seen as a method of reducing training costs. For pilot training it reduces the costs, of fuel for example, of allowing the trainee to learn by actually flying a plane. It also lessens the risk to human life, as trainees using simulation equipment can do no harm to themselves or their instructor when they make a potentially fatal mistake.

Simulation is used in a different form in business games and in-basket exercises. Business games simulate a competitive business environment. The trainees are divided into teams, each is given a role, and they then compete in a hypothetical business situation to see who can make the most effective decisions. In-basket exercises also simulate the business environment. Trainees are given a typical in-basket full of letters, memos, requests, problems to be solved, and so on. They have a brief like: 'At 11 a.m. this morning you are flying out to Morocco and will be out of the country for six months. It is essential that you deal with everything in your in-basket before you go.' These exercises are sometimes for assessment as well as training purposes. Role plays, where two or more individuals are assigned roles, such as interviewer and interviewee, or trade union representative, manager and employee are also forms of simulation. Role play sessions are often videotaped so that they can be re-run. One particular form of training that involves role plays is behaviour modelling, which is dealt with separately in this section. The advantage of these forms of simulation is that they allow the trainees to try out a range of behaviours and decisions in a work-like environment, giving them the opportunity to assess their effectiveness without having to face the consequences of doing this in a real situation.

Lectures

Lectures are particularly useful for imparting standard, basic information which can then be built upon by other training methods. For example, during induction it may be useful to have an introductory lecture about company procedures, rules and structure.

Demonstrations

Demonstrations are needed where 'telling' is not sufficient and 'showing' is more important. It is far more useful to show someone how to drive a car or use a computer system than it would be just to tell them how to do this.

Group methods

Group training methods can include group discussion, case studies, seminars and sensitivity training, for example, T-groups (an approach to human relations, the original emphasis of which was as a form of group therapy). Discussions, case studies and seminars have the benefit of encouraging participation and provide opportunities for trainees to learn from each other. T-groups are leaderless, unstructured groups designed to encourage learning from experience and group dynamics, and they provide a forum for the giving and receiving of personal feedback. T-groups were most popular in the 1970s and since that time there has been increasing scepticism about their value. Simpson (1984), however, argues that T-groups are alive and well and do have potential value.

Behaviour modelling

The use of behaviour modelling in training is based on social learning theory, which was described earlier in this chapter. It is a particularly effective method of interpersonal or social skills training. Traditional interpersonal skills training often incorporated videos of the John Cleese variety, which clearly demonstrated the wrong way to do things and that these behaviours should be avoided. Behaviour modelling is based on the demonstration of the right way to behave, and then providing facilities for trainees to practise this. The training process is well described by Roden, in an unpublished report of a interpersonal skills training programme developed at the Co-operative Bank in conjunction with UMIST:

> Target behaviours are selected and videos produced showing competent persons achieving success by following specific guidelines. Key points are displayed on screen and backed by trainer-led discussions – learning is then re-inforced by role-play. (Roden 1986, p. 1)

Another excellent example of the use of behaviour modelling is described by Grant (1984), where travel clerks learned how to resolve booking problems by this method.

Self-paced learning

There is a number of different terms for self-paced learning, such as distance learning, open learning and flexible learning. The critical features are that learners control the pace and the timing of their own learning and are not tutor-dependent. The most traditional version of self-paced learning is the correspondence course. These are still in use today, not because of their perceived excellence, but because of the difficulties of finding formal courses and meeting formal timetables. Developments from this include radio and television inputs leading to Open University-style open learning. Programmed instruction, either in the form of text or via teaching machines, was seen as the future of distance learning some fifteen to twenty years ago. This method has never really fulfilled its potential and further developments have concentrated on computer-based training and more recently on interactive video. Although such training is not trainer-dependent, the trainer plays a vital role in providing a reference point for the trainee, and in being someone who can provide help and encouragement.

The trainer also plays a vital role in ensuring that the learning materials and content are appropriate for and acceptable to the learners, which is a more difficult task when there is little contact with trainees. Webberley (1986) argues that the learning 'agenda' should be negotiated with the trainees where possible.

The design and conduct of training

All the foregoing information in this chapter influences the eventual design and conduct of the training programme. Decisions need to be made about:

1. The mix of training methods and media used.
2. The pacing and spacing of training: the speed at which the information should be put across, the length of sessions and the spacing between

sessions. Should the training be self-paced? The distribution of training is also important – would it be beneficial to concentrate the training over five consecutive days? Is this possible for the trainees? Would one day per week over five weeks be better?

3. The actual timing of training needs to be considered. When are the busy and slack periods for the potential trainees?
4. Whether there is sufficient training expertise in-house or whether outside speakers or instructors need to be brought in.
5. How much input will be expected from the trainees outside the normal working day?
6. The location of training needs to be considered. Is it to be on site, in the training centre, in a hotel?
7. How is the training to be evaluated? Swanson and Sleezer (1987) suggest a variety of methods by which training effectiveness might be evaluated, including performance tests, satisfaction ratings, assessment of the technology used, knowledge tests and cost-benefit analyses.

Summary propositions

25.1 No single theory of learning comprehensively explains how people learn.

25.2 Learning principles can be derived from a variety of learning theories and experiments. They can be used to guide the design of learning experiences.

25.3 Training needs should be investigated at the organizational level, department level, job level and individual level.

25.4 Training needs should be translated into training objectives. These are expressed in terms of the behaviour which is to be the end-result of training.

25.5 Training resources include both 'hard' training media (books, videos, etc.) and human resources.

25.6 There is no one best method of training. A method needs to be chosen which is appropriate to the trainees, the training objectives and the resources available.

References

Bandura, A., Ross, D. and Ross, S. A. (1963), 'A comparative test of the status envy and the secondary-reinforcement theories of identificatory learning', *Journal of Abnormal Psychology*, vol. 67, pp. 527–34.

Bass, B. M., and Vaughan, J. A. (1966), *Training in Industry: The management of learning*, Belmont, Calif.: Wadsworth/London: Tavistock.

Belbin, E. and Belbin, R. M. (1972), *Problems in Adult Retraining*, London: Heinemann.

Burgoyne, J. and Stuart, R. (eds.) (1978), 'Management development: context and strategies', *A Personnel Review Monograph*, Aldershot: Gower.

Flavell, J. H. (1963), *The Developmental Psychology of Jean Piaget*, New York: Van Nostrand Reinhold.

Gagne, R. (1965), *The Conditions of Learning*, New York: Holt, Rinehart & Winston.

Grant, D. (1984), 'A better way of learning from Nellie', *Personnel Management*, December.

Hergenhahn, B. R. (1982), *An Introduction to the Theories of Learning*, Englewood Cliffs, NJ: Prentice Hall.

Honey, P. and Mumford, A. (1989), *The Manual of Learning Opportunities*, Maidenhead: Peter Honey.

Hull, C. L. (1943), *Principles of Behavior*, New York: Appleton-Century-Crofts.

Kearsley, G. (1984), *Training and Technology: A handbook for HRD professionals*, Reading, Mass.: Addison-Wesley.

Kimble, G. A. (1961), in Hildegard and Marquis, *Conditioning and Learning* (2nd edition), Englewood Cliffs, NJ: Prentice Hall.

Kolb, D. A., Rubin, I.M. and McIntyre, J. M. (1984), *Organizational Psychology* (4th edition), Englewood Cliffs, NJ: Prentice Hall.

Laird, D. (1978), *Approaches to Training and Development*, Reading, Mass.: Addison-Wesley.

Mager, R. (1962), *Preparing Objectives for Programmed Instruction*; retitled 1975, *Preparing Instructional Objectives* (2nd edition), Belmont, Calif.: Fearson.

Mumford, A. (1971), *The Manager and Training*, London: Pitman.

Pavlov, I. P. (1941), *Conditional Reflexes and Psychiatry* (trans. and ed. W. H. Grant), New York: International Publishers.

Piaget, J. (1928), *Judgement and Reasoning in the Child*, New York: Harcourt Brace Jovanovich.

Rae, L. (1983), *The Skills of Training: A guide for managers and practitioners*, Aldershot: Gower.

Roden, J. (1986), *Interim Report to the Co-operative Bank on the Social Skills Project*, unpublished paper, UMIST.

Rogers, C. R. (1969), *Freedom to Learn*, Columbus, Ohio: Charles E. Merrill.

Simpson, B. (1984), 'T-groups, TA, NLP . . . What should we expect from human relations training?' *Personnel Management*, November.

Sims, R. R. (1989), 'Adapting training to trainee learning styles', *Journal of European Industrial Training*, vol. 14, no, 2, pp. 17–22.

Skinner, B. F. (1953), *Science and Human Behavior*, New York: Macmillan.

Stuart, R. (1984), 'Using others to learn: some everyday practice', *Personnel Review*, vol. 13, no. 4.

Swanson, R. A. and Sleezer, M. C. (1987), 'Training effectiveness evaluation', *Journal of European Industrial Training*, vol. 11, no. 4, pp. 7–16.

Thorndike, E. L. (1913), *The Psychology of Learning*, New York: Teachers College.

Walters, B. (1983), 'Designing and resourcing training'. In D. Guest and T. Kenny (eds.), *A Textbook of Techniques and Strategies in Personnel Management*, London: Institute of Personnel Management.

Watson, J. B. (1930), *Behaviorism* (2nd edition), Chicago: University of Chicago Press.

Webberley, R. (1986), 'The loneliness of the long-distance trainer', *Personnel Management*, June.

26

Management development

Is management development just another way of describing management training, to be used until a more desirable phrase can be coined, or until it becomes subsumed under the growing process of organizational development? Although new terminology is often used just as a refreshing change, or in order to make last year's history sound like this year's news, management development is distinct from both management training and organizational development.

In this chapter we consider the growth and identity of management development, its nature and goals, and the processes that contribute towards them.

The growth of management development

There is a strong myth-making tradition attached to the development of effective management as those senior in organizations have sought to preserve their elite status. Initially, there was no question of acquiring skill; entry to a management position came as part of the right of ownership, the favour of the owner or the natural entitlement of those in a particular social position. As the size of organizations and the number of managers began to increase, there was a move to professionalization to justify managerial status, with the development of professional or quasi-professional bodies, controlling entry by examination and election. This, together with organizational complexity, produced specialization and the longest-running feature of management development: management training courses. Run by educational establishments, professional bodies, employers or consultants, there is a wide range of courses which seek to

461

communicate some distilled wisdom relating to the management task. Although the training course is well established, it was joined during the 1960s by a fresh idea – that of developing individuals. Instead of managers being fed information in a course, their managerial capacity and potential would be developed by a wide variety of experiences, through which they would acquire greater under- standing, awareness, sensitivity, self-confidence and those other aspects of effectiveness that were regarded as most important but which could not be inculcated. This change of emphasis was accompanied by growing use of employee appraisal to determine individual development needs, rather than leaving trainers to produce universal programmes. There was also some move towards putting the control of the development programme in the hands of the individual being developed, instead of the experts. In reporting on one such experiment Graves concludes: 'managers are better able to develop their own skills if given development opportunities rather than training . . . training should be based on managerial needs as perceived by the managers rather than development needs perceived by the trainers' (Graves 1976, p. 15). Furthermore, such development may well take place on the job in the everyday ebb and flow of events rather than in the specially contrived circumstances beloved by trainers. In this way the learning is not only relevant to the job being done, it may also alter the manager's approach to his work as he becomes more questioning of events and more analytical of processes: 'The remarkable and persuasive reason for saying that nonetheless managers can become more effective as learners lies in the dedication to doing things, being active, that is the hallmark of so many of them' (Mumford 1981, p. 380). Mumford continues by suggesting that the art of encouraging learning is: 'to ask them to undertake activities associated with learning which build on existing managerial processes and rewards' (*ibid.*).

The focus in management development has moved to stress activities such as coaching, action learning and natural learning. In line with this increased emphasis on learning in the job, there has also been an upsurge of interest in mentoring, which like many of the best management development ideas describes a process long familiar to experienced managers, but substantially unrecognized and underused (Mumford 1985). This process is largely uncontrolled at present, but an understanding of mentoring and of the contributions of peers gives critical insight into the role of work relationships in the development of managers.

Interest in mentoring has also highlighted a particular problem for the development of women managers, that of finding a role model. It appears that, for the few women who are mentors or protégées, the nature of the relationship is different from that of men. This brings us to the thorny problem of whether the training and development needs of women managers are different from those of male managers and whether there should be separate development programmes especially for women.

One recent emphasis has been that on innovation and organization development, which for some is based on the premise that managers can only develop if the organization develops with them (and vice versa). Organization development takes various forms, but usually there is a focus on team-building exercises whereby the members of a team develop their capacity to work out their strategies for future development and the organizational change that this will involve.

The identity of management development

We can see from the above that management training contributes to management development but is not synonymous with it, as managers also learn and develop in many other ways. Management training and management development can be differentiated in four important ways:

1. Management development is a broader concept and is more concerned with developing the whole person rather than emphasizing the learning of narrowly defined skills.
2. Management development emphasizes the contribution of formal and informal work experiences.
3. The concept of management development places a greater responsibility on managers to develop themselves than is placed on most employees to train themselves.
4. Although in training generally there always needs to be a concern with the future, this is especially emphasized in management development. Managers are developed as much for jobs that they will be doing as for the jobs that they are doing. Both the organization and the managers benefit from this approach. Management development is a vital aspect of career management, and from the organization's point of view both are methods of satisfying human resource needs while allowing individuals to achieve their career goals.

Management development is also a separate entity from organization development. There are many other aspects to management development than can be provided for by organization development. Similarly, there is much more to organization development than management development. In fact, management development is not necessarily seen as an essential part of organization development, and Klatt *et al.* argue that 'once an overall OD strategy has been determined, it may be decided a part of this strategy should include the training and development of individuals' (Klatt *et al.* 1985, p. 271). It is, however difficult to envisage that organization development can take place without the development, at least informally, of management.

Review topic 26.1

How does management development differ from career development, career planning and career management?

What do managers do?

> The question 'what do managers do?' has an air of naïveté, insolence and even redundancy about it. Yet it is a question which is begged by many management-related issues. . . . The vast and growing industry of management education, training and development presumably rests upon a set of ideas about what managers do and, hence, what managers are being educated, trained and developed for. (Hales 1986, p. 88)

There has been much theorizing and uncertainty about the nature of managerial work. Managerial work has been studied from a variety of perspectives, including what managers do, how they distribute their time, with whom they interact, informal aspects of their work and themes that pervade management work (Hales 1986).

Among the mass of recent theorizing has been the research of Rosemary Stewart (1976) in analyzing work in terms of the relationships involved, and also some common recurrent management activities which are liaison, maintenance of work processes, innovation and setting the boundaries of the job. Minzberg (1973) suggests that managerial work comprises various combinations of ten distinct roles in three general categories: decision-making, interpersonal and information-processing. A little earlier, Scholefield (1968) had produced the suggestion that managers should do three things: operate the firm, make innovations and stabilize the organization. Other management researchers (for example, Torrington and Weightman 1982) have concentrated on the nature of the skills involved in management work, and have investigated how managers' time is allocated between the technical, administrative and managerial aspects of their jobs. Leavitt (1978) suggests four key ideas about the nature of the managing process. First, managing always includes some influencing and implementing activities, as managers have to get other people to do things. Secondly, managing also includes a lot of problem-solving, with managers not only having to work against tight deadlines, but also work on a dozen problems at the same time. Thirdly, managers have to be problem finders, and need to take an active rather than an entirely passive stance. Leavitt comments: 'He has to create problems, to set goals, to decide where he wants to go, even though he may have lots of trouble getting there and he may have to make painful compromises and many detours along the way (Leavitt 1978, p. 247.).

A final aspect of managing, as suggested by Leavitt, is that it takes place in an organization and that managers operate in a position that is peculiarly dependent, while seeming to be independent.

In the above quote, Leavitt points to one of the central themes of managerial work, that to a large extent managers define the work that they will do. This is undoubtedly one of the factors which makes managerial work so hard to characterize. Hales comments that: 'Managerial jobs seem, in general, to be sufficiently loosely defined to be highly negotiable and susceptible to choice of both style and content. (Hales 1986, p. 101). And Fletcher carries this point further: 'Management is neither art nor science nor skill. At base there is nothing to do. A manager is hired for what he knows other firms do, what he can find to do, and what he can be told to do' (Fletcher 1973, p. 136).

Hales (1986) comments that this opportunity for choice and negotiation, together with variation and contingency, pressure and conflict, and lack of opportunity for reflection are central themes in managerial work. All these ideas clearly have a bearing on the objectives of management development. However, a useful counterblast to all this theorizing is the iconoclasm of Alistair Mant (1977), whose scepticism is so perceptive and persuasive that one is left with the feeling that he might just be right when he argues that we tend to undervalue a large number of jobs that are of true social and economic importance, such as salesman and housewife, while ascribing enormous significance to the job of manager, which seems non-existent in some of the world's more successful industrial societies.

The goals of management development

Undoubtedly, those people who design management development programmes and experiences aim to encourage the development of effective managers. One of the greatest difficulties is that although there is a lot of research about what managers do, much less is written about the relationship between this and their effectiveness. Hales (1986) comments that some of the more celebrated writings on effective management are singularly reticent about specifying what effective managers are effective at. Since in any case there is much uncertainty about what managers do, it is not surprising that the goals of management development are often uncertain and frequently spurious. The goals of the organizers of development may differ markedly from those undergoing the process. Among the generalizations we can make are:

1. Management development has traditionally been an elitist process, although this may be changing with greater development for all.

2. Emphasis will be on skills at doing, rather than knowledge *about*.
3. Dominant will be the capacity of the individual manager to be socially adroit and to evaluate information as a preliminary to making choices between alternatives.

Following on from the last section we would suggest that it would be fruitful, among other things, to develop managers who can structure their own jobs and manage themselves and their careers. Much of the management development that takes place does so without any externally imposed goals – it takes place in the context of the job and is guided to a greater or lesser extent by managers themselves.

The elements of management development

It is not our aim in this section to make specific suggestions as to how to conduct the process of management development, but rather to review some aspects of organizing development experiences, including informal and formal training input and other aspects of managers' jobs which may contribute to their development as managers.

Selection

Those who undergo formal management development are nearly always selected by organizational superiors as being in need of the process. An undergraduate may take a degree in business studies without anyone else ever posing the question as to whether or not he or she is suited to a management post, and some people work very diligently at night school or on correspondence courses to obtain a qualification for some management specialism in an attempt to improve their employment prospects. These, however, are not processes of management development, to which entry depends on being chosen, but choice is sometimes made on strange criteria.

The greatest problems are those where someone is trying to correct a mistake for which management development is not the remedy. If job holders are underperforming because the job is beyond their basic ability, then the solution lies in rectifying the basic error – that they were appointed in the first place – rather than in elaborate procedures of courses, objective-setting and appraisal so that months later the continued inadequacy can be blamed on the individuals ('We really have done all we can to bring them up to scratch') and not on the people who wrongly appointed them in the first place.

Apart from the requisite ability and other qualities that are needed, it is important that the employee should be committed to the programme, seeing the benefits that will flow from it, and should have the opportunity to use and practise quickly the skills they hope to acquire.

Appraisal and individual development

Gradually, performance appraisal is being used in organizations as a means of determining development needs – or training needs – as well as or instead of a preliminary to a salary review. In this way the employees appraised are more likely to participate frankly and positively in the appraisal procedures so that their development programme is begun by an assessment, by themselves and others, of their current performance in relation to expected performance, and the implications of this for their development. Performance, as with other employees, is best defined in behavioural terms; Valerie and Andrew Stewart (1976) comment that this is possible, although what makes for effective management performance varies enormously from one job to another. The use of job competencies against which to analyze current behaviour is particularly helpful here. An appraisal also needs to be made of where the employee is at present and what they need to do to prepare for the type of future they envisage, if this is agreed to be feasible. Further information on appraisal will be found in the following chapter.

Education and training courses

A training course will usually be a key feature in a formal programme of development, and these may be standard offerings by various specialist bodies or in-house courses developed for their own specialist needs. Increasingly, these options are being combined so that there is the possibility of an externally provided course tailored to suit an organization's particular needs.

First are the pre-experience courses: full-time education leading to academic qualification with a management sciences or business studies label and undertaken by young people as a preliminary to a career. These have been developing in the United Kingdom since the middle 1960s and have proved very popular with students at universities and polytechnics. They are often described as 'vocational' and intended to be a practical preparation for a management-type occupation on completion. They can never, however, be vocational in the same sense as degrees in areas such as medicine or architecture because there is relatively little practical element in the course. The sandwich courses that incorporate periods of work in the 'real' world may help to bring the feet of students nearer to the ground, but they cannot give any meaningful experience in, and practice at, managerial work. The courses provide an education, normally based on a study of the academic disciplines of economics, mathematics, psychology and sociology and incorporating some work in the more specialized disciplines like industrial relations and organizational behaviour, as well as an introduction to the practical areas like accounting, marketing, personnel and production. The student should emerge with a balanced understanding of the workings of an industrial society and an industrial economy, and they will have some useful blocs of information which may well be at the frontiers of knowledge in management thought. The student should also have developed the more traditional qualities of maturity and the ability to analyze and debate that university education purports to nurture: they will not be trained to be a manager.

Second are the post-experience courses: full-time education usually leading to a diploma or master's degree with a management or business label and undertaken during a career. Although such courses were being run in this country early in this century, the great boom came after the establishment of the London and Manchester Business Schools and other management centres in the 1960s. The main difference is not only that students are older, but that they study on the basis of experience they have had and with the knowledge of the work to which they will return. Typically, the member of a course at a business school will be seconded by their employer at a time when they have already held a management post. The material of the course may not be very different from that of the pre-experience course, but the student's perception will be very different and their application of any new insights or skills will be more immediate.

Neither pre-experience nor post-experience courses of the type described here will feature strongly the skills element mentioned on page 465 in the listing of management development goals. It is interesting to see the quite different emphasis that is asserted by a past principal of the London Business School:

> I would argue that an essential basis for a flexible and adaptable industrial and commercial base must be a flexible and adaptable management. . . . [This] takes various forms. The first, which is evidently related to our place in the world economy, requires a greater awareness of the position of organizations in world markets and an increased capacity to think through problems on a wider canvas than in the past. Parochialism will not do as a basis for future prosperity. At the same time management will have to become more sensitive to changes in its immediate social environment. (Ball 1976)

The third category can be generally described as consultancy courses. Varying from a half-day to several weeks in length, they are run by consultants or professional bodies for all comers. They have the advantage that they bring together people from varying occupational backgrounds and are not, therefore, as introspective as in-house courses and are popular for topical issues. They are, however, often relatively expensive and superficial, despite their value as sources of industrial folklore, by which we mean the swapping of experiences among course members.

The most valuable courses of this type are those that concentrate on specific areas or knowledge, like developing interviewing skills or teaching special technical methods. This short-course approach is probably the only way for managers to come to terms with some new development, such as a change in legislation, because they need not only to find an interpretation of the development, they also need to share views and reactions with fellow managers to ensure that their own feelings are not idiosyncratic or perverse.

A fourth category is in-house courses which are often similar in nature to the consultancy courses. Such in-house courses are often run with the benefit of some external expertise, but this is not always the case. In-house courses can be particularly useful if the training needs to relate to specific organizational procedures and structures, or if it is geared to encouraging managers to work more effectively together in the organizational environment. For a development of this theme, see the section on organization development. The drawbacks.of in-house courses are that they suffer from a lack of breadth of both content and input from managers, and there is no possibility of learning from people in other organizations.

Lastly, and on the fringe of education and training courses, are outdoor (sometimes known as outward bound) – type courses. Outdoor courses attempt to develop such skills as leadership, getting results through people, self-confidence in handling people, and increasing self-awareness through a variety of experiences including outdoor physical challenges. One course brochure states:

> A range of intellectual, emotional and physical challenges is presented which involves working in a variety of environments; in group syndicate rooms, outdoor project areas, creative workshops, on rivers and lakes and in the hills and mountains. (Brathay 1986)

Action learning

The iconoclasm of Mant (1977), referred to earlier in this chapter, is mild compared with that of Revans (see, for example, Revans 1972, 1974), one of the great original thinkers to study management. As a professor of management he became more and more disenchanted with the world of management education, which he saw developing around him. Among the many aphorisms attributed to him was: 'If I teach my son to read, how do I know he will not read rubbish; if I teach him to write, how do I know that he will not write yet another book on management education?' Despairing of the way in which the London and Manchester Business Schools were established, Revans resigned his chair in Manchester and moved to Belgium to start his first action learning project. This was based on his conviction that managers do not need education but the ability to solve problems. His method has been basically to organize exchanges, so that a manager experienced in one organization is planted in another to solve a particular set of problems that is proving baffling. He or she brings a difference of experience, a freshness of approach, and they are not dependent on their new, temporary organizational peers for their career growth. They work on the problem for a period of months, having many sessions of discussion and debate with a group of other individuals similarly planted in unfamiliar organizations with a knotty problem to solve. The learning stems from the immediate problem that is presented, and from all the others that emerge, one by one, in the steps towards a solution. This presents a need that the student has to satisfy and all the learning is in terms of what they discover they need to know rather than what someone else feels is necessary. It is an idea of startling simplicity. Its relative unpopularity in academic circles is easy to understand, but in management circles there has been some diffidence because the action learning approach nearly always stirs something up, and not all organizations have the nerve to risk the soul-searching and upheaval that is caused.

Coaching

Coaching is an informal approach to management development based on a close relationship between the developing manager and one other person, usually their superior, who is experienced in management. The manager as coach helps trainees to develop by giving them the opportunity to perform an increasing range of management tasks, and by helping them to learn from their experiences. They work to improve the trainee's performance by discussion, exhortation, encouragement, understanding and counselling. It is vital that the coach is someone who has experienced those things which the trainee is now learning, as Henry Boettinger, that most elegant of writers on management, makes the point:

> Only someone who can actually perform in an art is qualified to teach it. There is no question that constructive criticism from an informed bystander is helpful; actors, for instance, can learn a great deal about human motivation from psychiatrists. Nevertheless, this kind of procedure is different from the one an actor goes through to show another how to express human feelings. (Boettinger 1975)

Mentoring

> As a training and development tool, it [mentoring] is not a new concept. For centuries wise men have offered counsel to the young. In ancient Greece, Odysseus entrusted the education of his son Telemachus to a trusted counsellor and friend. This trusted and wise friend, Mentor, reputedly became the counsellor, guide, tutor, coach, sponsor and mentor for his protégé, Telemachus. (Hunt and Michael 1983)

Mentoring is seen as offering a wide range of advantages for the development of the protégé, coaching as described above being just one of the benefits of the relationship. The mentor would occasionally be the individual's immediate manager, but more often it is a more senior manager in the same or a different function. Kram (1983) identifies two broad functions of mentoring, first, career functions, which are those aspects of the relationship that primarily enhance career advancement; secondly, psychosocial functions, which are those aspects of the relationship that primarily enhance a sense of competence, clarity of identity and effectiveness in the managerial role. Figure 26.1 shows these functions in more detail and compares them with the functions of peer relationships, which we discuss in the following section. There is a much greater stress in the mentoring relationship than in the coaching relationship, on career success, and individuals selected for mentoring, because, among other things, they are good performers, from the right social background, and know the potential mentors socially (Kanter 1977). There are advantages in the relationship for mentors as well as protégés – these include reflected glory from a successful protégé, the development of supporters throughout the organization, and the facilitation of their own promotion by adequate training of a replacement (Hunt and Michael 1983). Managers are also seen as responsible for developing talent, and mentorship may be encouraged or formalized as, for example, in the Bell Laboratories and some departments of the US Government (Stumpf and London 1981). The difficulties of establishing a formal programme include the potential mismatch of individuals, unreal expectations on both sides, and the time and effort involved. Burke and McKeen (1989) offer a thoughtful discussion of the advantages and disadvantages of formal programmes.

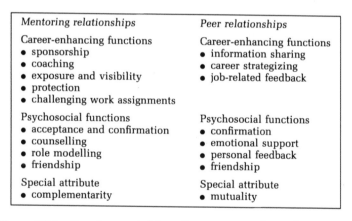

Figure 26.1 *Developmental functions – comparison of mentoring and peer relationships*
Source: Kram and Isabella (1985).

Peer relationships

Although mentor–protégé relationships have been shown to be related to high levels of career success, not all developing managers have access to such a relationship. Supportive peer relationships at work are potentially more available to the individual and offer a number of benefits for the development of both individuals. The benefits that are available depend on the nature of the peer relationship, and Kram and Isabella (1985) have identified three groups of peer relationships which are differentiated by their primary development functions and which can be expressed on a continuum from 'information peer' through 'collegial peer' to 'special peer'. Table 26.1 shows the developmental functions and the characteristics of each type of relationship. Most of us benefit from one or a number of peer relationships at work but often we do not readily appreciate their contribution towards our development. Peer relationships most often develop on an informal basis and provide mutual support. Some organizations, however, formally appoint an existing employee to provide such support to a new member of staff through their first 12–18 months in the organization. These relationships may, of course, continue beyond the initial period. The name for the appointed employee will vary from organization to organization, and sometimes the word 'coach' or 'mentor' is used – which can be confusing! Cromer (1989) discusses the advantages of peer relationships organized on a

Table 26.1 Peer relationships and the characteristics of each type

	Information peer	Collegial peer	Special peer
Primary functions	Information-sharing	Career strategizing Job-related feedback Friendship	Confirmation Emotional support Personal feedback Friendship
Level of commitment	Demands little, but offers many benefits	Information-sharing joined by increasing levels of self-disclosure and trust	Equivalent of best friend
Intensity of relationship	Social, but limited in sharing of personal experience	Allows for greater self-expression	Strong sense of bonding
Issues worked on	Increases individual's eyes and ears to organization (work only)	Limited support for exploration of family and work issues	Wide range of support and work issues
Needs satisfied	Source of information regarding career opportunities	Provides direct honest feedback	Offers chance to express one's personal and professional dilemmas, vulnerabilities and individuality

Source: Adapted from Kram and Isabella (1985, pp. 119–20).

formal basis and references the skills and qualities sought in peer providers, which include accessibility, empathy, organizational experience and proven task skills.

Review topic 26.2

Consider each significant peer relationship that you have at work. Where does each fit on the continuum of relationships shown in Figure 26.1, and what contributions does it make towards your development?

Natural learning

Natural managerial learning is learning that takes place on-the-job and results from managers' everyday experience of the tasks that they undertake. Natural learning is even more difficult to investigate than either coaching, mentoring or peer relationships, and yet the way that managers learn from everyday experiences, and their level of awareness of this, is very important for their development. Burgoyne and Hodgson (1983) collected information from managers by having them 'think aloud' while doing their work. They identified three levels of learning. The first level of learning is when the manager took in some factual information that had an immediate relevance but did not have any long-term effect on his view of the world in general. At the next level the manager learnt something that was transferable from the present situation to another – they had changed their conception about a particular aspect of their view of the world in general, this aspect being situation-specific. For example, managers use incidents to add to their personal stock of 'case law' and from this select models when dealing with future situations. In some cases managers specifically set aside time for reflective learning so that they can derive critical insights and new approaches for use in the future. Some managers also learnt through deliberate problem-solving: Burgoyne and Hodgson describe a manager who was unhappy with the way that he used his time, and who tried a new approach, was unsatisfied and so tried another, liked it and kept it. Level three learning was similar to level two, but was not situation-specific. Perhaps one of the most valuable insights from this research is that some learning occurred as a direct result of the research process, due to managers verbalizing what was happening or had happened, and thus becoming more conscious of the processes taking place. Mumford comments: 'In my view the focus should be on what managers do and how they can be helped to learn from what they do' (Mumford 1985, p. 30).

Self-development

To some extent self-development may be seen as a conscious effort to gain the most from natural learning in a job. The emphasis in self-development is that each individual is responsible for, and can plan, their own development, although they may need to seek help when working on some issues. Self-development involves individuals in analyzing their strengths, weaknesses and the way that they learn, primarily by means of questionnaires and feedback from others. This analysis may initially begin on a self-development course, or with the help of a facilitator, but would then be continued by the individual back on the job. From this analysis individuals, perhaps with some help at first, plan particular development opportunities and projects within their job, and are also better equipped to get more learning from all aspects of their job. They are also in a better position to seek appropriate opportunities and help, in their learning, from their manager.

Many of the activities included in self-development would be based on observation, collecting further feedback about the way they operate, experimenting with different approaches, and in particular reviewing what has happened, why and what they have learned. A managers' guide to self-development has been published by Pedler, Burgoyne and Boydell (1986), which provides some structured analyses and activities for managers to work through.

A logical extension of self-development within the job is the development of career planning where individuals can work through a guidebook which helps them identify their career goals, the ways they learn, and their development needs, liaising with their supervisor to check assumptions, share information and receive help. This process has been described by Burgoyne and Germain (1984) in relation to research staff at Esso.

Management learning groups

Management learning groups are another way in which managers can develop their natural learning from a job and also help other to learn. Typically, this involves a group of managers in a series of meetings where they would jointly discuss organizational issues and/or individual work problems. Groups may begin operating with a leader who is a process expert, not a content expert, and who therefore acts as a facilitator rather than a source of information. The group itself is the only source of information and as their process skills develop they may operate without outside help. The content and timings of the meetings can be very flexible, although clearly if they are to operate well they will require a significant level of energy and commitment. Blennerhasset (1988) gives an example of using such groups prior to further development of IT and demonstrates changes in individual attitudes and behaviour and beneficial effects for the organization.

Management by objectives

A particular formula, which has been widely used as a vehicle for management development, has been management by objectives, conveniently abbreviated to MbO. It is based on the elementary premise that unless you know where you are going you are unlikely to arrive, and unless you know what results you want to achieve you will not achieve them. This is applied to developing the effective management of an organization by a simple sequence of procedures which define objectives for individual managers in the context of a set of objectives for the organization as a whole. Once these have been established, and agreed by those who have to meet them, ways of meeting them are set down in statements with names like management guides and job improvement plans; the management guide specifying key results areas. Later comes the review of performance and the setting of fresh objectives. The initial attractiveness of this approach lay in the fact that it was relatively uncommon for such objectives to be set down for any individual in an organization and unlikely that any such individual would receive systematic feedback on the performance they were producing. One protagonist of MbO summarized the needs of the individual manager as follows:

1. 'Agree with me the results I am expected to achieve.'
2. 'Give me an opportunity to perform.'
3. 'Let me know how I am getting on.'
4. 'Give me guidance and training where I need it.'
5. 'Reward me according to my contribution.'

In many situations this was a major step forward to autonomy and self-control, and the excellent sense of the approach has influenced the nature of management development far beyond the number of organizations who formally adopted it. The difficulty lies in the tendency to expect too much and base future plans on specified performance standards of individuals rather than collectives. A set of objectives linked to sales volume of a new product for a sales manager will be of little value – perhaps even harmful – if a technical defect develops that the designers had not foreseen and cannot rectify. Every manager is vulnerable to the operation of *force majeure* in the form of the unpredictable and unexpected. Other difficulties are those of joint goal-setting between those who are not equal, so that the 'shared' objectives can easily be 'imposed' objectives. There is also a tendency to focus on short-term specific targets, like productivity targets or sales figures, at the expense of longer-term considerations that cannot be so precisely defined. However, the managerial needs identified in points 1–5 above are very real and also form the basis of more recent systems of performance management, which has some similarities with management by objectives and is discussed in the following chapter.

Organization development

The interaction between organizational structure and employee performance, as well as the interaction between organization and employee well-being, has been studied so closely as to bring a shift in thinking towards the idea that teams of managers and their organizations have to be developed simultaneously. This is much influenced by the concern with planned organizational change and the fear of organizational obsolescence because the methods of an organization are appropriate only for a situation that no longer exists. Organization development practitioners will focus on increasing organizational effectiveness and they may be particularly involved in the introduction of change, whether it be technical, cultural or organizational.

Compared with some of the approaches we have been discussing – like action learning and MbO – organization development lacks the basic simplicity to appeal to the imagination of many people, and its acceptance has been much bedevilled by uncertainty about what it is. This difficulty is compounded because organization development (inevitably abbreviated to OD) has a variety of gurus, each of whom has received a revelation about its nature that differs from all the others. One of the best summaries is by Bristow *et al.* (1978), who trace its development back to the United States (where else?) in the 1930s. OD is sometimes perceived as too 'touchy-feely' (Herman 1989), based on some of the softer OD practices, for example T-groups (see page 457), and this has persuaded some managers to avoid OD interventions.

OD's method of operation centres on not only objectives and aims, but on interpersonal behaviour, attitudes and values in the organization. There is usually an emphasis on openness between colleagues, improved conflict resolution methods, more effective team management and the collaborative diagnosis and solution of problems. As we have commented earlier in this chapter, OD does not necessarily include formalized training and development, although it is most likely that this will be incorporated.

Any training strategy typically centres on groups of managers, or directly on organizational processes with the assistance of the change agent or consultant, who helps the participants to perceive, face up to and resolve the behavioural problems experienced. OD is a 'macro' approach to development, as contrasted with individual training and development which is primarily a 'micro' approach.

Specific issues that OD practitioners may be involved with include:

- Developing processes for bringing about and implementing change.
- Assessing organizational effectiveness and developing improvement plans.
- Organization structure and design.
- Bringing about cultural change.
- Designing effective communication processes.
- Building effective work-groups and multidisciplinary teams.
- Managing the implementation and organizational implications of new technology.

- Effective work practices, such as clarification of roles and responsibilities in complex situations, work-group objective setting.
- Stimulating innovation and creativity.
- Problem-solving and effective decision-making processes.
- Managing interpersonal and inter-group conflict.

Source: Adapted from Purves (1989).

Van Eynde and Bledsoe (1990) found in their research that OD practitioners were now more likely to be working with client managers on more task-focused issues directly related to organizational effectiveness, and less on improvement of interpersonal relationships, than they were fifteen years ago. Team dynamics, for example, would now be dealt with inside the framework of helping a team to resolve a critical issue. Increasingly, OD consultants are involved in helping organizations to envisage the future. The researchers also found that there are increasing opportunities for OD practitioners to work with the highest levels in the organization, on changes that impact on the whole organization.

It is through these types of intervention, and from their experiences of the processes used, that managers develop further and are more able successfully to work through similar issues in the future.

Summary propositions

26.1 The emphasis on formal development programmes is declining in favour of greater interest in approaches to on-the-job development, such as mentoring, peer relationships and self-development.

26.2 The most effective management development combines both formal and informal methods.

26.3 Management development is different from management training as it is broader and geared more towards the future. It places a greater responsibility on managers to develop themselves.

26.4 Management development can be a critical aspect of organization development, career planning and career management, but it is not synonymous with any of these terms.

26.5 There is great uncertainty about what managers do, and to some extent managers define their own jobs. It would be fruitful to help them to develop the skills to do this. It would also be useful to help managers to learn from their own experiences.

References

Ball, R. J. (1976), 'Britain's economy: some implications for management and management education', *Personnel Review*. Autumn.

Blennerhasset, E. (1988), 'Research report: Management learning groups – a lesson in action', *Journal of European Industrial Training*, vol. 12, no. 8, pp. 5–12.

Boettinger, H. M. (1975), 'Is management really an art?' *Harvard Business Review*. January/February.

Brathay (1986), *Brathay Leadership and Development Training*, Ambleside, Cumbria: Brathay.

Bristow, J., Carby, K. and Thakur, M. (1978), 'An introduction to organization development'. In J. Bristow, K. Carby and M. Thakur, *Personnel in Change*, London: Institute of Personnel Management.

Burgoyne, J. G. and Germain, C. (1984), 'Self-development and career planning: an exercise in mutual benefit', *Personnel Management*, April.

Burgoyne, J. and Hodgson, V. E. (1983), 'Natural learning and managerial action: a phenomenological study in the field setting', *Journal of Management Studies*, vol. 20, no. 3.

Burke, R. J. and McKeen, C. A. (1989), 'Developing formal mentoring programs in organizations', *Business Quarterly*, vol. 53, pt. 3, pp. 76–9.

Cromer, D. R. (1989), 'Peers as providers', *Personnel Administrator*, vol. 34, pt. 5, pp. 84–6.

Fletcher, C. (1973), 'The end of management'. In J. Child (ed.), *Man and Organisations*, London: George Allen & Unwin.

Graves, D. (1976), 'The managers and management development', *Personnel Review*, Autumn.

Hales, C. P. (1986), 'What do managers do? A critical review of the evidence', *Journal of Management Studies*, vol. 53, no. 1.

Herman, S. M. (1989), 'Organisation development warts and all', *Organisation Development Journal*, Summer, pp. 16–20.

Hunt, D. M. and Michael, C. (1983), 'Mentorship: a career training and development tool', *Academy of Management Review*, vol. 8, no. 3.

Kanter, R. M. (1977), *Men and Women of the Corporation*, New York: Basic Books.

Klatt, L. A., Murdick, R. G. and Schuster, F. E. (1985), *Human Resource Management*, Columbus, Ohio: Charles E. Merrill.

Kram, K. E. (1983), 'Phases of the mentor relationship', *Academy of Management Journal*, vol. 26, no. 4.

Kram, K. E. and Isabella, L. A. (1985), 'Mentoring alternatives: the role of peer relationships in career development', *Academy of Management Journal*, vol. 28, no. 1.

Leavitt, H. J. (1978), *Management Psychology* (4th edition), Chicago: University of Chicago Press.

Mant, A. (1977), *The Rise and Fall of the British Manager*, Basingstoke: Macmillan.

Minzberg, H. (1973), *The Nature of Managerial Work*, London: Harper & Row.

Mumford, A. (1981), 'What did you learn today?' *Personnel Management*, August.

Mumford, A. (1985), 'What's new in management development?' *Personnel Management*, May.

Pedler, M., Burgoyne, J. and Boydell, T. (1986), *A Manager's Guide to Self-development*, London: McGraw-Hill.

Purves, S. (1989), 'Organization and Process Consultancy', unpublished paper.

Revans, R. W. (1972), 'Action learning – a management development programme', *Personnel Review*, Autumn.

Revans, R. W. (1974), 'Action learning projects'. In B. Taylor and G. L. Lippitt, *Management Development and Training Handbook*, Maidenhead: McGraw-Hill.

Scholefield, J. (1968), 'The effectiveness of senior executives', *Journal of Management Studies*, May.

Stewart, A. and V. (1976), *Tomorrow's Men Today*, London: Institute of Personnel Management.

Stewart, R. (1976), *Contrasts in Management*, Maidenhead: McGraw-Hill.

Stumpf, S. A. and London, M. (1981), 'Management promotions; individual and organizational factors influencing the decision process', *Academy of Management Review*.

Taylor, B. and Lippitt, G. L. (1974), *Management Development and Training Handbook*, Maidenhead: McGraw-Hill.

Torrington, D. and Weightman, J. (1982), 'Technical atrophy in middle management', *Journal of General Management*, vol. 7, no. 4.

Van Eynde, D. F. and Bledsoe, J. A. (1990), 'The changing practice of organisation development', *Leadership and Organisation Development Journal*, vol. 11, no. 2, pp. 25–30.

27

Performance assessment and the appraisal interview

As the internal mail arrived from the personnel department the manager groaned, 'Surely it's not time to fill in all those appraisal forms again, they'll have to wait, I'm just too busy at the moment; waste of time anyway, nothing ever happens to them.' Appraisal done badly is a waste of time for everyone involved; appraisal done well can improve motivation and performance for both appraiser and appraisee, and can greatly assist both individual development and organizational planning.

In this chapter we first consider what appraisal is and the importance of ongoing appraisal. We look at the varied uses of appraisal systems and at who appraises and what is being appraised, and then consider the development of appraisal criteria and approaches to appraisal interviews. We look at what can be done to make appraisal work, and in particular at performance management systems. We conclude with a contingency approach to appraisal.

Appraisal, performance assessment, performance evaluation, individual assessment, job appraisal and a number of other terms are used to refer to a similar organizational process. The terminology used sometimes indicates the approach adopted, and approaches vary considerably, but appraisal is something more than an organizational process. We all constantly appraise, consciously or unconsciously, objectively or subjectively. When we appraise something we rate its worth, its usefulness and the degree to which it displays various qualities. We appraise ourselves and other people; we appraise behaviour, personality and systems. Organizational appraisal systems are an attempt to formalize these activities for the benefit of both the individual and the organization. One of the loudest arguments that is heard against formal appraisal systems is from managers who assert that they appraise their staff continuously and therefore have no need of an externally imposed scheme. If this activity is done well, then managers have a valid argument from their own point of view. The problem is that this form of appraisal is often done unconsciously or badly, and a formal system can be used to improve the appraisal that already takes place. Formal appraisal systems should, therefore, support and encourage the manager in the continuous appraisal of staff. The other disadvantage of purely informal appraisal is that, however well it serves the needs of the individual and his boss, it does not satisfy the full range of organizational needs.

The uses of appraisal

The results of the appraisal process are often used for a number of different purposes, and frequently these purposes will conflict. Appraisal can be used to improve current performance, provide feedback, increase motivation, identify training needs, identify potential, let individuals know what is expected of them, focus on career development, award salary increases and solve job problems. It can be used to set out job objectives, provide information for human resource planning and career succession, assess the effectiveness of the selection process, and as a reward or punishment in itself. Fletcher and Williams (1985) have suggested two conflicting roles of judge and helper, which the appraiser may be called upon to play, depending on the purposes of the appraisal process. If a single appraisal system was intended both to improve current performance and to act as the basis for salary awards, the appraiser would be called upon to play both judge and helper at the same time. This makes it difficult for the appraiser to be impartial. It is also difficult for the appraisee, who may wish to discuss job-related problems, but is very cautious about what they say because of not wanting to jeopardize a possible pay rise. Randell *et al.* (1984) argue that the uses of appraisal can be divided into three broad categories, and that an appraisal system should attempt to satisfy only one of these. The categories they suggest are reward reviews, potential reviews and performance reviews. This implies that personnel managers need to think more carefully about the primary purpose of their appraisal system, and make sure that procedures, training and individual expectations of the system are not in conflict.

Given that there is a choice about the way the appraisal system will be used, Randell *et al.* argue that the greatest advantages will be gained by the use of performance reviews. Such reviews include appraisal of past performance, meeting of objectives, identification of training needs, problems preventing better performance, and so on. This poses a great problem, particularly for the private sector, but increasingly in the public sector, where there is a predilection to link pay directly to performance. Do these organizations settle just for reward reviews and forgo the advantages of performance reviews? Do they have two different appraisal systems, one for reward and one for performance at two distinctly different times of the year? Do they forget about linking performance and pay? These are key questions in relation to performance management systems, and are discussed later in this chapter.

Review topic 27.1

How do you think that a private organization should tackle the conflict between different potential uses of the appraisal system?

In our recent research we found that organizations were concentrating on 'performance' uses of their appraisal system, as shown in Table 27.1, but not to the exclusion of 'potential' and 'review' uses. Appraisal usually takes place yearly, sometimes at half-yearly intervals.

Table 27.1 Answers to the question: 'For which of the following is your performance appraisal system used?'

Uses	Blue-collar	White-collar	Management
To set performance objectives	35[a]	125	164
To assess past performance	72	189	208
To help improve current performance	77	197	214
To assess training and development needs	65	200	215
To assess increases or new levels of salary	35	92	104
To assess future potential	63	175	200
To assist in career planning decisions	35	139	168
Other	6	11	9

a. Figures indicate the number of times that this use was mentioned.

Not only does performance appraisal offer many advantages for the organization, but individuals often see benefits in the process for themselves, as suggested by Torrington and Weightman (1989). Performance appraisal may be seen as a time when they can gain feedback on their performance, reassurance, praise, encouragement, help in performing better, and some guidance on future career possibilities.

Who is appraised and who appraises?

Appraisal has traditionally been seen as most applicable to those in management and supervisory positions, but increasingly clerical and secretarial staff are being included in the process. Manual staff, particularly those who are skilled or have technical duties, are also subject to appraisal, although to a lesser extent than the other groups. Long (1986) notes that over the past decade there has been a substantial increase in performance reviews for non-managerial staff. Table 27.2 shows seven different categories of staff and the extent to which each were appraised by the 350 respondents of our survey. Some organizations have a flexible approach whereby individuals in certain grades, for example, secretarial and clerical, can elect whether or not to be included in the appraisal system. Other organizations allow those over a certain age to opt out of the system if they so wish. For some organizations, though, appraisal is a central process, and a mechanism through which they promote the organizational culture, and so the scheme applies to every single employee. The link between appraisal and culture is dealt with more fully in a later section of this chapter on the contingency approach to appraisal. Pervasive though appraisal might be in some organizations, there are others where it does not exist at all in a formal or acknowledged informal sense. Over a quarter of the respondent organizations to our survey carried out no appraisals at all. It is encouraging to note, however, that 140 organizations had increased the time that they spent on appraisal over the previous three years, compared with 112 organizations that spent the same amount of time, and only 29 organizations where the time spent had decreased.

Individuals are appraised by a variety of people, including their immediate supervisor, their superior's superior, a member of the personnel department, themselves, their peers or their subordinates. Sometimes, assessment centres are used to carry out the appraisal.

Table 27.2 Seven categories of staff and the number of organizations appraising each category

Categories of staff	Number of organizations appraising this category[a]
Manual unskilled and semi-skilled	92
Manual skilled and technical	119
Clerical/secretarial	189
Supervisory	215
Middle management/administrative	251
Technical/professional specialists	240
Senior management	229

a. Out of a total of 350 organizations.

Immediate superior

Most appraisals are carried out by the employee's immediate superior. The advantage of this is that the immediate supervisor usually has the most intimate knowledge of the tasks that an individual has been carrying out and how well they have been done. The annual appraisal is also the logical conclusion to the ongoing appraisal and feedback that should have been taking place throughout the year between the supervisor and the appraisee. Appraisal by immediate superior is sometimes called appraisal by 'father'.

Superior's superior

The level of authority above the immediate superior can be involved in the appraisal process in either of two different ways. First, they may be called upon to countersign the superior's appraisal of the employee in order to give a seal of approval to indicate that the process has been fairly and properly carried out. Secondly, the superior's superior may directly carry out the appraisal. This is known as the 'grandfather' approach to appraisal. This is more likely to happen when the appraisal process is particularly concerned with making comparisons between individuals and identifying potential for promotion. It helps to overcome the problem that superiors will all appraise by different standards, and minimizes the possibility that appraisees will be penalized due to the fact that their superior has very high standards and is a 'hard marker'. Grandfather appraisal is often used to demonstrate fair play.

Member of the personnel department

Much less frequently an employee will be appraised by a member of the personnel department. This happens when there is no logical immediate superior, or superior's superior, for example, in a matrix organization. Stewart and Stewart (1977) show how this can work in practice by the example of an accountancy and consultancy partnership where work teams are organized according to the particular project in hand. At the end of each project the team manager completes a summary of the performance of each member of the team. This is then forwarded to the 'development manager' in the personnel department. At the end of the appraisal year the development manager collates all the reports on a given employee and produces a composite performance appraisal which is then discussed with the individual. This type of appraisal can be tricky to organize and much depends on the skills of the co-ordinator in the personnel department.

Self-appraisal

There is increasing awareness of the biases that operate when we rate other people and the subjectivity of our judgements. There is more information about this in Chapter 10 on organizational and interpersonal communication. One way of eliminating these biases is for people to rate themselves. Fletcher (1984) argues that there is little doubt that people are capable of rating themselves, but the question is whether they are willing to do this, and will individuals rate themselves fairly? Meyer (1980) reports that when employees were asked to compare themselves with others they tended to overrate themselves; however, when individuals prepared self-appraisals for appraisal interviews they were more modest. Fletcher notes that one of the most fruitful ways for individuals to rate themselves is by rating different aspects of their performance relative to other aspects rather than relative to the performances of other people. He comments that by approaching self-appraisal in this way individuals are more discriminating.

Self-appraisal is relatively new and not heavily used at present. However, individuals do carry out an element of self-appraisal in some of the more traditional appraisal schemes. Some organizations encourage individuals to prepare for the appraisal interview by filling out some form of appraisal on themselves. The differences between the individual's own appraisal and the superior's appraisal can then be a useful starting point for the appraisal interview. The difference between this and self-appraisal is that it is still the superior's appraisal that officially counts, although in the light of the subordinate's comments they might amend some of the ratings that they have given. In many schemes appraisees are asked to sign the completed appraisal form to show that they agree with its conclusions. In the event of disagreement a space is provided for details of controversial items. At the other end of the scale there are 'closed' schemes which not only eschew any form of contribution from the appraisees, but also prevent the appraisees from knowing the ratings that they have been given by their appraiser.

Taylor, Lehman and Forde (1989) recommend a particularly constructive form of self-appraisal, where individuals do this as a mid-point evaluation and concentrate on development, improvement and enrichment strategies. Managers support this process and aid development by coaching. The formal appraisal by the manager does not take place until six months later.

Appraisal by peers

Latham and Wexley (1981) argue that peer ratings are both acceptably reliable and valid and have the advantage that peers have a more comprehensive view of the appraisee's job performance. They note the problem, though, that peers may be unwilling to appraise each other, as this can be seen as 'grassing' on each other. It is perhaps for this reason that peer appraisal is not often used, despite its claimed advantages. When peer rating is used an individual is rated by a group of peers and the results are averaged.

> **Review topic 27.2**
>
> Consider your peers. Think of the people who are most effective at their jobs. Without naming them, write down the behaviour and skills that characterize their job performance.

Appraisal by subordinates

Appraisal by subordinates is another less well used method of appraisal. It is more limited in its value than peer appraisal as subordinates are only acquainted with certain aspects of their superiors' work. Latham and Wexley (1981), however, argue that there are circumstances where it can be valuable and give an example of an organization where individuals were rated by both superiors and subordinates, and where any large discrepancies in ratings were seen as areas for follow-up investigation.

Assessment centres

Assessment centres are most often used in the appraisal of potential supervisors and managers. The advantage of assessment centres for this purpose is that ratings of potential can be assessed on the basis of factors other than current performance. It is well accepted that high performance in a current job does not mean that an individual will be a high performer if promoted to a higher level. It is also increasingly recognized that a moderate performer at one level may perform much better at a higher level. Assessment centres use tests, group exercises and interviews to appraise potential.

What is appraised?

Appraisal systems can measure a variety of things. They are sometimes designed to measure personality, sometimes behaviour or performance, and sometimes achievement of goals. These areas may be measured either quantitively or qualitatively. Qualitative appraisal often involves the writing of an unstructured narrative on the general performance of the appraisee. Alternatively, some guidance may be given as to the areas on which the appraiser should comment. The problem with qualitative appraisals is that they may leave important areas unappraised, and that they are not suitable for comparison purposes. When they are measured quantitatively some form of scale is used, often comprising five categories of measurement from 'excellent', or 'always exceeds requirements' at one end to 'inadequate' at the other, with the mid-point being seen as acceptable. Scales are, however, not always constructed according to this plan. Sometimes on a five-point scale there will be four degrees of acceptable behaviour and only one that is unacceptable. Sometimes an even-numbered (usually six-point) scale is used to prevent the central tendency. There is a tendency for raters to settle on the mid-point of the scale, either through lack of knowledge of the appraisee, lack of ability to discriminate, lack of confidence or desire not to be too hard on appraisees. Rating other people is not an easy task, but it can be structured so that it is made as objective as possible.

Avoidance of personality measures

Much traditional appraisal was based on measures of personality traits that were felt to be important to the job. These included traits such as resourcefulness, enthusiasm, drive, application and other traits such as intelligence. One difficulty with these is that everyone defines them differently, and the traits that are used are not always mutually exclusive. Raters, therefore, are often unsure of what they are rating. Ill-defined scales like these are more susceptible to bias and prejudice. Another problem is that since the same scales are often used for many different jobs, traits that are irrelevant to an appraisee's job may still be measured. One helpful approach is to concentrate on the job rather than the person. In an attempt to do this some organizations call their annual appraisal activity the 'job appraisal review'. The requirements of the job and the way that it is performed are considered, and the interview concentrates on problems in job performance which are recognized as not always being the 'fault' of the person performing the job. Difficulties in performance may be due to departmental structure or the equipment being used, rather than the ability or motivation of the employee. Other approaches concentrate on linking ratings to behaviour and performance on the job.

Behaviourally anchored rating scales

One way of linking ratings with behaviour at work is to use Behaviourally Anchored Rating Scales (BARS). These can be produced in a large organization by asking a sample group of raters independently to suggest examples of behaviour for each point on the scale in order to collect a wide variety of behavioural examples. These examples are then collated and returned to the sample raters without any indication of the scale point for which they were suggested. Sample raters allocate a scale point to each example, and those examples, which are consistently located at the same point on the scale, are selected to be used as behavioural examples for that point on the scale. Future raters then have some guidance as to the type of behaviour that would be expected at each point. BARS can be used in conjunction with personality scales, but are most helpful when using scales that relate more clearly to work behaviour. Figure 27.1 shows an example of a BARS in relation to 'relations with clients' – for the sake of clarity just one behavioural example is given at each point on the scale, whereas in a fully developed scale there may be several at each point. Another advantage of the development of BARS is that appraisers have been involved in the process and this can increase their commitment to the outcome.

Behavioural observation scales

Behavioural Observation Scales (BOS) provide an alternative way of linking behaviour and ratings. Fletcher and Williams (1985) comment that these scales are developed by lengthy procedures, and are similar in some ways to BARS. They indicate a number of dimensions of performance with behavioural statements for each. Individuals are appraised as to the extent to which they display each of the characteristics. Figure 27.2 gives an example.

Meeting objectives

Another method of making appraisal more objective is to use the process to set job objectives over the coming year and, a year later, to measure the extent to which these objectives have been met. The extent to which the appraisee is involved in setting these objectives varies considerably. If, as Stewart and Stewart (1977) suggest, these objectives are part of an organizational manage- ment by objectives scheme, then the individual may be given them, with limited negotiation available. Alternatively, if they are not part of a larger scheme there is a lot of scope for the individual to participate in the setting of such objectives. One of the biggest problems with appraisal on the basis of meeting objectives is that factors beyond the employee's control may make the objectives more difficult than anticipated, or even impossible. Another problem is that objectives will change over a period and so the original list is not so relevant a year later. Kane and Freeman (1986, p. 7) also highlight such difficulties as pressures to set 'easy' objectives, lack of comparability between the objectives of different individuals, unclear specification of measures and an emphasis on short-term, at the expense of long-term, accomplishments. They also discuss the 'fudge factor', where middle managers are pressured from the top to set challenging and stretching objectives for their people, and are pressured from below to set objectives that are not difficult to achieve. In order to please all, the middle manager fudges the issue rather than working it through. If suitable provision can be made for these contingencies and difficulties, appraisal by objectives can be effective and motivating.

Behavioural example:	Points of the rating scale
Often makes telephone calls on behalf of the client to find the correct office for him to go to even though this is not part of the job.	A
Will often spend an hour with a client in order to get to the root of a very complex problem.	B
Usually remains calm when dealing with an irate client.	C
If the answer to the client's problem is not immediately to hand he often tells them he has not got the information.	D
Sometimes ignores clients waiting at the reception desk for up to ten minutes even when he is not busy with other work.	E
Regularly keeps clients waiting for ten minutes or more and responds to their questions with comments such as 'I can't be expected to know that' and 'You're not in the right place for that'.	F

Figure 27.1 *An example of a behaviourally anchored rating scale: relations with clients*

Leadership/staff supervision

1 Provides help, training and guidance so that employees can improve their performance

Almost never   5   4   3   2   1   Almost always

2 Explains to staff exactly what is expected of them – staff know their job responsibilities

Almost never   5   4   3   2   1   Almost always

3 Gets involved in subordinates' work only to check it

Almost never   5   4   3   2   1   Almost always

4 Consults staff for their ideas on ways of making their jobs better

Almost never   5   4   3   2   1   Almost always

5 Praises staff for things they do well

Almost never   5   4   3   2   1   Almost always

6 Passes important information to subordinates

Almost never   5   4   3   2   1   Almost always

The number of behavioural statements to be rated for any one dimension will be determined through the job analysis used to identify the key dimensions of performance and behavioural statements.

Figure 27.2 *An example of a behavioural observation scale*
Source: Fletcher and Williams (1985, p. 45). Used with permission of
Century-Hutchinson Ltd.

Development of appraisal criteria

Stewart and Stewart (1977) suggest a variety of methods by which appraisal criteria can be identified. These include the use of the critical incident technique to identify particularly difficult problems at work, content analysis of working documents and performance questionnaires whereby managers and potential appraisees identify (anonymously) what characterizes the most effective job holder and the least effective job holder (see Stewart and Stewart 1977, pp. 37–59). We previously made the point that one of the advantages of BARS was that appraisers are involved in formulating the way that appraisal scales are used. There are, similarly, advantages in involving appraisers in the identification of appraisal criteria, as well as the advantages from an information point of view. There can also be advantages in involving potential appraisees in criteria identification (Silverman and Wexley 1984).

Job analysis

In addition to identifying appraisal criteria, job analysis is used to formulate key tasks and duties, and the performance standards that are expected. Appraisal is then based on a comparison between this and the performance actually achieved. This is similar to appraisal by objectives, but much broader. This type of job analysis and appraisal is a very useful approach in smaller organizations or those that cannot afford to invest in the development of sophisticated appraisal criteria. It is an approach that has apparent validity and clearly relates to job performance, and we would argue that no matter what other appraisal criteria are used, that this aspect of job analysis should also be included.

The appraisal interview

Where the appraisal process is completely 'closed', with appraisees not being told anything about how they have fared, it is very difficult to conduct an appraisal interview. Most employers, however, do incorporate an appraisal interview into the process. The purpose of the interview and the extent of the appraisee's participation will depend on the uses of the appraisal and the degree to which it is an 'open' process. Potentially, the interview can be used for the appraiser and appraisee to go through the appraiser's (and maybe appraisee's) performance ratings, or assessment. It provides an opportunity for the appraiser to explain the reasoning behind their judgements. The interview can also be used to focus on job problems and how these might be tackled. It provides a formal setting for both the appraiser and appraisee to feedback to the other about their expectations and their concerns related to the job. Additionally, it provides a forum for them to discuss training needs and development plans which may not crop up during day-to-day interaction.

Dangers to avoid include coming to firm conclusions about matters before hearing the appraisee's point of view, not being sufficiently prepared for the interview, not allowing the appraisee sufficient time to prepare and not allocating enough time for the interview.

Maier (1958) identified three types of performance appraisal interview, the tell-and-sell, tell-and-listen and the problem-solving styles. The tell-and-sell style was typified by an appraiser who told the appraisee their strengths and weaknesses and how they could improve on the weaknesses. The tell-and-listen style was typified by an appraiser who would not only do this but was also prepared to listen to how the appraisee saw things. In the problem-solving style, appraisee and appraiser came together to identify problems in the job and what could be done to tackle them jointly. It is this style that allows for the greatest participation from the appraisee in both defining the problems and suggesting their possible solutions. Maier's categorization had a significant influence on the way that appraisal has been approached. The problem-solving style was preferred by the majority of personnel managers who thought carefully about their performance appraisal schemes, and this approach was most often taught on training courses. Recently, however, these three approaches have been considered from a different angle, leading to a more flexible view, which is discussed in more detail in the last section of this chapter on the contingency approach to appraisal.

What can be said with confidence is that interviews need to be conducted in a sensitive manner, paying due regard to listening and other communication skills as we described in Chapter 10. Ideally, the appraisee should leave the interview content that any criticisms made of their performance were constructive and justified, and that any courses of action agreed are the right courses of action to which they feel committed. A recommended structure for a performance appraisal interview is shown in Figure 27.3. Alternative frameworks can be found in Torrington and Weightman (1989) and Dainow (1988).

1. Purpose and rapport	Agree purpose with employee Agree structure for meeting Check that pre-work is done
2. Ask their views	Ask employee to describe their work over the past year – what went well, went badly, what could be improved next year, what did they like, dislike, how can they develop over the next year, what should their objectives be for the next year
3. Offer your views	Show where agree and disagree with their views, offer own views and explain why
4. Explore disagreements	Explore the different views and agree how to resolve differences
5. Resolve differences	Resolve differences and note agreements and plans made
6. Close	Summarize, refer to follow up and close

Figure 27.3 *Structure for a performance appraisal interview*

Review topic 27.3

Many managers find appraisal interviewing a difficult task. Why do you think this is?

Making appraisal work

There are many reports of organizations installing an appraisal system only to find that they have to change it or completely abandon it after only a short time. Other organizations battle on with their systems, but recognize that they are ineffective or inadequate or disliked. What can be done to encourage the system to work as effectively as possible?

Purpose of the system

Effectiveness will be greater if all involved are clear about what the system is for. The personnel manager and senior managers need to work out what they want the appraisal system to achieve and how it fits in with the other personnel activities that feed into it and are fed by it, such as career planning, training and human resource planning. Those who have to operate the system also have to appreciate its objectives, otherwise they are just filling in forms to satisfy the irksome personnel people, as we saw at the opening of this chapter. Finally, those whose performance is to be appraised will answer questions and contribute ideas with much greater constructive candour if they understand and believe in the purposes of the scheme.

Management ownership

It is vital that the system is visibly owned by senior and line management in the organization, and that it is not something that is done for the personnel department. This may mean, for example, that appraisal forms are kept and used within the department and only selected times of data are fed through to the personnel function or other departments. Ideally, the form itself should be a working document used by appraiser and appraisee throughout the year.

Openness and participation

The more 'open' the appraisal system is, that is the more feedback that the appraisee is given about his or her appraisal ratings, the more likely the appraisee is to accept rather than reject the appraisal process. Similarly, the greater the extent to which the appraisee is allowed to participate in the system, the greater the chance of gaining his or her commitment.

Appraisal criteria

The involvement of both appraisers and appraisees in the identification of appraisal criteria has already been noted. Stewart and Stewart (1977) suggest that these criteria must be:

1. Genuinely related to success or failure in the job.
2. Amenable to objective, rather than subjective judgement, and helpful if they are:
   (a) Easy for the appraiser to administer.
   (b) Appear fair and relevant to the appraisee.
   (c) Strike a fair balance between catering for the requirements of the present job while at the same time being applicable to the wider organization.

Training

Appraisers need training in how to appraise and how to conduct appraisal interviews. Appraisees will also need some training if they have any significant involvement in the process. In our recent research we found that just over a third of the organizations that had appraisal systems trained all interviewers in appraisal interviewing. A further 18 per cent said that all interviewers had some training in interpersonal skills and that appraisal was included in this. Almost a quarter provided appraisal interviewing training for those who felt that they needed it. However, over 20 per cent provided no training at all. An excellent performance appraisal system is of no use at all if managers do not know how to use the system to best effect. Sims (1988) quotes an ineffective system which was sophisticated and well designed, but which line managers did not have the skills to use.

Administrative efficiency

The appraisal system needs to be administered so that it causes as few problems as possible for both parties. Form-filling should be kept to a minimum, and the time allocated for this activity should be sufficient for it to be done properly, but not so much that the task is seen as unimportant and low priority.

Action

Appraisal systems need to be supported by follow-up action. Work plans that are agreed by appraiser and appraisee need to be monitored to ensure that they actually take place, or that they are modified in accordance with changed circumstances or priorities. Training needs should be identified and plans made to meet those needs. Other development plans may involve the personnel department in arranging temporary transfers or moves to another department when a vacancy arises. In order to do this, it is vital that appraisal forms are not just filed and forgotten. Systems need to link in with other personnel systems, as we commented in the paragraph headed 'Purpose of the system'.

Culture and flexibility

The appraisal system needs to reflect the needs of the organization and be sufficiently flexible to meet the requirements of the individuals involved. This aspect is dealt with in more detail in the following section.

From appraisal to performance management

A further development which aims to ensure that the best and most effective use is made of the appraisal process is by tying it into a larger and more complete system of performance management. These systems, which are being increasingly used (see, for example, Fowler 1988), highlight appraisal as a central activity in the good management of staff. The difference from traditional appraisal is that the assessment process tends to be more rigorous and objective, and that this is clearly linked into precise job definition and organizational objective setting, individual development plans and the pay system. A typical system is shown in diagrammatic form in Figure 27.4.

Figure 27.4 *Four stages of a typical performance management system*

The stages of the system in more detail are:

1. Written and agreed job description, reviewed regularly. Objectives for the work-group which have been cascaded down from the organization's strategic objectives.
2. Individual objectives derived from the above, which are jointly devised by appraiser and appraisee. These objectives are results- rather than task-oriented, are tightly defined and include measures to be assessed. The objectives are designed to stretch the individual, and offer potential development as well as meeting business needs.
3. Development plan devised by manager and individual detailing development goals and activities designed to enable the individual to meet the objectives. The emphasis here is on managerial support and coaching.
4. Assessment of objectives. Ongoing formal reviews on a regular basis designed to motivate the appraisee and concentrate on developmental issues. Also, an annual asssessment which affects pay received depending on performance in achievement of objectives.

One of the major advantages of performance management is that as it is a comprehensive system of management, managers are forced to give emphasis to formal and planned employee development, and indeed a similar system described by Harper (1988) is referred to as Performance Review and Development. Another advantage is that it also enforces a clear role description and set of objectives agreed by managers and individuals. On the down side there is potential conflict between the aim of improving job performance, which requires openness and a developmental approach, and the link with pay (see the discussion on pages 481–2). This conflict is usually dealt with by separating, in time, the performance development and the performance pay reviews, an approach that is recommended by Taylor, Lehman and Forde (1989).

The contingency approach to appraisal

In 1978 Karen Legge urged a contingency approach to personnel management. A number of recent articles suggest how a contingency approach may be applied to the appraisal process. Much of what has been written concentrates on the personal interaction that is part of the appraisal process. George suggests that an effective appraisal scheme is dependent on the style and content of appraisal not conflicting with the culture of the organization. He suggests that the degree of openness that is required in the appraisal process is 'unlikely to materialize without an atmosphere of mutual trust and respect – something which is conspicuously lacking in many employing organizations' (George 1986, p. 32).

George also extends a previous point concerning the links between the appraisal system and other personnel and organizational systems when he comments:

> An investment in a system must involve statements about certain desired organizational characteristics and about the treatment of people in an organization. It is very mistaken, therefore, to regard appraisal as merely a technique or a discrete process with an easily definable boundary. (*ibid.*, p. 33)

The appraisal, therefore, needs to reflect wider values of the organization in order for it to be properly integrated into the organization and survive in an effective form. The appraisal system can in fact be used to display and support the culture and style of the organization. George suggests that it can be used to help integrate people into an explicit and purposeful culture. The appraisal process can also be used to help change the culture in an organization, but this would need to be done in conjunction with other supportive activities and be seen to be led from the top.

Other aspects of the contingency approach to appraisal include the appraiser's style in relation to their normal management style and in relation to the needs and personality of the appraisee. Pryor (1985) argues that appraisers should aim to achieve consistency between their normal day-to-day management style and the style that they adopt in appraisal interviews. George talks of the few really open relationships that individuals have at work and how in the appraisal situation we may be expecting interactions of a nature and quality which are not evident in most relationships. Pryor's ideas led to a reappraisal of the three interviewing styles defined by Maier (see page 491). In particular he re-evaluates the usefulness of the tell-and-sell and tell-and-listen styles, and suggests that they can be effectively adapted to the needs of appraisees with little experience who require less participation in the appraisal interview. Pryor suggests that the variety of interviewing styles can be illustrated by a participatory continuum, as shown in Figure 27.5. The appropriate style can be decided upon by considering the employees' 'readiness' to cope with a more participative style. Some factors which may be taken into account are also shown in Figure 27.5. One other important factor to be taken into account would be the appraisee's personality, which is somewhat more difficult to measure.

The contingency approach therefore takes into account the organizational culture and the characteristics of the appraiser and appraisee into account when an appraisal scheme is being formulated. The contingency approach should not, however, be used to bolster up the status quo when the status quo is clearly unsatisfactory. For example, it would be a mistake to design appraisal in line with the organizational culture if this has already been identified as undesirable. Similarly, we are not arguing that an appraiser should use an appraisal interviewing style that matches the management style, if that management style is clearly inappropriate. This is clearly a case for training and development, but not just training and development in appraisal.

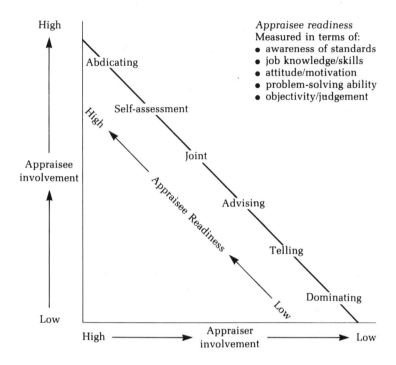

Figure 27.5 *Appraisal interaction model*
Source: Adapted from Fryer (1985, p. 38).

Summary propositions

27.1 Appraisal schemes formalize the ongoing appraisal that employers carry out.

27.2 Appraisal schemes serve a variety of purposes: it is not advisable to mix performance, potential and review purposes in the same scheme.

27.3 Self-appraisal is potentially useful, but there are still doubts about its validity, and it has been insufficiently used to be properly judged.

27.4 Appraisal schemes are most useful when they measure behaviour and performance rather than personality.

27.5 A contingency approach to appraisal takes account of the organiz-ation's culture and the characteristics of the appraiser and the appraisee.

References

Dainow, S. (1988), 'Goal-oriented appraisal', *Training Officer*, January, pp 6–8.

Fletcher, C. (1984), 'What's new in performance appraisal?' *Personnel Management*, February.

Fletcher, C. and Williams, R. (1985), *Performance Appraisal and Career Development*, London: Hutchinson.

Fowler, A. (1988), 'New directions in performance pay', *Personnel Management*, pp. 30–4.

George J. (1986), 'Appraisal in the public sector: dispensing with the big stick', *Personnel Management*, May.

Harper, S. C. (1988), 'A developmental approach to performance appraisal', *Business Horizons*, Sept./Oct. pp. 158–74.

Kane, J. S. and Freeman, K. A. (1986), 'MBO and performance appraisal; A mixture that's not a solution, Part 1', *Personnel*, December, pp. 26, 28, 30–6.

Kane, J. S. and Freeman, K. A. (1987), 'MBO and performance appraisal; A mixture that's not a solution, Part 2', *Personnel*, February, pp. 26–32.

Latham, G. P. and Wexley, K. N. (1981), *Increasing Productivity through Performance Appraisal*, Wokingham: Addison-Wesley.

Legge, K. (1978), *Power, Innovation and Problem-solving in Personnel Management*, Maidenhead: McGraw-Hill.

Long, P. (1986), *Performance Appraisal Revisited*, London: Institute of Personnel Management.

Maier, N. R. F. (1958), *The Appraisal Interview: Objectives methods and skills*, New York: John Wiley.

Maier, N. R. F. (1958), 'Three types of appraisal interview', *Personnel*, March/April, pp. 27–40.

Meyer, H. H. (1980), 'Self-appraisal of job performance', *Personnel Psychology*, vol. 33, pp. 291–5.

Pryor, R. (1985), 'A fresh approach to performance appraisal', *Personnel Management*, June.

Randell, G., Packard, P. and Slater, J. (1984), *Staff Appraisal*, London: Institute of Personnel Management.

Silverman, S. B. and Wexley, K. N. (1984), 'Reaction of employees to performance appraisal interviews as a function of their participation in rating scale development', *Personnel Psychology*, vol. 37.

Sims, R. R. (1988), 'Training supervisors in employee performance appraisals', *European Industrial Training*, vol. 12, no. 8, pp. 26–31.

Stewart, V. and Stewart, A. (1977), *Practical Performance Appraisal*, Aldershot: Gower.

Taylor, G. S., Lehman, C. M. and Forde, C. M. (1989), 'How employee self-appraisals can help', *Supervisory Management*, August, pp. 33–41.

Torrington, D. P. and Weightman, J. (1989), *The Appraisal Interview*, UMIST.

Part
V

Employee Relations

28

Trade union recognition and employee participation

Trade union recognition is widespread in Britain, although there has been a drop of over nearly three million union members since the peak figure of thirteen and a half million in 1979. Furthermore, much of the expansion in the economy has been in companies that are electing not to recognize trade unions. Some personnel managers are in establishments where unions are not recognized and where recognition is unlikely, some are in establishments where they are working towards recognition, but the great majority are in a situation where unions are recognized to some degree for at least part of the workforce. Thus most personnel managers are in a situation where they have to carry on managing recognition rather than initiating or rejecting it. In our research we found that 81 per cent of our respondents were in establishments with blue-collar employees in trade union membership; 72 per cent had white-collar employees in union membership and over half had management employees who were trade union members. Sixty per cent of respondent establishments had formal agreements for negotiating pay and conditions with blue- and white-collar union representatives, while 43 per cent had similar agreements with unions representing management employees.

This is one of the areas of personnel practice where there can be a marked difference in policy and approach between the public and private sectors of employment. One example is in Table 28.1, which shows a much higher density of union membership in the public sector than in the private.

The recent changes in union membership, employment legislation, high unemployment and economic recession have provided academic analysts with the challenge of describing how employee relations strategies have changed. We still lack a full explanation, but one of the best-known approaches has been the attempt of Purcell and Sisson (1983) to categorize management styles in industrial relations. These are summarized in Figure 28.1.

Table 28.1 Trade union membership in public and private sector establishments

	Private sector[a]		Public sector[a]	
	No trade union members (%)	Over 75% in trade unions (%)	No trade union members (%)	Over 75% in trade unions (%)
Blue-collar employees	28.6	55.9	3.6	81.0
White-collar employees	41.3	22.0	7.3	68.7
Management	74.6	12.2	15.3	59.8

a. Percentages of responses from 350 establishments.

Source: Mackay (1986).

Review topic 28.1

Which of the five categories in Figure 28.1 most closely fits your establishment? Does the category vary for different groups of employees?

Style	Characteristics
Traditional	Fire-fighting approach. Employee relations not important until there is trouble. Low pay. Hostile to trade unions. Authoritarian. Typical in small, owner-managed business.
Paternalist	Unions regarded as unnecessary because of employer's enlightenment. High pay. Concentration on encouraging employee identification with business objectives.
Consultative	Union participation encouraged through recognition. Problem-solving, informal approach to employee relations. Emphasis on two-way communications.
Constitutional	Similar to *consultative*, but emphasis on formal agreements to regulate relationship between two powerful protagonists.
Opportunistic	Large company devolving responsibility for employee relations to subsidiaries, with no common approach but emphasis on unit profitability.

Figure 28.1 *Categories of management styles in employee relations*
Source: Purcell and Sisson (1983, pp. 112–18).

This is a useful set of categories, although some organizations do not fit easily into any one of them. Most large, long-established companies will be in one of the last three; most public sector organizations will be in category four; and many of the newer businesses will be in some version of category two.

Collective consent

Taking a strictly managerial view of trade unions and their recognition, the interest is the degree to which recognition will deliver *collective consent* to a general framework of rules and guidelines within which management and employees operate.

Collective consent implies the acceptance of a situation, while agreement has the more positive connotation of commitment following some degree of initiative in bringing the situation into existence.

We are not, therefore, necessarily describing active employee participation in managerial decision-making. The range is wider, to include the variety of circumstances in which employees consent collectively to managerial authority, so long as they find it acceptable.

In order to couch the discussion in terms that can embrace a variety of styles, we set out seven *categories of consent*, in which there is a steadily increasing degree of collective employee involvement. We begin with a category in which there is straightforward and unquestioning acceptance of management authority, and then move through various stages of increasing participation in decision-making and the necessary changes in management style as the power balance alters and the significance of bargaining develops and extends to more and more areas of organizational life.

1. *Normative*: We use this term in the sense of Etzioni (1961), who described 'normative' organizations as being those in which the involvement of individuals was attributable to a strong sense of moral obligation. Any challenge to authority would imply a refutation of the shared norms and was therefore unthinkable.

2. *Disorganised*: In organizations that are not normative there may be collective consent simply because there is no collective focus for a challenge, so disorganized consent is where there may be discontent but consent is maintained through lack of employee organization.

3. *Organised*: When employees organize it is nearly always in trade unions and the first collective activities are usually in dealing with general grievances. It is very unlikely that there will be any degree of involvement in the management decision-making processes. Employees simply consent to obey instructions as long as grievances are dealt with.

4. *Consultative*: Consultation here is seen as a stage of development beyond initial trade union recognition, even though some organizations consult with employees before – often as a means of deferring – trade union recognition. Here is the first incursion into the management process as employees are asked for an opinion about management proposals before decisions are made, even though the right to decide remains with the management.

5. *Negotiated*: Negotiation implies that both parties have the power to decide and the power to withhold agreement, so that a decision can only be reached by some form of mutual accommodation. No longer is the management retaining all decision-making to itself; it is seeking some sort of bargain with employee representatives, recognizing that only such reciprocity can produce what is needed.

6. *Participative*: When employee representatives reach the stage of participating in the general management of the organization in which they are employed, there is a fundamental change in the control of that organization, even though this may initially be theoretical rather than actual. Employee representatives take part in making the decisions on major strategic issues like expenditure on research, the opening of new plants and the introduction of new products. In arrangements for participative consent there is a balance between the decision-makers representing the interests of capital and those representing the interests of labour, though the balance is not necessarily even.

7. *Controlling*: If the employees acquire control of the organization, as in a workers' co-operative, then the consent is a controlling type. This may sound bizarre, but there will still be a management apparatus within the organization to which employee collective consent will be given or from which it will be withheld.

All of the above categories require some management initiative to sustain· collective consent. In categories (1) and (2) it may be exhortation to ensure that commitment is kept up, or information supplied to defer organization. In each subsequent category there is an increasing bargaining emphasis that becomes progressively more complex.

The implication of the last few paragraphs is that there is a hierarchy of consent categories, through which organizations steadily progress. Although this has frequently been true in the past, it is by no means necessary. Some may begin at (6) or (7): there is no inflexible law of evolution and change can move in the opposite direction as well.

Trade union recognition and bargaining units

When a trade union has recruited a number of members in an organization, it will seek *recognition* from the employer in order to represent those members. The step of recognition is seldom easy but is very important as it marks an almost irrevocable movement away from unilateral decision-making by the management. We can examine some of the questions to be considered.

Why should a union be recognized at all?

If the employees want that type of representation they will not readily co-operate with the employer who refuses. In extreme cases this can generate sufficient antagonism to cause industrial action in support of recognition. A more positive reason is the benefits that can flow from recognition: there are employee representatives with whom to discuss, consult and negotiate so that communication and working relationships can be improved. The 1980s have, however, certainly seen a decline in union membership and effectiveness in resisting management initiatives. Employers are considering recognition claims more carefully, and collective consent can be achieved by other means in some situations, providing that the management work hard at the job of both securing and maintaining that consent.

When should a union be recognized?

When it has sufficient support from the employees. There is no simple way of determining what is sufficient. The Industrial Relations Act 1971 specified that 51 per cent of the employees must be in membership, but current legislation lays down no percentage. The first thirteen cases brought to ACAS (Advisory, Conciliation and Arbitration Service) after the passing of the Employment Protection Act 1975 produced recommendations for recognition where the level of membership varied from 21 to 100 per cent and in five cases the figure was below 40 per cent. Among the factors that influenced ACAS in whether or not to recommend recognition were the degree of union organization and efficiency, the number of representatives, the size of constituency and the degree of opposition to recognition from non-union employees. A frequent encouragement for the management of an organization to recognize a union relatively quickly is where there is the possibility of competing claims, with some employees seeking to get another union established because they do not like the first.

For whom should a union be recognized?

For that group of employees who have a sufficient commonality of interests, terms and conditions for one union to be able to represent them and the management be able to respond. This group of employees are sometimes described as those making up a *bargaining unit*; the boundaries of the units need careful consideration by the management to determine what is most appropriate and what consequent response to recognition claims they will make. There is a number of boundaries that are generally acknowledged: manual employees are usually represented by different unions from white-collar employees, and skilled employees are sometimes represented by a different union from the semi-skilled and unskilled as well as from those possessing different skills. Other boundaries are less easy, particularly where a distinction may be drawn on the grounds of hierarchical status, as between those who are paid monthly and those paid weekly. Where status is related to responsibility for subordinates there appears to be another accepted boundary: the supervisor will not be represented by the same union as the supervised, although one or two levels may be included sometimes in the same unit.

For what should a union be recognized?

The terms and conditions of employment of the employees who are members of the bargaining unit. A union can seek recognition on anything that might be covered in a contract of employment, but the employer may agree to recognition only for a limited range of topics. The irreducible minimum is assistance by a union representative for members with grievances, but the extent to which matters beyond that are recognized as being a subject of bargaining depends on which consent category the organization is in. It also depends on the possible existence of other agreements that could take some matters out of the scope of local recognition.

The legal position on recognition

Trade unions seek recognition from employers by the traditional means of recruiting members and making representations to the management. If they are not successful then they have to take risks by, for instance, calling on their members to take industrial action to persuade the employer into a position where he will grant recognition.

The Employment Protection Act 1975 provided an alternative method for trade unions to seek recognition via ACAS from an employer who was reluctant to recognize. These provisions were so unpopular that they were repealed by the Employment Act 1980, but it is worth a brief review to consider why the measures were originally introduced and what led to their repeal.

The 1975 legislation was based on the premise that an employer's right to refuse recognition to a trade union should be open to some question other than that of union bargaining power, in order to ensure basic rights of representation to employees and union members employed in situations where trade union organization was weak. Many unions ignored the 1975 measures entirely and most employers objected to the one-sided nature of legislation, whereby unions could ask for an investigation of an issue but employers could not. ACAS became concerned about the variety of hats they were being asked to wear. Their main duties are to improve industrial relations and to extend collective bargaining, but it was difficult to reconcile that with the compulsory arbitration that the 1975 provisions involved.

Although unions can no longer seek recognition by this method, it is still vital for them to be recognized if they are to enjoy other legal rights. The remaining provisions of the 1975 Act include rights for recognized trade unions only to receive collective bargaining information, time off for industrial relations, trade union and public duties, and consultation on proposed redundancies. The 1974 Health and Safety Act provisions for safety representatives only apply to recognized unions, as do the planning information rights under the 1975 Industry Act, and the workplace facilities and secret ballot provisions of the Employment Act 1980.

If an individual employer is a member of an employers' association that recognizes a particular union for national and collective bargaining, that does not mean that the individual employer necessarily recognizes the same union for any purpose at establishment level.

The correct legal definition of recognition is 'for the purpose of collective bargaining' with collective bargaining defined in sect. 29(1) of the Trade Union and Labour Relations Act 1974 as matters relating wholly or mainly to one of the following:

1. Terms and conditions of employment, or the physical conditions in which any workers are required to work.
2. Engagement or non-engagement, or termination or suspension of employment or the duties of employment of one or more workers.
3. Allocation of work or the duties of employment as between workers or groups of workers.
4. Matters of discipline.
5. The membership or non-membership of a trade union on the part of a worker.
6. Facilities for officials of trade unions.
7. The machinery for negotiation or consultation and other procedures, relating to any of the foregoing matters, including the recognition by employers or employers' associations of the right of a trade union to represent workers in any such negotiation or consultation or in the carrying out of such procedures.

The Transfer Regulations of 1981 require that union recognition continues and collective agreements remain in force after the transfer of an undertaking to new ownership providing that the transferred undertaking retains 'an identity distinct from the remainder of the transferee's undertaking'.

The union membership agreement ('the closed shop')

Another matter to consider is not only whether a trade union should be recognized but whether the employer should go further and make an agreement that all employees in a particular category should be members of that union. The principle is that of the closed shop, the technical term being 'union membership agreement'. A union membership agreement can be reached between an employer and a trade union that makes it a condition of employment for each employee in a particular category within the organization to be a member of that trade union. It is an aspect of employment practice that causes more interest than most. When the Trade Union and Labour Relations Act 1974 was making its way onto the Statute Book it was on this single point that modifications had to be made to satisfy members of the Commons who expressed serious alarm about individual freedom and the independent judgement of newspaper editors.

Those who are not involved in industrial relations, therefore, have an interest in this matter which ranges more broadly than considerations that are appropriate for the more specialized purview of this book. For those managing organizations we can see the issue of the closed shop as recognition writ large. To some extent it is the logical step beyond recognition in establishing the union as the mode of communication with, and representation of, employees. If this is the situation, runs the logical argument, all employees should support their union financially, exercise their right to vote and speak, and then be bound by the discipline of democratic control of the individual. Everyone is in the same position and there is no ill-feeling between members and non-members.

The other view of the matter is to question whether employees should be obliged to join a trade union against their will, especially if they have strong ideological objections, and whether there are some members of the organization for whom trade union membership provides serious role conflict, because their occupational life usually puts them in the position of representing employer interests in opposition to employee collective interests.

The 1980 and 1982 Employment Acts established new rights for the individual in relation to the closed shop. Previously the individual employee was obliged to be a member of the union if a union membership agreement existed between the employer and a recognized trade union, which made membership of that union a condition of employment. Anyone refusing to join or resigning from membership while employed in a category of work covered by the UMA (Union Membership Agreement) had no defence against dismissal by the employer on that ground. The single exception – long honoured by trade unions – was the employee who had genuine religious objections to trade union membership, and which has now been widened to include grounds of conscience or other grounds of deeply-held personal conviction as a basis for objecting either to membership of any union or to membership of a particular union.

Also, those who are not members of a union specified in a union membership agreement cannot be dismissed for remaining non-members. Any UMA coming into existence after August 1980 has to be approved by an 80 per cent vote in a secret ballot: furthermore the 80 per cent must be of those entitled to vote rather than of those actually voting. Dismissal for non-membership of a union will be unfair if there has not been a secret ballot before November 1983 or within intervals of five years after that date. In conjunction with the Act, the Department of Employment has issued a code of practice which sets out how the ballot should be conducted.

Management organization for recognition

The 'category of consent' for an organization will influence its style of management and the structure of its management organization, with the most important change coming when an organization moves from the second to the third category mentioned earlier in this chapter (see under Collective Consent). That is the point at which there is some guarantee of commitment by management to procedure and the acknowledgement that a limited range of management decisions could be successfully challenged by the employees, causing those decisions to be altered.

As personnel managers have become more dominant in the management handling of employee relations issues, the traditional pattern of personnel and line management has altered. The evidence from our research (in Table 28.2)

Table 28.2 Personnel management involvement in central employee relations issues. Answers from thirty respondents to the question: 'When procedures and agreements are being formulated and negotiated, which of the following comes closest to describing the nature of the personnel function's involvement?'

	Blue-collar	White-collar	Management
1. Complete responsibility to represent management and make decisions	22	23	18
2. Leading management role, but consulting with other managers prior to making decisions	127	142	120
3. Management representation and decision-making jointly with other managers	60	67	54
4. Advising other managers, who will make the management decisions	45	45	51
5. Providing information, if required	9	13	20
6. None	33	27	51
7. No reply	54	33	36

demonstrates the spread of personnel managers' experiences although these were answers to a question about the formulation of agreements rather than decisions on initial recognition. There is still, however, a notional distinction between the personnel and line roles.

The Commission on Industrial Relations has made this comment:

> 1.   The line manager is necessarily responsible for industrial relations within his particular area of operations. He needs freedom to manage his plant, department or section effectively within agreed policies and with access to specialist advice.
> 2.   The personnel manager should help by supplying expert knowledge and skill and by monitoring the consistent execution of industrial relations policies and programmes throughout the company. He needs the backing of top management and must establish the authority which comes from giving sound advice. (CIR 1973, p. 26)

The same publication indicates (*ibid.*, p. 13) that the simple distinction between advisory and executive roles is more useful as an instrument of analysis than as a means of describing current practice, which varies so much. Some organizations give full executive authority to industrial relations specialists. Parker, Hawes and Lumb illustrate the variation with two quotations from company policy statements:

> Management responsibility for the conduct of industrial relations is . . . delegated by the accountable line manager to his senior industrial relations executive who will make industrial relations decisions or review such decisions and ensure their consistency with established policy, practices and procedure. . . .
>
> The management of employees is the responsibility of line management; the role of personnel specialists is to advise and assist line management in the exercise of that responsibility and to provide requisite supporting services. (Parker *et al.* 1971, p. 23)

If we consider first the question of advice, we may say that the conception of advice used to be of the type offered by a well-meaning mother-in-law. It was thoughtful, genuinely intended to be helpful and was sometimes welcome, but its basis was simply general experience and good intentions. The recipient could use or ignore it at will, depending on the commonsense assessment of its value. Legislation has caused the need for advice of the type offered by a professional. This is thoughtful, intended to be helpful, but may not be welcome. It will be based on an informed examination of statute and precedent, and will carry a quite different type of authority. It may also be that people see the need not only for advice, but also for representation by someone who knows the esoteric rules of procedure and behaviour in a highly stylized form of discussion.

As well as advice, the employer needs to see that all employment matters are administered in a way that is consistent with the legislative framework, and part of that requirement is that managerial actions should be consistent with each other.

In many management decisions in relation to employees the correctness lies not only in the intrinsic quality of the decision but also in the consistency of management handling of similar matters previously and in other parts of the organization. In labour law consistency is an important feature of justice, and it can be achieved in an organization either by having inflexible rules or by having a single source of control on decisions made.

The need for specialist advice based on a sound knowledge of the law and the need for an associated control over a wide range of management decisions have changed the range of options open to the employer in deploying personnel experts. The personnel officer may be charged with the task of deciding action on all employment matters and then implementing those decisions. Alternatively, the officer may monitor tentative decisions by others, which are agreed or vetoed before they are confirmed and implemented by those who formulated them. There is no place for mothers-in-law.

Organizational strategy for union recognition

There is a sequence of steps in the strategy of an organization's management for union recognition.

Management attitudes

However dominant the personnel specialist may be on employee relations matters, the other members of management do not simply leave the officer to get on with trade union recognition while they pursue their other and more interesting preoccupations. The step of recognition, or the extension of recognition, and all that follows can affect other policy matters such as the introduction of new products, investment in new plant, the manning of equipment and the opening or closure of establishments.

Equally, policy decisions to do with marketing, manufacturing, financing or new technology are likely to have employment repercussions. Union recognition or extension of recognition represents the introduction of change that can have major implications in all parts of the life of the organization. Because of this it is important that collective management attitudes towards recognition should have as wide a degree of consensus as possible. Then policy on recognition and its consequences can be fully integrated with other aspects of policy.

The previous three sentences represent a homily that has been repeated for years, and managers are frequently sceptical about such bland exhortations to do something which they know to be extremely difficult. Some of the problems lie in the specialized nature of the issue. The very existence of trade unions is resented by some and the alleged behaviour of trade unionists has been given as the reason for the fall of governments, let alone managerial ineffectiveness. The reasons justifying trade union recognition in general, and on some contentious matters in particular, are not readily appreciated, and when understood may still be disputed. Another difficulty is the need for a positive rather than grudging approach to recognition. If the management of an organization recognize a trade union only because they feel there is no alternative, then they will derive scant benefit from the arrangement. As with other aspects of change in organizations it can be an initiative towards improvement and development or it can be a defensive reaction to something distasteful and unwanted. It is also typical for the new convert to trade union recognition to be disappointed with the outcome. The conventional illustration of this attitude is where management have been persuaded that rank-and-file employees will make a contribution to better management decisions if they are involved through their union being recognized. A few months later there are bitter, disillusioned remarks about the unwillingness of the employees to discuss anything other than trivial matters like the colour of their overalls.

These and other problems about the integration of policy and a management consensus on recognition can probably only be resolved by full and lengthy discussion by members of management to find and then agree on a collective view.

Preparing to recognize

Does a management respond or initiate on recognition? Does it wait for a claim and then treat it on its merits or does it invite a claim? The answer to this question will come from a consideration of timing. It has already been suggested in this chapter that care has to be taken with a recognition claim that the time is ripe, not too soon or too late. There is always a danger that recognition will be harder if deferred. The Commission on Industrial Relations (CIR) found several situations like this:

> the success of the company's products in the markets of the world meant that management had to concentrate, to the virtual exclusion of all else, on increasing output. . . . The problems arising from the needs and aspirations of a large number of people had been largely shelved under the presence of the more immediate need to meet production targets. (CIR 1973, p. 12)

Another argument in favour of a recognition initiative by the management is that most of the areas of employment where recognition has not yet been granted are white-collar; one of the traditional reasons for white-collar employees not joining unions is their feeling that the management do not approve. They may tend to identify with the management and do not want to do things that are disliked.

Preparing to recognize requires a decision on whether to wait or to initiate. It also requires decisions on strategy about which union would be most 'appropriate', what the boundaries of the bargaining units could be and on what matters recognition would be contemplated.

Organization, communication and responsibility

How are the management to organize themselves to make recognition work? This process will involve a re-examination of the decision-making processes so that the additional input of employee consent can be incorporated with the other variables to be evaluated. It does not mean that managers have to get permission from their employees before they do anything – even though this is how union recognition is often caricatured. The decision-making processes have to be examined and the boundaries of managerial roles redrawn. Any recognition step involves moving one or more items off the list that are customarily a subject for unilateral decision and onto the list of those for joint regulation. When that happens it will involve not only a different approach but also a different process of discussion and validation within the management ranks.

The contract for recognition

Ideally, there will be some written statement to which both parties assent; this will include the basic factual information about which union is a party to the agreement, what the bargaining unit is and what the subjects of recognition are. It may include much more, as it is an opportunity to declare aspects of the policy of the organization – either the policy of the organization's management or the policy of management and employee representatives combined. This can pave the way for openness between the parties, awareness of what is happening and consistency in management.

Such a statement will also have the advantage of focusing the attention of policy-makers on the purposes and implications of it. The drafting of the statement could well be the basis of the full and lengthy discussion suggested earlier in this chapter. The CIR give us a useful summary of the benefits of a written statement of policy:

> Firstly, the processes involved in producing the document will themselves have been valuable in focusing minds on the purpose of the policy. They clarify intentions and eliminate uncertainties which may exist when reliance is placed on custom and practice or when policy is a matter of surmise. Secondly, a written document provides an objective reference point in the communication of policy to managers, employees and their representatives. Thirdly, by making clear the starting point of policy it provides a basis for change. A written policy need not be inflexible but should be reviewed and adapted as circumstances require. By being written it should, in fact, be easier to change than policies which are embedded in custom and practice, tradition and precedent. (CIR 1973, p. 6)

One development in recent years has been the move by some employers to sign single-union agreements when setting up new plants. These avoid, on the one hand, a long-running series of arguments with unions seeking recognition and, on the other hand, the problems of fragmented bargaining arrangements. It also shifts any rivalry between unions to the stage before recognition. Pirelli General approached five different unions in south Wales:

> In each case the company outlined in some detail its proposed personnel philosophy and policies for the new factory, and each union was asked whether it wished to be considered for single recognition on those broad terms. All five unions . . . responded positively and enthusiastically. The prize . . . was the creation of new jobs and new union recruits in an area of very high unemployment. (Yeandle and Clark 1989, p. 37)

Employee involvement

During the 1970s there was a lively debate about industrial democracy and various forms of employee participation in the management decision-making processes of business. This was driven by the relatively strong position held by trade union leaders in the various industries and the need of a Labour government to gain their support at a time of a slender majority in the House of Commons. The most thorough-going idea was for the introduction of *industrial democracy*, which can take various forms, but essentially it is a form in which the participation of employees is developed via representative democracy at the boardroom level to influence, or to make, the major strategic decisions of the organization.

The main focus of the debate was the Committee of Inquiry on Industrial Democracy. Their majority proposal was that boards of companies should be reconstituted to give equal representation to shareholder and employee representatives, with a smaller number of independents holding the balance.

The proposals were met with varying degrees of horror in management circles and less than rapture among trade unions. The eventual government reaction to the ideas was contained in a White Paper over twelve months later, which declared that there would not be a standard form of participation, like that proposed by the Committee of Inquiry, imposed by law. Increased participation would result mainly from exhortation, although companies employing 5,000 people or more would be legally obliged to discuss with employees all major proposals affecting the workforce and those employing 2,000 or more would be required to concede a legal right to employee representation a few years later.

The 1979 change of government led to these proposals being shelved, but interest continues among both managers and trade unionists. Dowling *et al.,* surveyed the attitudes of executives in twenty-five large private companies and the regional officers of fourteen trade unions. Both groups were opposed to worker directors and were relieved that the likelihood of such legislation had receded: 'Managers tended to favour forms of "participation" which emphasized communication and consultation, whereas the trade union officials favoured extensions to the range of issues subject to collective bargaining or joint regulation' (Dowling *et al.* 1981, p. 190).

In 1984 Hanson and Rathkey published the results of a survey of shopfloor opinion they carried out in four different companies that would have been affected by the Bullock proposals to try to establish a shopfloor view of the industrial democracy idea. One of their most conclusive findings was that employees were very little interested in employees making decisions without management involvement. Also twice as many people wanted involvement *only* in matters concerning their own work and conditions as those who wanted involvement in both that and issues concerning the management of the company as a whole.

The managerial interest is usually in some form of sharing control in order to regain control and they are clearly committed to the idea that managers are the people to make decisions, although employees may be consulted and have things explained to them in order to obtain their commitment to management objectives. Difficult trading conditions have also increased managerial willingness to disclose information about company affairs. An amendment to the Employment Act 1982, introduced by the House of Lords, is a requirement for companies with more than 250 employees to include in their annual report a statement of action taken to introduce or develop arrangements for employee participation, specifically:

- Systematically providing employees with information on matters which concern them.
- Consulting with employees or their representatives on management decisions likely to affect employees' interests.
- Encouraging employee involvement through means such as shareholding.
- Providing information on financial and economic matters affecting the business.

Management interest has recently centred on the idea of *employee involvement* as a way of meeting the demands of the 1982 Act, although ACAS are not impressed:

> The pressing need is for employees to be further involved in consultative and decision-making processes in the organizations in which they work, if their talents and energies are to be released and their willing commitment secured to the measures necessary for economic recovery. ACAS officials report that progress in this area has been slow and there remains much to be done. (ACAS 1985, p. 16)

Another view of participation is that it should develop first at *the place of work* itself, with autonomous working groups taking over their own supervision, and with managers giving much more attention to the design of jobs and finding ways in which individual employees can participate more in the day-by-day decisions that affect their work. The argument supporting this is that board-level decisions are of little interest or immediacy to employees and that their participation will be apathetic or incompetent, while what they really care about is what they themselves do from day to day, as implied by the Hanson and Rathkey survey.

A third method is one that has been in operation for many years – *joint consultation*. This has been criticized as an avoidance of true participation, as it reserves all authority to decide to the management, who ask for employee comment if they want to.

Our own research shows a generally more assertive attitude among personnel specialists with a clear interest in activities to improve communications with the workforce as a whole and raise commitment. Forty per cent of respondents had taken initiatives such as communications exercises or team briefings with blue-collar employees, compared with only 4 per cent who had taken initiatives with the much-vaunted method of quality circles. Some form of direct participation had been attempted by 8 per cent of respondents.

Another type of initiative is *harmonization of terms and conditions* between different categories of employee. A third of our respondents had made some moves in this direction. Changes were mainly in holidays, hours and method of payment. Sound practical guidance on making moves towards harmonization is to be found in Roberts (1985).

The issue of trade union recognition is not as burning as it was in the 1970s, but most organizations have recognized unions and ACAS still has some 15 per cent of the collective conciliation workload in this area. Managements may recognize unions, they may involve employees, consult with them, participate with them or harmonize terms and conditions. After detailed examination of employee relations practice in four very different organizations, Marchington and Parker concluded that unions were becoming less central to employee relations, but not because of deliberate management attempts to 'take them on':

> unions were not on the whole central to workplace employee relations, and in some cases their role was becoming more marginal. This factor did not, however, arise from any concerted management strategy directed specifically at labour relations, but was more appropriately seen as a consequence of other actions taken in pursuit of wider corporate goals – in particular to increase employee commitment to product quality and customer service. (Marchington and Parker 1990, p. 257)

Management always needs the collective consent of its employees: it also needs a mandate to manage. In most situations this is at least partly delivered by trade union recognition.

Summary propositions

28.1 Employee consent to the exercise of management authority may be strengthened if the management recognize a trade union to provide a focused, collective questioning of that authority.

28.2 Management need to decide what bargaining units there should be, which union should be recognized for each unit, when it should be recognized and what the scope of recognition should be.

28.3 The step of recognition requires re-examination of management decision-making processes and will involve the personnel manager in taking the leading role in employment matters.

28.4 A written statement of policy on recognition can provide the basis for mutually beneficial development of collective consent.

28.5 Forms of industrial democracy involving employee control arouse little interest among employees or managers: there is greater interest in employee involvement.

References

ACAS (1985), *Annual Report, 1984*, London: HMSO.

Lord Bullock (1977), *Report of the Committee of Inquiry on Industrial Democracy*, London: HMSO.

Commission on Industrial Relations (1973), *The Role of Management in Industrial Relations*, London: HMSO.

Department of Employment (1983), *Code of Practice on Closed Shop Agreements and Arrangements*, London: HMSO.

Dowling, M., Goodman, J., Gotting, D. and Hyman, J. (1981), 'Employee participation: survey evidence from the north west', *Employment Gazette*, April.

Etzioni, A. (1961), *A Comparative Analysis of Complex Organizations*, New York: Free Press.

Hanson, C. and Rathkey, P. (1984), 'Industrial democracy: a post-Bullock shopfloor view', *British Journal of Industrial Relations*, vol. 22, no. 2, pp. 154–68.

Marchington, M. P. and Parker, P. S. (1990), *Changing Patterns of Employee Relations*, Hemel Hempstead, Harvester Wheatsheaf.

Purcell, J. and Sisson, K. (1983), 'Strategies and practice in the management of industrial relations'. In G. S. Bain (ed.), *Industrial Relations in Britain*, Oxford: Basil Blackwell.

Roberts, C. (ed.) (1985), *Harmonization: Whys and wherefores*, London: Institute of Personnel Management.

USDAW v. *Sketchley Ltd* [1981] IRLR 291.

J. Wilson Ltd v. *USDAW* [1978] IRLR 120.

Yeandle, D. and Clark, J. (1989), 'Growing a compatible IR set up', *Personnel Management*, vol. 21, no. 7, July, pp. 36–9.

29

Negotiating agreement

Negotiation is a longstanding art, which has developed into a major mode of decision-making in all aspects of social, political and business life, even though there is always a feeling that it is no more than a substitute for direct, decisive action. Henry Kissinger was US Secretary of State when protracted negotiations eventually brought to an end the war in Vietnam. He commented:

> A lasting peace could come about only if neither side sought to achieve everything that it had wanted; indeed, that stability depended on the relative satisfaction, and therefore the relative dissatisfaction, of all the parties concerned. (Kissinger 1973)

In employment we have acquired the institution of collective bargaining as a means of regulating the employment relationship between employer and organized employees. To some this is the cornerstone of industrial democracy and the effective running of a business, but to others it is seen as impairing efficiency, inhibiting change and producing the lowest, rather than the highest, common factor of co-operation between management and employees.

Is negotiation rightly viewed as an activity that is only second best to unilateral decision-making? If the outcome is no more than compromise, the choice seems to be between negotiation and capitulation. Some would argue that capitulation by one side would be a better outcome for *both* than a compromise that ignores the difficulties and dissatisfies both. There is, however, an alternative to splitting the difference in negotiation and that is where the differences in view and objective of the parties are accommodated to such an extent that the outcome for both is better than could have been achieved by the unilateral executive action of either.

Any negotiation is brought about by the existence of some goals that are common to both parties and some goals that conflict. Between employer and employees the desire to keep the business in operation is one of the goals they usually have in common, but there may be many that conflict, and the two parties negotiate a settlement because the attempt by one to force a solution on the other would either fail because of the other's strength or would not be as satisfactory a settlement without the approval of the other party. Both parties acknowledge that they will move from their opening position and that sacrifices in one area may produce compensating benefits in another. Many years ago G. C. Homans expressed the situation thus:

> The more the items at stake can be divided into goods valued more by one party than they cost to the other and goods valued more by the other party than they cost to the first, the greater the chances of a successful outcome. (Homans 1961, p. 62)

The nature of conflict in the employment relationship

The approach outlined later in this chapter depends on the view that conflict of interests is inevitable between employer and employee because there is an authority relationship in which the aims of the two parties will at least sometimes conflict (Dahrendorf 1959). A further assumption is that such conflict does not necessarily damage that relationship (Coser 1956).

This has led a number of commentators to discuss negotiation in terms of equally matched protagonists. The power of the two parties may not actually be equal, but they are both willing to behave as if it were. The negotiation situation thus has the appearance of power equalization, which can be real or illusory, due to the search for a solution to a problem. When both sides set out to reach an agreement that is satisfactory to themselves and acceptable to the other, then their power is equalized by that desire. Where the concern for acceptance by the other is lacking, there comes the use of power play of the forcing type described later in this chapter:

> negotiators seek to increase common interest and expand cooperation in order to broaden the area of agreement to cover the item under dispute. On the other hand, each seeks to maximize his own interest and prevail in conflict, in order to make the agreement more valuable to himself. No matter what angle analysis takes, it cannot eliminate the basic tension between cooperation and conflict that provides the dynamic of negotiation. (Zartman 1976, p. 41)

The relative power of the parties is likely to fluctuate from one situation to the next; this is recognized by the ritual and face-saving elements of negotiation, where a power imbalance is not fully used, both to make agreement possible and in the knowledge that the power imbalance may be reversed on the next issue to be resolved.

The classic work of Ann Douglas (1962) produced a formulation of the negotiating encounter that has been little modified by those coming after her. Blake, Shepard and Mouton (1964) are very well-known exponents of this view, and Walton (1969) has written a most helpful book, too little known in the United Kingdom, about the application of this thinking to the interpersonal relationships between equals in the management hierarchy. However, this needs further thought if it is to be applied to the negotiations that take place between representatives of management and representatives of employees about terms and conditions of employment. Cooper and Bartlett point out the difficulty:

> If equality is available to all . . . conflicting groups can meet. All they need to shed are their misperceptions and their prejudices. Any differences are psychological rather than economic. The truth of the matter is, of course, that . . . there are glaring inequalities of wealth and power. Each society contains its own contradictions which arise from the distribution of money, of status and control. So conflict resolution is not just a matter of clearing away mistrust and misunderstanding, replacing them with communication. It is also concerned with political matters such as the re-allocation of power. (Cooper and Bartlett 1976, p. 167)

Fox (1974) would make a clear distinction between the type of bargaining situation which forms the basis of the propositions set out by Walton and Blake *et al.* on the one hand, and British collective bargaining on the other. He describes the relationships between senior managers as relationships of *social exchange*, with high trust and discretion and tight specification of roles.

Sources of conflict in the collective employment relationship

Focusing our attention on the collective contract we can list some of the sources of conflict endemic in that situation.

The aggressive impulse

Those who have charted the evolution of *homo sapiens*, such as Konrad Lorenz (1966) and Robert Ardrey (1967), demonstrate for us the innate aggressiveness of man. Although the processes of civilization tend to constrain it there is a natural impulse to behave aggressively to some degree at some time. It has a number of outlets, for example, watching football, wrestling or boxing. Another outlet for aggression is in negotiations within the employing organization, which is a splendid arena for the expression of combat.

Divergence of interests

Probably the main source of industrial relations conflict is divergence of interests between those who are classified as managers and those who are seen as non-managers. One group is seeking principally such things as efficiency, economy, productivity and the obedience of others to their own authority. The members of the other group are interested in these things, but are more interested in features like high pay, freedom of action, independence of supervision, scope for the individual and leisure. To some extent these invariably conflict.

Potential benefits of such conflict

It is widely believed that conflict of the type described here – and described frequently and more luridly in the press – is counter-productive, and that all should make strenuous efforts to eliminate it. There are, however, some advantages.

Clearing the air

Many people feel that a conflict situation is improved by getting bad feelings 'off their chests' and bringing the matter into the open. Sometimes combatants feel closer as a result.

Introducing new rules

Employment is governed by a number of rules – formal rules that define unfair dismissal and the rate of pay for various jobs, as well as informal rules like modes of address. Management/union conflict is usually about a disagreement over the rules and the bargain that is struck produces a new rule: a new rate of pay, a new employment practice or whatever. It can be the only way of achieving that particular change, and it is a very authoritative source of rule-making because of the participation in its creation.

Modifying the goals

The goals that management set can be modified as a result of conflict with others. Ways in which their goals will be unpopular or difficult to implement may be seen for the first time and modifications made early instead of too late. A greater range and diversity of views are brought to bear on a particular matter so that the capacity for innovation is enhanced.

Clash of values

More fundamental is the possible clash of values, usually about how people should behave. These may be variations of allegiance to the positions of different political parties on questions like 'What is production for?', or differences of social class attitude to what constitutes courtesy. Most frequently the clash is about the issue of managerial prerogative. Managers are likely to believe and proclaim that management is their inalienable right, so that those who question the way their work is done are ignorant or impertinent. Non-managers may regard management as a job that should be done properly by people who are responsive to questioning and criticism.

Competitiveness

One of the most likely sources is the urge to compete for a share of limited resources. Much of the drive behind differential pay claims is that of competing with other groups at a similar level, but there may also be competition for finance, materials, security, survival, power, recognition or status.

Organizational tradition

If the tradition of an organization is to be conflict-prone, then it may retain that mode obdurately, while other organizations in which conflict has not been a prominent feature may continue without it. It is axiomatic that certain industries in the United Kingdom are much more likely to display the manifestations of extreme conflict in industrial relations than others. Indicators like the number of working days lost through strikes show a pattern of distribution which varies little between different industries year by year. The nature of the conflict can range between the extremes of pettiness, secrecy, fear and insecurity on the one hand, to vigorous, open and productive debate on the other, with many organizations exhibiting neither.

Understanding of respective positions

Combatants will come to a better understanding of their position on the issue being debated because of their need to articulate it, set it forth, develop supporting arguments and then defend those arguments against criticism. This enables them to see more clearly what they want, why they want it and how justifiable it is. In challenging the position of the other party, they will come to a clearer understanding of where they stand, and why.

Potential drawbacks of such conflict

These advantages may not be sufficient to balance the potential drawbacks.

Waste of time and energy

Conflict and the ensuing negotiations take a great deal of time and energy. Conflict can become attritive when over-personalized, and individuals become obsessed with the conflict itself rather than what it is about. Negotiation takes a lot longer than simple management decree.

Emotional stress for participants

People vary in the type of organizational stress to which they are prone. The need to be involved in negotiation is a source of stress which some people find very taxing, while others find it stimulating.

Organizational stress

Accommodating conflict often causes some inefficiency through the paraphernalia that can accompany it: striking, working to rule, working without enthusiasm, withdrawing co-operation or the simple delay caused by protracted negotiation.

Risks

Engaging in negotiation may be necessary as the only way to cope with a conflictual situation, but there is the risk of stirring up a hornets' nest. When conflict is brought to the surface it may be resolved or accommodated, or if the situation is handled badly it may get worse.

Worsening communications

The quality and amount of communication is impaired. Those involved are concerned more to confirm their own viewpoint than to convey understanding, and there are perceptual distortions like stereotyping and cognitive dissonance. The attitudes behind the communications may also become inappropriate as there are greater feelings of hostility and attempts to score off others.

Bargaining strategies

A reading of Schmidt and Tannenbaum (1960) and Lawrence and Lorsch (1972) helps us to identify various strategies that are adopted to cope with conflict and some of the likely effects.

Avoidance

To some extent conflict can be 'handled' by ignoring it. For a time this will prevent it surfacing so that it remains latent rather than manifest: the danger being that it is harder to deal with when it eventually does erupt. Opposing views cannot be heard unless there is apparatus for their expression. The management of an organization can fail to provide such apparatus by, for instance, not having personnel specialists, not recognizing trade unions and not recognizing employee representatives. If the management organize the establishment as if conflict of opinion did not exist, any such difference will be less apparent and its expression stifled. This is a strategy that is becoming harder and harder to sustain due to the developing legal support for employee representation.

Smoothing

A familiar strategy is to seek the resolution of conflict by honeyed words in exhortation or discussion where the emphasis is on the value of teamwork, the assurance that 'we all agree really' and an overt, honest attempt to get past the divergence of opinion, which is regarded as a temporary and unfortunate aberration. This is often an accurate diagnosis of the situation and represents an approach that would have broad employee support in a particular employment context.

Forcing

The opposite to smoothing is to attack expressions of dissent and deal with conflict by stamping it out. This is not easy and has innumerable, unfortunate precedents in the past and present.

Compromise

Where divergence of views is acknowledged and confronted, one possibility is to split the difference. If employees claim a pay increase of £10 and the management say they can afford nothing, a settlement of £5 saves the face of both parties *but satisfies neither*. However common this strategy may be – and sometimes there is no alternative – it has this major drawback: that both parties fail to win.

Confrontation

The fifth strategy is to confront the issue on which the parties differ. This involves accepting that there is a conflict of opinions or interests, exploring the scale and nature of the conflict and then working towards an accommodation of the differences which will provide a greater degree of satisfaction of the objectives of both parties than can be achieved by simple compromise. We suggest that this is the most productive strategy in many cases and offers the opportunity of both parties winning.

It is this fifth strategy which we consider in the remainder of this chapter.

Review topic 29.1

Consider an industrial dispute or disagreement which you have recently witnessed or read about.

1. Was the management strategy one of avoidance, smoothing, forcing, compromise or confrontation?
2. Was this an inappropriate strategy?
3. If the answer to the last question was 'yes', why was an inappropriate strategy used?

Bargaining tactics

In preparing for a bargaining encounter there are a number of things which bargainers must set in their minds before they begin.

Resolution or accommodation

Conflict can be *resolved* so that the original feelings of antagonism or opposition vanish, at least over the issue that has brought the conflict to a head. The schoolboy story of how two boys 'put on the gloves in the gym' after a long feud and thereafter shook hands and became firm friends is a theoretical example of a conflict resolved. This type of outcome has a romantic appeal and will frequently be sought in industrial relations issues because so many people feel acutely uncomfortable when involved in relationships of overt antagonism.

Alternatively, the conflict may be *accommodated,* so that the differences of view persist, but some *modus vivendi,* some form of living with the situation, is discovered. In view of the inevitability of the conflict that is endemic in the employment relationship, accommodation may be a more common prospect than resolution, but it is an interesting question for a bargainer to ponder when approaching the bargaining table: which is it – resolution or accommodation?

Tension level

Most bargainers feel that they have no chance to determine the timing of encounters. This is partly due to reluctance; managers in particular tend to resort to negotiation only when necessary, and the necessity is usually a crisis. A more proactive (instead of reactive) approach is to initiate encounters, to some extent at least trying to push them into favourable timings.

A feature of timing is the tension level. Too much, and the negotiators get the jitters, unable to see things straight and indulging in excessive interpersonal vituperation: too little tension, and there is no real will to reach a settlement. Ideal timing is to get a point when both sides have a balanced desire to reach a settlement.

Power balance

> Effective negotiation is rarely limited to the sheer exploitation of power advantage. The best settlement is one in which both sides can recognize their own and mutual advantages. (Fowler 1986, p. 132)

The background to any negotiation includes the relative power of the disputants. *Power parity is the most conducive to success*:

> Perceptions of power inequality undermine trust, inhibit dialogue, and decrease the likelihood of a constructive outcome from an attempted confrontation. Inequality tends to undermine trust on both ends of the imbalanced relationship, directly affecting both the person with the perceived power inferiority and the one with perceived superiority. (Walton 1969, p. 98)

The greater the power differential, the more negative the attitudes.

Synchronizing

The approaches and reciprocations of the two parties need a degree of synchronizing to ensure that an approach is made at a time when the other party is ready to deal with it. Management interpretation of managerial prerogative often causes managers to move quickly in the search of a solution, virtually pre-empting negotiation. When what they see as a positive overture is not reciprocated, then they are likely to feel frustrated, discouraged and cross; making themselves in turn unready for overtures from the other side.

Openness

Conflict handling is more effective if the participants can be open with each other about the facts of the situation and their feelings about it. The Americans place great emphasis on this and we must appreciate that openness is more culturally acceptable in the United States than in the United Kingdom, but we note their concern that negotiators should own up to feelings of resentment and anger, rather than masking their feelings behind role assumptions of self-importance.

The negotiating process

Having reviewed the background to bargaining and negotiation, .we now consider the various stages of the negotiating encounter in which aspects of ritual are especially important, making perhaps for formality and awkwardness rather than relaxed informality. However, the ritual steps are not time-wasting prevarication, but an inescapable feature of the process.

Agenda

The meeting needs an agenda or at least some form of agreement about what is to be discussed. In some quarters a naive conviction persists that there is some benefit in concealing the topic from the other party until the encounter begins, presumably because there is something to be gained from surprise. In fact this only achieves a deferment of discussion until the other party have had a chance to consider their position. The nature of the agenda can have an effect on both the conduct and outcome of the negotiations. It affects the conduct of the encounter by revealing and defining the matters that each side wants to deal with. It is unlikely that other matters will be added to the agenda, particularly if negotiations take place regularly between the parties, so that the negotiators can begin to see, before the meeting, what areas the discussions will cover.

The agenda will influence the outcome of negotiations as a result of the sequence of items on it as the possibilities of accommodation between the two positions emerge in the discussions. If, for instance, all the items of the employees' claim come first and all the management's points come later, the possibilities do not turn into probabilities until the discussions are well advanced. An agenda that juxtaposes management and employee 'points' in a logical fashion can enable the shape of a settlement to develop in the minds of the negotiators earlier, even though there would be no commitment until all the pieces of the jigsaw were available. Many negotiations take place without an agenda at all, sometimes because there is a crisis, sometimes because neither party is sufficiently well organized to prepare one. Morley and Stephenson (1977, pp. 74–8) review a number of studies to draw the conclusion that agreement between negotiators is facilitated when there is the opportunity for them to experience 'orientation' – considering on what to stand firm and on what to contemplate yielding – or where there is an understanding of the issues involved. An agenda is a prerequisite of orientation.

Information

Both parties will need facts to support their argument in negotiation. Some information will be provided to employee representatives for the purposes of collective bargaining and both sets of negotiators have to collect what they need, analyze it so that they understand it, and confirm that the interpretation is shared by each member of their team.

Strategy

The main feature of preparation is the determination of strategy by each set of negotiators. Probably the most helpful work on negotiation strategy has been done by Fowler (1990), with his careful analysis of bargaining conventions and possibilities. In this chapter we limit our considerations to four aspects of strategy.

Objectives

What do the negotiators seek to achieve? Here one would ask them to produce clear and helpful objectives. When the question has been put to management negotiators entering either real or contrived negotiations in recent years the following have been some of the statements of objectives:

- 'Get the best deal we possibly can.'
- 'Maintain factory discipline at all costs.'
- 'Remain dignified at all times.'
- 'Look for an opening and exploit it to the full.'

Apart from their general feebleness, all these declarations have a common, negative quality. The initiative is with the other party and the only strategy is to resist for as long as possible and to concede as little as possible. If this is the best management negotiators can contrive, then their prospects are indeed bleak. They are bound to lose; the only unresolved question is how much. They cannot gain anything because they do not appear to want anything.

More positive objectives are those that envisage improvements, which could flow from a changing of the employment rules – changes in efficiency, working practices, manning levels, shiftwork patterns, administrative procedures, flexibility, cost control, and so forth. Unless both parties to the negotiations want something out of the meeting there is little scope for anything but attrition.

Roles

Who will do what in the negotiations? A popular fallacy is that negotiation is best conducted by 'everyone chipping in when they have something to say' and 'playing it by ear'. This is the style for a brainstorming, problem-solving group discussion, and negotiation is quite different. Problem-solving implies common. interests; negotiation implies conflicting interests between groups who are opposed in debate. Negotiators need a specific role, that they stay in. The roles are:

1. *Chairman*: In the majority of cases the management provides this function, and one of the management team will chair the discussion and control the meeting.
2. *Advocate*: Each party requires one person who will be the principal advocate to articulate the case and to examine the opposing case. This provides focus to the discussion and control of the argument. Although it is common for the roles of chairman and advocate to be combined in one person for status reasons, this can put a great strain on the individual, who is bowling and keeping wicket at the same time.
3. *Specialists*: The third role is that of specialist. One person who fully understands the incentive scheme, another to provide expert comment on any legal points, and so forth. The important emphasis is on what the specialist does *not* do. One would not expect this particular negotiator to become involved in the general debate, as this is confusing and moves control from the advocate. The specialist's role is to provide advice when required. Negotiating does not benefit from free-for-all, unstructured discussion.
4. *Observers*: There is no need for all those attending to speak in order to justify their presence. There is an important part to be played by those who do no more than observe the discussions. They get less emotionally involved in the interplay and point-scoring, and are able to evaluate the situation as it develops. When there are adjournments the observers often initiate the discussions within their team as strategy is redefined and further tactics considered.

Predicting counter-claims

No strategy survives the first encounter with the opposition intact, but its chances are improved if the negotiators have tried to predict what they will hear from the opposition. In this way they will be prepared not only to advance their own arguments, but also to respond to arguments put to them.

Unity

Because negotiations are the confrontation of different sets of interests, each team works out a united position before negotiations begin and expresses that unity in negotiation. If the position is to be modified, then they will agree the modification. This is another aspect of the vital difference between this activity and problem-solving. It is the differences *between* the parties that have to be handled; differences *within* the parties are simply a nuisance.

Setting

The number of people representing each side will influence the conduct of negotiations. The larger the number the greater the degree of formality that is needed to manage the meeting; this is an argument in favour of negotiations between very small teams. On the other hand, meetings between two or three people in 'smoke-filled rooms' give rise to allegations of manipulation and are difficult for members of trade unions to countenance in view of their dependence on democratic support. Another problem is that different phases of negotiation call for different arrangements. Relatively large numbers can be an advantage at the beginning, but are often a hindrance in the later stages:

> it is not uncommon for the trade union side to field a sizeable team – a union official, perhaps, supported by a shop stewards' committee. It is unwise for a single manager to attempt to negotiate alone with such a team. Negotiation demands a high level of concentration and quick thinking and it is difficult for one person to maintain full attention to everything that is said, and to detect every nuance in the discussion. This does not mean that the management team must equal the trade union team in size. Indeed, to go beyond a fairly small number runs the risk of poor co-ordination between team members and the possibility that differing views will emerge within the team as negotiations proceed. (Fowler 1990, p. 35)

When asked to suggest an appropriate number, most experienced negotiators opt for three or four on each side.

The nature of the seating arrangements needs to reflect the nature of the meeting, and that means that the sides face each other, with the boundaries between the two being clear. The importance of the physical arrangements were demonstrated by the Paris peace talks, which were intended to bring an end to the Vietnam war. The start of talks was delayed for some weeks due to the delegations not being able to agree about the shape of the table.

Challenge and defiance

The somewhat melodramatic term 'challenge and defiance' is used to describe the opening stage of the negotiations, for the deliberate reason that there is a deal of theatricality about the various processes.

Negotiators begin by making it clear that they are representing the interests of people whose will and desire transcends that of the representatives themselves.

They also emphasize the strength of their case and its righteousness as weli as the impossibility of any movement from the position they are declaring. The theatricality lies in the realization by both sides that there *will* be movement from the relative positions that they are busy declaring to be immovable. The displays of strength are necessary for the negotiators to convince themselves that they are right and to convince the opposition.

The substantive element of this phase is to clarify what the differences are. By the time it draws to a close the negotiators should be quite clear on the matters that divide them, where and how. This, of course, is an important part of the process, differentiation precedes integration.

It is important for the participants to keep the level of interpersonal animosity down. This is a part of the emphasis on their representative role that has already been mentioned. Different behaviours are needed later that depend on an open, trusting relationship between the negotiators, so this must not be impaired by personal acrimony at the opening. It is similar to the ritual whereby a lawyer may refer to a legal adversary as 'my learned friend'.

Thrust and parry

After the differences have been explored, there is an almost instinctive move to a second, integrative stage of the encounter. Here negotiators are looking for possibilities of movement and mutual accommodation:

> Douglas distinguishes between the public role-playing activities of the first stage and the 'psychological' (individual) activities of the second stage as being concerned, respectively, with *inter-party* and *interpersonal exchange*. Behaviourally the inter-party exchange is characterized by *official* statements of position, ostensibly committing the party or parties to some future action congruent with that position. The interpersonal exchange, on the other hand, is characterized by *unofficial* behaviours which do not so commit the parties in question. (Morley and Stephenson 1970, p. 19)

Thus the statements made by negotiators are of a much more tentative nature than earlier, as they sound out possibilities, float ideas, ask questions, make suggestions and generally change style towards a problem-solving mode. This has to be done without any commitment of the party that is being represented, so the thrusts are couched in very non-committal terms, specifically exonerating the party from any responsibility. Gradually, the opportunities for mutual accommodation can be perceived in the background of the discussion. We can now incorporate the idea of target points and resistance points advanced by Walton and McKersie (1965).

The *target point* of a negotiating team is the declared objective – what they would really like to achieve. It will be spelled out in challenge and defiance. The *resistance point* is where they would rather break off negotiations than settle. This point is never declared and is usually not known either. Although negotiators frequently begin negotiations with a feeling of 'not a penny more than . . .', the point at which they would *actually resist* is seldom the same as that at which they *think they would resist*. Normally the resistance points for both parties slide constantly back and forth during negotiations.

Decision-making

Through thrust and parry all the variations of integration will have been considered and explored, even though negotiators will have veered away from making firm commitments. The third phase of their encounter is when they reach an agreement, and it is interesting to pause here with the comment that agreement is inevitable in all but a small minority of situations, because the bargainers need each other and they have no one else with whom to negotiate. The employees want to continue working for the organization. Even if they take strike action, they will eventually return to work. The management need the employees to work for them. Employees collectively cannot choose a different management with whom to negotiate and managers can seldom choose a replacement workforce with whom to bargain. They have to reach agreement, no matter how long it takes.

After an adjournment the management will make an offer. The decision about what to offer is the most difficult and important task in the whole process, because the offer can affect the resistance point of the other party. The way in which the other's resistance point will be affected cannot be predetermined. A very low offer could move the other's resistance point further away or bring it nearer; we cannot be sure until the negotiations actually take place.

The offer may be revised, but eventually an offer will be accepted and the encounter – not the negotiation – is over.

Negotiations on the contract for collective consent are thus significantly different from those other types of bargaining in which people engage. The negotiations to purchase a second-hand car or a house may seem at first sight to be similar, but in both those situations either party can opt out at any stage and cease to deal any further. The possibility of losing the other is always present, just as is the possibility of negotiating with a different 'opponent'. For this reason the political analogies are more helpful. A peace treaty has to be agreed between the nations that have been at war, and no one else.

Recapitulation

Once a bargain has been struck the tension of negotiation is released and the natural inclination of the bargainers is to break up and spread the news of the agreement that has been reached. It is suggested that they should first

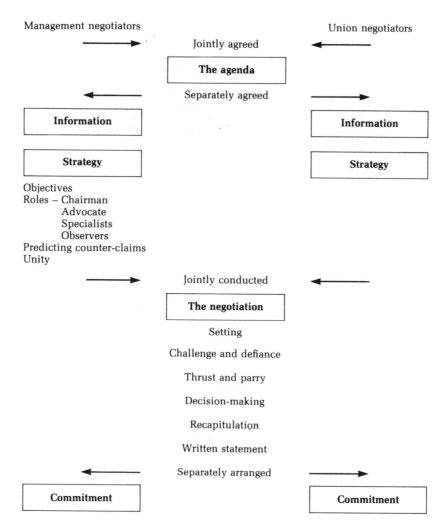

Management negotiators   Union negotiators

Jointly agreed

The agenda

Separately agreed

Information   **Information**

Strategy   **Strategy**

Objectives
Roles – Chairman
       Advocate
       Specialists
       Observers
Predicting counter-claims
Unity

Jointly conducted

The negotiation

Setting

Challenge and defiance

Thrust and parry

Decision-making

Recapitulation

Written statement

Separately arranged

Commitment   **Commitment**

Figure 29.1 *The negotiating process*

recapitulate all the points on which they have agreed and, if necessary, make arrangements on any minor matters still outstanding that everyone had forgotten.

In the wake of a settlement there is usually a number of such minor matters. If they are dealt with there and then they should be dealt with speedily because of the overriding feeling for agreement that has been established. If discussion of them is deferred because they are difficult, then agreement may be hard to reach later as the issues stand on their own, instead of in the context of a larger settlement.

Written statement

If it is possible to produce a brief written statement before the meeting is ended, both parties to the negotiations will be greatly helped. The emphasis here is on producing a brief written statement *before* the meeting ends, not as soon as possible afterwards. This will help all the negotiators to take away the same interpretation of what they have done and make them less dependent on recollection. In most circumstances it can also be used to advise non-participants: retyped as a memorandum to supervisors, put up on notice-boards, read out at union meetings, and so on. This will reduce the distortion that can stem from rumour. Until the agreement is in writing it rests on an *understanding*, and understanding can easily change.

Commitment of the parties

So far, agreement has been reached between negotiators only, and it is of no value unless the parties represented by those negotiators accept it and make it work. This requires acceptance at two levels: first in words and then in deeds.

Employee representatives have to report back to their membership and persuade them to accept the agreement. To some extent management representatives may have to do the same thing, but they customarily carry more personal authority to make decisions than do employee representatives.

Although this is a difficult and uncertain process, it is no more important than the final level of acceptance, which is where people make the agreement work. Benefits to the employees are likely to be of the type that are simple to administer – like an increase in the rates of pay – but benefits to the organization, like changes in working practices and the variation of demarcation boundaries, are much more difficult. They may quickly be glossed over and forgotten unless the changes are painstakingly secured after the terms have been agreed.

Boulwarism: a cautionary tale

Lemuel Boulware, Vice-President for Employee Relations in the General Electric Company of the United States, tried to side-step the ritual dance described above by developing a strategy which he called 'truth in bargaining'. The essence was that his first offer was also his last. He claimed that in conventional bargaining everyone knew that the first offer would be improved, so it was artificially low. He intended to be direct and truthful, making one offer that would not be varied so as to save time and speculation about the final outcome.

This policy had short-run success, but trade unions objected to Boulwarism on the grounds that it eliminated the constructive interchange of normal bargaining and diminished the importance of union representatives in negotiation. Eventually they challenged the policy successfully in the US courts on the grounds that it was not bargaining in good faith.

Review topic 29.2

1. What was Lemuel Boulware's mistake?
2. Why is the process (as well as the result) of negotiating important to both management representatives and employee representatives?
3. Is the process of negotiation important to the members of management and to the employees who are represented, but not participating in the negotiations; or are they only interested in the result?

Summary propositions

29.1 Conflict is inevitable in the employment relationship, but need not pose a threat to the relationship.

29.2 The optimum bargaining strategy will be to confront the issue on which the parties differ, to explore the reasons for the difference and to work towards an accommodation of those differences that will be acceptable to both parties.

29.3 Compared with other encounters at work, negotiating has a very high degree of ritualistic content, involving elaborate and artificial behaviours from the participants.

References

Ardrey, R. (1967), *The Territorial Imperative*, London: Collins.

Blake, R. R., Shepard, H. A. and Mouton, J. S. (1964), *Managing Intergroup Conflict in Industry*, Houston, Texas: Gulf Publishing.

Cooper, B. M. and Bartlett, A. F. (1976), *Industrial Relations: A study in conflict*, London: Heinemann.

Coser, L. A. (1956), *The Functions of Social Conflict*, New York: Free Press of Glencoe.

Dahrendorf, R. (1959), *Class and Conflict in Modern Society*, London: Routledge & Kegan Paul.

Douglas, A. (1962), *Industrial Peacemaking*, New York: Columbia University Press.

Fowler, A. (1986), *Effective Negotiation*, London: Institute of Personnel Management.

Fowler, A. (1990), *Negotiation Skills and Strategies*, London: Institute of Personnel Management.

Fox, A. (1974), *Work, Power and Trust Relations*, London: Faber & Faber.

Homans, G. C. (1961), *Social Behaviour: Its elementary forms*, London: Routledge & Kegan Paul.

Kissinger, H. (1973), in *New York Times*, 25 January.

Lawrence, P. R. and Lorsch, J. W. (1972), *Managing Group and Intergroup Relations*, Homewood, Ill.: Dorsey.

Lorenz, K. (1966), *On Aggression*, London: Methuen.

Morley, I. and Stephenson, G. M. (1970), 'Strength of case, communication systems and the outcomes of simulated negotiations', *Industrial Relations Journal*, Summer.

Morley, I. and Stephenson, G. M. (1977), *The Social Psychology of Bargaining*, London: George Allen & Unwin.

Schmidt, W. and Tannenbaum, R. (1960), 'Management of differences', *Harvard Business Review*, November/December, pp. 107–15.

Walton, R. E. (1969), *Interpersonal Peacemaking: Confrontations and third party consultation*, Reading, Mass.: Addison-Wesley.

Walton, R. E. and McKersie, R. B. (1965), *Towards a Behavioural Theory of Labour Negotiations*, London: McGraw-Hill.

Zartman, I. W. (1976), *The 50% Solution*, New York: Anchor Press/Doubleday.

Grievance and discipline

Grievance and discipline are solemn words to apply to the basic method of seeing fair play in the working relationship between employee and the employing organization. Both are seeking a good fit on the employment contract and this good fit is the foundation of the employment relationship. Both the manager (acting as the employer's agent) and the employee have the opportunity to remedy their dissatisfactions with each other. As a last resort either can terminate the contract, but there are many possibilities of mutual adjustment before that final step is taken. The employer seeks adjustment through processes of *discipline*; the employee seeks adjustment through processes of *grievance*.

Personnel managers and grievance and discipline

Personnel managers make one of their most significant contributions to organizational effectiveness by the way they facilitate and administer this interaction. First, they devise and negotiate the procedural framework of organizational justice on which both discipline and grievance depend. Secondly, they are much involved in the interviews and problem-solving discussions that eventually produce solutions to the difficulties that have been encountered. Thirdly, they maintain the viability of the whole process which forms an integral part of their work: they monitor grievances to make sure they are not overlooked and so that any general trend can be perceived, and they oversee the disciplinary machinery to ensure that it is not being bypassed or unfairly manipulated.

Grievance and discipline handling are one of the personnel roles that few other people want to take over. Ambitious line managers may want to select their own staff without personnel intervention or by using the services of consultants. They may try to brush their personnel colleagues aside and deal directly with trade union officials or organize their own management development, but grievance and discipline is too hot a potato.

Though it may seem like a thankless task that is 'pushed onto' personnel, it is now a major feature of personnel influence and power within the organization. The requirements of the law regarding explanation of grievance handling and the legal framework to avoid unfair dismissal combine to make this an area where personnel people must be both knowledgeable and effective. That combination provides a valuable platform for influencing other aspects of organizational affairs. The personnel manager who is *not* skilled in grievance and discipline is seldom in a strong organizational position.

What do we mean by discipline?

Discipline is regulation of human activity to produce a controlled performance. It ranges from the guard's control of a rabble to the accomplishment of lone individuals producing spectacular performance through self-discipline in the control of their own talents and resources.

First, there is *managerial discipline* in which everything depends on the leader from start to finish. There is a group of people who are answerable to someone who directs what they should all do. Only through individual direction can that group of people produce a worthwhile performance, like the person leading the community singing in the pantomime or the person conducting an orchestra. Everything depends on the leader.

Secondly, there is *team discipline*, whereby the perfection of the performance derives from the mutual dependence of all, and that mutual dependence derives from a commitment by each member to the total enterprise: the failure of one would be the downfall of all. This is usually found in relatively small working groups, like a dance troupe or an autonomous working group in a factory.

Thirdly, there is *self-discipline*, like that of the juggler or the skilled artisan, where a solo performer is absolutely dependent on training, expertise and self-control.

Discipline is, therefore, not only negative, producing punishment or prevention. It can also be a valuable quality for the individual subject to it, although the form of discipline depends not only on the individual employee but also on the task and the way it is organized. The development of self-discipline is easier in some jobs than others and many of the job redesign initiatives have been directed at providing scope for job holders to exercise self-discipline and find a degree of autonomy from managerial discipline. Figure 30.1 shows how the three forms are connected in a sequence or hierarchy, with employees finding one of three ways to achieve their contribution to organizational effectiveness.

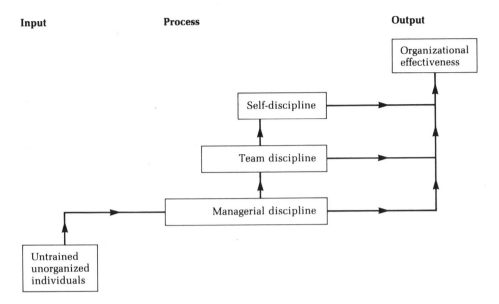

Figure 30.1 *Three forms of discipline*

However, even the most accomplished solo performer has been dependent on others for training, and advice, and every team has its coach.

Review topic 30.1

Note three examples of managerial discipline, team discipline and self-discipline from your own experience.

Managers are not dealing with discipline only when they are rebuking latecomers or threatening to dismiss saboteurs. As well as dealing with the unruly and reluctant, they are developing the co-ordinated discipline of the working team, engendering that *esprit de corps* which makes the whole greater than the sum of the parts. They are training the new recruit who must not let down the rest of the team, puzzling over the reasons why A is fitting in well while B is still struggling. Managers are also providing people with the equipment to develop the self-discipline that will give them autonomy, responsibility and the capacity to maximize their powers. The independence and autonomy that self-discipline produces also produces the greatest degree of personal satisfaction – and often the largest pay packet. Furthermore the movement between the three forms represents a declining degree of managerial involvement. If you are a leader of community singing, nothing can happen without you being present and the quality of the singing depends on your performance each time. If you train jugglers, the time and effort you invest pays off a thousand times, while you sit back and watch the show.

What do we mean by grievance?

Towards an understanding of grievance in employment

Pigors and Myers (1977, p. 229) give us a helpful approach to the question of grievances by drawing a distinction between the terms *dissatisfaction, complaint* and *grievance* as follows:

Dissatisfaction: Anything that disturbs an employee, whether or not the unrest is expressed in words.

Complaint: A spoken or written dissatisfaction brought to the attention of the supervisor and/or shop steward.

Grievance: A complaint that has been formally presented to a management representative or to a union official.

This provides us with a useful categorization by separating out *grievance* as a formal, relatively drastic step, compared with commonplace grumbling. It is much more important for management to know about *dissatisfaction*. Although nothing is being expressed, the feeling of hurt following failure to get a pay rise or the frustration about shortage of materials can quickly influence performance.

Much dissatisfaction never turns into complaint, as something happens to make it unnecessary. Dissatisfaction evaporates with a night's sleep, after a cup of coffee with a colleague, or when the cause of the dissatisfaction is in some other way removed. The few dissatisfactions that do produce complaint are also most likely to resolve themselves at that stage. The person hearing the complaint explains things in a way that the dissatisfied employee had not previously appreciated, or takes action to get at the root of the problem.

Grievances are rare since few employees will question their superior's judgement and fewer still will risk being stigmatized as a troublemaker. Also, many people do not initiate grievances because they believe that nothing will be done as a result of their attempt.

Personnel managers have to encourage the proper use of procedures to discover sources of dissatisfaction. Managers in the middle may not reveal the complaints they are hearing, for fear of showing themselves in a poor light. Employees who feel insecure, for any reason, are not likely to risk going into procedure, yet the dissatisfaction lying beneath a repressed grievance can produce all manner of unsatisfactory work behaviours from apathy to arson.

Individual dissatisfaction can lead to the loss of a potentially valuable employee; collective dissatisfaction can lead to industrial action.

Roethlisberger and Dickson (1939, pp. 225–69) differentiated three types of complaint, according to content.

The first kind referred to tangible *objects* in terms that could be defined by any competent worker and could be readily tested:

- 'The machine is out of order . . .'
- 'This tool is too dull . . .'
- 'The stock we're getting now is not up to standard . . .'
- 'Our cement is too thin and won't make the rubber stick . . .'

Second were those complaints based partly on sensory experience, but primarily on the accompanying, *subjective* reactions:

- 'The work is messy . . .'
- 'It's too hot in here . . .'
- 'The job is too hard . . .'

These statements include terms where the meaning is biologically or socially determined and can therefore not be understood unless the background of the complainant is known; seldom can their accuracy be objectively determined. A temperature of 18° Centigrade may be too hot for one person but equable for another.

The third type of complaint they differentiated were those involving the *hopes and fears of employees*:

- 'The supervisor plays favourites . . .'
- 'The pay rates are too low . . .'
- 'Seniority doesn't count as much as it should . . .'

These complaints proved the most revealing to the investigators as they showed the importance of determining not only what employees felt but also why they felt as they did; not only verifying the facts ('the manifest content') but also determining the feelings behind the facts ('the latent content').

Roethlisberger and Dickson concluded, for instance, that one employee who complained of his supervisor being a bully was actually saying something rather different, especially when he gave as his reason the fact that the supervisor did not say 'good morning'. Later, it was revealed that the root of his dissatisfaction was in his attitude to any authority figure, not simply the supervisor about whom he had complained.

Each of the types of dissatisfaction manifested in this analysis are important for the management to uncover and act upon, if action is possible. Action is likely to be prompt on complaints of this first type, as they are neutral: blame is being placed on an inanimate object and individual culpability is not an issue. Action may be taken on complaints of the second type where the required action is straightforward – such as opening a window if it is too hot – but the problem of accuracy is such that there may be a tendency to smooth over an issue or leave it 'to sort itself out' in time. The third type of complaint is the most difficult, and action is therefore less likely to be taken. Supervisors will often take complaints to be a personal criticism of their own competence, and employees will often translate the complaint into a grievance only by attaching it to a third party like a shop steward, so that the relationship between employee and supervisor is not jeopardized.

The framework of organizational justice

Now we have a basic understanding of grievance and discipline, we look at the ways of dealing with the dissatisfaction that causes them.

Review topic 30.2

Think of an example of employee dissatisfaction causing inefficiency in the organization that was not remedied because there was no complaint made. Why was there no complaint?

The organization requires a framework of justice to surround the everyday employment relationship so that managers and supervisors, as well as other employees, know where they stand when dissatisfaction develops.

Awareness of culture and appropriateness of style

The culture of an organization profoundly affects the behaviour of people within it and develops norms that are hard to alter. It is important to recognize the importance of this influence. If everyone is in the habit of arriving ten minutes late, a 'new broom' manager will have a struggle to change the habit. Equally, if everyone is in the habit of arriving punctually, then a new recruit who often arrives late will come under strong social pressure to conform, without need for recourse to management action. Culture also affects the freedom and candour with which people discuss dissatisfactions with their managers without allowing them to fester.

The style managers adopt in handling grievances and discipline will reflect their beliefs. The manager who sees discipline as being punishment and who regards grievances as examples of subordinates getting above themselves will behave in a relatively autocratic way, being curt in disciplinary situations and dismissive of complaints. The manager who sees disciplinary problems as obstacles to achievement that do not necessarily imply incompetence or ill-will by the employee will seek out the cause of the problem. The problem may then be revealed as one requiring firm, punitive action by the manager, but it may alternatively be revealed as a matter requiring management remedy of a different kind. In either case the manager will be supported by the bulk of the employees. The manager who listens out for complaints and grievances, gets to the bottom of the problems and finds solutions will run little risk of rumbling discontent from people obsessed by trivial problems.

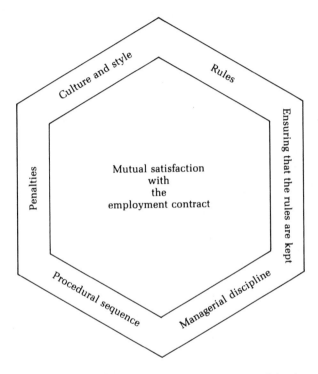

Figure 30.2 *The framework of organizational justice*

Rules

Every workplace has rules; the difficulty is to have rules that people will honour. Some rules come from statutes, like the tachograph requirement for HGV drivers, but most are tailored to meet the particular requirements of the organization in which they apply. For example, rules about personal cleanliness are essential in a food factory but less stringent in a garage.

Rules should be clear and readily understood. The number of rules should be sufficient to cover all obvious and usual disciplinary matters. To ensure general compliance it is helpful if rules are jointly determined, but it is more common for management to formulate the rules and for employee representatives eventually to concur with them. Employees should have ready access to the rules, through the employee handbook and noticeboard, and the personnel manager will always try to ensure that the rules are known as well as published.

The Department of Employment (1973) suggest that rules fall into six categories, relating to different types of employee behaviour:

1. *Negligence* is failure to do the job properly and is different from incompetence because of the assumption that the employee can do the job properly, but has not. The incompetent employee, unable to do the job properly, should not be subject to discipline.
2. *Unreliability* is failure to attend work as required, such as being late or absent.
3. *Insubordination* is refusal to obey an instruction or deliberate disrespect to someone in a position of authority. It is not to be confused with the use of bad language. Some of the most entertaining cases in industrial tribunals have involved weighty consideration of whether or not colourful language was intended to be insubordinate.
4. *Interfering with the rights of others* covers a range of behaviours that are deemed socially unacceptable. Fighting is clearly identifiable, but intimidation may be more difficult to establish. Less clear as a basis for rules that must be obeyed is the prohibition of practical jokes and pernicious gossip.
5. *Theft* is another clear-cut aspect of behaviour that is unacceptable when it is from another employee. Theft from the organization should be supported by very explicit rules, as stealing company property is regarded by many offenders as one of the perks of the job. How often have you taken home a box of paper clips or a felt tip pen without any thought that you were stealing from the employer?
6. *Safety offences* are those aspects of behaviour that can cause a hazard.

The Institute of Personnel Management conducted a survey (1979) of disciplinary practice in nearly 300 organizations and found that the three main reasons for disciplinary action were: poor timekeeping, unauthorized absence and poor standards of work. So the rules most frequently invoked were those relating to negligence and unreliability. Rules are not, however, just a basis for imposing penalties. Their greatest value is in providing guidelines on what people should do, and the majority will comply. The number of drivers killed on the roads has declined sharply because the great majority of drivers obey the law on wearing seat belts: there are very few prosecutions of drivers for failing to wear a belt.

Ensuring that the rules are kept

Although the majority of car drivers wear seat belts, the majority of dog owners do not have dog licences. It is not sufficient just to have rules, they are only effective if employees conform to their requirements.

1. *Information* is needed so that everyone knows what the rules are and why they should be obeyed. Written particulars may suffice in an industrial tribunal hearing, but most people follow the advice and behaviour of their colleagues in determining how they will behave, so informal methods of communication are just as important as formal statements.
2. *Induction* is a means of making the rules coherent and reinforcing their understanding. The background can be described and the reason for the rule explained, perhaps with examples, so that the new recruit not only knows the rules but understands why they should be obeyed.
3. *Placement* and relocation can both avoid the risk of rules being broken, by placing a new recruit with a working team that has high standards of compliance. If there are the signs of disciplinary problems in the offing, then a quick relocation can put the problem employee in a new situation where offences are less likely.
4. *Training* increases the new recruit's awareness of the rules, improving self-confidence and self-discipline. For established employees there will be new working procedures or new equipment from time to time and again training will reduce the risk of safety offences, negligence or unreliability.
5. *Review* of the rules periodically ensures that they are up-to-date, and also ensures that their observance is a live issue. If, for instance, there is a monthly meeting between management and stewards, it could be appropriate to have a rules review every twelve months. The simple fact that the rules are being discussed will keep up the general level of awareness of what they are.
6. *Penalties* make the framework of organizational justice firmer if there is an understanding of what penalties can be imposed, by whom and for what. It is not feasible or desirable to have a fixed scale, but neither is it wise for penalties to depend on individual managerial whim. This area has been partially codified by the legislation on dismissal, as described in Chapter 22, but the following are some typical forms of penalty:
   (a) *Rebuke*: This is probably used too little by managers nowadays. This is the simple 'Don't do that' or 'Smoking is not allowed in here' or 'If you're late again, you will be in trouble'. This is all that is needed in most situations, as someone has forgotten one of the rules, or had not realized it was to be taken seriously, or was perhaps testing the resolution of the management. Too frequently, managers are reluctant to risk defiance and tend to wait until they have a good case for more serious action rather than deploying their own, there-and-then authority.
   (b) *Caution*: Slightly more serious and formal is the caution, which is then recorded. This is not triggering the procedure for dismissal, it is just making a note of a rule being broken and an offence being pointed out.
   (c) *Warnings*: When the management begin to issue warnings, great care is required as the development of unfair dismissal legislation with its associated code of practice has made the system of warnings an integral part of disciplinary practice which has to be followed if the employer is to succeed in defending a possible claim of unfair

dismissal at tribunal. For the employer to show procedural fairness there should normally be a formal oral warning, or a written warning, specifying the nature of the offence and the likely outcome of the offence being repeated. It should also be made clear that this is the first, formal stage in the procedure. Further misconduct could then warrant a final written warning containing a statement that further repetition would lead to a penalty such as suspension or dismissal. All written warnings should be dated, signed and kept on record for a period agreed by rules known by both sides. Details must be given to the employee and to his or her representative, if desired. The means of appeal against the disciplinary action should also be pointed out.

(d) *Disciplinary transfer or demotion*: This is moving the employee to less attractive work, possibly carrying a lower salary. The seriousness of this is that it is public, as the employee's colleagues know the reason. A form of disciplinary transfer is found on assembly-lines, where there are some jobs that are more attractive and carry higher status than others. A rule-breaker may be 'pushed down the line' until his contempt is purged and he is able to move back up. Demotion is rare and seldom effective because the humiliation is so great. Those demoted usually either leave or carry on (probably because they cannot leave) with considerable resentment and having lost so much confidence that their performance remains inadequate.

(e) *Suspension*: A tactic that has the benefit of being serious and avoids the disadvantage of being long-lasting, like demotion. The employer has a contractual obligation to provide pay, but not to provide work, so it is easy to suspend someone from duty – with pay – either as a punishment or while an alleged offence is being investigated. If the contract of employment permits, it may also be possible to suspend the employee for a short period without pay.

(f) *Fines*: These are little used, because of contractual problems, but the most common is deduction from pay for lateness. Where employee attendance is controlled by time clock, 'quarter-houring' is still often used, so that the person who clocks in between one and fifteen minutes late will have fifteen minutes' pay deducted, those arriving between sixteen and thirty minutes late will have thirty minutes' pay deducted, and so on.

The important general comment about penalties is that they should be appropriate in the circumstances. Where someone is, for instance, persistently late or absent, suspension would be a strange penalty. In many factories the quarter-houring method has been found counter-productive as employees gradually evolve their own, personal version of flexible working hours. That may have many advantages but it fails completely to meet the apparent objective of ensuring that everyone starts work at the same time. Also penalties must be within the law. An employee cannot be demoted or transferred at managerial whim, and fines or unpaid suspension can only be imposed if the contract of employment allows such measures.

7. *Procedural sequence* is essential to the framework of organizational justice. It shall be the clear, unvarying logic of procedure, and be well known and trusted. Procedure makes clear, for example, who does and who does not have the power to dismiss. The dissatisfied employee who is wondering whether or not to turn a complaint into a formal grievance knows who will hear the grievance and where an appeal could be lodged. This security of procedure, where step B always follows step A, is needed by managers as well as by employees, as it provides them with their authority as well as limiting the scope of their actions.

8. *Managerial discipline.* Finally, managers must preserve general respect for the justice framework by their self-discipline in how they work within it. With very good intentions some senior managers maintain an 'open door' policy with the message: 'My door is always open . . . call in any time you feel I can help you.' This has many advantages and is often necessary, but it has danger for matters of discipline and grievance because it encourages people to bypass middle managers. They welcome the opportunity to talk to the organ grinder rather than the monkey. There is also the danger that employees come to see the settlement of their grievances as being dependent on the personal goodwill of an individual rather than on their human and employment rights.

Managers must also be consistent in their handling of discipline and grievance issues. Whatever the rules are, they will be generally supported only as long as they deserve such support. If they are enforced inconsistently they will soon lose any moral authority and depend only on the fear of penalties. Equally, the manager who handles grievances quickly and consistently is well on the way to enjoying the support of a committed group of employees.

The other need for managerial discipline is to test the validity of the discipline assumption. Is it a case for disciplinary action or for some other remedy? There is little purpose in suspending someone for negligence when the real problem is lack of training. Many disciplinary problems disappear under analysis, and it is sensible to carry out the analysis before making a possibly unjustified allegation of indiscipline.

Grievance procedure

The formality of the grievance procedure is often resented by managers, who believe that it introduces unnecessary rigidity into the working relationship: 'I see my people all the time. We work side by side and they can raise with me any issue they want, at any time they want. . . .' The problem is that many people will not raise issues with the immediate superior that could be regarded as contentious, in just the same way that managers, as was mentioned earlier, frequently shirk the rebuke as a form of disciplinary penalty. Formality in procedure provides a framework within which individuals can reasonably air their grievances and avoids the likelihood of managers dodging the issue when it is difficult. It avoids the risk of inconsistent *ad hoc* decisions and the employee knows at the outset that the matter will be heard and where it will be heard. The key features of grievance procedure are fairness, facilities for representation, procedural steps and promptness.

1. *Fairness* is needed not only to be just but also to keep the procedure viable. If employees develop the belief that the procedure is only a sham, then its value will be lost and other means will be sought to deal with grievances. Fairness is best supported by the obvious even-handedness of the ways in which grievances are handled, but it will be greatly enhanced if the appeal stage is either to a joint body or to independent arbitration, as the management is then relinquishing the chance to be judge of its own cause. It is rare for a joint body of management and employee representatives to be the final appeal body, but external arbitration – usually by ACAS – is more widely adopted.

2. *Representation* can be of help to the individual employee who lacks the confidence or experience to take on the management single handedly. A representative, such as a shop steward, has the advantage of having dealt with a range of employee problems and may be able to advise the person with the grievance whether the claim is worth pursuing. There is always the risk that the presence of the representative produces a defensive management attitude affected by a number of other issues on which the manager and shop steward may be at loggerheads, so the managers involved in hearing the grievance have to cast the representative in the correct role for the occasion.

3. *Procedural steps* should be limited to three. There is no value in having more just because there are more levels in the management hierarchy. This will only lengthen the time taken to deal with matters and will soon bring the procedure into disrepute. The reason for advocating three steps is that three types of management activity are involved in settling grievances.

   The first step is the *preliminary*, when the grievance is lodged with the immediate superior of the person with the complaint. In the normal working week most managers will have a variety of queries from members of their departments, some of which could become grievances, depending on the manager's reaction. Mostly the manager will either satisfy the employee or the employee will decide not to pursue the matter. Sometimes, however, a person will want to take the issue further. This is the preliminary step in procedure, but it is a tangible step as the manager has the opportunity to review any decisions made causing the dissatisfaction, possibly enabling the dissatisfied employee to withdraw the grievance.

The hearing is when the complainant has the opportunity to state the grievance to a more senior manager, who is able to take a broader view of the matter than the immediate superior and who may be able both to see the issue more dispassionately and to perceive solutions that the more limited perspective of the immediate superior obscured. It is important for the management that the hearing should finalize the matter whenever possible, so that recourse to appeal is not automatic. The hearing should not come to be seen by the employees as no more than an irritating milestone on the way to the real decision-makers. This is why procedural steps should be limited to three.

If there is an *appeal*, this will usually be to a designated more senior manager, and the outcome will be either a confirmation or modification of the decision at the hearing.

4. *Promptness* is needed to avoid the bitterness and frustration that can come from delay. When an employee 'goes into procedure', it is like pulling the communication cord in the train. The action is not taken lightly and it is in anticipation of a swift resolution. Furthermore, the manager whose decision is being questioned will have a difficult time until the matter is resolved. The most familiar device to speed things up is to incorporate time limits between the steps, specifying that the hearing should take place no later than, say, four working days after the preliminary notice and that the appeal should be no more than five working days after the hearing. This gives time for reflection and initiative by the manager or the complainant between the stages, but does not leave time for the matter to be forgotten.

Where the organization has a collective disputes procedure as well as one for individual grievances, there needs to be an explicit link between the two so that individual matters can be pursued with collective support if there is not a satisfactory outcome. The 1972 Industrial Relations Code of Practice contains suggestions about handling individual grievances, which are shown in Figure 30.3. An outline grievance procedure is in Figure 30.4.

Disciplinary procedure

Procedures for discipline are very similar to those for grievance and depend equally on fairness, promptness and representation. There are some additional features.

Extracts from the *Industrial Relations Codes of Practice* (HMSO 1972)

All employees have a right to seek redress for grievances relating to their employment. Each employee must be told how he can do so.

Management should establish, with employee representatives or trade unions concerned, arrangements under which individual employees can raise grievances and have them settled fairly and promptly. There should be a formal procedure, except in very small establishments where there is close personal contact between the employer and his employees.

Individual grievances and collective disputes are often dealt with through the same procedure. Where there are separate procedures they should be linked so that an issue can, if necessary, pass from one to the other, since a grievance may develop into a dispute.

The aim of the procedure should be to settle the grievance fairly and as near as possible to the point of origin. It should be simple and rapid in operation.

The procedure should be in writing and provide that:

(a) the grievance should normally be discussed first between the employee and his immediate superior;

(b) the employee should be accompanied at the next stage of the discussion with management by his employee representative if he so wishes;

(c) there should be a right of appeal.

Figure 30.3   *Individual grievance procedures*

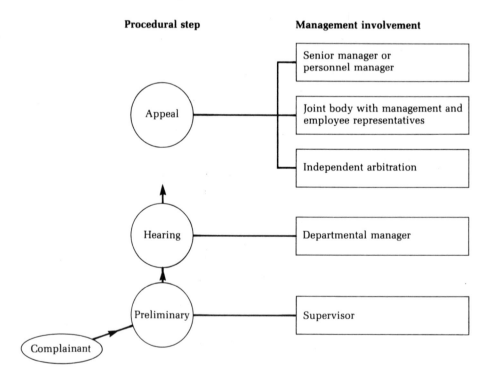

Figure 30.4   *Outline grievance procedures*

Authorization of penalties

The law requires that managers should not normally have the power to dismiss their immediate subordinates without reference to more senior managers. Whatever tangible penalties are to be imposed, they should only be imposed by people who have that specific authority delegated to them. Usually this means that the more serious penalties can only be imposed by more senior people, but there are many organizations where such decisions are delegated to the personnel department.

Investigation

The procedure should also ensure that disciplinary action is not taken until it has been established that an offence has been committed that justifies the action. The possibility of suspension on full pay is one way of allowing time for investigation of dubious allegations, though the stigma attached to this should not be forgotten.

Information and explanation

If there is the possibility of disciplinary action, the person to be disciplined should be told of the complaint, so that an explanation can be made, or the matter denied, before any penalties are decided. If an employee is to be penalized, then the reasons for the decision should be explained to make sure that cause and effect are appreciated. The purpose of penalties is to prevent a recurrence.

The Advisory Conciliation and Arbitration Service has produced a code of practice for disciplinary practice and procedures, extracts of which appear in Figure 30.5. An outline disciplinary procedure is in Figure 30.6.

Disputes

Procedures for the avoidance of disputes are mainly drawn up in national negotiations between employers' associations and trade unions or between single employers and unions. Disputes can arise for a wide range of reasons, but their essence is that they are *collective*: employees are acting in concert, and nearly always using union machinery, to persuade the management to alter a decision. Sometimes the grievance of an individual can escalate into a collective dispute if employees together feel that a matter of principle is at stake. Disciplinary penalties, especially dismissals, can also become matters for collective

Extracts from *Disciplinary Practice and Procedures in Employment* (ACAS 1977)

Disciplinary procedures should:

(a) Be in writing.
(b) Specify to whom they apply.
(c) Provide for matters to be dealt with quickly.
(d) Indicate the disciplinary actions which may be taken.
(e) Specify the levels of management which have the authority to take the various forms of disciplinary action, ensuring that immediate superiors do not normally have the power to dismiss without reference to senior management.
(f) Provide for individuals to be informed of the complaints against them and to be given an opportunity to state their case before decisions are reached.
(g) Give individuals the right to be accompanied by a trade union representative or by a fellow employee of their choice.
(h) Ensure that, except for gross misconduct, no employees are dismissed for a first breach of discipline.
(i) Ensure that disciplinary action is not taken until the case has been carefully investigated.
(j) Ensure that individuals are given an explanation for any penalty imposed.
(k) Provide a right of appeal and specify the procedure to be followed.

Figure 30.5 *Disciplinary procedures*

employee action, when the dismissal is regarded as unfair or victimization.

There are usually more steps in a procedure for collective dispute than for individual grievances and provisions to preclude strikes, lock-outs or other forms of industrial action before procedure is exhausted.

The general issue of dealing with discipline must also take account of the legal aspects of dismissal, as was discussed in Chapter 19, and the operation of tribunals, as set out in the next chapter.

Are grievance and discipline processes equitable?

For these processes to work they must command support, and they will only command support if they are seen as equitable, truly just and fair. At first it would seem that it is concern for the individual employee that is paramount, but the individual cannot be isolated from the rest of the workforce. Fairness should therefore be linked to the interests that all workers have in common in the organization, and to the managers who must also perceive the system as equitable if they are to abide by its outcomes.

Procedures have a potential to be fair in that they are certain. The conduct of industrial relations becomes less haphazard and irrational; people 'know where they stand'. The existence of a rule cannot be denied and opportunities for one party to manipulate and change a rule are reduced. Procedures also have the advantage that they can be communicated. The process of formalizing a procedure that previously existed only in custom and practice clarifies the

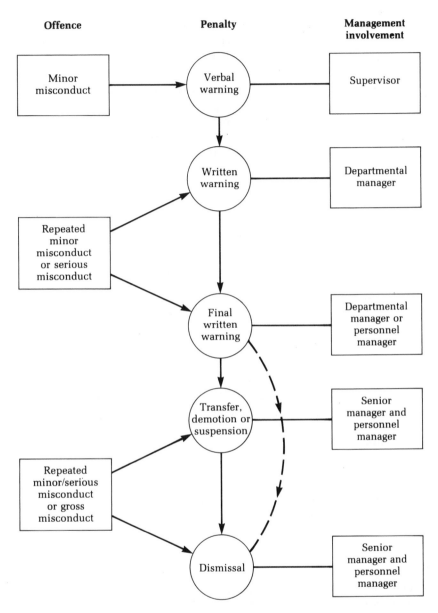

Figure 30.6 *Outline disciplinary procedure*

ambiguities and inconsistencies within it and compels each party to recognize the role and responsibility of the other. By providing pre-established avenues for responses to various contingencies there is the chance that the response will be less random and so more fair. The impersonal nature of procedures offers the possibility of removing hostility from the workplace, since an artificial social situation is created in which the ritual displays of aggression towards management are not seen as personal attacks on managers.

The achievement of equity may not match the potential. Procedures cannot, for instance, impart equitability into situations that are basically unfair. Thus attempting to cope with an anomalous pay system through grievance procedure may be alleviating symptoms rather than treating causes. It is also impossible to overcome accepted norms of inequity in a plant, such as greater punctuality being required of manual employees than of white-collar employees.

A further feature of procedural equity is its degree of similarity to the judicial process. All adopt certain legalistic mechanisms, like the right of individuals to be represented and to hear the case against them, but some aspects of legalism, such as burdens of proof and strict adherence to precedent, may cause the application of standard remedies rather than the consideration of individual circumstances.

Review topic 30.3

The 'red-hot stove' rule of discipline offers the touching of a red hot stove as an analogy for effective disciplinary action:

1. The burn is immediate. There is no question of cause and effect.
2. You had warning. If the stove was red-hot, you knew what would happen if you touched it.
3. The discipline is consistent. Everyone who touches the stove is burned.
4. The discipline is impersonal. A person is burned not because of who he is, but because he touched the stove.

Think of an attempt at disciplinary action that went wrong. Which of the features of the red-hot stove rule were missing?

Notions of fairness are not 'givens' of the situation; they are socially constructed and there will never be more than a degree of consensus on what constitutes fairness. Despite this, the procedural approach can exploit standards of certainty and consistency which are widely accepted as elements of justice. The extent to which a procedure can do this will depend on the suitability of its structure to plant circumstances, the commitment of those who operate it and the way that it reconciles legalistic and bargaining elements.

Summary propositions

30.1 Grievance and discipline handling are two areas of personnel work that few other people want to take over and provide personnel managers with some of their most significant contributions to organizational effectiveness.

30.2 Discipline can be understood as being either managerial, team or self-discipline, and they are connected hierarchically.

30.3 Dissatisfaction, complaint and grievance is another hierarchy. Unresolved employee dissatisfaction can lead to the loss of potentially valuable employees. In extreme cases it can lead to industrial action.

30.4 Grievance and disciplinary processes both require a framework of organizational justice.

References

ACAS (1977), *Disciplinary Practice and Procedures in Employment*, London: ACAS.

ACAS (1985), *Disciplinary and Other Procedures in Employment (Draft Code of Practice)*, London: ACAS.

Department of Employment (1973), *In Working Order*, London: HMSO.

Industrial Relations Code of Practice (1972), London: HMSO.

Institute of Personnel Management (1979), *Disciplinary Procedures and Practice*, London: Institute of Personnel Management.

Pigors, P. and Myers, C. S. (1977), *Personnel Administration* (8th edition), Maidenhead: McGraw-Hill.

Roethlisberger, F. J. and Dickson, W. J. (1939), *Management and the Worker*, Cambridge, Mass.: Harvard University Press.

31

Preparing for tribunal

For most personnel managers, dealing with tribunal matters is an occasional, but important, activity. Evans *et al.* (1985, p. 41) found that 30 per cent of their respondents had had some experience with industrial tribunals. Over 10 per cent of our questionnaire respondents had modified their procedures as a result of a complaint made to a tribunal, and 55 per cent of them would be the person to represent their organization at a tribunal hearing. Although 60 per cent of all complaints are settled by conciliation officers, as well as an unknown proportion by independent resolution between the employer and the ex-employee, although two-thirds of complaints reaching tribunal are unsuccessful, and although successful claimants rarely receive more than £1,500 in settlement, tribunal hearings remain important to management. The financial cost to the employer may be substantial and the opprobrium of being adjudged by a tribunal as in some way unfair to employees could be damaging to recruitment and morale.

Personnel managers, therefore, always need to regard the possibility of a tribunal appearance as one of the yardsticks of personnel management effectiveness. They need first to make sure that such appearances will not occur because of any laxity in personnel practice or inadequacy in procedure. Secondly, they have to handle everything to do with a hearing, or a possible hearing, when it occurs.

Personnel managers need also to consider the implications for the ex-employee in bringing an unsuccessful claim to a tribunal hearing.

Tribunals and their scope

Industrial tribunals were first established by the 1964 Industrial Training Act and now have a wide range of matters within their jurisdiction. Each tribunal consists of a legally qualified chairman who sits with two lay members.

> The presence of lay members, it was hoped, would help maintain the desired informality, make tribunal decisions more acceptable to employers and workers affected by them and, above all, enable the tribunals to bring both legal and industrial or commercial expertise and experience to bear on deciding employment cases. (Dickens 1983, p. 28)

Lay members are usually trade union officials or personnel specialists and are nominated by one 'side' of industry or the other, but they are not supposed to act as representatives of the interests nominating them. Their purpose is to serve only the interests of justice, and in this they act as equals with the chairman, not as advisers: 'Those who chair tribunals have no doubt that lay members are very influential in decision-making, a view shared, slightly less emphatically, by the lay members themselves. (Dickens 1983, p. 31).

Personnel managers need to appreciate that tribunal proceedings are run by people concerned with justice and the procedures of the law, and one of them will be legally qualified, but the others will have experience of industrial matters. Even though the lay representation is to ensure that the realities of the workplace are not overlooked, the guidance for the tribunal's decision will be the wording of the statute on the basis of which the complaint has been laid, rather than finding a viable compromise for the place of work.

The scope of tribunals is greater than many people realize. The main workload is dealing with complaints of unfair dismissal (63 per cent), but they also deal with unequal pay (3.3 per cent), discrimination (7.2 per cent), and many of the other issues in the Employment Protection Consolidation Act 1978 and the Employment Acts 1980 and 1982 (such as rights in union membership and non-membership, particulars of terms and conditions of employment, maternity rights, guarantee payments, time off for public duties, redundancy and employer insolvency). Where industrial training boards survive, employers can appeal to a tribunal about their levy assessment, as they can against an improvement or prohibition notice from a health and safety inspector under the Health and Safety at Work Act 1974. Employees can use a tribunal for a complaint that an employer is not allowing equal access for men and women to an occupational pension scheme, and a recognized independent trade union can complain of not being consulted by an employer intending to contract out of the State Earnings Related Pension Scheme (SERPS). An area where tribunals do *not* have jurisdiction is in claims for damages for breach of contract of employment through alleged wrongful dismissal.

Basic procedure

Tribunal procedure is governed by the Industrial Tribunals (Rules of Procedure) Regulations 1985 (Sl 1985, no. 16).

The originating application

First, the complainant has to make an originating application to the Secretary of the Tribunals. This has to be in writing, specifying the name and address of the applicant, the name of the employer against whom relief is sought and the grounds on which the relief is sought.

Normally, this application is made on form IT1, but there is no procedural requirement for this, providing that the correct information is provided. The application is lodged with the Secretary at the Central Office of the Industrial Tribunals (COIT) in London or Glasgow. After vetting to ensure that the applicant is entitled to claim (for example, not over the age of retirement), the COIT will send a copy on to the appropriate regional office. The employer against whom the complaint is made will receive a leaflet explaining procedure, a copy of the IT1, a form IT2 and a form IT3.

IT2 is a formal notification of the claim, stating that the employer (now known as the respondent) is required to enter an appearance within fourteen days of receiving the IT2.

IT3 is the notice of appearance, a form to be filled in by the employer and returned to the tribunal.

The employer's response

It is necessary to study the IT1 and the IT2 carefully, as there may be points of fact that disqualify the applicant from making a claim. An obvious example is the ex-employee claiming unfair dismissal who has entered dates of employment that are incorrect.

The next step for the employer is to decide whether or not to resist the claim. This will involve not only whether or not the employer accepts the merits of the case, but also whether it is worth the time and expense of resisting it. It has been estimated that it costs an employer anything between £1,000 and £15,000 to *win* a case.

It may be that extra time is needed to examine the matters before that decision is made. In that case a request for further time should be made to the tribunal office. Eventually, however, the IT3 must be returned, otherwise the employer cannot take any further part in the proceedings.

Further and better particulars

If the substance of the case against the company is not clear from the IT1, or if more information from the applicant is required, this can be sought providing that they are: 'further particulars of the grounds on which he or it relies and of any facts or contentions relevant thereto (Industrial Tribunals Regulations 1985, sect. 4).

It is not permitted to ask for the evidence, only for more particulars of the grounds. This is an important distinction, which needs to be appreciated as the applicant does not have to produce any evidence until requested by the tribunal at a public hearing. The request for further and better particulars should be sent directly to the complainant, with a copy to the tribunal office. If the information is not voluntarily supplied to the respondent in reasonable time, the respondent can then ask the tribunal to make an order requiring the applicant to provide the information.

It is also possible to require copies of documents from the complainant if they are necessary for the respondent's case. In practice, however, this request is much more likely to come from the complainant, asking for copies of company documents, such as written warnings and company rules, which the employer is then obliged to supply.

Pre-hearing assessments

> A tribunal may at any time before the hearing . . . consider, by way of a pre-hearing assessment, the contents of the originating application and entry of appearance, any representations in writing which have been submitted and any oral argument advanced by or on behalf of a party. (Industrial Tribunals Regulations 1985, sect. 6).

This is a means of saving time and trouble in proceeding with a claim that lacks substance. It is possible to ask the tribunal office for a pre-hearing assessment (PHA), and this will normally be granted by the chairman, providing that the reasons advanced are persuasive. The applicant or the COIT can also initiate a pre-hearing assessment.

> Of the 7,606 PHAs to October 1982, 2,505 were withdrawn (8 per cent) or settled (21 per cent) after the notice but before the actual assessment was held. The notice itself, therefore, seems to have the effect of encouraging a determination on average of some 29 per cent of the cases where a PHA was ordered. (Angel 1984, p. 82).

The average time taken by a pre-hearing assessment is less than thirty minutes, and the members of the tribunal may decide to issue a warning that costs will be considered if either party proceeds. They will only do this if they believe that the case of either side lacks merit. It does not prevent the case proceeding, but discourages the majority of those that appear at an early stage to be without merit.

The hearing

If a matter is to proceed to a hearing, the tribunal office will give fourteen days' notice to both parties, although either party could ask for an adjournment to a more convenient date if there are reasonable grounds for such an application.

There is also the possibility of a preliminary hearing to determine whether or not the tribunal is qualified to deal with the matter. This is different from a pre-hearing assessment as it is not dealing with the merits of the case, but with the question of whether or not the tribunal has jurisdiction. An example could be where a complainant claiming unfair dismissal had a contract of employment for less than sixteen hours a week and was therefore not covered by unfair dismissal protection. Either party can apply for a preliminary hearing and the decision of the tribunal can end the case there and then. Such a peremptory conclusion cannot be guaranteed by a pre-hearing assessment.

Although it is intended that tribunal proceedings should be informal, most lay people visiting a tribunal for the first time find the procedure forbiddingly legalistic. Individual chairmen have the discretion to conduct proceedings in the way they regard as most appropriate in the circumstances but the usual routine is as set out in Figure 31.1. This imposes a sequence of events that is familiar and comfortable for those accustomed to court proceedings, but that is uncomfortable for other people who are inhibited by being restrained from interrupting or debating the rights and wrongs of issues as they are raised.

The purpose of the procedure is to help the members of the tribunal to understand the matters involved and to marshal the data for their eventual judgment in a way that they find logical and constructive.

The decision

Normally the decision of the tribunal will be announced by the tribunal chairman after the tribunal members have retired and considered the evidence. Sometimes the deliberations may require further consideration and in complex matters there may be a *reserved decision*, where the decision is not made until after those attending have dispersed and applicant and respondent are informed by post. Where the decision is announced at the conclusion of the hearing, the parties are still advised by post of the decision and the grounds on which it was based.

If the applicant is successful the tribunal will order one of a range of remedies specified in the relevant statutes. There is a summary of these in Angel (1984, pp. 195–212).

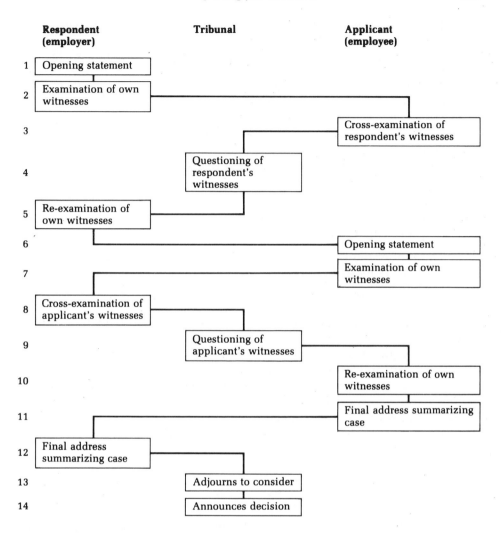

Figure 31.1 *Normal procedure for tribunal hearing*

Review and appeal

The decision of the tribunal can be challenged by asking for a review or by making an appeal. Either party can ask for a review at the time the decision is announced or by writing within fourteen days of receiving the postal notification of the decision, but the request must be accompanied by a statement of reasons for believing that the decision was not well founded. The grounds on which a review can be considered are:

The decision was wrongly made as a result of an error on the part of the tribunal staff; or

A party did not receive notice of the proceedings leading to the decision; or

The decision was made in the absence of a party or person entitled to be heard; or

New evidence has become available since the making of the decision provided that its existence could not have been reasonably known of or foreseen; or

The interests of justice require such a review.
(Industrial Tribunals Regulations 1985, sect. 10(1))

Review topic 31.1

Think of examples of each of the five grounds on which a review might be requested.

On review a tribunal is empowered to order a re-hearing or to change its decision.

An appeal always lies to a higher body, the Employment Appeals Tribunal or the High Court, and must be on matters of law rather than on matters of fact. An appeal cannot be used simply as a means of trying to reach a different group of people in the hope of a more sympathetic hearing. Determining the difference between matters of fact and matters of law is not a straightforward decision for a layman and it is probable that you would seek legal advice before lodging an appeal.

Legal representation

Although tribunals are intended to be informal, employers elect to have representation in approximately half of all the cases that are heard. Many people believe that it is this tendency to choose legal representation that has led to the perceived preoccupation with legalism for which tribunal proceedings are often criticized. There is no limitation to the right of audience, so a party in a tribunal hearing can be represented by: 'counsel or by a solicitor or by a representative of a trade union or an employers' association or by any other person whom he desires to represent him (Industrial Tribunals Regulations 1985, sect. 7 (6)).

It does not seem necessary for employers to be legally represented so often, although there may be instances where the matter involves difficult evidence and some doubt as to what can be properly construed as evidence, or where the interpretation of the law is difficult. In most instances, however, the only difficulty presented to the personnel manager is the tribunal procedure for the hearing itself. As has already been said, this can be inhibiting for those who are not familiar with it. The sequence set out in Figure 31.1 is similar to that in a magistrates' court, with the advocates bearing the responsibility for the conduct of the cases, while the members of the bench listen and intervene rarely. According to Angel (1984 op. cit., p. 49) there is a tendency for practice to change in some tribunals, with the chairman taking on the main responsibility for the conduct of the case, ensuring that all relevant matters are aired and properly presented. This makes it less necessary for either party to be legally represented.

Preparing the case

In preparing for a hearing it is necessary to be clear about the law on the matter which is the subject of the complaint. The easiest source of information is in the free explanatory leaflets, which are available from the Department of Employment. Specific information is also available from the Commission for Racial Equality and the Equal Opportunities Commission, or from the Health and Safety Executive. There are also books, such as Lewis (1983) or Selwyn (1985), which provide detailed guidance both on the statutes and the developing cases and judgments.

It is also vital to be clear about the evidence. Did the alleged action take place at the time and in the manner alleged? Was procedure properly followed? Are the necessary documents available? If witnesses are needed, are they willing and able to attend the tribunal?

Paynter makes the point that the collection and organization of documentary evidence can be invaluable and will carry more weight than oral evidence:

> Put the exhibits into one bundle using a single binding. Have three available for the tribunal, one for use by witnesses, one (or two) for your opponent, and sufficient for your own purposes. Number the pages consecutively. The order is not of vital importance, but aim to put them in the same order as you will use them, which is generally chronological order. (Paynter 1985, p. 36).

Presentation of the case

Throughout presentation the most useful material will be the documents already prepared. If these are distributed to the tribunal members and to the applicant, it is then possible to refer tribunal members to particular documents and features of those documents at any time in the development of the case.

Opening statement

If invited by the chairman to introduce the case, the respondent's introduction should be brief, indicating what are thought to be the main legal points and the general background. It can also be helpful to explain how many witnesses there are to be called upon and what their evidence will be about, as well as the documents which have been brought along.

Examination of own witnesses

The case is opened by examining the witnesses on the respondent's side. Once the witness has been introduced by the respondent, the clerk will call that person to the stand and administer the oath. The evidence of the witness is then produced; the answers constitute evidence. The questions need to be precise and short, so that what the witness says is relevant to the way in which the respondent develops the story. Witnesses who ramble or 'want to put their side of the story' can be a nuisance, as they may be much more concerned about other aspects of an incident than that which the tribunal is considering.

Rules are not as precise as in other courts so hearsay evidence is often allowed and some leading questions are permitted, although one must always be careful not to put words into the mouths of witnesses ('I think you would agree that Mr X was unpopular with all his colleagues and you were all very glad when he was dismissed?').

Some of the evidence prepared may be readily admitted as accurate by the respondent, so a written statement of it could be read to the tribunal instead of calling the witness to give verbal evidence, but tribunals will not normally allow witnesses to give evidence by reading from a prepared statement. Although it might be more convenient for a witness who is not used to speaking in public, it runs counter to the legal precept that evidence must be that which the witness can personally recall unaided.

After each witness has given evidence the respondent has the right to cross-examine them on what they have said, and the members of the tribunal may also ask questions. Before they leave the stand the respondent might want to put further questions to them to clarify matters which have been raised in cross-examination.

Cross-examination of applicant's witnesses

Although the applicant's witnesses may well be hostile towards the respondent, they are under oath to tell the truth and the respondent is entitled to ask questions relevant to the case, provided that only factual matters are brought up. It is not a debate; the chance to comment on what the witness has said comes later.

The tribunal wants to ascertain facts, and 95 per cent of the basic facts will probably not be in dispute, only the interpretation or emphasis to be put on them. It is usually not helpful to try to show up a witness as a liar by means of clever or fierce cross-examination. (Paynter 1985, p. 37)

Review topic 31.2

Practise cross-examination by 'cross-examining' a friend or relative on some matter of which you both have knowledge, and with the collaboration of another friend who knows nothing of the matter. Remember that you are producing 'evidence' for a third party. Make your questions brief and concise, without leading. Then ask the other friend to recount the matter to you. How accurate is this version?

Final address

After the evidence has been heard from both sides, there are summary statements from both advocates. The personnel manager representing the organization against which the complaint has been laid will speak last. There is now the opportunity to summarize the evidence which challenges the application and to present the legal reasons why the matter should be resolved in favour of the respondent.

The amateur advocate should remember that the tribunal will only need to have pointed out that which is salient and in contention, especially where there is a conflict of evidence.

The tribunal award

The decision of the tribunal will be an award, as mentioned earlier in this chapter. Figure 31.2 summarizes the range of options available to a tribunal in cases of unfair dismissal.

Of the 2,254 unfair dismissal claims upheld by tribunals during 1984, 1,244 were settled by compensation, 46 by reinstatement and 32 by re-engagement. In 132 cases there was a redundancy payment and in 800 cases the remedy was left to the parties (Department of Employment 1986, p. 49). The average compensation was £1,345. A basic award only was made in 90 cases and the maximum compensatory award was made in 16 (*Ibid.*, p. 50).

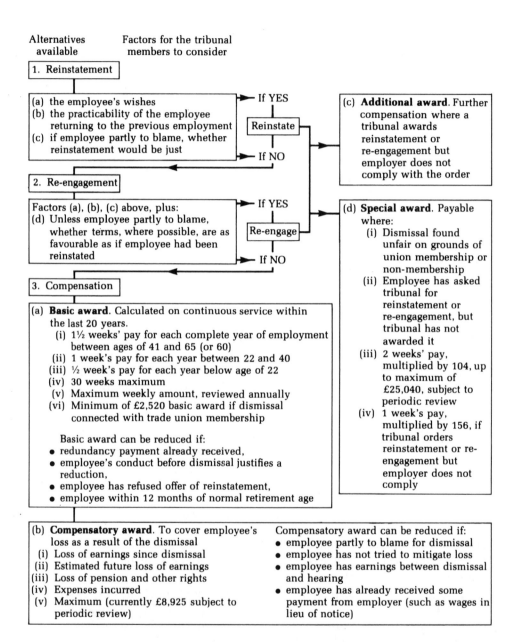

Figure 31.2 *Remedies available to a tribunal after finding a claimant to have been unfairly dismissed*

Summary propositions

31.1 Many personnel managers have experience of tribunal proceedings. This is both a way in which the effectiveness of personnel management can be assessed and one of the areas of specialized personnel management expertise.

31.2 Although the scope of industrial tribunals is wide, 90 per cent of their cases deal with alleged unfair dismissal, unequal pay or discrimination.

31.3 The basic procedure of tribunals is: originating application, employer's response, hearing and decision. Other possible features are further and better particulars, pre-hearing assessment, review and appeal.

31.4 Employers are legally represented in approximately half of the cases coming to tribunal, but often the personnel manager could handle the case without such assistance.

31.5 The tribunal will make their decision on the basis of evidence, which may be in documents produced for their scrutiny or in answer to questions put by advocates to witnesses.

References

Angel, J. (1984), *Industrial Tribunals: Preparing and presenting your case*, Croydon: Tolley.

Department of Employment. (1986), 'Work of the industrial tribunals and the Employment Appeal Tribunal in 1984', *Employment Gazette*, February. London: HMSO.

Dickens, L. (1983), 'Do lay members influence tribunal decisions?' *Personnel Management*, November.

Evans, S., Goodman, J. and Hargreaves, L. (1985), *Unfair Dismissal Law and Employment Practice*, Department of Employment Research paper no. 53, London: HMSO.

Industrial Tribunals (Rules of Procedure) Regulations 1985 (SI 1985, no. 16), London: HMSO.

Janner, G. (1988), 'Dealing with industrial tribunals', In B. Livy (ed.), *Corporate Personnel Management*, London: Pitman.

Lewis, D. (1983), *Essentials of Employment Law*, London: Institute of Personnel Management.

Paynter, G. (1985), 'How to tackle a tribunal case', *Personnel Management*, February.

Selwyn, N. (1985), *Employment Law* (5th edition), London: Butterworths.

Part
VI

Pay

32

Payment administration

A strange thing about payment is that managers seem to shy away from actually using the word. We hear about 'compensation', 'reward' or 'remuneration', yet the idea of *compensation* is making amends for something that has caused loss or injury. Do we want to suggest that work necessarily causes loss or injury? *Reward* suggests a special payment for a special act. Much current management thinking on pay issues is to induce more special effort by employees, but the bulk of the pay bargain for an individual is not affected by performance. *Remuneration* is a more straightforward word which means exactly the same as payment but has five more letters and is misspelt (as renumeration) more often than most words in the personnel manager's lexicon. *Payment* seems to us a good, solid, clear word to encompass all that is involved from basic rates to pensions.

Fairness and performance in payment

One basis for deciding who should be paid what is an assessment of fairness – 'a fair day's pay for a fair day's work'. The employer believes that the employee should be paid a fair amount in relation to the skill and effort that has to be exercised, and employees feel there is a reasonable level of payment that can be expected for the contribution made. When both sets of expectations can be satisfied, then we have in place a further dimension of the employment contract described in the first chapter.

The axiom of a fair day's pay for a fair day's work is not necessarily either fair or just. Karl Marx described it as a conservative motto and it undoubtedly impedes change in pay arrangements. What is seen as fair is putting something back to what it used to be: the restoration of a differential or the rectification of an anomaly. Change is almost defined as unfair because it undermines the status quo and reduces standards. By inhibiting change, the fairness principle also impedes restructuring.

Another criticism is that any differences in relative payment are related to the work undertaken, yet that is intrinsically no more logical than the quite different concept of 'from each according to his ability: to each according to his needs'.

Despite these criticisms of the fairness principle, it remains the most useful basis for any discussion of payment because it is the notion used by both employers and employees in considering the acceptability of payment arrangements, actual or proposed, although the other principle of supply and demand is always present. 'Supply and demand have long been held to be at the heart of the wage determination process, at least in the opinion of economists. The supply of manpower should be equated with the organization demand if performance is to be underpinned' (Smith 1983, p. 26). Supply and demand remains only a partial explanation of pay determination, even in the more sophisticated formulas of marginal productivity theory or wages fund theory. Whatever limited validity these economists' explanations may have in explaining national labour market behaviour, the mutual assessment of what is fair remains the most useful starting point for the personnel manager assessing what is to be done within the organization and for individual employees deciding the acceptability of their level of payment. A group of employees strongly persuaded that they are underpaid will not change their minds if it is explained to them that: 'wages had to be paid out of a fund from the accummulated revenues deriving from past production, and the size of fund, and therefore wages, were determined by the ratio of supply to amounts of revenue set aside for labour' (*ibid.*, p. 29).

The other basis for deciding relative payment is performance, with above-average performance producing above-average pay and above-average increases in pay. This has certainly been very popular in the late 1980s for payment arrangements related to management posts, and a development of the earlier notion of management by objectives: 'The trend towards performance, rather than merit, assessment is a trend towards rewarding output rather than input. It stems from the concept of performance management – a much wider development than just a change in payment practices' (Fowler 1988).

Neither fairness nor performance are easy principles to implement. Judgements of fairness are typically supported by pay systems based on incremental scales and job evaluation, yet the most widespread reason for industrial action is dissatisfaction with relative pay. Performance-related payment arrangements are only relatively easy to run when everyone is doing better. The difficulty of below-average pay for below-average performers is indicated by the fact that schemes typically deliver enhanced pay even when performance by objective criteria like company profitability declines. In press comment on accelerating pay levels for company directors in 1990, it was pointed out that directors of

Midland Bank had all enjoyed substantial increases at a time when the bank was reporting record losses.

Employee objectives for the contract for payment

Those who are paid, and those who administer payment schemes, have objectives for the payment contract which differ according to whether one is the recipient or the administrator of the payments. The contract for payment will be satisfactory in so far as it meets the objectives of the parties. Therefore we consider the range of objectives, starting with employees.

First objective: purchasing power

The absolute level of weekly or monthly earnings determines the standard of living of the recipient, and will therefore be the most important consideration for most employees. How much can I buy? Employees are rarely satisfied about their purchasing power, and the annual pay adjustment will do little more than reduce dissatisfaction. The two main reasons for this are inflation and rising expectations.

Second objective: felt-fair

We have already discussed the notion of fairness in payment. Here we have the term 'felt-fair', which was devised by Elliott Jaques (1962), who averred that every employee had a strong feeling about the level of payment that was fair for the job. Here we move away from the absolute level of earnings to the first of a series of aspects of relative income. In most cases this will be a very rough personalized evaluation of what is seen as appropriate.

The employee who feels underpaid is likely to demonstrate the conventional symptoms of withdrawal from the job: looking for another, carelessness, disgruntlement, lateness, absence, and the like. Those who feel they are overpaid (as some do) may simply feel dishonest, or may seek to justify their existence in some way, like trying to look busy, that is not necessarily productive.

Third objective: rights

A different aspect of relative income is that concerned with the rights of the employee to a particular share of the company's profits or the nation's wealth. The employee is here thinking about whether the division of earnings is providing fair shares of the Gross National Product. 'To each according to his needs' is overlaid on 'a fair day's pay . . .' This is a strong feature of most trade union arguments and part of the general preoccupation with the rights of the individual. Mainly this is the longstanding debate about who should enjoy the fruits of labour.

Fourth objective: relativities

'How much do I (or we) get relative to . . . group X?' This is a version of the 'felt-fair' argument. It is not the question of whether the employee feels the remuneration to be reasonable in relation to the job done, but in relation to the jobs other people do.

There are many potential comparators, and the basis of comparison can alter. The Pay Board (1974) pointed out three. First is the definition of pay. Is it basic rates or is it earnings? Over how long is the pay compared? Many groups have a level of payment that varies from one time of the year to another. Second is the method of measuring the changes: absolute amount of money or percentage. £5 is 10 per cent of £50 but 5 per cent of £100. Third is the choice of pay dates. Most groups receive annual adjustments to their pay, but not at the same time and the period between settlements can be crucial to perceived relativities.

Fifth objective: recognition

Most people have an objective for their payment arrangements of their personal contribution being recognized. This is partly seeking reassurance, but is also a way in which people can mould their behaviour and their career thinking to produce progress and satisfaction. It is doubtful if financial recognition has a significant and sustained impact on performance, but providing a range of other forms of recognition while the pay packet is transmitting a different message is certainly counter-productive.

Sixth objective: composition

How is the pay package made up? The growing complexity and sophistication of payment arrangements raises all sorts of questions about pay composition. Is £200 pay for 60 hours' work better than £140 for 40 hours' work? The arithmetical answer that the rate per hour for the 40-hour arrangement is marginally better than for 60 hours is only part of the answer. The other aspects will relate to the individuals, their circumstances and the conventions of their working group and reference groups. Another question about composition might be: Is £140 per week plus a pension better than £160 per week without? Such questions do not produce universally applicable answers because they can be quantified to such a limited extent, but some kernels of conventional wisdom can be suggested as generalizations:

1. Younger employees are more interested in high direct earnings at the expense of indirect benefits, like pensions, which will be of more interest to older employees.
2. Incentive payment arrangements are likely to interest employees who either see a reliable prospect of enhancing earnings through the ability to control their own activities, or who see the incentive scheme as an opportunity to wrest control of their personal activities (which provide little intrinsic satisfaction) away from management by regulating their earnings.
3. Married women are seldom interested in payment arrangements that depend on overtime.
4. Overtime is used by many men to produce an acceptable level of purchasing power, particularly among the lower-paid.
5. Pensions and sickness payment arrangements beyond statutory minima are a *sine qua non* of white-collar employment, and are of growing importance in manual employment.

Employer objectives for the contract for payment

In looking at the other side of the picture, we consider the range of objectives in the thinking of employers, or those representing an employer interest *vis-à-vis* the employee.

First objective: prestige

There is a comfortable and understandable conviction among managers that it is 'a good thing' to be a good payer. This seems partly to be simple pride at doing better than others, but also there is sometimes a feeling that such a policy eliminates a variable from the contractual relationship. In conversation with one of the authors a chief executive expressed it this way:

> I want to find out the highest rates of pay, job-for-job, within a fifty-mile radius of my office. Then I will make sure that all my boys are paid 20 per cent over that. Then I know where I am with them as I have taken money out of the equation. If they want to quit they can't hide the real reason by saying they're going elsewhere for more cash: they can't get it. Furthermore, if I do have to fill a job I know that we won't lose a good guy because of the money not being right.

Whether high pay rates succeed in getting someone the reputation of being a good employer is difficult to see. What seems much more likely is that the low-paying employer will have the reputation of being a poor employer.

Second objective: competition

More rational is the objective of paying rates that are sufficiently competitive to sustain the employment of the right numbers of appropriately qualified and experienced employees to staff the organization. A distinction is drawn here between competition thinking and prestige thinking, as the former is more designed to get a good fit on one of the employment contract dimensions rather than simply overwhelm it. It permits consideration of questions such as: How selective do we need to be for this range of jobs? And: How can we avoid over-paying people and inhibiting them from moving on? Every employer has this sort of objective, even if only in relation to a few key posts in the organization.

Third objective: control

There may be ways of organizing the pay packet that will facilitate control of operations and potentially save money. The conventional approach to this for many years was the use of piecework or similar incentives, but this became difficult due to the unwillingness of most employees to see their payment fluctuate wildly at the employer's behest. Theoretically, overtime is a method of employer control of output through making available or withholding additional payment prospects. In practice, however, employees use overtime for control more extensively than employers. Gradually, other ways in which employers could control their payroll costs are being eliminated or made more difficult by legislation. Redundancy, short-term lay-off and dismissal are all now more expensive, and women are less readily seen as a reservoir of inexpensive, temporary labour.

Fourth objective: motivation and performance

There is a widespread conviction about the motivational effect of payment that rests on oversimplistic assumptions about amounts and methods of payment. Some features of payment and its influence on performance are worth mentioning here.

Incentive payment schemes have been extensively used in manufacturing as the basis for paying manual employees, and they have a built-in bias towards volume rather than quality of output. Two extreme examples indicate the weakness of this approach. Someone engaged in manufacture of diamond-tipped drilling bits would serve the employer poorly if payment were linked to output. If it were possible to devise a payment system that contained an incentive element based on high quality of workmanship or on low scrap value that might be more effective. If school-teachers were paid a 'quantity bonus' it would presumably be based either on the number of children in the class or on some indicator like the number of examination passes. The first would encourage teachers to take classes as large as possible, with probably adverse results in the quality of teaching. The second might increase the proportion of children succeeding in examinations, but would isolate those who could not produce impressive examination performance.

There has been a marked increase in employer use of performance-related pay for management and professional staff, especially for senior managers;

> organizations have sought either to re-establish or to introduce for the first time schemes which reinforce the messages required to produce improved performance and increased productivity. Private sector employers in particular now increasingly believe that they are not providing an appropriate or competitive package for their directors and senior executives unless there is some element of risk money to add on to the basic salary and reward the achievement of company growth, profitability and success. At the same time, companies have been re-examining the use of bonus schemes for more junior employees in order to increase motivation and to reward them for their contribution. (Armstrong and Murlis 1988, p. 203)

Fifth objective: cost

Just as employees are interested in purchasing power, the absolute value of their earnings, so employers are interested in the absolute cost of payment, and its bearing on the profitability or cost-effectiveness of their organization. The importance of this varies with the type of organization and the relative cost of employees, so that in the refining of petroleum employment costs are modest, in teaching or nursing they are substantial. The employer interest in this objective is long-term as well as short. Not only do employees expect their incomes to be maintained and carry on rising, rather than fluctuating with company profitability, but also the indirect costs of employing people can be substantial. In some organizations there is greater interest in head-count than in costs.

The elements of payment

The payment of an individual will be made up of one or more elements from those shown in Figure 32.1. Fixed elements are those that make up the regular weekly or monthly payment to the individual, and which do not vary other than

Bonus	Profit allocation		Variable elements	The total potential pay package
Bonus	Discretionary sum		• Irregular	
Incentive	Group calculation basis		• Variable amount	
Incentive	Individual calculation basis		• Usually discretionary	
Overtime payment				
Premia	Occasional			
Premia	Contractual		Fixed elements	
Benefits	Fringe benefits		• Regular	
Benefits	Payment in kind	Other	• Rarely variable	
Benefits	Payment in kind	Accommodation	• Usually contractual	
Benefits	Payment in kind	Car		
Benefits	Benefit schemes	Other		
Benefits	Benefit schemes	Pension		
Benefits	Benefit schemes	Sick pay		
Plussage	'Fudge' payments			
Plussage	Special additions			
Basic rate of payment			Basic	

Figure 32.1 *The potential elements of payment*

in exceptional circumstances. Variable elements can be varied either by the
employee or the employer.

Basic

The irreducible minimum rate of pay is the basic. In most cases this is the
standard rate also, not having any additions made to it. In other cases it is a basis
on which earnings are built by the addition of one or more of the other elements
in payment. One group of employees – women operatives in footwear – have
little more than half of their earnings in basic, while primary and secondary
schoolteachers have virtually all their pay in this form.

Plussage

Sometimes the basic has an addition to recognize an aspect of working
conditions or employee capability. Payments for educational qualifications and
for supervisory responsibilities are quite common. There is also an infinite range
of what are sometimes called 'fudge' payments, whereby there is an addition to
the basic as a start-up allowance, mask money, dirt money, and so forth.

> ## Review topic 32.1
>
> If your employer offered you a 'remuneration package', which could be made up from any of the items in Figure 32.1 provided that the total cost was no more than £x, what proportion of each item would you choose and why? Does your answer suggest ideas for further development of salary policies?

Benefits

Extras to the working conditions that have a cash value are categorized as benefits and can be of great variety. Some have already been mentioned; others include luncheon vouchers, subsidized meals, discount purchase schemes and the range of welfare provisions like free chiropody and cheap hairdressing.

Premia

Where employees work at inconvenient times, like shifts or permanent nights, they receive a premium payment as compensation for the inconvenience. This is for inconvenient rather than additional hours of work. Sometimes this is built into the basic rate or is a regular feature of the contract of employment so that the payment is unvarying. In other situations shift working is occasional and short-lived, making the premium a variable element of payment.

Overtime

It is customary for employees working more hours than are normal for the working week to be paid for those hours at an enhanced rate, usually between 10 and 50 per cent more that the normal rate according to how many hours are involved. Seldom can this element be regarded as fixed. No matter how regularly overtime is worked, there is always the opportunity for the employer to withhold the provision of overtime or the employee to decline the extra hours.

Incentive

Incentive is here described as an element of payment linked to the working performance of an individual or working group, as a result of prior arrangement. This includes most of the payment by results schemes that have been produced by work study, as well as commission payments to salespeople. The distinguishing feature is that the employee knows what has to be done to earn the payment, though he or she may feel very dependent on other people, or on external circumstances, to receive it.

Bonus

A different type of variable payment is the gratuitous payment by the employer that is not directly earned by the employee: a bonus. The essential difference between this and an incentive is that the employee has no entitlement to the payment as a result of a contract of employment and cannot be assured of receiving it in return for a specific performance. The most common example of this is the Christmas bonus.

We include profit sharing under this general heading although the share ownership confers a clear entitlement. The point is that the level of the benefit cannot be directly linked to the performance of the individual but to the performance of the business. In some cases the two may be synonymous, with one dominant individual determining the success of the business, but there are very few instances like this, even in the most feverish imaginings of tycoons. Share ownership or profit sharing on an agreed basis can greatly increase the interest of the employees in how the business is run and can increase their commitment to its success, but the performance of the individual is not directly rewarded in the same way as in incentive schemes.

The difference between wages and salaries

The divide between wages and salaries is gradually lessening, but there remains a number of major differences in emphasis that affect not only the payer of the wages or the salary, but also the attitude of the recipient. This tends both to emphasize and reflect the tendency to identify core and peripheral workforces as we saw in our discussion of labour markets.

There has recently been much enthusiasm for the notion of harmonization of terms and conditions across different categories of employee (Roberts 1985) and we have found that many of our respondents have made moves in this direction, with a third of them making changes to remove differential treatment between manual and white-collar employees on holidays, hours and method of payment. Although there are changes being made, we review here the nature of the differences that exist, so that those seeking to remove the differences know what lies beneath them. Some of the more obvious differences between the two methods of payment can be outlined here. An alternative discussion can be found in Lupton and Bowey (1974, pp. 106–15).

Periodicity

Conventionally, wages are paid more frequently than salaries, so that most wage-earners will be paid weekly while most salary-earners are paid monthly. The unit of time for which the wage-earner is paid will probably be much shorter, so that five or ten minutes' lateness will often be penalized by a deduction of pay for that period. Rates are usually expressed as hourly rates, with that figure remaining the standard reference point in any discussion or negotiation, so that weekly earnings are seen as a variable figure based on the rate multiplied by 38 (or whatever the normal weekly hours are) with possible subtractions for lateness or absence and possible additions for overtime, shift working, incentives, and the like.

The salaried employee's monthly payments are usually expressed as an annual figure, which is the reference point in comparisons and negotiations. Implicit in this is that the salary-earner cannot provide services to the employer that are readily susceptible to division into small segments. It is very rare for lateness and short-term absence to be penalized by salary deductions, leading to the wage-earner's assertion that the salaried are paid 'work or play'.

Pensions and fringe benefits

The difference in the periodicity of payment leads to another variable: the importance that is attached to benefits other than cash-in-hand. Until the 1970s pension provision, other than by the state, for the wage-earner was unusual outside public sector employment, whereas it was the *sine qua non* for the salaried. There are other common fringe benefits that usually feature in the remuneration package for the salaried, such as luncheon vouchers, additional payments for extra qualifications, company cars and the generally grey area of 'expenses'. Those receiving wages are less likely to have these fringe advantages and have traditionally been very unwilling to receive them instead of cash.

Method of payment

One of the great dividers has been the method of payment, with salary-earners nearly always being paid by bank transfer or cheque while wage-earners are still often paid in cash. It emphasizes the expected dominance of short-term thinking on financial matters by wage-earners in contrast to the longer-term concern with financial security by the salaried. The immediate payment in cash is a method kept alive in the black economy.

The nature of the incentive

Incentives for wage-earners are required to be precise, comprehensible, fair and quick. Apart from the minority of the salaried who receive add-on incentives of this type, the incentive principle for them is of a fundamentally different nature: *prospects*. Salaries are geared to the career principle so that their recipients are always encouraged to look ahead to the possibility of the salary going up. Like their wage-earning colleagues they expect increases to compensate for changes in the cost of living, but they are encouraged to look to the future in three other ways. First, they may be on incremental scales carrying definite expectations of a future salary level with a precise cash value. Secondly, there is a stronger element of discrimination between salary-earners on the basis of individual performance or merit assessment than with wage-earners, where consistency or uniformity are more common. Thirdly, salary scales are the visual representation of career growth. There is always a better-paid job in the future with the individual reaching the ceiling relatively late and the different career ladders being adjacent to each other, requiring little more, in the eyes of the employee, than persistence, hard work and good behaviour to ensure access. Wage-earners see themselves reaching the peak of their earning power much earlier, probably in their twenties, and will see the initiatives required to get onto another ladder as being very demanding because wage-earners are not defined in the social system as ladder-climbers.

Identification

The last difference to mention is probably the most important, as it is a part of all the others. Those receiving salaries are likely to identify with the management interest in the organization. This was suggested by the studies by Batstone and his colleagues (1977), and Bain (1972) has pointed out that management encouragement is one of the features that needs to be present before white-collar unions expand. Salaried employees are most likely to see themselves doing a piece of the job of management, which has had to be split up because it – and the organization – have grown too big for top management to handle alone, but unquestionably it is a part of management. Wage-earners see themselves as doing the work that the management would never do and which is independent of management apart from the labour-hiring contract.

Review topic 32.2

Some employers who have moved wage-earners to salaried status have been surprised that the employees do not assume the same attitudes to work as those who are already salaried. Why do you think this is?

The identification of the salaried with management interests is closely related to their dependence on those senior to them in the hierarchy. Fringe benefits will sometimes depend on the favour of someone else, who will query an item on an expense sheet or let it pass; or who will decide the priority sequence for company cars to be replaced. Principally, however, salary-earners depend on their superiors for the most significant determinants of their future: merit payments and promotion. These will result from hard work and good behaviour, as was mentioned above, but there are no absolute standards of good behaviour. Work study officers do not measure it and produce a standard for the employee to use. Merit lies in the eye of the beholder, whose subjective evaluation will dominate any system if peer rating, performance management or any other scheme which can only modify – not eliminate – the degree of subjective judgement. Also, promotion depends not on merit alone, however it is judged, but on competition; this makes the competitors dependent on those who declare the winner.

The foregoing paragraphs show us that the difference in the nature of salary against wages reflects a difference in attitude to the employment contract. The contract of the wage-earner emphasizes insecurity and the here-and-now, while the contract for the salaried employee emphasizes a long-term relationship between employer and employee. The employee looks forward to terms and conditions of employment steadily improving over a long career path, and the employer can anticipate ready compliance with employer objectives for the organization because of the employee's interest in the future.

The relationship also reflects the difficulty of measuring the performance of salaried employees, whose contribution is usually not immediate and tangible. Some critics would argue that the emphasis on career growth is counter-productive because it encourages job holders to behave in a way that will demonstrate their potential for the next job rather than their competence in the current position. A slightly different version of this question is posed in the famous Peter Principle (Peter and Hull 1969), which states that 'each employee is promoted to the level of his own incompetence'. In attacking the hierarchical idea, Dr Peter argued that the effect of the career pyramid on employees was to encourage performance that would ensure promotion, which was sensibly based on competence, so that competence in one job leads to being promoted out of it. Further success in the next job leads to further promotion, which only stops when you reach a position in which you cannot cope – the level of your own incompetence. Because your performance is now incompetent it does not justify further promotion, leaving you stuck in a job you cannot do. Most of those engaged in organizing schemes of management development and making promotion decisions would argue that this is too simplistic a criticism, since the criteria for promotion are more those of potential for the future than past performance, even though the evidence of future potential must be distilled from achievements so far.

The salary structure

A typical organization will have a salary structure of groups, ladders and steps.

Groups

The first element of the structure is the broad groupings of salaries, each group being administered according to the same set of rules. The questions in making decisions about this are to do with the logical grouping of job holders, according to their common interests, performance criteria, qualifications and – perhaps – bargaining arrangements and trade union membership. The British Institute of Management study (1973) used a framework of four groups:

1. *Senior and middle management*: Directors, heads of major functions and their immediate subordinates.
2. *Junior management*: Responsible to the above and including supervisory staff.
3. *Technical and specialist*: Personnel with technical or professional skills and/ or qualifications (excluding those working in a managerial capacity), e.g. work study officer, technician, draughtsman/woman.
4. *Clerical*: All clerical occupations including secretarial staff. (British Institute of Management 1973)

There are various alternatives to this now rather dated type of arrangement, such as separating senior and middle management; incorporating technical and specialist personnel into appropriate management groups according to seniority; including manual employees as a salaried group. Another alternative is not to have groups at all, but simply a single system of ladders and steps, so that all salaried employees have their payment arrangements administered according to one set of criteria. The argument against such a system is that it applies a common set of assumptions that may be inappropriate for certain groups. In general management, for instance, it will probably be an assumption that all members of the group will be interested in promotion and job change; this will be encouraged by the salary arrangements, which will encourage job holders to look for opportunities to move around. In contrast, the research chemist will be expected to stick at one type of job for a longer period, and movement into other fields of the company's affairs, like personnel or marketing, will often be discouraged. For this reason it will be more appropriate for the research chemist to be in a salary group with a relatively small number of ladders, each having a large number of steps; while a general management colleague will be more logically set in a context of more ladders, each with fewer steps.

The broad salary ranges are then set against each group, to encompass either the maximum and minimum of the various people who will then be in the group or – in the rare circumstance of starting from scratch – the ideal maximum and minimum levels.

As the grouping has been done on the basis of job similarity, the attaching of maximum and minimum salaries can show up peculiarities, with one or two jobs far below a logical minimum and others above a logical maximum. This requires the limits for the group to be put at the 'proper' level, with the exceptions either being identified as exceptions and the incumbents being paid a protected rate or being moved into a more appropriate group.

Salary groups will not stack neatly one on top of another in a salary hierarchy. There will be considerable overlap, recognizing that there is an element of salary growth as a result of experience as well as status and responsibility. A typical set of groups could be as illustrated in Figure 32.2.

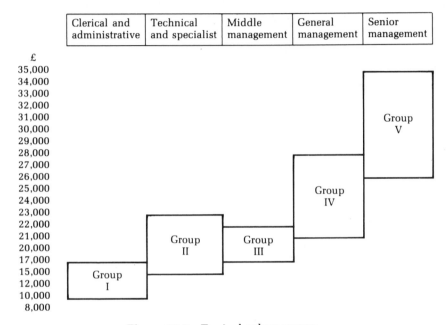

Figure 32.2   *Typical salary groups*

Another way of dealing with specialists is to take them out of the corporate salary structure altogether and pay them according to salaries prescribed by an acknowledged outside body. This is done most frequently for nurses working in industry, who are often paid according to scales published by the Royal College of Nursing. A device like this can solve the problem of one or two specialized employees whose general rank or standing in the organization is not consistent with the necessary level of payment.

The grouping stage in salary administration has thus identified a number of employees whose remuneration will be organized along similar lines.

Ladders and steps

Because the salaried employee is assumed to be career-oriented, salary arrangements are based on that assumption, so each salary group has several ladders within it and each ladder has a number of steps (often referred to as 'scales' and

Pay

'points'). As with groups there is considerable overlap, the top rung of one ladder being much higher than the bottom rung of the next. Taking the typical general management group that was mentioned above, we could envisage four ladders, as shown in Figure 32.3. The size of the differential between steps varies from £200 to £600 according to the level of the salary and the overlapping could be used in a number of ways according to the differing requirements. Steps 6 and 7 on each ladder would probably be only for those who had reached their particular ceiling and were unlikely to be promoted further, while steps 4 and 5 could be for those who are on their way up and have made sufficient progress up one ladder to contemplate seeking a position with a salary taken from the next higher ladder.

Annual salary (£)	A	B	C	Ladders D
17,100				7
16,500				6
15,900				5
15,300			7	4
14,800			6	3
14,300			5	2
13,800		7	4	1
13,400		6	3	
13,000		5	2	
12,600	7	4	1	
12,300	6	3		
12,000	5	2		
11,700	4	1		
11,500	3			
11,300	2			
11,100	1			

Figure 32.3 *Ladders and steps in a salary group*

The figures attached to the ladders in this example are round, in the belief that salaries are most meaningful to recipients when they are in round figures. However, ladders are sometimes developed with steps having a more precise arithmetical relationship to their relative position, so that each step represents the same percentage increase. Equally, some ladders have the same cash amount attached to each step.

Some commentators place importance on the relationship of the maximum to the minimum of a ladder, described as *the span*, and the relationship between the bottom rung of adjacent ladders, referred to as *the differential*. Bowley (1972) suggests that the most logical arrangement is a 50 per cent span and a 20 per cent differential. There is no inscrutable logic behind those precise figures, so that 49 per cent and 21 per cent would not be 'wrong', but they have a similar value to the use of round figures referred to in the last paragraph. There is a neatness and symmetry about the method, which can commend itself to salary recipients.

The self-financing increment principle

It is generally believed that fixed incremental payment schemes are self-regulating, so that introducing incremental payment schemes does not mean that within a few years everyone is at the maximum. The assumption is that just as some move up, others retire or resign and are replaced by new recruits at the bottom of the ladder:

> The position can best be illustrated in terms of a single group of staff paid within the same salary range. The normal movement of salaries for the individual members of such a group set up what might be described as a circular process. While some individuals progress upwards, others leave the group by retirement or resignation or promotion and are replaced by newcomers who usually start lower down the pay range. The process of 'attrition' can mean that in certain circumstances the payment of increments is completely self-financing and leads to no increase in the salary bill. (National Board for Prices and Incomes 1969, pp. 25–6)

This thinking was born in a period when salary-earners were moving relatively frequently in an active labour market. Once the buoyancy of that market lessens then the effect of attrition is less also and the incremental pay scheme becomes an escalator not only for the individual, but also for the salary costs of the organization. The Office of Manpower Economics survey (1973) suggested that the level of attrition will fluctuate more with variable schemes than with fixed schemes, and an article by Boddy (1977) produced evidence of incremental payment schemes showing considerable increases in cost.

The way in which such movements are measured is by a device known as the compa-ratio, which compares all the salaries being received by individuals on a particular ladder with the middle point of the ladder, viz.:

$$\frac{\text{Average of all salaries on the ladder}}{\text{Middle rung of the ladder}} \times 100$$

Assuming that all salaries should average out at the mid-point, this provides a means of control.

Review topic 32.3

If incremental scales cease to be self-financing through lack of labour market movement, what advantage is there to the employer in keeping them?

Pay comparisons

Salary structures have to have an internal logic that makes sense to at least the majority of the salary recipients, but they also have to be consistent with what is being paid elsewhere, as was considered in the chapter on labour markets. There are a number of ways in which comparisons can be made. The most reliable is to use salary surveys, which are carried out by consultants. The method is to obtain information from a number of employers and then arrange the anonymous information into a range of categories for comparison, such as size of company by turnover and number of employees. More difficult is to define the jobs for which salaries are being compared, both in terms of the job specialization and the degree of responsibility and accountability of the post holder. *Incomes Data Services* and *Industrial Relations Services* publish regular reviews of what the surveys are saying.

Salary clubs are informal collections of employers who meet periodically to share information about relative rates of pay for categories of staff they all employ.

A service found especially valuable by its users is the pay comparison information provided by the Hay-MSL management consultancy, where the regular pay reports are based on jobs evaluated by the Hay-MSL system, so there is an unusual degree of reliability in the like-for-like comparisons.

Salary decisions

Who decides where in the salary structure the individual fits? The answer to that question at one extreme is 'job evaluation and fixed increments' and at the other extreme it is the capricious whim of another individual. The first means that decisions are not made about individuals but about systems, and the individual salary emerges from the inexorable process of increments. The second means that decisions on salaries are made without constraint and, perhaps, without logic. Between these two extremes we can list the sequence of decisions that are involved in a typical annual salary review:

1. *How much the salary budget for the next year will be*: Decision made by the senior decision-making individual or coalition after submissions of evidence from personnel, finance and other specialists, including an interpretation of labour market indicators and trade union negotiations, if any.
2. *How the additional budget provision is to be divided between general increases (cost-of-living) and individual increases (merit)*: This decision probably made at the same time as the first, but evidence and advice from personnel given more weight than any other. Possibly a wholly personnel decision.
3. *How merit increases are decided*: Recommendation from individual's superior, according to clear-cut rules, vetted by personnel to ensure consistency of approach by all superiors and that no previous undertakings are overlooked.
4. *How individuals hear the news*: Face-to-face by line superior, written confirmation from personnel.

The remaining chapters in this final part of our book deal with some of the key sub-features of payment arrangements, including the approach to performance management, which appears in the closing chapter.

Summary propositions

32.1 For both parties to the employment contract the main consideration is that the payment arrangement should be 'fair'.
32.2 Employee and employer have different frames of reference that determine their respective views of fairness.
32.3 The main elements of payment are basic rate, plussage, benefits, premia, overtime, incentive and bonus.
32.4 Despite moves towards harmonization, there remain major differences between wages and salaries.
32.5 Salaried status reflects and reinforces the commitment of the salaried person to career orientation and identification with management interests.
32.6 A typical salary structure has groups, ladders and steps which interconnect to describe and encourage career progression.
32.7 The idea that incremental salary systems keep the total cost of salaries stable around the mid-point of scales is seldom correct when there is little staff turnover.

References

Armstrong, M. and Murlis, H. (1988), *Reward Management: A handbook of salary administration*, London: Kogan Page.

Bain, G. S. (1972), *White Collar Unions: A review*, London: Institute of Personnel Management.

Batstone, E., Boraston, I. and Frenkel, S. (1977), *Shop Stewards in Action*, Oxford: Basil Blackwell.

Boddy, D. (1977), 'Salary payment and salary costs', *British Journal of Industrial Relations*, March.

Bowley, A. (1972), *Salary Structures for Management Careers*, London: Institute of Personnel Management.

British Institute of Management (1973), *Salary Administration. Survey report no. 16*, London: British Institute of Management.

Fowler, A. (1988), 'New directions in performance pay', *Personnel Management*, November, vol. 20, no. 11.

Jaques, E. (1962), 'Objective measures for pay differentials', *Harvard Business Review*, January/February, pp. 133–7.

Lupton, T. and Bowey, A. M. (1974), *Wages and Salaries*, Harmondsworth: Penguin Books.

National Board for Prices and Incomes Report no. 132 (1969), *Salary Structures*, Cmnd 4187, London: HMSO.

Office of Manpower Economics (1973), *Incremental Payment Schemes*, London: HMSO.

Pay Board (1974), *Relativities*, London: HMSO.

Peter, L. J. and Hull, R. (1969), *The Peter Principle*, New York: Morrow.

Roberts, C. (ed.) (1985), *Harmonization Whys and Wherefores*, London: Institute of Personnel Management.

Smith, I. (1983), *The Management of Remuneration: Paying for effectiveness*, London: Institute of Personnel Management.

33

Job evaluation

One of the main tasks of payment administration is setting the differential gaps. It is necessary always to juggle the three factors of performance, market rate and equity. It is rarely possible or wise to pay people only according to their performance or contribution, and linking payment only to developments in the labour market can make working relationships very difficult. There is always the vexed question of how much more than Y and how much less than Z should X receive? The relative contribution of each individual of the three is difficult to measure, so some acceptable assessment of each job is made. The difficult problem of assessing performance is overlaid with the even more difficult problem of making comparisons.

The standard way of tackling this problem is using a form of job evaluation. Half our questionnaire respondents used job evaluation for white-collar and management employee groupings and a third used it for blue-collar employees. The number of jobs being covered by this method was reported as increasing in sixty-four establishments and reducing in only twenty-one, while the majority reported the number of evaluated jobs as being unchanged. In reporting the results of a survey of 371 organizations, Spencer (1990) shows that the reason for introducing job evaluation, both now and in the past, is overwhelmingly to achieve fair pay, although there is an increasing interest in using it as a basis of performance pay.

The application of job evaluation has been intensified by the implications of the Equal Pay Act, as modified in 1984, which places as central in assessing equal pay claims the question of whether or not a job-evaluated payment scheme is in use.

In this chapter we consider first the background to the problems of getting relative payment right and then the job evaluation methods available. Finally, we consider especially the equal pay aspects.

591

Relativities and differentials

There are four different types of pay relationship that personnel managers need to understand, as dissatisfaction with relative pay can come from any of these sources.

Differentials

Differentials is the term used to describe pay differences within a single group of people whose jobs are sufficiently similar in content for comparisons to be logical. This will either be by unilateral management decision, by following agreed procedures probably involving members of the group whose jobs are being compared, or by agreement between one set of negotiators representing management interests and one representing employee interests – the simple model of the bargaining relationship. If the management of an organization negotiates with one bargaining agent on behalf of, say, manual employees who are skilled, semi-skilled and unskilled, then any disagreement about different levels of pay between the different categories of employee are for those two parties to resolve. The resolution is normally within their competence, unless the negotiators are so unresponsive to the feelings of their members that one category of employees withdraws its support and seeks separate representation.

Internal relativities

A more difficult type of pay relationship to control is that of internal relativity. Here the employer is constant, but the employees are represented by different agents as a result of being in different bargaining units. The most common internal relativity problem is between manual and non-manual employees, where one union or group of unions represents the manual employees and another represents the non-manuals, although bargaining may be much more fragmented in many organizations – the problem of multi-unionism. Although more difficult to control than differentials, there is at least one common factor, the employer.

External relativities

Employees do not, however, restrict themselves to making comparisons between their own pay and that of others within their organizations, even though this may be the most cogent comparison. They will compare themselves with those in other companies, industries and services. Occasionally there will be a common element in the union, which negotiates better terms with one employer than another for groups of employees who see themselves as being similar.

More often the comparison is with completely different groups of employees. The long-running industrial dispute involving ambulance crews at the end of 1989 centred on the question of external relativity between them and members of the police and fire services.

The difficulty is shown most sharply in public sector pay bargaining, where there are large numbers of employees doing apparently similar work with pay scales that are broadly the same in all parts of the country. Every recipient of the pay is likely to make comparisons with friends and neighbours who are better off, or who seem to be better off. Public sector employees are extensively unionised and union research departments prepare detailed analyzes of comparative pay rates, again picking those comparators that produce comparisons most favourable to their own cause. Any pay claim always has some comparator, as this is what gives it credibility.

A potential problem of external relativity is in the employment of peripheral employees by contractors of consultants, who may be working alongside permanent staff enjoying less attractive (or apparently attractive) terms and conditions.

External identification

In one specialized category the employee identifies with an external employee grouping for purposes of determining the appropriate pay level. These people are usually taken out of intra-organizational bargaining. The obvious examples are company doctors and nurses, where the appropriate rates of pay are determined by bodies external to the company which proceeds to pay on that basis, unless there is some wish to pay above that rate. Other examples would be such professional groups as solicitors, surveyors and architects, and there will be many others where the number of employees will be so small as well as specialized that some external reference is the most appropriate way of determining the rate. The company employing one or two chemists or actuaries or other specialists would probably accept scales of pay published by the appropriate professional body rather than try to produce a pay structure that accommodated a range of specialists all identifying with an external professional grouping.

Review topic 33.1

Taking your own job, score from 0 to 5 the relative importance to you of the four types of pay relationship described in the 'Relativities and Differentials' section of this chapter. 0 = no importance, 5 = very important. Now do the same exercise with three or four other jobs and job holders that you know, such as members of your own family. How do you explain any differences?

Limitations on management action

If managers can accept and understand the range of limitations upon their actions in connection with pay comparisons, they can begin to develop a strategy to deal with them. There are five major constraints upon management action.

The product market

The influence of the product market varies according to how important labour costs are in deciding product cost, and in how important product cost is to the customer. In a labour-intensive and low-technology industry like catering, there will usually be such pressure on labour costs that the pay administrator has little freedom to manipulate pay relationships. In an area like magazine printing, the need of the publisher to get his product on time is so great that labour costs, however high, may concern him relatively little. In this situation the pay negotiators have much more freedom to deal at least with differentials.

In their analysis of the footwear industry, Goodman and his colleagues (1977) found that a major reason why the industry was characterized by peace rather than conflict was the need for employer collaboration on labour matters because of the intensive competition in the product market.

The labour market

We have suggested that external relativity is the most intractable type of pay relationship for personnel specialists because it is so completely beyond their control. It may not be beyond their understanding, and understanding could offer the opportunity at least to pre-empt some problems so as to deal with them before or when they arise rather than being taken by surprise. Accountants and craftworkers, for instance, come very close in our categorization to those who identify with an external employee grouping, as their assessment of their pay level will be greatly influenced by the 'going rate' in the trade or the district. A similar situation exists with jobs that are clearly understood and where skills are readily transferable, particularly if the employee is to work with a standard piece of equipment. Driving heavy goods vehicles is an obvious example, as the vehicles are common from one employer to another, the roads are the same, and only the loads vary. Other examples are typists, telephone operators, card punchers and computer operators. Jobs that are less sensitive to the labour market are those that are organizationally specific, like most semi-skilled work in manufacturing, general clerical work and nearly all middle-management positions.

Collective bargaining

Perhaps the most obvious constraint for management is the operation of collective bargaining. Employees do not join trade unions in order to comply with managerial wishes, but to question them, and the differential structure that fits in with management requirement will not necessarily fit in with employee expectations. The study by Metcalf (1977) tries to assess the effect of unionization on relative wages and concludes that it is significant, even if less dramatic than some have argued previously.

Gradually, the extension of collective bargaining to white-collar and managerial groups has reduced the scope for unilateral decisions about differential structures. One of the influences of collective bargaining is in the use of internal relativities as the basis for negotiations. The members of a low-pay group will narrow the gap between themselves and those in a high-pay group; whereupon the higher-paid will seek to widen the gap again by 'restoring the differential'. Before long there will follow more arguments from the lower-paid that the gap has widened – and should be narrowed.

Technology

Technology has an effect on most things, and pay is no exception. As technology changes so there will arise the need for new skills in the organization and people who are recruited possessing those skills will tend to import a pay level with them. The external identification principle may justify special treatment for one or two such employees, but once the numbers begin to increase, then they must be assimilated into the pay structure, almost certainly upsetting it in the process.

Internal labour market

Just as there is a labour market of which the company is a part, so there is a labour market within the organization. This is mainly in the constraining influence of custom and practice, so that any substantive and permanent change in the internal relativities needs considerable justification. One pair of commentators, Doeringer and Piore (1971), have classified different types of internal labour market. First is the *enterprise market*, so-called because the enterprise or organization defines the boundaries of the market itself. Such will be the situation of manual workers engaged in production processes, for whom the predominant pattern of employment is one in which jobs are formally or informally ranked, with those jobs of the highest pay or prestige usually being filled by promotion from within and those at the bottom of the hierarchy usually being filled only from outside the enterprise. It is, therefore, those at the bottom that are most sensitive to the external labour market. Doeringer and Piore point out that there is a close parallel with managerial jobs, the main ports of entry being from management trainees or supervisors in the organization, and the number of appointments from outside gradually reducing as jobs become more senior. This *modus operandi* is one of the main causes of the problems that redundant executives face. The second type of market is the *craft*, where there are rigid rules of entry – usually a combination of time-served apprenticeship plus an appropriate union card – but the allocation of jobs to people tends to be much more flexible, emphasizing equality of employment experience among the workforce rather than the considerations of seniority and ability which are predominant in enterprise markets.

The situation in internal labour markets may be the most important in attitude formulation on pay relationships:

> Feelings of being inadequately paid usually arise as a result of highly localized anomalies. The macro-system of pay differentials, the argument runs, is generally accepted as just. Therefore, in evaluating their own pay, individuals make the critical comparisons not with levels of earnings throughout society as a whole, but with more restricted 'reference groups'. Individuals compare their earnings against those of people in the same or broadly similar occupations. (Roberts *et al.* 1975, p. 31)

The authors of the article from which this extract is taken go on to question this assumption, on the basis that people are generally ill-informed on what relative pay levels are, but concede that the view expressed represents 'conventional wisdom'. Coates and Silburn (1970) have demonstrated that even the poorest are able to feel satisfaction with their lot if they select appropriate comparators. An opinion, advanced with little supporting argument, suggests that the internal labour market may be the most important influence on attitudes about pay relationships:

> It seems to us at least arguable that most people are little interested in whether other people are better off, or whether they have become better off than others, provided they themselves are treated fairly in relation to most of those with whom they work. No grand design here. (IDS 1977, p. 17)

Management policy decisions and pay relationships

Although there are limitations to managerial freedom of action on pay relationships, there is still a need for managerial initiative in policies to influence differentials and relativities. These are mostly to do with employee groupings or deciding on *job families*.

The job family is a collection of jobs which have sufficient common features for them to be considered together when differential gaps are being set. What are the management decisions to be made?

Why not one big (happy) family?

The first question is whether there should be sub-groupings within the organization at all, or whether all employees should be paid in accordance with one overall salary structure. Internal relativities disappear; there is only a differential structure. This arrangement has many attractions, as it emphasizes the integration of all employees and may encourage them to identify with the organization as a whole, it is administratively simple and can stimulate competition for personal advancement. Two well-publicized schemes of pay structuring have been built on the principle of a single pay structure, and each has used a single-factor scheme of job evaluation to determine the differentials. In Paterson's (1972) decision-band method, the single factor is the nature of the decisions taken by the employee in Jaques' scheme (1961) it is the timespan of the discretion that the employee is expected to exercise.

There are undoubtedly organizations with a single pay structure, and the Paterson and Jaques methods of determining differentials have been adopted, but they remain rare because of the reservations that are expressed about such integration. The more diverse the skills, values and union affiliation of the employees, the more difficult is such a single job family. In the National Health Service, for instance, there is a diversity of skills that can probably not be matched in any other area of occupational life. While it might be possible to structure a single system of payment to encompass doctors, nurses and ancillary staff, it would be extremely difficult to extend such a scheme to include administrators and paramedical cadres. The factors used to compare job with job will always tend to favour one grouping at the expense of another: one job at the expense of another. The wider the diversity of jobs that are brought within the purview of a single scheme, the wider will be the potential dissatisfaction, with the result that the payment arrangement is one that at best is tolerated because it is the least offensive rather than being accepted as satisfactory. The limitations of the single-factor evaluation scheme have been pungently criticized by Alan Fox (1972) on the grounds that it discriminates in favour of those in posts that are traditionally better paid anyway and therefore inhibits change of pay differentials towards a more broadly acceptable structure.

Other difficulties about a single, integrated system of payment are those of responding to the external labour market and the impact of collective bargaining. If the only variables to control were within the organization, it would be easier to sustain than in a situation where sectional interests are actively seeking to alter the structure specifically in their favour.

There has recently been renewed interest in the idea of what is now called 'integrated' job evaluation, with blue-collar and white-collar employees in the same scheme, to deal with equal value issues. This can avoid problems of, for instance, secretaries comparing their payment unfavourably with that of technicians. A helpful case history of the introduction of such a scheme has been produced by ACAS (1983). Spencer (1990) reports an interesting development. When referring to existing schemes of job evaluation, his respondents reported 19 per cent of schemes as covering all employees. For new schemes that proportion doubled to 38 per cent. This suggests that the one big happy family approach is increasing significantly in popularity.

Review topic 33.2

In what type of situations do you think a single, integrated job evaluated pay structure would be appropriate? Where would such a pay structure be inappropriate? What are the most likely management problems in each case?

Bargaining units

In our chapter on trade union recognition there was mention of the need to decide the boundaries of bargaining units. A job family and a bargaining unit will normally coincide, as the matter principally being discussed – pay – is common to both concepts. However, job families are created to deal with differential gaps rather than internal relativities even though they influence the internal relativity structure, and it is quite feasible to have bargaining units with more than one job family within them. A company might, for instance, negotiate with a trade union to determine a single salary scale for clerical, computer and administrative staff and then evaluate jobs in two separate families in the bargaining unit to determine the place within the scale for the different jobs. This procedure would be justified by the argument that the skills and requirements of computing staff are specialized, so that differentials are appropriately decided only by comparison with other computing jobs, while the relative position of computing staff is settled by collective bargaining.

There is again a need to make sure that the use of bargaining units as a means of determining job families is consistent with equal pay legislation:

> as a general rule all groups should be included at the outset wherever practicable, and then good reasons put forward for any exclusions. Trade unions and employers should appreciate that problems can be created if bargaining units are used as the sole basis for the scope of jobs to be covered. (Equal Opportunities Commission 1982, pp. 9–10)

The family structure

Another decision to be made is whether there will be any degree of overlap on the pay scales that relate to each family. There is no right answer to this question, although some overlap is usual, as suggested in the last chapter. No overlap at all (a rare arrangement) emphasizes the hierarchy, encouraging employees to put their feet on the ladder and climb, but the clarity of internal relativities may increase the dissatisfaction of those on the lower rungs and put pressure on the pay system to accommodate the occasional anomaly. Overlapping grades blur the edges of relativities and can reduce dissatisfaction at the bottom, but introduce dissatisfaction higher up.

Another reason why pay scales for different job families usually overlap is to accommodate scales of different length. A family with a flat hierarchy will tend to have a small number of scales with many steps, while the steep hierarchy will tend to have more scales, but each with fewer steps. One of the main drawbacks of overlapping scales is the problem of migration, where an employee regards the job as technical at one time and makes a case for it to be reclassified as administrative at another time, because there is no further scope for progress in the first classification.

Another aspect of migration is the more substantive case of employees seeking transfer to other jobs as a result of changes in the relative pay scales, which reduce rigidity in the internal labour market.

Are executives a special case?

It is usual for executive pay to be discussed and administered differently from the pay of other employees. This is largely because traditional theoretical formulations of economists have no place for executives, who are neither wage-earners in the normal sense nor owners, yet they are both earners and acting on behalf of the owner(s).

A further reason for regarding executives as a special case is the result of a number of investigations that have demonstrated a relationship between executive pay and organizational features such as sales turnover and number of employees. An admirable summary is to be found in Husband (1976) of work by analysts who argue that there is a typical relationship between the number of earners and the number of salaries at different levels.

In recent years the moves towards performance-related pay have been much greater for executives than for other categories of employee and they are rarely included in job evaluation.

Job evaluation methods

Job evaluation is the most common method used to compare the relative values of different jobs in order to provide the basis for a rational pay structure. Among the many definitions is this one form ACAS:

> Job evaluation is concerned with assessing the relative demands of different jobs within an organization. Its usual purpose is to provide a basis for relating differences in rates of pay to different in-job requirements. It is therefore a tool which can be used to help in the determination of a pay structure. (ACAS 1984)

It is a well-established technique, having been developed in all its most common forms by the 1920s. In recent years it has received a series of boosts. First, various types of incomes policy between 1965 and 1974 either encouraged the introduction of job evaluation or specifically permitted expenditure above the prevailing norm by companies wishing to introduce it. More recently the use of job evaluation is the hinge of most equal pay cases. Despite its popularity it is often misunderstood, so the following points have to be made:

1. Job evaluation is concerned with the job and not the performance of the individual job holder. Individual merit is not assessed.
2. The technique is systematic rather than scientific. It depends on the judgement of people with experience, requiring them to decide in a planned and systematic way, but it does not produce results that are infallible.
3. Job evaluation does not eliminate collective bargaining. It determines the differential gaps between incomes; it does not determine pay level.
4. Only a structure of pay rates is produced. Other elements of earnings, such as premia and incentives, are not determined by the method.

There are many methods of job evaluation in use and they are summarized in Smith (1983, pp. 68-106) and in Armstrong and Murlis (1988, pp. 75–85). We have already seen the problems connected with the single-factor schemes, like those of Jaques and Paterson. Some of the more complex schemes have been developed in order to improve the reliability of the outcome, usually by the use of a computer, but they have the problems of being harder to understand and depend on mechanical decision-making rather than on human judgement. This may produce 'better' decisions, which are less acceptable. Cynical, and possibly unfair, criticisms of complex schemes range from accusations that they are means for consultants to make money to statements that they are devices to blind shop stewards with science.

The most popular scheme is that of *points rating*, under which a number of factors (such as skill, effort and responsibility) are identified as being common to all the jobs being evaluated. Each factor is given a weighting indicating its value relative to the others and for each factor there are varying degrees. A job description is prepared for each job and a committee then considers each description in turn, comparing it, factor by factor, with the degree definitions. Points are allocated for each factor and the total points value determines the relative worth of each job. The best-known set of factors, weightings and degrees is that devised for the National Electrical Manufacturers Association of the United States, but the International Labour Organization has produced a list of the factors used most frequently:

Accountability	Mental fatigue
Accuracy	Physical demands
Analysis and judgement	Physical skills
Complexity	Planning and co-ordination
Contact and diplomacy	Problem-solving
Creativity	Resources control
Decision-making	Responsibility for cash/materials/
Dexterity	confidential information
Education	equipment or process, records
Effect of errors	and reports
Effort	Social skills
Initiative	Supervision given/received
Judgement	Task completion
Know-how	Training and experience
Knowledge and skills	Work conditions
Mental effort	Work pressure

The points values eventually derived for each job can be plotted on a graph or simply listed from the highest to the lowest to indicate the ranking. Then – and only then – are points ratings matched with cash amounts, as decisions are made on which points ranges equate with various pay levels.

It is virtually inevitable that some jobs will be found to be paid incorrectly after job evaluation has been completed. If the evaluation says that the pay rate should be higher then the rate duly rises, either immediately or step by step, to the new level. The only problem is finding the money and introducing job evaluation always costs money. More difficult is the situation where evaluation shows the employee to be overpaid. It is not feasible to reduce the pay of the job holder without breaching the contract of employment. There have been two approaches. The first, which was never widespread and appears almost to have disappeared, is *buying out*. The overpaid employee is offered a large lump sum in consideration of the fact of henceforth being paid at the new, lower rate. The second and more general device used is that of the personal rate or *red circling*. An example could be where the rate for the job would be circled in red on the salary administrator's records to show that the employee should continue at the present level while remaining in that post, but a successor would be paid at the lower job-evaluated rate.

Our research showed that, although points rating is the most widely used scheme, the Hay-MSL *Guide Chart Profile Method* is the most popular method for evaluating management jobs (see Table 33.1 for an example of some of the methods). This proprietary method is based on assessing three main factors: know-how, problem-solving and results. Jobs are assessed by using each of three guide charts, one for each factor. A profile is then developed for the job showing the relationship between the factors, a ranking is eventually produced and the rates of the jobs considered in order to produce a new pay structure. At this stage comes one of the greatest advantages of this system. The proprietors have available a vast amount of comparative pay data on different organizations using their system, so their clients cannot only compare rates of pay within the organization (differentials and internal relativities); they can also examine their external relativities. The method of operating this system and several other consultants' methods is described by Armstrong and Murlis (1988, pp. 459–95).

Table 33.1   The use of different methods of job evaluation. Answers from 350 questionnaire respondents to the question: 'What types of job evaluation scheme are used for the various categories of jobs in this establishment?'

	Blue-collar workers	White-collar workers	Management
Hay-MSL	9	26	49
Ranking	13	20	16
Grading or classification	31	46	30
Factor comparison	21	31	24
Points rating	26	76	45
Other	4	4	8

Employee participation in job evaluation

The degree of participation by non-managerial employees in job evaluation varies from one organization to another. In some cases the entire operation is conducted from start to finish without any employee participation at all. Some degree of participation is more common. Apart from negotiating on pay levels and bargaining units, the main opportunities for employee contribution are as follows.

Job families

Employees collectively need to consent to the family structure and they can probably add to the deliberations of managers about what that structure should be, as they will be well aware of the sensitive points of comparison.

Job descriptions

Job descriptions are crucial to the evaluation and it is common for job holders to prepare their own, using a pro-forma outline, or for supervisors to prepare them for jobs for which they are responsible. Spencer (1990) reports 88 per cent of his respondents answering that job descriptions were prepared by involving job holders and 94 per cent involved supervisors. Superficially, this is an attractive method, as there is direct involvement of the employee, who cannot claim to have been misrepresented. Also, it delegates the task of writing job descriptions, enabling it to be completed more quickly. The drawback is similar to that of character references in selection. Some employees write good descriptions and some write bad ones: some overstate while others understate. Inconsistency in job descriptions makes consistency in evaluation difficult.

An alternative is for job descriptions to be compiled by job analysts after questioning employees and their supervisors, who subsequently initial the job description which the analyst produces, attesting to its accuracy.

Evaluation

The awarding of points is usually done by a panel of people who represent between them the interests and expertise of management and employee. This is not only being 'democratic', it is acknowledging the need for the experience and perspective of job holders as well as managers in arriving at shrewd judgements of relative worth. Naturally, panel memberships alter so that employees are not asked to evaluate their own jobs. Although there is an understandable general tendency for employee representatives to push ratings up, and for management representatives to try to push them down, this usually smooths out because both parties are deriving differential rankings and not pay levels. The only potential conflict of interest will be if employee representatives and managers have divergent objectives on the shape of the eventual pay structure, with big or small differential gaps.

Equal value

The whole issue of job evaluation is brought into sharp focus by the recent amendments to the Equal Pay Act, so that since 1984 it has been possible for a case to be brought to an industrial tribunal claiming equal pay if the work done by the claimant is equal, in terms of the demands made upon them, to the work done by a higher-paid man employed in the same establishment. This is in addition to the two previous rights established by the Act of a right to equal pay on the basis of having the same or broadly similar work or work of equal value.

The same or broadly similar work

The work does not have to be identical to that done by men to justify equal pay: it has to be either the same or of a broadly similar nature. Any difference in pay or terms of employment can only be justified if there is a difference in the work done that is substantial or of *practical importance*. The frequency with which the difference occurs will influence the assessment of what is 'like work'. If, for instance, a male supervisor is better qualified and therefore able to exercise a greater flexibility and mobility of supervision than a woman supervisor doing the same job, there could be a case for a discriminatory payment as the difference can be judged as of practical importance. Another justification for discriminatory payment is where there is a *material difference*:

> A man and a woman were employed on broadly similar work as audit clerks, but she complained because she was paid less. The man carried more responsibility and did more complex work (difference of practical importance) but there was also a material difference in that clients of the employer could be charged more for the services of the man than the woman, thus entitling him to be paid more. (*Oakes* v. *Lester Beasley 1976*)

Work of equal value

This relates to jobs that are substantially different, but that are rated as equivalent by the process of job evaluation, which is intended to provide a standard method of comparing the contents of widely differing jobs. In this situation the job content is not important in justifying or resisting an equal pay claim. It is important that the scheme of job evaluation should be fair and without sex bias. The Act provides the definition of job evaluation to be used:

> A woman is to be regarded as employed on work rated as equivalent with that of any man if her job and his job have been given an equal value, in terms of the demand made on a worker under various headings (for instance, effort, skill, decision), on a study undertaken with a view to evaluating in those terms the jobs to be done by all or any of the employees in an undertaking . . . or would have been given an equal value but for the evaluation being made on a system setting different values for men and women on the same demand under any heading. (Equal Pay Act 1970, Sect. 1 (5))

Equal value

If an employee makes a complaint to an industrial tribunal and normal ACAS conciliation cannot resolve the matter, the tribunal may refer the matter for investigation by an independent expert: 'The expert will be drawn from a list of persons designated by ACAS. It may not be necessary for them to use formal job evaluation techniques but their assessments will need to consider the various demands made on the employees in the jobs being compared' (Lowry 1983, p. 27). The report of the independent expert will then be used by the tribunal as a basis of their decision on whether or not to make an award of equal pay to the complainant.

By far the best known case is that of *Julie Hayward* v. *Cammell Laird* (1984), where a cook was awarded pay equal to that of men employed as joiners and laggers, but only after appeal to the House of Lords three years after making the initial complaint. A number of other cases have been dealt with successfully. There were 200 applications to tribunal in 1984 and over 300 in each year from 1985 to 1987. Perhaps the most significant results of the legislation was the substantial pay increases awarded to check-out operators in Sainsbury's in 1990 after an extensive job evaluation review. Employer action is best reviewed by Wainwright (1985) and Gill and Ungerson (1984).

Summary propositions

33.1 The personnel manager needs to understand four types of pay comparison: differentials, internal relativities, external relativities and external identification.

33.2 Management freedom of action in deciding relative pay rates is constrained by the product market, the labour market, collective bargaining, technology and the internal labour market.

33.3 Management policy decisions about organizing pay relationships relate mainly to job families, bargaining units, the structure of job families and deciding whether or not executives are a special case.

33.4 The most popular method of job evaluation is points rating, although the Hay-MSL Guide Chart profile method is more widely used for management jobs.

33.5 Employees participate in the job evaluation process at any or all of the following stages: job families, job descriptions, evaluation.

33.6 Under the amended Equal Pay Act, women may claim equal pay with that of a man if the work is the same or broadly similar, of equal value or equal in the demands made on them.

References

ACAS, (1983), *Integrated Job Evaluation at Continental Can*, London: Advisory Conciliation and Arbitration Services. (This was earlier produced as no. 291 of *Industrial Relations Review and Report*, March 1983.)

ACAS, (1984), *Job Evaluation*, London: Advisory, Conciliation and Arbitration Services.

Armstrong, M. and Murlis, H. (1988), *Reward Management: A handbook of salary administration*, London: Kogan Page.

Coates, K. and Silburn, R. (1970), *Poverty: The forgotten Englishman*, Harmondsworth: Penguin Books.

Doeringer, P. B. and Piore, M. J. (1971), *Internal Labor Markets and Manpower Analysis*, Lexington: Heath.

Equal Opportunities Commission (1982), *Job Evaluation Schemes Free of Sex Bias*, Manchester: Equal Opportunities Commission.

Fox, A. (1972), 'Time span of discretion theory: an appraisal'. In T. Lupton, (ed.), *Payment Systems*, Harmondsworth: Penguin Books.

Gill, D. and Ungerson, B. (1984), *Equal Pay: The challenge of equal value*, London: Institute of Personnel Management.

Goodman, J. F. B., Armstrong, E. G. A., Wagner, A. and Davies, J. E. (1977), *Rule-making and Industrial Peace*, Beckenham: Croom Helm.

Hayward v. *Cammell Laird Shipbuilders Ltd* [1984] TLR 52.

Husband, T. M. (1976), *Work Analysis and Pay Structure*, Maidenhead: McGraw-Hill.

IDS Focus (1977), *The Pay Merry-go-round*, London: Incomes Data Services Ltd.

IDS Study (1985), *Blue Collar Job Evaluation*, London: Incomes Data Services Ltd.

International Labour Organization, (1986), *Job Evaluation*, Geneva, ILO.

Jaques, E. (1961), *Equitable Payment*, London: Heinemann.

Lowry, P. (1983), 'Equal pay for work of equal value: how the new regulations will work,' *Personnel Management*, September.

Lupton, T. and Bowey, A. M. (1974), *Wages and Salaries*, Harmondsworth: Penguin Books.

Metcalf, D. (1977), 'Unions, incomes policy and relative wages in Britain', *British Journal of Industrial Relations*, July, pp. 157–75.

Oakes v. *Lester Beasley and Co.* [1976] IRLR 172.

Paterson, T. T. (1972), *Job Evaluation*, London: Business Books. (This method has now been adopted and developed by the consultants Arthur Young as their own proprietary method.)

Roberts, K., Clark, S. C., Cook, F. G. and Semeonoff, E. (1975), 'Unfair or unfounded pay differentials and incomes policy', *Personnel Management*, August, pp. 29–37.

Smith, I. (1983), *The Management of Remuneration: Paying for effectiveness*, London: Institute of Personnel Management.

Spencer, S. (1990), 'Devolving job evaluation,' *Personnel Management*, 1990.

Wainwright, D. (1985), 'Equal value in action: the lessons from Laird's', *Personnel Management*, January.

34

Pensions and Sick Pay

The provision of pensions and sick pay has been viewed as the mark of a 'good' employer, and yet employees have not until recently seen these as benefits which attracted their interest. There is now, however, an increasing public awareness of pensions matters, stimulated by governmental actions, the media and the pensions industry. Sick pay too has attracted greater attention since statutory sick pay was introduced in 1986.

This chapter is organized into two major sections. In the first we look at the reasons for increased awareness about pensions provision, various categories of pension schemes, pensions information and the role of the personnel department. In the second part we discuss the role of the personnel department in state and occupational sick pay, and then look at sick pay and absence monitoring and control.

Increased awareness about pensions provision

Pensions are increasingly seen as 'deferred pay' rather than a reward for a lifetime of employment (IDS 1982), and as such are attracting more attention from employees and trade unions, and are seen as more negotiable than in the past. As the state pension scheme is changed and changed again, and its future form becomes more uncertain, greater attention is being paid to company schemes. The proposals concerning the future of the State Earnings Related Pension Scheme have directed attention to other schemes, including both occupational and personal schemes. The nature of work has changed dramatically since the first company pension schemes emerged. There has been a move from lifetime employment with one employer towards greater job mobility for all groups of employees. Sometimes this movement is deliberate, for example, the young executive who joins a new company to further her career; sometimes it is involuntary, as in the case of redundancy. This has prompted an interest in the way that company pension schemes provide for those employees who have had more than one, frequently many, employers. The increasing likelihood of fairly lengthy unemployment between one job and the next, together with increasing attention to the role of women who characteristically have broken records of employment due to family commitments, have highlighted the assumptions on which most company pension schemes are based. The plight of those who, having been made redundant at fifty are never to find work again, has made people more aware of the potential role of pensions schemes.

Our expectations in general have risen, with ideas of early retirement from choice, 'while you're still young enough to enjoy it', and increasing expectations that retirement should not necessarily be a time for 'tightening your belt', but a time to reap the rewards from one's work and to do things that there was never time for before. Retirement is now seen more as a beginning than an end, and consequently the pensions that support this new beginning are seen as more important at an earlier age than before. In addition to this, as information is more generally available, employees expect more information about their pension schemes and about the benefits to which they will eventually become entitled.

Review topic 34.1

Robert Noble-Warren (1986) talks about 'lifetime planning' as a series of 'rest and recuperation' periods throughout life as well as the planning of financial provision. Lifetime planning has to start with a statement of your life's objectives.

What are your life's objectives and what work, rest and financial plans can you make to achieve these?

Types of pension scheme

There are four levels of pension schemes: state schemes, company pension schemes, industry pension schemes and individual schemes.

State schemes

The state runs two schemes: a basic scheme and SERPS (State Earnings Related Pension Scheme). Every employee is obliged to contribute a standard amount to the basic scheme which provides an old age pension on reaching the age of 65 for men and 60 for women. For those employees who earn over a certain amount (known as the lower earnings limit) a percentage of salary earned between this limit and a higher salary level (known as the upper earnings limit) is also payable. Both these payments are deducted from wages as part of the national insurance contribution. The individual who has paid into SERPS as well as the basic scheme will receive a higher pension from the state on retirement in proportion to the additional amount that they have contributed. The employer also makes a contribution into the state pension scheme in a way similar to the individual employee. The state pension scheme is organized on a pay-as-you-go basis. This means that there is no state pension fund as such, and the money that is paid to today's pensioners comes from today's taxes and national insurance contributions. The money that will be paid to today's contributors, when they become pensioners, will come not from the investment of their and their employers' contributions, but from the contributions of the workforce and their employers in the future. There has been much criticism of the state pension scheme (see, for example, Butler and Pirie, 1983), and the government has put forward proposals for the abolition of SERPS. The 1986 Social Security Act brought in a phased reduction of benefits under SERPS from April 1988. Implications of this and other aspects of the Act are discussed in Amy (1986).

Company schemes

There is a number of advantages to companies in setting up pensions schemes. Nash (1989) gives a good description of these, which include pensions as part of the mechanism to recruit and retain good people, the generation of goodwill and loyalty, the improvement of industrial relations, and a mechanism for managing early retirement and redundancy. In addition to these the provision of such a scheme enhances the employer's image, which can have pay-offs in many areas.

Company schemes vary considerably, and we shall consider their specific arrangements in more depth in the section on 'Varieties of Company Pension Schemes'. They are normally funded by contributions from the employee (say, 6 per cent of salary) and a similar contribution from the employer. Sometimes large companies and public sector organizations offer non-contributory pensions, in which case the employee pays nothing. In general, company schemes provide an additional retirement pension on top of the basic state pension, and sometimes on top of SERPS. Most often, however, the company will avoid employee and employer payments into SERPS by means of 'contracting out'. A company can contract out of SERPS only if its pension scheme meets certain requirements. The Occupational Pensions Board (OPB) will decide whether contracting out will be allowed, and if so they will issue a contracting out certificate.

Company schemes generally provide better and wider-ranging benefits than the state schemes and they provide some flexibility. They are most often found in large organizations and the public sector, but some smaller organizations also run such schemes. Garlick (1986) reports that over eleven million employees are members of company pension schemes, but Hayward (1989) records that there are still around ten million employees who are solely dependent on state provision. Men and women have equal access to company schemes, and the Social Security Act 1989 brought further changes which enforced equal treatment of men and women in the schemes. However, differences in pensionable age, survivors' benefits and optional provisions are still allowable in law at the moment (see Industrial Relations Review and Report 1989). There is a tendency for a higher proportion of managerial workers than other groups to be in pensions schemes. Blue-collar workers are least likely to be in schemes. Part-time employees are sometimes excluded, as are those on temporary contracts, although this very much depends on the employer.

Company schemes rarely pay their pensioners in the pay-as-you-go manner operated by the state, but create a pension fund, which is managed separately from the business. The advantage of this is that should the company go broke, the pension fund cannot be seized to pay debtors because it is not part of the company. The money in the pension fund is invested and held in trust for the employees of the company at the time of their retirement. Very large organizations will self-administer their pension fund, and appoint an investment manager or a fund manager. The manager will plan how to invest the money in the fund to get the best return and to ensure that the money that is needed to pay pensions and other benefits will be available when required. An actuary can provide mortality tables and other statistical information in order to assist planning. Smaller organizations may appoint an insurance company or a bank to administer their pension funds, and so use their expertise. Pension funds can be invested in a variety of different ways, and Garlick comments that: 'They often deploy assets greater than the market capitalization of the companies that sponsor them and have come to dominate investment on the stock market' (Garlick 1986, p. 7)

The fund may also be used to purchase property and lend mortgages to others. Government and local government stock with specified redemption dates are also useful forms of investment as they may be selected to provide cash when claims are expected. Toulson argues that the investments made by the pension fund should meet the following criteria: 'Wise investment includes at least three criteria. Investments must be safe; they must be profitable; they must also be capable of being realized when cash is required to pay benefits (Toulson 1982, p. 8). Booth (1986), however, notes that an increasing number of funds are investing in venture capital projects, which is basically investment in new businesses. This long-term investment is much more risky, and Booth does suggest that only a small proportion of overall funds should be invested in this manner. The structure of some pension schemes and the success of the investments have meant large surpluses of money building up in the scheme. This has enabled both employer and employee to take a contributions holiday, as at Lucas Industries who have taken a two-year contribution holiday (quoted in Garlick 1986).

Another advantage of setting up a pension fund, apart from the protection of the money, is that if the scheme is approved by the Superannuation Funds Office (SFO) of the Inland Revenue, various tax advantages can be claimed. Both employer and employee can claim tax relief on the contributions that they make to the scheme, and there are also tax advantages for the pensions benefits that are paid out.

Industry-wide schemes

Sometimes employers and employees will contribute to an 'industry-wide' pension scheme, as an alternative to a company scheme. The reasoning behind these schemes is described very well by Incomes Data Services when they say:

> These schemes are particularly useful in industries where there is a large number of small companies, and employees tend to be mobile within the confines of the industry. The companies would not be large enough to run their own schemes, and the employees would not welcome being tied to a company pension scheme (IDS 1982, p. 13)

The operation of such schemes is very similar to company schemes except that a number of different companies contribute to the same scheme.

Personal pensions

Increasing attention is being paid to the possibility of personal pensions. Self-employed people have always needed to be concerned with making their own provisions for retirement, as they are excluded from joining SERPS. More general attention has been focused on this area due to increasing job mobility and the perceived greater portability of personal pensions. A personal pension is arranged, usually through an insurance company, and the individual pays regular amounts into their own 'pension fund' in the same way that they would with a company fund. The employer may or may not also make a contribution to the fund. At present there are very few employers who take part in this arrangement, but in July 1984 the government issued a consultative document on personal pensions (DHSS 1984), suggesting that all employees should have the right to make their own pension arrangements, and from 1988 these recommendations have become operational. There has been a very mixed reaction to the proposals. The Institute of Directors, for example, has been in favour. Moody comments on less favourable responses when he says:

> The concerns seem to be about whether occupational schemes will be damaged, whether there will be administrative chaos, whether individuals will be misled by plausible salesmen and finish up with

inadequate pensions, whether personal pensions will prove to be an irrelevance for pension scheme members or even whether they could result in the erosion of the state earnings-related scheme (Moody 1984, p. 34)

The IPM working party, in response to the government's consultative document, suggested that a better solution would be to allow members of company pension schemes to make additional pension provision via personal schemes (quoted in Moody 1984).

Varieties of company pension scheme

We have already looked at the ways that money is paid into the pension fund, and we shall now look at the way that money is paid out in the form of a pension. There is a variety of schemes which each pay out money to pensioners on a different basis. The most common type of scheme is that based on the final salary of the employee, but there are three other forms of well-known scheme. These are a flat rate scheme, an average salary scheme and a money purchase scheme. Figure 34.1 shows all these schemes and other forms of pension that are available.

Provider	Type of scheme	Additional benefits
State provision	Basic pension	No facility for additional benefits on top of SERPS
	Earnings related pension SERPS	
Company provision	Flat rate scheme	Sometimes additional benefits provided by 'top hat' scheme or additional voluntary contributions
	Average salary scheme	
	Money purchase scheme	
	Final salary scheme	
Industry-wide provision	Flat rate scheme	Sometimes additional benefits provided by 'top hat' scheme or additional voluntary contributions
	Average salary scheme	
	Money purchase scheme	
	Final salary scheme	
Personal provision	Employee funded money purchase scheme	Sometimes additional benefits provided by further investment in the scheme
	Employee and employer funded money purchase scheme	

Figure 34.1   *Pensions provision*

Flat rate schemes

Flat rate schemes take into account the length of service of the employee, but not the wage or salary that they were earning prior to retirement. A fixed rate of money is payable each year on retirement which is determined purely by the employee's length of service.

Average salary schemes

Average salary schemes take into account both length of service and the salary that the employee has earned in each of those years. The critical figure is the average of all the yearly salaries that the employee has earned. They are usually worked out at one fiftieth of each annual salary the employee has earned. If there was little inflation and the employee had only made a short trip up the promotion ladder, the average salary would be close to the final salary of the employee. In this case a pension that equated to a proportion of the average salary may be quite acceptable. In a case of high inflation and an employee who had started at the bottom and worked her way up to the top, a pension that equated to a proportion of her average salary would be less than acceptable. Some companies will now re-evaluate in line with inflation the contributions made into such a scheme, but many do not, and re-evaluation takes no account of career progression. See Figure 34.2 for an example of an average salary scheme.

```
25 year period
Final salary                                  = £12,000
(for 4 years)

Salary                                        = £10,000
(for 10 years)

Salary                                        = £ 6,000
(for 11 years)

 4 years' contribution at £12,000 =    1/50 of £12,000 ×  4 = £   950
10 years' contribution at £10,000 =    1/50 of £10,000 × 10 = £2,000
11 years' contribution at £ 6,000 =    1/50 of £ 6,000 × 11 = £1,320
                                       Pension per annum of  £3,070

40 year period
Final 25 years as above                                    = £3,070

Salary                                  = £4,000
(for 8 years)

Salary                                  = £2,000
(for 7 years)

8 years' contribution at £4,000 =      1/50 of £4,000 × 8 = £  640
7 years' contribution at £2,000 =      1/50 of £2,000 × 7 = £  280
                                       Pension per annum of £3,990
```

Figure 34.2 *Average salary schemes: over a 25-year and a 40-year period*

Final salary schemes

A final salary scheme, as the name suggests, takes into account the employees' final salary as well as the length of time that they have contributed to the pension fund. For each year of contribution employees earn the right to receive a specified proportion of their final salary as a pension. The better schemes offer one sixtieth. This means that for each year of contribution to the fund the employee is entitled to receive one sixtieth of their final salary in the form of a pension. Some worked examples are shown in Figure 34.3. The other commonly used fraction is one eighteenth. Employees in schemes that are based on one sixtieth would, after forty years of contribution, be able to receive two-thirds their final salary as a pension, and this is the maximum that is allowable (Toulson 1982). Employees in schemes that are based on one eightieth would receive half their final salary as a pension after forty years of contributions.

1/60 Scheme
Final salary   = £12,000

Contributions for 25 years   = 1/60 of £12,000 × 25

                                      = £5,000 per annum to be paid as a pension

Final salary   = £12,000

Contributions for 40 years   = 1/60 of £12,000 × 40

                                      = £8,000 per annum to be paid as a pension

1/80
Final salary   = £12,000

Contributions for 25 years   = 1/80 of £12,000 × 25
                                      = £3,750 per annum to be paid as a pension

Final salary   = £12,000

Contributions for 40 years   = 1/80 of £12,000 × 40

                                      = £6,000 per annum to be paid as a pension

---

Figure 34.3 *Final salary schemes: examples of various contribution periods with a 1/60 scheme and a 1/80 scheme*

Money purchase schemes

Money purchase schemes are organized in a totally different way from the schemes above, and there are no promises about what the final level of pension will be. Employees and employers contribute to these schemes in much the same way as to the other types of these schemes – that is, a certain percentage of current salary. The pension benefits from the scheme are entirely dependent on the money that has been contributed and the way that it has been invested. If investments have been very profitable and there has been little inflation, then the final pension may turn out to be adequate. Money purchase schemes result in a lump sum available at retirement and this is used to buy a pension. However, in times of very high inflation this type of scheme has severe drawbacks, and this accounted for their decline in popularity in the 1970s. Money purchase schemes are, however, seen as more flexible and more easily transferable, and there has been a revival of interest in such schemes (IDS 1982) as the most suitable basis for personal, portable pensions. The 1986 Social Security Act simplified the requirements for opting out of SERPS, which facilitated the use of money purchase and other personal schemes.

In addition to the pension scheme, which forms the major investment for retirement purposes, there are two other types of contribution which may be made for this purpose.

Top-hat schemes

Noble-Warren (1986) notes that top-hat schemes were originally used to top up an individual's pension entitlements with a new employer to ensure that they matched what the individual would have received with the old employer. Top-hat schemes are operated like money purchase schemes, and are particularly flexible because they may be funded by a single or occasional payment, and there is no commitment to pay a certain amount each month while in employment.

Additional voluntary contributions

Additional voluntary contributions are a different way of improving retirement benefits. Incomes Data Services points out that although this may well be an efficient form of saving, there are a number of disadvantages:

- There is normally no employer's contribution.
- Once a person starts contributing, he is not usually allowed to stop unless he leaves the company.
- He cannot normally get the money back until retirement age.
  (IDS 1982, pp. 15–16)

Company pension schemes and the problem of early leavers

We mentioned at the beginning of this chapter that pensions were traditionally seen as a reward for a lifetime's employment, and the way that pensions are structured reflects this. Early leavers may have one or more of three options in making their pension arrangements when they begin work for a new employer. One option can be claiming back the contributions that the individual has made into the pension scheme, and sometimes interest may be paid on these. Deductions are also made in accordance with tax laws, and of course, the employer's contribution is lost. Another alternative may be opting for a preserved pension. With a final salary scheme, if there were no inflation, and if the individual progressed very little up the career ladder, a preserved pension from an old employer plus a pension from the recent employer would equate well with the the pension they would have received had they been with the new employer for the whole period. However, if these conditions are not met, which in recent times they have not been, individuals who have had more than one employer lose out on the pension stakes. In some cases it is possible to transfer pension contributions to another scheme, and a transferred pension is often financially the best option. However, transfer value is not necessarily the same as original value, due to the way schemes use different sets of actuarial assumptions.

The disadvantages of leaving one employer's pension scheme and joining a new one have been one of the driving forces behind the recent interest in personal, portable pensions.

Pensions information and the role of the personnel department

Employees expect more information about their pensions, both in general terms and about their specific circumstances. The personnel department has become increasingly involved in pensions, which until recently have been mainly the province of the finance department or the secretariat. This involvement partly stems from increasing use of the computer, and the development of integrated, or at least linked systems, covering personnel, pensions and payroll. It also stems from greater trade union and employee interest in, and awareness of, pensions, and the potential of pensions to become another area for negotiation. As information becomes ever increasingly available, employees expect to know more about the benefits to which they will become entitled at retirement. The computer is ideal to provide up-to-date statements of contributions and entitlements, and many employers now send these to employees on an annual basis. Pensions modelling also enables employees to be given information about the pension consequences of selecting certain leaving dates. Pensions is increasingly becoming an area where choices have to be made and personnel managers can be in a good position to provide information and advice. The importance of pensions information, and a user-friendly approach to presenting it, is described by Hunt (1988).

Some employers provide an annual report of the pension fund for employees, but many do not. Garlick notes that accountants suggest that there should be four essential components in this annual report:

1. The general activity, history and development of the scheme contained in a trustee's report.
2. The value and transactions of the fund covered by audited accounts.
3. The actuary's report showing the progress of a scheme towards meeting its potential liabilities and obligations to members.
4. A separate report setting out the investment policy of the fund and its performance relative to its stated policy. (Garlick 1986, p. 10)

- Are pensions related to final salary?
- If so, is the fraction used both adequate and competitive?
- Do portions of a year count for benefit?
- Is entry to the scheme monthly, quarterly or must people wait until the scheme anniversary?
- Does the scheme provide immediate cover for lump sum death benefits on joining service (if otherwise eligible)?
- Is the lump sum death benefit payable under discretionary trust thereby avoiding delay or capital transfer tax?
- Can part-time staff join the scheme? If so, is membership compulsory and how are benefits calculated when members change from full to part-time status or vice versa?
- Can life cover continue for a period after leaving service for people made redundant?
- Does the scheme provide for the maximum cash permitted in lieu of pension on retirement?
- Does the scheme give fair value for money to people leaving service before retirement?
- Do the rules contain the requisite transfer-in and out provisions?
- Are the definitive deed and rules available or, as is often the case, are they still in draft form?
- Is there a simplified and readable explanatory booklet describing the scheme?
- Are members given any form of annual report from the trustees and regular statements of their benefits?
- Are members in any way involved in the running of the pension scheme?
- Is the personnel department closely involved in pensions policy and the running of the scheme?
- Is the scheme used positively as an aid to recruitment and are leavers fully aware of what they may be losing?
- Is there a pre-retirement training scheme?
- Is there any form of post-retirement escalation on pensions in course of payment or pre-retirement escalation for people who have left service?
- Does the scheme contain the flexibility to cope with early retirement problems?
- Are there provisions for pensions to be augmented at the discretion of the trustees?
- Do the rules permit members to make additional voluntary contributions (which attract full tax relief) to augment their benefits in whatever way they choose?

Figure 34.4 *A pensions checklist: How far does the scheme achieve benefits for the company?*
Source: Moody (1983, pp. 316–17). Used with the permission of
the Institute of Personnel Management.

Pension schemes need to be reviewed frequently to ascertain what benefits they are providing for the company in the light of changing circumstances. Personnel managers can draw on their specialist knowledge of labour markets, the changing nature of employment and the characteristics of the company's manpower to help assess the appropriateness of the pension scheme. Moody (1983) suggests that a pensions checklist could be used, such as that in Figure 34.4 on p. 617.

Sick pay and the role of the personnel department

As with pensions schemes, the provision of sick pay is seen as the mark of a good employer. The personnel manager and the personnel department have a variety of roles to play in relation to sick pay, particularly since the introduction of statutory sick pay in 1983 when state sick pay in additional to occupational sick pay have been administered by the employer.

Advice

The personnel manager is the most appropriate person to advise employees about SSP and the occupational scheme (if there is one) and how these schemes apply in individual circumstances. In particular, managers may need to advise staff who are nearing the end of their sick pay entitlement as to the remainder of their benefit and what special arrangements may be made in their case.

Home visits

Personnel managers, or welfare officers, may visit employees, at home, who have been away sick for a considerable period. Such visits are partly intended just to keep in touch with the employee and his progress, but also for the advisory purposes outlined above, and for planning purposes. For example, it might be appropriate to discuss with the employee the possibility of early retirement when sick pay runs out. These visits are sometimes organized on a more regular basis, say every month, and may be included as part of the sick pay procedure. In these circumstances they are intended partly as a deterrent to those claiming sick pay under false pretences. Because of this, trade union officials are generally unenthusiastic about home visits.

Dismissal and transfer

The personnel manager will be involved in the dismissal of those employees who are unlikely to be able to return. Dismissal would be on the grounds of incapability. This is a serious step for the personnel manager to consider, and Incomes Data Services suggest the following aspects are worthy of consideration:

- The nature, length and effect of the illness or disability on the employee's past and likely future service to the company.
- The importance of the job and the possibilities of temporary replacement.
- Whether it is against the employee's, the organization's or even the public's interest to go on employing the individual.

In many circumstances the personnel manager will be able to investigate a much happier option, that of finding suitable alternative work in the organization to which the employee may be transferred when sufficiently fit.

Sick pay and absence policy and procedures

Personnel managers are well placed to contribute to or instigate the development of occupational sick pay policy and of the procedures used to administer both occupational sick pay and SSP. Personnel managers, too, have a part to play in such procedures, apart from the obvious administrative role, as for example they may be involved in interviewing employees with a high level of absence prior to the initiation of disciplinary procedures.

Administrative procedures

The personnel manager will be the organization's expert on SSP, and will normally be responsible for its administration, collating information from line managers and feeding relevant information into the payroll section, unless this is done electronically. There is a number of specialized computer packages available to assist personnel departments with this administrative responsibility, and the introduction of SSP spurred many departments into purchasing a computer. Absence and sick pay recording is particularly important as the DSS may ask to inspect records going back for up to three years. Where possible the records kept for the DSS should be combined with any additional absence and sick pay information so that there is only one sick pay record for each individual, thus avoiding the problems of duplication.

Monitoring of sick pay and absence

The monitoring and analysis of absence and sick pay is an important aspect of personnel work. Based on this information the personnel manager will be able to assist line managers by providing guidelines along which to take action regarding such matters as suspected abuse of the sick pay system.

Disciplinary procedures

The personnel manager will be involved at some stage in disciplinary matters resulting from the abuse of the sick pay scheme, depending on the requirements of the organization's disciplinary procedure.

State sick pay

State or statutory sick pay was first administered by employers in April 1983 as a result of the Housing Benefits Act 1982. Since then the administration of the scheme has been amended by the Health and Social Security Act 1984 and the Social Security Act 1985. The changes came into force in April 1986. Under the SSP scheme the employer pays the employee, when sick, an amount equivalent to that which he would in the past have received from the DSS. The employer reclaims the money that has been paid out from national insurance contributions which would normally have been forwarded to the government. Although low, state sickness benefit does take into account the needs of the person involved, so that a married person with two children would receive more pay than a single person. Most employees are entitled to state sickness benefit; however, there are some exceptions which include employees who fall sick outside the EC, employees who are sick during an industrial dispute, employees over pension-able age and employees whose earnings are below the earnings limit. SSP is built around the concepts of qualifying days, waiting days, certification, linked periods, transfer to the DSS and record periods.

Qualifying days

Qualifying days are those days on which the employee would normally have worked, except for the fact that he or she was sick. For many Monday to Friday employees this is very straightforward. However, it is more complex to administer for those on some form of rotating week or shift system. Sick pay is only payable for qualifying days.

Waiting days

Three waiting days have to pass before the employee is entitled to receive sick pay. These three days must be qualifying days, and on the fourth qualifying day the employee is entitled to sickness benefit, should he or she still be away from work due to sickness.

Certification

A doctor's certificate for sickness is required after seven days of sick absence. Prior to this the employee provides self-certification. This involves notifying the employer of absence due to sickness by the first day on which benefit is due – that is immediately following the three waiting days.

Linked periods

The three waiting days do not always apply. If the employee has had a period of incapacity from work (PIW) within the previous eight weeks, then the two periods are linked and treated as just one period for SSP purposes, and so the three waiting days do not have to pass again.

Transfer to the DSS

The employer does not have to administer SSP for every employee indefinitely. Where the employee has been absent due to sickness for a continuous or linked period of twenty-eight weeks the responsibility for payment passes from the employer to the DSS. A continuous period of twenty-eight weeks' sickness is clearly identifiable. It is not so clear when linked periods are involved. An employee who was sick for five days, back at work for four weeks, sick for one day, at work for seven weeks and then sick for two days would have a linked period of incapacity of eight days. Alternatively, an employee who was sick for four days, back at work for ten weeks and then sick for five days would have a period of incapacity this time of five days.

Record periods

The DSS requires employers to keep SSP records for three years so that these can be inspected. Gill and Chadwick (1986) point out that the new linking and transfer rules mean that, in theory, an employer could be paying SSP to an individual for almost ten years before twenty-eight weeks' linked PIW came to an end. The DSS, however, do not require records for the whole of a linked PIW if this is greater than three years.

Occupational sick pay

Occupational sick pay (OSP) is administered in a variety of different ways and the employee's pay while sick can vary between state benefit (as above) and full normal pay. Most schemes are individual to the employer and are administered according to different rules from state sick pay. However, with the introduction of SSP, Chadwick argues: 'However, as I hope I have illustrated, two different schemes, OSP and SSP, with totally differing sets of rules and regulations, can only cause confusion for your employees and, perhaps, additional employee relations problems (Chadwick 1983, p. 29).

The introduction of SSP was an ideal opportunity for employers to review their sick pay arrangements, tighten up procedures and reconsider benefits. A number of employers, however, take the view that occupational sick pay will be abused and either fail to introduce a system or are very cautious about improving it. Employers are understandably concerned about the effects of high absence levels, which increase costs due to temporary cover, overtime or overmanning, and due to delayed or lost production. Additional problems are created by the need for reorganization when employees are absent. However some authors argue that this problem is exaggerated or has only a temporary effect: 'A common myth, often elevated into a "fact" by certain employers during negotiations, is that the introduction of, or improvement to an occupational sick-pay scheme will result in increased absenteeism' (Cunningham 1981, p. 55). Incomes Data Services have a slightly different view: 'Any increase in benefit or a reduction of waiting days is normally matched by a marked rise in absenteeism from the date of implementation, but this tends to fall back towards previous levels after a number of months' (IDS 1979, p. 12).

Some industries are better than others in the provision of sick pay, for example shipbuilding, leather and textiles, clothing and footwear are less well provided for than insurance, banking, gas, electricity, water, mining and public administration (DHSS 1977). Similarly, some grades of employee fare better than others. Higher-paid workers are more likely to be in a scheme (DHSS 1977), and, in particular, white-collar and management staff are still better provided for than most manual workers, with a number of employers running two separate sick pay schemes.

Review topic 34.2

- How would you argue in favour of harmonization of sick pay provision?
- What objections may be raised against such a scheme and how would deal with these?

Occupational sick pay schemes vary according to waiting days, period of service required, amount of benefit available, length of benefit entitlement, the funding of the scheme and administrative procedures.

Waiting days

Many occupational sick pay schemes have no waiting days at all, and the employee is paid from the first day of sickness. This is one area where there is a clear difference between manual and non-manual schemes, and Incomes Data Services comment: 'The manual unions, in particular, see the use of waiting days as the most obvious difference between staff and manual sick-pay schemes' (IDS 1979, p. 57). Many manual schemes still have three waiting days in line with the SSP regulations.

Period of service required

Some employers provide sick pay for sickness absence from the first day of employment. Others require a qualifying period to be served. For some this is a nominal period of four weeks, but the period may be three or six months, or a year or more. There is a major difference here from SSP which is available immediately after employment has begun.

Amount of benefit

Some employers offer a flat rate benefit which is paid in addition to the money provided via SSP. Others, however, link benefits to level of pay. The problem with flat rate schemes is that they quickly become out of date and need to be renegotiated from time to time. The best schemes offer normal pay for a specified period (minus the amount received via SSP). This is very straightforward for those staff who receive a basic salary with no other additions. It is more difficult to define for those whose pay is supplemented by shift allowances or productivity bonuses. Some employers will pay basic pay only with no additions, others may pay basic plus some or all additions, or give an average of the pay that has been earned over the weeks prior to sickness.

The amount of benefit may not be the same throughout the whole period of sickness. Sometimes an employer will pay a period on full pay, and then a period on half-pay, or some other combination.

Length of entitlement

The length of entitlement to sick pay varies considerably and is often dependent on the employee's length of service, so that entitlement to sick pay gradually increases in line with total length of service. Entitlement can vary between a few weeks and a year or more. Very often smaller entitlements will be expressed in terms of the number of weeks payable within any one year. However, unused entitlement can often be carried forward from one year to the next. Public sector employees are often well-off in respect of length of benefit and many employers provide six months' full pay followed by six months' half-pay after three years of service.

Funding of schemes

Most employers run non-contributory sick pay schemes. However, a few do require contributions from their employees. The majority of sick pay schemes are based on the individual employer, but there are some industry-wide schemes. Some employers provide sick pay schemes via insurance companies by paying premiums so that employees claim their sick pay from the insurance company. There is a number of disadvantages with these schemes, including the loss of future entitlement to some state benefits.

Administrative procedures

Each employer will develop administrative procedures which suit their own particular sick pay scheme. However, a number of general points have to be considered when designing procedures, as shown in Figure 34.5.

Absence and sick pay monitoring and control

The personnel department has a distinct role to play in the monitoring and control of absence levels and sick pay. In addition to the practical problems, high absence is bad for morale and suggests an employer unconcerned about the employees' behaviour. Control begins with formulating administrative procedures, as outlined in Figure 34.5. Procedures, however, are useless unless they are recognized and adhered to. It is, therefore, essential that employees know what is expected of them when they are sick – that they know whom to

- How, to whom and when should employees notify they are sick?
- When is a doctor's certificate required, to whom should it go?
- Any arrangements for return to work interviews?
- How is absence information to be transferred from the line manager to personnel, and from personnel to payroll?
- What should happen if employees are sick whilst on holiday or on a bank holiday?
- What sickness and absence records are to be kept and who will keep them, in what form?
- How are poor attenders to be identified, and what investigations should be made and action taken?
- What methods should be used to keep in touch with long-term sick employees?
- What arrangements are there to transfer older long-term sick employees on to a retirement pension?
- How will the OSP procedures integrate with the SSP procedures?

Figure 34.5 *A checklist for occupational sick pay procedures*

inform, when they need to do this and what information they need to give. If there is an employee handbook, the rules of the sick pay scheme and absence procedures should be included, and this information should be emphasized by line managers. Employees need to be aware of sick pay policy, and what is regarded as acceptable and unacceptable behaviour in relation to the scheme. They need to know how the disciplinary procedure will be implemented with regard to abuse of the sick pay scheme, and the type of information that management will use in order to decide when to invoke the procedure. Sick pay should not, however, be presented in a completely negative way, and the reasons why the organization provides sick pay and the benefits available should be clearly presented to encourage the employee to take a responsible attitude towards the scheme, so that the use of disciplinary procedures is a rare rather than a frequent event.

Managers also need to be very clear about their role in absence and sick pay procedures, in particular regarding the transfer of information and the interviewing of absentees on their return or after a certain level of absence has been reached. Some form of periodic check needs to be made to ensure that these features are working properly and not being buried under the heavy demands of the production schedule.

A further aspect of control is the monitoring of sick absence and other absence. Information for this monitoring can be used in the development of control procedures. For example, lists may be produced of those employees claiming most sick pay entitlement and managers may be asked to interview these employees in order to provide further information and explanation. Monitoring of sick absence is entirely dependent on the keeping of complete and reliable records. Useful analyses of this information can be produced by comparing different individuals; groups, such as age groups or skill level groups; departments; times of year; or comparing absence over a few years to identify trends. Comparison with the absence levels of other employers may also be illuminating. It is helpful to look at total amount of absence, number of spells of absence and length of each spell of absence. An excellent guide to the monitoring of absence is by Behrend (1978). An example of the type of analysis that Behrend has used with the help of computers is illustrated in Figure 34.6.

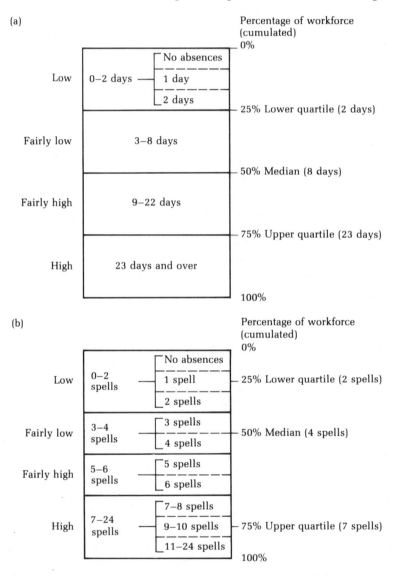

Figure 34.6 *An example of the analysis of absence: (a) classification of employees by number of days lost; (b) classification of employees by number of absence spells*
Source: Behrend (1978, p. 13).

The computer has also been used quite extensively in absence analysis, and one example of this is by Fell (1983).

Another important factor in absence control is to consider whether sick pay policy and procedures encourage longer spells of absence than necessary due to the use of waiting periods and the back-dated payment for waiting periods if they are part of a longer period of absence.

Review topic 34.3

Suggest an absence monitoring and control system for your organization, describing the role of the line manager and the personnel department.

Summary propositions

34.1 The personnel department is becoming increasingly involved in the area of pensions.

34.2 Both the personnel manager and the line manager have a key role to play in absence control.

34.3 Pensions are still seen as the mark of a good employer, and are increasingly seen as deferred pay rather than a reward for long service.

34.4 Many employers feel a moral obligation to provide for employees when they are sick. There are also practical advantages such as a healthier workforce, being seen as a caring employer and being more able to attract new employees.

34.5 Pensions have traditionally been an area where employees have been allowed little choice. The opportunities for choice are gradually increasing.

35.6 Some pension schemes have difficulty in coping with inflation and career progression, and most schemes fail to provide adequately for early leavers.

34.7 Absence control is important, as high absence levels cost money, lower morale and suggests an employer's lack of interest in their employees.

References

Amy, R., (1986), 'Pensions after 1988: sizing up the options', *Personnel Management* December.

Behrend, H. (1978), *How to Monitor Absence from Work: from head-count to computer*, London: Institute of Personnel Management.

Booth, G. (1986), 'Choosing an investment manager'. In the Institute of Directors, *The Directors' Guide to Pensions*, London: The Director Publications Ltd.

Brown, T. (1987), 'Pensions: A fund of crucial decisions', *Personnel Management*, August.

Butler, G. and Pirie, M. (1983), *The Future of Pensions*, London : Adam Smith Institute.

Central Statistical Office (1985), *Social Trends*, no. 15, London: HMSO.

Chadwick, K. (1983), 'A prescription for statutory sick pay and the supplementary benefits', *Personnel Management*, March.

Cunningham, M. (1981), *Non-wage Benefits*, London: Pluto Press.

DHSS (1977), *Report on a Survey of Occupational Sick Pay Schemes*, London: HMSO.

Fell, A. (1983), 'Putting a price on lost time', *Personnel Management*, April.

Garlick, R. (1986), 'The case for company pensions'. In the Institute of Directors, *The Directors' Guide to Company Pensions*, London: The Director Publications Ltd.

Gill, D. and Chadwick, K. (1986), 'The new prescription for SSP', *Personnel Management*, April.

Hayward, S. (1989), 'Coping with pensions changes', *Director*, December

Hunt, P. (1988), 'Must pensions always be a turn-off?', *Personnel Management*, November.

Incomes Data Services, (1979), *IDS Guide to Sick Pay and Absence*, London: Incomes Data Services.

Incomes Data Services (1982), *Pensions for Early Leavers: IDS study, no. 274*, London: Incomes Data Services.

Institute of Directors (1986), *The Directors' Guide to Pensions*, London; The Director Publications Limited.

McGoldrick, A. (1984), *Equal Treatment in Occupational Pension Schemes*, Research Report, Manchester: Equal Opportunities Commission.

Moody, C. (1984), 'Pensions and other forms of non-cash remuneration'. In D. Guest, and T. Kenny, (eds.), *A Textbook of Techniques and Strategies in Personnel Management*, London: Institute of Personnel Management.

Moody, C. (1984), 'The perils of portable pensions', *Personnel Management*, December.

Nash, T. (1989), 'Know your own pension', *Director*, January.

Noble-Warren, R. (1986), 'Lifetime planning'. In the Institute of Directors, *The Directors' Guide to Pensions*, London: The Director Publications Ltd.

Toulson, N. (1982), *Modern Pensions*, Cambridge: Woodhead-Faulkner.

35

Incentives, performance pay and fringe benefits

Incentive payments remain one of the ideas that fascinate managers as they search for the magic formula. Somewhere there is a method of linking payment to performance so effectively that their movements will coincide, enabling the manager to leave the workers on automatic pilot, as it were, while attending to more important matters such as strategic planning or going to lunch. This conviction has sustained a continuing search for this elusive formula, which has been hunted with all the fervour of those trying to find the Holy Grail or the crock of gold at the end of the rainbow.

Performance-related pay is the topical version of this idea, with a significant change of emphasis. Incentives are to stimulate performance, while performance pay is to reward it; incentives are for the rank and file, while performance payments are for the managerial elite. Incentive thinking is preoccupied with the problem of control and avoiding costs getting out of hand, because 'they' will take the management to the cleaners if they are given half a chance. Performance pay thinking is dominated by the need to reward the deserving so that they too can share in the prosperity of the business at the same time as creating it.

Incentives and performance pay are part of a complex arrangement to express and to maintain the working relationship between the employer and the employee. They demonstrate not just what the management is trying to achieve, but also what the managers believe about the relationship. Elaborate incentive systems frequently represent a working relationship in which manager and worker are far apart with considerable mutual mistrust and little common interest. Elaborate systems of fringe benefit often represent a situation in which management is attempting to emphasize the degree of common interest, although they do not always succeed in overcoming mistrust. Schemes of performance pay typically carry the implicit view that those who may receive the payments are loyal, keen and hard-working: the possibility of the scheme being manipulated to achieve levels of payment which are not justified is never mentioned.

The key ideas in understanding the history of incentives are manipulation and luck. Those receiving incentive payment have had a clear, unshakeable conviction that the scheme was a managerial manipulative device to do the worker down. Those administering payment schemes have developed an equally clear conviction that workers have manipulated payment schemes to frustrate managerial objectives for efficiency and increased productivity in order to optimize employee earnings 'unfairly'. The idea of luck has been used both to explain and to rationalize variations in incentive payment by attributing the variation not to effort but to events not directly under the employee's control, like the level of orders, the share-out of the jobs that can produce high levels of earnings and those that do not, availability of materials, administrative delays, and so on.

Despite the disenchantment, incentive schemes persist, with over a third of male manual employees and over 16 per cent of non-manual males receiving incentive payments in 1988. The proportion of earnings that were incentives was usually between 15 and 25 per cent. The reasons why they persist include some of the reasons why they have lost favour, such as the way in which managements frequently avoid a problem by buying a way past it through juggling with the incentive arrangement. If there were not an incentive pay scheme in existence it could not be used for that sort of short-circuiting operation. Other reasons are their use to overcome resistance to change, the attractiveness sometimes to employees who feel they are gaining an element of control over their own workplace, the possible help from a supervisory point of view and – probably more important than any of these – a deep-seated conviction in the minds of many managers that incentive schemes ought to work as they seem basically sensible.

Table 35.1   Percentage of workers receiving incentive payments

	1984 (%)	1986 (%)	1988 (%)
Male manual workers	46.5	42.8	39.0
Male non-manual workers	19.1	16.7	16.3
Female manual workers	35.3	32.3	29.8
Female non-manual workers	13.4	11.4	12.0

Source: *New Earnings Survey* (1984, 1986, 1988).

Managerial expectations of incentive schemes

There is no single managerial view and there is no standard working situation in which managers have to organize payment arrangements. The need for managers to adopt varying opinions is set out by Lupton and Bowey:

In order to be sure of the outcome of a scheme the manager needs to consider the particular circumstances of his firm. From a contingency perspective we are now able to understand the apparently conflicting prescriptions of people like R. M. Currie who advocated incentive-bonus schemes of various kinds, and Wilfred Brown who recommended that piecework be abandoned. They had each been observing situations in which the particular system they were proposing had been successful, but were not aware that there was something peculiar about those circumstances which contributed to the success of the scheme. (Lupton and Bowey 1975, p. 79)

Motivational theories

The opinion of managers will first be influenced by the personal theory of motivation they hold. McGregor's Theory X (McGregor 1970), for instance, describes the average human being as having an inherent dislike of work, which he will avoid if he can. The manager agreeing with that point of view may well regard incentive schemes as necessary to control workers who will otherwise tend to idle. McGregor's Theory Y, on the other hand, describes the average human being as able to exercise self-control in the pursuit of objectives and to accept responsibility, finding physical and mental effort as natural as play or rest. The manager subscribing to that point of view will be less likely to look for incentives for control and more concerned with clarity, reasonableness and employee involvement. Some managers certainly hold a Theory X point of view about some of the people in the business and a Theory Y point of view about the others, leading to drastically different approaches to payment arrangements.

Control

Control thinking is expressed in the view that the output of individuals has to be measured for incentive payments to be made, and that these measurements provide a useful set of control information for the manager, either to see who is working hard and who is idling, or in order to build up data on how best to distribute tasks among a group of people so that they can all work optimally. This type of information can also demonstrate where there are weaknesses in departmental organization, and provide some basis for controlling labour costs.

There is much managerial cynicism about control through incentive schemes because employees, individually or collectively, set out to beat the system. A control system implies rules, and most human beings accept the validity of rules at the same time as they seek to test their flexibility. Especially if the incentive scheme is a management scheme with limited employee involvement in its creation and maintenance, the controlling rules will stimulate a competitive claim for control from employees seeking to optimize their benefits from the scheme rather than those of the management:

> The practical logic of incentives is that people want money, and that they will work harder to get more of it. Incentive plans do not, however, take account of several other well-demonstrated characteristics of behaviour in the organizational setting:
> 1. that most people also want the approval of their fellow workers and that, if necessary, they will forgo increased pay to obtain this approval;
> 2. that no managerial assurances can persuade workers that incentive rates will remain inviolate regardless of how much they produce;
> 3. that the ingenuity of the average worker is sufficient to outwit any system of controls devised by management. (McGregor 1970, p. 71)

Cost

Incentive arrangements are built on the principle that the cost of increasing output through incentive payments will decline with volume, so that the unit costs for each of 100 units of output will be less than the unit cost for each of 99 such units. There can be a situation in which this only appears to happen, as the scheme is manipulated to produce a rather different result. A remark attributed to a Midlands shop steward sums up the reason: 'When we get control of the piecework scheme, management lose control of their labour costs.' All but the most crude methods of incentive payment incorporate an element to compensate employees for an inability to earn an incentive because of delays beyond their control, usually known as waiting time. Few schemes can get round the problem of employees assigning as much output as possible to the productive periods of the day at the same time as recording as much waiting time as possible. There are many other ways in which direct labour costs can increase as a result of incentive arrangements, not least of which is the bargaining of local representatives to increase the cash pay-off. Also the scheme may require high indirect labour costs in clerical and related staff to keep all the records that the scheme requires.

Employee expectations of incentive schemes

Just as there is no single set of managerial expectations, so there is no single set of employee expectations surrounding incentives. The contingency approach is as relevant for them as it is for managers:

It is dangerous to make broad generalizations regarding British workers' attitudes to incentive systems. In some industries their use is taken for granted by the workers. This is probably the case, for example, with female operatives in the hosiery industry. In other industries there is great suspicion of incentive schemes on the part of workers. A typical case is probably the printing industry. (Husband 1976, p. 73)

Orientation to work

What employees expect from work will influence what they expect of the payment arrangements. If there is a strong instrumental orientation, then there will be a stronger interest in the financial arrangements, although the interest may lead to compliance with management objectives for the scheme or frustration of those objectives, according to whichever provides the best pay-off. Lawler examined a wide range of research studies before producing the conclusion:

pay can be instrumental for the satisfaction of most needs but it is most likely to be seen as instrumental for satisfying esteem and physiological needs, secondarily to be seen as instrumental for satisfying autonomy or security needs and least likely for satisfying social or self-actual needs. (Lawler 1971, p. 121)

Autonomy

Incentive pay programmes can give employees scope for autonomy in providing a satisfactory basis on which to determine a rate and level of application to the job rather than having it determined by others and mediated via close supervision. It may sound contradictory in view of earlier remarks about management control to suggest here that it can be the employees who gain control of their work as well as of the payment scheme, but the reason is that the incentive scheme takes the form of objective setting. It is somewhat analogous to Management by Objectives in that the scheme will normally provide an open-ended objective with the implication: 'It's up to you: you can earn as much as you like.' The responsibility for exactly when the work is done and how the individual work space is organized is partly transferred from the management to the employee, and supervision is more remote.

Interest

It is not always recognized that the incentive pay structure can be welcome as a source of interest in an otherwise monotonous occupation. Casual conversation with anyone holding a job with a strong element of routine shows how they tend to set up milestones to look forward to. The coffee break is not just a break and a chance to drink coffee; it is also a marker that the morning is half over. Others are such events as the arrival of the post, the bell sounding at the nearby school, the plane from New York flying overhead, the Pullman going past on the way to London, and many more. Financial incentives can build another marker element into the day's routine as people check how close they have come to the target for the day.

Typical problems with incentive schemes

The satisfaction of one party may be the dissatisfaction of the other, so that, for instance, the expectation of the management that control of labour costs will be improved will be disappointed if that control is lost to union negotiators. There are, however, various other problems to mention.

Operational inefficiencies

For incentives to work to the mutual satisfaction of both parties, there has to be a smooth operational flow, with materials, job cards, equipment and storage space all readily available exactly when they are needed, and an insatiable demand for the output. Seldom can these conditions be guaranteed and when they do exist they seldom last without snags. Raw materials run out, job cards are not available, tools are faulty, the stores are full, customer demand is fluctuating or there is trouble with the computer. As soon as this sort of thing happens the incentive-paid worker has an incentive to fiddle the scheme for protection against operational vagaries.

Fluctuation in earnings

Any payment method that is truly linked to performance must result in a level of earnings that will fluctuate in all but the most unusual circumstances, as demand will vary, operations will be spasmodically inefficient or the operator's effectiveness will alter from time to time. If the fluctuations are considerable then the employees will be encouraged to try to stabilize them, either by pressing for the guaranteed element to be increased, or by storing output in the good times to prevent the worst effects of the bad, or by social control of high-performing individuals to share out the benefits of the scheme as equally as possible. Any one of these tactics reduces the potential management advantages quite considerably, but has relatively less effect on the employee advantages suggested above.

Quality of work

The stimulus to increase volume of output can adversely affect the quality of output, as there is an incentive to do things as quickly as possible. If the payment scheme is organized so that only output meeting quality standards is paid for, there may still be the tendency to produce expensive scrap. Operatives filling jars with marmalade may break the jars if they work too hurriedly. This means that the jar is lost and the marmalade as well, for fear of glass splinters.

Quality of working life

Financial incentives in industry today probably yield a net gain in productivity, but most of them fail to release more than a small fraction of the energy and intelligence workers have to give to their jobs. Even when the financial incentive yields higher productivity, it may also generate such conflicts within the organization that we must wonder whether the gains are worth the costs. (Whyte 1972, p. 115)

In our industrial consciousness payment by results is associated with the worst aspects of rationalized work: routine, tight control, hyper-specialization and mechanistics. The worker is characterized as an adjunct to the machine, or as an alternative to a machine. Although this may not necessarily be so, it is usually so, and generally expected. The quality of working life for the individual employee is impaired. In a more general way the quality of working life is impaired because of the mechanical element in the control of working relationships.

The selective nature of incentives

Seldom do incentive arrangements cover all employees. Typically, groups of employees are working on a payment basis which permits their earnings to be geared to their output, while their performance depends on the before or after processes of employees not so rewarded, such as craftsmen making tools and fixtures, labourers bringing materials in and out, fork-truck drivers, store-keepers and so forth. This type of problem is illustrated most vividly by Angela Bowey's study of a garment factory, where employees 'on piecework' were set against those who were not, by the selective nature of the payment arrangement (Lupton and Bowey 1975, pp. 76–8).

One conventional way round the problem is to pay the 'others' a bonus linked to the incentive earned by those receiving it. The reasoning for this is that those who expect to earn more (like the craftsmen) have a favourable differential guaranteed as well as an interest in high levels of output, while that same interest in sustaining output is generated in the other employees (like the labourers and the storekeepers) without whom the incentive-earners cannot maintain their output levels. The drawbacks are obvious. The labour costs are increased by making additional payments to employees on a non-discriminating basis, so that the storekeeper who is a hindrance to output will still derive benefit from the efforts of others, and the employees whose efforts are directly rewarded by incentives feel that the fruits of their labour are being shared by those whose labours are not so directly controlled.

Obscurity of payment arrangements

Because of these difficulties, incentive schemes are constantly modified or refined in an attempt to circumvent fiddling or to get a fresh stimulus to output, or in response to employee demands for some other type of change. This leads to a situation in which the employees find it hard to understand what behaviour by them leads to particular results in payment terms.

Is performance-related pay any different?

From the hype one would assume that performance-related pay or merit pay is a splendid new invention. As was indicated at the opening of this chapter, and in Chapter 32, there are differences in emphasis, but what do these amount to in practice?

The long history of incentive schemes, and particularly of trade union involvement in their development, has been to make them collective and impersonal. The idea of performance pay is usually to make it individual and personal, so that some do better than others – or some do worse than others. Therein lies the problem. If the performance pay arrangement is to be effective, it must have an apparent impact on individual performance, but selective individual reward can be divisive and lead to overall ineffectiveness unless everyone perceives the rules to be fair. Consider the following practical problems that have been encountered recently:

> Peter and Patrick are sales consultants for a financial services company and both had business targets for a six month period. Peter met his target comfortably and received the predetermined bonus of £6,000 for reaching on-target earnings. Patrick failed to reach his

target because his sales manager boss left the company and poached two of Patrick's prime customers just before they signed agreements with Patrick, whose bonus was therefore £2,000 instead of £6,250.

Joy-Anne was a sales consultant for the same company as Peter and Patrick. Before the sales manager left, he made over to her several promising clients with whom he had done considerable preparatory work and who were not willing to be 'poached' by his new employer. All of these signed agreements and one of them decided to increase the value of the deal ten-fold without any reference to Joy-Anne until after that decision was made, and without knowing that she was now the appropriate contact. Her bonus for the period was £23,400.

Henry is a production manager in a light engineering company with performance pay related to a formula combining output with value-added. Bonus payments were made monthly *in anticipation* of what they should be. One of Henry's initiatives was to increase the gearing of the payment by results scheme in the factory. Through peculiarities of company accounting his bonus payments were 'justified' according to the formula, but later it was calculated that the production costs had risen by an amount that cancelled out the value-added benefits. Also 30 per cent of the year's output had to be recalled due to a design fault.

Peter had his bonus made up to £6,250. Joy-Anne had her bonus reduced to £8,000, but took legal advice and had the cut restored, whereupon Peter and Patrick both threatened to resign until mollified by ex-gratia payments of £2,000 each. Peter resigned three months later. Henry was dismissed.

These are not unusual difficulties and may be tolerable in an organization that is doing well, but. . . .

> Individualized pay seems tailor-made for a period of competitive expansion. . . . By all accounts this has had a considerable initial effect on company performance. But at the same time it produced a tremendous inflationary spiral. The systems introduced have generally been highly geared, with a high pay threshold as a carrot to attract employees and secure acceptance of the new arrangements. Awards for below standard performance have often been higher than the general run of increases in other industries.' (IDS 1988, p.5)

When schemes are individualized, it is always difficult to keep pay rises down for the poorer performer. Few managers have the stomach for passing on the bad news and then hoping to get a satisfactory working performance out of the person who has not had a pay rise. If a business is struggling, it cannot afford unfettered performance pay. Sometimes, there is a management justification for performance payments being made only to those in key management posts on the grounds that only they can initiate significant change and improvement in overall business performance. Furthermore the payments made to this small number of individuals amount to a small proportion of the organization's total expenditure. The payments are still likely to be inflationary, as the hankering after equity by others in the organization will put strong pressure on pay levels at every point.

Twenty years ago, inflation was sometimes attributed to 'consolidation', as progressively the proportion of pay that was basic as opposed to payment by results was increased, the rewards for the performance gradually being consolidated in the pay that people received regardless of the performance. Currently, this can be seen happening in a very public way in the published accounts of private companies, which include directors' emoluments. There have been several instances of company chairmen having a significant proportion of their income linked to company performance, yet the other directors decide to reward the chairman with a special payment as compensation for the fact that the success of the business has faltered.

The more exuberant schemes are gradually being replaced by arrangements that are better controlled, but the problems remain and it seems as if performance pay still suffers many of the weaknesses that were found in incentive payment schemes during the 1920s and 1930s.

An interesting account of performance pay in the Civil Service is to be found in Brindle (1987), and an approach in the National Health Service is in Fowler (1988). We should not, however, overlook a news item in the May 1990 issue of *Personnel Management*: 'Coventry City Council, one of the first councils to introduce performance-related pay for top managers, has abandoned it . . . it was seen as an exercise justifying increased levels of pay, whereas the council wanted to concentrate on building up teamwork.'

Payment by results schemes

The largest number of people paid incentives are paid through payment by results schemes, which are set out here.

Individual time-saving

It is rare for a scheme to be based on the payment of x pence per piece produced, as this provides no security against external influences which depress output. The type of scheme most in use, and the type against which most of the earlier criticisms in this chapter have been levelled, is one whereby the incentive is paid for time saved in performing a specified operation. A standard time is derived for a work sequence and the employee receives an additional payment for the time saved in completing a number of such operations. If it is not possible to work due to shortage of materials or some other reason, the time involved is not counted when the sums are done at the end of the day.

Standard times are derived by the twin techniques of method study and work measurement which are the skills of the work study engineer. By study of the operation, the work study engineer decides what is the most efficient way to carry it out and then times an operator actually doing the job over a period, so as to measure the 'standard time'.

Despite the criticisms, a payment method of this sort can suit a situation where people are employed on short-cycle manual operations with the volume of output varying between individuals depending on their skill or application.

Group incentives

Sometimes the principles of individual time-saving are applied to group rather than individual output. The argument is that in many circumstances it is fruitless to operate a scheme encouraging individuals who are working in harmony to compete in increasing their individual output. Where jobs are interdependent, group incentives can be appropriate, but it may also put great pressure on the group members, aggravating any interpersonal animosity that exists and increasing the likelihood of stoppages for industrial action.

Measured daywork

To some people the idea of measured daywork provides the answer to the shortcomings of individual incentive schemes. Instead of employees receiving a variable payment accordance with the output achieved, they are paid a fixed sum as long as they maintain a predetermined and agreed level of working. A useful summary of this method was provided by the Office of Manpower Economics (1973).

Theoretically, this deals with the key problem of other schemes by providing for both stable earnings and stable output instead of 'as much as you can, when you can, if you can', but the (National Board for Prices and Incomes found that productivity declined in some instances when this method was introduced, although there were also instances of lower labour cost per unit (NBPI 1968, p. 38). It seems that there is a greater degree of effective management control of these schemes than there is of conventional payment by results arrangements. IDS quote from a TUC working party on productivity techniques:

> There can be no doubt that management techniques reduce signifi-
> cantly workers' control over some important aspects of their employ-
> ment, e.g. the pace and method of work. A payment scheme such as

measured daywork involves the use of several of these techniques including work study and job evaluation, and trade unions are right to be cautious in their acceptance of it. There is good reason to conclude that the growth in the use of measured daywork indicates its value, whether real or apparent, permanent or temporary, for employers. (IDS 1977, p. 6)

Husband, however, speaks of 'a happier industrial relations climate' and 'less expenditure on dealing with grievances' as being among the many benefits that can come from measured daywork. He then sounds a note of caution:

Unless sound production engineering, production scheduling and supervisory practices are developed there is no reason to suppose that a measured daywork pay structure will remain undistorted over time. The pay structure is subject to many of the same pressures under measured daywork as it is under conventional bonus systems. Measured daywork provides a sound base, but management need to strengthen the base by effective training of foremen and careful analysis of their production control systems. (Husband 1976, p. 81)

Plant-wide schemes

A variant on the group incentive is the plant-wide bonus scheme, under which all employees in a plant or other organization share in a pool bonus that is linked to the level of output, the value added by the employees collectively or some similar formula. The attraction of these methods lies in the fact that the benefit to the management of the organization is 'real' because the measurement is made at the end of the system, compared with the measurements most usually made at different points within the system, whereby wages and labour costs can go up while output and profitability both come down. Theoretically, employees are also more likely to identify with the organization as a whole, they will co-operate more readily with the management and each other, and there is even an element of workers' control.

The difficulties are that there is no tangible link between individual effort and individual reward, so that those who are working hard can have their efforts nullified by others working less hard or by misfortunes elsewhere.

Review topic 33.1

Where manual employees are employed on some form of payment by results, New Earnings Survey shows that the percentage of average earnings made up by incentive payments is under 20 per cent for men and over 30 per cent for women. How would you explain this difference?

Commission

The payment of commission on sales is a widespread practice about which surprisingly little is known as these schemes have not come under the same close scrutiny that has been put on incentive schemes for manual employees. They suffer from most of the same drawbacks as manual incentives, except that they are linked to business won rather than to output achieved.

Tips

The practice of tipping is generally criticized as being undesirable for those receiving tips – it requires them to be deferential and obsequious – and for those giving them – because it is an unwarranted additional charge for a service they have already paid for. It is also often described as an employer device to avoid the need to pay realistic wages. Despite the criticism the practice persists, although it is of varying significance in different countries of the world.

The attraction of tipping is the feeling by employees that they can personally influence the level of their remuneration by the quality of service they give, and the feeling by the tipper of providing personal recognition for service received. This does not answer the criticism that tipping is usually for reasons of convention rather than direct acknowledgement of special service. From the employer's point of view the tipping convention can help ensure application to customers' wishes by employees, but can present problems in coping with known 'bad tippers'.

Fringe benefits

Features of payment other than wages or salary have grown in importance steadily since the 1960s, and the United Kingdom has a level of provision that is not found in other western countries. This is especially marked in the executive, management and professional area. Figure 35.1 is an example of how the

---

1. Starting salary of £13,400, to be reviewed after six months
2. Free private medical insurance
3. 25 days' annual holiday in addition to statutory days
4. Non-contributory pension scheme
5. Interest-free season ticket loan
6. Personal loan facility at reduced rate of interest
7. Free membership of three London clubs
8. Participation in annual performance rewards competition
9. Profits-related bonus scheme, paid monthly in advance

Figure 35.1 *Features of an offer to a 21-year-old graduate joining a graduate training programme in October 1989*

remuneration package can become very elaborate as the employer adds on benefits which are cheaper than actually paying money.

Gill (1989) quotes the exceptional case of a retired company chairman who was made a consultant with a package that included £92 a day for lunch, four centre court tickets for Wimbledon every year and four tickets for each opera season at Covent Garden. A less unusual example is: 'A banker's £35,000 salary typically brings with it a bonus averaging about £9,000 a year, a car and petrol, free health insurance, life insurance cover of £100,000, an interest-free loan of £6,000 and a £60,000 mortgage at 5 per cent interest.'

This type of development has been mainly due to taxation advantages, either to the employer or the employee, although there is a further refinement, known as the cafeteria approach, whereby the employee can choose between alternatives in putting together a personalized pay and benefits package. This idea has been current for some time without being widely adopted:

> While some UK employers do offer an element of choice over individual elements of the benefits package, very few have adopted a more structured approach where individual choice is seen as a benefit in its own right. Some companies have toyed with the idea of flexible compensation but have not, up to now, regarded the potential advantages as sufficient to outweigh the complexity involved. (Woodley 1990, p. 42).

Over recent years we have all begun to reflect on our payment arrangements in a more calculated way than before with the introduction, for instance, of the option to change from an employer's pension arrangements to a private pension plan, to make additional voluntary contributions, various possibilities of share ownership, and so forth. Perhaps the cafeteria approach to benefits is an idea whose time has at last come.

Despite their great attraction, fringe benefits can exacerbate status problems, with the have-nots bitterly resenting the privilege of the haves. A few years ago one of the authors was involved in conciliation to find a resolution to a long-running industrial dispute at a small industrial plant where closure was likely with the consequent redundancy of the workforce. The three senior managers at the plant were all geographically mobile, awaiting their next career move to greener pastures. They all also enjoyed the benefit of company cars. In the second week of the dispute all the cars were renewed. In the third week a man from 'Central Personnel', in London, arrived for discussions with the local management team and shopfloor assumptions were that this discussion was to find a solution to the strike. It later transpired that it was to explain why the cars were 1,600 cc instead of 2,000 cc; the issue being discussed between 12.15 and 2.45 p.m. over lunch in a nearby hotel. In the fifth week outside contractors arrived to lay a strip of tarmacadam from the factory gates across a muddy works yard to the office block in the centre, with a final strip outside the offices wide enough for three cars to be parked.

Cars

The Automobile Association calculated that in 1986 the cost of owning a car for the 10,000-mile-a-year driver is £3,700 annually. Provision of a car by the employer is clearly a major attraction:

> The company car is a cherished symbol of power, status and prestige. From the most junior commercial traveller to the chairman of a major industrial concern, his metal overcoat says more about him than the cut of his suit, and while that attitude persists, then so will the poor management of this almost anachronistic device continue. (Blauth 1986)

As that extract demonstrates, the attraction of the benefit is accompanied by significant management problems and the management of their provision is beset with almost as much power, status and prestige as their possession. In October 1988 *Personnel Management* magazine estimated that a car was 'a standard element in the remuneration package' for executives earning about £16,000 upwards. Out of our 350 research respondents, 209 indicated that company cars were provided for management employees (54 for white-collar and 6 for blue-collar), but the personnel manager was seldom closely involved in their allocation.

The company car is not a free benefit for the user, who pays tax on both the car and on the fuel that it uses. The method of tax collection is a reduction of the personal allowance, depending on the amount of business mileage, the original market value of the car, its age and cubic capacity. Details change with each Budget, but they are set out in booklet IR47, available free of charge from offices of the Inland Revenue. An alternative to the company car is a mileage allowance, more widely used in the public sector of employment. This is usually either a standard rate or a rate that varies with engine size. IDS Study 332 (1985) gives examples of mileage rates varying between 17 and 46 pence a mile.

Profit sharing

Whether profit sharing is an incentive or a fringe benefit depends partly on your point of view and partly on whether or not you feel you can influence the level of company profitability. The typical arrangement is simply to pay employees a cash bonus, calculated as a proportion of annual profits, on which the employee incurs both a PAYE and national insurance liability:

> Profit sharing is not widespread and suffers several limitations, not least of which is the absence of the main requirement of incentive schemes: that payment be made close to achieved performance . . . . Also ineffective workers share equally with the effective employees, the payments are often very small and lack significance in the mind of

the employee. The payment may fluctuate from year to year, and thus may become an unreliable element of earnings. (Smith 1983, p. 159)

An alternative is the Approved Deferred Share Trust (ADST) which was established under the Finance Act 1978. In this arrangement the company allocates the proportion of profit not in cash to employees, but to a trust fund which purchases company shares on behalf of the employees. The shares are then allocated to eligible employees on some agreed formula. The employee shareholder only pays tax when the shares are sold, and there is no additional national insurance contribution by employee or employer. ADST schemes seldom allow shares to be sold in the first two years after purchase and if they are sold in the following two years the employee pays tax on one of two values – either the price paid originally or the final selling price. If the shares are sold during the fourth year of ownership the tax obligation reduces to three quarters of what it would have been the year earlier, and after five years of ownership there is no tax obligation at all. Share dividends are received and taxed in the normal way. A variant of this arrangement was made possible by the Finance Act 1980 under which Save As You Earn Schemes can be established, enabling employees, if they wish, to purchase company shares through monthly deductions from salary.

A further alternative is a Profit-related Pay Plan (PRP), introduced in the 1987 budget. When a scheme is registered with the Inland Revenue, a part of the employee's pay is linked automatically with the profits of the business and tax relief is available on that proportion, up to a point where PRP is the lower of either 20 per cent of the employee's total pay or £3,000. Half of that sum would be available for tax relief, so the person earning £21,000 a year, of which 10 per cent (£2,100) was PRP, would have £1,050 on which tax was not payable.

Review topic 35.2

In view of the comments by Ian Smith (1983) about profit-sharing, what are the advantages to the employer of ADST and PRP schemes?

Other benefits

Employers provide a wide range of other benefits, from free hairdressing in company time to loans to buy season tickets. Table 35.2 shows the number of establishments participating in our research which provided any of nineteen different fringe benefits. Answers to other questions showed that over half provided private medical insurance to management employees (seventy-six provided it for blue-collar employees) and time off for medical and dental appointments was common. One-third of all respondents said that the proportion of employment costs devoted to fringe benefits was increasing, yet the general area of fringe benefits was the one where personnel specialists felt they had least discretion.

A benefit not included in Table 35.2 is the London allowance. This reached over £3,000 for some employees working in Inner London at the end of 1989, having been increasing steadily for some time. Some employers also have a lower 'ROSELAND' (rest of south-east England) payment. For clearing banks this is £750. There is an increasing practice of fitting the allowance to a particular location instead of to a general geographical area: 'A number of retailers have moved away from strict geographical zoning towards a 'nominated stores' approach, under which individual stores can be switched easily from one level of payment to another as the labour market dictates.' (IDS 1989, p. 1).

Table 35.2   The range of fringe benefits provided. Number of respondent organizations, out of a total of 350, providing the following fringe benefits for three categories of employee

	Blue-collar	White-collar	Management
Relocation expenses	124	237	290
Subsidized meals	211	246	245
Long-service awards	228	246	244
Company car	6	54	209
Medical facilities	94	103	180
Car servicing	6	40	152
Subscription to professional bodies	29	87	141
Employee discount on products	118	139	136
Personal loans	56	81	95
Petrol credit card	3	22	83
Share option scheme	64	70	75
Mortgage facilities	30	45	53
Christmas bonus	45	56	47
Company-owned housing	38	42	43
Transport to and from work	42	32	27
Clothing allowance	92	44	24
Service-related shareholding	14	18	19
Subsidized holidays	14	18	19
Share incentive scheme	11	11	15

Some employees jealously guard the 'benefit' of being paid in cash rather than by bank giro credit. This right of manual workers was protected by the Truck Acts 1940 and the Payment of Wages Act 1960, but there has been a long-running campaign to eliminate cash payment in order to save administrative time in making up pay packets and to overcome security problems. The Wages Act 1986 removed the entitlement to be paid in 'coin of the realm' for employees engaged after 1 January 1987 and makes it doubtful that an existing employee could claim a contractual right to continue being paid this way.

Review topic 35.3

What are the advantages to the employee and to the employer of payment being weekly in cash rather than monthly by bank giro credit?

Incentives, fringe benefits and personnel management

The very costly aspects of remuneration discussed in this chapter are seldom managed in a positive way with a sense of purpose about why they are provided and what they are to achieve. Usually, an extra is provided because it is a good bargain. Membership of the local health club can be obtained at half price by the employer, so it seems like too good an opportunity to miss. Many benefits are provided simply because it is the accepted practice, like the company car. Incentive schemes are set up in the belief that they should work, but without any evidence that the method actually proposed will work in that situation. The various schemes are seldom co-ordinated, with different executives responsible for different features. Sometimes the responsibility of the personnel manager is total, sometimes it is nil, yet all these features affect the basic activity of personnel work: matching the expectations of employer with the expectations of employee. Furthermore they form an increasing proportion of employment costs.

Incentives and fringe benefits need to be firmly incorporated within payment policy with the personnel manager reviewing everything that is provided and proposed. What is it? What is it for? Does it achieve its purpose? Is that purpose worth achieving? Does it fit within the overall payment policy? Who administers the feature being considered? Is that the appropriate person? How much does each feature cost? How much trouble does it cause? What benefit does it confer?

Unless incentive and fringe benefit provision are positively managed, they can become an expensive and ineffective element in the employment relationship.

Summary propositions

35.1 Incentives cannot be understood in isolation from the whole of the working relationship between employer and employee. Incentive arrangements demonstrate what managers believe about that relationship.

35.2 Typical problems with incentive schemes include having to cope with operational inefficiencies, fluctuation in earnings, the effect of incentives on the quality of work produced and on the quality of working life for the producers, as well as the selective nature of incentives and the frequent obscurity of the incentive arrangement itself.

35.3 Performance-related payments tend to be inflationary and present operational problems when overall organizational effectiveness declines.

35.4 Methods of payment by results include individual time-saving, group incentives, measured daywork, plant-wide schemes, productivity schemes, commission and tipping.

35.5 Fringe benefits are not intended to have a direct motivational effect, but are tax-efficient ways of providing additions to the remuneration package and some degree of choice within it. They are more common and diverse for management employees than for others and can cause considerable problems of relative status.

35.6 Fringe benefits include cars, mileage allowance, profit-sharing and many other small perquisites.

35.7 Fringe benefits are an area where personnel managers feel they have little discretion and influence.

35.8 Unless incentive payments and fringe benefits are managed positively, this increasingly costly aspect of the remuneration package can become an expensive and ineffective element in the employment relationship.

References

Automobile Association (1986), *Schedule of Estimated Standing and Running Costs*, Basingstoke: Automobile Association.

Blauth, J. (1986), 'Button up your metal overcoat', *Guardian*, 13 June.

Brindle, D. (1987), 'Will performance pay work in Whitehall?', *Personnel Management*, August.

Fowler, A. (1988), 'New directions in performance pay', *Personnel Management*, November

Gill, L. (1989), 'Fitting the perk to the person', *The Times*, October 31.

Husband, T. M. (1976), *Work Analysis and Pay Structure*, Maidenhead: McGraw-Hill.

Incomes Data Services (1977), *Incentive Pay Schemes*, IDS Study 140, London: Incomes Data Services.

Incomes Data Services (1985), *Improving Productivity*, IDS Study 331, London: Incomes Data Services.

Incomes Data Services: (1985), *Staff Benefits and Allowances*, IDS Study 332, London: Incomes Data Services.

Incomes Data Services, (1988), *Performance Pay*, IDS Focus 49, London: Incomes Data Services.

Incomes Data Services, (1989), *Incentive Bonus Schemes*, IDS Study 443, London: Incomes Data Services.

Incomes Data Services, (1989), *London and South East Allowances*, IDS Study 445, London: Incomes Data Services.

Lawler, E. E. Jnr. (1971), *Pay and Organizational Effectiveness*, New York: McGraw-Hill.

Lupton, T. and Bowey, A. M. (1975), *Wages and Salaries*, Harmondsworth: Penguin Books.

McGregor, D. (1970), *The Human Side of Enterprise*, Maidenhead: McGraw-Hill.

National Board for Prices and Incomes, (1968), *Payment by Results Systems*, Report no. 65. London: HMSO.

Office of Manpower Economics, (1973), *Measured Daywork*, London: HMSO.

Smith, I. (1983), *The Management of Remuneration: Paying for effectiveness*, London: Institute of Personnel Management.

White, M. (1985), 'What's New in Pay?', *Personnel Management*, February.

Whyte, W. F. (1972), 'Economic incentives and human relations'. In T. Lupton, (ed.), *Payment Systems*, Harmondsworth: Penguin Books.

Woodley, C. (1990), 'The cafeteria route to compensation', *Personnel Management*, May, pp. 42–5.

Index